I have to recommend . . . *Nourishing Traditions* by Sally Fallon. The first chapter of her book is so right on target that I feel a little guilty for taking her ideas. But what she pointed out is that independent producers of food—such as people who present us with meat, poultry, eggs and butter—provide the lowest profit margin in the industry. People who put out junk food . . . have an incredible return on invested capital because they are putting out low-cost items and making a very high profit.

Robert C. Atkins, MD
Author of *The Atkins' New Diet Revolution*

Nourishing Traditions is more than a cookbook—it's an *education* that will lead you to "cook with pride," as you will know that you are giving your family the proper nourishment for a lifetime of vigorous good health. Now *that* is the real "joy of cooking!"

William Campbell Douglass, MD
Author of *The Milk Book*

Nourishing Traditions . . . is a work of genius . . . richly encyclopedic. . . . Run, don't walk to the nearest phone and order *Nourishing Traditions.*

Clara Felix
Author of the *Felix Letter*

This cookbook is unique. . . . *Nourishing Traditions* throws down the gauntlet to challenge the "Diet Dictocrats."

Beatrice Trum Hunter
Author of *Consumer Beware*

As a convinced vegetarian of some 25 years, I opened Sally Fallon's book to her many meat recipes and immediately closed it again. But then I figured that there must be more to it than that. There is. . . . I was surprised at the wealth of information to help me (even as a vegetarian) make better food choices and prepare the ones I have chosen to get the most nourishment from them.

Peter Hinderberger, MD, Past President
Physicians Association for Anthroposophical Medicine

I figured it would be only a matter of time before people would realize that lowfat and low-cholesterol diets were highly overrated for healthfulness. Now comes a cookbook author and food writer who is well aware of the politically correct nutrition misinformation, but who also has the knowledge and courage to challenge its assumptions.

Gene Logsdon
Author of the *Contrary Farmer*

NOURISHING TRADITIONS

The Cookbook that Challenges Politically Correct Nutrition and the Diet Dictocrats

REVISED SECOND EDITION

Sally Fallon

with Mary G. Enig, Ph.D.

Cover Design by Kim Waters Murray
Illustrations by Marion Dearth

NOURISHING TRADITIONS

The Cookbook that Challenges
Politically Correct Nutrition
and the Diet Dictocrats

REVISED SECOND EDITION

Sally Fallon

with Mary G. Enig, Ph.D.
Cover Design by Kim Waters Murray
Illustrations by Marion Dearth

A Note to the Reader: The ideas and suggestions contained in this book are not intended as a substitute for appropriate care of a licensed health care practitioner.

Published by:
NewTrends Publishing, Inc.
Washington, DC 20007

US and Canada Orders (877) 707-1776
Overseas Orders: (574) 268-2601
www.newtrendspublishing.com newtrends@kconline.com

Available to the trade through
Biblio Distribution (a division of NBN) 800-462-6420

First Edition: 16,000
Second Edition: 29,000
Revised Second Edition: 40,000; 25,000

ISBN
0-9670897-3-5

PRINTED IN THE UNITED STATES OF AMERICA

For Sarah, Nicholas, James and Davidson
and their children

ACKNOWLEDGMENTS

The authors are grateful to Marianne Gregory, whose suggestion planted the seed for this book; to those who watered it with their encouragement and help including Dr. Alsop Corwin, H. Leon Abrams, Jr., Steven Acuff, Patrick Von Mauck, Dr. Meira Fields, Leyla Uran, Zeynep Gur, Tamas and Hajna Dakun, Pam Howar, Jeffrey Dearth, Valerie Curry, Charlie Votaw, Richard Thomas, Tom Dix, Cy Nelson, Randolph and Ginny Aires, Carmen and George Denby, Trudy Fallon, Jon Cutler, Supat Sirivicha, Ira Wexler, Chris Archilla, Vladimir Ratsimer, Lynn Greaves, Kurt Reiman, Fred Gregory, Dr. Artemis Simopoulos, William Shawn, Christopher Hartman, Bob White, Diana Vivian, Mary Hudson and Milka Halama; and to John Fallon whose support and enthusiasm never faltered.

Particular thanks goes to Maggie Wetzel who always used butter.

We also wish to thank those who contributed recipes: Maggie Wetzel, Harry Wetzel and Katie Wetzel; Marianne Gregory; John Desmond; Rosemary Barron; Sally Hazel Fallon, Anne Marie Fallon and Tom Fallon; Philomena Aparicio; Madeline Curry; Moustafa and Lynn Soliman; Sue Rogers; Carole Valentine; Audrey Powell; Maribel Kim; Vivian Mason; June Shields; Marie Meyer; Taiwo Obi; Thomas Connelly; Isabel Molin; Maria de Lourdes Campos; Tony Rossi, Mary Jo Bierline; Emily Sagar; Karen Acuff; Soroor Ehteshami; Maria Noguera and Marie Claude Leduc.

We are also grateful to the many individuals who contributed to the second edition. Jenny Mathau, Kasia Welin Grossman and Valerie Mortensen helped immeasurably with their detailed lists of questions and recipe suggestions. Thank you also to Tom Cowan, Jan LaTourette, Geoffrey Morell, Jake McGuire, Rebeccah and Eugene Yen, Donna Gates, Sandy Cameron, Lee Clifford, Julie Thomas, Lisa Millimet, Ali-Reza Fassihi, Betsy Pryor, Steve Foxman, Valerie McBean, Walter Scharrer, Maury Silverman, Trauger Groh, John MacArthur, Walter Felber, Louise Dwyer, Pilar Bastida, Marguerite Wyner, David Morris, Cynthia Renfrow, Nee Sinclair, Jayne Taylor, Richard Dobbs, Sally Eauclaire Osborne, Christian Elwell, El King, Renee Bartol, Zahra Partovi, Robert Irons, Terence Martin, Harley Lyons, Maryanna Erzinger, Eva Holland, Joe Hilgendorf, Stephen Byrnes, Winnie Barker, Roberto Aparacio, Loren Zanier, Karine Bauch, Brenda Ruble, Chuck Eisenstein, Deanna Buck, Hy Lerner, Tom Heinrichs, Becky Mauldin, Josh Knox, Marie Bishop and Christopher Cogswell; with particular thanks to Nancy Morris and Catherine Czapp for their herculean proofreading labors and to Harry Wetzel for his help in taking the manuscript to production.

❧ CONTENTS ❧

❧ PREFACE ❧

Technology is a generous benefactor. To those who have wisely used his gifts he has bestowed freedom from drudgery; freedom to travel; freedom from the discomforts of cold, heat and dirt; and freedom from ignorance, boredom and oppression. But father technology has not brought us freedom from disease. Chronic illness in industrialized nations has reached epic proportions because we have been dazzled by his stepchildren—fast foods, fractionated foods, convenience foods, packaged foods, fake foods, embalmed foods, ersatz foods—all the bright baubles that fill up the shelves at our grocery stores, convenience markets, vending machines and even health food stores.

The premise of this book is that modern food choices and preparation techniques constitute a radical change from the way man has nourished himself for thousands of years and, from the perspective of history, represent a fad that not only has severely compromised his health and vitality but may well destroy him; and that the culinary traditions of our ancestors, and the food choices and preparation techniques of healthy nonindustrialized peoples, should serve as the model for contemporary eating habits, even and especially during this modern technological age.

The first modern researcher to take a careful look at the health and eating habits of isolated traditional societies was a dentist, Dr. Weston Price. During the 1930's, Dr. Price traveled the world over to observe population groups untouched by civilization, living entirely on local foods. While the diets of these peoples differed in many particulars, they contained several factors in common. Almost without exception, the groups he studied ate liberally of seafood or other animal proteins and fats in the form of organ meats and dairy products; they valued animal fats as absolutely necessary to good health; and they ate fats, meats, fruits, vegetables, legumes, nuts, seeds and whole grains in their whole, unrefined state. All primitive diets contained some raw foods, of both animal and vegetable origin.

Dr. Price found fourteen groups—from isolated Irish and Swiss, from Eskimos to Africans—in which almost every member of the tribe or village enjoyed superb health. They were free of chronic disease, dental decay and mental illness; they were strong, sturdy and attractive; and they produced healthy children with ease, generation after generation.

Dr. Price had many opportunities to compare these healthy so-called "primitives" with members of the same racial group who had become" civilized" and were living on the products of the industrial revolution—refined grains, canned foods, pasteurized milk and sugar. In these peoples, he found rampant tooth decay, infectious disease, degenerative illness and infertility. Children born to traditional peoples who had adopted the industrialized diet had crowded and crooked teeth, narrowed faces, deformities of bone structure and susceptibility to every sort of medical problem. Studies too numerous to count have confirmed Dr. Price's observations that the so-called civilized diet, particularly the Western diet of refined carbohydrates and devitalized fats and oils, spoils our God-given genetic inheritance of physical perfection and vibrant health.

Later research on the diets of traditional and nonindustrialized peoples has focused on their food preparation techniques. Almost universally, these societies allow grains, milk products and often vegetables, fruits and meats to ferment or pickle by a process called lacto-fermentation. These pickling techniques preserve foods so that they are available during periods of scarcity, but unlike modern preservation methods, which deaden and denature our foods, lacto-fermentation makes nutrients in these foods more available and supplies the intestinal tract with health-promoting lactic acid and lactic-acid-producing bacteria.

Another technique found universally in ethnic cuisines is the use of bone broths, rich in gelatin as well as in calcium and other minerals. The archives of our medical libraries contain many studies on the beneficial effects of gelatin taken on a daily or frequent basis, but these studies are ignored even as traditional methods for making rich stocks are forgotten.

Technology can be a kind father but only in partnership with his mothering, feminine partner—the nourishing traditions of our ancestors. These traditions require us to apply more wisdom to the way we produce and process our food and, yes, more time in the kitchen, but they give highly satisfying results—delicious meals, increased vitality, robust children and freedom from the chains of acute and chronic illness. The wise and loving marriage of modern invention with the sustaining, nurturing food folkways of our ancestors is the partnership that will transform the Twenty-First Century into the Golden Age; divorce hastens the physical degeneration of the human race, cheats mankind of his limitless potential, destroys his will and condemns him to the role of undercitizen in a totalitarian world order.

❧ INTRODUCTION ❧

In no period of our history as a nation have Americans been so concerned about the subject of diet and nutrition. Yet if we accept the premise that what we eat determines our health, then we must add the observation that in no period of our history as a nation have Americans eaten so poorly, a statement that the most cursory survey of current statistics can prove.

Although heart disease and cancer were rare at the turn of the century, today these two diseases strike with increasing frequency, in spite of billions of dollars in research to combat them, and in spite of tremendous advances in diagnostic and surgical techniques. In America, one person in three dies of cancer, one in three suffers from allergies, one in ten will have ulcers and one in five is mentally ill. Continuing this grim litany, one out of five pregnancies ends in miscarriage and one quarter of a million infants are born with a birth defect each year. Other degenerative diseases—arthritis, multiple sclerosis, digestive disorders, diabetes, osteoporosis, Alzheimer's, epilepsy and chronic fatigue—afflict a significant majority of our citizens, sapping the energy and the very life blood of our nation. Learning disabilities such as dyslexia and hyperactivity afflict seven million young people. These diseases were also extremely rare only a generation or two ago.

Today, chronic illness afflicts nearly half of all Americans and causes three out of four deaths in the United States. Most tragically, these diseases, formerly the purview of the very old, now strike our children and those in the prime of life.

Americans spend one dollar out of every fourteen for medical services, or over $800 billion yearly—more than the national deficit, the food bill and the profits of all U.S. corporations combined—yet we have little to show for this tremendous drain on our resources. Medical science has not even been able to lengthen our life span. Fewer persons alive at 70 today survive until 90 than forty years ago. And those who do survive past 70 are often a helpless burden to their families, rather than useful members of society. Credit for today's relatively long life span belongs to improved sanitation and the reduction of infant mortality.

New killer viruses now command newspaper headlines and even infectious diseases such as tuberculosis are making a comeback, this time in forms resistant to allopathic drugs. Chemical sensitivities and problems with the immune system abound. We have almost forgotten that our natural state is one of balance, wholeness and vitality.

POLITICALLY CORRECT NUTRITION

Clearly something is very wrong, even though many Americans have been conscientious about following orthodox dietary advice. They take exercise seriously, many have stopped smoking, consumption of fresh vegetables has increased, many have reduced their intake of salt, and a good portion of America has cut back on red meats and animal fats. But none of these measures has made a dent in the ever-increasing toll of degenerative disease. We buy foods labeled lowfat, no cholesterol, reduced sodium, thinking they are good for us. Why, then, are we so sick?

The premise of this book is that the advice of the Diet Dictocrats—what they tell us and, just as important, what they don't tell us—is wrong. Not 100 percent wrong. There is a certain amount of truth in their pronouncements, enough to give them credibility, but not enough to save us from the sufferings of chronic disease.

Who are the Diet Dictocrats? In general they are doctors, researchers and spokesmen for various government and quasi-government agencies, such as the Food and Drug Administration; the American Medical Association (AMA); the American Dietetic Association (ADA); prestigious hospitals and research centers, such as Sloan-Kettering, the National Institutes of Health (NIH) and the National Heart, Lung and Blood Institute (NHLBI); university medical schools and nutrition departments; the National Academy of Science (NAS); and large so-called philanthropic organizations like the American Cancer Society (ACS) and the American Heart Association (AHA), ostensibly dedicated to combatting our most serious diseases. Based on what we read in the newspapers and national magazines, these organizations speak with one voice. "Exercise, eat vegetables, stop smoking, reduce salt," they say, "and cut back or eliminate animal fats and red meat." Recently, the US Department of Agriculture (USDA) issued new nutritional guidelines in the form of a pyramid, calling for a diet based on grains—bread, pasta, cereal and crackers—along with fruits and vegetables. The guidelines recommend only small amounts of protein foods—meat, fowl, fish, nuts and legumes—and strictly limited consumption of sweets and fats.

The new guidelines have their good points. The experts are right, for example, in calling for a reduction in sweets in the American diet. We must recognize and applaud progress wherever we find it. Since 1923, when a US Farmers Bulletin recommended one pound of sugar per person per week, consumers have heard numerous government reassurances that sugar is harmless. During the last few years these soothing voices have fallen quiet as the evidence against sugar continues to mount. The new Department of Agriculture guidelines represent a rare establishment warning against eating too much sugar but it is doubtful that the popular press will emphasize this feature of the Food Pyramid.

The new food guidelines rightly stress the importance of fruits and vegetables; for many years, the medical establishment ignored their value. The American Cancer Society even denied the role of fresh vegetables in preventing cancer, in spite of considerable evidence to the contrary. The new guidelines reflect the fact that this evidence can no longer be ignored.

Unfortunately, several dangerous errors are built into the edifice of the USDA Food Pyramid. First, the new guidelines imply that everyone can eat the same foods in the same proportions and be healthy. According to the recommendations, grains should be the basis of our diet; but many people do very poorly on grains. Others have a low tolerance for dairy products. These intolerances are due to a number of factors, including ethnic background and genetic inheritance. Secondly, the pyramid calls for reduced fats without addressing the dangers of lowfat diets. Finally, the new guidelines perpetuate the myth that fats, carbohydrates and proteins have equal nutritional properties no matter how much or how little they are processed. The experts make no distinction between whole grains and refined, between foods grown organically and those grown with pesticides and commercial fertilizers, between unprocessed dairy products from pasture-fed cows and pasteurized dairy products from confined animals raised on processed feed, between fresh and rancid fats, between traditional fresh fruits and vegetables and those that have been irradiated or genetically altered, between range-fed meats and those from animals raised in crowded pens; between natural and battery-produced eggs; in short, between the traditional foods that nourished our ancestors and newfangled products now dominating the modern marketplace.

This is Politically Correct Nutrition. It singles out foods grown by independent producers—eggs and beef—but spares the powerful and highly profitable grain cartels, vegetable oil producers and the food processing industry; it sacrifices old-fashioned butter on the altar of the latest nutritional fad but spares pasteurized milk products and processed cheese; it gives lip service to the overwhelming evidence implicating sugar as a major cause of our degenerative diseases but spares the soft drink industry; and it raises not a murmur against refined flour, hydrogenated vegetable oils and foods adulterated with harmful preservatives, flavorings and coloring agents.

The Diet Dictocrats are strangely silent about the ever increasing trend toward food processing and the devitalization of America's rich agricultural bounty. Food processing is the largest manufacturing industry in the country and hence the most powerful. This industry naturally uses its financial clout to influence the slant of university research and the dictates that come from government agencies. A 1980 study showed that almost half the leading officials at the FDA had previously worked for organizations the agency is mandated to regulate. The universities have equally powerful ties to the food processing industry. A good example is Harvard University where Dr. Frederick Stare, head of the nutrition department for many years, began his career with several articles delineating nutritional deficiencies caused by white flour and a study on Irish brothers that positively correlated a high intake of vegetable oils—not animal fats—with heart disease. Soon after he became department head, however, the university received several important grants from the food processing industry. Dr. Stare's articles and weekly newspaper columns then began assuring the public that there was nothing wrong with white bread, sugar and highly processed foods. He recommended one cup of corn oil per day to prevent heart disease, and in one article he even suggested Coca-Cola as a snack!

Most "nutritional" cookbooks follow the Diet Dictocrats' politically correct guidelines, including all those approved by the American Heart Association. A good example is the bestselling *Eater's Choice* by Dr. Ron Goor and Nancy Goor. A brief introduction rehashing a few politically correct studies, said to implicate saturated fats as the cause of heart disease, is followed by pages of recipes just loaded with sugar and white flour. The authors assure us that the best thing we can do for our hearts is to replace butter with margarine and eliminate eggs and red meat from our diet, in spite of the fact that most studies, honestly evaluated, show that such a diet is not only useless but also harmful.

FATS

Fats from animal and vegetable sources provide a concentrated source of energy in the diet; they also provide the building blocks for cell membranes and a variety of hormones and hormone-like substances. Fats as part of a meal slow down nutrient absorption so that we can go longer without feeling hungry. In addition, they act as carriers for important fat-soluble vitamins A, D, E and K. Dietary fats are needed for the conversion of carotene to vitamin A, for mineral absorption and for a host of other processes.

Politically Correct Nutrition is based on the assumption that we should reduce our intake of fats, particularly saturated fats from animal sources. Fats from animal sources also contain cholesterol, presented as the twin villain of the civilized diet.

The theory—called the lipid hypothesis—that there is a direct relationship between the amount of saturated fat and cholesterol in the diet and the incidence of coronary heart disease was proposed by a researcher named Ancel Keys in the late 1950s. Numerous subsequent researchers have pointed out the flaws in his data and conclusions. Nevertheless, Keys received far more publicity than those presenting alternative views. The vegetable oil and food processing industries, the main beneficiaries of any research that could be used to demonize competing traditional foods, worked behind the scenes to promote further research that would support the lipid hypothesis.

The most well-known advocate of the lowfat diet was Nathan Pritikin. Actually, Pritikin advocated elimination of sugar, white flour and all processed foods from the diet and recommended the use of fresh raw foods, whole grains and a strenuous exercise program, but it was the lowfat aspects of his regime that received the most attention in the media. Adherents found that they lost weight and that their cholesterol levels and blood pressure declined. The success of the Pritikin diet was probably due to a number of factors having nothing to do with reduction in dietary fat—weight loss alone, for example, will lower cholesterol, at least at first—but Pritikin soon found that the fat-free diet presented many problems, not the least of which was the fact that people had trouble staying on it. Those who possessed enough will power to remain fat-free for any length of time developed a variety of health problems including low energy, difficulty in concentration, depression, weight gain and mineral deficiencies.[1] Pritikin may have saved himself from heart disease but his lowfat diet did not help him recover from leukemia. He died, in the prime of life, of suicide when he realized that his Spartan regime was not working. We shouldn't have to die of either heart disease or cancer—or consume a diet that makes us depressed.

When problems with the no-fat regime became apparent, Pritikin introduced a small amount of fat from vegetable sources into his diet—about 10 percent of the total caloric intake. Today the Diet Dictocrats advise us to limit fats to 25-30 percent of the caloric intake, which is about 2 1/2 ounces or 5 tablespoons per day for a diet of 2400 calories. Careful reckoning of fat intake and avoidance of animal fats, they say, is the key to perfect health.

These "experts" assure us that the lipid hypothesis is backed by incontrovertible scientific proof. Most people would be surprised to learn that there is, in fact, very little evidence to support the contention that a diet low in cholesterol and saturated fat actually reduces death from heart disease or in any way increases one's life span. Consider the following:

Before 1920 coronary heart disease was rare in America; so rare that when a young internist named Paul Dudley White introduced the German electrocardiograph to his colleagues at Harvard University, they advised him to concentrate on a more profitable branch of medicine. The new machine revealed the presence of arterial blockages, thus permitting early diagnosis of coronary heart disease. But in those days clogged arteries were a medical rarity, and White had to search for patients who could benefit from his new technology. During the next forty years, however, the incidence of coronary heart disease rose dramatically, so much so that by the mid-1950s heart disease was the leading cause of death among Americans. Today heart disease causes at least 40 percent of all US deaths. If, as we have been told, heart disease is caused by consumption of saturated fats, one would expect to find a corresponding increase in animal fat in the American diet. Actually, the reverse is true. During the sixty-year period from 1910 to 1970, the proportion of traditional animal fat in the American diet declined from 83 percent to 62 percent, and butter consumption plummeted from 18 pounds per person per year to four. During the past eighty years, dietary cholesterol intake has increased only 1 percent. During the same period the percentage of dietary vegetable oils in the form of margarine, shortening and refined oils increased about 400 percent while the consumption of sugar and processed foods increased about 60 percent.[2]

The Framingham Heart Study is often cited as proof of the lipid hypothesis. This study began in 1948 and involved about 6,000 people from the town of Framingham, Massachusetts. Two groups were compared at five-year intervals—those who consumed little cholesterol and saturated fat and those who consumed large amounts. After 40 years, the director of this study had to admit: "In Framingham, Mass., the more saturated fat one ate, the more cholesterol one ate, the more calories one ate, the lower the person's serum cholesterol. . . we found that the people who ate the most cholesterol, ate the most saturated fat, ate the most calories, weighed the least and were the most physically active."[3] The study *did* show that those who weighed more and had abnormally high blood cholesterol levels were slightly more at risk for future heart disease, but weight gain and cholesterol levels had an inverse correlation with fat and cholesterol intake in the diet.[4]

In a multi-year British study involving several thousand men, half were asked to reduce saturated fat and cholesterol in their diets, to stop smoking and to increase consumption of unsaturated oils such as margarine and vegetable oils. After one year, those on the "good" diet had 100 percent more deaths than those on the "bad" diet, in spite of the fact that those on the "bad" diet continued to smoke! But in describing the study, the author ignored these results in favor of a politically correct conclusion: "The implication for public health policy in the UK is that a preventive programme such as we evaluated in this trial is probably effective. . . ."[5]

The Multiple Risk Factor Intervention Trial, (MRFIT) sponsored by the National Heart, Lung and Blood Institute, compared mortality rates and eating habits of over 12,000 men. Those with "good" dietary habits (reduced saturated fat, reduced cholesterol and reduced smoking) showed a marginal reduction in total coronary heart disease, but their overall mortality from all causes was higher. Similar results have emerged in several other studies. The few trials that indicate a correlation between fat reduction and a decrease in coronary heart disease mortality also document a concurrent increase in deaths from cancer, brain hemorrhage, suicide and violent death.[6]

The Lipid Research Clinics Coronary Primary Prevention Trial (LRC-CPPT), which cost 150 million dollars, is the study most often cited by the experts to justify lowfat diets. Actually, dietary cholesterol and saturated fat were not tested in this study as all subjects were given a low-cholesterol, low-saturated-fat diet. Instead, the study tested the effects of a cholesterol-lowering drug. Their statistical analysis of the results implied a 24 percent reduction in the rate of coronary heart disease in the group taking the drug compared with the placebo group; however, non-heart disease deaths in the drug group increased—deaths from cancer, stroke, violence and suicide.[7] Even the conclusion that lowering cholesterol reduces heart disease is suspect. Independent researchers who tabulated the results of this study found *no* significant statistical difference in coronary heart disease death rates between the two groups.[8] However, both the popular press and medical journals touted the LRC-CPPT as the long-sought proof that animal fats are the cause of heart disease, America's number-one killer.

While it is true that researchers have induced heart disease in some animals by giving them extremely large dosages of oxidized or rancid cholesterol—amounts ten times that found in the ordinary human diet—several population studies squarely contradict the cholesterol-heart disease connection. A survey of 1700 patients with hardening of the arteries, conducted by the famous heart surgeon Michael DeBakey, found no relationship between the level of cholesterol in the blood and the incidence of atherosclerosis.[9] A survey of South Carolina adults found no correlation of blood cholesterol levels with "bad" dietary habits, such as use of red meat, animal fats, fried foods, butter, eggs, whole milk, bacon, sausage and cheese.[10] A Medical Research Council survey showed that men eating butter ran half the risk of developing heart disease compared to those using margarine.[11]

Mother's milk provides a higher proportion of cholesterol than almost any other food. It also contains over 50 percent of its calories as fat, much of it saturated fat. Both cholesterol and saturated fat are essential for growth in babies and children, especially the development of the brain.[12] Yet, the American Heart Association is now recommending a low-cholesterol, lowfat diet for children! Most commercial formulas are low in saturated fats and soy formulas are completely devoid of cholesterol. A recent study linked lowfat diets with failure to thrive in children.[13]

Numerous surveys of traditional populations have yielded information that is an embarrassment to the Diet Dictocrats. For example, a study comparing Jews when they lived in Yemen, whose diets contained fats solely of animal origin, to Yemenite Jews living in Israel, whose diets contained margarine and vegetable oils, revealed little heart disease or diabetes in the former group but high levels of both diseases in the latter.[14] (The study also noted that the Yemenite Jews consumed no sugar but those in Israel consumed sugar in amounts equaling 25-30 percent of total carbohydrate intake.) A comparison of populations in northern and southern India revealed a similar pattern. People in northern India consume 17 times more animal fat but have an incidence of coronary heart disease seven times lower than people in southern India.[15] The Masai and kindred African tribes subsist largely on milk, blood and beef. They are free from heart disease and have low cholesterol levels.[16] Eskimos eat liberally of animal fats from fish and marine animals. On their native diet they are free of disease and exceptionally hardy.[17] An extensive study of diet and disease patterns in China found that the region in which the populace consumes large amounts of whole milk had half the rate of heart disease as several districts in which only small amounts of animal products are consumed.[18] Several Mediterranean societies have low rates of heart disease even though fat—including highly saturated fat from lamb, sausage and goat cheese—comprises up to 70 percent of their caloric intake. The inhabitants of Crete, for example, are remarkable for their good health and longevity.[19] A study of Puerto Ricans revealed that, although they consume large amounts of animal fat, they have a very low incidence of colon and breast cancer.[20] A study of the long-lived inhabitants of Soviet Georgia revealed that those who ate the most fatty meat lived the longest.[21] In Okinawa, where the average life span for women is 84 years—longer than in Japan—the inhabitants eat generous amounts of pork and seafood and do all their cooking in lard.[22] None of these studies is mentioned by those urging restriction of saturated fats.

The relative good health of the Japanese, who have the longest life span of any nation in the world, is generally attributed to a lowfat diet. Although the Japanese eat few dairy fats, the notion that their diet is low in fat is a myth; rather, it contains moderate amounts of animal fats from eggs, pork, chicken, beef, seafood and organ meats. With their fondness for shellfish and fish broth, eaten on a daily basis, the Japanese probably consume more cholesterol than most Americans. What they do *not* consume is a lot of vegetable oil, white flour or processed food (although they do eat white rice). The life span of the Japanese has increased since World War II along with an increase in animal fat and protein in the diet.[23] Those who point to Japanese statistics to promote the lowfat diet fail to mention that the Swiss live almost as long on one of the fattiest diets in the world. Tied for third in the longevity stakes are Austria and Greece—both with high-fat diets.[24]

As a final example, let us consider the French. Anyone who has eaten his way across France has observed that the French diet is loaded with saturated fat in the form of butter, eggs, cheese, cream, liver, meats and rich patés. Yet the French have a lower rate of coronary heart disease than many other western countries. In the United States, 315 of every 100,000 middle-aged men die of heart attacks each year; in France the rate is 145 per 100,000. In the Gascony region, where goose and duck liver form a staple of the diet, this rate is a remarkably low 80 per 100,000.[25] This phenomenon has recently gained international attention and was dubbed the French Paradox. (The French do suffer from many degenerative diseases, however. They eat large amounts of sugar and white flour and in recent years have succumbed to the timesaving temptations of processed foods.)

A chorus of establishment voices, including the American Cancer Society, the National

Cancer Institute and the Senate Committee on Nutrition and Human Needs, claims that animal fat is linked not only with heart disease but also with cancers of various types. Yet when researchers from the University of Maryland analyzed the data they used to make such claims, they found that vegetable fat consumption was correlated with high rates of cancer and animal fat was not.[26]

Clearly something is wrong with the theories we read in the popular press—and used to bolster sales of lowfat concoctions and cholesterol-free foods. The notion that saturated fats *per se* cause heart disease as well as cancer is not only facile, it is just plain wrong. But it *is* true that some fats are bad for us. In order to understand which ones, we must know something about the chemistry of fats.

Fats—or lipids—are a class of organic substances that are not soluble in water. In simple terms, fatty acids are chains of carbon atoms with hydrogen atoms filling the available bonds. Most fat in our bodies and in the food we eat is in the form of triglycerides, that is, three fatty-acid chains attached to a glycerol molecule. Elevated triglycerides in the blood have been positively linked to proneness to heart disease, but these triglycerides do not come directly from dietary fats; they are made in the liver from any excess sugars that have not been used for energy. The source of these excess sugars is any food containing carbohydrates, particularly refined sugar and white flour.

Fatty acids are classified in the following way:

- **Saturated:** A fatty acid is saturated when all available carbon bonds are occupied by a hydrogen atom. They are highly stable, because all the carbon-atom linkages are filled—or saturated—with hydrogen. This means that they do not normally go rancid, even when heated for cooking purposes. They are straight in form and hence pack together easily, so that they form a solid or semisolid fat at room temperature. Saturated fatty acids are found mostly in animal fats and tropical oils, and your body also makes them from carbohydrates.

- **Monounsaturated:** Monounsaturated fatty acids have one double bond in the form of two carbon atoms double-bonded to each other and therefore lack two hydrogen atoms. Your body makes monounsaturated fatty acids from saturated fatty acids and uses them in many ways. Monounsaturated fats have a kink or bend at the position of the double bond so that they do not pack together as easily as saturated fats and therefore tend to be liquid at room temperature. Like saturated fats, however, they are relatively stable. They do not go rancid easily and hence can be used in cooking. The monounsaturated fatty acid most commonly found in our food is oleic acid, the main component of olive oil as well as the oils from almonds, pecans, cashews, peanuts and avocados.

- **Polyunsaturated:** Polyunsaturated fatty acids have two or more pairs of double bonds and therefore lack four or more hydrogen atoms. The two polyunsaturated fatty acids found most frequently in our foods are double unsaturated linoleic acid, with two double bonds—also called omega-6; and triple unsaturated linolenic acid, with three double bonds—also called omega-3. (The omega number indicates the position of the first double bond.) Your body cannot make these fatty acids and hence they are called "essential." We must obtain our essential fatty acids or EFAs from the foods we eat. Polyunsaturated fatty acids have kinks or turns at the position of the double bond and hence do not pack together easily. They remain liquid, even when refrigerated. The unpaired electrons at the double bonds make these oils highly reactive. They go rancid easily, particularly omega-3 linolenic acid, and must be treated with care. Polyunsaturated oils should never be heated or used in cooking. In nature, polyunsaturated fatty acids are usually found in the *cis* form, which means that both hydrogen atoms at the double bond are on the same side.

All fats and oils, whether of vegetable or animal origin, are some combination of saturated fatty acids, monounsaturated fatty acids and polyunsaturated linoleic acid and linolenic acid. In general, animal fats such as butter, lard and tallow contain about 40-60 percent saturated fat and are solid at room temperature. Vegetable oils from northern climates contain a preponderance of polyunsaturated fatty acids and are liquid at room temperature. But vegetable oils from the tropics are highly saturated. Coconut oil, for example, is 92 percent saturated. These fats are liquid in the tropics but hard as butter in northern climates. Vegetable oils are more saturated in tropical regions because the increased saturation helps maintain stiffness in plant leaves. Olive oil with its preponderance of oleic acid is the product of a temperate climate. It is liquid at warm temperatures but hardens when refrigerated.

Researchers classify fatty acids not only according to their degree of saturation but also by their length.

- **Short-chain** fatty acids have four to six carbon atoms. These fats are always saturated. Four-carbon butyric acid is found mostly in butterfat from cows, and six-carbon capric acid is found mostly in butterfat from goats. These fatty acids have antimicrobial properties—that is, they protect us from viruses, yeasts and pathogenic bacteria in the gut. They do not need to be acted on by the bile salts but are directly absorbed for quick energy. For this reason, they are less likely to cause weight gain than olive oil or commercial vegetable oils.[27] Short-chain fatty acids also contribute to the health of the immune system.[28]

- **Medium-chain** fatty acids have eight to twelve carbon atoms and are found mostly in butterfat and tropical oils. Like the short-chain fatty acids, these fats have antimicrobial properties, are absorbed directly for quick energy, and contribute to the health of the immune system.

- **Long-chain** fatty acids have from 14 to 18 carbon atoms and can be either saturated, monounsaturated or polyunsaturated. Stearic acid is an 18-carbon saturated fatty acid found chiefly in beef and mutton tallows. Oleic acid is an 18-carbon monounsaturated fat which is the chief component of olive oil. Another monounsaturated fatty acid is the 16-carbon palmitoleic acid which has strong antimicrobial properties. It is found almost exclusively in animal fats. The two essential fatty acids are also long chain, each 18 carbons in length. Another important long-chain fatty acid is gamma-linolenic acid (GLA) which has 18 carbons and three double bonds. It is found in evening primrose, borage and black currant oils. A healthy body can make GLA out of omega-6 linoleic acid. GLA is used in the production of substances called prostaglandins, localized tissue hormones that regulate many processes at the cellular level.

- **Very-long-chain** fatty acids have 20 to 24 carbon atoms. They tend to be highly unsaturated, with four, five or six double bonds. Some people can make these fatty acids from EFAs, but others, particularly those whose ancestors ate a lot of fish, lack enzymes to produce them. These "obligate carnivores" must obtain elongated fatty acids from animal foods like organ meats, egg yolks, butter and fish oils. The most important very-long-chain fatty acids are dihomo-gamma-linolenic acid (DGLA) with 20 carbons and three double bonds, arachidonic acid (AA) with 20 carbons and four double bonds, eicosapentaenoic acid (EPA) with 20 carbons and five double bonds, and docosahexaenoic acid (DHA) with 22 carbons and six double bonds. All of these except DHA are used in the production of prostaglandins. In addition, AA and DHA play important roles in the function of the nervous system.[29]

Politically correct dietary gurus tell us that polyunsaturated oils are good for us and that saturated fats cause cancer and heart disease. Such misinformation about the relative virtues of saturated fats versus polyunsaturated oils has caused profound changes in western eating habits. At the turn of the century, most of the fatty acids in the diet were either saturated or monounsaturated, primarily from butter, lard, tallows, coconut oil and small amounts of olive oil. Today most of the fats in the diet are polyunsaturated, primarily from vegetable oils derived from soy, as well as from corn, safflower and canola.

Modern diets can contain as much as 30 percent of calories as polyunsaturated oils, but scientific research indicates that this amount is far too high. The best evidence indicates that our intake of polyunsaturates should not be much greater than 4 percent of the caloric total, in approximate proportions of 1.5 percent omega-3 linolenic acid and 2.5 percent omega-6 linoleic acid.[30] Consumption in this range is found in native populations in temperate and tropical regions whose intake of polyunsaturated fatty acids comes from the small amounts found in legumes, grains, nuts, green vegetables, fish, olive oil and animal fats—not from commercial vegetable oils.

Excess consumption of polyunsaturated oils has been shown to contribute to a large number of disease conditions including increased cancer and heart disease, immune system dysfunction, damage to the liver, reproductive organs and lungs, digestive disorders, depressed learning ability, impaired growth, and weight gain.[31]

One reason the polyunsaturates cause so many health problems is that they tend to become oxidized or rancid when subjected to heat, oxygen and moisture as in cooking and processing. Rancid oils are characterized by free radicals—that is, single atoms or clusters with an unpaired electron in an outer orbit. These compounds are extremely reactive chemically. They have been characterized as "marauders" in the body for they attack cell membranes and red blood cells, causing damage in DNA/RNA strands that can trigger mutations in tissue, blood vessels and skin. Free radical damage to the skin causes wrinkles and premature aging, free radical damage to the tissues and organs sets the stage for tumors, and free radical damage in the blood vessels initiates the buildup of plaque. Is it any wonder that tests and studies have repeatedly shown a high correlation between cancer and heart disease with the consumption of polyunsaturates?[32] New evidence links exposure to free radicals with premature aging, with autoimmune diseases such as arthritis and with Parkinson's disease, Lou Gehrig's disease, Alzheimer's and cataracts.[33]

Problems associated with an excess of polyunsaturates are exacerbated by the fact that most polyunsaturates in commercial vegetable oils are in the form of double unsaturated omega-6 linoleic acid, with very little of vital triple unsaturated omega-3 linolenic acid. Recent research has revealed that too much omega-6 in the diet creates an imbalance that can interfere with production of important prostaglandins.[34] This disruption can result in increased tendency to form blood clots and to inflammation, high blood pressure, irritation of the digestive tract, depressed immune function, sterility, cell proliferation, cancer and weight gain.[35]

A number of researchers have argued that along with a surfeit of omega-6 fatty acids, the American diet is deficient in the more unsaturated omega-3 linolenic acid. This fatty acid is necessary for cell oxidation, for metabolizing important sulphur-containing amino acids and for maintaining proper balance in prostaglandin production. Deficiencies have been associated with asthma, heart disease and learning deficiencies.[36] Most commercial vegetable oils contain very little omega-3 linolenic acid and large amounts of the omega-6 linoleic acid. In addition, modern agricultural and industrial practices have reduced the amount of omega-3 fatty acids in commercially available vegetables, eggs, fish and meat. For example, organic eggs from hens allowed to feed on insects and green plants can contain omega-6 and omega-3 fatty acids in the beneficial ratio of approximately one-to-one, but commercial supermarket eggs from hens fed mostly grain can contain as much as nineteen times more omega-6 than omega-3![37]

The demonized saturated fats—which Americans are trying to avoid—are *not* the cause of our modern diseases. In fact, they play many important roles in the body chemistry:

- Saturated fatty acids constitute at least 50 percent of the cell membranes, giving them necessary stiffness and integrity so they can function properly.

- They play a vital role in the health of our bones. For calcium to be effectively incorporated into the skeletal structure, at least 50 percent of the dietary fats should be saturated.[38]

- They lower Lp(a), a substance in the blood that indicates proneness to heart disease.[39]

- They protect the liver from alcohol and other toxins, such as Tylenol.[40]

- They enhance the immune system.[41]

- They are needed for the proper utilization of essential fatty acids. Elongated omega-3 fatty acids are better retained in the tissues when the diet is rich in saturated fats. [42]

- Saturated 18-carbon stearic acid and 16-carbon palmitic acid are the preferred foods for the heart, which is why the fat around the heart muscle is highly saturated.[43] The heart draws on this reserve of fat in times of stress.

- Short- and medium-chain saturated fatty acids have important antimicrobial properties. They protect us against harmful microorganisms in the digestive tract.

The scientific evidence, honestly evaluated, does not support the assertion that "artery-clogging" saturated fats cause heart disease.[44] Actually, evaluation of the fat in artery clogs reveals that only about 26 percent is saturated. The rest is unsaturated, of which more than half is polyunsaturated.[45]

And what about cholesterol? Here, too, the public has been misinformed. Our blood vessels can become damaged in a number of ways—through irritations caused by free radicals or viruses, or because they are structurally weak—and when this happens, the body's natural healing substance steps in to repair the damage. That substance is cholesterol. Cholesterol is a high-molecular-weight alcohol that is manufactured in the liver and in most human cells. Like saturated fats, the cholesterol we make and consume plays many vital roles:

- Along with saturated fats, cholesterol in the cell membrane gives our cells necessary stiffness and stability. When the diet contains an excess of polyunsaturated fatty acids, these replace saturated fatty acids in the cell membrane, so that the cell walls actually become flabby. When this happens, cholesterol from the blood is "driven" into the tissues to give them structural integrity. This is why serum cholesterol levels may go down temporarily when we replace saturated fats with polyunsaturated oils in the diet.[46]

- Cholesterol acts as a precursor to vital corticosteroids, hormones that help us deal with stress and protect the body against heart disease and cancer; and to the sex hormones like androgen, testosterone, estrogen and progesterone.

- Cholesterol is a precursor to vitamin D, a vital fat-soluble vitamin needed for healthy bones and nervous system, proper growth, mineral metabolism, muscle tone, insulin production, reproduction and immune system function.

- The bile salts are made from cholesterol. Bile is vital for digestion and assimilation of dietary fats.

- Recent research shows that cholesterol acts as an antioxidant.[47] This is the likely explanation for the fact that cholesterol levels go up with age. As an antioxidant, cholesterol protects us against free radical damage that leads to heart disease and cancer.

- Cholesterol is needed for proper function of serotonin receptors in the brain.[48] Serotonin is the body's natural "feel-good" chemical. Low cholesterol levels have been linked to aggressive and violent behavior, depression and suicidal tendencies.

- Mother's milk is especially rich in cholesterol and contains a special enzyme that helps the baby utilize this nutrient. Babies and children need cholesterol-rich foods throughout their growing years to ensure proper development of the brain and nervous system.

- Dietary cholesterol plays an important role in maintaining the health of the intestinal wall.[49] This is why low-cholesterol vegetarian diets can lead to leaky gut syndrome and other intestinal disorders.

Cholesterol is not the cause of heart disease but rather a potent antioxidant weapon against free radicals in the blood, and a repair substance that helps heal arterial damage (although the arterial plaques themselves contain very little cholesterol). However, like fats, cholesterol may be damaged by exposure to heat and oxygen. This damaged or oxidized cholesterol seems to promote both injury to the arterial cells as well as pathological buildup of plaque in the arteries.[50] Damaged cholesterol is found in powdered eggs, in powdered milk (added to reduced-fat milks to give them body) and in meats and fats that have been heated to high temperatures in frying and other high-temperature processes.

High serum cholesterol levels often indicate that the body needs cholesterol to protect itself from high levels of altered, free radical-containing fats. Just as a large police force is needed in a locality where crime occurs frequently, so cholesterol is needed in a poorly nourished body to protect the individual from a tendency to heart disease and cancer. Blaming coronary heart disease on cholesterol is like blaming the police for murder and theft in a high crime area.

Poor thyroid function (hypothyroidism) will often result in high cholesterol levels. When thyroid function is poor, usually due to a diet high in sugar and low in usable iodine, fat-soluble vitamins and other nutrients, the body floods the blood with cholesterol as an adaptive and protective mechanism, providing a superabundance of materials needed to heal tissues and produce protective steroids. Hypothyroid individuals are particularly susceptible to infections, heart disease and cancer.[51]

The cause of heart disease is not animal fats and cholesterol but rather a number of factors inherent in modern diets, including excess consumption of vegetable oils and hydrogenated fats; excess consumption of refined carbohydrates in the form of sugar and white flour; mineral deficiencies, particularly low levels of protective magnesium and iodine; deficiencies of vitamins, particularly of vitamin A, C and D, needed for the integrity of the blood vessel walls, and of antioxidants like selenium and vitamin E, which protect us from free radicals; and, finally, the disappearance of antimicrobial fats from the food supply, namely, animal fats and tropical oils.[52] These once protected us against the kinds of viruses and bacteria that have been associated with the onset of pathogenic plaque leading to heart disease.

While serum cholesterol levels do not provide an accurate indication of future heart disease, high levels of a substance called homocysteine has been positively correlated with pathological buildup of plaque in the arteries and the tendency to form clots—a deadly combination. Folic acid, vitamin B_6, vitamin B_{12} and choline are nutrients that lower serum homocysteine levels.[53] These nutrients are found mostly in animal foods.

Prevention of heart disease will not be achieved with the current focus on lowering cholesterol—either by drugs or diet—but by consuming a diet that provides animal foods rich in protective fats and vitamins B_6 and B_{12}; by bolstering thyroid function through daily use of natural sea salt, a good source of usable iodine; by avoiding vitamin and mineral deficiencies that make the artery walls more prone to ruptures and the buildup of plaque; by including antimicrobial fats in the diet; and by eliminating processed foods containing refined carbohydrates, oxidized cholesterol and free-radical-containing vegetable oils that cause the body to need constant repair.

It is important to understand that, of all substances ingested by the body, it is polyunsaturated oils that are rendered most dangerous by food processing, especially unstable omega-3 linolenic acid. Consider the following processes inflicted upon naturally occurring fatty acids before they appear on our tables:

    Extraction: Oils naturally occurring in fruits, nuts and seeds must first be extracted. In the old days this extraction was achieved by slow-moving stone presses. But oils processed in large factories are obtained by crushing the oil-bearing seeds and heating them to 230 degrees Farenheit. The oil is then squeezed out at pressures from 10 to 20 tons per inch, thereby generating more heat. During this process the oils are exposed to damaging light and oxygen. In order to extract the last 10 percent of the oil from crushed seeds, processors treat the pulp with one of a number of solvents—usually hexane. The solvent is then boiled off, although up to 100 parts per million may remain in the oil. Such solvents, themselves toxic, also retain the toxic pesticides adhering to seeds and grains before processing begins.

High-temperature processing causes the weak carbon bonds of unsaturated fatty acids, especially triple unsaturated linolenic acid, to break apart, thereby creating dangerous free radicals. In addition, antioxidants, such as fat-soluble vitamin E, which protect the body from the ravages of free radicals, are neutralized or destroyed by high temperatures and pressures. BHT and BHA, both suspected of causing cancer and brain damage, are often added to these oils to replace vitamin E and other natural preservatives destroyed by heat.

There *is* a safe modern technique for extraction that drills into the seeds and extracts the oil and its precious cargo of antioxidants under low temperatures, with minimal exposure to light and oxygen. These expeller-expressed, unrefined oils will remain fresh for a long time if stored in the refrigerator in dark bottles. Extra virgin olive oil is produced by crushing olives between stone or steel rollers. This process is a gentle one that preserves the integrity of the fatty acids and the numerous natural preservatives in olive oil. If olive oil is packaged in opaque containers, it will retain its freshness and precious store of antioxidants for many years.

Hydrogenation: This is the process that turns polyunsaturates, normally liquid at room temperature, into fats that are solid at room temperature—margarine and shortening. To produce them, manufacturers begin with the cheapest oils—soy, corn, cottonseed or canola, already rancid from the extraction process—and mix them with tiny metal particles—usually nickel oxide. The oil with its nickel catalyst is then subjected to hydrogen gas in a high-pressure, high-temperature reactor. Next, soap-like emulsifiers and starch are squeezed into the mixture to give it a better consistency; the oil is yet again subjected to high temperatures when it is steam-cleaned. This removes its unpleasant odor. Margarine's natural color, an unappetizing grey, is removed by bleach. Dyes and strong flavors must then be added to make it resemble butter. Finally, the mixture is compressed and packaged in blocks or tubs and sold as a health food.

Partially hydrogenated margarines and shortenings are even worse for you than the highly refined vegetable oils from which they are made because of chemical changes that occur during the hydrogenation process. Under high temperatures, the nickel catalyst causes the hydrogen atoms to change position on the fatty acid chain. Before hydrogenation, pairs of hydrogen atoms occur together on the chain, causing the chain to bend slightly and creating a concentration of electrons at the site of the double bond. This is called the *cis* formation, the configuration most commonly found in nature. With hydrogenation, one hydrogen atom of the pair is moved to the other side so that the molecule straightens. This is called the *trans* formation, rarely found in nature. Most of these man-made *trans* fats are toxins to the body, but unfortunately your digestive system does not recognize them as such. Instead of eliminating them, your body incorporates *trans* fats into the cell membranes as though they were *cis* fats—your cells actually become partially hydrogenated! Once in place, *trans* fatty acids wreak havoc with cell metabolism because chemical reactions can take place only when electrons in the cell membranes are in certain arrangements or patterns, which the hydrogenation process has disturbed.

During the 1940s, researchers found a strong correlation between cancer and the consumption of fat—the fats used were hydrogenated fats although the results were presented as though the culprit were saturated fats.[54] In fact, until recently saturated fats were usually lumped together with *trans* fats in the various US data bases that researchers use to correlate dietary trends with disease conditions.[55] Thus, natural saturated fats were tarred with the black brush of unnatural hydrogenated vegetable oils.

Altered partially hydrogenated fats made from vegetable oils actually block utilization of essential fatty acids, causing many deleterious effects including sexual dysfunction, increased blood cholesterol and paralysis of the immune system.[56] Consumption of hydrogenated fats is associated with a host of other serious diseases, not only cancer but also atherosclerosis, diabetes, obesity, immune system dysfunction, low-birth-weight babies, birth defects, decreased visual acuity, sterility, difficulty in lactation and problems with bones and tendons.[57] Yet hydrogenated fats continue to be promoted as health foods. The popularity of margarine and shortening over butter represents a triumph of advertising duplicity over common sense. Your best defense is to avoid them like the plague.

❧ **Homogenization:** This is the process whereby the fat particles of cream are strained through tiny pores under great pressure. The resulting fat particles are so small that they stay in suspension rather than rise to the top of the milk. This makes the fat and cholesterol more susceptible to rancidity and oxidation, and some research indicates that homogenized fats may contribute to heart disease.[58]

The media's constant attack on saturated fats is extremely suspect. Research does not support the claim that butter causes chronic high cholesterol values—although some studies show that butter consumption causes a small, temporary rise. In fact, stearic acid, the main component of beef fat, actually lowers cholesterol.[59] Margarine, on the other hand, provokes chronic high levels of cholesterol and has been linked to both heart disease and cancer.[60] The new soft margarines or tub spreads, while lower in hydrogenated fats, are still produced from rancid vegetable oils and contain many additives.

The Diet Dictocrats have succeeded in convincing Americans that butter is dangerous, when in fact it is a valued component of many traditional diets and a source of the following nutrients:

❧ **Fat-Soluble Vitamins:** These include true vitamin A or retinol, vitamin D, vitamin K and vitamin E as well as all their naturally occurring cofactors needed to provide maximum benefit. Butter is America's best source of these important nutrients. In fact, vitamin A is more easily absorbed and utilized from butter than from other sources.[61] The fat-soluble vitamins occur in large amounts only when the butter comes from cows eating green grass.

When Dr. Weston Price studied isolated traditional peoples around the world, he found that butter was a staple in many native diets. (He did not find any isolated peoples who consumed polyunsaturated oils.) The groups he studied particularly valued the deep yellow butter produced by cows feeding on rapidly growing green grass. Their natural intuition told them that its life-giving qualities were especially beneficial for children and expectant mothers. When Dr. Price analyzed this deep yellow butter he found that it was exceptionally high in all fat-soluble vitamins, particularly vitamin A. He called these vitamins "catalysts" or "activators." Without them, according to Dr. Price, we are not able to utilize the minerals we ingest, no matter how abundant they may be in our diets. He also believed the fat-soluble vitamins to be necessary for absorption of the water-soluble vitamins. Vitamins A and D are essential for growth, for healthy bones, for proper development of the brain and nervous systems and for normal sexual development. Many studies have shown the importance of butterfat for reproduction; its absence results in "nutritional castration," the failure to bring out male and female sexual characteristics. As butter consumption in America has declined, sterility rates and problems with sexual development have increased. In calves, butter substitutes are unable to promote growth or sustain reproduction.[62]

Not all the societies Dr. Price studied ate butter; but all the groups he observed went to great lengths to obtain foods high in fat-soluble vitamins—fish, shellfish, fish eggs, organ meats, blubber of sea animals and insects. Without knowing the names of the vitamins contained in these foods, isolated traditional societies recognized their importance in the diet and liberally ate animal products containing them. They rightly believed such foods to be necessary for fertility and the optimum development of children. Dr. Price analyzed the nutrient content of native diets and found that they consistently provided about *ten* times more fat soluble vitamins than the American diet of the 1930s. This ratio is probably more extreme today as Americans have deliberately reduced animal-fat consumption. Dr. Price realized that these fat-soluble vitamins promoted the beautiful bone structure, wide palate, flawless uncrowded teeth and handsome, well-proportioned faces that characterized members of isolated traditional groups. American children in general do not eat fish or organ meats, at least not to any great extent, and blubber and insects are not a part of the western diet; many will not eat eggs. The only good source of fat-soluble vitamins in the American diet, one sure to be eaten, is butterfat. Butter added to vegetables and spread on bread, and cream added to soups and sauces, ensure proper assimilation of the minerals and water-soluble vitamins in vegetables, grains and meat.

The Wulzen Factor: Called the "antistiffness" factor, this compound is present in raw animal fat. Researcher Rosalind Wulzen discovered that this substance protects humans and animals from calcification of the joints—degenerative arthritis. It also protects against hardening of the arteries, cataracts and calcification of the pineal gland.[63] Calves fed pasteurized milk or skim milk develop joint stiffness and do not thrive. Their symptoms are reversed when raw butterfat is added to the diet. Pasteurization destroys the Wulzen factor—it is present only in *raw* butter, cream and whole milk.

The Price Factor or Activator X: Discovered by Dr. Price, Activator X is a powerful catalyst which, like vitamins A and D, helps the body absorb and utilize minerals. It is found in organ meats from grazing animals and some seafood. Butter can be an especially rich source of Activator X when it comes from cows eating rapidly growing grass in the spring and fall seasons. It disappears in cows fed cottonseed meal, high protein soy-based feeds or even hay.[64] Fortunately, Activator X is not destroyed by pasteurization.

Arachidonic Acid: A 20-carbon polyunsaturate containing four double bonds, found in small amounts only in animal fats. Arachidonic acid (AA) plays a role in the function of the brain, is a vital component of the cell membranes and is a precursor to important prostaglandins. Some dietary gurus warn against eating foods rich in AA, claiming that it contributes to the production of "bad" prostaglandins, ones that cause inflammation. But prostaglandins that counteract inflammation are also made from AA.

Short- and Medium-Chain Fatty Acids: Butter contains about 12-15 percent short- and medium-chain fatty acids. This type of saturated fat does not need to be emulsified by bile salts but is absorbed directly from the small intestine to the liver, where it is converted into quick energy. These fatty acids also have antimicrobial, antitumor and immune-system-supporting properties, especially 12-carbon lauric acid, a medium-chain fatty acid not found in other animal fats. Highly protective lauric acid should be called a conditionally essential fatty acid because it is made only by the mammary gland and not in the liver like other saturated fats.[65] We must obtain it from one of two dietary sources—small amounts in butterfat or large amounts in coconut oil. Four-carbon butyric acid is practically unique to butter. It has antifungal properties as well as antitumor effects.[66]

Omega-6 and Omega-3 Essential Fatty Acids: These occur in butter in small but nearly equal amounts. This excellent balance between linoleic and linolenic acid prevents the kind of problems associated with overconsumption of omega-6 fatty acids.

Conjugated Linoleic Acid (CLA): Butter from pasture-fed cows also contains a form of rearranged linoleic acid called CLA, which has strong anticancer properties. It also encourages the buildup of muscle and prevents weight gain. CLA disappears when cows are fed even small amounts of grain or processed feed.[67]

Lecithin: Lecithin is a natural component of butter that assists in the proper assimilation and metabolization of cholesterol and other fat constituents.

Cholesterol: Mother's milk is high in cholesterol because it is essential for growth and development. Cholesterol is also needed to produce a variety of steroids that protect against cancer, heart disease and mental illness.

Glycosphingolipids: This type of fat protects against gastrointestinal infections, especially in the very young and the elderly. For this reason, children who drink skimmed milk have diarrhea at rates three to five times greater than children who drink whole milk.[68]

Trace Minerals: Many trace minerals are incorporated into the fat globule membrane of butterfat, including manganese, zinc, chromium and iodine. In mountainous areas far from the sea, iodine in butter protects against goiter. Butter is extremely rich in selenium, a trace mineral with antioxidant properties, containing more per gram than herring or wheat germ.

One frequently voiced objection to the consumption of butter and other animal fats is that they tend to accumulate environmental poisons. Fat-soluble poisons such as DDT do accumulate in fats; but water-soluble poisons, such as antibiotics and growth hormones, accumulate in the water fraction of milk and meats. Vegetables and grains also accumulate poisons. The average plant crop receives ten applications of pesticides—from seed to storage—while cows generally graze on pasture that is unsprayed. Aflatoxin, a fungus that grows on grain, is one of the most powerful carcinogens known. It is correct to assume that all of our foods, whether of vegetable or animal origin, may be contaminated. The solution to environmental poisons is not to eliminate animal fats—so essential to growth, reproduction and overall health—but to seek out organic meats and butter from pasture-fed cows, as well as organic vegetables and grains. These are becoming increasingly available in health food stores and supermarkets and through mail order and cooperatives.

Before leaving this complex but vital subject of fats, it is worthwhile examining the composition of other dietary fats and oils in order to determine their usefulness and appropriateness in food preparation:

- **Duck and Goose Fat** are semisolid at room temperature, containing about 35 percent saturated fat, 52 percent monounsaturated fat (including small amounts of antimicrobial palmitoleic acid) and about 13 percent polyunsaturated fat. The proportion of omega-6 to omega-3 fatty acids depends on what the birds have eaten. Duck and goose fat are quite stable and are highly prized in Europe for frying potatoes.

- **Chicken Fat** is about 31 percent saturated, 49 percent monounsaturated (including moderate amounts of antimicrobial palmitoleic acid) and 20 percent polyunsaturated, most of which is omega-6 linoleic acid, although the amount of omega-3 can be raised by feeding chickens flax or fish meal, or allowing them to range free and eat insects. Although widely used for frying in kosher kitchens, it is inferior to duck and goose fat, which were traditionally preferred to chicken fat in Jewish cooking.

- **Lard** or pork fat is about 40 percent saturated, 48 percent monounsaturated (including small amounts of antimicrobial palmitoleic acid) and 12 percent polyunsaturated. Like the fat of birds, the amount of omega-6 and omega-3 fatty acids in lard will vary according to the diet of the pigs. In the tropics, lard may also be a source of lauric acid if the pigs have eaten coconuts. Like duck and goose fat, lard is stable and a preferred fat for frying. It was widely used in America at the turn of the century. It is an excellent source of vitamin D, especially in third-world countries where other animal foods are likely to be expensive. Some researchers believe that pork products should be avoided because they may contribute to cancer. Others suggest that only pork *meat* presents a problem and that pig *fat* in the form of lard is safe and healthy.

- **Beef and Mutton Tallows** are 50-55 percent saturated, about 40 percent monounsaturated and contain small amounts of the polyunsaturates, usually less than 3 percent. Suet, which is the fat from the cavity of the animal, is 70-80 percent saturated. Suet and tallow are very stable fats and can be used for frying. Traditional cultures valued these fats for their health benefits. They are a good source of antimicrobial palmitoleic acid.

- **Olive Oil** contains 75 percent oleic acid, the stable monounsaturated fat, along with 13 percent saturated fat, 10 percent omega-6 linoleic acid and 2 percent omega-3 linolenic acid. The high percentage of oleic acid makes olive oil ideal for salads and for cooking at moderate temperatures. Extra virgin olive oil is also rich in antioxidants. It should be cloudy, indicating that it has not been filtered, and have a golden yellow color, indicating that it is made from fully ripened olives. Olive oil has withstood the test of time; it is the safest vegetable oil you can use, but don't overdo. The longer-chain fatty acids found in olive oil are more likely to contribute to the buildup of body fat than the short- and medium-chain fatty acids found in butter and coconut oil.

- **Peanut Oil** contains 48 percent oleic acid, 18 percent saturated fat and 34 percent omega-6 linoleic acid. Like olive oil, peanut oil is relatively stable and therefore appropriate for stir-frys on occasion. But the high percentage of omega-6 presents a potential danger, so use of peanut oil should be strictly limited.

- **Sesame Oil** contains 42 percent oleic acid, 15 percent saturated fat, and 43 percent omega-6 linoleic acid. Sesame oil is similar in composition to peanut oil. It can be used for frying because it contains unique antioxidants that are not destroyed by heat. However, the high percentage of omega-6 militates against exclusive use.

- **Safflower, Corn, Sunflower, Soybean and Cottonseed Oils** all contain over 50 percent omega-6 and, except for soybean oil, only minimal amounts of omega-3. Safflower oil contains almost 80 percent omega-6. Research continues to accumulate on the dangers of excess omega-6 oils in the diet, whether rancid or not. Use of these oils should be strictly limited. They should never be consumed after they have been heated, as in cooking, frying or baking. High oleic safflower and sunflower oils, produced from hybrid plants, have a composition similar to olive oil, namely, high amounts of oleic acid and only small amounts of polyunsaturated fatty acids and thus are more stable than traditional varieties. However, it is difficult to find truly cold-pressed versions of these oils.

- **Canola Oil** contains 5 percent saturated fat, 57 percent oleic acid, 23 percent omega-6 and 10-15 percent omega-3. The newest oil on the market, canola oil was developed from the rape seed, a member of the mustard family. Rape seed is considered unsuited to human consumption because it contains a long-chain fatty acid called erucic acid, which under some circumstances is associated with fibrotic heart lesions. Canola oil was bred to contain little if any erucic acid and has drawn the attention of nutritionists because of its high oleic-acid content. But there are some indications that canola oil presents dangers of its own. It has a high sulphur content and goes rancid easily. Baked goods made with canola oil develop mold very quickly. During the deodorizing process, the omega-3 fatty acids of processed canola oil are transformed into *trans* fatty acids, similar to those in margarine and possibly more dangerous.[69] A recent study indicates that "heart healthy" canola oil actually creates a deficiency of vitamin E, a vitamin required for a healthy cardiovascular system.[70] Other studies indicate that even low-erucic-acid canola oil causes heart lesions, particularly when the diet is also low in saturated fat.[71]

❧ **Flax Seed Oil** contains 9 percent saturated fatty acids, 18 percent oleic acid, 16 percent omega-6 and 57 percent omega-3. With its extremely high omega-3 content, flax seed oil provides a remedy for the omega-6/omega-3 imbalance so prevalent in America today. Not surprisingly, Scandinavian folk lore values flax seed oil as a health food. New extraction and bottling methods have minimized rancidity problems. It should always be kept refrigerated, never heated, and consumed in *small* amounts in salad dressings and spreads.

❧ **Tropical Oils** are more saturated than other vegetable oils. Palm oil is about 50 percent saturated, with 41 percent oleic acid and about 9 percent linoleic acid. Coconut oil is 92 percent saturated with over two-thirds of the saturated fat as medium-chain fatty acids (often called medium-chain triglycerides). Of particular interest is lauric acid, found in large quantities in both coconut oil and in mother's milk. This fatty acid has strong antifungal and antimicrobial properties. Coconut oil protects tropical populations from bacteria and fungus so prevalent in their food supply; as third-world nations in tropical areas have switched to polyunsaturated vegetable oils, the incidence of intestinal disorders and immune deficiency diseases has increased. Because coconut oil contains lauric acid, it is often used in baby formulas. Palm kernel oil, used primarily in candy coatings, also contains high levels of lauric acid. These oils are stable and can be kept at room temperature for many months without becoming rancid. Highly saturated tropical oils do not contribute to heart disease but have nourished healthy populations for millennia.[72] It is a shame we do not use these oils for cooking and baking—the bad rap they have received is the result of intense lobbying by the domestic vegetable oil industry.[73] Red palm oil has a strong taste that most will find disagreeable—although it is used extensively throughout Africa—but clarified palm oil, which is tasteless and white in color, was formerly used as shortening and in the production of commercial French fries, while coconut oil was used in cookies, crackers and pastries. The saturated fat scare has forced manufacturers to abandon these safe and healthy oils in favor of hydrogenated soybean, corn, canola and cottonseed oils.

In summary, our choice of fats and oils is one of extreme importance. Most people, especially infants and growing children, benefit from *more* fat in the diet rather than less. But the fats we eat must be chosen with care. Avoid all processed foods containing newfangled hydrogenated fats and polyunsaturated oils. Instead, use traditional vegetable oils like extra virgin olive oil and small amounts of unrefined flax seed oil. Acquaint yourself with the merits of coconut oil for baking and with animal fats for occasional frying. Eat egg yolks and other animal fats with the proteins to which they are attached. And, finally, use as much good quality butter as you like, with the happy assurance that it is a wholesome—indeed, an essential—food for you and your whole family.

Organic butter, extra virgin olive oil, and expeller-expressed flax oil in opaque containers are available in health food stores and gourmet markets. Edible coconut oil can be found in Indian and Caribbean markets. (See Sources for good quality fats and oils by mail order.)

CARBOHYDRATES

All green plants produce carbohydrates—starch and sugar—in their leaves through the action of sunlight, carbon dioxide and water. Sugar comes in many forms. Sucrose, or common table sugar, is a disaccharide which breaks down during digestion into the simple sugars glucose and fructose. Glucose is the primary sugar in the blood; fructose is the primary sugar in fruit and high fructose corn syrup. Other common disaccharides are maltose (malt sugar) and lactose (milk sugar). Chemical terms ending in -*ose* indicate a sugar.

Complex sugars are longer-chain sugars composed of fructose and other simple sugars. Relatively short complex sugars called stachynose and raffinose occur in beans and other legumes; longer ones occur in certain plant foods like the Jerusalem artichoke and seaweed. Unlike herbivorous animals, humans lack digestive enzymes needed to break down these sugars into their simple components. However, some individuals have certain beneficial flora in the large intestine that break down complex sugars with innocuous carbon dioxide as a by-product; other people have flora in the large bowel that produce embarrassing methane as a by-product. Cooking also breaks down these complex sugars to a certain extent.

In contrast, most humans are able to digest starch, a polysaccharide composed exclusively of glucose molecules. During the process of cooking, chewing and especially through prolonged enzymatic action during digestion, the starches are broken into separate glucose molecules. Glucose enters the bloodstream via the small intestine where it supplies energy wherever the body needs it—for accomplishing cellular processes, for thinking or for moving an arm or a leg. As the body uses glucose for all its processes, it can be said that sugar is essential to life. But the body does not need to ingest sugar, or even large quantities of carbohydrates, to produce it. Certain isolated traditional groups, such as the Eskimos, the pre-Columbian plains Indians and the medieval inhabitants of Greenland, subsisted on diets composed almost entirely of animal products—protein and fats. Examination of the skulls of these groups shows a virtual absence of tooth decay, indicative of a high general level of health on a diet almost completely devoid of carbohydrate foods.

Only during the last century has man's diet included a high percentage of *refined* carbohydrates. Our ancestors ate fruits and grains in their whole, unrefined state. In nature, sugars and carbohydrates—the energy providers—are linked together with vitamins, minerals, enzymes, protein, fat and fiber—the bodybuilding and digestion-regulating components of the diet. In whole form, sugars and starches support life, but refined carbohydrates are inimical to life because they are devoid of bodybuilding elements. Digestion of refined carbohydrates calls on the body's own store of vitamins, minerals and enzymes for proper metabolization. When B vitamins are absent, for example, the breakdown of carbohydrates cannot take place, yet most B vitamins are removed during the refining process.

The refining process strips grains, vegetables and fruits of both their vitamin and mineral components. Refined carbohydrates have been called "empty" calories. "Negative" calories is a more appropriate term because consumption of refined calories depletes the body's precious reserves. Consumption of sugar and white flour may be likened to drawing on a savings account. If continued withdrawals are made faster than new funds are put in, the account will eventually become depleted. Some people may go longer than others without overt suffering, but eventually all will feel the effects of this inexorable law. If you were fortunate enough to be born with an excellent constitution, you may be able to eat unlimited quantities of sugar with relative impunity, but your children's or your grandchildren's inheritance will be one of impoverished reserves.

The all-important level of glucose in the blood is regulated by a finely tuned mechanism involving insulin secretions from the pancreas and hormones from several glands, including the adrenal glands and the thyroid. When sugars and starches are eaten in their natural, unrefined form, as part of a meal containing nourishing fats and protein, they are digested slowly and enter the bloodstream at a moderate rate over a period of several hours. If the body goes for a long time without food, this mechanism will call upon reserves stored in the liver. When properly working, this marvelous blood sugar regulation process provides our cells with a steady, even supply of glucose. The body is kept on an even keel, so to speak, both physically and emotionally.

But when we consume *refined* sugars and starches, particularly alone, without fats or protein, they enter the blood stream in a rush, causing a sudden increase in blood sugar. The body's regulation mechanism kicks into high gear, flooding the bloodstream with insulin and other hormones to bring blood sugar levels down to acceptable levels. Repeated onslaughts of sugar will eventually disrupt this finely tuned process, causing some elements to remain in a constant state of activity and others to become worn out and inadequate to do the job. The situation is exacerbated by the fact that a diet high in refined carbohydrates will also be deficient in vitamins, minerals and enzymes, those bodybuilding elements that keep the glands and organs in good repair. When the endocrine system thus becomes disturbed, numerous other pathological conditions soon manifest— degenerative disease, allergies, obesity, alcoholism, drug addiction, depression, learning disabilities and behavioral problems.

Disrupted regulation results in blood sugar that habitually remains either higher or lower than the narrow range under which the body is designed to function. A person with abnormally high blood sugar is a diabetic; a person whose blood sugar regularly drops below normal is hypoglycemic. These two diseases are really two sides of the same coin and both stem from the same cause— excess consumption of refined carbohydrates. The diabetic lives in danger of blindness, gangrene in the limbs, heart disease and diabetic coma. Insulin injections can protect the diabetic from sudden death by coma but, unless the diet improves, cannot halt the progressive deterioration of the cornea, the tissues and the circulatory system. Low blood sugar opens a veritable Pandora's box of symptoms ranging from seizures, depression and unfounded phobias to allergies, headaches and chronic fatigue.

Hypoglycemics are often advised to eat something sweet when they feel the symptoms of low blood sugar, for sugar rushes into the bloodstream and gives a temporary lift. This policy is misguided for several reasons. First, as the calories are empty, the bodybuilding reserves are further depleted. Second, the roller-coaster cycle of high blood sugar, sent too low by a faulty regulating mechanism, is further perpetuated. And finally, the brief period of high blood sugar sets in motion a harmful process called glycation, the bonding of amino acids to sugar molecules when blood-sugar levels are too high. These abnormal proteins are then incorporated into the tissues and can do enormous damage, especially to the long-lived proteins in the lens of the eye and the myelin sheath around the nerves.[74] The collagen of skin, tendons and membranes is also damaged by these glycated proteins. This process takes place in everyone who eats sugar, not just in diabetics.

Strict abstinence from refined sugar and very limited use of refined flour is good advice for everyone. We must remember that these skeletonized products were virtually unknown in the human diet before 1600 and never used in great quantities before the 20th century. Our physical nature is such that we need foods that are whole, not refined and denatured, to grow, prosper and reproduce. As the consumption of sugar has increased, so have all the "civilized" diseases. In 1821, the average sugar intake in America was 10 pounds per person per year; today it is 170 pounds per person, representing over one-fourth the average caloric intake. Another large portion of total calories comes from white flour and refined vegetable oils.[75] This means that less than half the diet must provide all the nutrients to a body that is under constant stress from its intake of sugar, white flour and rancid and hydrogenated vegetable oils. Herein lies the root cause of the vast increase in degenerative diseases that plague modern America.

Until recently, the Diet Dictocrats denied the role of sugar as a cause of disease. Few establishment spokesmen will admit that sugar consumption has anything to do with heart disease, and some have adopted the breathtaking stance that sugar does not cause diabetes. The food industry is not embarassed to jusfity its use of sugar. "If we didn't prefer foods with added sugar, it would not be added," says Dr. Frederick Stare, former chairman of the Department of Nutrition at Harvard University's School of Public Health. "Remember, eating is one of the real pleasures of life. . . for most people, sugar helps other things taste better. . . . Sugar calories are not different from other calories, from calories obtained from protein, starch, fat or alcohol." Harvard's Department of Nutrition receives the bulk of its funding from the food industry, and nothing contributes to the profits of the big processing conglomerates so much as sugar—cheap, easily produced and stored, of infinite shelf life, its sweetness a convenient mask for the flavorless, overprocessed concoctions to which it is added. Sugar is the food processors' best preservative because it blocks various forms of spoilage bacteria by tying up the water in which they grow.

Scientific evidence against sugar has been mounting for decades. As early as 1933, research showed that increased consumption of sugar caused an increase in various disease conditions in school children.[76] Sugar, especially fructose, has been shown to shorten life in numerous animal experiments.[77] Sugar consumption has recently been cited as the root cause of anorexia and eating disorders.[78] In the 1950s, British researcher Yudkin published persuasive findings that excessive use of sugar was associated with the following conditions: release of free fatty acids at the aorta, rise in blood cholesterol, rise in triglycerides, increase in adhesiveness of the blood platelets, increase in blood insulin levels, increase in blood corticosteroid levels, increase in gastric acidity, shrinkage of the pancreas and enlargement of the liver and adrenal glands.[79]

Numerous subsequent studies have positively correlated sugar consumption with heart disease.[80] These results are far more unequivocal than the presumed association of heart disease with saturated fats. Researchers Lopez in the 1960s and Ahrens in the 1970s have repeatedly pointed out the role of sugar as a cause of coronary heart disease, but their work has not received recognition by government agencies or by the press. The food processing industry—America's largest industry—has a tremendous interest in confining this research to scientific publications stored in the basements of our medical libraries. If the public were made aware of the dangers of refined carbohydrate consumption and took steps to reduce it, this powerful industry would shrink to a fraction of its size. The food fabricators don't need animal fats to produce junk food for a profit; but they do need vegetable oils, white flour and sugar.

More plagues than heart disease can be laid at sugar's door. A survey of medical journals in the 1970s produced findings implicating sugar as a causative factor in kidney disease, liver disease, shortened life span, increased desire for coffee and tobacco, atherosclerosis and coronary heart disease.[81] Sugar consumption is associated with hyperactivity, behavior problems, lack of concentration and violent tendencies.[82] Sugar consumption encourages the overgrowth of *candida albicans*, a systemic fungus in the digestive tract, causing it to spread to the respiratory system, tissues and internal organs. Sugar consumption is positively associated with cancer in humans and test animals.[83] Tumors are known to be enormous sugar absorbers. Research indicates that it is the fructose, not the glucose, moiety of sugar that is the most harmful, especially for growing children.[84] Yet the greatest increase in sugar consumption during the last two decades is from high fructose corn syrup used in soft drinks, ketchup and many other fabricated foods aimed at children.

Last but not least, sugar consumption is the cause of bone loss and dental decay. Tooth decay and bone loss occur when the precise ratio of calcium to phosphorus in the blood varies from the normal ratio of four parts phosphorus to ten parts calcium. At this ratio, all blood calcium can be properly utilized. Dr. Melvin Page, a Florida dentist, demonstrated in numerous studies that sugar consumption causes phosphorus levels to drop and calcium to rise.[85] Calcium rises because it is pulled from the teeth and the bones. The drop in phosphorus hinders the absorption of this calcium, making it unusable and therefore toxic. Thus, sugar consumption causes tooth decay not because it promotes bacterial growth in the mouth, as most dentists believe, but because it alters the internal body chemistry.

Orthodox nutritionists admit that sugar causes tooth decay—although they may be mistaken about just why this is so—but their warnings to avoid tooth decay by limiting sweets are disingenuous. Most people would be willing to pay the price for bad teeth as long as they did not have to stop eating sugar. After all, teeth can be repaired or replaced. But poor teeth are always the outward sign of other types of degeneration in the body's interior, degeneration that cannot be repaired in the dentist's chair.

Sweetness in fruits, grains and vegetables is an indication that they are ripe and have reached maximum vitamin and mineral content. The naturally sweet foods from which sugar is extracted—sugar beet, sugar cane and corn—are particularly high in nutrients such as B vitamins, magnesium and chromium. All of these seem to play an important role in the blood sugar regulation mechanism. These nutrients are discarded—or made into animal feed—when the raw product is refined into sugar. Refining strips foods of vital nutrients while concentrating sugars, thus allowing us to fulfill our body's energy requirements without obtaining the nutrients needed for bodybuilding, digestion and repair.

Whole grains provide vitamin E, B vitamins in abundance, and many important minerals, all of which are essential to life. These are also discarded in the refining process. Fiber—indigestible cellulose that plays an important role in digestion and elimination—is also removed. Refined flour is commonly fortified, but this is of little value. Fortification adds a handful of synthetic vitamins and minerals to white flour and polished rice after a host of essential factors have been removed or destroyed. Some of the vitamins added during the fortification process may even be dangerous. Some researchers believe that excess iron from fortified flour can cause tissue damage, and other studies link excess or toxic iron to heart disease.[86] Vitamins B_1 and B_2 added to grains without B_6 lead to imbalances in numerous processes involving B vitamin pathways. The safety of bromating and bleaching agents, almost universally applied to white flour, has never been established.

Moderate use of natural sweeteners is found in many traditional societies. Thus it is perfectly acceptable to satisfy your sweet tooth by eating fully ripened fruit in season and limited amounts of certain natural sweeteners high in vitamins and minerals, such as raw honey, date sugar, dehydrated cane sugar juice (commercially available as Rapadura, made by Rapunzel Corporation) and maple syrup. (See Guide to Natural Sweeteners, page 536.) Avoid all refined sugars including table sugar, so-called raw sugar or brown sugar (both composed of about 96 percent refined sugar), corn syrup, fructose and large amounts of fruit juice.

We recommend the use of a variety of whole grains but with an important caveat. Phosphorus in the bran of whole grains is tied up in a substance called phytic acid. Phytic acid combines with iron, calcium, magnesium, copper and zinc in the intestinal tract, blocking their absorption.[87] Whole grains also contain enzyme inhibitors that can interfere with digestion. Traditional societies usually soak or ferment their grains before eating them, processes that neutralize phytates and enzyme inhibitors and, in effect, predigest grains so that all their nutrients are more available.[88] Sprouting, overnight soaking and old-fashioned sour leavening can accomplish this important predigestion process in our own kitchens. Many people who are allergic to grains will tolerate them well when they are prepared according to these procedures. Proper preparation techniques also help break down complex sugars in legumes, making them more digestible.

Whole grains that have been processed by high heat and pressure to produce puffed wheat, oats and rice are actually quite toxic and have caused rapid death in test animals.[89] We do not recommend rice cakes, a popular snack food. Breakfast cereals that have been slurried and extruded at high temperatures and pressures to make little flakes and shapes should also be avoided. Most, if not all, nutrients are destroyed during processing, and they are very difficult to digest. Studies show that these extruded whole grain preparations can have even more adverse effects on the blood sugar than refined sugar and white flour![90] The process leaves phytic acid intact but destroys phytase, an enzyme that breaks down some of the phytic acid in the digestive tract.

Most grains and legumes available in supermarkets have been treated numerous times with pesticides and other sprays that inhibit mold and vermin. Genetically modified grains contain foreign proteins that are likely to be highly irritating to the digestive tract. It therefore pays to purchase organically or biodynamically grown cereals and legumes. (See Sources.) Grains will be fresher if packaged in cellophane or plastic, rather than taken from open bins.

Most people who have "got religion" about nutrition have learned through experience that sugar and white flour are inimical to good health, and they know how difficult it is to give these things up in a society whose eating habits are based on them. It is relatively easy to replace margarine with butter and refined polyunsaturates with extra virgin olive oil because these fats taste so much better; but sugar and white flour, being mildly to severely addictive, are harder to renounce. Try replacing white flour products with a variety of properly prepared whole grains and limiting sweets to occasional desserts made from natural sweeteners. It may take time, and you will almost certainly have setbacks, but in the end your willpower and persistence will reward you with greatly improved health and stamina.

PROTEINS

Proteins are the building blocks of the animal kingdom. The human body assembles and utilizes about 50,000 different proteins to form organs, nerves, muscles and flesh. Enzymes—the managers and catalysts of all our biochemical processes—are specialized proteins. So are antibodies.

All proteins are combinations of just 22 amino acids, eight of which are "essential" nutrients for humans, meaning that the human body cannot make them. When the essential amino acids are present in the diet, the body can usually build the other "nonessential" amino acids; but if just one essential amino acid is low or missing, the body is unable to synthesize the other proteins it needs, even when overall protein intake is high. Of particular importance to the health of the brain and nervous system are the sulphur-containing amino acids—methionine, cysteine and cystine—found most plentifully in eggs and meat. Some individuals cannot manufacture amino acids considered "nonessential," such as taurine and carnitine, but must obtain them from dietary sources, namely red meat.

Protein is essential for normal growth, for the formation of hormones, for the process of blood clotting and for the formation of milk during lactation. Protein helps regulate the acid-alkaline balance of tissues and blood. When protein is lacking in the diet, there is a tendency for the blood and tissues to become either too acid or too alkaline, depending on the acidity or the alkalinity of the foods we eat. Improper acid-alkaline balance is often a problem among vegetarians.

Just as animal fats are our only sources of vitamins A and D and other bodybuilding factors, so also animal protein is our only source of complete protein. All of the essential amino acids, and many considered "nonessential," are present in animal products. Sources of protein from the vegetable kingdom contain only incomplete protein; that is, they are low in one or more essential amino acids, even when overall protein content is high. The body must ingest all the essential amino acids in order to use any of them. The two best sources of protein in the vegetable kingdom are legumes and cereal grains, but all plant foods are low in tryptophan, cystine and threonine. Legumes, such as beans, peanuts and cashews are high in the amino acid lysine but low in methionine. Cereal grains have the opposite profile. In order to obtain the best possible protein combination from vegetable sources, pulses and grains should be eaten together and combined with at least a small amount of animal protein. Most grain-based cuisines instinctively incorporate this principle. For example, animal products plus corn and beans are staple fare in Mexican cuisine, as are chick peas and whole wheat in the Middle East and rice and soybean products in Asia.

Vegetarianism has recently achieved political correctness, and nutritionists advocating a restriction or complete elimination of animal products garner good reviews in the popular press. Their influence is reflected in the new Food Pyramid with its emphasis on grains; but the scientific evidence, honestly evaluated, argues against relying too heavily on grains and legumes as sources of protein or for severely reducing animal products in the diet.

Our primitive ancestors subsisted on a diet composed largely of meat and fat, augmented with vegetables, fruit, seeds and nuts. Studies of their remains reveal that they had excellent bone structure, heavy musculature and flawless teeth. Agricultural man added milk, grains and legumes to this diet. These foods allowed him to pursue a more comfortable life style than the hunter-gatherer, but at a price. In his studies of isolated "primitive" peoples, Dr. Weston Price found that those whose diets consisted largely of grains and legumes, while far healthier than civilized moderns, had, nevertheless, more caries than those living primarily on meat and fish. Skulls of prehistoric peoples subsisting almost entirely on vegetable foods have teeth containing caries and abscesses and show evidence of bone problems and tuberculosis as well.[91]

A more recent study by Dr. Emmanuel Cheraskin corroborates Dr. Price's observations. He surveyed 1040 dentists and their wives. Those who had the fewest problems and diseases as measured by the Cornell Medical Index had the most protein in their diets.[92] The claim that high-protein diets cause bone loss is supported neither by scientific research nor by anthropological surveys.[93] Inadequate protein intake leads to loss of myocardial muscle and may therefore contribute to coronary heart disease.[94] However, protein cannot be adequately utilized without dietary fats. That is why protein and fats occur together in eggs, milk, fish and meats. A high-protein, lowfat diet can cause many problems including too rapid growth and depletion of vitamin A and vitamin D reserves.[95]

Studies of Mayan remains lead to interesting conclusions about the long-term effects of a diet devoid of animal products. Archeologists found that the average male skeleton was about 165 centimeters during the early period of Mayan civilization, when meat was readily available. During later periods, the height of the average lower class male declined to 157 centimeters—about the height of the average Pygmy. At the same time, the average height of males from the ruling class increased to about 170 centimeters. The lower class subsisted mostly on corn and beans while the ruling classes were able to supplement their diet with small amounts of scarce animal protein.[96] Will such extreme class differentiation divide the American population if it follows the guidelines of the new Food Pyramid—either through ignorance or by necessity?

Vegetarians often claim that animal products shorten life span, but the most cursory look at long-lived ethnic groups proves that this is not the case. Russians from the Caucasus Mountains, an area famous for longevity, eat lots of fatty meat and whole milk products. Studies of Soviet Georgian populations show that those who have the most meat and fat in their diets live the longest.[97] Inhabitants of Vilcabamba in Equador, known for their longevity, consume a variety of animal foods including whole milk and fatty pork. The long-lived people of Hunza consume animal protein in the form of high-fat goat milk products. On the other hand, the vegetarian inhabitants of southern India have one of the shortest life spans in the world.[98]

Not only is it difficult to obtain adequate protein on a diet devoid of animal products, but such a diet often leads to deficiencies in many important minerals as well. This is because a largely vegetarian diet lacks the fat-soluble catalysts needed for mineral absorption. Furthermore, phytates in grains block absorption of calcium, iron, zinc, copper and magnesium. Unless grains are properly prepared to neutralize phytates, the body may be unable to assimilate these minerals. Zinc, iron, calcium and other minerals from animal sources are more easily and readily absorbed. We should not underestimate the dangers of deficiencies in these minerals. The effects of calcium and iron deficiency are well known, those of zinc less so. Even a minor zinc deficiency in pregnant animals results in offspring with deformities, such as club feet, cleft palates, domed skulls and fused and missing ribs. In humans, zinc deficiency can cause learning disabilities and mental retardation. In men, zinc depletion decreases fertility. Man's best source of zinc is animal products, particularly oysters and red meat.

Usable vitamin B_{12} occurs *only* in animal products. The body stores a supply of vitamin B_{12} that can last from two to five years. When this supply is depleted, B_{12} deficiency diseases result. These include pernicious anemia, impaired eyesight, panic attacks, schizophrenia, hallucinations and nervous disorders, such as weakness, loss of balance and numbness in the hands and feet. One study found that a very high percentage of inmates in psychiatric wards suffers from low serum levels of B_{12}.[99] Vitamin B_{12} deficiency has been found in breast-fed infants of strict vegetarians.[100] Fermented soy foods and spirulina contain compounds that resemble B_{12} but these forms are not absorbed by humans because they are not picked up by the "intrinsic factor," a specialized protein secreted in the stomach that allows B_{12} to be assimilated. In fact, the plant forms of B_{12} may even create B_{12} deficiencies.[101] (Viability of the intrinsic factor depends on a number of factors including calcium status, pancreatic enzymes and proper pH in the upper intestine. The ability to assimilate B_{12} frequently declines with age so that many elderly people suffer from B_{12} deficiency even though they continue to eat animal products.)

Because grains and pulses eaten alone cannot supply complete amino acids, vegetarians must take care to balance the two at every meal. Vegetarian diets also tend to be deficient in phosphorus as meat is the principle source of phosphorus for most people. This is another reason that vegetarianism has been linked to tooth decay. Vegetarians often have difficulty maintaining the proper acid-alkaline balance in the blood and tissues because adequate protein and minerals are needed for this complex regulation mechanism.

Careful examination of mammalian physiology and eating habits reveals that none of the higher animals is strictly vegetarian. All primates eat some form of animal food. Gorillas—mistakenly labeled vegetarian—eat insect eggs and larvae that adhere to leaves and fruit. Other primates eat crickets, flies, rodents, small antelope and other animals. Neither can cattle and other ruminants be labeled strictly vegetarian because they always take in insect life adhering to the plants they eat, and because their stomachs and intestinal tracts contain enormous amounts of protozoa. These microscopic animals help digest grasses and in turn are digested and utilized by the cow. Only during the present modern age has any group of humans been able to follow a diet strictly free of animal products. In less sanitary times, there were always insect parts in the food supply. Small insects with their larvae or eggs left on plant foods prevent B_{12} deficiency anemia among Hindus in India. Hindus also eat milk products, and some sects consume termites. When these Hindus move to England, where the food supply is subject to strict sanitary regulations, the incidence of pernicious anemia increases dramatically.[102]

Current wisdom dictates that Americans should at least reduce their consumption of red meats and the dark meat of birds because these meats contain more saturated fat than fish or white poultry meat; but even this stricture is ill-advised, especially for those who tend to be anemic. Red meat is rich in iron and zinc, both of which play important roles in the body's use of essential fatty acids; and, as we have seen, consumption of saturated fat poses no threat to our health.

A few highly publicized studies have claimed a link between consumption of meat and saturated fats with cancer, especially cancer of the colon.[103] Studies claiming a correlation of animal product consumption with cancer do not stand up to careful scrutiny. In many of these studies, the data bases combined saturated fats from animal sources with hydrogenated vegetable oils, known to be carcinogenic.[104] Furthermore, these studies did not include sugar and white flour in their surveys, even though researcher Lopez and others have shown that in so-called civilized countries high meat consumption and high sugar intake often occur together.[105] Actually, the pathway for colon cancer is well understood. It involves high levels of omega-6 linoleic acid and hydrogenated fats, which in the presence of carcinogens and acted on by certain enzymes in the cells lining the colon lead to tumor formation.[106] This explains why colon cancer is prevalent in some industrialized countries where there are many carcinogens in the diet and where consumption of vegetable oils and sugar is high; but in traditional societies, where sugar and vegetable oils are absent and the food is free of additives, meat-eating is not associated with cancer.

We have already seen that both fats and carbohydrates can be devitalized by processing and refining. The same can be said of proteins. Isolated protein powders made from soy, whey, casein and egg whites are currently popular as basic ingredients in diet beverages and many so-called health food products. These protein isolates are usually obtained by a high-temperature process that over-denatures the proteins to such an extent that they become virtually useless[107] while increasing nitrates and other carcinogens.[108] Protein powders are often consumed as part of a lowfat diet and can thereby lead to depletion of vitamin A and D reserves. Soy protein isolates are high in mineral-blocking phytates, thyroid-depressing phytoestrogens and potent enzyme inhibitors that depress growth and cause cancer.[109]

Diets in which unnatural isolated powdered proteins from soy, eggs or milk are fed to animals or humans cause a negative calcium balance that can lead to osteoporosis. Critics of meat-eating have seized on these results to claim that meat causes bone loss. But meat or milk—as opposed to protein powders—fed to human subjects do not cause calcium loss nor do they contribute to osteoporosis.[110] The healthy meat-eating groups studied by Weston Price did not show any evidence whatsoever of osteoporosis.

In summary, animal products are important sources of bodybuilding elements in the diet. Furthermore, animal fats supply vitamin A and vitamin D and animal protein is rich in minerals, vitamin B_6 and vitamin B_{12}. The primitive tribes studied by Dr. Price especially valued certain high-vitamin animal products like organ meats, butter, fish eggs and shellfish for growing children and for parents of both sexes during the childbearing years. They also ate some animal food raw.

We cannot stress too highly that animal protein foods—meat, eggs and milk—always come with fat and this is how we should eat them. Animal fat supplies vitamins A and D needed for the assimilation of protein. Consumption of lowfat milk products, egg whites and lean meat can lead to serious deficiencies of these vital fat-soluble nutrients.[111]

Animal fats and gelatin-rich bone broths both spare protein, which means that meat goes a lot further when eaten in a broth or combined with animal fat.[112] Individuals who must restrict protein consumption for budgetary reasons should include liberal amounts of good quality animal fats and budget-sparing bone broth in their diets.

Any discussion of meat-eating should include the observation that temporary abstinence from animal products has been traditionally valued as a cleansing, healing practice. This is reflected in the dietary laws of many religions and in the practices of primitive peoples who engage in periods of sparse eating or complete fasting, often in late winter or early spring when food is scarce. This wisdom is justified by the fact that meatless diets often prove beneficial in the treatment of cancer and other diseases such as arthritis, kidney problems and gout. But problems arise when the practice is continued too long. These include caries, bone loss, nervous disorders and reproductive ailments. Strict vegetarianism is particularly dangerous for growing children and for women—and men—during their child-producing years.

We must be careful, as well, not to blindly extrapolate from the habits of carnivorous primitive peoples. There is a great deal to be learned from their dietary habits, but the fact is that we are not fundamentally cave men but beings with a divine component to our being. The desire to abstain from animal products, found so often in those of a spiritual nature, may reflect a longing to return to a former, more perfect state of consciousness that was ours before our souls took embodiment in physical bodies on the material plane. This longing attracts many to the belief that our bodies and souls can be purified, or that we can achieve spiritual enlightenment, through a meatless diet. Saintly individuals are often drawn to strict vegetarian habits, and some have been able to sustain themselves on a diet free of animal products for fairly long periods of time. (Some have even lived on no food at all; for many years St. Therese Neumann of Bavaria consumed only the consecrated host. Similar well-documented examples are found in the lives of Catholic and Hindu saints.) Even so, it is a mistake to think that meat-eaters lack spirituality—many highly spiritual people eat meat regularly. Perhaps they instinctively realize that when we eat animal products we are accepting, reverently and humbly, the requirements of the earthly body temple in which the soul is temporarily housed, even as we look forward to the day when we have completed our earthly assignment and our souls will be free to return to a higher condition, one in which we will no longer be dependent on foods provided by the animal kingdom. Seen in this light, strict vegetarianism can be likened to a kind of spiritual pride that seeks to "take heaven by force," and to shirk the earthly duties for which the physical body was created.

The rare St. Thereses on our planet usually lead celibate and contemplative lives. But most of us were born to live and work in the world and share the responsibility for producing healthy children. Animal products are essential for optimum growth and healthy reproduction. If you feel compelled to adopt the life of a saint or a sage and are attracted to vegetarianism, we urge you to wait until your later years to do so, when the period of growth and procreation is accomplished, and then to avoid fanaticism in its practice. If you choose not to eat red meat nor to serve it to your family, make sure to provide your loved ones with good quality dairy products and an adequate supply of seafood. If your religious beliefs proscribe both fish and meat, then a good supply of high-quality dairy products and eggs is essential. Raw milk or cheese must be used to provide vitamin B_{12}, as this essential nutrient is virtually destroyed by pasteurization. If your budget prevents plentiful consumption of animal products, it is important to supplement a balance of grains and pulses with at least a small amount of animal products each day, including animal fats rich in vitamins A and D. Animal studies indicate that animal protein in the amount of one sardine per person per day, combined with protein from grains and pulses, is generally sufficient to maintain reproduction and adequate growth,[113] but not necessarily to achieve robust good health.

The amount of meat you include in your diet depends on your genetic makeup and on hormonal factors. Some people require lots of meat while others do not produce enough hydrochloric acid in their stomachs to handle large amounts very well. Some researchers claim that our need for protein declines in later years. Requirements for individual essential amino acids vary enormously. For example, dark-skinned people may need more tryptophan, found in eggs and dairy products, as this essential amino acid is used in the production of melanin; deficiencies may lead to insomnia, hyperactivity and other nervous disorders. Some individuals have high requirements for carnitine, a nonessential amino acid found plentifully in lamb or beef, because they have difficulty manufacturing enough of it for proper functioning of the heart.

Our endorsement of animal products must be tempered with this important caveat: The meat, milk and eggs in our supermarkets are highly contaminated and vastly inferior in nutritional quality to those available to our ancestors just a few decades ago. Modern cattle-raising techniques include the use of steroids to make meat more tender and antibiotics that allow cattle to survive in crowded feedlots. Many cattle supplying steaks to the American table have never seen the open range, and calves raised for veal are often confined to crates for the whole of their pathetic short lives. Diseased animals routinely pass inspection and find their way into the food supply. Chickens are raised in crowded pens, often under artificial light both night and day, and fed on substandard food. They, too, must be guarded from infection by antibiotics. Their eggs are inferior in nutritional qualities to those of free-range, properly nourished hens. According to the renowned cancer specialist Virginia Livingston-Wheeler, most chicken and nearly half the beef consumed in America today is cancerous and pathogenic. Her research has convinced her that these cancers are transmissible to man.[114]

Some have argued that cows and sheep require pasturage that could be better used to raise grains for starving millions in Third World countries. This argument ignores the fact that a large portion of our earth's land is unsuited to cultivation. The open range and desert and mountainous areas yield their fruits in grazing animals. Grasslands perfectly suited to grazing cover an area in China's interior equal to *three* times the entire amount of land under cultivation in the rest of the country.[115] Citing the arguments of vegetarians, the Chinese government has opted to more intensely cultivate existing agricultural lands rather than to develop those untapped regions as grazing lands, a measure that would supply much-needed animal products to the Chinese diet.

A far more serious threat to humanity is the monoculture of grains and legumes, which tends to deplete the soil and requires the use of artificial fertilizers and pesticides. The educated consumer and the enlightened farmer together can bring about the return of the mixed farm, where cultivation of fruits and vegetables is combined with the raising of livestock and fowl in a manner that is efficient, economical and environmentally friendly. Cattle providing rich manure are the absolute basis for healthy, sustainable farming. Moreover, chickens allowed access to pasture eat worms and insects whose nutrients end up in high-quality eggs; sheep grazing in orchards obviate the need for herbicides; and livestock foraging in woodlands and other marginal areas provide rich, unpolluted meat and milk, making these lands economically viable for the farmer. It is not animal cultivation that leads to hunger and famine but unwise agricultural practices and monopolistic distribution systems.

We don't recommend that you stop eating meat, but we do suggest that you be careful of your supply. Make an effort to obtain organic beef, lamb and chicken. Range-fed beef that is finished with several weeks of grain feeding is fine, as long as the grains are organic and no cottonseed meal or soy protein are added to the feed. Grain finishing merely imitates the natural feeding habits of cattle and other ruminants, which get fat in the late summer and fall when they are feeding on natural grains in the field. The use of small quantities of animal parts in livestock rations allows the rancher to shorten the feedlot period, because this practice imitates nature as well. Animal-based supplements replace insects that cattle consume in the field. Outbreaks of scrapie and mad cow disease are most likely caused by neurotoxic pesticides and toxic mineral overload, rather than the inclusion of animal parts in feeding, a practice that dates back almost 100 years.[116] When animal-part feeding is prohibited, soy meal is used as an inferior replacement.

Other good meat choices include buffalo and wild game such as deer and antelope as well as game birds like duck, geese, pheasant and wild turkey. These are rich in nutrients and add variety to the diet.

Learn to eat the organs of land animals as well as their muscle meats—traditional peoples studied by Dr. Price consistently prized organ meats for their health-giving properties.

Eggs from pasture-fed chickens are available at many health food stores. They constitute the most complete, nutritious and economical form of animal protein available and are valued by traditional cultures throughout the world.

Make a habit of eating fish, especially cold-water deep-sea fish, as often as possible. They are rich in omega-3 fatty acids, fat-soluble vitamins and many important minerals including iodine, selenium and magnesium. Dr. Price was amazed to find that primitive landlocked peoples made great efforts to obtain food from the sea. However, we recommend avoidance of farm-raised fish—which often receive antibiotics inappropriate feed, such as soy meal—as well as scavenger-type fish like carp and catfish, which test high in PCBs and other contaminants.

Two types of meat require further discussion—pork and shellfish. Investigation into the effects of pork consumption on blood chemistry has revealed serious changes for several hours after pork is consumed.[117] The pork used was organic, free of trichinosis, so the changes that occurred in the blood were due to some other factor, possibly a protein unique to pork. In the laboratory, pork is one of the best mediums for feeding the growth of cancer cells. The prohibitions against pork found in the Bible and the Koran thus may derive from something other than a concern for parasite contamination. However, in fairness it must be noted that many groups noted for longevity, such as the inhabitants of Soviet Georgia and Okinawa, consume pork meat and lard in their diet on a daily basis. Lard is an excellent source of vitamin D.

Shellfish such as scallops, clams, mussels, oysters, shrimp, crab and lobster are highly prized by traditional peoples. They are rich sources of fat-soluble nutrients, particularly vitamin D. They should be eaten very fresh and in season, as they are subject to rapid spoilage. Some people are highly allergic to shellfish and should avoid them completely.

Ocean fish that contain mercury also contain substances called alkylglycerols that remove mercury from the body, but organically bound mercury in fish from industrially polluted waters is toxic and has caused deformities and mental deficiencies in the children of Japanese women who ate mercury-contaminated fish from Minamata Bay. A similar contamination poisoned natives near the Hudson Bay in Canada.

Research indicates that meats cooked at very high temperatures contain elevated amounts of carcinogens.[118] Meat should be eaten raw, rare or braised in water or stock. Avoid processed meats such as sausage, luncheon meats and bacon that have been preserved with nitrites, nitrates and other common meat preservatives. These are potent carcinogens that have been linked to cancer of the esophagus, stomach, large intestine, bladder and lungs. Traditionally, sausage was a healthy, high-fat product containing nutrient-dense organ meats and preserved through lacto-fermentation, a process that actually increases nutrients; while bacon was preserved through salt curing and smoking. These delicious old-fashioned products will return to the marketplace with consumer demand.

Charcoal grilled meats and smoked foods contain chemicals called polycyclic aromatic hydrocarbons that are used to induce cancer in laboratory animals, yet our ancestors ate liberally of smoked meats and fish without suffering from high levels of cancer. There are probably factors in traditional diets that protect against these carcinogens. Modern man is best advised to eat smoked and barbecued meats sparingly.

MILK & MILK PRODUCTS

What about milk? Among nutritionists, there is no other subject that arouses so much controversy—even animosity—as the debate on milk consumption. While our hunter-gatherer ancestors did not use milk products, there are many healthy nomadic and agricultural societies, dating back as far as 9,000 years, that depend on milk of cattle, sheep, goats, horses, water buffalo and camels for their animal protein and fat and value this "white blood" for its life-sustaining properties. Just a few decades ago, Americans accepted without question the premise that milk was good for us and that a safe, plentiful supply was actually vital to our national security. Today milk consumption is blamed for everything from chronic ear infections in children to cancer and diabetes in adults.

Some people have a low tolerance to milk because they lack intestinal lactase, an enzyme that digests lactose, or milk sugar. All baby mammals produce lactase but production of the enzyme declines and may even disappear after weaning. In humans, a mutation or recessive gene allows the continued production of lactase in some individuals. In an isolated population that depends on milk products for animal protein, those with this gene would have an advantage. If a gene for the persistence of lactase had a frequency of 5 percent in such a population, in 400 generations its frequency would have risen to 60 percent assuming that those who possessed it had 1 percent more children per generation than intolerant individuals.[119] Natural selection is the mechanism for adapting isolated populations to the food available to them. But modern man is highly peripatetic, and no society in the western world is composed entirely of people whose ancestors come from the immediate region.

By some estimates, only 30-40 percent of the world's population produces lactase in adulthood. Overuse of antibiotics also contributes to lactose intolerance. However, most lactose intolerant individuals can consume milk products in small quantities without problems.[120] Asians are said to be lactose intolerant but many of the inhabitants of Japan and China drink milk and eat milk products like cheese, yoghurt and ice cream when they can obtain them.

In addition, some people are allergic to a milk protein called casein, which is one of the most difficult proteins for the body to digest. Once again, the process of natural selection will result in a population more able to digest casein if milk and milk products are part of the traditional diet.

The practice of fermenting or souring milk is found in almost all traditional groups that keep herds. This process partially breaks down lactose and predigests casein. The end products, such as yoghurt, kefir and clabber, are often well tolerated by adults who cannot drink fresh milk. Butter and cream contain little lactose or casein and are usually well tolerated in their natural state, even by those who are lactose intolerant. Even so, fermented or soured butter and cream are more digestible. Those with an extreme intolerance for milk protein can take butter in the form of ghee or clarified butter from which the milk solids have been removed. Cheese, which consists of highly concentrated casein, is well tolerated by some and best completely avoided by others. Cheeses made from raw milk contain a full complement of enzymes and are therefore more easily digested than cheeses made from pasteurized milk. Natural cheeses, whether from pasteurized or unpasteurized milk, will be more digestible when eaten unheated. Processed cheeses contain emulsifiers, extenders, phosphates and hydrogenated oils; they should be strictly avoided.

While some lucky people are genetically equipped to digest milk in all its forms, the milk sold in your supermarket is bad for everybody, partly because the modern cow is a freak of nature. A century ago cows produced two or three gallons per day; today's Holsteins routinely give three or four times as much. This is accomplished by selective breeding to produce cows with abnormally active pituitary glands and by high-protein feeding. The pituitary gland not only produces hormones that stimulate the production of milk, it also produces growth hormones. Recently the FDA approved a genetically engineered growth hormone for cows. These hormones are identical to those produced by the pituitary gland in today's high-production cows. This practice will simply add to the high level of bovine growth hormones that have been present in our milk for decades. These hormones are present in the water fraction of the milk, not in the butterfat. Babies receive growth hormones from their mothers through their mothers' milk. Small amounts of these hormones are necessary and moderate amounts are not harmful, but a superfluity can result in growth abnormalities. Excessive pituitary hormones are also associated with tumor formation, and some studies link milk consumption with cancer. The freak-pituitary cow is prone to many diseases. She almost always secretes pus into her milk and needs frequent doses of antibiotics.

Another serious problem with today's dairying methods is the feeding of high-protein soybean meal to the cows. This stimulates them to produce large quantities of milk but contributes to a high rate of mastitis and other problems that lead to sterility, liver problems and shortened lives. Little research has been done to determine what these soy feeds do to the kind and quality of protein in cow's milk. Is the current high rate of milk-protein allergies due to the use of inappropriate feed in our dairy herds? The proper food for cows is green plants, especially the rapidly growing green grasses in the early spring and fall. Milk from properly fed cows will contain the Price Factor and cancer-fighting CLA as well as a rich supply of vitamins and minerals. Unfortunately, under the current system, farmers have little incentive to pasture-feed their herds nor to follow other practices that result in high quality milk.

Another factor contributing to the degradation of today's milk is pasteurization. We have been taught that pasteurization is beneficial, a method of protecting ourselves against infectious disease, but closer examination reveals that its merits have been highly exaggerated. The modern milking machine and stainless steel tank, along with efficient packaging and distribution, make pasteurization totally unnecessary for the purposes of sanitation. And pasteurization is no guarantee of cleanliness. All outbreaks of salmonella from contaminated milk in recent decades—and there have been many—have occurred in pasteurized milk. This includes a 1985 outbreak in Illinois that struck over 14,000 people causing at least one death. The salmonella strain in that batch of pasteurized milk was found to be genetically resistant to both penicillin and tetracycline.[121] Raw milk contains lactic-acid-producing bacteria that protect against pathogens. Pasteurization destroys these helpful organisms, leaving the finished product devoid of any protective mechanism should undesirable bacteria inadvertently contaminate the supply. Raw milk in time turns pleasantly sour, while pasteurized milk, lacking beneficial bacteria, will putrefy.

But that's not all that pasteurization does to milk. Heat alters milk's amino acids lysine and tyrosine, making the whole complex of proteins less available; it promotes rancidity of unsaturated fatty acids and destruction of vitamins. Vitamin C loss in pasteurization usually exceeds 50 percent; loss of other water-soluble vitamins can run as high as 80 percent; the Wulzen or anti-stiffness factor is totally destroyed as is vitamin B_{12}, needed for healthy blood and a properly functioning nervous system. Pasteurization reduces the availability of milk's mineral components, such as calcium, chloride, magnesium, phosphorus, potassium, sodium and sulphur, as well as many trace minerals. There is some evidence that pasteurization alters lactose, making it more readily absorbable. This, and the fact that pasteurized milk puts an unnecessary strain on the pancreas to produce digestive enzymes, may explain why milk consumption in civilized societies has been linked with diabetes.[122]

Last but not least, pasteurization destroys all the enzymes in milk—in fact, the test for successful pasteurization is absence of enzymes. These enzymes help the body assimilate all bodybuilding factors, including calcium. That is why those who drink pasteurized milk may suffer from osteoporosis. Lipase in raw milk helps the body digest and utilize butterfat.

After pasteurization, chemicals may be added to suppress odor and restore taste. Synthetic vitamin D_2 or D_3 is added—the former is toxic and has been linked to heart disease[123] while the latter is difficult to absorb.[124] The final indignity is homogenization, which has also been linked to heart disease.

Powdered skim milk is added to the most popular varieties of commercial milk—one-percent and two-percent milk. Commercial dehydration methods oxidize cholesterol in powdered milk, rendering it harmful to the arteries. High temperature drying also creates large quantities of cross-linked proteins and nitrate compounds, which are potent carcinogens, as well as free glutamic acid, which is toxic to the nervous system.[125]

Modern pasteurized milk, devoid of its enzyme content, puts an enormous strain on the body's digestive mechanism. In the elderly, and those with milk intolerance or inherited weaknesses of digestion, this milk passes through not fully digested and can build up around the tiny villi of the small intestine, preventing the absorption of vital nutrients and promoting the uptake of toxic substances.[126] The result is allergies, chronic fatigue and a host of degenerative diseases.

All the healthy milk-drinking populations studied by Dr. Price consumed raw milk, raw cultured milk or raw cheese from normal healthy animals eating fresh grass or fodder. It is very difficult to find this kind of milk in America. In California, New Mexico and Connecticut, raw milk is available in health food stores, although such milk often comes from cows raised in confinement.

In many states you can buy raw milk at the farm. If you can find a farmer who will sell you raw milk from old-fashioned Jersey or Guernsey cows (or from goats), tested free of tuberculosis and brucellosis and allowed to feed on fresh pasturage, then by all means avail yourself of this source.

Some stores now carry pasteurized but not homogenized milk from cows raised on natural feed. Such milk may be used to make cultured milk products such as kefir, yoghurt, cultured buttermilk and cultured cream. Traditionally cultured buttermilk, which is low in casein but high in lactic acid, is often well tolerated by those with milk allergies and gives excellent results when used to soak whole grain flours for baking. If you cannot find good quality raw milk, you should limit your consumption of milk products to cultured milk, cultured buttermilk, whole milk yoghurt, butter, cream and raw cheeses—all of which are available in all states. Much imported cheese is raw—look for the words "milk" or "fresh milk" on the label—and of very high quality.[127]

For butter from pasture-fed cows and organic ghee by mail order, see Sources. See also www.Realmilk.com for a listing of raw milk and milk products from pasture-fed animals.

VITAMINS

The discovery of the first vitamins, in the early 1900s, began the era of modern interest in diet and nutrition. Pioneering chemists found that certain "unknown substances" in food were essential to life. They discovered that fat-soluble vitamin D and water-soluble B vitamins were necessary to prevent diseases like rickets, beriberi and pellagra; and that vitamin C, a factor present in many fresh foods, prevented scurvy. By the 1930s, scientists had discovered many more vitamins and had catalogued their effects. Public interest in the subject was intense, and articles on vitamins often appeared in magazines and newspapers.

The study of vitamins has not waned since the early days of research, and the subject of food science has proved to be far more complex than scientists at first imagined. The early discoveries led some researchers to conclude that all vitamins necessary to life could be supplied in their isolated factory-produced form as vitamin pills. We now know that vitamins do not exist as single components but as parts of a complex of compounds, each part contributing to the whole. For example, vitamin C used to treat scurvy and other deficiency conditions is more effective when given as a natural food concentrate, which includes minerals, rutin and other analogs.[128]

As many as seventeen water-soluble vitamins labeled B have been discovered, present in different proportions in different foods, but all working together synergistically; vitamin D may have as many as twelve components of which several are active;[129] vitamin P has at least five components. Most vitamins produce optimum results in the presence of certain naturally occurring "cofactors," such as trace minerals, enzymes and coenzymes, as well as other vitamins.

The bewildering array of factors in foods now known to be essential has led well-informed nutritionists to recognize the futility of providing all factors necessary to life in pill form. While supplementing the diet with certain isolated vitamins has proven temporarily beneficial for many disease conditions, the best source of vitamins for most of us in the long term is properly prepared whole foods. For this reason, the importance of eating nutrient-dense meals, rich in vitamins and their cofactors, cannot be underestimated.

Vitamin and mineral content of food varies enormously with farming methods.[130] Nitrogen fertilizers produce initial high yields, in part by pulling minerals from the soil. In time, commercially fertilized soils become depleted, and the foods grown on them suffer accordingly. Overall, vitamin and mineral content of American fruits and vegetables has declined significantly during the last fifty years.[131] The revival of interest in compost and natural fertilizers, rich in minerals including trace minerals, is due in part to the realization that healthy soil is the basis of health for all life forms. Scientific assays have shown large differences in vitamin and mineral content between foods grown with nitrogen fertilizers and food grown organically. For example, cabbage can vary in its iron content from 94 parts per million to 0 parts per million; tomatoes can vary in iron content from 1,938 parts per million to 1 part per million. Vitamin A content of butterfat varies with the season as well as the soil; even the protein portion of grains and legumes will vary with soil fertility. Some commercially raised oranges have been found to contain *no* vitamin C!

Food processing affects vitamin content to varying extents. Some vitamins are heat-sensitive while others survive heating fairly well. Steaming and waterless methods of cooking preserve vitamins better than rapid boiling, and vegetables cooked in an acidic liquid preserve vitamins better than those cooked in an alkaline medium. Oxidation is a prime cause of vitamin loss. Long periods of high heat used in canning are destructive to some vitamins but not all. On the other hand, cold temperatures and freezing have little effect on vitamin content, and air or sun drying preserves or even enhances nutrient content. Some methods of food preservation and processing actually make nutrients more available—these include simmering bones in acidic liquid to make broth, culturing of dairy products, sprouting and traditional methods of pickling, fermenting and leavening.

The Diet Dictocrats have set minimum daily requirements for a few key vitamins and minerals, but many investigators feel that these standards are far too low. These critics contend that minimum daily requirements are sufficient to prevent acute deficiencies but not enough to support optimum health, especially as individual requirements for specific vitamins and minerals vary widely. In fact, a typical profile of nutrient requirements is one in which the individual has average needs with respect to most vitamins and minerals but requirements far in excess of average for a few specific nutrients.[132] Consumption of sugar, refined flour and hydrogenated fats, and of alcohol, tobacco and many drugs, depletes the body of nutrients, resulting in higher vitamin and mineral requirements for users. Stress of any sort causes the body to use up available nutrients at a faster-than-normal rate.

Space permits only a most cursory summary of the major nutrients in our food.

Vitamin A: This all-important vitamin is a catalyst on which innumerable biochemical processes depend. According to Dr. Price, neither protein, minerals nor water-soluble vitamins can be utilized by the body without vitamin A from animal sources.[133] Vitamin A also acts as an antioxidant, protecting the body against pollutants and free radicals, hence against cancer. Vitamin A stimulates the secretion of gastric juices needed for protein digestion, plays a vital role in building strong bones and rich blood, contributes to the production of RNA and is needed for the formation of visual purple. Sources of preformed vitamin A (called retinol) include butterfat, egg yolks, liver and other organ meats, seafood and fish liver oils. Provitamin A or carotene is also a powerful antioxidant. It is found in all yellow, red, orange or dark green fruits and vegetables. Carotenes are converted to vitamin A in the upper intestine. Vegetarians claim that the body's requirements for vitamin A can be met with carotenes from vegetable sources, but many people—particularly infants, children, diabetics and individuals with poor thyroid function—cannot make this conversion.[134] Furthermore, studies have shown that our bodies cannot convert carotenes into vitamin A without the presence of fat in the diet.[135] Dr. Price discovered that the diets of healthy isolated peoples contained at least *ten* times more vitamin A from animal sources than found in the American diet of his day. The high vitamin A content of their diets insured them excellent bone structure, wide handsome faces with plenty of room for the teeth and ample protection against stress of all types. It is best to obtain vitamin A from natural sources like yellow butter, egg yolks, organ meats, fish, shellfish and cod liver oil as high amounts of synthetic vitamin A from supplements can be toxic, especially to those with impaired liver function and to those whose diets are otherwise poor. High levels of natural vitamin A have no toxic effects, in spite of the medical establishment's dire warnings to the contrary. Antibiotics, laxatives, fat substitutes and cholesterol-lowering drugs interfere with vitamin-A absorption.

Vitamin B Complex: All the water-soluble B vitamins work as a team to promote healthy nerves, skin, eyes, hair, liver, muscle tone and cardiovascular function; they protect us from mental disorders, depression and anxiety. Deficiency of the B vitamin complex can result in the enlargement and malfunction of almost every organ and gland in the body. The best source of B vitamins is whole grains—refinement thus wastes this essential source. They are also found in fresh fruits, vegetables, nuts, legumes, seafood and organ meats; they can also be produced by intestinal bacteria. B_1 (thiamine) was the first water-soluble vitamin to be discovered. Deficiency leads to the disease beriberi. Recent evidence indicates that B_1 deficiency is the root cause of anorexia and other eating disorders.[136] It is essential for the manufacture of hydrochloric acid and has been used to treat constipation, fatigue, herpes and multiple sclerosis. Sugar consumption rapidly depletes vitamin B_1. B_2 or riboflavin is found in a variety of whole foods. Frequent cracks in the lips and corners of the mouth is a sign of deficiency. Deficiency of B_3 or niacin results in the disease pellagra, characterized by dermatitis, dementia, tremors and diarrhea. The amino acid tryptophan can be converted to niacin and has been used to treat a variety of symptoms indicative of niacin deficiency. Pantothenic acid, vitamin B_5, found in organ meats, egg yolks and whole grains, is essential for the proper function of the adrenal glands. It plays a vital role in cell metabolism and cholesterol production. Pantothenic acid can improve the body's ability to withstand stress. Recent studies have revealed that vitamin B_6 or pyridoxine, found mostly in animal products, contributes to the proper functioning of over one hundred enzymes. Deficiencies in B_6 have been linked to diabetes, nervous disorders and coronary heart disease. They are widespread in the US because excess B_1 and B_2, added to white flour, interferes with B_6 function and because Americans no longer have access to one of the best sources of this heat-sensitive nutrient—raw milk. The B vitamin folic acid counteracts cancer by strengthening the chromosomes; folic acid deficiency can result in babies born with neural tube deformities like spinal bifida. B_{12} is needed to prevent anemia and nervous disorders as well as to maintain fertility and promote normal growth and development. Usable B_{12} is found *only* in animal foods. An early symptom of B_{12} deficiency is a tendency to irrational anger. B_{15} (pangamic acid) and B_{17} (nitrilosides) protect against cancer; the former is found in grains and seeds; the latter in grasses, sprouts, buckwheat, legumes and many fruit seeds. Traditional diets were much richer in nitrilosides than our own.

Vitamin C: A water-soluble vitamin best known for its use in treatment of the common cold, it is also needed for a host of processes including tissue growth and repair, strength of capillary walls, lactation and adrenal gland function. It is vital for the formation of collagen, the body's structural substance. It promotes healing of wounds and is a powerful antioxidant. Dr. Linus Pauling and others have promoted megadoses of Vitamin C for cancer while others have used large doses to treat schizophrenia and drug addiction. But megadoses of isolated ascorbic acid may lead to imbalances and deficiencies in vitamin P. New evidence suggests that vitamin C works synergistically with vitamin E. Hypoglycemics and individuals on a high-protein diet require more vitamin C as these conditions interfere with the metabolism of ascorbic acid. It is found in many fruits and vegetables and in certain animal organs. Vitamin C is destroyed by heat. Alcohol and many common drugs including aspirin and oral contraceptives may reduce vitamin C levels in the body.

- **Vitamin D:** Like vitamin A, vitamin D is needed for calcium and phosphorus absorption and thus is essential for strong bones, healthy teeth and normal growth. It seems to protect against cancer and multiple sclerosis. Deficiency can cause rickets and myopia. The body manufactures vitamin D_3 out of cholesterol in the presence of sunlight. Although some claim that we can obtain all the vitamin D we need by spending a short amount of time each day in the sun, Price found that healthy primitive diets were rich in vitamin D-containing foods like butterfat, eggs, liver, organ meats, marine oils and seafood, particularly shrimp and crab. Synthetic D_2 has been linked to hyperactivity, coronary heart disease and other allergic reactions, while synthetic vitamin D_3 is poorly absorbed. New research indicates that optimal intake should be ten times higher than the US Recommended Daily Allowance, thus confirming the findings of Dr. Price.

- **Vitamin E:** This fat-soluble vitamin is needed for circulation, tissue repair and healing. It seems to help in the treatment of fibrocystic conditions, sterility, PMS and muscular dystrophy. It seems to retard the aging process. A vital role of vitamin E is the deactivation of free radicals. This powerful antioxidant works in concert with certain trace elements, notably selenium and zinc, to prevent cancer and cardiovascular disease. Increased ingestion of polyunsaturated oils requires greater amounts of vitamin E in the diet. It is found in unrefined vegetable oils, butter, organ meats, grains, nuts, seeds, legumes and dark green leafy vegetables.

- **Vitamin K:** This fat-soluble compound is needed for blood clotting and plays an important role in bone formation. Vitamin K given to postmenopausal women helps prevent bone loss. It is found in liver, egg yolks, butter, grains, dark leafy vegetables, vegetables of the cabbage family and fermented soy foods like miso.

- **Vitamin P:** Also called the bioflavonoids, these water-soluble compounds enhance the absorption of vitamin C to promote healing and protect the structure of blood capillaries. Bioflavonoids stimulate bile production, lower cholesterol levels, regulate menstrual flow, help prevent cataracts and have antibacterial effects. One of the bioflavonoids, rutin, has been shown to have a sedative-stimulant effect on the brain. Sources include peppers, grapes, buckwheat and the white peel of citrus fruits.

- **Coenzyme Q_{10}:** Coenzyme Q_{10}, sometimes called vitamin Q, is a nutrient that every cell in the body must have in order to produce energy. It also serves as an antioxidant and has been particularly effective in the treatment of cardiovascular disease and periodontal problems. Sources include all animal products, particularly heart meat. Cholesterol-lowering drugs interfere with absorption of coenzyme Q_{10}.

- **Activator X or the Price Factor:** Discovered by Weston Price, this fat-soluble nutrient is a potent catalyst to mineral absorption. It is found in certain fatty parts of animals that feed on young green growing plants or microorganisms, such as organ meats, fish and shellfish, fish eggs and butter from cows eating rapidly growing green grass of spring and fall pasturage. Largely absent today, the Price Factor was present in all traditional diets.

MINERALS

As the remarkable properties of vitamins have revealed themselves to investigators, so too have those of the various minerals in our food and water. The seven macrominerals—calcium, chloride, magnesium, phosphorus, potassium, sodium and sulphur—now share the research spotlight with a longer list of essential trace minerals. These are needed only in minute amounts, but their absence results in many disease conditions. The number of trace minerals known to be essential to life now exceeds thirty, and some researchers believe that for optimum health we need to take in every substance found in the earth's crust. Along with familiar trace minerals, such as iron and iodine, the body also needs others less well known, like cobalt, germanium and boron.

Mankind ingests minerals in a number of different forms. He can take them in as salts; that is, as molecules in which a negatively charged atom is bonded ionically to a positively charged atom as in common table salt (sodium chloride) or less well-known salts such as magnesium chloride, calcium phosphate or zinc sulfate. In water and other liquids, these form a solution as the salts dissolve into positively and negatively charged mineral ions.

Minerals are also ingested as integral parts of the foods we eat, in which case the minerals are held ionically in a claw-like way or "chelated" by a large molecule. Examples include chlorophyll (which chelates a magnesium atom), hemoglobin (which chelates an iron atom) and enzymes that chelate copper, iron, zinc and manganese.

Minerals are usually absorbed in ionic form. If they are not in ionic form when consumed, they are ionized in the gut, with salts dissolving into their two components or chelates releasing their key elements. The system by which mineral ions are then absorbed is truly remarkable. If, for example, the body needs calcium, the parathyroid gland will send a signal to the intestinal wall to form a calcium-binding protein. That calcium-binding protein will then pick up a free calcium ion, transport it through the intestinal mucosa and release it into the blood.[137] Manganese and magnesium have similar carriers and their absorption, retention and excretion is likewise governed by complex feedback mechanisms involving other nutrients and hormonal signals. Absorption and excretion of phosphorus is regulated in part by activity of the adrenal glands and vitamin D status.

There are a number of factors that can prevent the uptake of minerals, even when they are available in our food. The glandular system that regulates the messages sent to the intestinal mucosa require plentiful fat-soluble vitamins in the diet to work properly. Likewise, the intestinal mucosa requires fat-soluble vitamins and adequate dietary cholesterol to maintain proper integrity so that it passes only those nutrients the body needs, while at the same time keeping out toxins and large, undigested proteins that can cause allergic reactions. Minerals may "compete" for receptor sites. Excess calcium may impede the absorption of manganese, for example. Lack of hydrochloric acid in the stomach, an over-alkaline environment in the upper intestine or deficiencies in certain enzymes, vitamin C and other nutrients may prevent chelates from releasing their minerals. Finally, strong chelating substances, such as phytic acid in grains, oxalic acid in green leafy vegetables and tannins in tea may bind with ionized minerals in the digestive tract and prevent them from being absorbed.

Several types of mineral supplements are available commercially including chelated minerals, mineral salts, minerals dissolved in water and "colloidal" mineral preparations. A colloid is a dispersion of small particles in another substance. Soap, for example, forms a colloidal dispersion in water; milk is a dispersion of colloidal fats and proteins in water, along with dissolved lactose and minerals. Colloidal mineral preparations presumably differ from true solutions in that the size of the dispersed particles is ten to one thousand times larger than ions dissolved in a liquid. Colloidal dispersions tend to be cloudy; or they will scatter light that passes through them. Shine a flashlight through water containing soap or a few drops of milk and its path can be clearly seen, even if the water seems clear.

There is no evidence that the body absorbs colloidal mineral preparations any better than true solutions of mineral salts or minerals in chelated form. Many so-called "colloidal" formulas often contain undesirable additives, including citric acid, that prevent the mineral particles from settling to the bottom of the container. Furthermore, these products may contain an abundance of minerals that can be toxic in large amounts, such as silver and aluminum. Even mineral preparations in which the minerals are in true solution may contain minerals in amounts that may be toxic. If a product tastes very bitter, it probably should be avoided.

Some commercial interests sell minerals chelated to amino acids which they claim do not break down in the gut, but which pass in their entirety through the mucosa and into the blood, thus bypassing certain blocks to mineral absorption. However, such products, if they work, bypass the body's exquisitely designed system for taking in just what it needs and may cause serious imbalances. Obviously, such formulations should be taken only under the supervision of an experienced health care practitioner.

The proper way to take in minerals is through mineral-rich water; through nutrient-dense foods and beverages; through mineral-rich bone broths in which all of the macrominerals—sodium, chloride, calcium, magnesium, phosphorus, potassium and sulphur—are available in ready-to-use ionized form as a true electrolyte solution; through the use of unrefined sea salt; and by adding small amounts of fine clay or mud as a supplement to water or food, a practice found in many traditional societies throughout the world. Analysis of clays from Africa, Sardinia and California reveals that clay can provide a variety of macro- and trace minerals including calcium, phosphorus, magnesium, iron and zinc.[138] Clay also contains aluminum, but silicon, present in large amounts in all clays, prevents absorption of this toxic metal and actually helps the body eliminate aluminum that is bound in the tissues.[139]

When mixed with water, clay forms a temporary colloidal system in which fine particles are dispersed throughout the water. Eventually the particles settle to the bottom of the container, but a variety of mineral ions will remain in the water. These mineral ions are available for absorption, while other minerals that form an integral part of the clay particles may, in some circumstances, be available for absorption through ionic exchange at the point of contact with the intestinal villi.

Clay particles, defined as having a size less than 1-2 microns, have a very large surface area relative to their size. They carry a negative electric charge and can attract positively charged pathogenic organisms along with their toxins and carry them out of the body,[140] Thus, clay compounds not only provide minerals but also can be used as detoxifying agents. As such, they facilitate assimilation and can help prevent intestinal complaints, such as food poisoning and diarrhea. They also will bind with antinutrients found in plant foods, such as bitter tannins, and prevent their absorption.

The seven macrominerals, needed in relatively large amounts, are as follows:

❧ **Calcium:** Not only vital for strong bones and teeth, calcium is also needed for the heart and nervous system and for muscle growth and contraction. Good calcium status prevents acid-alkaline imbalances in the blood. The best sources of usable calcium are dairy products and bone broth. In cultures where dairy products are not used, bone broth is essential. Calcium in meats, vegetables and grains is difficult to absorb. Both iron and zinc can inhibit calcium absorption as can excess phosphorus and magnesium. Phytic acid in the bran of grains that have not been soaked, fermented, sprouted or naturally leavened will bind with calcium and other minerals in the intestinal tract, making these minerals less available. Sufficient vitamin D is needed for calcium absorption as is a proper potassium/calcium ratio in the blood. Sugar consumption and stress both pull calcium from the bones.

❧ **Chloride:** Chloride is widely distributed in the body in ionic form, in balance with sodium or potassium. It helps regulate the correct acid-alkaline balance in the blood and the passage of fluids across cell membranes. It is needed for the production of hydrochloric acid and hence for protein digestion. It also activates the production of amylase enzymes needed for carbohydrate digestion. Chloride is also essential to proper growth and functioning of the brain. The most important source of chloride is salt, as only traces are found in most other foods. Lacto-fermented beverages (page 583) and bone broths (page 116) both provide easily assimilated chloride. Other sources include celery and coconut.

❧ **Magnesium:** This mineral is essential for enzyme activity, calcium and potassium uptake, nerve transmission, bone formation and metabolism of carbohydrates and minerals. It is magnesium, not calcium, that helps form hard tooth enamel, resistant to decay. Like calcium and chloride, magnesium also plays a role in regulating the acid-alkaline balance in the body. High magnesium levels in drinking water have been linked to resistance to heart disease. Although it is found in many foods, including dairy products, nuts, vegetables, fish, meat and seafood, deficiencies are common in America due to soil depletion, poor absorption and lack of minerals in drinking water. A diet high in carbohydrates, oxalic acid in foods like raw spinach and phytic acid found in whole grains can cause deficiencies. An excellent source of usable magnesium is beef, chicken or fish broth. High amounts of zinc and vitamin D increase magnesium requirements. Magnesium deficiency can result in coronary heart disease, chronic weight loss, obesity, fatigue, epilepsy and impaired brain function. Chocolate cravings are a sign of magnesium deficiency.

❧ **Phosphorus:** The second most abundant mineral in the body, phosphorus is needed for bone growth, kidney function and cell growth. It also plays a role in maintaining the body's acid-alkaline balance. Phosphorus is found in many foods, but in order to be properly utilized, it must be in proper balance with magnesium and calcium in the blood. Excessive levels of phosphorus in the blood, often due to the consumption of soft drinks containing phosphoric acid, can lead to calcium loss and to cravings for sugar and alcohol; too little phosphorus inhibits calcium absorption and can lead to osteoporosis. Best sources are animal products, whole grains, legumes and nuts.

❧ **Potassium:** Potassium and sodium work together—inner cell fluids are high in potassium while fluids outside the cell are high in sodium. Thus, potassium is important for many chemical reactions within the cells. Potassium is helpful in treating high blood pressure. It is found in a wide variety of nuts, grains and vegetables. Excessive use of salt along with inadequate intake of fruits and vegetables can result in a potassium deficiency.

❧ **Sodium:** As all body fluids contain sodium, it can be said that sodium is essential to life. It is needed for many biochemical processes including water balance regulation, fluid distribution on either side of the cell walls, muscle contraction and expansion, nerve stimulation and acid-alkaline balance. Sodium is very important to the proper function of the adrenal glands. However, excessive sodium may result in high blood pressure, potassium deficiency, and liver, kidney and heart disease; symptoms of deficiency include confusion, low blood sugar, weakness, lethargy and heart palpitations. Meat broths and zucchini are excellent sources.

❧ **Sulphur:** Part of the chemical structure of several amino acids, sulphur aids in many biochemical processes. It helps protect the body from infection, blocks the harmful effects of radiation and pollution and slows down the aging process. Sulphur-containing proteins are the building blocks of cell membranes, and sulphur is a major component of the gel-like connective tissue in cartilage and skin. Sulphur is found in cruciferous vegetables, eggs, milk and animal products.

Although needed in only minute amounts, trace minerals are essential for many biochemical processes. Often it is a single atom of a trace mineral, incorporated into a complex protein, that gives the compound its specific characteristic—iron as a part of the hemoglobin molecule, for example, or a trace mineral as the distinguishing component of a specific enzyme. The following list is not meant to be exhaustive but merely indicative of the complexity of bodily processes and their dependence on well-mineralized soil and food.

❧ **Boron:** Needed for healthy bones, boron is found in fruits, especially apples, leafy green vegetables, nuts and grains.

❧ **Chromium:** Essential for glucose metabolism, chromium is needed for blood sugar regulation as well as for the synthesis of cholesterol, fats and protein. Most Americans are deficient in chromium because they eat so many refined carbohydrates. Best sources are animal products, molasses, nuts, whole wheat, eggs and vegetables.

❧ **Cobalt:** This mineral works with copper to promote assimilation of iron. A cobalt atom resides in the center of the vitamin B_{12} molecule. As the best sources are animal products, cobalt deficiency occurs most frequently in vegetarians.

❧ **Copper:** Needed for the formation of bone, hemoglobin and red blood cells, copper also promotes healthy nerves, a healthy immune system and collagen formation. Copper works in balance with zinc and vitamin C. Along with manganese, magnesium and iodine, copper plays an important role in memory and brain function. Nuts, molasses and oats contain copper but liver is the best and most easily assimilated source. Copper deficiency is widespread in America. Animal experiments indicate that copper deficiency combined with high fructose consumption has particularly deleterious effects on infants and growing children.

Germanium: A newcomer to the list of trace minerals, germanium is now considered to be essential to optimum health. Germanium-rich foods help combat rheumatoid arthritis, food allergies, fungal overgrowth, viral infections and cancer. Certain foods will concentrate germanium if it is found in the soil—garlic, ginseng, mushrooms, onions and the herbs aloe vera, comfrey and suma.

Iodine: Although needed in only minute amounts, iodine is essential for numerous biochemical processes, such as fat metabolism, thyroid function and the production of sex hormones. Muscle cramps are a sign of deficiency as are cold hands and feet, proneness to weight gain, poor memory, constipation, depression and headaches. It seems to be essential for mental development. Iodine deficiency has been linked to mental retardation, coronary heart disease, susceptibility to polio and breast cancer. Sources include most sea foods, unrefined sea salt, kelp and other sea weeds, fish broth, butter, pineapple, artichokes, asparagus and dark green vegetables. Certain vegetables, such as cabbage and spinach, can block iodine absorption when eaten raw or unfermented. Requirements for iodine vary widely. In general, those whose ancestors come from seacoast areas require more iodine than those whose ancestors come from inland regions. Proper iodine utilization requires sufficient levels of vitamin A, supplied by animal fats. In excess, iodine can be toxic. Consumption of high amounts of inorganic iodine (as in iodized salt or iodine-fortified bread) as well as of organic iodine (as in kelp) can cause thyroid problems similar to those of iodine deficiency, including goiter.[141]

Iron: As part of the hemoglobin molecule, iron is vital for healthy blood; iron also forms an essential part of many enzymes. Iron deficiency is associated with poor mental development and problems with the immune system. It is found in eggs, fish, liver, meat and green leafy vegetables. Iron from animal protein is more readily absorbed than iron from vegetable foods. The addition of fat-soluble vitamins found in butter and cod liver oil to the diet often results in an improvement in iron status. Recently, researchers have warned against inorganic iron used to supplement white flour. In this form, iron cannot be utilized by the body and its buildup in the blood and tissues is essentially a buildup of toxins. Elevated amounts of inorganic iron have been linked to heart disease and cancer.

Manganese: Needed for healthy nerves, a healthy immune system and blood sugar regulation, manganese also plays a part in the formation of mother's milk and in the growth of healthy bones. Deficiency may lead to trembling hands, seizures and lack of coordination. Excessive milk consumption may cause manganese deficiency as calcium can interfere with manganese absorption. Phosphorus antagonizes manganese as well. Best sources are nuts (especially pecans), seeds, whole grains and butterfat.

- **Molybdenum:** This mineral is needed in small amounts for nitrogen metabolism, iron absorption, fat oxidation and normal cell function. Best sources are lentils, liver, grains, legumes and dark green leafy vegetables.

- **Selenium:** A vital antioxidant, selenium acts with vitamin E to protect the immune system and maintain healthy heart function. It is needed for pancreatic function and tissue elasticity and has been shown to protect against radiation and toxic minerals. High levels of heart disease are associated with selenium-deficient soil in Finland and a tendency to fibrotic heart lesions is associated with selenium deficiency in parts of China. Best sources are butter, Brazil nuts, seafood and grains grown in selenium-rich soil.

- **Silicon:** This much neglected element is needed for strong yet flexible bones and healthy cartilage, connective tissue, skin, hair and nails. In the blood vessels, the presence of adequate silicon helps prevent atherosclerosis. Silicon also protects against toxic aluminum. Good sources are grains with shiny surfaces, such as millet, corn and flax, the stems of green vegetables and homemade bone broths in which chicken feet or calves' feet have been included.

- **Vanadium:** Needed for cellular metabolism and the formation of bones and teeth, vanadium also plays a role in growth and reproduction and helps control cholesterol levels in the blood. Deficiency has been linked to cardiovascular and kidney disease. Buckwheat, unrefined vegetable oils, grains and olives are the best sources. Vanadium is difficult to absorb.

- **Zinc:** Called the intelligence mineral, zinc is required for mental development, for healthy reproductive organs (particularly the prostate gland), for protein synthesis and collagen formation. Zinc is also involved in the blood sugar control mechanism and thus protects against diabetes. Zinc is needed to maintain proper levels of vitamin E in the blood. Inability to taste or smell and loss of appetite are signs of zinc deficiency. High levels of phytic acid in cereal grains and legumes block zinc absorption. Zinc deficiency during pregnancy can cause birth defects. As oral contraceptives diminish zinc levels, it is important for women to wait at least six months after discontinuing the pill before becoming pregnant. Best sources include red meat, oysters, fish, nuts, seeds and ginger.

Not all minerals are beneficial. Lead, cadmium, mercury, aluminum and arsenic, while possibly needed in minute amounts, are poisons to the body in large quantities. These come from polluted air, water, soil and food; lead finds its way into the water supply through lead pipes. Sources of aluminum include processed soy products, aluminum cookware, refined table salt, deodorants and antacids. Baking powder can be another source of aluminum and should be avoided. Amalgam fillings are the principle source of toxic mercury in the system—linked to Alzheimer's and a number of other disease conditions. Minerals like calcium and magnesium, and the antioxidants—vitamin A, carotenes, vitamin C, vitamin E and selenium—all protect against these toxins and help the body to eliminate them. Adequate silicon protects against aluminum.

ENZYMES

An important branch of twentieth-century nutritional research, running parallel to and equal in significance to the discovery of vitamins and minerals, has been the discovery of enzymes and their function. Enzymes are complex proteins that act as catalysts in almost every biochemical process that takes place in the body. Their activity depends on the presence of adequate vitamins and minerals, particularly magnesium. Many enzymes incorporate a single molecule of a trace mineral—such as manganese, copper, iron or zinc—without which the enzyme cannot function. In the 1930s, when enzymes first came to the attention of biochemists, some 80 were identified; today, over 5,000 have been discovered.

Enzymes fall into one of three major classifications. The largest is the metabolic enzymes, which play a role in all bodily processes including breathing, talking, moving, thinking, behavior and maintenance of the immune system. A subset of these metabolic enzymes acts to neutralize poisons and carcinogens, such as pollutants, DDT and tobacco smoke, changing them into less toxic forms, which the body can then eliminate. The second category is the digestive enzymes, of which there are about 22 in number. Most of these are manufactured by the pancreas. They are secreted by glands in the duodenum (the upper part of the small intestine) and work to break down the bulk of partially-digested food leaving the stomach.

The enzymes we need to consider when planning our diets are the third category, the food enzymes. These are present in ample amounts in many raw foods, and they initiate the process of digestion in the mouth and stomach. Food enzymes include proteases for digesting protein, lipases for digesting fats and amylases for digesting carbohydrates. Amylases in saliva contribute to the digestion of carbohydrates while they are being chewed, and all enzymes found in food continue this process while it is mixed and churned by contractions in the stomach. The glands in the stomach secrete hydrochloric acid and pepsinogen, which initiate the process of protein digestion, as well as the intrinsic factor needed for vitamin B_{12} absorption; but the various enzymes needed for complete digestion of our food are not secreted until further down the line, in the small intestine. However, while food is held in the stomach, the enzymes present in what we have consumed can do their work before this more or less partially-digested mass passes on to the enzyme-rich environment of the small intestine.

Enzyme research has revealed the importance of certain raw and fermented foods in the diet. The enzymes in raw food, particularly raw fermented food, help start the process of digestion and reduce the body's need to produce digestive enzymes. All enzymes are deactivated at a wet-heat temperature of 118 degrees Fahrenheit and a dry-heat temperature of about 150 degrees. It is one of those happy designs of nature that foods and liquids at 117 degrees can be touched without pain, but liquids over 118 degrees will burn. Thus, we have a built-in mechanism for determining whether or not the food we are eating still contains its enzyme content.

A diet composed exclusively of cooked food puts a severe strain on the pancreas, drawing down its reserves, so to speak. If the pancreas is constantly overstimulated to produce enzymes that ought to be in foods, the result over time will be inhibited function. Humans eating an enzyme-poor diet, comprised primarily of cooked food, use up a tremendous amount of their enzyme potential in the outpouring of secretions from the pancreas and other digestive organs. The result, according to the late Dr. Edward Howell, a noted pioneer in the field of enzyme research, is a shortened life span, illness and lowered resistance to stress of all types. He points out that humans and animals on a diet comprised largely of cooked food, particularly grains, have enlarged pancreas organs while other glands and organs, notably the brain, actually shrink in size.[142]

Dr. Howell formulated the following Enzyme Nutrition Axiom: The *length of life* is inversely proportional to the rate of exhaustion of the *enzyme potential* of an organism. The increased use of food enzymes promotes a *decreased rate* of exhaustion of the enzyme potential.[143] Another rule can be expressed as follows: Whole foods give good health; enzyme-rich foods provide limitless energy.

Almost all traditional societies incorporate raw, enzyme-rich foods into their cuisines—not only vegetable foods but also raw animal proteins and fats in the form of raw dairy foods, raw fish and raw muscle and organ meats. These diets also traditionally include a certain amount of cultured or fermented foods, which have an enzyme content that is further enhanced by the fermenting and culturing process. The Eskimo diet, for example, is composed in large portion of raw fish that has been allowed to "autolate" or "predigest;" that is, become putrefied or semirancid; to this predigested food they ascribe their stamina. The culturing of dairy products, found almost universally among preindustrialized peoples, enhances the enzyme content of milk, cream, butter and cheese. Ethnic groups that consume large amounts of cooked meat usually include fermented vegetables or condiments, such as sauerkraut and pickled carrots, cucumbers and beets, with their meals. Cultured soybean products from Asia, such as *natto* and *miso*, are another good source of food enzymes if these foods are eaten unheated. Even after being subjected to heat, fermented foods are more easily assimilated because they have been predigested by enzymes. In like manner, cooked meats that have first been well aged or marinated present less of a strain on the digestive mechanism because of this predigestion.

Grains, nuts, legumes and seeds are rich in enzymes, as well as other nutrients, but they also contain enzyme inhibitors. Unless deactivated, these enzyme inhibitors can put great strain on the digestive system. Sprouting, soaking in warm acidic water, sour leavening, culturing and fermenting—all processes used in traditional societies—deactivate enzyme inhibitors, thus making nutrients in grains, nuts and seeds more readily available.

Most fruits and vegetables contain few enzymes; exceptional plant foods noted for high enzyme content include extra virgin olive oil and other unrefined oils, raw honey, grapes, figs and many tropical fruits including avocados, dates, bananas, papaya, pineapple, kiwi and mangos.

While we should include a variety of raw foods in our diets, we need to recognize that there are no traditional diets composed exclusively of raw foods. Even in the tropics, where fires are not needed for warmth, the inhabitants build a fire every day to cook their foods. Some nutrients are made more available through cooking and cooking also neutralizes naturally occurring toxins in plant foods. In general, grains, legumes and certain types of vegetables should be cooked. Animal foods should be consumed both raw and cooked. Some people do very poorly on raw foods—or find raw foods unappetizing—in which case they should emulate the Asians by including small amounts of enzyme-rich condiments with a diet of cooked foods.

SALT, SPICES & ADDITIVES

Many topics under the rubric of nutrition are fraught with controversy and the subject of salt is no exception. It has been fashionable in recent years for nutritionists to restrict the use of salt and this is one proscription endorsed by medical orthodoxy. Early research uncovered a correlation of salt intake with high blood pressure, but subsequent studies indicated that salt restriction may harm more people than it helps. A large study conducted in 1983 found that dietary salt did not have any significant effect on blood pressure in the majority of people. In some cases, salt restriction actually raised blood pressure.[144] A 1930s study found that salt deficiency led to loss of taste sensation, cramps, weakness, lassitude and severe cardiorespiratory distress on exertion.[145]

With few exceptions, all traditional cultures use some salt. Isolated primitive peoples living far from the sea or other salt sources burn sodium-rich marsh grasses and add the ash to their food. Salt provides not only sodium but also chloride, needed for the manufacture of hydrochloric acid, proper functioning of the brain and nervous system and for many other processes. The chloride component of salt also activates amylases, needed for the digestion of carbohydrate foods.

The need for salt varies according to the individual. People with weak adrenal glands lose salt in their urine and must have plentiful salt in the diet, but for others excessive salt consumption causes calcium to be excreted in the urine and may contribute to osteoporosis. Excessive salt in the diet also depletes potassium.

Some nutritionists contend that salt stimulates the glands in much the same way that sugar does and can thus lead to a host of degenerative illnesses. A salt-free diet will often cure acne and oily skin. On the other hand, salt is a powerful enzyme activator. Dr. Edward Howell, noted enzyme researcher, observed that those whose diets are composed almost entirely of raw foods, like the Eskimos, do not need much salt; but those who subsist on a diet composed largely of cooked foods, like the Chinese, require greater amounts of salt to activate enzymes in the intestines.

Most discussions of salt ignore the issue of salt processing. Few people realize that our salt—like our sugar, flour and vegetable oils—is highly refined; it is the product of a chemical and high-temperature industrial process that removes all the valuable magnesium salts as well as trace minerals naturally occurring in the sea. To keep salt dry, salt refiners adulterate this "pure" product with several harmful additives, including aluminum compounds. To replace the natural iodine salts that are removed during processing, potassium iodide is added in amounts that can be toxic. To stabilize the volatile iodide compound, processors add dextrose which turns the iodized salt a purplish color. A bleaching agent is then necessary to restore whiteness to the salt.

Sun dried sea salt contains traces of marine life that provide organic forms of iodine. Some researchers claim that this form of iodine remains in the bodily fluids for many weeks, whereas the iodine released from iodide salts passes through very quickly.[146] This may be why the late physician Henry Bieler found evidence of sodium starvation in the tissues of people who consumed large amounts of refined salt.[147]

Even most so-called sea salt is produced by industrial methods. The best and most health-promoting salt is extracted by the action of the sun on seawater in clay-lined vats. Its light grey color indicates a high moisture and trace mineral content. This natural salt contains only about 82 percent sodium chloride; it contains about 14 percent macro-minerals, particularly magnesium, and nearly 80 trace minerals. The best and purest commercially available source of unrefined sea salt is the natural salt marshes of Brittany, where it is "farmed" according to ancient methods. (See Sources.) Red sea salt from Hawaii is also an excellent product, but it is not readily available in the continental US. Unrefined salt mined from ancient seabeds contains many trace minerals and is theoretically acceptable as long as it comes from areas where nuclear testing has not occurred nor where nuclear wastes are stored. However, it will lack organic iodine from the minute bits of plant life that are preserved in moist Celtic sea salt.

Both surfeit and deficiency of iodine can lead to problems with the thyroid gland, including goiter, hyperthyroidism and hypothyroidism. Iodized salt will often relieve the overt symptoms of goiter—it will cause the thyroid gland to shrink back to normal or near-normal size—but it does not prevent other thyroid problems, such as obesity, low vitality, fragile teeth and bones, various sexual and mental problems, as well as heart disease and cancer.

Broth made from meat and animal bones is another good source of sodium, chloride and iodine as well as magnesium, potassium and important trace minerals. Broth made from fish carcasses and fish heads is rich in additional substances that nourish the thyroid gland. Properly made, broth is also a source of gelatin, which research has shown to be an excellent aid to digestion and assimilation of cooked foods.[148] The food provider with an eye for nutrition, as well as good taste, will make these broths a staple in her repertoire.

What about spices? Once again there is debate among nutritionists. One school of thought claims that spices stimulate the glands and should always be avoided; others point out that spices make our food taste good and render it more digestible by stimulating the saliva. Spices are good sources of magnesium and other minerals. As a general rule, the hotter the spice, the more magnesium it contains. Certainly it would be a shame to forego the rich cornucopia of spices that modern transport brings to our markets. A compromise position allows spicy foods in moderation to those who are healthy; but those whose glands have been worn out by many years of poor diet may have to adopt bland fare in order to regain and maintain their well-being. Fresh herbs are less stimulating and should be used whenever possible—they are rich in vitamins, minerals and other health-promoting factors. Always buy herbs and spices labeled nonirradiated. (See Sources)

Monosodium glutamate is an additive that has been soundly condemned by knowledgeable researchers—for good reason. Manufactured glutamate is a neurotoxic substance that causes many adverse reactions. In sensitive individuals these can manifest as dizziness, violent diarrhea and even anaphylactic shock. Longer term and more insidious consequences of MSG ingestion include Parkinson's and Alzheimer's in adults and neurological damage in children. Animal studies have linked MSG with brain lesions, retinal degeneration and obesity.[149]

The powerful MSG industry lobby has been able to allay public fears about MSG by pointing out that monosodium glutamate contains glutamic acid, a nonessential amino acid that occurs plentifully in meat broths and naturally fermented products like soy sauce and *miso*. It is glutamic acid that gives these foods their rich, meat-like taste. However, the form of glutamic acid in these foods is a naturally occurring isomer that is not toxic, except to hypersensitive individuals; but the glutamic acid in MSG is an unnatural isomer that causes dangerous neurological reactions in many individuals.[150] All foods containing MSG should be avoided. Hydrolyzed protein also includes large amounts of unnatural glutamic acid and produces the same effects.[151] Recently a growth enhancer called Auxigro has been approved as a spray for crops like apples and beans. It contains 30 percent

MSG![152] Yet another reason to choose organically raised produce!

A great many processed foods contain MSG or hydrolyzed protein, especially soy-based concoctions and those sold as meat broth substitutes. Unfortunately, MSG and related substances are not always labeled. Calcium caseinate, sodium caseinate, textured protein, hydrolyzed protein, and citric acid always contain MSG; soy foods, nutritional yeasts, protein powders, malt flavorings, amino acids and various mixes labeled "flavorings," "natural flavors" or "seasonings" usually contain MSG. MSG is frequently formed during processing even if not deliberately added to a food product—just one more reason to avoid processed foods.

About the hundreds of other additives, preservatives, colorings and artificial flavorings added to processed foods, we can only counsel you to avoid them as much as possible. The healthy body produces enzymes that deactivate many of these substances; but when the body is overloaded with junk food, and its enzyme production overtaxed, it cannot marshal the resources needed to neutralize this onslaught of poisons. Research indicates that while small amounts of additives taken one at a time may be relatively harmless, taken together they can have severely toxic effects.[153]

It is important to distinguish between food processing techniques that preserve or enhance the nutrients in food and those that deplete them. In general, freezing preserves most nutrients; pickling, fermenting and culturing according to traditional methods enhance the availability of many nutrients by increasing enzyme activity. Sun drying is an age-old method for preserving foods that conserves and even enhances nutrients. But we should avoid foods processed by methods involving high temperatures, including pasteurization, high-temperature drying, high-temperature and high-pressure processing of grains (extrusion) and high-temperature and solvent extraction of oils.

Irradiation does not heat foods to high temperatures but it does nevertheless alter their nutrients.[154] Feeding studies show that irradiated foods cause mutagenic blood abnormalities in children.[155] Irradiated seeds will not sprout. Most commercial spices are irradiated.

Canned foods should play a limited role in your cooking, not only because vitamins are destroyed but because canned foods lack enzymes. Fresh vegetables are almost always preferable with the exception of tomatoes. Tomatoes for canning are picked at the peak of ripeness with a carotene content much higher than most fresh tomatoes sold in stores. Carotenes survive the canning process although some other vitamins may not. Thus, limited use of canned tomato products is acceptable. The canning process reduces phytate content in legumes, such as kidney beans and chick peas, but the prolonged heat involved in the process may overdenature some of the proteins contained in these foods.

Whenever possible, buy organically raised meats and produce although you needn't make a fetish about it. It is particularly important to buy organic potatoes and onions. Regular commercial potatoes and onions have been treated with sprout inhibitors that cause cellular changes in test animals. Avoid thin-skinned fruits that have come from long distances—they usually have been treated with chemicals of questionable safety.

Organically produced food is generally richer in nutrient content and free from most toxic residues. The highest quality organic standards are those practised by biodynamic farmers who fertilize with composted manure and have revived ancient methods of revitalizing the soil.

Organically produced foods are becoming more available. You can now purchase organic grains and legumes at farmers' markets and most health food stores. Even better, support the efforts of conscientious local farmers by joining a local group or co-op that buys directly from organic or biodynamic farms.

BEVERAGES

Most books on nutrition have little to say about what we drink, yet our choice of beverage plays an important role in determining our health.

A primary factor contributing to the scourge of degenerative diseases plaguing America is the national love affair with soft drinks. Americans consumed 43 gallons of soft drinks per person in 1990, nearly double the amount of 1970. Soft drinks have found their way into the hands of tiny children and into vending machines in our public schools. We have become the Pepsi degeneration.

What's wrong with soft drinks? Just about everything. First, they are loaded with sweeteners—usually high fructose corn syrup—or sugar substitutes, notably aspartame. We have already discussed the deleterious effects of refined sugar, particularly fructose, on every organ and system in the body. The sugar in soda pop is nothing but naked calories and acts as an antinutrient. Sugar in soft drinks accounts for 35 percent of all US sugar consumption and, more than any other source, contributes to what has become a national addiction to sweet foods of all kinds.

Sugar substitutes do nothing to reduce the dependence or craving for sweet-tasting foods, and tests have shown that sugar substitutes don't even help you lose weight—some people actually gain weight when they drink diet sodas.[156] Furthermore, they have their own dangers. The most widely used artificial sweetener—aspartame or Nutra-sweet—is a neurotoxic substance that has been associated with numerous health problems including dizziness, visual impairment, severe muscle aches, numbing of extremities, pancreatitis, high blood pressure, retinal hemorrhaging, seizures and depression. It is suspected of causing birth defects and chemical disruptions in the brain.[157] Researchers at Utah State University found that even at low levels aspartame induces adverse changes in the pituitary glands of mice.[158] The pituitary gland is the master gland upon which the proper function of all biochemical processes depend.

When aspartame is digested it breaks down into the amino acids phenylalanine and aspartic acid, plus methanol. Methanol, or wood alcohol, is a known poison. Methanol is also found in fruit juices, and our regulatory agencies have seized upon this fact to assure us that the methanol by-product of aspartame is not harmful. They fail to point out that the methanol content of diet soft drinks is 15 to 100 times higher than that of fruit juices. In any event, the safety level of methanol has never been determined.

In addition to sugar or sugar substitutes, most soft drinks contain phosphoric acid—this is what gives them their kick. Phosphoric acid blocks the absorption of calcium and magnesium in the intestines, thus contributing directly to fragile, easily fractured bones in children and osteoporosis or bone loss in adults. Magnesium deficiency contributes to impairment of the immune system, fatigue, high blood pressure and many other ailments. Phosphoric acid may also be a major cause of kidney stones.

Many soft drinks also contain caffeine. Caffeine and its related substance theobromine (from tea and cocoa) are like sugar in their effects on the body. They stimulate the adrenal glands to release an adrenaline-like substance, which in turn causes the liver to release sugar into the blood stream. This is what gives you the "lift" when you drink coffee, tea or caffeinated soft drinks. The problem is that the delicate blood-sugar-regulation mechanism cannot long tolerate the constant stimulation of habitual caffeine ingestion. Often the blood sugar lowering mechanisms overreact, causing low blood sugar and its concomitant complaints of chronic fatigue, dizziness, depression, allergies and behavioral disorders. Caffeine-containing drinks irritate the lining of the stomach and cause an increase in stomach acid. They affect the nervous system, leading to insomnia and restlessness. Prolonged use of caffeine can contribute to any one of a number of serious diseases, such as cancer, bone loss, mental disorders and birth defects. Caffeine's effects on the nervous system are most pronounced in children—yet cola drinks have become standard fare for our youth. It has been said that if coffee were introduced as a new drug today, it would not receive FDA approval. It is best to avoid all sources of caffeine and related substances—not just colas but also coffee and tea, decongestants, pep pills, aspirin, diuretics and—we're sorry to say—chocolate.

As a final blow, soft drink manufacturers polish off their creation with a variety of artificial flavorings, colorings and preservatives, most of which have dubious claims to safety. The entire brew is a concoction of chemicals designed to sap our physical and mental health. Soda pop is the veritable drink of the devil. If you choose to improve the eating habits of your family, here is your starting point, the first place to take a stand. Don't buy soft drinks, don't keep them around and do everything you can to discourage your children from drinking them.

The list of drinks to avoid is a long one—soft drinks, sugared drinks and milk that has been pasteurized or homogenized. Coffee, tea, and cocoa are traditional drinks but they contain stimulants that are best avoided. To this group must be added yet another—fruit juice—because the process of juicing fruit concentrates its sweetness. There is as much sugar in a glass of orange juice as there is in a candy bar—and most of it is fructose, which is more harmful than the sucrose of sugar. Consumption of apple juice has been linked to failure to thrive in infants.[159] Excessive consumption of fruit juice can also upset the acid-alkaline balance of the body, causing the urine to become alkaline rather than acid. Even overconsumption of vegetable juices, which are not sweet, can cause an imbalance. Fresh fruit is delicious and healthful in moderate amounts, but even overindulgence in fruit can lead to severe mineral deficiencies. Our natural "appestats" usually prevent us from eating too much fruit at one time, but in fruit juice we get concentrated sweetness—the equivalent of several pieces of fruit—in several quick gulps. Furthermore, most fruit juice is filtered and pasteurized, hence skeletonized, much like refined sugar and white flour. Fruit juice consumption should be limited to an ounce or two at a time, diluted with water, so that you do not take in any more fructose than you would consume in one piece of fruit.

What about water? Should we drink distilled or purified, bottled or tap, hard or soft? The evidence points to hard water, which is water rich in mineral ions, as being of great value in promoting overall health. Several studies have shown that the rate of coronary heart disease is lower in localities where hard water is available. Areas of the world noted for the longevity of local inhabitants—notably the Caucasus, Hunzaland and Vilcabamba in South America—are all watered by richly mineralized runoff from the grinding action of high mountain glaciers.

A comparative study of the water in Deaf Smith County, Texas with that of Dallas produced an interesting profile of drinking water's ideal components. Deaf Smith County residents are famous for their good teeth and bone structure; they have few fractures even in advanced age. X-rays of both people and cattle show unusual bone size and density; cross sections of long bones are approximately 50 percent greater in thickness than those of people living in other regions. By contrast, bones of Dallas County residents break easily and heal slowly. Analysis of the water in both counties reveals the surprising fact that the calcium content of Dallas County water is six times higher than that of Deaf Smith County. But Deaf Smith County water is eight times richer in iodine, two times higher in magnesium and contains numerous trace minerals that are absent from Dallas County water.[160] It seems that the magnesium and trace minerals, especially iodine, contribute to enzymatic processes that go into creating strong and healthy bones; and magnesium is incorporated into the bone itself, contributing to its strength.

Water that has been softened is water that has been shorn of its valuable mineral content. Water softeners function by exchanging sodium ions for ions of other minerals, so that the end product is high in sodium but low in minerals. The use of softened water is highly correlated with an increased incidence of cancer, heart attacks and strokes.[161]

Unfortunately, most water supplies are contaminated by a number of harmful chemicals, either as a result of runoff from farms and gardens or because they are deliberately treated with chlorine or fluorides. Fluoridated water should be avoided at all costs. Fluoride is an enzyme inhibitor that contributes to bone loss, bone deformities, cancer and a host of other illnesses. It offers little real protection against tooth decay.[162] Bottled mineral water varies widely in quality and is not necessarily free from contaminants.

So what is the solution? There is no perfect source of water for most of us, but the best solution seems to be tap water that has been treated with a filter. A ceramic or compressed carbon filter removes all heavy metals, chlorine and other impurities but leaves valuable mineral ions, such as calcium, magnesium, iodine, silicon and selenium. Unfortunately, these types of filters are less effective for removing fluorides and nitrates. Some filtering systems run the water through two different filters, one ceramic or charcoal filter that removes heavy metals and chlorine, and one that removes some of the fluoride. (See Sources.) Fluorides and nitrates can also be completely removed with a reverse osmosis water treatment unit. Unfortunately, this process is said to denature the water, such that plants do not grow as well when watered with reverse osmosis water. State-of-the-art reverse osmosis units "restructure" the water by running it through pebbles. Reverse osmosis also removes beneficial minerals, but these can be restored to the diet with a mineral supplement of fine clay or mineral ions added to the water. (See Sources.)

How much water should we drink? Conventional wisdom calls for six to eight large glasses per day, but Oriental medicine teaches that this is a dangerous practice that puts undue strain on the kidneys. In fact, when we drink plain water with few electrolytes, the body tries to excrete it as quickly as possible in order to maintain homeostasis in the blood.[163] Researchers from both East and West warn that excessive liquids taken at meals dilute stomach acid and put undue strain on the digestive process. On the other hand, large amounts of purified or distilled water taken throughout the day as a temporary measure have been used successfully to treat a number of disease conditions, such as kidney stones and toxemia. A good rule is to avoid drinking too much liquid from one-half hour before a meal to two hours after and to sip beverages slowly with meals. It is also wise to avoid liquids that are too hot or too cold. Iced water with a meal makes digestion very difficult. Water to which a squeeze of fresh lemon or lime juice has been added will quench thirst and aid digestion better than plain water.

Water is a by-product of carbohydrate and fat metabolism. Thus, a diet that is high in protein but low in fat and carbohydrates can lead to excessive thirst.

A study of beverages from around the world reveals that traditional societies frequently consume lacto-fermented beverages made from fruits, milk, sap, herbs and grains.[164] Lacto-fermentation is a process whereby special bacteria transform sugars and starches into beneficial acids. These drinks are valued for medicinal qualities including the ability to relieve intestinal problems and constipation. They encourage lactation, strengthen the sick, enhance digestion and promote overall well-being and stamina. Above all, these drinks are considered superior to plain water in their ability to relieve thirst during physical labor. Many vitamins and minerals are lost through perspiration. Modern research has discovered that a liquid containing small amounts of sugars along with minerals in ionic form is actually absorbed faster than plain water, is retained more thoroughly and has the added advantage of rapidly replacing minerals lost in sweat.[165] This research has been used to promote commercial sports drinks—high-sugar, additive-laced concoctions containing small amounts of electrolytes. But natural lactic-acid fermented drinks contain numerous valuable minerals in ionized form and small amounts of natural sugars along with lactic acid and beneficial *lactobacilli*, all of which promote good health in many ways, while at the same time satisfying the sensation of thirst.

Both modern soft drinks and plain water are poor substitutes for these health-promoting traditional beverages. Taken with meals, they contribute to thorough and easy digestion of food; taken during physical labor, they rapidly replace lost mineral ions to give an energizing lift that renews rather than depletes the body's reserves. The day when every town and hamlet in America produces its own distinctive lacto-fermented brew, made from the local products of woods and fields, will be the day when Americans see the dawning of a new age of good health and well-being—along with a new era of economic vitality based on small-scale local production rather than on large-scale monopolistic control of the food processing industry.

On the subject of alcoholic beverages, the evidence is also inconsistent. Certainly the problem of alcoholism is enormous, particularly in the United States where there are some 15 to 20 million alcoholics, or about one in every ten people. Alcoholics are more prone to disease and to accidents than the normal population and tend to die young. On the other hand, several traditional societies, noted for the longevity and good health of their citizens, consume moderate amounts of beer or wine made from grapes, bananas and other fruits. These wines tend to have a lower alcohol content than modern wines and beers. Research indicates that moderate consumption of alcohol, particularly wine, may prevent heart disease; one oft-quoted study indicates that those who drink moderately— one to two glasses of wine per day—in general live longer than those who overindulge, and than those who do not drink at all, but this may be due to the fact that such people tend to be moderate in *all* their habits and may be better able to afford a more nutritious diet. Other studies link even moderate alcohol consumption with breast cancer.[166]

The religions of the world differ in their laws on alcohol consumption, but most are in agreement that those on a spiritual path, or those who have chosen a life of devoted service, should refrain from alcoholic beverages. If you do drink, we urge you to partake only of wine or unpasteurized beer with meals in very moderate amounts and to abstain from all alcoholic beverages from time to time. Pregnant women should not consume alcohol. (If you use wine in cooking but want to be sure that the alcohol has evaporated, boil the sauce to which it has been added, uncovered, for about ten minutes.)

The problem of alcoholism is allied to the problem of nutrition in general. The root cause of alcohol cravings is a deficiency of B vitamins, trace minerals and the amino acid glutamine.[167] Some practitioners find that alcoholics improve when grains are removed from their diets.[168] Thus, the best diet for the alcoholic is one that is high in B vitamins, devoid of all grains and sugars and rich in high-protein foods such as eggs and meat—not exactly the diet promoted by the Department of Agriculture and its new food pyramid!

Alcoholics tend to lack alcohol dehydrogenase, an enzyme that gets rid of alcohol. This implies deficiencies in magnesium and zinc as well as an overload on the pancreas, all of which can be ameliorated by a diet of nutrient-rich and enzyme-rich foods. Homemade bone broths and lacto-fermented beverages can be particularly beneficial to the alcoholic because they aid digestion and the assimilation of much-needed nutrients.

Former alcoholics often replace alcoholic drinks with sweets and sodas without realizing that sugar plays havoc with the intestinal flora, fostering overgrowth of *candida albicans* and other fungi. Under certain conditions these pathogenic yeasts actually convert sugars in the gut to alcohol! There are well-documented cases of inebriation caused by sugar consumption and candida overgrowth in persons who do not drink alcohol.[169] The alcoholic, in turning to sugar, is often supplying himself with alcohol throughout the day!

Alcohol-free beer and wine are high in carbohydrates and should also be avoided by those attempting to give up alcoholic beverages. Often they still contain 0.5 percent alcohol, and the taste of these wines and beers may perpetuate the longing for alcohol. As they have been boiled to remove alcohol, they have been shorn of their enzyme content, which is a health-promoting, compensating factor in wine and unpasteurized beer.

The recipes for traditional lacto-fermented beverages we present in this book constitute an alternative not only to soft drinks but to alcoholic beverages as well. We offer the theory that the craving for alcohol, as well as the craving for soft drinks, stems from an ancient collective memory of the kind of lacto-fermented beverages still found in traditional societies. These beverages give a lift to the tired body by supplying mineral ions depleted through perspiration and make food taste more agreeable and satisfying by supplying *lactobacilli*, lactic acid and enzymes needed for easy and thorough digestion.

ABOUT FOOD ALLERGIES & SPECIAL DIETS

For many people, the presence of food allergies and the necessity to restrict food choices present an unwelcome barrier to the joy of eating. Food allergies afflict a large portion of our population and can cause such diverse complaints as sneezing, itching, arthritis, nervous disorders, concentration problems, insomnia, headaches and chronic fatigue. More recently, diseases like cancer, diabetes, multiple sclerosis and schizophrenia have been linked to food allergies. Often allergy sufferers find that they are allergic to the very foods they eat frequently and like the most.

Allergy tests have revealed sensitivities to every food commonly eaten, but most prevalent are allergies to milk products and grains—precisely the two foods added to man's diet when he changed from a hunter-gatherer life style to one of cultivation and domestication. The proteins of grain and milk, namely gluten and casein, are two of the hardest proteins for humans to digest. This is one reason that traditional cultures usually soak or sprout grains and culture their dairy products before eating them. Problems with milk also stem from the body's inability to produce the enzyme lactase, required to break down lactose or milk sugar. The process of fermenting or culturing milk products breaks down a portion of the lactose; even so, large numbers cannot tolerate milk products in any form. Some people are sensitive to the high levels of the amino acid tyramine found in cheddar-type cheeses. Asians, in general, tolerate milk products less well than Westerners.

On the other hand, Asians tolerate grains better than other population groups, probably because of the length of time they have subsisted on grains. Those members of Asian societies unable to thrive on grains have long since been selected out through shortened life span and reduced fertility. This selection process may be the reason that Asians have pancreas organs and salivary glands up to 50 percent larger as a function of body weight that those of Westerners.[170] These traits allow them to digest grains more fully and contribute to their high tolerance for rice, millet and wheat. The comparatively smaller salivary glands and pancreas of the Westerner often make it difficult for him to digest grains, especially gluten-containing grains such as wheat, corn, oats, rye and barley. Gluten intolerance is associated with a family history of alcoholism, arthritis, Down's syndrome and mental disorders such as schizophrenia and dementia.[171] Gluten intolerance has been linked with vitamin B_6 deficiency.

People with poor adrenal function are often unable to tolerate carbohydrates in any form. Others cannot digest meat very well, due to suppressed or absent hydrochloric acid production in the stomach. This may be due to a deficiency of vitamin B_6 and zinc, both needed for the production of pancreatic enzymes, or of insufficient chloride due to a low-salt diet. Hydrochloric acid production often decreases with age, rendering meats less well tolerated by the older generation. Some individuals are sensitive to foods from the nightshade family—tomatoes, potatoes, eggplant and peppers—and react with sore and painful joints, leading to arthritis. Certain fruits, such as tomatoes, almonds, apricots, peaches and nectarines, contain aspirin-like compounds called salicylates, which have been shown to contribute to hyperactivity and asthma in some children. Citrus fruits frequently cause allergies. Heavily yeasted foods, such as vinegar, barley malt, alcoholic beverages, commercially pickled foods, soy sauce, Worcestershire sauce and aged cheeses, often exacerbate the symptoms of chronic yeast infection.[172]

An easy way to determine whether you are allergic to a certain food is the following: Avoid the suspected food for at least four days. Then eat a moderate amount of it on an empty stomach. Test your pulse before and after eating the food. If your pulse rises more than a few beats per minute, or if you have any adverse reaction, you are probably allergic to it.[173] We should always be alert to symptoms of food intolerance, such as rashes, fatigue, insomnia, headaches, joint pain and hoarseness. These are nature's warning signals, and it is the wise individual who heeds them.

Genetic predisposition is a major cause of allergies; another is poor diet in general, resulting in digestion that is less than thorough. A diet deficient in animal fats and other bodybuilding factors during infancy and childhood may lead to weaknesses in the intestinal walls, the so-called "leaky gut syndrome" in which partially digested food particles pass into the blood stream. Another contributing factor is enzyme exhaustion from a diet composed primarily of cooked foods. Consumption of sugar and caffeine leads to adrenal exhaustion, a prime cause of allergies. Sugar and refined carbohydrates in the gut can stimulate an overgrowth of *candida albicans*, naturally occurring fungi that break down dead or inert foods in the intestines. With overconsumption of dead foods, such as refined carbohydrates, these organisms multiply uncontrollably. Vinegar and other heavily yeasted foods also encourage candida overgrowth in some people. These yeasts actually change form, attach themselves to the walls of the intestine and grow into the intestine, causing holes in the intestinal wall that allow undigested food and toxins, including toxins produced by candida itself, to enter the bloodstream. These toxins and food particles will then trigger allergic reactions, especially when the immune system is weak or the body is under stress.

A final cause of food allergies is the present-day tendency to eat exclusively foods from just a few types or families. Of the 4,000 or so edible plant species that have fed human societies at one time or another in the past, only 150 are widely cultivated today and just three of them provide 60 percent of the world's food.[174] Today our choice of foods is limited to about thirty species, and for many the choice is even more restricted. It is not unusual for some children to eat nothing but pizza, hot dogs and peanut butter sandwiches, or for those following the macrobiotic diet to consume mostly rice and soybean products with a few vegetables. Such diets will not only be deficient in many nutrients, but the constant call for enzymes needed to digest those particular foods can lead to the exhaustion of that specific digestion mechanism. The exclusive use of just a few foods can lead to severe food addictions—every bit as harmful and as difficult to break as addictions to drugs or alcohol. These food addictions, with their concomitant allergic reactions, nurture the biochemical disruptions that lead to more serious degenerative diseases.

If you have food allergies or sensitivities, you will need to eliminate some categories of food from your diet. The best defense against allergies to begin with is a varied and healthful diet from which all refined and stimulating foods—sugar, white flour, refined and hydrogenated vegetable oils, refined salt and caffeine—have been eliminated, and which supplies the intestinal tract with lactic-acid producing bacteria and food enzymes on a frequent basis.

Along with allergies, our genetic inheritance, constitutional type, age, race, occupation, climate and overall state of health all have a bearing on what we should eat. Elderly people and invalids, whose digestive mechanisms have been compromised or are in decline, should pay special attention to getting a good supply of enzymes in their diet and should favor foods that have been puréed, prepared with meat broths or predigested, like soaked gruels and porridges. Growing children and pregnant women need plenty of fat-soluble vitamins found in butter, cream, fish and fish eggs, eggs and organ meats. Those living in cold climates also need more foods rich in vitamin

A. Those who do hard physical labor may need a steady supply of animal products in the diet; but those who lead a contemplative life often find overconsumption of animal products, especially red meat, a hindrance. People who suffer from an underactive thyroid condition often do best on a diet in which fats, especially unsaturated fats, are restricted; while others, notably hypoglycemics and individuals prone to seizures, benefit from a diet that is comparatively high in fats.

The wisdom of the ancients teaches us that there are appropriate times for both feasting on rich foods and for fasting on the simplest of fare. Periodic fasting is an age-old method for restoring and maintaining health. Fasting on meat or vegetable broth or on lacto-fermented vegetable juices allows our enzyme-producing and digestive mechanisms to rest so that other enzyme systems can work at repair, detoxification and healing. Many ancient physicians recommended a monodiet for the sick, such as ten days of rice gruel. Hippocrates often prescribed a diet consisting only of raw milk for those suffering from TB or psoriasis. Healing fasts work best when carried out in conjunction with a program of intestinal cleansing through enemas or colonics.

The danger of fasting is that it can be continued too long. The body temple may benefit from the occasional application of mops and brooms—broths and vegetable preparations—but this magnificent edifice is built strong and kept in good repair with bricks and mortar—nutrient-dense proteins and fats.

There has been much debate about the ideal proportions of protein, carbohydrate and fat in our diets. The Politically Correct diet is one that is high in carbohydrates and low in protein and fat; others suggest a diet in which carbohydrates are all but eliminated, especially for weight loss. Another school of thought suggests that a certain precise balance of macronutrients (40 percent carbohydrates, 30 percent protein and 30 percent fat) is the key to perfect health. Traditional diets, when analyzed, reveal approximate proportions of 40 percent carbohydrate foods, 20 percent protein foods and 40 percent fats,[175] with the exception of arctic regions and certain cattle-herding groups that do not use much in the way of plant foods and whose diets can be as high as 80 percent fat.[176] (Fats have twice as many calories per unit of weight as protein and carbohydrates. As protein and carbohydrate foods are more than 80 percent water, the amount of fat by weight in a diet that yields 40 percent of total calories is actually quite small. Thus, a lightly marbled steak with a mere 1/4 inch of fat around the edge will contain about 50 percent of calories as fat.) These proportions should serve as guidelines only and not as rigid dogma that causes us to make a fetish of our eating habits. Systems that stress macronutrient *quantities* often overlook the importance of the food *quality*. A snack bar composed of protein powder, refined sugars and cheap oils should not considered an appropriate food, whatever claims are made for its macronutrient balance.

A recent popular book urges specific diets based on blood types, arguing, for example, that all people of Type A blood should be vegetarians and that only those with Type B blood should consume dairy products.[177] This system is based on theories of human evolution that are impossible to prove and on research that is difficult to validate.[178] Diet systems that emphasize high quality ancestral foods and proper preparation techniques have better chances for long-term success than those that assign the earth's entire population to one of four food lists, particularly when those lists include questionable foods like soy and exclude nourishing fats like coconut oil.

Other dietary systems that have enjoyed some popularity are those that deal with the acid- and alkaline-forming characteristics of our foods and their supposed effects on the pH value of the blood and tissues. When entirely burned, foods leave an ash or residue that is either acidic, alkaline or neutral. Breads, cereals, fish, meats, eggs and poultry usually leave an acid-ash residue

due to high amounts of chlorine, sulphur (in the case of meats and eggs) and phosphorus (in the case of meat and whole grains). Alkaline-ash foods are those in which the elements potassium, sodium, calcium and magnesium predominate, including most vegetables and fruits—even fruits with a high acid component like citrus and tomatoes, because these acids can be completely metabolized in the body into carbon dioxide, water and energy. As for nuts, almonds, chestnuts and coconuts are alkaline-ash foods, while Brazil nuts, peanuts and walnuts yield an acid ash. Most legumes are alkaline-ash foods except for lentils which yield an acid ash. Neutral-ash foods are the pure fats like butter and lard, because they can be completely burned, and refined carbohydrates like white sugar and cornstarch, because they contain no minerals. Milk products yield an alkaline ash due to high levels of calcium. Phytates in whole grains complicate the picture because they bind with alkaline-ash minerals and carry them out of the body. Additives found in various foodstuffs have an unpredictable effect on the food residue.

Under normal conditions, the blood, saliva and extracellular fluids are slightly alkaline, while the urine is slightly acidic. The pH value of these fluids is maintained by a series of complex feedback mechanisms in the body and, in general, is not dependent on dietary excesses of either acid or alkaline foods. After a meal rich in proteins, the blood will become more alkaline for a short period, which is in effect a balancing reaction to the secretion of large amounts of hydrochloric acid in the stomach. Following this the blood then undergoes a short-lived increase in acidity, which is again a balancing reaction to the heavy secretion of alkaline enzyme-rich solutions from the pancreas. These reactions are completely normal and should in no way be interpreted as justification for avoiding high-protein, "acid-forming" foods.

In the most simple terms, the normal, slightly alkaline condition of the blood is maintained primarily by the action of the kidneys and the lungs regulating the balance between the amount of carbon dioxide and bicarbonate ions in the blood. Problems with the kidneys or lungs, dehydration, ingestion of certain drugs, diabetic conditions or other causes may lead to acidosis, with symptoms of drowsiness, progressing to stupor and coma. This acute condition may be relieved by taking an alkaline solution, such as bicarbonate of soda. The condition of alkalosis may likewise be caused by impaired kidney function as well as hyperventilation, ingestion of certain drugs such as diuretics or steroids, and loss of acid from the body due to vomiting or gastric drainage. Symptoms include cramps, muscle spasms, irritability and hyperexcitability. Treatment of this acute condition may include breathing expired carbon dioxide from a paper bag or taking an acidic solution, such as ammonium chloride.

Unusual chronic or long-term conditions of acidosis or alkalosis *may* be relieved by stressing more acid-forming or alkaline-forming foods in the diet, but such regimes can also lead to deficiencies that further exacerbate the condition. Many people with perfectly normal blood pH values have followed "alkalinizing diets" without realizing that there is no particular need to do so. One particularly dangerous theory suggests that the human diet should be composed entirely of alkaline-forming fruits and vegetables to the exclusion of protein-rich "acid-forming" foods. Under the vast majority of conditions, high-protein foods, such as meat and eggs, do not cause the blood to be pathologically acidic. On the contrary, good quality protein is needed for the body to maintain the proper pH values of the blood and extracellular fluids and to maintain the health and integrity of the lungs and kidneys, those organs which have the most to do with regulating the pH values of the blood. Phosphorus in whole grains, which is an "acid-forming" mineral, actually plays an important role in preventing the blood from becoming too acid. Dr. Weston Price found that the

Eskimo, living on a diet composed almost exclusively of "acid-forming" high-protein foods, showed no signs of acidosis. When he analyzed the diets of healthy primitive people, free of tooth decay and disease, he found that they were high in both acid-ash and alkaline-ash foods, with acid-ash foods predominating.[179]

An unbalanced diet consisting mainly of "alkaline-forming" fruits and vegetables, while possibly useful in the short term as a fast, can lead to serious deficiencies in the long run—and for diabetics and hypoglycemics a diet composed exclusively of fruits and vegetables can be dangerous even in the short term.

A variation of acid-alkaline dietary formulations is the diet that prohibits the combination of protein foods, which require acid for digestion, with sugars and starches, which are digested in an alkaline environment. This diet was introduced at turn of the century by Dr. W. H. Hay and received renewed interest with the publication of *Fit for Life* by Harvey and Marilyn Diamond. The authors advocate eating starches and proteins at different meals; further, they recommend beginning the day with fruit only, eating starches at lunch, and saving protein foods for the evening meal. As proof of the importance of proper food combining, they cite research showing that protein and starches taken together are not fully digested. To clinch their argument, they point out that legumes—foods that contain both starch and protein—often cause indigestion.

There are several problems with the assumptions behind this food-combining system. The assertion that the body is unable to digest protein and starches together is just plain wrong. The healthy body is entirely equipped to do just that. Protein digestion begins in the acidic environment of the stomach; alkaline-dependent enzymes then digest starches in the small intestine while other alkaline-dependent enzymes complete the process of protein digestion. In addition, food enzymes help predigest both protein and starches in the stomach, and this digestion is more or less thorough in relation to the enzymes available from food and saliva. Gelatin-rich broth taken with a meal also contributes to a thorough digestion of both proteins and starches.

Beans cause digestive problems not because they contain protein and starches together, but because they contain two complex sugars, farrinose and stachyose, which are not easily broken down by enzymes normally found in the intestines. Beans and other legumes will be more digestible if soaked for a long period before cooking as this process begins the breakdown of these starches. Beans properly prepared have provided nourishment to human beings all over the globe and can be easily digested by most people. Actually, there is no food on earth that is a pure starch or a pure protein. Even meat contains some sugar, and all acidic fruits contain starch.

A final argument against food combining notes that we find no such strictures among traditional societies whose intuitive wisdom has dictated the food choices that kept them healthy for generations. A few examples culled from the research of Dr. Price will suffice: Isolated Swiss villagers ate milk products with rye bread; primitive Gaelic peoples subsisted on fish and oats; natives of the Caribbean consumed seafood along with starchy tubers of the manioc family; Indians in the Andes mountains ate potatoes with small animals and seafood; Polynesians consumed starchy tubers, fruit and seafood. Semitic peoples combined meat and milk products with grains. Primitive peoples, with their unerring native wisdom, put no restrictions on combining starches and proteins or even fruits and proteins—they couldn't afford to and they didn't need to.

It must be said, however, that some people find they have more energy when they avoid certain food combinations, possibly a sign that their digestive systems have been compromised through poor diet and improper food preparation techniques. Milk products with meat and citrus fruits with grains seem to be the most frequent problem-causing combinations. Many find they do not tolerate raw fruit eaten with other foods. An individual determination of improper food combinations can only be accomplished on a trial and error basis.

No discussion of special diets would be complete without a consideration of the macrobiotic diet system, said to be based on the ancient Chinese text *The Yellow Emperor's Classic of Internal Medicine*. Macrobiotics was introduced to the West by George Ohsawa and popularized by several gifted writers. It is an extension of the ancient Chinese world view that all energies and all objects in the cosmos can be classified as either yin (female) or yang (male). With its system of facial diagnosis and treatment based upon correspondences of specific foods to various organs and conditions, it has many similarities to the medieval doctrine of the four humors, which has recently enjoyed something of a resurgence in Europe. Such intuitive and noninvasive methods can be very useful to the medical practitioner, especially when combined with more orthodox diagnostic techniques that are grounded in the scientific method.

According to the marcobiotic system, sugar is the most yin food, followed by fruit juices, honey, tropical fruits, acid fruits, dairy products and vegetables of the nightshade family; pork is the most yang food, followed by beef, game, poultry, eggs and fish. Vegetables and legumes are slightly yin while grains are slightly yang. Rice, revered by Asians as the perfect food, is said to be in the center—with perfect balance of yin and yang energies.

Ohsawa repeatedly warned about dangers of refined foods like sugar and white flour. He had excellent short-term results with this diet—in spite of the fact that it did not eliminate smoking—both in Japan and in the West. Unfortunately, Ohsawa confused many people by his extreme statements and unclear food guidelines—only a small portion of his writing was directly concerned with food—and he is generally remembered for the strict brown rice diet, a cleansing regime for the sick. Michio Kushi then developed his "standard macrobiotic diet," which gave more precise macrobiotic food recommendations. People more easily understood the Kushi presentation, which mentions but does not stress natural sea salt, fish broth and fermented vegetables as necessary components of the diet. Kushi permitted a small portion of white meat fish occasionally, *if desired*, claiming that a totally vegetarian fare would cover all nutritional needs. This claim cannot be supported by scientific evidence and, in fact, directly contradicts *The Yellow Emperor's Classic of Internal Medicine,* which lists the five meats as essential, strengthening components of the diet.

Kushi's more extreme claims—that a strict brown rice diet confers spiritual enlightenment, and that diets based entirely on local foods bring peace to the planet—defy common sense. In many parts of the world, the two principles are impossible to implement jointly. Rice-eating macrobiotic disciples living in Montana must rely on foods imported from distant lands in order to practice their search for enlightenment, but in order to achieve world peace they would need to give up rice-eating for a diet of local beef.

The particulars of Kushi's diet can be faulted on several counts. First, as many adherents omit fish broth and fermented vegetables, it often lacks both gelatin and food enzymes and can therefore be difficult to digest, especially for the Westerner who, with a smaller pancreas and salivary gland than the Asian, fares better on grains that have been soaked, fermented or cooked in gelatin-rich broth. For this reason, candida infection, intestinal discomfort and low energy are frequent complaints among macrobiotic adherents. Dishes containing *seitan*—unfermented wheat gluten—can pose real problems to those with gluten intolerance. Secondly, this restrictive version of macrobiotics does not supply all-important fat-soluble vitamins A and D. Predictably, children born and raised in households where this diet was rigorously applied suffered from small stature and rickets.[180] In adults, dangerously low cholesterol levels resulting in depression, poor concentration and even strokes and cancer have been associated with diets that call for the elimination of animal proteins and fats and an over reliance on vegetable oils—diets found in many macrobiotic cookbooks and, indeed, in numerous health-oriented cookbooks. A third problem is the danger of mineral deficiencies, especially zinc deficiency, from a heavy reliance on grains that have not been soaked or fermented. In short, second generation macrobiotics is an artificial diet not found in any traditional society anywhere in the world, which as an alternative to junk food often gives good results at first, but which leads to widespread deficiencies in the long term.

A new breed of macrobiotic practitioners has bravely admitted the faults of Kushi's interpretation and now sees macrobiotics as an open-ended system, subject to progressive revelation. Many macrobiotic cookbooks now include recipes for oily fish and eggs; and a number of counselors have begun to recommend butter and other dairy products, especially for children. We submit that the principles presented in this book, including the use of gelatinous broth, fermented foods, soaked and soured grains, natural sea salt and a more scientific approach to the subject of fats, would ensure Ohsawa's promised benefits without requiring those drawn to macrobiotics to abandon any of their basic principles.

Two important foods in the macrobiotic diet require additional comment: soybeans and seaweed. Soybeans are high in phytates and contain potent enzyme inhibitors that are only deactivated by fermentation and not by ordinary cooking.[181] These inhibitors can lead to protein assimilation problems in those who consume unfermented soy products frequently.[182] Soybeans must not be used like other legumes in soups and other dishes but only as fermented products like *miso*, *natto* and *tempeh*. It is also a mistake to rely on tofu or bean curd as a protein food because of its high phytate content.[183] Those who wish to eat tofu would be wise to imitate the Japanese who eat small amounts of tofu in fish broth and not as a substitute for animal foods. Soy milk, often substituted for cow's milk, also has a high phytate content and can lead to mineral deficiencies.[184] Phytoestrogens found in soy foods, although touted as panaceas for heart disease, cancer and osteoporosis, are potent endocrine disrupters as well as goitrogens—substances that depress thyroid function.[185] Phytoestrogens are not removed by fermenting or modern processing.

Seaweeds are found in many native diets. They are an excellent source of minerals but may contribute to iodine poisoning if overconsumed. They also contain long-chain complex sugars, similar to those found in the Jerusalem artichoke, which some individuals are unable to digest. Furthermore, many commercial seaweeds are treated with pesticides and fungicides on drying racks. Those who consume seaweeds frequently should be careful of their supply and should simmer them for a long period to begin the breakdown of the long-chain sugars found in all sea vegetables. (For unsprayed seaweeds, see Sources.)

Nourishing traditional foodways—which include traditional animal fats, a wide variety of properly prepared whole foods, some raw foods, homemade fish and meat broths and lacto-fermented grains, vegetables and beverages—can and should be incorporated not only into macrobiotics, but into *every* diet—Asian, Middle Eastern, African, Latin American, European and plain old American. The living laboratory of human society has demonstrated that diets based on these wise and ancient principles, regardless of specific ingredients, promote optimum physical and mental well-being and healthy offspring, generation after generation.

PARTING WORDS

Twentieth-century men and women, faced with a dazzling array of modern food products, are naturally tempted by their convenience and glitz. They would prefer not to worry about how their foods are processed or what they contain; they would prefer not to spend time in food preparation the way their ancestors did. But the inevitable consequence of this insouciance is the host of the debilitating diseases now endemic in our society.

With traditions forgotten, the tool that allows modern men and women to regain their health and vitality is knowledge—knowledge of the fruits of honest scientific inquiry as well as renewed familiarity with culinary customs of times past. The cook, the food provider and parents of young children can no longer afford to be misled by what passes for nutritional wisdom in the popular press, especially as so much orthodox advice—magnified, simplified and twisted by publicity for processed foods—is partially or totally wrong. We urge you to keep abreast of research conducted by independent researchers and holistic doctors, especially as it sheds light on the nourishing traditions of our ancestors.

Then call on your reserves of ingenuity and creativity to translate that knowledge into delicious meals in whatever culinary tradition may appeal to you and your family. We must not lose sight of the fact that the fundamental requirement of the food we eat is that we like it. The healthiest food in the world does us no good if we must gag it down because it tastes bad.

Our food should satisfy our four basic tastes—salt, sour, bitter and sweet. These tastes are meant to guide us to the foods we need, but they are easily suborned by ignorance or lack of will. Satisfy the salt taste with natural sea salt or traditional meat broths, which also provide magnesium and vital trace minerals, instead of products laced with MSG or drenched in commercial salt; please the sour taste bud with old-fashioned fermented foods that provide the enzymatic by-products of the culturing process, rather than with pasteurized condiments and alcohol; gratify the bitter taste bud with the dark green vegetables and bitter herbs that are valued in every traditional society, so rich in vitamins and minerals, instead of coffee and tea; and delight the sweet tooth with fruits at their peak of ripeness and with natural sweeteners high in nutrients, rather than refined sugar products.

The challenge to every individual is to determine the diet that is right for him and to implement that diet in a way that does not divorce him from the company of fellow human beings at mealtimes. Each person's ideal diet is usually discovered through a combination of study, observation and intuition, a process designed to replace that mysterious infallible instinct that guided primitive man to the foods he needed to keep him healthy and strong.

To make us healthy, our food must taste good; it must be digestible, and it must be eaten in peace. Even whole foods, properly prepared according to traditional methods, do us no good if we eat them with a grudge; they will not confer health on the man who does not forgive. It is the loving heart who will find, in the pages that follow, guidelines for providing an abundance of all the nutrients we need to live healthy, happy and productive lives.

GUIDE TO FOOD SELECTION

A sound approach to food selection, one that will serve you better than the USDA Food Pyramid, divides our choices into three distinct categories: **Nourishing Traditional Foods**, **Compromise Foods** and **Newfangled Foods**. Eat a varied diet of foods chosen from the **Nourishing Traditional Foods** category. The proportion of animal foods, grains, dairy products, fruits and fats you choose will depend on your ethnic heritage, your constitution, your age, your occupation, the climate in which you live and your specific food sensitivities and allergies. Healthy people can eat **Compromise Foods** in moderate amounts. **Newfangled Foods** are best avoided by everybody.

NOURISHING TRADITIONAL FOODS

Proteins: Fresh, pasture-raised meat including beef, lamb, game, chicken, turkey, duck and other fowl; organ meats from pastured animals; seafood of all types from deep sea waters; fresh shellfish in season; fish eggs; fresh eggs from pastured poultry; organic fermented soy products in small amounts.

Fats: Fresh butter and cream from pasture-fed cows, preferably raw and cultured; lard and beef, lamb, goose and duck fat from pastured animals; extra virgin olive oil; unrefined flax seed oil in small amounts; coconut oil and palm oil.

Dairy: Raw, whole milk and cultured dairy products, such as yoghurt, piima milk, kefir and raw cheese, from traditional breeds of pasture-fed cows and goats.

Carbohydrates: Organic whole grain products properly treated for the removal of phytates, such as sourdough and sprouted grain bread and soaked or sprouted cereal grains; soaked and fermented legumes including lentils, beans, and chickpeas; sprouted or soaked seeds and nuts; fresh fruits and vegetables, both raw and cooked; fermented vegetables.

Beverages: Filtered, high-mineral water; lacto-fermented drinks made from grain or fruit; meat stocks and vegetable broths.

Condiments: Unrefined sea salt; raw vinegar; spices in moderation; fresh herbs; naturally fermented soy sauce and fish sauce.

❦ COMPROMISE FOODS ❧

Protein: Pork, fish from shallow waters, commercially raised beef, lamb, turkey and chicken; barbecued or smoked meats; traditionally made, additive-free sausage; additive-free bacon; battery eggs; tofu in very small amounts.

Fats: Unrefined peanut and sesame oils.

Dairy: Raw, whole, uncultured milk from conventional dairies; pasteurized, cultured milk products; pasteurized cheeses; melted cheeses.

Carbohydrates: Whole grains not treated for phytates, such as quick-rise breads and pasta; unbleached white flour; canned legumes; thin-skinned fruits and vegetables imported from long distances; canned tomato products; well-cooked, unsprayed seaweeds; natural sweeteners, such as honey, maple syrup, Rapadura, and date sugar.

Beverages: Wine or unpasteurized beer in moderation with meals; diluted fruit juices; herb teas.

Condiments: Commercial salt; pasteurized vinegar; canned condiments without MSG.

❦ NEWFANGLED FOODS ❧

Protein: Processed meats containing additives and preservatives, such as luncheon meat, salami and bacon; hydrolyzed protein and protein isolates; soy milk.

Fats: All highly processed vegetable oils, margarine, tub spreads and vegetable shortenings; fat substitutes; foods fried in vegetable oils; lowfat products.

Dairy: Pasteurized, homogenized commercial milk; ultrapasteurized cream and milk; processed cheeses; reduced-fat dairy products.

Carbohydrates: Bleached and "fortified" white flour products; commercial dry cereals; granolas; refined sugar in all forms, such as dextrose, fructose and high fructose corn syrup; irradiated and genetically modified grains, fruits and vegetables; most canned products; chocolate.

Beverages: Soda pop; distilled or pasteurized alcohol products; full strength fruit juices; commercial rice and oat milks; coffee, tea and cocoa.

Condiments: Commercial baking powder; MSG; artificial flavors, additives and colors; chemically produced food preservatives; aspartame.

A WORD on EQUIPMENT

Modern equipment takes old-fashioned drudgery out of traditional cooking—but it is important to make wise choices. The following is a suggested list, in order from most to least essential.

- **Stainless Steel Cookware:** Choose stainless steel rather than aluminum cookware. Acidic or salty foods cooked in aluminum will cause this toxic metal to be dissolved into food. Recent research has linked aluminum with Alzheimer's disease and many investigators feel that aluminum from cookware contributes to other diseases as well.[186] Unfortunately, as some people have gotten the message about aluminum and have exchanged their inexpensive aluminum pans for the more expensive stainless steel variety, aluminum cookware has crept back in at the top end, so to speak, in the form of spun aluminum pots and pans for the gourmet market. Don't buy them. They look great, but aluminum is highly reactive, even in high-tech form.

- **Stockpot:** A large stockpot made of stainless steel or good quality enamel is a must.

- **Cast-Iron Skillets:** Heavy, old-fashioned cast-iron frying pans are great for all sautéing and stir-frys. These pans should not be washed with soap but merely rinsed in hot water and dried with paper towels. A cast-iron pan, well seasoned in this manner, will never stick; and food cooked in heavy cast iron is much less likely to burn than food cooked in the thickest stainless steel.

- **Flameproof Casseroles:** Casseroles that can be used on the stove burner or in the oven come in a variety of sizes. Choose casseroles made of good quality enamel over cast iron, or simply the less expensive uncoated cast-iron varieties.

- **Good Knives:** Serrated knives of various lengths are best for bread and vegetables—those made by Cutco (see Sources) are excellent and keep their cutting edge for years. Tempered steel knives that can be honed are best for meats, including a fish filleting knife with a medium-length, flexible blade and a long, flexible round-ended carving knife. A large chopping knife should be included your collection.

- **Kitchen Scissors:** Sturdy kitchen scissors come in handy for a variety of tasks, from snipping herbs to carving chickens. Cutco makes excellent kitchen scissors. (See Sources.)

- **Wooden Cutting Boards:** Wooden cutting boards are much less likely to harbor pathogenic bacteria than plastic ones. You should have two—one for meats and one for vegetables and fruits.

- **Handheld Blender:** This low-cost appliance makes soup-making a breeze. The soup is blended right in the pot, thus saving time and dishes to wash.

- **Glass and Stainless Steel Food Containers:** Glass or stainless steel containers are less likely to promote contamination of refrigerated food than plastic ones. But plastic is fine for storing dry foods like grains and crispy nuts and frozen foods like stocks.

- **Wide-Mouth, Quart-Size Mason Jars:** These are the best containers for lacto-fermented vegetables and chutneys. They are inexpensive and widely available. Special pickling crocks, for making large amounts of sauerkraut and other fermented foods, are available through catalog order. (See Sources.)

- **Glass Beverage Containers:** For lacto-fermented beverages you will need two-quart glass containers with airtight seals. For ginger beer and small beer you will need bottles with wire-held corks or stoppers.

- **Food Processor:** What did we do before this labor-saving device made its way into our kitchens? For slicing, grating, chopping, mixing and blending, the food processor is invaluable, allowing us to prepare traditional dishes that once required extensive hand labor—chopping parsley for tabouli, grinding chickpeas for hummus, making a julienne of vegetables, processing perfect mayonnaise. The food processor handles these prosaic chores with ease. Choose one that comes with a variety of blades and an attachment that allows you to add oils drop by drop—essential for making mayonnaise and pesto sauce.

- **Stainless Steel Baking Pans and Cookie Sheets:** These are made by Enko and are available at some cookware stores, at a cost not much greater than the aluminum and coated varieties. (See Sources.)

- **Handheld Mixer:** This is a handy gadget to have if you do any baking, but a wire whisk and a little muscle power will accomplish the same tasks.

- **Grain Mill:** If you bake frequently, you will want to buy a grain mill. This allows you to have fresh flour when you need it. (Whole grain flour quickly goes rancid after grinding.) A small hand mill can be bought for about $100. Motor-driven mills are more expensive, but serious cooks will find that they are worth it. The grinding surface should be true stone and not a synthetic version. A good choice is the Jupiter mill, manufactured in Germany. (See Sources.) The grinding surface is hard granite and it has adjustable settings, which allow you to both crack grains and grind them into fine flour. A stainless steel milling attachment allows you to grind oily seeds and sprouted grains.

- **Grain Roller:** If you want rolled oats and rye flakes that are absolutely fresh, a grain roller will do the job. (See Sources.)

- **Corn Mill:** The Jupiter mill will grind corn kernels with a little coaxing, but corn bread aficionados may wish to obtain a mill designed specifically for corn. (See Sources.)

- **Mini Mill:** This is useful for grinding spices and flax seeds.

- **Ice Cream Maker:** Modern ice cream makers, with quart-sized containers that are stored in the freezer, eliminate the need for ice and salt and make ice cream making a breeze.

- **Food Mill:** This is an inexpensive gadget useful for blending apple sauce and several soups and sauces that require the removal of skins. Highly recommended is the French *Moulin a Legumes*, with a removable blade. Less satisfactory is the Foley Food Mill, an American version.

- **Stoneware:** Stoneware muffin tins and bread pans give very satisfactory results for the soaked flour recipes in this book.

- **Juicer:** A juicer is needed for several beverage recipes. Many food processors come with juicer attachments.

- **Popcorn Maker:** An electric popcorn maker allows children to prepare this nutritious snack by themselves. (Store bought popped popcorn is not only rancid—it is loaded with commercial salt and partially hydrogenated vegetable oils.)

- **Dehydrator:** Dehydrators are good for drying crispy nuts and other foods, but a warm oven works just as well.

- **Jet Stream Oven:** If you must have some rapid-cooking mechanism, try the Jet Stream oven. (See Sources.) It cooks food quickly using convection currents and is a healthy alternative to the microwave. The Jet Stream does not compromise the taste of food as the microwave does, and it will even brown chickens and roasts.

Equipment that should *not* be found in the kitchens of conscientious cooks includes:

- **Microwave Oven:** Unfortunately, the microwave achieved instant popularity without much prior research to study the effects of eating microwaved food. In consequence, one large experiment involving an unwitting populace is now in progress. The small amount of research done on the effects of eating microwaved food has shown that the microwave may have unfavorable effects on fats and proteins, making them more difficult to assimilate. More recent studies carried out in Switzerland revealed that the microwave caused changes in vitamin content and availability. Eating microwaved food results in abnormal blood profiles, similar to those that occur in the early stages of cancer.[187] An especially dangerous practice is using the microwave for heating baby's bottle. Altered amino acids in microwaved milk can be toxic to the liver and nervous system, especially for infants.[188] We recommend that you resist using the microwave at all costs.

- **Pressure Cooker:** This is another relative newcomer to the culinary scene. The danger is that pressure cookers cook foods too quickly and at temperatures above the boiling point. A flameproof casserole is ideal for grains as well as for stews. Traditional cuisines always call for a long, slow cooking of grains and legumes.

KITCHEN TIPS AND HINTS

- To remove insects from organic or homegrown Brussels sprouts, cauliflower, artichokes, etc., soak thirty minutes in water to which 2 tablespoons of salt and vinegar have been added. Rinse well and proceed with cooking.

- Wash all fruits and vegetables to remove pesticides and other impurities in Dr. Bonner's Sal Suds (see Sources), hydrogen peroxide or plain Chlorox bleach (1 teaspoon per gallon). Soak about 10 minutes and then rinse well.

- To ripen tomatoes, peaches and other thin-skinned fruits, set them well separated in a sunny spot on a tray lined with paper towels. When soft enough, transfer to refrigerator.

- Do not add garlic to sautéing onions or other vegetables, because it has a tendency to burn. Add garlic after you have added your liquid—stock, wine, stir-fry sauce, tomatoes, etc.

- Always use unsalted butter. Those who like their butter salty can sprinkle sea salt on later.

- Use only unrefined salt, preferably Celtic sea salt.

- Use extra virgin olive oil and butter for cooking. Occasional use of peanut oil for stir-frying is permissible. Use lard or duck fat for stove-top potato frying.

- Always skim foam off stock, sauces, soups, legumes and stews. Many impurities rise to the top with the foam. Add spices and seasoning to stock, sauces, soups, legumes and stews after skimming.

- Grated lemon and orange rind should come from organic lemons. If not, wash the skins well with soap, rinse and dry before grating.

- Sauces and stews containing wine should be allowed to boil, uncovered, for at least 10 minutes to ensure all alcohol has evaporated.

- Grow your own herbs if you have garden space. If not, at least grow thyme in a pot. Nothing beats fresh thyme for flavor.

- To dry lettuce, watercress, spinach or parsley, wash well, shake dry and place in a pillow case (in the case of lettuce) or small cloth bag (in the case of watercress or parsley.) Tie up and place in your washing machine. Run on the last spin cycle to remove water by centrifugal force.

- To peel tomatoes and other thin-skinned fruits, bring a pan of filtered water to a boil. Using a slotted spoon, dip tomatoes in, one at a time, for about 5 seconds each. The skin should peel off easily. To seed tomatoes, cut in half at the equator, hold tomato half in the palm of your hand and gently squeeze out seeds.

- To peel large amounts of garlic, place whole bulbs in the oven and bake at 300 degrees until the individual cloves open. Remove from oven and pick out individual cloves.

- Always dry meat well before browning or it will stew rather than brown. Throw out browning fat when all pieces have browned and add more fat to pan, if necessary, to sauté vegetables.

- Always put meat juices back into sauces and stews—they are rich in important amino acids.

- When beating egg whites and cream, best results will be obtained by using a wire whisk rather than an electric beater. Beat egg whites in a very clean stainless steel or glass bowl with a pinch of salt.

≈ Keep your kitchen uncluttered and your counters clear. Store only frequently used items in your kitchen cupboards and leave as much working space as possible on your counters. Wipe counters after each task to provide a clean space for the next. Easy access to the tools and utensils you need and clean, clear counter space help make cooking a joy rather than a chore.

≈ Dishwasher powder is extremely poisonous and should be used with great care. Use half the recommended amount and only for one cycle of the dishwasher. Do not fill the second cycle receptacle with dish powder, but let it be a rinse cycle so that your dishes are rinsed twice. If you are caring for a cancer patient or anyone who is very sick, wash their dishes by hand in a mild liquid soap and rinse well.

≈ When preparing a meal, always think ahead to what must be done for the next two meals; put grains and pulses to soak and meats to marinate, as necessary. Our readers will notice that the food preparation methods we recommend call for considerable advance planning—not a bad habit to cultivate in life.

≈ Throw away all boxed breakfast cereals—the flakes, shapes and puffed grains produced by the extrusion process. Start your day with soaked oatmeal or other grain, whole grain dishes such as pancakes or muffins, eggs, fish, nut milks, broth or homemade soup.

≈ Aim for a diet that is 50 percent raw or enzyme-enhanced. Raw foods include vegetables, fruits, meats, fats and milk products.

≈ A good rule is to start your evening meal with a dish containing enzymes—either a salad with homemade dressing, raw meat or fish, or soup containing cultured cream. If your next course includes a sauce made from gelatin-rich stock, easy digestion and a peaceful night's sleep will be assured.

≈ If the meal you serve consists entirely of cooked foods, then a lacto-fermented condiment is a must.

≈ Keep sweets to a minimum, even natural sweets.

REFERENCES

1. Gittleman, Ann Louise, MS, *Beyond Pritikin*, 1980, Bantam Books, New York, NY.

2. Enig, Mary G, PhD, <u>*Trans*</u> *Fatty Acids in the Food Supply: A Comprehensive Report Covering 60 Years of Research*, 2nd Edition, Enig Associates, Inc., Silver Spring, MD, 1995, 4-8.

3. Castelli, William, *Archives of Internal Medicine*, Jul 1992, 152:7:1371-1372.

4. Hubert H, et al, *Circulation*, 1983, 67:968; Smith, R and E R Pinckney, *Diet, Blood Cholesterol and Coronary Heart Disease: A Critical Review of the Literature*, Vol 2, 1991, Vector Enterprises, Sherman Oaks, CA.

5. Rose G, et al, *The Lancet*, 1983, 1:1062-1065.

6. "Multiple Risk Factor Intervention Trial; Risk Factor Changes and Mortality Results," *Journal of the American Medical Association*, September 24, 1982, 248:12:1465.

7. "The Lipid Research Clinics Coronary Primary Prevention Trial Results. I. Reduction in Incidence of Coronary Heart Disease," *Journal of the American Medical Association*, 1984, 251:359.

8. Kronmal, R, *Journal of the American Medical Association*, April 12, 1985, 253:14:2091.

9. DeBakey, M, et al, *Journal of the American Medical Association*, 1964, 189:655-59.

10. Lackland, D T, et al, *Journal of Nutrition,* Nov 1990, 120:11S:1433-1436.

11. *Nutrition Week,* Mar 22, 1991, 21:12:2-3.

12. Alfin-Slater, R B, and L Aftergood, "Lipids," *Modern Nutrition in Health and Disease*, 6th ed, R S Goodhart and M E Shils, eds, Lea and Febiger, Philadelphia, 1980, 131.

13. Smith, M M, and F Lifshitz, *Pediatrics,* Mar 1994, 93:3:438-443.

14. Cohen, A, *American Heart Journal,* 1963, 65:291.

15. Malhotra, S, *Indian Journal of Industrial Medicine*, 1968, 14:219.

16. Kang-Jey Ho, et al, *Archeological Pathology*, 1971, 91:387; Mann, G V, et al, *American Journal of Epidemiology*, 1972, 95:26-37.

17. Price, Weston, DDS, *Nutrition and Physical Degeneration,* 1945, Price-Pottenger Nutrition Foundation, San Diego, CA, 59-72.

18. Chen, Junshi, *Diet, Life-Style and Mortality in China: A Study of the Characteristics of 65 Chinese Counties,* Cornell University Press, Ithica, NY.

19. Willett, W C, et al, *American Journal of Clinical Nutrition*, June 1995, 61(6S):1402S-1406S; Perez-Llamas, F, et al, *Journal of Human Nutrition and Diet*, Dec 1996, 9:6:463-471; Alberti-Fidanza, A, et al, *European Journal of Clinical Nutrition*, Feb 1994, 48:2:85-91.

20. Fernandez, N A, *Cancer Research,* 1975, 35:3272; Martines, I, et al, *Cancer Research,* 1975, 35:3265.

21. Pitskhelauri, G Z, *The Long Living of Soviet Georgia*, 1982, Human Sciences Press, New York, NY.

22. Franklyn, D, *Health*, September 1996, 57-63.

23. Koga, Y et al, "Recent Trends in Cardiovascular Disease and Risk Factors in the Seven Countries Study: Japan," *Lessons for Science from the Seven Countries Study*, H Toshima, et al, eds, Springer, New York, NY, 1994, 63-74.

24. Moore, Thomas J, *Lifespan: What Really Affects Human Longevity*, 1990, Simon and Schuster, New York, NY.

25. O'Neill, Molly, *New York Times*, Nov 17, 1991.

26. Enig, Mary G, Ph D, et al, *Federation Proceedings*, Jul 1978, 37:9:2215-2220.

27. Portillo, M P, et al, *International Journal of Obesity and Related Metabolic Disorders*, Oct 1998, 22(10):947-9; Dulloo, A G, et al, *Metabolism*, Feb 1995, 44(2):273-9.

28. Kabara, J J, *The Pharmacological Effects of Lipids*, The American Oil Chemists' Society, Champaign, IL, 1978, 1-14; Cohen, L A, et al, *Journal of the National Cancer Institute*, 1986, 77:43.

29. *Preventive Medicine,* Mar-Apr 1998, 27(2); 189-94; *The Lancet*, 1998, 352:688-91; "Good Fats Help Children's Behavioral Problems," *Let's Live*, September 1997, 45.

30. Lasserre, M, et al, *Lipids*, 1985, 20:4:227.

31. A general review of citations for problems with polyunsaturate consumption is found in Pinckney,

Edward R, MD, and Cathey Pinckney, *The Cholesterol Controversy*, 1973, Sherbourne Press, Los Angeles, 127-131; Research indicating the correlation of polyunsaturates with learning problems is found in Harmon, D, et al, *Journal of the American Geriatrics Society,* 1976, 24:1: 292-8; Meerson, Z, et al, *Bulletin of Experimental Biology and Medicine,* 1983, 96:9:70-71; Regarding weight gain, levels of linoleic acid in adipose tissues reflect the amount of linoleic acid in the diet, Valero, et al, *Annals of Nutrition and Metabolism,* Nov/Dec 1990, 34:6:323-327; Felton, C V, et al, *The Lancet,* 1994, 344:1195-96.

32. Pinckney, Edward R, MD, and Cathey Pinckney, *The Cholesterol Controversy*, 1973, Sherbourne Press, Los Angeles, 130; Enig, Mary G, PhD, et al, *Federation Proceedings,* July 1978, 37:9:2215-2220.

33. Machlin, I J, and A Bendich, *Federation of American Societies for Experimental Biology (FASEB) Journal,* 1987, 1:441-445.

34. Kinsella, John E, *Food Technology*, October 1988, 134 ; Lasserre, M, et al, *Lipids*, 1985, 20:4:227.

35. Horrobin, D F, *Reviews in Pure and Applied Pharmacological Sciences,* Vol 4, 1983, Freund Publishing House, 339-383; Devlin, T M, ed, *Textbook of Biochemistry*, 2nd Ed, 1982, Wiley Medical, 429-430; Fallon, Sally, and Mary G Enig, PhD, "Tripping Lightly Down the Prostaglandin Pathways," *Price-Pottenger Nutrition Foundation Health Journal*, 1996, 20:3:5-8, also posted at www.westonaprice.org.

36. Okuyama, H, et al, *Progresive Lipid Research*, 1997, 35:4:409-457.

37. Simopoulos, A P, and Norman Salem, *American Journal of Clinical Nutrition,* 1992, 55:411-4.

38. Watkins, B A, et al, "Importance of Vitamin E in Bone Formation and in Chrondrocyte Function" Purdue University, Lafayette, IN, *American Oil Chemists Society Proceedings*, 1996; Watkins, B A, and M F Seifert, "Food Lipids and Bone Health," *Food Lipids and Health*, R E McDonald and D B Min, eds, p 101, Marcel Dekker, Inc, New York, NY, 1996.

39. Dahlen, G H, et al, *Journal of Internal Medicine*, Nov 1998, 244(5):417-24; Khosla, P, and K C Hayes, *Journal of the American College of Nutrition,* 1996, 15:325-339; Clevidence, B A, et al, *Arteriosclerosis, Thrombosis and Vascular Biology,* 1997, 17:1657-1661.

40. Nanji, A A, et al, *Gastroenterology*, Aug 1995, 109(2):547-54; Cha, Y S, and D S Sachan, *Journal of the American College of Nutrition,* Aug 1994, 13(4):338-43; Hargrove, H L, et al, *Federation of American Societies for Experimental Biology (FASEB) Journal*, Meeting Abstracts, Mar 1999, #204.1, p A222.

41. Kabara, J J, *The Pharmacological Effects of Lipids*, The American Oil Chemists Society, Champaign, IL, 1978, 1-14; Cohen, L A, et al, *Journal of the National Cancer Institute,* 1986, 77:43.

42. Garg, M L, et al, *Federation of American Societies for Experimental Biology (FASEB) Journal,* 1988, 2:4:A852; Oliart Ros, R M, et al, "Meeting Abstracts," *American Oil Chemists Society Proceedings*, May 1998, 7, Chicago, IL.

43. Lawson, L D and F Kummerow, *Lipids*, 1979, 14:501-503; Garg, M L, *Lipids*, Apr 1989, 24(4):334-9.

44. Ravnskov, U, *Journal of Clinical Epidemiology*, Jun 1998, 51:(6):443-460. See also http://home2.swipnet.se/~w-25775/.

45. Felton, C V, et al, *The Lancet*, 1994, 344:1195.

46. Jones, P J, *American Journal of Clinical Nutrition*, Aug 1997, 66(2):438-46; Julias, A D, et al, *Journal of Nutrition*, Dec 1982, 112(12):2240-9.

47. Cranton, E M, MD, and J P Frackelton, MD, *Journal of Holistic Medicine*, Spring/Summer 1984, 6-37.

48. Engelberg, Hyman, *The Lancet*, Mar 21, 1992, 339:727-728; Wood, W G, et al, *Lipids*, Mar 1999, 34(3):225-234.

49. Alfin-Slater, R B, and L Aftergood, "Lipids," *Modern Nutrition in Health and Disease*, 6th ed, R S Goodhart and M E Shils, eds, Lea and Febiger, Philadelphia 1980, 134.

50. Addis, Paul, *Food and Nutrition News*, March/April 1990, 62:2:7-10.

51. Barnes, Broda, and L Galton, *Hypothyroidism, The Unsuspected Illness*, 1976, T Y Crowell, New York, NY.

52. Fallon, Sally, and Mary G Enig, PhD, "Diet and Heart Disease—Not What You Think," *Consumers' Research*, July 1996, 15-19. See also, "What Causes Heart Disease," posted at www.westonaprice.org.

53. Ubbink, J B, *Nutrition Reviews,* Nov 1994, 52:11:383-393.

54. Enig, Mary G, PhD, *Nutrition Quarterly*, 1993, 17:(4):79-95.

55. Enig, Mary G, PhD, _Trans Fatty Acids in the Food Supply: A Comprehensive Report Covering 60 Years of Research_, 2nd Edition, Enig Associates, Inc, Silver Spring, MD, 1995, 148-154; Enig, Mary G, PhD, et al, _Journal of the American College of Nutrition_, 1990, 9:471-86.

56. Holman, R T, _Geometrical and Positional Fatty Acid Isomers_, E A Emkin and H J Dutton, eds, 1979, American Oil Chemists Society, Champaign, IL, 283-302; _Science News Letter_, Feb 1956; Schantz, E J, et al, _Journal of Dairy Science,_ 1940, 23:181-89.

57. Enig, Mary G, PhD, _Trans Fatty Acids in the Food Supply: A Comprehensive Report Covering 60 Years of Research_, 2nd Edition, Enig Associates, Inc, Silver Spring, MD, 1995; Watkins, B A et al, _Broiler Poultry Science_, Dec 1991, 32(5):1109-1119.

58. Zikakis, et al, _Journal of Dairy Science_, 1977, 60:533; Oster, K, _American Journal of Clinical Research_, Apr 1971, Vol II(I).

59. Bonanome, A, and S C Grundy, _New England Journal of Medicine,_ 1988, 318:1244.

60. _Nutrition Week,_ Mar 22, 1991, 21:12:2-3.

61. Fraps, G S, and A R Kemmerer, _Texas Agricultural Bulletin_, Feb 1938, No 560.

62. Schantz, E J, et al, _Journal Dairy Science,_ 1940, 23:181-89.

63. van Wagtendonk, W J and R Wulzen, _Archives of Biochemistry,_ Academic Press, Inc, New York, NY, 1943, 1:373-377.

64. Personal communication, Pat Connolly, Executive Director, Price-Pottenger Nutrition Foundation.

65. Enig, Mary G, PhD, "Health and Nutritional Benefits from Coconut Oil," _Price-Pottenger Nutrition Foundation Health Journal_, 1998, 20:1:1-6.

66. Prasad, K N, _Life Science_, 1980, 27:1351-8; Gershon, Herman, and Larry Shanks, _Symposium on the Pharmacological Effect of Lipids_, Jon J Kabara, ed, American Oil Chemists Society, Champaign, IL, 1978, 51-62.

67. Belury, M A, _Nutr Rev,_ April 1995, 53:(4)83-89; Kelly, M L, et al, _Journal of Dairy Science_, Jun 1998, 81(6):1630-6.

68. Koopman, J S, et al, _American Journal of Public Health,_ 1984, 74:12:1371-1373.

69. Personal communication, Mary G Enig, PhD.

70. Sauer, F D, et al, _Nutrition Research_, 1997, 17:2:259-269.

71. Kramer, J K G, et al, _Lipids_, 1982, 17:372-382; Trenholm, H L, et al, _Canadian Institute Food Science Technology Journal_, 1979, 12:189-193.

72. Prior, I, et al, _Am Journal of Clinical Nutrition,_ 1981, 34:1552.

73. Personal communication, Mary G Enig, PhD. This lobbying against tropical oils is largely channeled through the Institute for Shortening and Edible Oils.

74. Furth, Anna, and John Harding, _New Scientist_, September 1989, 44-47.

75. Beasley, Joseph D, MD, and Jerry J Swift, MA, _The Kellogg Report_, 1989, The Institute of Health Policy and Practice, Annandale-on-Hudson, NY, 144-145.

76. Paton, J, _British Medical Journal,_ 1933, 1:738.

77. Howell, Edward, MD, _Enzyme Nutrition,_ 1985, Avery Publishing, Wayne, NJ, 88, 104; Fields, M, _Proc Soc Exp Biol Med_, 1984, 175:530-537.

78. Douglas, W C, MD, _Second Opinion_, Atlanta, GA, May 1995, Vol V, No 5.

79. Yudkin, J, _The Lancet,_ 1957, 11:155-62; Yudkin, J, et al, _Annals of Nutrition and Metabolism,_ 1986, 30:4:261-66; Yudkin, J, et al, _Sugar: Chemical, Biological and Nutritional Aspects of Sucrose,_ 1971, Daniel Davey, Hartford, CT.

80. Lopez, A, _American Journal of Clinical Nutrition_, 1966, 18:149-153.

81. Howell, Edward, MD, _Enzyme Nutrition,_ 1985, Avery Publishing, Wayne, NJ, 88, 104.

82. Beasley, Joseph D, MD, and Jerry J Swift, MA, _The Kellogg Report_, 1989, The Institute of Health Policy and Practice, Annandale-on-Hudson, NY, 132; Yudkin, John, Dr, _Sweet & Dangerous_, 1973, Bantam Books, New York, NY.

83. Beasley, Joseph D, MD, and Jerry J Swift, MA, _The Kellogg Report_, 1989, The Institute of Health Policy and Practice, Annandale-on-Hudson, NY, 129.

84. Fields, M, _Proceedings of the Society of Experimental Biology and Medicine,_ 1984, 175:530-537.

85. Page, Melvin, DDS, _Degeneration, Regeneration_, 1949, Price-Pottenger Nutrition Foundation, San Diego, CA.

86. Sullivan, J L, *The Lancet*, June 13, 1981, 1239; Gutteridge, J M, et al, *Biochemical Journal*, 1982, 206:605-9.

87. Reinhold, John G, *Ecology of Food and Nutrition*, 1972, I:187-192; Reddy, N R, et al, *Phytates in Cereals and Legumes*, 1989, CRC Press, Boca Raton, FL.

88. Aubert, Claude, *Les Aliments Fermentés Traditionnels. Une Richesse Meconnue,* 1985, Terre Vivante, Mens, France, 35; Steinkraus, Keith H, ed, *Handbook of Indigenous Fermented Foods*, 1983, Marcel Dekker, Inc, New York, NY.

89. Stitt, Paul, *Fighting the Food Giants*, 1981, Natural Press, Manitowoc, WI, 62.

90. Jenkins, David J A, et al, *American Journal of Clinical Nutrition*, March 1981, 34:362-366.

91. Abrams, H Leon, *Journal of Applied Nutrition*, 1980, 32:2:70-71.

92. Cheraskin, E, et al, *Journal of Orthomolecular Psychiatry*, 1978, 7:150-155.

93. Spencer, H, et al, *Federation Proceedings,* Nov 1986, 45:12:2758-2762 ; Spencer, H and L Kramer, *American Journal of Clinical Nutrition,* June 1983, 37:6:924-929; Fallon, Sally, and Mary G Enig, PhD, "Dem Bones—Do High Protein Diets Cause Bone Loss?" *Price-Pottenger Nutrition Foundation Health Journal*, 1996, 20:2:1-4, also posted at www.westonaprice.org.

94. Webb, J G, et al, *Canadian Medical Association Journal*, Oct 1, 1986, 135:7:753-8.

95. Fallon, Sally, "Vitamin A Vagary," *Price-Pottenger Nutrition Foundation Health Journal*, 1995, 19:2:1-3, also posted at www.westonaprice.org; Jennings, I W, *Vitamins in Endocrine Metabolism*, 1970, Heineman, London, UK.

96. Haviland, W A, *American Antiquity*, 1967, 32:316-325.

97. Pitskhelauri, G Z, MD, *The Long Living of Soviet Georgia*, 1982, Human Sciences Press, New York, NY.

98. Abrams, H Leon, *Journal of Applied Nutrition*, 1980, 32:2:70-71.

99. Lindenbaum, J, et al, *New England Medical Journal*, June 30, 1988, 318:26:1720-1728.

100. *Nutrition Reviews*, 1979, 37:142-144.

101. Specker, B L, et al, *American Journal of Clinical Nutrition* 1988, 47:89-92; Berg H van den, et al, *The Lancet,* 1988, 1:242-3; Herbert, V, *American Journal of Clinical Nutrition,* 1987, 46:387-402; Murray, M T, *American Journal of Natural Medicine*, April 1996, 3:(3):10-15; Ensminger, A H, et al, *Encyclopedia of Foods & Nutrition*, 1994, CRC Press, Boca Raton, FL, 1284.

102. *Nature's Way,* 1979, 10:20-30.

103. A good example is the Haenszel, et al study of Japanese American men which showed a correlation with consumption of beef and colon cancer, but stronger correlations with consumption of macaroni, green beans and peas. Extensive press coverage emphasized the connection of beef and colon cancer but ignored the stronger correlation with other Western foods. The study used the questionable technique of dietary recall and did not have matched controls. Haenszel, W, et al, *Journal of the National Cancer Institute*, Dec 5, 1973, 51(6):1765-79.

104. Enig, Mary G, PhD, *Townsend Letter for Doctors,* December 1993, 1214-1215.

105. Lopez, A, *American Journal of Clinical Nutrition*, 1996, 18:149.

106. Merrill, Alfred J, et al, *Annual Reviews of Nutrition,* 1993, 13:539-559.

107. Wallace, G M, *Journal of the Science of Food and Agriculture,* Oct 1971, 22:526-35.

108. Rackis, J J, et al, *Qualitative Plant Foods in Human Nutrition,* 1985, 35:225.

109. Rackis, J J, et al, *Qualitative Plant Foods in Human Nutrition,* 1985, 35:232; Fallon, Sally, and Mary G Enig, PhD, "Soy Products for Dairy Products - Not So Fast," *Health Freedom News*, Sept 1995, 12-20; Fallon, Sally and Mary G Enig, PhD, *The Ploy of Soy*, Price-Pottenger Nutrition Foundation, San Diego, CA. See also Soy Alert! at www.westonaprice.org.

110. Fallon, Sally, and Mary G Enig, PhD, "Dem Bones—Do High Protein Diets Cause Bone Loss?" *Price-Pottenger Nutrition Foundation Health Journal*, 1996, 20:2:1-4, also posted at www.westonaprice.org.

111. Fallon, Sally, "Vitamin A Vagary," *Price-Pottenger Nutrition Foundation Health Journal*, 1995, 19:2:1-3, also posted at www.westonaprice.org; Jennings, I W, *Vitamins in Endocrine Metabolism*, 1970, Heineman, London, UK.

112. Burton, B T, and W R Foster, *Human Nutrition,* 4th ed, 1988, McGraw-Hill Book Co, 85; Gotthoffer, N R, *Gelatin in Nutrition and Medicine*, 1945, Grayslake Gelatin Co, Greyslake, IL.

113. Aubert, Claude, *Dis-Moi Comment Tu Cuisines, Je Te Dirais Comment Tu Te Portes,* 1987, Terre

Vivant, Mens, France, 114.

114. Livingston-Wheeler, Virginia, MD, *Conquest of Cancer: Vaccines and Diet,* 1984, F Watts, New York, NY.

115. Simoons, F J, *Food in China: A Cultural and Historical Inquiry*, 1991, CRC Press, Boca Raton, FL, 462.

116. Purdy, Mark, *Journal of Nutritional Medicine*, 1994, 4:43-82.

117. Personal communication, Dr Olympia Pinto, Rio de Janeiro. Using both phase contour and dark field microscopy, Dr. Pinto studied the blood profiles of patients and medical students consuming pork. He had difficulty finding subjects for long term studies because test subjects voluntarily discontinued pork consumption after initial blood asseys.

118. Adamson, R H, *Cancer Prevention,* Nov 1990, 1-7; Bjeldanes, L F, et al, *Journal of Agriculture and Food Chemistry,* 1983, 31:18-21.

119. Holzman, Neil A, et al, *Modern Nutrition in Health and Disease*, 6th ed, Goodhart and Shils, eds, 1980, Lea and Febiger, Philadelphia, PA, 1193-1219.

120. Shils, M E, et al, *Modern Nutrition in Health and Disease,* 8th ed, 1994, Goodhart and Shils, eds, Lea and Febiger, Philadelphia, PA, 40.

121. Douglass, William Campbell, MD, *The Milk Book,* 1994, Second Opinion Publishing, Atlanta, GA; Beasley, Joseph D, MD, and Jerry J Swift, MA, *The Kellogg Report*, 1989, The Institute of Health Policy and Practice, Annandale-on-Hudson, NY, 174.

122. Maclaren, N, et al, *New England Journal of Medicine*, Jul 1992, 327:5:348-9.

123. Fraser, DR, *The Lancet*, Jan 14, 1995, 345:8942:104-105; Buist, RA, *International Clinical Nutrition Reviews*, 1984, 4:4:159-171.

124. Thomas, M K, et al, *New England Jounral of Medicine*, Mar 19, 1998, 338(12):777-83

125. Samuels, J L, "MSG Dangers and Deceptions," *Health and Healing Wisdom*, Price-Pottenger Nutrition Foundation, 1998, 22:2:28. See also www.truthinlabeling.com.

126. Personal communication, Francis Woidich, MD.

127. For further sources of high quality milk products, see www.realmilk.com or contact a local chapter of the Weston A. Price Foundation listed at www.westonaprice.org.

128. Baker, H, and O Frank, *Journal of the International Associates of Preventive Medicine*, Jul 1982, 19-24.

129. Price, Weston, DDS, *Nutrition and Physical Degeneration,* 1945, Price-Pottenger Nutrition Foundation, San Diego, CA, 278.

130. Smith, B, *Journal of Applied Nutrition,* 1993, 45:1.

131. Bergner, Paul, *The Healing Power of Minerals, Special Nutrients and Trace Elements*, 1997, Prima Publishing, Rocklin, CA.

132. Burton, B T, ed, *The Heinz Handbook of Nutrition*, 1959, McGraw Hill, New York, NY.

133. Price, Weston, DDS, *Nutrition and Physical Degeneration,* 1945, Price-Pottenger Nutrition Foundation, San Diego, CA. Dr. Price referred to vitamins A and D as "fat-soluble activators."

134. Dunne, Lavon J, *Nutrition Almanac*, 3rd ed, 1990, McGraw Hill, New York, NY; Jennings, I W, *Vitamins in Endocrine Metabolism*, 1970, Heineman, London, UK.

135. Solomans, N W, and J Bulox, *Nutrition Reviews,* Jul 1993, 51:199-204.

136. Douglas, W C, MD, *Second Opinion*, Atlanta, GA, May 1995, Vol V, No 5.

137. Linder, Maria C, ed, *Nutritional Biochemistry and Metabolism with Clinical Applications*, 2nd ed, 1991, Appleton & Lange, Norwalk, CT, 191-212.

138. Johns, T, and M Duquette, *American Journal of Clinical Nutrition*, 1991, 53:448-56.

139. Jacqmin-Gada, H, et al, *Epidemiology*, 1996, 7(3):281-85; Bellia, J P, et al, *Annals of Clinical Laboratory Science*, 1996, 26(3):227-33.

140. Damrau, F, *Medical Annals of the District of Columbia*, Jun 1961, 30:(6):326-328.

141. Ensminger, A H, et al, *The Concise Encyclopedia of Foods & Nutrition*, 1995, CRC Press, Boca Raton, FL, 586.

142. Howell, Edward, MD, *Enzymes for Health and Longevity*, 1980, Omangod Press, Woodstock Valley, CT.

143. Howell, Edward, MD, *Enzyme Nutrition*, 1985, Avery Publishing Group, Wayne, NJ, xv.

144. Holden, Robert A, et al, *Journal of the American Medical Association,* Jul 15, 1983, 250:3:356-369.

145. McCance, RA, *Nutrition Reviews*, Mar 1990, 48:145-147.

146. DeLangre, Jacques, *Seasalt's Hidden Powers,* 1992, Happiness Press, Magnolia, CA.

147. Bieler, H, MD, *Food is Your Best Medicine,* 1965, Ballantine Books, New York, NY.

148. These studies are summarized in Gotthoffer, NR, *Gelatin in Nutrition and Medicine*, 1945, Grayslake Gelatin Co, Greyslake, IL.

149. Samuels, J L, and A Samuels, Ph D, *Search for Health,* Sep/Oct 1993, 2:1:28-47; Blaylock, Russell, L, MD, *Excitotoxins: The Taste that Kills*, 1996, Health Press, Santa Fe, NM.

150. Samuels, J L, "MSG Dangers and Deceptions," *Health and Healing Wisdom*, Price-Pottenger Nutrition Foundation, 1998, 22:2:3. See also www.truthinlabeling.com.

151. Samuels, J L, and A Samuels, Ph D, *Search for Health,* Sep/Oct 1993, 2:1:28-47; Samuels, J L, and A Samuels, Ph D, *Townsend Letter for Doctors,* Nov 1995.

152. Samuels, J L, " MSG Update," *Health and Healing Wisdom*, Price-Pottenger Nutrition Foundation, 1998, 22:3:22.

153. Ershoff, B H, *Journal of Nutrition*, 1977, 107: 822-828.

154. Elias, P S, and A J Cohen, *Radiation Chemistry of Major Food Components,* 1977, Elsevier Biomedical Press, NY.

155. Bhaskaram, C, and G Sadasivan, *American Journal of Clinical Nutrition,* Feb 1975, 28:130-35.

156. Stellman, S D, and L Garfinkel, *Appetite,* 1988, 11:85-91.

157. Blaylock, Russell, L, MD, *Excitotoxins: The Taste that Kills*, 1996, Health Press, Santa Fe, NM.

158. Roberts, H J, MD, *Natural Food and Farming,* Mar/Apr 1992, 23-34.

159. Smith, M M, and F Lifshitz, *Pediatrics,* Mar 1994, 93:3:438-443.

160. Myers, John, MD, *Metabolic Aspects of Health,* 1979, Price-Pottenger Nutrition Foundation, San Diego, CA.

161. Sherman, W C, *Food and Nutrition News,* Feb 1977, 48:3:3; Foster, H D, *The Lancet,* Sep 12, 1987, 2(8559):633.

162. Yiamouyiannis, J, *Fluoride, The Aging Factor*, 1986, Health Action Press, Dellaware, OH.

163. Linder, Maria C, ed, *Nutritional Biochemistry and Metabolism with Clinical Applications*, 2nd ed, 1991, Appleton & Lange, Norwalk, CT, 9.

164. Steinkraus, Keith H, ed, *Handbook of Indigenous Fermented Foods*, 1983, Marcel Dekker, Inc, New York, NY.

165. American Gastroenterological Association, *Physiology of Intestinal Fluid and Electrolyte Absorption*, 1980, Milner-Fenwick, Baltimore, MD.

166. Hiatt, R A, et al, *Preventive Medicine,* Academic Press, Nov 1988, 17:(6):683-685.

167. Williams, Roger J, MD, *The Prevention of Alcoholism Through Nutrition*, 1981, Bantam Books, New York, NY.

168. Igram, C, MD, *Eat Right or Die Young,* 1989, Literary Visions, Inc, Cedar Rapids, IA, 134.

169. Crook, William G, *The Yeast Connection*, Random House, New York, NY, 1983, 221-222.

170. Howell, Edward, *Enzymes for Health and Longevity*, 1980, Omangod Press, Woodstock Valley, CT, 111.

171. Reading, Chris, MD, *Your Family Tree Connection: Genealogy and Health,* 1984, Keats Publishing, Inc, New Canaan, CT.

172. Lorenzani, Shirley S, Ph D, *Candida, A Twentieth Century Disease*, 1986, Keats Publishing, New Canaan, CT .

173. Coca, Arthur F, *The Pulse Test*, 1982, Lyle Stuart, Inc, Secaucus, NJ.

174. "Nuturing a Cornucopia of Potential," *Washington Post*, Oct 26, 1993.

175. Fallon, Sally, and Mary G Enig, PhD, "Americans Now and Then," *Price-Pottenger Nutrition Foundation Health Journal*, 1996, 20:4:3, also posted at www.westonaprice.org.

176. Stefansson, Vilhjalmur, *The Fat of the Land*, 1956, The MacMillan Co, New York, NY.

177. D'Adamo, P J, *Eat Right For Your Type*, 1996, G P Putnam's Sons, New York, NY.

178. Valentine, T and C Valentine, *True Health*, Winter 1998, p 1-6, Valentine Communication Corp. Naples, FL; Osborne, S E, "Eat Right for Your Type Hype," *Health and Healing Wisdom*, Price-Pottenger Nutrition Foundation, San Diego, CA, 1998, 22:(4):3-8, also posted at www.westonaprice.org.

179. Price, Weston A, DDS, "Acid-Base Balance of Diets which Produce Immunity to Dental Caries among the South Sea Islanders and other Primitive Races," Dec 1934, *Price-Pottenger Nutrition Foundation Health Journal*, 1997, 21:4:10-11.

180. Abrams, H Leon, *Journal of Applied Nutrition*, 1980, 32:2:70-71; Dagnelie, Pieter C, et al, *American Journal of Clinical Nutrition,* 1990, 51:202-208.

181. Ologhobo, A D, and B L Fetuga, *Journal of Food Science,* Jan/Feb, 1984, 49:1:199-201; Fallon, Sally and Mary G Enig, PhD, *The Ploy of Soy*, Price-Pottenger Nutrition Foundation, San Diego, CA. See also Soy Alert! at www.westonaprice.org.

182. Katz, S, *Nutritional Anthropology*, 1987, Alan R. Lin, Inc, NY, New York, 47.

183. *Nutrition Research* Jan 1989 9:1:127-132.

184. Lonnerdal, Bo, PhD, *American Journal of Clinical Nutrition* November 1984, 40:1064;

185. Divi, R L, et al, *Biochemical Pharmacology*, 1997, 54:1087-1096.

186. Weiner, Dr. Michael, *Reducing the Risk of Alzheimer's,* 1987, Scarborough House Publishers, Chelsea, MI.

187. Valentine, Tom, *Search for Health,* Sept/Oct 1992, 1:1:2-13.

188. Lubec, G, *The Lancet*, Dec 9, 1989, 1392-3.

MASTERING
THE BASICS

CULTURED DAIRY PRODUCTS

Cultured or fermented dairy products play a role in many traditional cuisines. In fact, only in the West is milk consumed in a "natural" or unfermented state, and this Occidental practice is relatively new. Before the age of industrialization, Europeans consumed milk as yoghurt, cheese, clabber, or curds and whey. Without pasteurization or refrigeration, milk sours and separates spontaneously. This is due to the process of lacto-fermentation during which lactic-acid-producing bacteria begin digesting or breaking down both milk sugar (lactose) and milk protein (casein). When these friendly bacteria have produced enough lactic acid to inactivate all putrefying bacteria, the milk is effectively preserved from spoilage for several days or weeks and in the case of cheese, which undergoes further fermentation of a different type, for several years.

Yoghurt is the fermented milk product with which we are most familiar in the West. It comes originally from Bulgaria. Unlike spontaneously soured milk, yoghurt is produced by first heating milk and then adding a culture. In Russia, a popular beverage is *kefir*, a slightly effervescent beverage, sometimes mildly alcoholic, of fermented cow, goat or sheep milk. *Koumiss*, another Russian beverage popular in the eastern regions, is made from mare's milk. Scandinavian countries produce a cultured milk product in wooden barrels called *longfil,* which keeps for many months. The Norwegians make a variety of *longfil* called *kjaeldermelk,* which they produce in caves. In the Middle East, milk is soured in special containers to produce *laban*. In India, milk from cows or water buffalo is soured to produce *dahi*, which the Indians consume with every meal. The Masai tribesmen of Africa consume milk as their principal food—always in soured or cultured form.

In Europe, soured milk products are still extensively used. Sour or fermented cream—*creme fraiche*—is an indispensable ingredient in soups and sauces. The delicious sour butter of France and Germany is made from churning fermented cream. Cultured butter needs no salt and its high enzyme content makes it easy to digest. Cream cheese and cottage cheese are traditionally made by allowing the fermentation process to continue for several days until the white curds or casein-containing portion of the milk separates from the whey. When this cream cheese is weighted down or inoculated with further cultures, it undergoes an additional fermentation process resulting in many different types of cheese. Modern cheese makers consider whey a waste product, but in earlier times it was used to produce a variety of other fermented foods and beverages.

Like the process of sprouting grains, fermentation of milk results in numerous beneficial changes. Fermentation breaks down casein, or milk protein, one of the most difficult proteins to digest. Culturing restores many of the enzymes destroyed during pasteurization including lactase, which helps digest lactose or milk sugar, and numerous enzymes, which help the body absorb calcium and other minerals. Lactase produced during the culturing process allows many people who are sensitive to fresh milk to tolerate fermented milk products. Both vitamin B and vitamin C content of milk increase during fermentation.

Research has shown that regular consumption of cultured dairy products lowers cholesterol and protects against bone loss. In addition, cultured dairy products provide beneficial bacteria and lactic acid to the digestive tract. These friendly creatures and their by-products keep pathogens at bay, guard against infectious illness and aid in the fullest possible digestion of all food we consume. Perhaps this is why so many traditional societies value fermented milk products for their health-promoting properties and insist on giving them to the sick, the aged and nursing mothers. In the absence of high-technology sanitation systems, lacto-fermented dairy foods, as well as lacto-fermented beverages and vegetables, provide essential protection against infectious disease.

A great many recipes in this book call for fermented dairy products in the form of cultured milk, cultured cream cheese, yoghurt, kefir, whey and cultured cream. Cultured sour cream can be made using a Finnish culture called *piima* (see Sources), or with cultured buttermilk to produce a European-style sour cream called *creme fraiche*. *Creme fraiche* is available commercially in many gourmet or specialty food shops. In sauces, cultured cream gives heavenly results.

Homemade cultured whey is indispensable for making fermented vegetables, chutneys, beverages and grain dishes. It can be made from various types of cultured milk, good quality yoghurt or even fresh raw milk, which will sour and separately naturally when left at room temperature for several days.

The recipes presented here are designed to allow you to produce fermented dairy products from cow or goat milk with a minimum of difficulty. Start with the best quality milk you can find, preferably clean raw milk from pasture-fed animals.

Milk culturing is an art and the recipes presented here may need adjusting to individual circumstances. The *piima* culture is the most temperature-sensitive, requiring a constant ambient temperature of 72 to 75 degrees. The kefir culture, which produces a thicker sour milk, is not as temperature-sensitive as *piima* culture, making it easier to use, but the grains must be added to new milk frequently to keep them active. A kefir powder has been developed which is very easy to use and stores well, but it requires a new packet for each culture. The buttermilk culture is also relatively foolproof, is not temperature-sensitive and remains active for many weeks without reculturing.

It pays to make milk culturing part of your routine so that you always have on hand the products you need for healthy snacks and appetizing meals.

The tradition of preserving foods, enhancing their nutritive value, and making them more interesting to eat through fermentation is a very ancient one. A form of yoghurt was said to have been revealed to Abraham by an angel; and the starter particles of kefir, a substance similar to yogurt but thin enough to be drinkable, are called "grains of the Prophet Mohammed," the Prophet having been credited with their introduction. William H. Lee, PhD *The Friendly Bacteria*

The fermentation of milk makes it more assimilable to persons with lactose intolerance because a large part of the lactose is transformed into lactic acid, and because the presence of the enzyme lactase in fermented milk products helps break down lactose in the digestive tract. Furthermore, a portion of the milk protein (casein) is decomposed, liberating the amino acids of which it is formed. Research shows that proteins in yoghurt are digested twice as quickly as those of nonfermented milk. Claude Aubert *Les Aliments Fermentés Traditionnels*

During fermentation of milk products, thirty to forty percent of the lactose is broken down so that the high lactose content is reduced. However, a special enzyme activity also takes place. Fermented products that are not pasteurized or heated in ways that destroy enzyme activity have significant levels of enzymes that contribute to the digestion of lactose in the intestine. Dr. Betty Kamen *Health Freedom News*

PIIMA STARTER CULTURE
Makes 1 cup

1 cup good quality cream
1 envelope piima powder (see Sources)

Piima culture (also called *vili* or Finnish culture) is derived from the milk of cows that feed on the butterwort plant. Centuries ago, Scandinavian farmers discovered that milk clabbered better when their cows consumed this herb.

Start with the best quality cream you can find, such as the thick old-fashioned cream available at health food stores and gourmet food shops. Raw cream is best, but pasteurized cream will do. Do not use ultrapasteurized cream—it does not contain enough nutrients to support your culture.

Using a room thermometer, find a place in your house where the temperature is a fairly constant 72-75 degrees, such as a closet or cupboard with a light bulb or a shelf over a refrigerator or near a heating vent. If the temperature is below 69 degrees, the culture will become stringy and slimy. If the temperature is more than 75 degrees, the culture will separate and sour.

Place the cream in an impeccably clean glass jar. It is very important to avoid contamination by airborne bacteria or by aerosols, sprays, paint fumes, dusts, molds, yeast and insecticides. Stir in the *piima* powder and cover tightly. Leave in a spot that is 72-75 degrees for about 24 hours until it thickens slightly. Transfer to refrigerator, where it will become firm. The culture will keep well chilled for several months. Always test it with your nose before using. If it smells bad, throw it out and start again.

PIIMA MILK
Makes 1 quart

1 quart fresh whole milk, nonhomogenized
1 tablespoon starter culture (page 82)

This is a good way to add enzymes and restore nutrients to pasteurized milk. The resultant product is not too thick and can be drunk like milk and used in infant formula (page 602). Try to find milk from a dairy that allows its cows (or goats) to pasture feed. Do not use ultrapasteurized or homogenized milk.

Place milk in a clean glass container. Add the starter, stir or shake well, cover tightly and place in a spot where the temperature is a stable 72-75 degrees for 20 to 24 hours. Chill well.

CULTURED BUTTER AND BUTTERMILK
Makes 1/2 pound butter and 2 cups buttermilk

1 quart piima cream or creme fraiche (page 84)
*   or 1 quart raw cream left at room temperature*
for   about 8 hours to sour

Place cultured or soured cream in a food processor fitted with a steel blade and process until butter forms. Turn butter and buttermilk into a strainer set over a container. Transfer butter to a stainless steel or wooden bowl and press out buttermilk with a wooden spoon or paddle, adding to buttermilk already in the container by pouring through a strainer. Wash the butter by adding a little water and pressing some more. Repeat until butter no longer exudes buttermilk. Form butter into a ball, lift it out of the bowl and pat it dry with paper towels. Place butter in a crock or container and buttermilk in glass containers, cover and chill well. (Butter may be frozen for long-term storage.)

Variation: Sweet Butter

Use fresh cream that has not been soured. You may add *1/2 teaspoon sea salt* if desired.

Each isolated Swiss valley or village has its own special feast days of which athletic contests are the principal events. The feasting in the past has been largely on dairy products. The athletes were provided with large bowls of cream as constituting one of the most popular and healthful beverages, and special cheese was always available. . . their cream products took the place of our modern ice cream. . . it is reported that practically all skulls that are exhumed in the Rhone Valley and, indeed, practically throughout all of Switzerland, where graves have existed for more than a hundred years, are found with relatively perfect teeth; whereas the teeth of people recently buried have been riddled with caries or lost through this disease. Weston Price, DDS *Nutrition and Physical Degeneration*

[The Rosickys] had been at one accord not to hurry through life, not to be always skimping and saving. They saw their neighbours buy more land and feed more stock than they did, without discontent. Once when the creamery agent came to the Rosickys to persuade them to sell him their cream, he told them how much the Fasslers, their nearest neighbours, had made on their cream last year. "Yes," said Mary, "and look at them Fassler children! Pale, pinched little things, they look like skimmed milk. I'd rather put some colour into my children's faces than put money into the bank." Willa Cather *Neighbour Rosicky*

In isolated Swiss villages, a limited amount of garden stuff is grown, chiefly green foods for summer use. While the cows spend the warm summer on the verdant knolls and wooded slopes near the glaciers and fields of perpetual snow, they have a period of high and rich productivity of milk. The milk constitutes an important part of the summer's harvesting. While the men and boys gather in the hay and rye, the women and children go in large numbers with the cattle to collect the milk and make and store cheese for the following winter's use This [raw] cheese contains the natural butter fat and minerals of the splendid milk and is a virtual storehouse of life for the coming winter.

These people. . . recognize the presence of Divinity in the life-giving qualities of the butter made in June when the cows have arrived for pasturage near the glaciers. [The priest] gathers the people together to thank the kind Father for the evidence of His Being in the life-giving qualities of butter and cheese made when the cows eat the grass near the snow line. This worshipful program includes the lighting of a wick in a bowl of the first butter made after the cows have reached the luscious summer pasturage. This wick is permitted to burn in a special sanctuary built for that purpose. The natives of the valley are able to recognize the superior quality of their June butter, and, without knowing exactly why, pay it due homage. Weston Price, DDS *Nutrition and Physical Degeneration*

Myth: Saturated fat clogs arteries.
Truth: The fatty acids found in artery clogs are mostly unsaturated (74%) of which 41% are polyunsaturated. (*Lancet* 1994 344:1195)

CREME FRAICHE
(European Style Sour Cream)
Makes 2 cups

1 pint good quality cream
1 tablespoon commerical or whole-milk buttermilk or commercial creme fraiche

European-style sour cream, called *creme fraiche*, (and pronounced "crem fresh") is a key ingredient in French cooking. It has a delicious flavor and is wonderful in creamed soups and sauces. In larger cities, *creme fraiche* is available at gourmet and health food stores.

To make *creme fraiche* at home, start with the best quality cream you can find. Raw cream is best but pasteurized will do. Do not use ultrapasteurized cream. Place in a clean glass container. Add buttermilk or *creme fraiche*, stir well, cover tightly and place in a warm spot for 20 to 24 hours. Chill well.

Note: If you can find neither good quality cream nor *creme fraiche*, use the best quality American-style, additive-free sour cream you can find in all recipes that call for *creme fraiche* or *piima* cream.

PIIMA CREAM
Makes 2 cups

1 pint good quality cream
1 tablespoon starter culture (page 82)

Cream cultured with the piima culture is similar to European-style *creme fraiche*. Use the best quality cream you can find. Raw cream is best but pasteurized will do. Do not use ultrapasteurized cream. Place cream in a clean glass container. Add the starter, cover tightly and place in a spot where the temperature is a stable 72-75 degrees for 20 to 24 hours. It will have thickened slightly. Chill well. When cool the cream becomes quite firm. Piima cream will keep in the refrigerator for several weeks. It may develop a thin yellowish or pinkish crust—simply remove this with a spoon.

WHOLE-MILK BUTTERMILK

Makes 1 quart

1 quart whole milk, preferably raw
but not ultrapasteurized
about 1/4 cup buttermilk culture (see Sources)

This is the easiest of all the cultured milks. Place milk in a glass container, add the buttermilk culture, stir well and cover. Keep at room temperature (but not higher than 80 degrees) until the milk thickens and curdles slightly. Chill well. Reserve 1/4-1/2 cup in a separate jar in the refrigerator for the next culture. Note: A similar culture from Sweden is called *fil mjolk*.

YOGHURT

Makes 1 quart

1/2 cup good quality commercial plain yoghurt,
or 1/2 cup yoghurt from previous batch
1 quart pasteurized whole milk, nonhomogenized
a candy thermometer

Yoghurt is easy to make—neither a yoghurt-maker nor a special culture is necessary. The final product may be thinner in consistency than commercial yoghurt.

Gently heat the milk to 180 degrees and allow to cool to about 110 degrees. Stir in yoghurt and place in a shallow glass, enamel or stainless steel container. Cover the container and place in a warm oven (about 150 degrees, or a gas oven with a pilot light) overnight. In the morning transfer to the refrigerator. (Throughout the day, use paper towels to mop up any whey that exudes from the yoghurt.)

Variation: Raw Milk Yoghurt

Place *1 quart raw milk* in a double boiler and heat to 110 degrees. Remove *2 tablespoons of the warm milk* and add *1 tablespoon yoghurt* (commercial or from previous batch). Stir well and pour into a quart-sized wide-mouth mason jar. Add a further *2 table-spoons plus 2 teaspoons yoghurt* to the jar and stir well. Cover tightly and place in a dehydrator set at 95 degrees for 8 hours. Transfer to the refrigerator.

Metchnikoff attributed the relatively long life span and freedom from disease of Bulgarian peasants to their consumption of sour milk containing a lactic acid bacillus. . . . However, his assumption took no account of a far better explanation. Dairy products form a large proportion of the diet in certain countries. Before the era of pasteurization, dairy products were utilized in the raw condition, since their palatability does not improve by heat-treatment, as is the case with many food materials. When a large share of the calorie requirement was supplied by raw milk, raw butter and raw cheese, not only did the organism receive a daily quota of enzymes, but the enzyme content of the tissues was not so heavily drawn upon as in those countries where the preponderance of the diet consisted of heat-treated foods. Therefore, the Bulgarian peasants, many of whom Metchnikoff found to live to the century mark in their mountainous abode, might be expected to have a long life span because their enzyme reserve is more slowly used up during the course of living. Edward Howell, MD *Food Enzymes for Health and Longevity*

Various researchers have learned that children and certain adults can beat allergies by taking the supplement *lactobacillus acidophilus*, the friendly bacteria found in yoghurt [and other fermented foods]. One published study revealed that every allergic child who volunteered to be tested was deficient in *lactobacillus acidophilus*, a condition corrected, in most instances, by taking this supplement. John Shelly *Health Freedom News*

Kefir is a cultured and microbial-rich food that helps restore the inner ecology. It contains strains of beneficial yeast and beneficial bacteria (in a symbiotic relationship) that give kefir antibiotic properties. A natural antibiotic—and it is made from milk! The finished product is not unlike that of a drink-style yogurt, but kefir has a more tart, refreshing taste and contains completely different microorganisms. . . kefir does not feed yeast, and it usually doesn't even bother people who are lactose intolerant. That's because the friendly bacteria and the beneficial yeast growing in the kefir consume most of the lactose and provide very efficient enzymes (lactase) for consuming whatever lactose is still left after the culturing process. . . kefir is mucous-forming, but. . . the slightly mucus-forming quality is exactly what makes kefir work for us. The mucus has a "clean" quality to it that coats the lining of the digestive tract, creating a sort of nest where beneficial bacteria can settle and colonize. . . .

Kefir is made from gelatinous white or yellow particles called "grains." The grains contain the bacteria/yeast mixture clumped together with casein (milk proteins) and polysaccharides (complex sugars). They look like pieces of coral or small clumps of cauliflower and range from the size of a grain of wheat to that of a hazelnut. Some grains have been known to grow in large flat sheets that can be big enough to cover your hand. No other milk culture forms grains. . . making kefir truly unique. Once the grains ferment the milk by incorporating their friendly organisms into the final product, you remove these grains with a strainer before drinking the kefir. The grains are then added to a new batch of milk, and the process continues indefinitely. Donna Gates *The Body Ecology Diet*

KEFIR
Makes 2 cups

2 cups fresh whole milk, nonhomogenized
and preferably raw
1/2 cup good quality cream (optional)
1 tablespoon kefir grains or
1 package kefir powder (see Sources)

Kefir is thicker than piima milk or buttermilk and has a wonderful tart flavor.

If using kefir grains, place them in a fine strainer and rinse with filtered water. Place milk and optional cream in a clean wide-mouth, quart-size mason jar. If milk is cold, place jar in a pan of simmering water until milk reaches room temperature. Add kefir grains or powder to milk, stir well and cover loosely with a cloth. Place in a warm place (65 to 76 degrees) for 12 hours to 2 days.

If using the powder, kefir is ready when it thickens, usually within 24 hours.

If using grains, stir vigorously occasionally to redistribute the grains. Every time you stir, taste the kefir. When it achieves a tartness to your liking, the kefir is ready. The kefir may also become thick and effervescent, depending on the temperature, incubation time and the amount of curds you use. Pour the kefir through a strainer into another jar to remove the grains. Store in refrigerator. Use the grains to make another batch of kefir, or prepare them for storage by rinsing them well with water and placing in a small jar with about 1/2 cup filtered water. They may be stored in the refrigerator several weeks or in the freezer for several months. If they are left too long in storage, they will lose their culturing power.

WHEY AND CREAM CHEESE

Makes 5 cups whey and 2 cups cream cheese

2 quarts piima milk (page 83),
whole-milk buttermilk (page 85),
yoghurt (page 85) or raw milk

We call for the use of whey in many recipes throughout this book—as a starter culture for lacto-fermented vegetables and fruits, for soaking grains and as a starter for many beverages. The cream cheese, which is a by-product, is far superior to the commercial variety, which is produced by putting milk under high pressure and not by the beneficial action of lactic-acid-producing bacteria.

If you are using piima milk or whole-milk buttermilk, let stand at room temperature 1-2 days until the milk visibly separates into white curds and yellowish whey. If you are using yoghurt, no advance preparation is required. You may use homemade yoghurt or good quality commercial plain yoghurt. If you are using raw milk, place the milk in a clean glass container and allow it to stand at room temperature 1-4 days until it separates.

Line a large strainer set over a bowl with a clean dish towel. Pour in the yoghurt or separated milk, cover and let stand at room temperature for several hours (longer for yoghurt). The whey will run into the bowl and the milk solids will stay in the strainer. Tie up the towel with the milk solids inside, being careful not to squeeze. Tie this little sack to a wooden spoon placed across the top of a container so that more whey can drip out. When the bag stops dripping, the cheese is ready. Store whey in a mason jar and cream cheese in a covered glass container. Refrigerated, the cream cheese keeps for about 1 month and the whey for about 6 months.

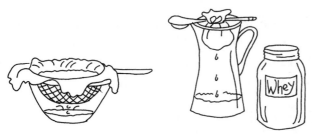

Whey is such a good helper in your kitchen. It has a lot of minerals. One tablespoon of whey in a little water will help digestion. It is a remedy that will keep your muscles young. It will keep your joints movable and ligaments elastic. When age wants to bend your back, take whey. . . . With stomach ailments, take one tablespoon whey three times daily, this will feed the stomach glands and they will work well again. Hanna Kroeger *Ageless Remedies from Mother's Kitchen*

Old Par, [an English peasant] who lived to the age of 152 years and 9 months, existed and even thrived on a diet of "subrancid cheese and milk in every form, coarse and hard bread and small drink, generally sour whey," as William Harvey wrote. . . . "On this sorry fare, but living in his home, free from care, did this poor man attain to such length of days." Terence McLaughlin *A Diet of Tripe*

In Iceland. . . . whey accumulated as a by-product of curd-making and was kept in barrels, where a fermentation process began. It was then called *syra*. Syra was either diluted with water and drunk, or used for the preservation of food. Many kinds of food were preserved in this manner, such as blood sausage, liver sausage, sheep's heads, lamb's testicles, fatty meat, whale meat and blubber and seal flippers. Syra was the most common beverage of Icelanders for many centuries and can in effect be said to have replaced ale, as lack of grain prevented us from brewing much ale. The whey was poured into huge barrels in the larder . . . and the blanket that developed on the surface of a syra barrel was called *jastur*, which is the same word as yeast in English. Syra was also used to marinate food. Nanna Rognvaldardottir *Matarast*

Traditional Gaelic society supported a system of seminomadic pastoral farming because Ireland was climatically suited to the rearing of livestock. Meat of all types was eaten in large quantities. Milk in liquid, solid and semisolid forms was an important adjuvant and sour milk, in varying degrees of viscosity, was consumed. Especially popular were curds called "bonaclabbe." Butter also formed an essential part of the daily diet. People ate fistfuls of rancid butter rolled in oats, spread butter on oatcakes and even ate butter on its own. The importance of butter is indicated by the practice of burying stores for future consumption in cool, damp bogs. S. J. Connolly *The Oxford Companion to Irish History*

I have followed for many years the sickening effect of soy on ruminants. Cows that formerly could easily reach the age of 15 years and have 12 calves have on average now less than three calves and reach hardly the age of 6. One main reason is the high percentage of soy in the rations. It works into the buildup of ammonia in the rumen. This affects negatively the liver and then shows up in mastitis and sterility. Off they go to the butcher. Only there can a vet identify the defective livers. The soybean, bringing about high milk yields in the first two lactations—is the curse of our cattle herds. And the milk achieved through it is not health promoting either. . . . If awake consumers, environmentalists, nutritionists and farmers do not work concretely together in the future, there will not be any healthy farms and healthy foods. Trauger Groh *PPNF Health Journal*

CULTURED MILK SMOOTHIE
Makes about 3 cups

1 1/4 cups whole-milk buttermilk (page 85),
     kefir (page 86) or yoghurt (page 85)
1 ripe banana or 1 cup berries (fresh or frozen)
2 tablespoons coconut oil (see Sources)
2 egg yolks
3-4 tablespoons maple syrup or raw honey
     or 1/4 teaspoon stevia powder
1 teaspoon vanilla extract (omit with berries)
pinch of nutmeg (omit with berries)

Smoothies made with good quality cultured milk make a wonderful snack, quick breakfast or strengthening meal for invalids. Unfortunately, most commercial smoothies contain soy protein powder and problematic sweeteners. Fortunately, smoothies are easy and quick to make at home.

Place banana or berries in food processor or blender and process until smooth. Add remaining ingredients and process until well blended.

RAW MILK WARMER
Makes about 2 cups

1 1/2 cups raw milk
2 tablespoons carob powder
3-4 tablespoons maple syrup or
     1/4 teaspoon stevia powder
1 teaspoon vanilla extract
1 teaspoon chocolate extract
1-2 tablespoons nutritional yeast flakes (see Sources)

Place all ingredients in a glass container and mix well with a wire whisk. Place in a pan of simmering water and stir occasionally until the mixture becomes warm. Do not overheat!

FERMENTED VEGETABLES & FRUITS

It may seem strange to us that, in earlier times, people knew how to preserve vegetables for long periods without the use of freezers or canning machines. This was done through the process of lacto-fermentation. Lactic acid is a natural preservative that inhibits putrefying bacteria. Starches and sugars in vegetables and fruits are converted into lactic acid by the many species of lactic-acid-producing bacteria. These *lactobacilli* are ubiquitous, present on the surface of all living things and especially numerous on leaves and roots of plants growing in or near the ground. Man needs only to learn the techniques for controlling and encouraging their proliferation to put them to his own use, just as he has learned to put certain yeasts to use in converting the sugars in grape juice to alcohol in wine.

The ancient Greeks understood that important chemical changes took place during this type of fermentation. Their name for this change was "alchemy." Like the fermentation of dairy products, preservation of vegetables and fruits by the process of lacto-fermentation has numerous advantages beyond those of simple preservation. The proliferation of *lactobacilli* in fermented vegetables enhances their digestibility and increases vitamin levels. These beneficial organisms produce numerous helpful enzymes as well as antibiotic and anticarcinogenic substances. Their main by-product, lactic acid, not only keeps vegetables and fruits in a state of perfect preservation but also promotes the growth of healthy flora throughout the intestine. Other alchemical by-products include hydrogen peroxide and small amounts of benzoic acid.

A partial list of lacto-fermented vegetables from around the world is sufficient to prove the universality of this practice. In Europe the principle lacto-fermented food is sauerkraut. Described in Roman texts, it was prized for both for its delicious taste as well as its medicinal properties. Cucumbers, beets and turnips are also traditional foods for lacto-fermentation. Less well known are ancient recipes for pickled herbs, sorrel leaves and grape leaves. In Russia and Poland one finds pickled green tomatoes, peppers and lettuces. Lacto-fermented foods form part of Asian cuisines as well. The peoples of Japan, China and Korea make pickled preparations of cabbage, turnip, eggplant, cucumber, onion, squash and carrot. Korean *kimchi,* for example, is a lacto-fermented condiment of cabbage with other vegetables and seasonings that is eaten on a daily basis and no Japanese meal is complete without a portion of pickled vegetable. American tradition includes many types of relishes—corn relish, cucumber relish, watermelon rind—all of which were no doubt originally lacto-fermented products. The pickling of fruit is less well known but, nevertheless, found in many traditional cultures. The Japanese prize pickled *umeboshi* plums, and the peoples of India traditionally fermented fruit with spices to make chutneys.

Lacto-fermented condiments are easy to make. Fruits and vegetables are first washed and cut up, mixed with salt and herbs or spices and then pounded briefly to release juices. They are then pressed into an air tight container. Salt inhibits putrefying bacteria for several days until enough lactic acid is produced to preserve the vegetables for many months. The amount of salt can be reduced or even eliminated if whey is added to the pickling solution. Rich in lactic acid and lactic-acid-producing bacteria, whey acts as an inoculant, reducing the time needed for sufficient lactic acid to be produced to ensure preservation. Use of whey will result in consistently successful pickling; it is essential for pickling fruits. During the first few days of fermentation, the vegetables are kept at room temperature; afterwards, they must be placed in a cool, dark place for long-term preservation.

It is important to use the best quality organic vegetables, sea salt and filtered or pure water for lacto-fermentation. *Lactobacilli* need plenty of nutrients to do their work; and, if the vegetables are deficient, the process of fermentation will not proceed. Likewise if your salt or water contains impurities, the quality of the final product will be jeopardized.

Lacto-fermentation is an artisanal craft that does not lend itself to industrialization. Results are not always predictable. For this reason, when the pickling process became industrialized, many changes were made that rendered the final product more uniform and more saleable but not necessarily more nutritious. Chief among these was the use of vinegar for the brine, resulting in a product that is more acidic and not necessarily beneficial when eaten in large quantities; and of subjecting the final product to pasteurization, thereby effectively killing all the lactic-acid-producing bacteria and robbing consumers of their beneficial effect on the digestion.

The recipes presented here are designed to be made in small quantities in your own kitchen. They require no special equipment apart from a collection of wide-mouth, quart-sized mason jars and a wooden pounder or a meat hammer. (For special sauerkraut crocks that enable you to make large quantities, see Sources.)

We recommend adding a small amount of homemade whey (page 87) to each jar of vegetables or fruit to ensure consistently satisfactory results. Whey supplies *lactobacilli* and acts as an inoculant. *Do not use commercial concentrated whey or dried whey.* You may omit whey and use more salt in the vegetable recipes, but whey is essential in the recipes calling for fruit.

About one inch of space should be left between the top of your vegetables with their liquid and the top of the jar, as the vegetables and their juices expand slightly during fermentation. Be sure to close the jars very tightly. Lacto-fermentation is an anaerobic process and the presence of oxygen, once fermentation has begun, will ruin the final product.

We have tried to keep these recipes as simple as possible without undue stress on ideal temperatures or precise durations. In general, a room temperature of about 72 degrees will be sufficient to ensure a lactic-acid fermentation in about two to four days. More time will be needed if your kitchen is colder and less if it is very warm. After two to four days at room temperature, the jars should be placed in a dark, cool spot, ideally one with a temperature of about 40 degrees. In days gone by, crocks of lacto-fermented vegetables were stored in root cellars or caves. A wine cellar or small refrigerator kept on a "warm" setting is ideal; failing that, the top shelf of your refrigerator will do. Lacto-fermented fruit chutneys need about two days at room temperature and should always be stored in a refrigerator.

Lacto-fermented vegetables increase in flavor with time—according to the experts, sauerkraut needs at least six months to fully mature. But they also can be eaten immediately after the initial fermentation at room temperature. Lacto-fermented vegetable condiments will keep for many months in cold storage but lacto-fermented fruits and preserves should be eaten within two months of preparation.

Some lacto-fermented products may get bubbly, particularly the chutneys. This is natural and no cause for concern. And do not be dismayed if little spots of white foam appear at the top of the pickling liquid. They are completely harmless and can be lifted off with a spoon. The occasional batch that goes bad presents no danger—the smell will be so awful that nothing could persuade you to eat it. The sign of successful lacto-fermentation is that the vegetables and fruits remained preserved over several weeks or months of cold storage.

Lactic-acid fermented vegetables and fruit chutneys are not meant to be eaten in large quantities but as condiments. They go beautifully with meats and fish of all sorts, as well as with pulses and grains. They are easy to prepare, and they confer health benefits that cannot be underestimated.

Scientists and doctors today are mystified by the proliferation of new viruses—not only the deadly AIDS virus but the whole gamut of human viruses that seem to be associated with everything from chronic fatigue to cancer and arthritis. They are equally mystified by recent increases in the incidence of intestinal parasites and pathogenic yeasts, even among those whose sanitary practices are faultless. Could it be that in abandoning the ancient practice of lacto-fermentation and in our insistence on a diet in which everything has been pasteurized, we have compromised the health of our intestinal flora and made ourselves vulnerable to legions of pathogenic microorganisms? If so, the cure for these diseases will be found not in vaccinations, drugs or antibiotics but in a restored partnership with the many varieties of *lactobacilli*, our symbionts of the microscopic world.

Of all the organic acids, lactic acid is the one that best inhibits the proliferation of bacteria that cause putrefaction, but it does not bring about in the body the over-acidifying action of certain other acids . . . . While other products of the fermentation process, like alcohol and acetic acid, must be decomposed and eliminated, lactic acid can in large part be used by the body. Annelies Schoneck *Des Crudités Toute L'Année*

Organic acids present in fermented milk and vegetable products play an important role in the health of old people as they aid a digestive system that is growing more and more feeble. Annelies Schoneck *Des Crudités Toute L'Année*

After two or three days of lacto-fermentation, vegetables begin to soften and certain substances in them begin to decompose. If the vegetables contain nitrates—often the case after a summer with little sun—they are broken down. . . . If all goes well, the lactic-acid producing bacteria take over and the process of acidification begins. New substances are formed, notably . . . choline and, above all, lactic acid. This acidification ensures the conservation of the vegetables . . . but the fermentation of the aromas doesn't come about until a later stage, during storage. Lacto-fermentation is not only a means of conserving foods but also a procedure for ennobling them, as proved by their taste and aroma. Annelies Schoneck *Des Crudités Toute L'Année*

SAUERKRAUT

Makes 1 quart

1 medium cabbage, cored and shredded
1 tablespoon caraway seeds
1 tablespoon sea salt
4 tablespoons whey (page 87) (if not available,
*   use an additional 1 tablespoon salt)*

In a bowl, mix cabbage with caraway seeds, sea salt and whey. Pound with a wooden pounder or a meat hammer for about 10 minutes to release juices. Place in a quart-sized, wide-mouth mason jar and press down firmly with a pounder or meat hammer until juices come to the top of the cabbage. The top of the cabbage should be at least 1 inch below the top of the jar. Cover tightly and keep at room temperature for about 3 days before transferring to cold storage. The sauerkraut may be eaten immediately, but it improves with age.

LATIN AMERICAN SAUERKRAUT

(Cortido)
Makes 2 quarts

1 large cabbage, cored and shredded
1 cup carrots, grated
2 medium onions, quartered lengthwise
    and very finely sliced
1 tablespoons dried oregano
1/4-1/2 teaspoon red pepper flakes
1 tablespoon sea salt
4 tablespoons whey (page 87) (if not available,
    use an additional 1 tablespoon salt)

This delicious spicy condiment goes beautifully with Mexican and Latin American food of all types. It is traditionally made with pineapple vinegar but can also be prepared with whey and salt. Like traditional sauerkraut, cortido improves with age.

In a large bowl mix cabbage with carrots, onions, oregano, red chile flakes, sea salt and whey. Pound with a wooden pounder or a meat hammer for about 10 minutes to release juices. Place in 2 quart-sized, wide-mouth mason jars and press down firmly with a pounder or meat hammer until juices come to the top of the cabbage. The top of the cabbage mixture should be at least 1 inch below the top of the jars. Cover tightly and keep at room temperature for about 3 days before transferring to cold storage.

Variation: Traditional Cortido

Omit salt and whey and use *4-6 cups pineapple vinegar (page 156)*. Mix all ingredients except pineapple vinegar together in a large bowl and pound lightly. Stuff cabbage loosely into 3 quart-sized, wide-mouth mason jars and add enough vinegar to cover the cabbage. The top of the cabbage mixture should be at least 1 inch below the top of the jars. Cover tightly and keep at room temperature for about 3 days before transferring to cold storage.

Among all the vegetables that one can conserve through lacto-fermentation, cabbage has been man's preferred choice. . . . Here is how it was prepared in the olden days, according to Anna Nilssonn: "As children, we always looked forward to the day they made sauerkraut. Two men seated themselves face to face and, straddling a barrel, held between them a large tool for shredding the cabbage. The little box that the cabbage fell into went back and forth between them to the rhythm of a song they chanted. Then arrived the moment that all of us children were waiting for. When they sang the refrain, one of the men would jump nimbly into the cask, scatter a handful of salt over the grated cabbage, and stamp down with his feet." But sauerkraut was known at a much more ancient time. . . . In China, they fermented cabbage 6000 years ago. In ancient Rome, sauerkraut had a reputation as a food that was easy to digest. Even at that period, there were already two known methods for lacto-fermenting vegetables according to descriptions. . . given by Pliny (about 50 BC). The first method consisted in mashing the shredded cabbage in great earthenware containers, which were then hermetically sealed. The second consisted of mixing different vegetables, including wild herbs, and covering them with a solution of salt water. This mixture was called *compositur* or "mixture." Tiberius always carried a barrel of sauerkraut with him during his long voyages to the Middle East because the Romans knew that the lactic acid it contained protected them from intestinal infections. Annelies Schoneck *Des Crudités Toute L'Année*

One striking observation [of ethnic cuisines] is that rarely are meals eaten without at least one fermented food, often a drink. In France, if one took away bread, cheese, ham, sausage, wine and beer, all produced through fermentation, our meals would be much impoverished. In colder countries sauerkraut, cucumbers, *cornichons* (always fermented in the old days), other vegetables and many types of fish preserved by fermentation are always served. In Japan, it's not a meal without *miso*, soy sauce and pickles, all fermented products. In India, they drink soured milk every day, practically at every meal. In Indonesia they eat *tempeh*, in Korea *kimchi* (a kind of sauerkraut) and in Africa porridge of fermented millet or cereal beers. In Moslem countries these fermented drinks are forbidden but they eat bread, dishes made with fermented pulses and milk products. Without being indispensable, a small amount of some raw fermented food (preferably lacto-fermented) helps the digestion. This is especially true when the meal is a bit heavy. It isn't by chance, nor merely for the pleasure of taste, that we eat *cornichons* with *charcuterie*. Claude Aubert *Dis-Moi Comment Tu Cuisines*

KOREAN SAUERKRAUT
(Kimchi)
Makes 2 quarts

1 head Napa cabbage, cored and shredded
1 bunch green onions, chopped
1 cup carrots, grated
1/2 cup daikon radish, grated (optional)
1 tablespoon freshly grated ginger
3 cloves garlic, peeled and minced
1/2 teaspoon dried chile flakes
1 tablespoon sea salt
4 tablespoons whey (page 87) (if not available, use an additional 1 tablespoon salt)

Place vegetables, ginger, garlic, red chile flakes, sea salt and whey in a bowl and pound with a wooden pounder or a meat hammer to release juices. Place in a quart-sized, wide-mouth mason jar and press down firmly with a pounder or meat hammer until juices come to the top of the cabbage. The top of the vegetables should be at least 1 inch below the top of the jar. Cover tightly and keep at room temperature for about 3 days before transferring to cold storage.

JAPANESE SAUERKRAUT
(Tsukemono)
Makes 1 quart

1 head Napa cabbage, cored and shredded
1 bunch green onions, chopped
2 tablespoons naturally fermented soy sauce
2 tablespoons fresh lemon juice
1 teaspoon sea salt
2 tablespoons whey (page 87) (if not available, use an additional 1 teaspoon salt)

This is traditionally made with a culture derived from rice bran, but whey serves an identical purpose and is more easily obtained. Place all ingredients in a bowl, mix well and pound with a wooden pounder or a meat hammer to release juices. Place in a quart-sized, wide-mouth mason jar and press down firmly with a pounder or meat hammer until juices come to the top of the cabbage. The top of the vegetables should be at least 1 inch below the top of the jar. Cover tightly and keep at room temperature for about 3 days before transferring to cold storage.

GINGER CARROTS

Makes 1 quart

4 cups grated carrots, tightly packed
1 tablespoon freshly grated ginger
2 tablespoons sea salt
4 tablespoons whey (page 87) (if not available,
    use an additional 1 tablespoon salt)

These are the best introduction to lacto-fermented vegetables we know; the taste is delicious; and the sweetness of the carrots neutralizes the acidity that some people find disagreeable when they are first introduced to lacto-fermented vegetables. Ginger carrots go well with rich foods and spicy meats.

In a bowl, mix all ingredients and pound with a wooden pounder or a meat hammer to release juices. Place in a quart-sized, wide-mouth mason jar and press down firmly with a pounder or meat hammer until juices cover the carrots. The top of the carrots should be at least 1 inch below the top of the jar. Cover tightly and leave at room temperature about 3 days before transferring to cold storage.

Sauerkraut owes its reputation in part to the famous navigators of past centuries. For his second round-the-world voyage, Captain Cook loaded 60 barrels of sauerkraut onto his ship. After 27 months at sea, 15 days before returning to England, he opened the last barrel and offered some sauerkraut to some Portuguese noblemen who had come on board . . . they carried off the rest of the barrel to give some to their friends. This last barrel was perfectly preserved after 27 months, in spite of changes in climate and the incessant rocking of the ship. The sauerkraut had also preserved sufficient quantities of vitamin C to protect the entire crew from scurvy. Not one case occurred during the long voyage even though this disease usually decimated crews on voyages of this length. Claude Aubert *Les Aliments Fermentés Traditionnels*

A certain amount of raw, uncooked food in the diet is indispensable to the highest degree of health. Assuming that the proteins, fats, carbohydrates, minerals, and vitamins are equally available for nutrition in raw and cooked food, any demonstrable nutritional superiority of raw food must then be ascribed to the "live" quality of raw food, and when this live quality is subjected to analysis, it is shown to consist of. . . no other property than that possessed by enzymes. Edward Howell, MD *Food Enzymes for Health and Longevity*

According to orthodox Hindu and Buddhist philosophies, onions and garlic were believed to have the quality of *tamas* or "darkness," and were forbidden to upper-cast and respectable persons because they brought on "ignorance, sloth, fear and lewdness" in humans. They were also forbidden to celibates because of their supposed aphrodisiac effect. The high sulphur content of garlic has a heating effect upon the blood, according to medievalists.

Nevertheless, garlic and onions have long been valued for their use in cooking, as pickled snacks and for medicinal purposes. Studies have corroborated the belief that these foods hinder the growth of intestinal parasites and germs and help fight off infections, both in the digestive tract and in the lungs. Garlic, and to a lesser extent onions, are rich dietary sources of sulphur and selenium.

The traditional use of garlic for the prevention of blood clots also has recently been corroborated by science. Researches have identified a substance called adenosine in garlic oil that breaks down a blood-clot-promoting protein called fibrin. SWF

Using the food of the host as a culture medium, the quantity of enzymes produced by these countless bacteria must be considerable and they are placed at the selective disposal of the organism. It cannot be denied that bacteria are efficient and prolific enzyme producers since highly active bacterial enzymes are being used regularly in industry. Edward Howell, MD *Food Enzymes for Health and Longevity*

PICKLED PEARL ONIONS
Makes 1 quart

2 pounds pearl onions
1 cinnamon stick
1 small nutmeg, cracked open
2 teaspoons whole cloves
1 tablespoon juniper berries
1 teaspoon green peppercorns
several sprigs fresh tarragon
1 tablespoon sea salt
4 tablespoons whey (page 87) (if not available, use an additional 1 tablespoon salt)
1 cup filtered water

Loosen skin on onions by plunging them into boiling water for about 10 seconds. Remove, peel and place in a quart-sized, wide-mouth mason jar. Combine remaining ingredients and pour mixture over onions, adding more water if necessary to cover them. The top of the liquid should be at least 1 inch below the top of the jar. Cover tightly and keep at room temperature for about 3 days before transferring to cold storage.

PICKLED GARLIC
Makes 1 quart

about 12 heads garlic
2 teaspoons dried oregano
2 teaspoons sea salt
2 tablespoons whey (page 87) (if not available, use an additional 2 teaspoons salt)

Set garlic heads in a 300 degree oven and bake until heads open and cloves can be easily removed. Place cloves in a quart-sized, wide-mouth mason jar. Mix oregano, salt and whey with 1/2 cup of water. Pour over garlic, adding more water if necessary to cover the garlic. The top of the liquid should be at least 1 inch below the top of the jar. Cover tightly and keep at room temperature for about 3 days before transferring to cold storage.

PICKLED CUCUMBERS

Makes 1 quart

4-5 pickling cucumbers or 15-20 gherkins
1 tablespoon mustard seeds
2 tablespoons fresh dill, snipped
1 tablespoon sea salt
4 tablespoons whey (page 87) (if not available,
    use an additional 1 tablespoon salt)
1 cup filtered water

Wash cucumbers well and place in a quart-sized, wide-mouth mason jar. Combine remaining ingredients and pour over cucumbers, adding more water if necessary to cover the cucumbers. The top of the liquid should be at least 1 inch below the top of the jar. Cover tightly and keep at room temperature for about 3 days before transferring to cold storage.

Variation: Pickled Cucumber Slices

Wash cucumbers well and slice at 1/4 inch intervals. Proceed with recipe. Pickles will be ready for cold storage after about 2 days at room temperature.

PEASANT LUNCH

*Sour Dough Bread
with Cultured Butter*

❧❦❧

Raw Cheddar Cheese

❧❦❧

Pickled Herring

❧❦❧

*Pickled Garlic
Pickled Cucumbers*

❧❦❧

Kvass

Lacto-fermented cucumbers and *cornichons* [small cucumbers] are very refreshing and far less acid than pickles conserved in vinegar—one never grows tired of them. In classic cooking, these cornichons always go with meat courses and with sausages and preserved meats; a wise habit since this vegetable is able to dissolve precipitates of uric acid and thus prevents the formation of stones, often caused by meats and sausages, foods rich in uric acid. Claude Aubert *Les Aliments Fermentés Traditionnels*

A 1999 study published in the *Lancet* found that consumption of lacto-fermented vegetables was positively associated with low rates of asthma, skin problems and autoimmune disorders in Swedish children attending a Waldorf school. The same study found that use of raw milk and avoidance of vaccinations added to the protective effects. SWF

Almanzo felt a little better when he sat down to the good Sunday dinner. Mother sliced the hot rye'n'injun bread on the breadboard by her plate. Father's spoon cut deep into the chicken pie; he scooped out big pieces of thick crust and turned up their fluffy yellow undersides on the plate. He poured gravy over them; he dipped up big pieces of tender chicken, dark meat and white meat sliding from the bones. He added a mound of baked beans and topped it with a quivering slice of fat pork. At the edge of the plate he piled dark-red beet pickles. And he handed the plate to Almanzo. Laura Ingalls Wilder *Farmer Boy*

The daikon radish is greatly prized as a digestive aid in the Orient where it is eaten in a great variety of ways— fresh or preserved, dried, salted and added to soup or meat dishes. Fermented daikon radish, or *takuan*, is commonly served with macrobiotic food. Tests have shown it to be especially high in *lactobacilli*. It is also valued as a diuretic, as a decongestant and as a source of substances that inhibit cancer. Folk wisdom claims the daikon rids the body of accumulated fats. The root is an excellent source of vitamin C. SWF

PICKLED BEETS
Makes 1 quart

12 medium beets
seeds from 2 cardamom pods (optional)
1 tablespoon sea salt
4 tablespoons whey (page 87) (if not available,
    use an additional 1 tablespoon salt)
1 cup filtered water

Prick beets in several places, place on a cookie sheet and bake at 300 degrees for about 3 hours, or until soft. Peel and cut into a 1/4-inch julienne. (Do not grate or cut the beets with a food processor—this releases too much juice and the fermentation process will proceed too quickly, so that it favors formation of alcohol rather than lactic acid.) Place beets in a quart-sized, wide-mouth mason jar and press down lightly with a wooden pounder or a meat hammer. Combine remaining ingredients and pour over beets, adding more water if necessary to cover the beets. The top of the beets should be at least 1 inch below the top of the jar. Cover tightly and keep at room temperature for about 3 days before transferring to cold storage.

PICKLED DAIKON RADISH
Makes 1 quart

3 pounds daikon radish, peeled and grated
1 tablespoon sea salt
4 tablespoons whey (page 87) (if not available,
    use an additional 1 tablespoon salt)

Place all ingredients in a bowl, mix well and pound with wooden pounder or meat hammer to release juices. Place radish mixture in a quart-sized, wide-mouth mason jar and press down lightly with a wooden pounder or a meat hammer until juices come to the top of the radish mixture. The top of the radish mixture should be at least 1 inch below the top of the jar. Cover tightly and keep at room temperature for about 3 days before transferring to cold storage.

PICKLED TURNIPS

Makes 1 quart

2 1/2 cups turnips, peeled, quartered and sliced
3/4 cup beets, peeled, quartered and sliced
1 medium onion, peeled, quartered and sliced
1 tablespoon sea salt
4 tablespoons whey (page 87) (if not available,
    use an additional 1 tablespoon salt)
1 cup filtered water

Mix vegetables and place in a quart-sized, wide-mouth mason jar. Press down lightly with a wooden pounder or a meat hammer. Mix water with salt and whey and pour over vegetables, adding more water if necessary to cover the turnip mixture. The top of the vegetables should be at least 1 inch below the top of the jar. Cover tightly and keep at room temperature for about 3 days before transferring to cold storage.

When we buy vegetables, we are often deceived by their color and appearance whereas their aroma, taste and consistency tell us more about their quality. And quality is of paramount importance if we want to preserve these vegetables through lacto-fermentation; lactic-acid-producing bacteria need a great many vitamins and minerals that only vegetables rich in these elements can supply. This is why when foods are successfully lacto-fermented, we can be assured of their inherent nutritional quality. Annelies Schoneck *Des Crudités Toute L'Année*

PICKLED RED PEPPERS

Makes 1 quart

about 12 thick red bell peppers, seeded
    and cut into quarters
1 tablespoon sea salt
4 tablespoons whey (page 87) (if not available,
    use an additional 2 teaspoons salt)
1/2-1 cup filtered water

Place peppers skin side up in oiled pyrex dishes and bake at 450 degrees about 10 minutes. Turn pepper pieces over and bake another 10 minutes or so until skins are browned and begin to buckle. Remove pepper pieces to a platter and cover with a plastic bag. Let cool about 10 minutes and carefully remove skin. Pack the peppers into a quart-sized, wide-mouth mason jar. Mix whey and salt with water and pour into jar, adding more water if necessary to cover the peppers. The top of the peppers should be at least 1 inch below the top of the jar. Cover tightly and keep at room temperature for about 3 days before transferring to cold storage.

*EGYPTIAN
SUPPER*

Mazalika
❦
Falafel
❦
*Tahini Sauce
Pita Bread*
❦
*Tomato Cucumber
Salad*
❦
Pickled Turnips
❦
Rice Milk

The digestive process has two distinct features: one is the breaking down of ingested foods; the other is the building up of nutrients needed by the body. If the breaking down is incomplete, the building up cannot proceed correctly. In reality we nourish ourselves not by what we eat but by what we are capable of breaking down and transforming into nutrients the body can use. Of great importance in this process is the role played by the aromatic substances that are formed during lacto-fermentation. The aroma of lacto-fermented foods is the by-product of certain substances present in infinitesimal amounts but essential for the ultimate assimilation of the food to the body. Hippocrates expressed this principle with the words *Suavia nutriunt*—that which smells good nourishes and promotes healing and health. Thus, the role of these substances that make fermented foods taste good goes far beyond that of gustatory pleasure and the stimulation of digestion to our general well being.

What is astonishing is that lactic acid contributes to both processes—that of decomposition and that of reconstruction. On the one hand it supplies digestive juices in the form of organic acids that help break down the foods we eat, and on the other it activates the metabolic processes

PICKLED GINGER
Makes 1 quart

about 3 pounds fresh ginger root
1 tablespoon sea salt
4 tablespoons whey (page 87) (if not available, use an additional 1 tablespoon sea salt)
1 cup filtered water

Peel ginger and slice very thinly. Place in a large bowl and pound lightly with a wooden pounder or a meat hammer to release juices. Place in a quart-sized, wide-mouth mason jar and press down lightly with a pounder or meat hammer. Mix water with salt and whey and pour into jar, adding more water if necessary to cover the ginger. The top of the ginger should be at least 1 inch below the top of the jar. Cover tightly and keep at room temperature for about 3 days before transferring to cold storage.

CORN RELISH
Makes 1 quart

3 cups fresh corn kernels
1 small tomato, peeled, seeded and diced
1 small onion, finely diced
1/2 red pepper, seeded and diced
2 tablespoons cilantro leaves, chopped
1/4-1/2 teaspoon red pepper flakes
1 tablespoon sea salt
4 tablespoons whey (page 87)

To peel tomatoes, see page 70. In a large bowl mix all ingredients. Pound lightly with a wooden pounder or a meat hammer to release juices. Place in a quart-sized, wide-mouth mason jar and press down with a pounder or meat hammer until juices cover the relish. The top of the vegetables should be at least 1 inch below the top of the jar. Cover tightly and keep at room temperature for about 3 days before transferring to cold storage.

PICKLED GRAPE LEAVES

Makes 1 quart

2 dozen grape leaves
1 tablespoon sea salt
4 tablespoons whey (page 87) (if not available,
*   use an additional 1 tablespoon salt)*
2 cups filtered water

If you have a grape vine in your garden or live near a vineyard, you may want to try these. Pickled grape leaves are used to make dolmas (page 253).

Wash leaves well. Place water, salt and whey in a large bowl. Soak grape leaves in the liquid for about 1 hour. Place all the leaves together and roll up. Stuff into a quart-sized, wide-mouth mason jar. Pour in enough soaking liquid to cover leaves. The top of the liquid should be at least 1 inch below the top of the jar. Cover tightly and keep at room temperature for about 3 days before transferring to cold storage.

TOMATO PEPPER RELISH

Makes 1 quart

4 ripe tomatoes, peeled, seeded and chopped
1 bunch green onions, chopped
1 green pepper, seeded and chopped
1-2 jalapeno chiles, seeded and chopped
1 bunch cilantro, chopped
2 cloves garlic, mashed
4 tablespoons whey (page 87)
1 tablespoon sea salt
1/2 cup filtered water

To peel tomatoes, see page 70. Mix all vegetables in a bowl and pound lightly with a wooden pounder or a meat hammer. Place in a quart-sized, wide-mouth mason jar and press down lightly with a pounder or meat hammer until the liquid completely covers the tomato mixture. The top of the vegetables should be at least 1 inch below the top of the jar. Cover tightly and keep at room temperature for about 2 days before transferring to cold storage.

whereby these foods are transformed into new living substances.

Lacto-fermented foods normalize the acidity of the stomach. If stomach acidity is insufficient, it stimulates the acid producing glands of the stomach, and in cases where acidity is too high it has the inverse effect. Lactic acid helps break down proteins and thus aids in their assimilation by the body. It also aids the assimilation of iron. The decomposition in the stomach of the organic forms of iron depends on the quantity of hydrochloric acid present as well as the amount of vitamin C, which is why sauerkraut and other lacto-fermented vegetables rich in this vitamin have such a favorable influence. . . . Lactic acid activates the secretions of the pancreas, which is particularly important for diabetics. . . . Sauerkraut contains large quantities of choline, a substance that lowers blood pressure and regulates the passage of nutrients into the blood. . . . Choline has another interesting property in that it aids the body in the metabolism of fats. If choline is lacking, fats accumulate in the liver. . . . Sauerkraut also contains acetylcholine which has a powerful effect on the parasympathetic nervous system. It helps reduce blood pressure, slows down the rate of heartbeat, and promotes calmness and sleep. As acetylcholine is destroyed by cooking, raw sauerkraut and its juice is preferable to cooked. Acetylcholine also has a beneficial effect on the peristaltic movements of the intestine. Sauerkraut and other lacto-fermented vegetables thus are recommended for constipation.
Annelies Schoneck *Des Crudités Toute L'Année*

There is often the tendency to look for exterior infectious agents as the cause of illness. We forget that the intestine that is functioning poorly leads to serious consequences for the whole body. This is why, since most ancient times, lactic acid was used to clean the intestine. Different types of lacto-fermented juices were used as preferred remedies against typhus and other illnesses of this type. The most recent research has confirmed this beneficial action of lactic-acid-producing bacteria. . . . The mucus membranes of the intestinal tract are protected by bacteria which create an acid environment in which the pathogenic bacteria cannot multiply. The whole digestive tract harbors a complex bacteriological flora that varies from one part to the next. The lactic-acid-producing bacteria are characterized by the fact that they survive the transition from the stomach to the small intestine and they are still active when they reach the large intestine. . . . Recent research has shown that lactic-acid-producing bacteria can prevent the growth of coliform bacteria and agents of cholera from establishing themselves in the intestine. Even certain carcinogenic substances are inhibited and inactivated. . . . In effect, the state of our intestinal flora contributes not only to the absorption of nutrients and the functioning of the intestine but also to our ability to resist infections. Annelies Schoneck *Des Crudités Toute L'Année*

FERMENTED TARO ROOT

(Poi)
Makes about 3 cups

2 pounds taro root
1 tablespoon sea salt
4 tablespoons whey (page 87)

Taro and related tubers are found throughout the tropical world—in Africa, the West Indies and Polynesia. Explorers discovered that the natives ate root vegetables after they had been buried in the ground and fermented for several days to several months!

Poke a few holes in the tubers and bake in an oven at 300 degrees for about 2 hours or until soft. Peel and mash with salt and whey. Place in a bowl, cover and leave at room temperature for 24 hours. Place in an airtight container and store in the refrigerator. This may be spread on bread or crackers like cream cheese. It also makes an excellent baby food.

Variation: Fermented Sweet Potato
Use *2 pounds sweet potatoes* instead of taro root.

POTATO CHEESE

Makes about 4 cups

4 cups cooked potatoes, peeled
2 cups piima milk (page 83) or kefir (page 86)
1 tablespoon sea salt

This recipe for fermented potatoes comes from *The American Frugal Housewife*, published in 1833. Mix ingredients well in food processor. Place in a covered bowl and leave at room temperature for about 2 days. Place in a large strainer, lined with a clean linen towel. Tie the towel in a bundle to a spoon, hung over a jug or bowl, so the "cheese" can drain. When draining stops, transfer to an airtight container and store in the refrigerator.

FERMENTED BEAN PASTE

Makes 1 quart

3 cups basic beans (page 496), cooked and drained
1 onion, peeled and coarsely chopped
3 cloves garlic, peeled
1 tablespoon sea salt
4 tablespoons whey (page 87)

Place onion and garlic in food processor and process until well chopped. Add remaining ingredients and process until smooth. Place in a quart-sized, wide-mouth mason jar, leaving 1 inch of space between the top of the beans and the top of the jar. Cover tightly and leave at room temperature for about 3 days before transferring to the refrigerator. Serve as a dip with pita chips (page 521) or baked or fried tortillas (page 519).

SALSA

Makes 1 quart

4 medium tomatoes, peeled, seeded and diced
2 small onions, finely chopped
3/4 cup chopped chile pepper, hot or mild
6-8 cloves garlic, peeled and finely chopped
*   (optional)*
1 bunch cilantro, chopped
1 teaspoon dried oregano
juice of 2 lemons
1 tablespoon sea salt
4 tablespoons whey (page 87) (if not available,
*   use an additional 1 tablespoon salt)*
1/4 cup filtered water

To peel tomatoes, see page 70. Mix all ingredients and place in a quart-sized, wide-mouth mason jar. Press down lightly with a wooden pounder or a meat hammer, adding more water if necessary to cover the vegetables. The top of the vegetables should be at least 1 inch below the top of the jar. Cover tightly and keep at room temperature for about 2 days before transferring to cold storage.

There is something fascinating about microorganisms. They are everywhere: in the air, in water, in our food, on our bodies, in our bodies, invisible and without number, capable of multiplying with extraordinary rapidity, agents of illness and even of death, but also the foundation of life and health. Microorganisms frighten us: aren't these germs responsible for deadly scourges (tuberculosis, plague, cholera, typhoid)? Aren't they responsible for serious food contamination?

Down with the one-celled organism, we say! Long live disinfection! Germicides, fungicides, antibiotics, antiseptics, sterilization, freezing—we lack no weapons in the war against germs. Medicine, agriculture and the food industry make use of them all. [We should] consider not how to kill microorganisms but rather how to make them our friends and allies; how to use them in ways that encourage their proliferation in our foods. We should consider how to put to use the numerous types of microorganisms that, far from contaminating what we eat, improve its flavor and nutritive value in such a way as to turn simple foodstuffs into true natural remedies. Grains, pulses, vegetables, fruits and milk—these are the foods that can be transformed by fungus and bacteria, using very ancient procedures, in such a way as to confer on them qualities they initially lacked, as well as to preserve them without the aid of modern industrial processes. Claude Aubert *Les Aliments Fermentés Traditionnels*

Use of mustard seed dates back to antiquity, both for its epicurean and medicinal properties. A member of the brassica family, related to broccoli and cabbage, mustard is valued for its seed, which contains a compound called sinigrin. During grinding, enzymatic action liberates the pungent principle from the sugar molecule to which it is attached. Sulphur compounds and oils are also released. These compounds have a penetrating odor and an irritating effect on the skin and mucous membranes. Paradoxically, mustard compounds have been used throughout the world for the treatment of diseases of the lungs and sinuses. During the Tang Dynasty in China, mustard was used as a treatment for pulmonary diseases. The Egyptians recommended mustard in respiratory therapy, and in the Middle Ages mustard was used against asthma, coughs and chest congestion. The English physician Herberden also recommended mustard seed to treat asthma. SWF

Ketchup provides us with an excellent example of a condiment that was formerly fermented and therefore health promoting, but whose benefits were lost with large scale canning methods and a reliance on sugar rather than lactic acid as a preservative.

The word "ketchup" derives from the Chinese Amoy dialect *ke-tsiap* or pickled fish-brine or sauce, the universal condiment of the ancient world. The English added foods like mush-

MUSTARD
Makes 2 cups

1 1/2 cup (4 ounces) ground mustard
1/2 cup filtered water
2 tablespoons whey (page 87)
2 teaspoons sea salt
juice of 1 lemon
2 cloves garlic, mashed (optional)
1 tablespoon honey (optional)
2 tablespoons whole mustard seeds (optional)

Mix all ingredients together until well blended, adding more water if necessary to obtain desired consistency. Place in a pint-sized jar or two 8-ounce jars. The top of the mustard should be at least 1 inch below the top of the jar. Cover tightly and keep at room temperature for about 3 days before transferring to cold storage.

KETCHUP
Makes 1 quart

3 cups canned tomato paste, preferably organic
1/4 cup whey (page 87)
1 tablespoon sea salt
1/2 cup maple syrup
1/4 teaspoon cayenne pepper
3 cloves garlic, peeled and mashed
1/2 cup homemade fish sauce (page 157)
*   or commercial fish sauce*

Mix all ingredients until well blended. Place in a quart-sized, wide-mouth mason jar. The top of the ketchup should be at least 1 inch below the top of the jar. Leave at room temperature for about 2 days before transferring to refrigerator.

MINT CHUTNEY

Makes 3 cups

2 cups fresh mint leaves
1 medium onion, peeled and coarsely chopped
4 cloves garlic, peeled and coarsely chopped
4 jalapeno chiles, seeded and chopped
2 teaspoons cumin seeds, toasted in oven
2/3 cup crispy almonds (page 515), chopped
1 tablespoon sea salt
4 tablespoons whey (page 87)
1 cup filtered water

Place all ingredients except salt, whey and water in food processor and pulse a few times until finely chopped but not paste-like. Place in a quart-sized, wide-mouth mason jar and press down lightly. Mix salt and whey with water and pour into jar, adding more water if necessary to cover the chutney. The top of the chutney should be at least 1 inch below the top of the jar. Cover tightly and keep at room temperature for 2 days before transferring to refrigerator. This should be eaten within 2 months.

CHERRY CHUTNEY

Makes 1 quart

4 cups ripe cherries, pitted and quartered
1/2 teaspoon coriander seeds
1/2 teaspoon whole cloves
grated rind and juice of 1 orange
1/8 cup Rapadura (see page 536)
1/4 cup whey (page 87)
2 teaspoons sea salt
1/2 cup filtered water

Mix cherries with spices and orange rind, place in a quart-sized, wide-mouth mason jar and press down lightly. Mix remaining ingredients and pour into jar, adding more water if necessary to cover the cherries. The top of the chutney should be at least 1 inch below the top of the jar. Cover tightly and keep at room temperature for 2 days before transferring to refrigerator. This should be eaten within 2 months.

rooms, walnuts, cucumbers and oysters to this fermented brew; Americans added tomatoes from Mexico to make tomato ketchup.

Writing in 1730, Dean Swift mentions ketchup as one of several fermented foods favored by the English. "And for our home-bred British cheer, Botargo (fish roe relish), catsup and cabiar (caviar)."

Americans consume one-half billion bottles of ketchup per year. The chief ingredient of the modern version, after tomatoes, is high fructose corn syrup. A return to ancient preservation methods would transform America's favorite condiment from a health liability (produced in huge factories) to a beneficial digestive aid (produced as an artisanal product in farming communities). SWF

JUNE DINNER

Summer Salad

Basic Baked Chicken

Cherry Chutney

Corn on the Cob

Sautéed Zucchini

Strawberry Delights

The pineapple is a native of South America. It is an unusual fruit in that it forms when the fruits of a hundred or more separate flowers coalesce. It has a high sugar content and a delicious flavor. Pineapple is high in fiber and contains carotenoids, B-complex vitamins and vitamin C. Organically grown pineapple from selenium-rich soil also contains a unique enzyme called bromelain that helps digest protein—but the enzyme is absent in many commercially available varieties of the fruit. This enzyme works not only in the acid present in the stomach but also in the alkaline environment of the intestine and has been used to treat a number of diseases including heart disease, rheumatoid arthritis, injuries, edema, pneumonia and scleroderma. It is claimed to shorten labor and reduce appetite.

According to Professor Francisco Villaroel of Bolivia, pineapple is a powerful remedy for chest ailments, jaundice, arteriosclerosis, anemia and cerebral problems, such as neurasthenia, melancholia and loss of memory.

Pineapple is rich in manganese, which is necessary for strong bones and a healthy nervous system. Recent studies have revealed that women with osteoporosis have about one-third less manganese in their blood than healthy women. The manganese in pineapple is in a particularly absorbable form.

The enzyme bromelain in pineapple is what makes other fruit become soggy when mixed with pineapple. Surprisingly, pineapple that has been lacto-fermented does not become soggy but retains its crispness. With its protein-digesting bromelain content, lacto-fermented pineapple chutney is the perfect accompaniment for meat dishes of all types. SWF

FRUIT CHUTNEY
Makes 1 quart

3 cups fresh peaches, pears, apples, mango
  or papaya
1/2 cup filtered water
grated rind of 2 lemons
juice of 2 lemons
1/8 cup Rapadura (see page 536)
2 teaspoons sea salt
1/4 cup whey (page 87)
1/2 cup crispy pecans (page 513), chopped
1/2 cup dark raisins
1 teaspoon ground cumin
1/2 teaspoon red pepper flakes
1/2 teaspoon dried green peppercorns, crushed
1/2 teaspoon dried thyme
1 teaspoon fennel seeds
1 teaspoon coriander seeds

Mix water, lemon juice, lemon rind, Rapadura, salt and whey. Peel fruit and cut up into lemon juice mixture. Mix with nuts, raisins, herbs and spices and place in a quart-sized, wide-mouth mason jar. Press down lightly with a wooden pounder or a meat hammer, adding more water if necessary to cover the fruit. The mixture should be at least 1 inch below the top of the jar. Cover tightly and keep at room temperature for 2 days before transferring to refrigerator. This should be eaten within 2 months.

PINEAPPLE CHUTNEY
Makes 1 quart

1 small pineapple
1 bunch cilantro, coarsely chopped
1 tablespoon freshly grated ginger
2 tablespoons fresh lime juice
1 teaspoon sea salt
1/4 cup whey (page 87)
1/2 cup filtered water

Mix pineapple, cilantro and ginger and place in a quart-sized, wide-mouth mason jar. Press down lightly with a wooden pounder or a meat hammer. Mix lime juice, sea salt and whey with water and pour over pineapple, adding more water if necessary to cover the pineapple. The chutney should be at least 1 inch below the top of the jar. Cover tightly and keep at room temperature for 2 days before transferring to refrigerator. This should be eaten within 2 months.

Variation: Hot Pineapple Chutney
Add *1 small red onion, 1 jalapeno pepper* and *1/2 red pepper,* all finely chopped.

PAPAYA CHUTNEY
Makes 1 quart

3 cups ripe papaya, peeled and cubed
1 tablespoon freshly grated ginger
1 red pepper, seeded and cut into a julienne
1 small onion, chopped
1 jalapeno chile, seeded and chopped (optional)
1/2 cup fresh mint leaves, cut into pieces
1 bunch cilantro, chopped
1/8 cup Rapadura (see page 536)
1/2 cup lime juice
2 teaspoons sea salt
1/4 cup whey (page 87)
1/2 cup filtered water

Mix papaya with ginger, peppers, onion, mint and cilantro and place in a quart-sized, wide-mouth mason jar. Press down lightly with a wooden pounder or a meat hammer. Mix remaining ingredients and pour into jar, adding more water if necessary to cover the fruit. The chutney should be at least 1 inch below the top of the jar. Cover tightly and leave at room temperature for 2 days before transferring to refrigerator. This should be eaten within 2 months.

Variation: Mango Chutney
Use *3 cups firm mango, peeled and cubed,* instead of papaya.

Know Your Ingredients
Name This Product # 1

Imported mangoes, corn syrup, sugar, distilled vinegar, salt, raisins, lime juice, dextrose, tamarind extract, caramel coloring, spices, natural flavors and dehydrated onions.

See Appendix B for Answer

The papaya hails from the American tropics. The papaya tree is fast growing and short lived; it looks like a palm tree with a tuft of large leaves at the top. Some papayas weigh as much as twenty pounds—perhaps this is why Columbus called the papaya tree the "melon tree." Most commercially available papayas in America come from Hawaii; but they are also grown in Florida, Mexico and Puerto Rico. Papayas picked green will ripen at room temperature. They are rich in carotenoids and vitamin C as well as potassium and phosphorus. They contain a unique protein digestion enzyme, which is used commercially as a meat tenderizer—hence the wisdom of taking papaya chutney with meats. Save the papaya seeds to make papaya pepper (page 157), which is also rich in enzymes and an excellent substitute for black pepper. SWF

There is a large difference between the vitamins found in foods and many of the vitamins sold in pill form in our health food stores and drugstores. Vitamins in foods come with many cofactors—such as related vitamins, enzymes, and minerals—which act with the vitamin to ensure that it is absorbed and properly used. Most commercially produced supplements contain vitamins that are either crystalline or synthetic. Crystalline vitamins are those that have been separated from natural sources by chemical means; synthetic vitamins are produced "from scratch" in the laboratory. Both are purified or fractionated concentrates of the vitamin, which act more like drugs than nutrients in the body. They can actually disrupt the body chemistry and cause many imbalances. An additional danger with synthetic vitamins is that they can be the mirror image of what is found in nature, a form that may actually be patently harmful.

Natural vitamins obtained from whole foods, food concentrates and superfoods like yeast, spirulina, bee pollen and cod liver oil work in small quantities with almost magical effects. But crystalline or synthetic vitamins may not work at all. For example, synthetic B_1 derived from coal tar did not cure beriberi in Korean prisoners-of-war but rice polishings with natural vitamin B complex did; synthetic vitamin C is not as effective in curing scurvy as fresh citrus juice; and synthetic betacarotene given to smokers actually increased their risk of cancer, while the natural forms found in fruits and vegetables are protective. SWF

RAISIN CHUTNEY

Makes 1 quart

3 cups raisins, soaked in warm water for 1 hour
4 cloves garlic, peeled and coarsely chopped
1 bunch cilantro, stems removed
20 black peppercorns
1/2 teaspoon red pepper flakes
2 tablespoons coriander seeds
1 tablespoon cumin seeds
1 tablespoon anise seeds
1 tablespoon freshly grated ginger
2 teaspoons sea salt
1/4 cup whey (page 87)
1 cup filtered water

Place garlic and cilantro in food processor and pulse a few times. Drain raisins and add to food processor along with peppercorns, red pepper flakes, seeds and ginger. Pulse a few times until the mixture becomes a coarse paste. Transfer to a quart-sized, wide-mouth mason jar and press down lightly with a wooden pounder or a meat hammer. Mix salt and whey with water and pour into jar. You may need to poke a few holes in the chutney to allow liquid to percolate through. Add more water if necessary to cover the chutney. The top of the chutney should be at least 1 inch below the top of the jar. Cover tightly and keep at room temperature for about 2 days before transferring to refrigerator. The chutney should be eaten within 2 months.

PRESERVED LEMON

Makes 1 quart

5 *organic lemons, preferably thin-skinned variety*
3 *tablespoons sea salt*
3 *cinnamon sticks, broken up*
2 *tablespoons whey (page 87)*
juice of 2 lemons

Wash lemons well, slice thinly and cut slices into quarters. Toss in a bowl with salt and cinnamon sticks. Place in a quart-sized, wide-mouth mason jar and press down lightly with a wooden pounder or a meat hammer. Mix lemon juice with whey and add to jar, pressing down so that the liquid completely covers the lemons. Lemons should be at least 1 inch below the top of the jar. Cover tightly and keep at room temperature for up to 2 weeks, turning jar once a day, before transferring to cold storage. When adding to recipes, remove pulp and cut skin into a julienne.

ORANGE MARMALADE

Makes 1 quart

3-4 *organic oranges*
1 *tablespoon salt*
1/4 *cup whey (page 87)*
1/2 *cup filtered water*
1/4 *cup Rapadura (see page 536)*

This makes a marmalade that is liquid rather than thick. Slice oranges very thinly and cut slices into quarters. Place in a quart-sized, wide-mouth mason jar and press down lightly with a wooden pounder or a meat hammer. Combine remaining ingredients and pour over oranges, adding more water if necessary to cover them. Marmalade should be at least 1 inch below the top of the jar. Cover tightly and keep at room temperature for about 3 days before transferring to cold storage. If marmalade develops spots of white mold on the top, simply remove them with a spoon.

Variation: Kumquat Marmalade

Use *about 2 dozen kumquats* instead of oranges.

Lemons are native to southeastern Asia. They were introduced to the Mediterranean about 1000 AD and thence taken to Europe and the United States. They are valued for their strongly flavored peel—used in many medicinal and cosmetic preparations—and above all for their juice, rich in vitamin C and citric acid. Lemon and lime juice have long been used to treat scurvy; lemon juice is also an effective diuretic. In tests of plant extracts, lemon extract was found to be effective in killing roundworms. The high acidity of lemon juice, and its disinfectant and antimicrobial properties, make it ideal for marinating raw fish. The Romans believed that lemon was an antidote for all poisons, including venomous snake bites.

Most commercial lemons and other citrus fruits are treated with neurotoxic cholinesterase inhibitors to prevent spoilage, so it pays to seek out organic lemons, oranges and grapefruit. SWF

Oranges are famous for their high vitamin C content. They also contain potassium and some calcium. The interior white membrane is an excellent source of bioflavonoids, so essential to the health of the blood capillaries. Seville oranges are prized for the flavor of their skin, which folklore claims has medicinal properties. Before the days of refrigerated ships, oranges from Spain came to Northern Europe in the form of marmalade. Originally marmalade was a lacto-fermented food! The oranges were mixed with salt water and pressed into large casks. The long sea voyage gave them plenty of time to ferment and develop rich flavors. Sugar was too expensive to be added in large quantities, so marmalade was traditionally quite tart. SWF

Native of China, and cousin to almonds, cherries, peaches and plums, the apricot was valued by ancient cultures both for its delicious fruit and tasty seed. Chinese "almond cakes" and "almond soup" were actually made of apricot seeds. The apricot is especially cherished in the Himalayan kingdom of Hunza where the inhabitants eat large amounts of a wild variety as a source of health and exceptional longevity. In 1934, the Nobel-prize winner G. S. Whipple praised the apricot as "equal to liver in hemoglobin regeneration." Apricots are rich in betacarotene, an antioxidant that helps prevent cancer, as well as magnesium, potassium, calcium and especially iron. Dried Turkish apricots are one of the very few wild fruits available commercially in American markets. SWF

The education of the young in the tribal groups Weston Price studied included instruction in dietary wisdom as a way of ensuring the health of future generations and the continuance of the tribe in the face of the constant challenges of finding food and defending the group against warring neighbors. Modern parents, living in times of peace and abundance, face an altogether different challenge, one of discrimination and cunning. For they must learn to discriminate between hyperbole and truth when it comes to choosing foods for themselves and their family; and to practice cunning in protecting their children from those displacing products of modern commerce that prevent the optimal expression of their genetic heritage—foodstuffs made of sugar, white flour, vegetable oils and products that imitate the nourishing foods of our ancestors—margarine, shortening, egg replacements, meat extenders, fake broths, ersatz cream,

APRICOT BUTTER
Makes 2 quarts

4 cups unsulphured dried apricots
1 tablespoon sea salt
1/4 cup whey
1/4-1/2 cup raw honey

Cook apricots in filtered water until soft. Let cool slightly and transfer with a slotted spoon to food processor. Process with remaining ingredients. Taste for sweetness and add more honey if necessary. Place in quart-sized, wide-mouth mason jars. The apricot butter should be at least 1 inch below the tops of the jars. Cover tightly and keep at room temperature for about 2 days before transferring to refrigerator. This should be eaten within 2 months. It is excellent with breakfast porridge (page 455) or on pancakes (page 478).

Variation: Apple Butter
Use *dried apples* instead of apricots

Variation: Pear Butter
Use *dried pears* instead of apricots.

BERRY PRESERVES

Makes 1 quart

4 cups fresh berries, such as bosenberries,
  blackberries or raspberries, or a mixture
2 teaspoons sea salt
1/4 cup Rapadura (see page 536)
1/4 cup whey
2 teaspoons Pomona's Universal Pectin (available at
  gourmet markets and health food stores)
2 teaspoons calcium water
  (see instructions in Pomona Pectin package)

You may use any summer berry except strawberries, which are too acid for lacto-fermentation purposes.

Wash berries and place in a bowl with remaining ingredients. Carefully mash down with a wooden pounder or a meat hammer until berries are well crushed. Mix thoroughly and place a quart-sized, wide-mouth mason jar. The top of the preserves should be at least 1 inch below the top of the jar. Cover tightly and keep at room temperature for 2 days before transferring to the refrigerator. Use within 2 months.

Variation: Berry Syrup

Omit pectin and calcium water. Place berries in a quart-sized, wide-mouth mason jar and press down lightly. Mix remaining ingredients and pour into jar. Add enough filtered water to bring level of the liquid to the top of the berries. Proceed with recipe. This is delicious on vanilla ice cream (page 550) or pancakes (page 478).

processed cheese, factory farmed meats, industrially farmed plantfoods, protein powders and packets of stuff that never spoils.

For a future of healthy children—for any future at all—we must turn our backs on the dietary advice of sophisticated medical orthodoxy and return to the food wisdom of our so-called primitive ancestors, choosing traditional whole foods that are organically grown, humanely raised, minimally processed and above all not shorn of their vital lipid component. *Ancient Dietary Wisdom for Tomorrow's Children*

The best reason for eating berries is that they taste so good—but there are many others. Berries are good sources of minerals, vitamin C and carotenoids. Wild or organically grown berries will supply nitrilosides, an anticancer member of the B complex family.

Berries, particularly strawberries, blackberries and raspberries, contain a compound called ellagic acid, which is an antioxidant that helps detoxify carcinogens. Researchers have found that it works in several ways—by blocking the activation of carcinogens, by inhibiting the carcinogen itself and by preventing DNA in cells from undergoing mutation.

Strawberries are the richest source of ellagic acid, which is in both the pulp and the seeds; but strawberries, unfortunately, do not take well to lacto-fermentation. Other berries, however, can be made into delicious fermented preserves or beverages.

Berries with cream for breakfast, berries with whipped cream for dessert and berry ice cream are delicious, synergistic combinations of water-soluble nutrients and minerals with fat-soluble activators. SWF

SPROUTED GRAINS, NUTS & SEEDS

Credit for discovering the value of sprouted seeds traditionally goes to the Chinese, who learned to germinate legumes many centuries ago. They carried mung beans on their ocean-going ships, sprouted them throughout their voyages and consumed them in sufficient quantities to prevent scurvy. The Chinese instinctively knew that an important factor missing in nongerminated seeds was produced during the sprouting process—that substance is vitamin C.

But it is a mistake to think that the value of sprouted grain was unknown in the West. For centuries, beers of all sorts have been made with germinated grains. Certain old French cookbooks recommend sprouting dried peas before using them in soups. Bulgur, used extensively in Middle Eastern cooking, is made from coarsely ground sprouted wheat. According to enzyme specialist Dr. Edward Howell, in the past we ate most of our grains in partially germinated form. Grain standing in sheaves and stacks in open fields often began to sprout before it was brought into storage. Modern farming techniques prevent grains from germinating before they reach our tables.

The process of germination not only produces vitamin C but also changes the composition of grain and seeds in numerous beneficial ways. Sprouting increases vitamin B content, especially B_2, B_5 and B_6. Carotene increases dramatically—sometimes eightfold. Even more important, sprouting neutralizes phytic acid, a substance present in the bran of all grains that inhibits absorption of calcium, magnesium, iron, copper and zinc; sprouting also neutralizes enzyme inhibitors present in all seeds. These inhibitors can neutralize our own precious enzymes in the digestive tract. Complex sugars responsible for intestinal gas are broken down during sprouting, and a portion of the starch in grain is transformed into sugar. Sprouting inactivates aflatoxins, potent carcinogens found in grains. Finally, numerous enzymes that help digestion are produced during the germination process.

Sprouted grains should be a regular feature of the diet, and they can be used in numerous ways—in salads, sandwiches, vegetable dishes, as breakfast cereals and as additions to breads and baked goods. However, we must warn against overconsumption of *raw* sprouted grains as raw sprouts contain irritating substances that keep animals from eating the tender shoots. These substances are neutralized in cooking. Sprouted grains should usually be eaten lightly steamed or added to soups and casseroles.

No special equipment is required to transform grains and seeds into sprouts—just wide-mouth, quart-sized mason jars with a round of window screen material cut to fit into the lid of the jar, replacing the solid insert. For seeds that sprout easily, see Sources.

The method for sprouting all grains and seeds is the same—only the length of time needed to accomplish full germination varies with the size and nature of the seed. Simply fill a mason jar one-third full with any grain or seed. Add filtered water to the top of the jar and screw on the top with its screen insert. Allow the seeds to soak overnight and pour off the water. Rinse the seeds well—you can do this without removing the top. Invert the jar and let it sit at an angle so it can drain, and to allow air to circulate. The seeds should be rinsed every few hours, or at least twice a day. In one to four days the sprouts will be ready. Rinse well, shake out excess moisture, and replace the screen insert with the solid section of the lid. Store the sprouts in the refrigerator.

Almost any grain or seed can be sprouted—wheat, barley, dried beans, radish seeds, onion seeds, chia seeds, chick peas and almonds. Fragile seeds such as pumpkin and sunflower also sprout nicely. Hulled seeds should be purchased in tightly sealed packages and not from open bins, so that oxidation is minimized.

Seeds that are difficult to sprout include flax seeds, which become too mucilaginous to rinse properly, and oat seeds, which will not sprout once they have been separated from their outer hulls. Seeds that have been irradiated, such as those sold as spices, will not sprout.

Nuts like pecans and walnuts that have been removed from their shells cannot be sprouted, but an overnight soaking in warm, salted filtered water will neutralize sprout inhibitors. (See Snacks, page 512.) Skinless almonds and peanuts will often sprout, an indication that their skins have been removed by mechanical means and not by a process involving boiling or roasting.

There is only one seed we do *not* recommend in sprouted form (or in any form) and that is—surprisingly—alfalfa! After mung beans, alfalfa is the variety of sprout that has caught on in the health food world. Unfortunately, it seems that all the praise heaped on the alfalfa sprout was ill advised. Tests have shown that alfalfa sprouts inhibit the immune system and can contribute to inflammatory arthritis and lupus. Alfalfa seeds contain an amino acid called canavanine that can be toxic to man and animals when taken in quantity. (Canavanine is not found in mature alfalfa plants; it is apparently metabolized during growth.)

Germination increases the enzyme activity as much as six times. This is due to proteolytic release of the enzymes by inactivation of the enzyme inhibitors found in all seeds. Soaking the seeds allows proteases within to neutralize the inhibitor and release the enzymes from bondage. During the years 1930 to 1940 chemists spoke of free and bound enzymes in seeds. It was found that such enzymes as protease and papaine soaked in water with the seeds, released the "sleeping" enzymes from bondage. In 1944 when enzyme inhibitors were discovered in seeds the mystery was cleared up. Edward Howell, MD *Food Enzymes for Health and Longevity*

Any seed can be made to germinate [unless it has been irradiated] by increasing its moisture and holding it at the proper temperature. Resting seeds contain starch, which is a storage product and a source of future energy when conditions become ideal for the seed to germinate and grow into a plant. In nature, seeds sometimes must rest or hibernate for months or years before conditions become satisfactory for them to grow. Enzymes are present in the resting seed but are prevented from being active by the presence of enzyme inhibitors. Germination neutralizes the inhibitors and releases the enzymes. Enzyme inhibitors are part of the seed machinery and serve a purpose. But these inhibitors are out of place in our bodies. They could stop our own enzymes from working. Edward Howell, MD *Food Enzymes for Health and Longevity*

GRAINS (WHEAT, RYE, BARLEY)

Rinse 2 to 3 times per day. Sprouts are tiny and white. They will be ready in 3 to 4 days, reaching a maximum length of 1/4 inch. Use to make bulgur (page 460) and whole grain casseroles, or add to bread.

BUCKWHEAT

Begin with whole buckwheat seeds that have *not* been toasted. Rinse 2 to 3 times per day. Tiny sprouts are ready in 2 days. Use to make kasha (page 464).

BEANS (MUNG AND ADZUKI)

Fill jar only 1/4 full. Rinse 4 or more times per day. Sprouts will be ready in about 4 days. Mung bean sprouts are ready when 2 inches long; the adzuki bean sprout is ready at 1 inch.

BEANS (KIDNEY, LIMA, BLACK)

Rinse 3 to 4 times per day. Sprouts are ready in about 3 days, when sprout is 1/4-inch long. Beans should then be cooked. Sprouted beans will cook in much less time than beans that have been merely soaked.

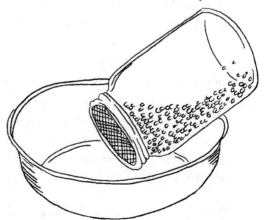

ALMONDS

Use either whole or skinless almonds. Rinse 3 times per day. Sprouts are ready in 3 days. Sprout is merely a tiny white appendage, about 1/8-inch long.

LENTILS

Rinse 3 times a day. Sprout 2 to 3 days until sprout is 1/4-inch long. Steam or cook lightly.

SUNFLOWER SEEDS

These are among the most satisfactory seeds for sprouting. Sunflower sprouts are just delicious in salads, but they must be eaten shortly after sprouting is accomplished as they soon go black. Use hulled sunflower seeds purchased in airtight packages. Rinse 2 times per day. Sprouts are ready in 12 to 18 hours, when the sprout is just barely showing. Use in high enzyme salad (page 193).

PUMPKIN OR MELON SEEDS

Use hulled seeds. Rinse 3 times per day and sprout for about 3 days until sprout is 1/4-inch long. Seeds merely soaked for 12 hours and then lightly toasted are a traditional Mexican food called pepitas (page 513).

SESAME SEEDS

Use unhulled sesame seeds. Rinse 4 times daily. Tiny sprouts are ready in 2 to 3 days.

SMALL SEEDS (CHIA, ONION, CRESS, RADISH, FENUGREEK & POPPY)

Rinse several times per day. Sprouts are ready in 3 to 4 days when they are 1-inch to 2-inches long. Sprouted small seeds are wonderful on sandwiches.

Before the advent of factory farms, grain was partially germinated, but modern grain consists of dormant (resting) seeds. . . . In former times grain was harvested and sheaved. The sheaves were put into shocks and were gathered and built into stacks which stood in the field for several more weeks before threshing. During this period of weathering in the field the grain seeds were exposed to rain and dew which soaked into the sheaves. The grain could pick up this moisture and, with heat from the sun, conditions were ideal for favoring a degree of germination and enzyme multiplication in the grain. The modern combine harvester removes the grain from the stalk immediately after cutting and permits it to be hauled away to the granary. Hence, there is no weathering and consequent enzyme development, resulting in a mature but dormant seed. Edward Howell, MD *Food Enzymes for Health and Longevity*

The sprouting of seeds is one of the most fascinating natural phenomena. From this minuscule appendage, tiny part of a seed even tinier, is born the plant. That this sprout has exceptional nutritional value is thus not surprising. But even more remarkable is the ability of this sprout to produce a whole range of substances—principally vitamins and enzymes—that are completely absent, or present only in extremely small amounts, in the unsprouted seed. The seed becomes hardly recognizable and transforms itself into something new, which is less energetic but richer in nutrients. Claude Aubert *Dis-Moi Comment Tu Cuisines*

STOCKS

A lamentable outcome of our modern meat processing techniques and our hurry-up, throwaway lifestyle has been a decline in the use of meat, chicken and fish stocks. In days gone by, when the butcher sold meat on the bone rather than as individual filets and whole chickens rather than boneless breasts, our thrifty ancestors made use of every part of the animal by preparing stock, broth or bouillon from the bony portions.

Meat and fish stocks are used almost universally in traditional cuisines—French, Italian, Chinese, Japanese, African, South American, Middle Eastern and Russian; but the use of homemade meat broths to produce nourishing and flavorful soups and sauces has almost completely disappeared from the American culinary tradition.

Properly prepared, meat stocks are extremely nutritious, containing the minerals of bone, cartilage, marrow and vegetables as electrolytes, a form that is easy to assimilate. Acidic wine or vinegar added during cooking helps to draw minerals, particularly calcium, magnesium and potassium, into the broth. Dr. Francis Pottenger, author of the famous cat studies as well as articles on the benefits of gelatin in broth, taught that the stockpot was the most important piece of equipment to have in one's kitchen.

It was Dr. Pottenger who pointed out that stock is also of great value because it supplies hydrophilic colloids to the diet. Raw food compounds are colloidal and tend to be hydrophilic, meaning that they attract liquids. Thus, when we eat a salad or some other raw food, the hydrophilic colloids attract digestive juices for rapid and effective digestion. Colloids that have been heated are generally hydrophobic—they repel liquids, making cooked foods harder to digest. However, the proteinaceous gelatin in meat broths has the unusual property of attracting liquids—it is hydrophilic—even after it has been heated. The same property by which gelatin attracts water to form desserts, like Jello, allows it to attract digestive juices to the surface of cooked food particles.

The public is generally unaware of the large amount of research on the beneficial effects of gelatin taken with food. Gelatin acts first and foremost as an aid to digestion and has been used successfully in the treatment of many intestinal disorders, including hyperacidity, colitis and Crohn's disease. Although gelatin is by no means a complete protein, containing only the amino acids arginine and glycine in large amounts, it acts as a protein sparer, allowing the body to more fully utilize the complete proteins that are taken in. Thus, gelatin-rich broths are a must for those who cannot afford large amounts of meat in their diets. Gelatin also seems to be of use in the treatment of many chronic disorders, including anemia and other diseases of the blood, diabetes, muscular dystrophy and even cancer.

Other important ingredients that go into broth are the components of cartilage, which recently have been used with remarkable results in the treatment of cancer and bone disorders, and of collagen, used to treat rheumatoid arthritis and other ailments.

In folk wisdom, rich chicken broth—the famous Jewish penicillin—is a valued remedy for the flu. The 12th-century physician Moses Maimonides prescribed chicken broth as a treatment for colds and asthma. Modern research has confirmed that broth helps prevent and mitigate infectious diseases. The wise food provider, who uses gelatin-rich broth on a daily or frequent basis, provides continuous protection from many health problems.

Another traditional belief is that fish head broth contributes to virility. Fish stock, made from the carcasses and heads of fish, is especially rich in minerals including all-important iodine. Even more important, stock made from the heads, and therefore the thyroid glands of the fish, supplies thyroid hormone and other substances that nourish the thyroid gland. Four thousand years ago, Chinese doctors rejuvenated aging patients with a soup made from the thyroid glands of animals. According to ancient texts, this treatment helped patients feel younger, gave them more energy and often restored mental abilities. During the reign of Queen Victoria, prominent London physicians prescribed special raw thyroid sandwiches to failing patients. Very few of us could eat such fare with relish, but soups and sauces made from fish broth are absolutely delicious—a remedy that no convalescent could refuse. According to some researchers, at least 40 percent of all Americans suffer from a deficiency of the thyroid gland with its accompanying symptoms of fatigue, weight gain, frequent colds and flu, inability to concentrate, depression and a host of more serious complications like heart disease and cancer. We would do well do imitate our brothers from the Mediterranean and Asian regions by including fish broth in the diet as often as possible.

The wonderful thing about fish and meat stocks is that, along with conferring many health benefits, they also add immeasurably to the flavor of our food. In European cuisines, rich stocks form the basis of those exquisite, clear, thick, smooth, satisfying and beautifully flavored sauces that seem to be produced by magic. The magic is in the stock, made from scratch with as much care and attention to detail as the final dish. Those who have had the privilege of visiting the kitchens of fine restaurants in France have observed pots of pale broth simmering on the back burners of huge cookstoves. When this insipid-looking liquid is enriched with herbs or wine and reduced by boiling down, the effects of the gelatin and flavors of meat and bone become concentrated. The result is a wonderful sauce, both nutritious and delicious. It is worth taking time and putting effort into making meat stocks on a regular basis. Your family will gain innumerable health benefits, and you will earn a reputation of an excellent cook.

The test of whether your stock contains liberal amounts of gelatin is carried out by chilling the broth. It should thicken, even to the point of jelling completely, when refrigerated. If your broth is still runny when chilled, you may add a little powdered gelatin (see Sources) to thicken it. Bear in mind, however, that some people have reactions to commercially prepared gelatin, which will contain small amounts of free glutamic acid, similar to MSG. Your stock will also thicken more when it is reduced by boiling down.

Stock can be made in bulk and stored until needed. Clear stock will keep about five days in the refrigerator, longer if reboiled, and several months in the freezer. You may find it useful to store stock in pint-sized or quart-sized containers in order to have appropriate amounts on hand for sauces and stews. If space is at a premium in your freezer, you can reduce the stock by boiling down for several hours until it becomes very concentrated and syrupy. This reduced, concentrated stock—called *fumet* or *demi-glace*—can be stored in small containers or zip-lock bags. Frozen *fumet* in zip-lock bags is easily thawed by putting the bags under hot running water. Add water to thawed *fumet* to turn it back into stock. Be sure to mark the kind of stock or *fumet* you are storing with little stick-on labels—they all look alike when frozen.

FISH STOCK

*3 or 4 whole carcasses, including heads, of non-oily
    fish such as sole, turbot, rockfish or snapper*
2 tablespoons butter
2 onions, coarsely chopped
1 carrot, coarsely chopped
several sprigs fresh thyme
several sprigs parsley
1 bay leaf
1/2 cup dry white wine or vermouth
1/4 cup vinegar
about 3 quarts cold filtered water

Ideally, fish stock is made from the bones of sole or turbot. In Europe, you can buy these fish on the bone. The fish monger skins and filets the fish for you, giving you the filets for your evening meal and the bones for making the stock and final sauce. Unfortunately, in America sole arrives at the fish market preboned. But snapper, rock fish and other non-oily fish work equally well; and a good fish merchant will save the carcasses for you if you ask him. As he normally throws these carcasses away, he shouldn't charge you for them. Be sure to take the heads as well as the body—these are especially rich in iodine and fat-soluble vitamins. Classic cooking texts advise against using oily fish such as salmon for making broth, probably because highly unsaturated fish oils become rancid during the long cooking process.

Melt butter in a large stainless steel pot. Add the vegetables and cook very gently, about 1/2 hour, until they are soft. Add wine and bring to a boil. Add the fish carcasses and cover with cold, filtered water. Add vinegar. Bring to a boil and skim off the scum and impurities as they rise to the top. Tie herbs together and add to the pot. Reduce heat, cover and simmer for at least 4 hours or as long as 24 hours. Remove carcasses with tongs or a slotted spoon and strain the liquid into pint-sized storage containers for refrigerator or freezer. Chill well in the refrigerator and remove any congealed fat before transferring to the freezer for long-term storage.

When he was a boy in Japan, Itoh learned from his mother to use all parts of a fish, including the eyes, roe and bones. After World War II it was necessary to conserve food, so they made broth from bones that were then retrieved, dried, eaten salted as a crispy snack. . . . One type of appetizer, *Nimono*, means "cooked in broth." This is one of the most difficult skills to acquire and each chef takes much pride in developing an individual style with broths. *Palisades Citizens News*

The beginnings of gelatin therapy are buried in antiquity; reference to its use as a hemostatic agent in China in the first century is found in the writings of San Han Ron (204 AD). . . stating that gelatin has been used as a hemostatic agent in China and Japan from prehistoric times. Homberger also referred to its use in China and Japan during the first century for stopping nose bleeding by inhaling the powdered form and for "bleeding of the stomach, the urogenital organs, the uterus. . . the intestines and the rectum." Dutton likewise noted frequent reference to the early use of gelatin, both internally and externally, in the Chinese pharmacology. . . . In 1759 a report was made by an anonymous writer in Nuremberg on the use of gelatin in dysentery, at the same time indicating that gelatin had been employed for a long time as a source of nourishment for weak patients. Bishoff in 1805 referred to its use in wasting away diseases and in dysentery and deplored the forgotten use of "this ancient remedy." N. R. Gotthoffer *Gelatin in Nutrition and Medicine*

If man did not cook his food, there would be no need for the addition of any hydrophilic colloid [gelatin] to his dietary. Uncooked foods contain sufficient hydrophilic colloids to keep gastric mucosa in excellent condition. As we live largely on cooked food, problems arise. An old description of the stomach contents portrays them in layers, each layer assuming its position by virtue of its specific gravity: meat first, then vegetables and fruits . . .and finally the water layer with its scum of fat. According to this view, these layers churn around in sufficient gastric juices to digest the meal in one and one-half hours to four hours if all goes well. If these gastric contents are then removed and examined, the aqueous layer is strongly acid, though the degree of acidity differs with the individual. If we add a hydrophilic colloid of excellent hydration capacity to the diet portrayed above, a definite change takes place in the stomach contents. If they are withdrawn for analysis, a gluey mass is recovered. It is not sour as are the stomach contents without the gelatin; it does not show any acidity until the colloid is broken down. Under these conditions, digestion is generally distributed throughout the mass rather than layered. F. M. Pottenger, Jr., MD *Hydrophilic Colloid Diet*

> Fish broth will cure anything.
> *South American Proverb*

ORIENTAL FISH STOCK

2 medium fish carcasses, including heads,
*   of non-oily fish such as turbot, rockfish*
*   or snapper*
shells (and heads if available) from 3/4 pound
*   fresh shrimp (reserve shrimp for other uses)*
2-3 quarts cold filtered water
1/4 cup vinegar
3 sticks celery, chopped
4 cloves garlic, peeled and chopped
1 inch fresh ginger, peeled and chopped
1 teaspoon black pepper corns

Place carcasses, shrimp shells, water and vinegar in a large stainless steel pot. Bring to a boil and skim. Add remaining ingredients. Simmer, covered, for at least 4 hours or as long as 24 hours. Strain into storage containers for the refrigerator or freezer. Chill well in the refrigerator and remove any congealed fat before transferring to the freezer for long-term storage.

BONITO BROTH
Makes 2 quarts

about 1 cup shaved dried bonito (available in
*   Asian markets)*
2 quarts cold filtered water
1/4 cup vinegar

This is an easy version of fish stock from Japan. Place all ingredients in a stainless steel pot, bring to a boil and skim. Cover and simmer for several hours. There is no need to strain this stock as the bonito flakes disintegrate in the broth.

SHRIMP STOCK

about 4 ounces small dried shrimp
*   (available from Asian markets)*
6 tablespoons extra virgin olive oil or
*   cold-pressed peanut oil*
1 cup dry white wine or vermouth
2 quarts cold filtered water
1/4 cup vinegar
1 carrot, peeled and coarsely chopped
5-6 cloves garlic, peeled
3 small pieces lemon rind
several sprigs fresh thyme, tied together

All Asian markets sell tiny dried shrimp, which are a staple of Oriental cuisine. Generally, the smaller the shrimp, the more expensive and the better the quality. Buy shrimp as small as you can afford, preferably without added salt.

Heat olive oil or peanut oil in a large stainless steel pot. Add shrimp and sauté for several minutes over medium-high heat, stirring constantly. (Sautéing in oil helps remove the fishy taste.) Add wine and bring to a rapid boil. Add cold water and vinegar, bring to a boil and skim. Add remaining ingredients, reduce heat, cover and simmer for several hours.

Strain stock into storage containers for the refrigerator or freezer, reserving the contents of the strainer. Refrigerate stock until cold and remove any fat that congeals on the surface before transferring to the freezer for long-term storage

When the shrimp have cooled, pick out the carrot pieces, garlic cloves, lemon rind and thyme. The cooked shrimp may now be used to make shrimp butter or fermented shrimp paste (p).e 158.)

Variation: Crawfish or Prawn Stock

Use *shells and heads from about 2 pounds of fresh crawfish or prawns* instead of dried shrimp. Place in batches in food processor and process briefly to break shells up into small pieces. Proceed from beginning of the recipe.

The value of gelatin in the treatment of diseases of the digestive system has long been recognized. Uffelmam, in 1891, referred to the use of gelatin in certain cases of gastric catarrh, especially in hyperacidity. Weil, Lumiere and Pehu found, by direct clinical practice, that gelatin acted better and more rapidly than bismuth and tannin and their derivatives in remedying infant diarrhea, which had not developed as far as infant cholera. . . . These workers believed that gelatin acted to cause a mechanical neutralization of the intestinal poisons. . . . Mann was impressed with the value of gelatin in the cure of colitis. Herzberg pointed out that he had employed gelatin, in the simple form of a concentrated calves' foot broth, with excellent results in diuretic condition of children and adults, in cases of abdominal typhus and in dysentery. N. R. Gotthoffer *Gelatin in Nutrition and Medicine*

American cooking, tumbling as fast as it is toward a totally takeout cuisine, retains two potent images that can still revivify our appetite for good, homemade food: baked goods, which stand for the gift of pleasure, and meat-based broths, from which all the kitchen's healing goodness flows. Not too long ago, this image reflected a truth: a continuous river of broth spilled from the stockpot to inspirit soups, enhance pasta and rice, baste the roast, sauce the vegetables and provide a sop for bread. And, most important of all, its aroma filled the house, cosseting all who inhaled it with deep well-being, as if the very air were filled with nurture. The chef may have transmogrified his meat waters into gold; the housewife transmuted them into a far more essential nutrient: love. John Thorne *Outlaw Cook*

BEEF STOCK

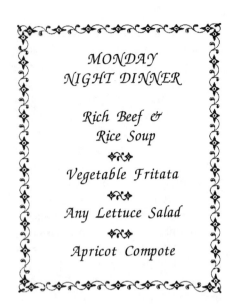

about 4 pounds beef marrow and knuckle bones
1 calves foot, cut into pieces (optional)
3 pounds meaty rib or neck bones
4 or more quarts cold filtered water
1/2 cup vinegar
3 onions, coarsely chopped
3 carrots, coarsely chopped
3 celery sticks, coarsely chopped
several sprigs of fresh thyme, tied together
1 teaspoon dried green peppercorns, crushed
l bunch parsley

The essential premise of stock is a good one: letting nothing go to waste. This means, first, finding a way to eat animals that, while edible, have not been raised strictly to be eaten. Once, not so long ago, much of the meat served on all but the tables of the rich came from animals that had already led useful lives as beasts of burden or wool producers, or careerists who had sent eggs and milk to the table before arriving there themselves.

Furthermore, in those days, because of the vexing problems of spoilage, animals were slaughtered locally, sometimes even at home, supplying ample trimmings and bones (not to mention offal). A cuisine based on stock begins with such butcher's leavings—bones, especially, but also cuts of meat too tough to eat. Butchers then had whole carcasses to contend with, not cartons of selected parts. To keep the profitable cuts moving they had to shift all the rest, too, for such price as they could get. John Thorne
Outlaw Cook

Good beef stock must be made with several sorts of bones: knuckle bones and feet impart large quantities of gelatin to the broth; marrow bones impart flavor and the particular nutrients of bone marrow; and meaty rib or neck bones add color and flavor.

Place the knuckle and marrow bones and optional calves foot in a very large pot with vinegar and cover with water. Let stand for one hour. Meanwhile, place the meaty bones in a roasting pan and brown at 350 degrees in the oven. When well browned, add to the pot along with the vegetables. Pour the fat out of the roasting pan, add cold water to the pan, set over a high flame and bring to a boil, stirring with a wooden spoon to loosen up coagulated juices. Add this liquid to the pot. Add additional water, if necessary, to cover the bones; but the liquid should come no higher than within one inch of the rim of the pot, as the volume expands slightly during cooking. Bring to a boil. A large amount of scum will come to the top, and it is important to remove this with a spoon. After you have skimmed, reduce heat and add the thyme and crushed peppercorns.

Simmer stock for at least 12 and as long as 72 hours. Just before finishing, add the parsley and simmer another 10 minutes.

You will now have a pot of rather repulsive-looking brown liquid containing globs of gelatinous and fatty material. It doesn't even smell particularly good. But don't despair. After straining you will have a delicious and nourishing clear broth that forms the basis for many other recipes in this book.

Remove bones with tongs or a slotted spoon. Strain the stock into a large bowl. Let cool in the refrigerator and remove the congealed fat that rises to the top. Transfer to smaller containers and to the freezer for long-term storage.

Note: The marrow may be removed from the bones and spread on whole grain sourdough bread. Your dog will love the leftover meat and bones. The congealed fat can be used to make pemmican (page 525) or put outside to feed the birds.

Variation: Lamb Stock

Use *lamb bones*, especially lamb neck bones and riblets. This makes a delicious stock.

Variation: Venison Stock

Use *venison meat and bones*. Be sure to use the feet of the deer and a section of antler if possible.

Broth isn't much: a chicken back, some parsley sprigs, a carrot, a celery stalk and time, of course, to bring the flavors out. And after hours of simmering, its life begins, for broth is not a finished food—it is just the start of culinary magic. And it is the crux of all cooking. With it, the sauce is a snap and the soup is practically made.

The words "broth" and "stock" are used interchangeably in many cookbooks, and for good reason, because the differences between the two are hair-splittingly small. In general usage "broth" is a home-cooking term, while "stock" is the province of professional kitchens. Broth is made from spits and spots of leftovers, and its nature changes according to what's on hand. Stock follows a prescribed formula. It is made on a regular basis and forms the groundwork for all of the sauces, soups and simmerings that are the mainstays of a classic kitchen.

There is yet another distinction. The meaty element of stock is predominantly bone, while broth is typically made with meat. This difference changes the finished products in two significant ways. The large proportion of bone gives stock a more gelatinous texture and greater clarity. Broths tend to be thinner and cloudier.

Essential to all broths is starting with cold water. As the ingredients warm in the water, their fibers open slowly, releasing their juices to add flavor. Off flavors can result if the broth is not skimmed.

The broth must be kept at a bare simmer throughout the cooking process to ensure clarity. Andrew Schloss
The Washington Post

> Indeed, stock is everything in cooking. . . without it nothing can be done.
>
> *Auguste Escoffier*

Why is chicken soup superior to all the things we have, even more relaxing than "Tylenol?" It is because chicken soup has a natural ingredient which feeds, repairs and calms the mucous lining in the small intestine. This inner lining is the beginning or ending of the nervous system. It is easily pulled away from the intestine through too many laxatives, too many food additives. . . and parasites. Chicken soup. . . heals the nerves, improves digestion, reduces allergies, relaxes and gives strength. Hanna Kroeger *Ageless Remedies from Mother's Kitchen*

CHICKEN STOCK

1 whole free-range chicken or 2 to 3 pounds of bony chicken parts, such as necks, backs, breastbones and wings
gizzards from one chicken (optional)
feet from the chicken (optional)
4 quarts cold filtered water
2 tablespoons vinegar
1 large onion, coarsely chopped
2 carrots, peeled and coarsely chopped
3 celery sticks, coarsely chopped
1 bunch parsley

If you are using a whole chicken, cut off the wings and remove the neck, fat glands and the gizzards from the cavity. By all means, use chicken feet if you can find them—they are full of gelatin. (Jewish folklore considers the addition of chicken feet the secret to successful broth.) Even better, use a whole chicken, with the head on. These may be found in Oriental markets. Farm-raised, free-range chickens give the best results. Many battery-raised chickens will not produce stock that gels.

Cut chicken parts into several pieces. (If you are using a whole chicken, remove the neck and wings and cut them into several pieces.) Place chicken or chicken pieces in a large stainless steel pot with water, vinegar and all vegetables except parsley. Let stand 30 minutes to 1 hour. Bring to a boil, and remove scum that rises to the top. Reduce heat, cover and simmer for 6 to 24 hours. The longer you cook the stock, the richer and more flavorful it will be. About 10 minutes before finishing the stock, add parsley. This will impart additional mineral ions to the broth.

Remove whole chicken or pieces with a slotted spoon. If you are using a whole chicken, let cool and remove chicken meat from the carcass. Reserve for

other uses, such as chicken salads, enchiladas, sandwiches or curries. (The skin and smaller bones, which will be very soft, may be given to your dog or cat.) Strain the stock into a large bowl and reserve in your refrigerator until the fat rises to the top and congeals. Skim off this fat and reserve the stock in covered containers in your refrigerator or freezer.

Variations: Turkey Stock and Duck Stock

Prepare as chicken stock using *turkey wings and drumsticks* or *duck carcasses from which the breasts, legs and thighs have been removed.* (See page 295.) These stocks will have a stronger flavor than chicken stock and will profit from the addition of *several sprigs of fresh thyme, tied together,* during cooking. Be sure to refrigerate and defat these stocks before using. The reserved duck fat is highly prized for cooking purposes.

CLARIFIED STOCK

2 quarts defatted stock
2 egg whites, lightly beaten

For most recipes, clarification is unnecessary. If you want a perfectly clear stock, however, add egg whites and bring to a boil, whisking with a wire whisk. When the stock begins to boil, stop whisking. Let boil for 3 to 5 minutes. A white foam, gradually becoming a spongy crust, will form on the surface. Off heat, lift off the crust and strain the stock through a strainer lined with a kitchen towel.

QUICK STOCK

1 can Health Valley chicken or beef stock or
*   frozen, store-bought beef, chicken or*
*   fish stock*
1 teaspoon gelatin (see Sources)

This lacks the flavor and nutritive properties of homemade stock, but will do in emergencies. Mix liquid stock with gelatin, bring to a boil and proceed with your recipe.

> Good broth resurrects the dead.
> *South American Proverb*

It was a rare winter when there was not an outbreak of diphtheria in Hayfield or Back Creek or Timber Ridge. . . . Doctor Brush rode with his saddlebags all day long from house to house, never bothering to wash his hands when he came or went. His treatment was to scour throats with a mixture of sulphur and molasses and to forbid his patients both food and water. [Both of Mrs. Blake's girls, Betty and Mary, got diphtheria that winter.] While Fairhead was walking up and down the yard, he kept an eye on the windows of Mrs. Blake's upstairs bedroom. As soon as the candle-light shone there, it would be time for him to go help with the girls. He circled the house, picked up some sticks from the woodpile, and was about go into the kitchen when he saw through the window something which startled him. A white figure emerged from the stairway and drifted across the indoor duskiness of the room. It was Mary, barefoot, in her nightgown, as if she were walking in her sleep. She reached the table, sank down on a wooden chair, and lifted the bowl of chicken broth in her two hands. . . . She drank slowly, resting her elbows on the table. . . . Fairhead knew he ought to go in and take the soup from her. But he was unable to move or to make a sound. . . .

Mary slept all night. When Mrs. Blake came in at four in the morning and held her candle before the girl's face, she knew that she was better . . . .But Betty died, just slipped away without a struggle, like she was dropping asleep. Willa Cather *Sapphira and the Slave Girl*

ABOUT STOCK-BASED SAUCES

There need be no mystery about meat sauces—quite simply, they are made from stocks that have been flavored and thickened in some way. Once you have learned the technique for making sauces—either clear sauces or thick gravies—you can ignore the recipe books and be guided by your imagination.

Reduction Sauces: The principle here is to thicken the gelatinous stock by evaporation through rapid boiling. The first step is to "deglaze" coagulated meat juices in the roasting pan or skillet by adding *1/2 cup to 1 cup wine or brandy*, bringing to a boil and stirring with a wooden spoon to loosen pan drippings. Then add *3 to 4 cups stock*, bring to a boil and skim. (Use chicken stock for chicken dishes, beef stock for beef dishes, etc.) The sauce may now be flavored with any number of ingredients, such as *vinegar, mustard, herbs, spices, fresh orange or lemon juice, naturally sweetened jam, garlic, tomato paste, grated ginger, grated lemon rind, creamed coconut, whole coconut milk* (see page 160) or *cultured cream* (page 84). Let sauce boil vigorously, uncovered, until reduced by at least one-half, or until desired thickness is achieved. You may add about *1-2 teaspoons gelatin* (see Sources) to promote better thickening, Another way to thicken is to mix *2 tablespoons arrowroot powder* with *2 tablespoons water*. Gradually add this to the boiling sauce until the desired thickness is obtained. If sauce becomes too thick, thin with a little water. Fish sauce thickens very nicely with the addition of *1-2 tablespoons shrimp butter* (page 158). The final step in sauce-making is to taste and add *sea salt* if necessary. Note: Gelatin does contain small amounts of MSG and should be avoided by those with extreme MSG sensitivities.

Gravies: Gravies are thickened with flour rather than by the reduction process. They are suitable for meats like roast chicken, turkey or leg of lamb, which drip plenty of fat into the pan while cooking. After removing the roasting meat and roasting rack, place pan on a burner. You should have at least *1/2 cup good fat drippings*—if not, add some butter, goose fat or lard. Add about *1/2 cup unbleached flour* to the fat and cook over medium high heat for several minutes, stirring constantly, until the flour turns light brown. Add *4 to 6 cups warm stock*, bring to a boil and blend well with the fat-flour mixture, using a wire whisk. Reduce heat and simmer 10 minutes or so. Check for seasonings and add *sea salt* and *pepper* if necessary. You may also add *herbs, cream, butter, whole coconut milk* or *creamed coconut* (see page 160).

SALAD DRESSINGS

In recent decades, misinformation and confusion about fats has led many dieticians and nutritionists to advise against salad dressings. Our salads should be dressed with plain lemon juice, they say, in order to avoid an excess of fats and oils in the diet. The problem is that a salad with nothing more than a squeeze of lemon juice is virtually inedible. As a result of this well-meaning advice, many health conscious individuals avoid salads, rather than enjoy them with relish.

It is certainly true that we should avoid all *bottled and commercial* salad dressings, which are invariably made with cheap, low-quality oils that have been stripped of their nutrients and rendered dangerously rancid by high-temperature or solvent extraction processes. Bottled dressings are further adulterated with many ingredients that should not pass between human lips, including stabilizers, preservatives, artificial flavors and colors, not to mention refined sweeteners. These expensive blends of empty calories are bad for everybody, young and old, and should not be allowed in our cupboards.

Almost all bottled salad dressings—particularly the lowfat varieties—contain neurotoxic MSG, hydrolyzed vegetable protein or similar substances. These flavor enhancers are not always listed on the label. Ingredients listed as "natural flavors" or "spices" may contain MSG!

But homemade salad dressings, made with extra virgin olive oil plus raw vinegar or lemon juice, are the best coat that any self-respecting salad can put on. Olive oil supplies vitamin E and a cornucopia of antioxidants, while both olive oil and raw vinegar provide a wide spectrum of enzymes, right at the start of your meal where they belong. Fresh herbs and garlic, anchovies, cultured cream, raw cheese, raw egg yolk and homemade mayonnaise added to dressings all have a contribution to make, both to enzyme and vitamin content and to exciting flavors that whet the appetite and encourage us to eat our salads down to the last bite.

Good dressings take very little time to make. Our basic salad dressing can be put together in less than half a minute and requires no more equipment than a fork and a small bowl. With a little practice you will learn to make it without measuring. Most of our other dressings are variations on the basic recipe. Salad dressings are one of the easiest things in the whole culinary repertoire to master, and they pay substantial dividends in health benefits for very little effort expended.

For all of our dressings we recommend extra virgin olive oil (see Sources) as a base, along with a small amount of unrefined flax seed oil. Olive oil provides oleic acid, a very stable monounsaturated fatty acid. Studies have repeatedly shown that olive oil provides numerous health benefits, including protection from heart disease. If the oil has been correctly processed, it will still contain its original content of antioxidants, which protect the oil's fatty acids from rancidity. According to Dr. Edward Howell, cold-pressed or expeller-expressed oils also contain lipases that can be activated in the stomach to facilitate the breakdown of triglycerides to free fatty acids. Use Italian olive oil for the best taste. Look for olive oil that is cloudy—a sign that it has not been filtered—and golden yellow in color—a sign that it has been pressed from ripe olives.

Along with olive oil, we recommend adding a small amount of unrefined flax seed oil, the best vegetable source of omega-3 fatty acids (linolenic acid). Flax oil is extremely susceptible to rancidity so be sure to buy unrefined flax seed oil in dark bottles that have been kept in cold storage. (For reputable suppliers of flax oil, see Sources.) Don't be tempted, however, to use or consume large amounts of flax oil as a surfeit of omega-3 fatty acids can cause imbalances on the cellular level, just as much as a surfeit of omega-6 fatty acids.

We strongly advise you to avoid the many polyunsaturated oils touted as health foods, such as soy, cottonseed, corn and safflower, even cold-pressed versions of these products. These oils are almost always rancid and most have a very high omega-6 component. Surfeit of omega-6 interferes with enzymes needed to produce important prostaglandins, and thus may contribute to impaired immune function and to a host of other diseases. Canola oil is high in omega-3, but research indicates that the oil contributes to vitamin E deficiency. Because it goes rancid easily, it must be deodorized to hide the telltale odor of rancidity; and during this process a particularly dangerous form of *trans* fat is formed.

Two of our dressings offer a particularly synergistic combination of omega-3 fatty acids and sulphur-containing proteins—our blue cheese dressing and the tahini dressing. Roquefort cheese made from sheep milk is a good source of protective lauric acid.

Americans and Europeans differ on the question of proportions of oil to vinegar in salad dressings. Americans tend to make their dressings in a proportion of three parts oil to one part vinegar; the French use five parts olive oil to one part vinegar, a combination that most Americans find too oily. We have taken the middle ground and give proportions of four parts oil to one part vinegar. You can adjust these proportions to suit your taste. Those who wish to avoid vinegar may substitute cultured whey (page 87), beet kvass (page 608) or fresh lemon juice in many of these recipes.

We have not listed salt and pepper in our dressing recipes. Sea salt and pepper or papaya pepper can be added according to your taste. Remember that mustard preparations tend to be rather salty. Most dressings prepared with mustard will not need additional salt. Culinary enthusiasts may wish to make their own mustard (page 104).

BASIC DRESSING
Makes about 3/4 cup

1 teaspoon Dijon-type mustard, smooth or grainy
2 tablespoons plus 1 teaspoon raw wine vinegar
1/2 cup extra virgin olive oil
1 tablespoon expeller-expressed flax oil

Dip a fork into the jar of mustard and transfer about 1 teaspoon to a small bowl. Add vinegar and mix around. Add olive oil in a thin stream, stirring all the while with the fork, until oil is well mixed or emulsified. Add flax oil and use immediately.

HERB DRESSING
Makes about 3/4 cup

3/4 cup basic dressing
1 teaspoon finely chopped fresh herbs, such as
  parsley, tarragon, thyme, basil or oregano

Prepare basic dressing and stir in herbs.

GARLIC DRESSING
Makes about 3/4 cup

3/4 cup basic dressing
1 clove garlic

Prepare basic dressing. Peel garlic clove and mash in a garlic press. Stir into dressing. Let sit a few minutes to allow amalgamation of garlic flavor.

Know Your Ingredients
Name This Product #3

Soybean oil, high fructose corn syrup, water, pickle relish, vinegar, tomato paste, salt, dehydrated egg yolk, algin derivative and xanthan gum (for consistency), mustard flour, natural flavors, dehydrated onion, spice, calcium disodium EDTA (to preserve freshness).

See Appendix B for Answer

The underlying cause of modern chronic disease can be summed up as the change in our environment and food supply due to the unwise application of technology to farming and food production, the abandonment of traditional foodways and above all the insidious penetration of processed and imitation foods into the food supply of western nations.

Oils stripped of precious nutrients and altered in structure, a penny's worth of grains puffed and flaked and sold for hundreds of pennies per box, fragile, life-giving milk subjected to high-temperature processing, sweet foods denuded of vitamins and minerals—this is the witch's brew that leads to physical and spiritual degeneration. SWF

And I heard a voice in the midst of the four beasts say, A measure of wheat for a penny, and three measures of barley for a penny; and see thou hurt not the oil and the wine.

Rev 6:6

The amounts of MSG and similar additives being added to foods increased throughout the postwar period. In fact, the amount of MSG alone added to foods has doubled in every decade since the 1940's. By 1972, 262,000 metric tons of MSG were produced.... Throughout this period, few suspected that these taste enhancing additives could be doing serious harm to individuals eating these foods.... Until this time, neuroscientists assumed that glutamate supplied the brain with energy. Based on this idea, scientists in one clinical study, fed large doses of MSG to retarded children to see if it would improve their IQ. The experiment failed. Then, in 1957, two ophthalmologists, Lucas and Newhouse, decided to test MSG on infant mice in an effort to study an eye disease known as hereditary retinal dystrophy. But, when they examined the eye tissues of the sacrificed animals, they made a startling discovery. The MSG had destroyed all of the nerve cells in the inner layers of the animal's retina, which are the visual receptor cells of the eye. Despite this frightening discovery, MSG continued to be added to food in enormous amounts and cookbooks continued to recommend it as a taste enhancing additive for recipes. But the worst was yet to be disclosed about this compound. Some ten years later John W. Olney, MD, a neuroscientist working at the Department of Psychiatry at Washington University in St. Louis, repeated Lucas and Newhouse's experiment in infant mice. His findings indicated that MSG was not only toxic to the retina but also to the brain. When he examined the animals' brains he discovered that specialized cells in a critical area of the animals' brains, the hypothalamus, were destroyed after a single dose of MSG. Russell L Blaylock, MD *Excitotoxins: The Taste That Kills*

BALSAMIC DRESSING
Makes about 3/4 cup

1 teaspoon Dijon-type mustard, smooth or grainy
2 tablespoons plus 1 teaspoon balsamic vinegar
1/2 cup extra virgin olive oil
1 tablespoon expeller-expressed flax oil

Balsamic vinegar is a red wine vinegar that has been aged in wooden casks. It has a delicious, pungent flavor that goes well with dark greens, such as watercress or lamb's lettuce.

Dip a fork into the jar of mustard and transfer about 1 teaspoon to a small bowl. Add vinegar and mix around. Add olive oil in a thin stream, stirring all the while with the fork, until oil is well mixed or emulsified. Add flax oil and use immediately.

SUN DRIED TOMATO DRESSING
Makes about 3/4 cup

3/4 cup basic dressing (page 129)
1 teaspoon sun dried tomato flakes (see Sources)
1 teaspoon chives or green onion, finely chopped

Prepare basic dressing. Add tomato flakes and let stand a few minutes to allow dried tomatoes to soften. Just before serving add chopped chives or green onion.

WALNUT DRESSING
Makes about 1/2 cup

2 tablespoons sherry vinegar
2 tablespoons unrefined walnut oil
6 tablespoons extra virgin olive oil

Like flax oil, walnut oil is rich in omega-3 fatty acids. Buy unrefined walnut oil in dark cans and store in the refrigerator.

Place all ingredients in a bowl and stir with a fork.

CREAMY DRESSING

Makes about 1 cup

3/4 cup basic or herb dressing (page 129)
1/4 cup piima cream or creme fraiche (page 84)

This is a traditional recipe of the Auvergne region in France. Prepare basic or herb dressing. Blend in cream with a fork.

ROASTED TOMATO DRESSING

Makes about 2 cups

1 pound firm plum tomatoes
1 cup extra virgin olive oil
1/4 cup balsamic vinegar
1/4 cup shallots or green onions, finely chopped
1 teaspoon raw honey
2 tablespoons fresh basil, finely chopped
    (or 2 teaspoons dried basil)
1 teaspoon fresh oregano, finely chopped
    (or 1/4 teaspoon dried oregano)
1 tablespoon parsley, finely chopped
2 tablespoons expeller-expressed flax oil

This is a delicious dressing for salads in winter! Wash and dry the tomatoes. Brush with olive oil and set in a shallow glass pan. Roast in a 400 degree oven about 30 minutes until skin begins to blister. Cool completely. Chop and set aside.

Whisk remaining ingredients except flax oil together in a bowl and season to taste with sea salt and pepper. Stir in tomatoes. Let dressing sit an hour or so to amalgamate flavors. Just before serving, stir in flax oil. Store leftover dressing in refrigerator.

A study has shown that boys born to mothers who experience post-partum depression later display behavioral problems in school. Inhibited emotional development, caused by Mom's post-pregnancy blues, is the accepted explanation. Much more likely is the fact that the same deficiencies that cause new mothers to be depressed also inhibit full development of the nervous system in their infants. The solution is proper prenatal nutrition, including plenty of foods rich in nutrients that feed the nervous system, such as eggs, shellfish, fish eggs, liver, cod liver oil, butter and cream. SWF

In numerous reviews written by upholders of the diet-heart idea it is often said that this idea is based on "strong scientific data," the evidence is "overwhelming" or "powerful" and "controversy is unjustified" . . . . nothing could be further from the truth. To use such vocabulary it has been necessary to exaggerate trivial, apparently supportive findings; to belittle or ignore the wealth of controversial and disproving evidence; and to quote unsupportive results as if they were supportive. . . .

Observations that are totally devastating for the diet-heart idea are mostly ignored. A good example is the fact that if we exclude individuals with the rare disease familial hypercholesterolemia (less than 0.5 percent of mankind suffer from it), there is no association between the level of blood cholesterol and the degree of vascular atherosclerosis. Uffe Ravnskov, MD, PhD *The Cholesterol Myths*

Unpasteurized milk and butter were used for thousands of years, with a history of conferring good health on their users. Since the time of Hippocrates, physicians used raw milk and raw butter as therapeutic agents to treat disease. Whole nations formerly depended upon dairy products as major sources of food. But when pasteurization was introduced, dairy products strangely and precipitously lost their health charms, almost as if somebody waved an evil wand and, presto, dairy products were instantly cursed. For example, in the days before milk and butter lost their lipase due to the heat of pasteurization, millions of people lived on dairy products without getting atherosclerosis (clogged arteries due to cholesterol deposits) because lipase knows how to handle cholesterol.

We have lost our ability to tame this killer. Lipase was also a valued guest in olive oil and other oils when they were thick and opaque but had to give up its residence when the factories made them clear. The commercial production of these oils coincides with the rise of cancer-related deaths in modern society. These strong indications of the value of lipase offer reasons why lipase should be given high priority in research to test its capacity to neutralize pathogenic effects. Edward Howell, MD *Enzyme Nutrition*

Publications almost beyond counting have studied the prognostic value of the "good" HDL-cholesterol. The reason is, of course, that it is hard to find any prognostic value. If HDL-cholesterol had a heart-protecting effect of real importance, it would not be necessary to use the tax payer's money to demonstrate the effect again and again in expensive studies. Uffe Ravnskov, MD, PhD *The Cholesterol Myths*

CREAMY MAYONNAISE DRESSING
Makes about 1 1/4 cups

3/4 cup basic dressing (page 129)
1/4 cup piima cream or creme fraiche (page 84)
1/4 cup mayonnaise (page 137)
1 tablespoon fresh herbs, finely chopped

Place all ingredients in a jar and shake vigorously, or blend in a bowl with a whisk.

CILANTRO LIME DRESSING
Makes about 3/4 cup

1/2 cup extra virgin olive oil
1 tablespoon expeller-expressed flax oil
3 tablespoons fresh lime juice
1 tablespoon cilantro, finely chopped
1/4 teaspoon dried oregano
dash cayenne pepper
pinch stevia powder

Place all ingredients in a bowl and stir vigorously with a fork.

MEXICAN DRESSING
Makes about 3/4 cup

1/2 cup extra virgin olive oil
1 tablespoon expeller-expressed flax oil
3 tablespoons raw wine vinegar
pinch stevia powder
1 clove garlic, peeled and mashed
1/2 teaspoon dried oregano
1/4 teaspoon chile powder

Place all ingredients in a bowl and stir vigorously with a fork.

BLUE CHEESE DRESSING

Makes about 1 cup

3/4 cup basic dressing (page 129)
2-4 tablespoons crumbled blue cheese

If possible, use genuine Roquefort cheese made from sheep milk, which is rich in lauric acid. Place all ingredients in a food processor and pulse a few times until blended; or mash cheese into dressing with a fork.

ANCHOVY DRESSING

Makes about 1 1/4 cups

1 can anchovies packed in olive oil
3/4 cup extra virgin olive oil
1 tablespoon expeller-expressed flax oil
1 clove garlic, peeled and mashed
1 teaspoon Dijon-type mustard
1/4 cup raw wine vinegar
1 tablespoon fresh lemon juice

Place all ingredients in food processor and blend until smooth.

CAESAR DRESSING

Makes about 3/4 cup

1/2 to 1 teaspoon Dijon-type mustard
1 tablespoon raw wine vinegar
1 tablespoon fresh lemon juice
1 tablespoon finely grated Parmesan cheese
1/2 cup extra virgin olive oil
1 tablespoon expeller-expressed flax oil
1 egg yolk
2 anchovy filets
1 clove garlic, peeled and mashed

Place all ingredients in food processor and blend until smooth.

"LDL has the strongest and most consistent relationship to individual and population risk of CHD, and LDL-cholesterol is centrally and causally important in the pathogenetic chain leading to atherosclerosis and CHD." These words you will find in a large review *Diet and Health*.

Reviews by distinguished scientific bodies are supposed to meet high standards. . . [but] the "large body of evidence" was cooked down to one single study, which showed a predictive value for LDL-cholesterol but for a few age groups only. LDL-cholesterol is neither centrally nor causally important, it has not the strongest and most consistent relationship to risk of CHD, it has not a direct relationship to the rate of CHD, and it has not been studied in more than a dozen randomized trials. . .

Thus, the experimenters claim support from unsupportive epidemiological and clinical studies, and the epidemiologists and the clinicians claim support from inconclusive experimental evidence. The victims of this miscarriage of justice are an innocent and useful molecular construction in our blood, producers and manufacturers of animal fat all over the world, and millions of healthy people who are frightened and badgered into eating a tedious and flavorless diet that is said to lower their bad cholesterol. Uffe Ravnskov, MD, PhD *The Cholesterol Myths*

Highly charged with energy and unstable and unpredictable as a madman who runs amuck in a crowd, molecules with an unpaired electron are called free radicals. . . . Longevity authorities claim that these enemies shorten our lives by attacking cell membranes, injuring cells, impairing their function, damaging and often reprogramming genetic material, opening the way for cancer. In a frenzied attempt to recover their missing electron, free radicals steal an electron from the next molecule, forcing it to become a free radical; and the process continues, causing a domino effect. Results differ in different parts of the body. In the skin, collagen is destroyed, causing wrinkling. There and in the body, fat becomes rancid and in time whole body organs or systems can be sabotaged. Synovial fluid (the natural lubrication in joints) thickens, making joint movement difficult and painful, a condition called arthritis.

More than 60 degenerative diseases common to aging can be caused by free radicals. The worst ones are atherosclerosis and the blocking of blood flow in arteries; Alzheimer's and Parkinson's disease, excessive loss of brain cells; cancer when genetic material is damaged and normal body materials are converted to carcinogens; cataracts caused by sunlight and oxidation; emphysema, inflammation and breaking down of lung tissue; heart disease, damage to heart muscle and stroke. James F. Scheer *Health Freedom News*

LEMON HONEY DRESSING
Makes about 3/4 cup

1/3 cup fresh lemon juice
1/3 cup extra virgin olive oil
1 teaspoon expeller-expressed flax oil
1 tablespoon or more raw honey

Mix lemon juice with olive oil and flax oil. Whisk in 1 tablespoon honey. Add more honey if more sweetness is desired.

LEMON PEPPER DRESSING
Makes about 3/4 cup

2 tablespoons fresh lemon juice
1 tablespoon raw wine vinegar
1/4 teaspoon sea salt
1/2 teaspoon cracked pepper
dash stevia powder
1 clove garlic, peeled and mashed
1/2 cup extra virgin olive oil
1 tablespoon expeller-expressed flax oil

Place all ingredients in a bowl and stir vigorously with a fork.

ORANGE DRESSING
Makes about 3/4 cup

3 tablespoons fresh orange juice
1/2 teaspoon finely grated orange rind
1 tablespoon raw wine vinegar
1/2 cup extra virgin olive oil
1 tablespoon expeller-expressed flax oil

It is best to use an organic orange, so there will be no pesticides on the rind. Wash the rind well before grating.

Place all ingredients in bowl and stir vigorously with a fork.

ORIENTAL DRESSING
Makes about 1 1/4 cup

4 tablespoons rice vinegar
2 tablespoons naturally fermented soy sauce
2 teaspoons freshly grated ginger
2 teaspoons toasted sesame oil
2 teaspoons green onions or chives, finely chopped
1 clove garlic, peeled and mashed (optional)
1 teaspoon raw honey
2/3 cup extra virgin olive oil
    or cold-pressed peanut oil
2 teaspoons expeller-expressed flax oil

Place all ingredients in a jar and shake vigorously.

TAHINI DRESSING
Makes about 2 cups

1 small onion, coarsely chopped
1 stalk celery, coarsely chopped
2 tablespoons naturally fermented soy sauce
juice of 2 lemons
1/2 cup tahini
4 tablespoons extra virgin olive oil
1 tablespoon expeller-expressed flax oil
1/8 to 1/4 cup water

Place celery and onion in food processor and pulse until finely chopped. Add remaining ingredients except water and process until well blended. Thin with water as necessary to achieve desired consistency.

Myth: Americans do not consume enough essential fatty acids.

Truth: Americans consume far too much of one kind of EFA (omega-6 EFA's found in most polyunsaturated vegetable oils) but not enough of another kind of EFA (omega-3 EFA's found in fish, fish oils, eggs from properly fed chickens, dark green vegetables and herbs, and oils from certain seeds such as flax and chia, nuts such as walnuts and in small amounts in all whole grains.) (*Am J Clin Nutr* 1991 54:438-63)

Know Your Ingredients
Name This Product #4

Water, corn syrup, cultured lowfat buttermilk, vinegar, garlic juice, cellulose gel, sugar, salt, skim milk, sour cream (dried), onion (dried), xanthan gum, malto-dextrin, monosodium glutamate with potassium sorbate and calcium disodium EDTA as preservatives, lactic acid, natural flavor, propylene glycol alginate, cultured skim milk (dried), artificial color, phosphoric acid, lemon juice concentrate, green onion (dried), spice, Dl-alpha-tocopherol acetate (vitamin E)

See Appendix B for Answer

SAUCES, MARINADES & CONDIMENTS

Our collection of sauces and condiments can be divided into two groups: those composed of raw ingredients and therefore valuable as sources of enzymes; and those that have been heated. The first category includes various types of mayonnaise and marinades. Store-bought versions of these condiments have invariably been pasteurized and the vital enzyme component destroyed. But when you make these accompaniments yourself, taking care to use only raw, high-enzyme ingredients, such as extra virgin olive oil, organic eggs, whey and cultured cream, your condiments will not only add taste to your meals but will also serve as rich sources of vital nutrients. Whey added to mayonnaise promotes lacto-fermentation, thus augmenting enzyme content and increasing shelf life of this useful condiment.

Our heated sauces for meats, fish and South-of-the-Border foods are made with homemade stocks so that, although the enzyme component may be lacking, the hydrophilic colloids of the gelatinous broth will contribute to digestibility, both of the sauce and the dish it accompanies.

Marinades that feature raw ingredients, particularly raw oils with their full complement of lipase, begin the digestive process of meats. Although the meats are usually cooked after several hours of steeping, their nutrients are nevertheless more available due to this predigestion; and, of course, they are more tender and flavorful as well.

Politically correct nutrition eschews sauces, thereby implying that food that is good for us must necessarily be dry and bland. We submit that the right use of sauces, containing either rich stock or enzymes from whole raw ingredients, not only makes our food more appetizing but also promotes easy digestion and assimilation.

We cannot stress too highly that commercially prepared sauces and condiments invariably contain neurotoxic additives to make them palatable—MSG, hydrolyzed vegetable protein and related substances—often deceptively labeled as "natural flavorings" or "spices."

MAYONNAISE
Makes 1 1/2 cups

1 whole egg, at room temperature
1 egg yolk, at room temperature
1 teaspoon Dijon-type mustard
1 1/2 tablespoons lemon juice
1 tablespoon whey (page 87), optional
3/4-1 cup extra virgin olive oil or
  expeller-expressed sunflower oil (see Sources)
  or a combination
generous pinch sea salt

Homemade mayonnaise imparts valuable enzymes, particularly lipase, to sandwiches, tuna salad, chicken salads and many other dishes and is very easy to make in a food processor. The addition of whey will help your mayonnaise last longer, adds enzymes and increases nutrient content. Use sunflower oil if you find that olive oil gives too strong a taste. Homemade mayonnaise will be slightly more liquid than store-bought versions.

In your food processor, place egg, egg yolk, mustard, salt and lemon juice and optional whey. Process until well blended, about 30 seconds. Using the attachment that allows you to add liquids drop by drop, add olive oil and/or sunflower oil with the motor running. Taste and check seasoning. You may want to add more salt and lemon juice. If you have added whey, let the mayonnaise sit at room temperature, well covered, for 7 hours before refrigerating. With whey added, mayonnaise will keep several months and will become firmer with time. Without whey, mayonnaise will keep for about 2 weeks.

By adding extra bacteria to Waldorf-like salad and letting it ferment, its shelf life is extended to five weeks. Untreated, such salads are soon contaminated by microorganisms and spoil. . . . The new process, devised at the University of Wageningen, uses a naturally occurring *lactobacillus* isolated from the water in which soy curd has been soaked. Often used to make yoghurt and salami, these bacteria grow well at 40-50 degrees C, producing lactic acid at the same time. Most organisms that spoil salads fail to grow at such high temperatures.

The bacteria are mixed into the salad dressing, inoculated for seven hours at 45 degrees C, and then refrigerated. The lactic acid produced by the bacteria during incubation prevent the growth of other bacteria at low temperatures. Fermentation delays the oxidation of unsaturated oils, which form the basis of the dressing, because the added bacteria consume all the oxygen. Fermentation also produces a pleasant, mildly sour taste many consumers prefer. *New Scientist*

Animal tissue fat, cream and olives have been found by a number of investigators to contain sizable quantities of lipase if examined before the materials were subjected to heat treatment. On the other hand it has been reported that in human obesity the lipase content of the fat is decreased. Dell'Acqua found the lipase content of adipose tissue from cases of human obesity and from lipomas was less than normal. Edward Howell, MD *Food Enzymes for Health and Longevity*

Know Your Ingredients
Name This Product #5

Water, soybean oil, sugar, vinegar, food starch-modified, salt, cellulose gel (microcrystaline cellulose), mustard flour, egg white, artificial color, sodium caseinate, xanthan gum, cellulose gum, spice, paprika, natural flavor, betacarotene (color)

See Appendix B for Answer

Keeping up a high enzyme potential is the one way the body has to deal with tobacco smoke, short wave radiation, toxic chemicals and the prevention and cure of disease. There is no other mechanism in the body except enzyme action to protect the body from any hazard. It is ambiguous to say that nature cures, when we must know that the only machinery in the body to do anything is enzyme action. Hormones do not work. Vitamins cannot do any work. Minerals were not made to do any work. Proteins cannot work. Nature does not work. Only enzymes are made for work. So it is enzymes that cure. Therefore, the ability of the body to make any of the numerous enzymes needed for good health and long life must be kept at a high level by the methods incorporated in The Food Enzyme Concept. Edward Howell, MD *Food Enzymes for Health and Longevity*

HERBED MAYONNAISE
Makes 1 1/2 cup

1 1/2 cup mayonnaise (page 137)
1/2 cup fresh herbs, finely minced

We suggest dill as the best addition to mayonnaise, but you may also add basil, tarragon or parsley. Chop or snip herbs finely and stir thoroughly into mayonnaise.

SPICED MAYONNAISE
Makes 2 cups

1 small onion, coarsely chopped
2 tablespoons extra virgin olive oil
1 tablespoon curry powder
1/4 teaspoon ground cloves
1 teaspoon freshly grated ginger
2 tablespoons tomato paste
1 cup chicken stock (page 124)
1 teaspoon raw honey
1/2 teaspoon sea salt
1 cup mayonnaise (page 137)
1/2 cup piima cream or creme fraiche (page 84)

This elegant sauce is used for curried chicken platter (page 415).

Sauté onion in olive oil. Add spices and cook gently. Add tomato paste and chicken stock. Blend well. Bring to a boil and allow the liquid to reduce to about 1/2 cup. Strain into a bowl. Let cool and whisk in honey until well blended. Blend in salt, mayonnaise and cultured cream. The final sauce should be the consistency of thick cream.

CREOLE MAYONNAISE

Makes 1 1/2 cups

2 egg yolks, at room temperature
2 tablespoon fresh lemon juice
2 tablespoons whey (page 87), optional
1 teaspoon Dijon-type mustard
1 clove garlic, peeled and crushed
1/2 teaspoon sea salt
1/2 teaspoon dried thyme
1/2 teaspoon dried basil
1/2 teaspoon dried oregano
1/4 teaspoon paprika
1/4 teaspoon tabasco sauce
1/8 teaspoon cayenne pepper
2/3 cup extra virgin olive oil,
     or 2/3 cup expeller-expressed sunflower oil
     (see Sources) or a mixture

Place all ingredients except olive oil and/or sunflower oil into food processor and blend thoroughly. Using the attachment that allows you to add liquids drop by drop, add olive oil and/or sunflower oil with the motor running. Check for seasonings. You may want to add more salt or lemon juice. If you have added whey, let the mayonnaise sit at room temperature, well covered, for 7 hours before refrigerating. With whey added, the mayonnaise will keep at least 5 weeks, refrigerated; without, for about 2 weeks.

CURRIED MAYONNAISE

Makes 2 cups

1 cup mayonnaise (page 137)
1/2 cup piima cream or creme fraiche (page 84)
3 tablespoons extra virgin olive oil
3 tablespoons raw vinegar
3 tablespoons curry powder

Blend all ingredients with a whisk. Use in curried chicken salad (page 414).

The available evidence does not justify a placid continuance of a nihilistic attitude toward the vital forces operating in the living organism. It is a motif of science to reduce complex phenomena to simple integral units. Enzymes emerge as the true yardstick of vitality. Enzymes offer the only means of calculating the vital energy of an organism. That which has been referred to as "vitality," "vital force," "vital energy," "vital activity," "nerve energy," "vital resistance," "life energy," "life" and "life force" may be and probably is synonymous with that which has been known as "enzyme activity," "enzyme value," "enzyme energy," "enzyme vitality" and "enzyme content." The available evidence does not permit further procrastination but requires that what is known, vaguely and incomprehensibly, as life force or activity be defined in terms of concrete and measurable enzyme units. Edward Howell, MD *Food Enzymes for Health and Longevity*

Many years ago, one of my good friends described his memories of a banquet given to welcome him and his fellow captives after their release from a Japanese prisoner-of-war camp. The buffet was laden with roasts, vegetables, assorted breads, pies, salads, enticing desserts and fresh fruits, the likes of which they had not seen for several years. What did these men grab first? The butters, margarines, salad oils and creams. They were after fats. They consumed nothing else until the bare fats were gone. With such primordial craving for the substance, does it not make sense to honor our bodies with the purest our purse will allow? Valerie MacBean *Coconut Cookery*

Back in 1967 or so. . .a food technologist told me how he thought the term "plastic food" must have originated. Some biochemist, he speculated, must have observed that when looked at through a microscope, a hydrogenated fat molecule looks very much like a plastic molecule. . . ."Lipid chemists," he explained, "actually talk about plasticizing oils". . . .I decided to discontinue selling margarine—as well as products containing vegetable shortening, margarine's cousin—and to perform a little experiment.

It was quite nontechnical. . . . I put a cube of margarine, the kind I had been selling, on a saucer and placed the saucer on the window sill in the back room of my store. I reasoned that if I made it readily available and if it was real food, insects and microorganisms would invite themselves to the feast. Flies and ants and mold would be all over it just as if it were butter . . . . That cube of margarine became infamous. I left it sitting on the window sill for about two years. Nobody ever saw an insect of any description go near it. Not one speck of mold ever grew on it. All that ever happened was that it kind of half-puddled down from the heat of the sun beating through the windowpane, and it got dusty— very dusty, a cube of margarine doesn't clean up very well. Finally, it got to looking so revolting that I decided to terminate the experiment. For me, the experiment had not been foreshortened; I had reached the conclusion long ago that margarine basically is not food, whether or not it's like plastic. Fred Rohe *PPNF Health Journal*

GREEN GELATIN MAYONNAISE
Makes 1 1/4 cups

1 bunch parsley, stems removed
1 whole egg, at room temperature
1 egg yolk, at room temperature
1 teaspoon Dijon-type mustard
1 1/2 tablespoons lemon juice
1 cup extra virgin olive oil or
    1 cup expeller-expressed sunflower oil
    (see Sources) or a mixture
generous pinch sea salt
2 tablespoons gelatin (see Sources)
1/2 cup water

Place parsley in a large strainer and dip into boiling water. Drain and squeeze dry. Place parsley in food processor and pulse a few times. Add egg, egg yolk, mustard, salt and lemon juice. Process until well blended, about 30 seconds. Using the attachment that allows you to add liquids drop by drop, add the olive oil and/or sunflower oil with the motor running. Melt gelatin in water over lowest heat and stir into mayonnaise. Use for glazing poached salmon (page 269).

SOUR CREAM SAUCE
Makes 1 1/2 cup

1 cup piima cream or creme fraiche (page 84)
2 egg yolks
1/4 cup extra virgin olive oil
1/4 cup raw vinegar
1-2 tablespoons Dijon-type mustard
1/2 teaspoon sea salt
1/4 teaspoon pepper
pinch of stevia powder

This is an excellent substitute for mayonnaise—it is higher in fat-soluble vitamins and is quicker and easier to make. Mix all ingredients together with a wire whisk.

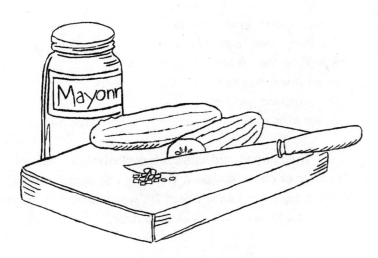

When Adelle Davis, the famous nutrition writer, appeared on the Johnny Carson show, she was asked to give a "rule of thumb" for healthy eating. She said, "If it is advertised in the media, don't buy it." An excellent rule indeed. Unfortunately the TV station blipped her out. Viewers never heard the comment.

When money goes into advertising, cuts must be made elsewhere so the cheapest ingredients are used—hydrogenated vegetable oils, high fructose corn syrup, white flour and additives that mimic the taste of properly prepared whole food. SWF

TARTAR SAUCE

Makes 1 1/2 cups

1 cup mayonnaise (page 137)
1/2 cup minced pickled cucumber (page 97)
2 tablespoons minced green onion
2 tablespoons finely chopped parsley
2 tablespoons small capers, rinsed in a strainer
     and dried with paper towels
1 tablespoon lemon juice
1/4 teaspoon sea salt
1/4 teaspoon pepper
pinch of cayenne pepper

This is wonderful with fish—and so much better than store-bought varieties. Blend all ingredients well. Check seasonings. Store in refrigerator, but serve at room temperature.

Know Your Ingredients
Name This Product #6

Enriched long grain rice, enriched vermicelli, dehydrated cream cheese, (sweet cream, dehydrated nonfat milk, cheese culture), dehydrated nonfat milk, salt, monosodium glutamate (natural flavor enhancer), dehydrated asparagus, dextrose, natural flavors, onion powder, partially hydrogenated soybean oil, dehydrated egg, dehydrated butter, dehydrated parsley, garlic powder, turmeric and paprika extractives (for color), sodium caseinate.

See Appendix B for Answer

What if someone were to tell you that a chemical added to food could cause brain damage in your children, and that this chemical could effect how your children's nervous systems formed during development so that in later years they may have learning or emotional difficulties? What if there was scientific evidence that these chemicals could damage a critical part of the brain known to control hormones so that later in life your child might have endocrine problems? How would you feel?

Suppose evidence was presented to you strongly suggesting that the artificial sweetener in your diet soft drink may cause brain tumors to develop, and the number of brain tumors reported since the widespread introduction of this artificial sweetener has risen dramatically? Would that affect your decision to drink these products and especially to allow your children to drink them? What if you could be shown overwhelming evidence that one of the main ingredients in this sweetener (aspartame) could cause the same brain lesions as MSG? Would that affect your buying decisions?

And finally, what if it could be demonstrated that all of these types of chemicals (called excitotoxins) could possibly aggravate or even precipitate many of the neurodegenerative brain diseases, such as Parkinson's disease, Huntington's disease, ALS and Alzheimer's disease? Would you be concerned if you knew that these excitotoxin food additives are a particular risk if you have ever had a stroke, brain injury, brain tumor, seizure or have suffered from hypertension, diabetes, meningitis or viral encephalitis?

I would think that all of us would be more than just concerned to learn that well-known powerful brain toxins were being added to our food and

CREAMY DILL SAUCE
Makes 1 1/2 cups

1 egg
1 tablespoon grated onion
4 tablespoons lemon juice
4 tablespoons finely chopped dill
1 teaspoon sea salt
1/4 teaspoon pepper
1 cup piima cream or creme fraiche (page 84)

This is wonderful with cold poached salmon, salmon mousse or cold roast beef. Beat egg and combine with remaining ingredients. Check for seasonings. You may want to add more salt and lemon juice.

HORSERADISH SAUCE
Makes 1/2 cup

1/4 cup fresh horseradish
1/4 cup piima cream or creme fraiche (page 84)

Mix together with a fork. Serve with roast beef.

SHRIMP COCKTAIL SAUCE
Makes 1 cup

1/4 cup fresh horseradish
3/4 cup ketchup (page 104)

Mix together with a fork.

EGG MUSTARD SAUCE

Makes 1 cup

1/2 cup mayonnaise (page 137)
2-3 egg yolks
1 tablespoon Dijon-type mustard
2 tablespoons snipped dill
sea salt and pepper

Blend mayonnaise, egg yolks, mustard and dill together and season to taste. Excellent with salmon or raw beef, Italian style (page 234).

YOGHURT SAUCE

Makes 2 cups

1 1/2 cups plain, whole yoghurt
1/4 cup lemon juice
1/4 cup water
3 cloves garlic, peeled and mashed
sea salt

Blend yoghurt, lemon juice, water and garlic together and season to taste.

ANCHOVY PASTE

(Anchoiade)
Makes 1/2 cup

2 cloves garlic
4 ounces canned anchovies with olive oil
1 tablespoon extra virgin olive oil
1/2 teaspoon raw vinegar

Place all ingredients in food processor and pulse to achieve a coarse paste. This is excellent spread on round croutons (page 520) or with Variety Salad for Grown-Ups (page 186).

drink to boost sales. We would be especially upset to learn that these additives have no other purpose than to enhance the taste of food and the sweetness of various diet products.

You would also be upset to learn that many of these brain lesions in your children are irreversible and can follow a single exposure of a sufficient concentration. And I would bet that you would be incredulous to learn that the food industry disguises many of these "excitotoxin additives" so that they will not be recognized. In fact, many foods that are labeled "No MSG" not only contain MSG but also contain other excitotoxins of equal potency. Russell L. Blaylock, MD *Excitotoxins: The Taste That Kills*

Know Your Ingredients
Name This Product #7

Natural flavoring, modified corn starch, wheat flour, salt, maltodextrin, sweet cream, green peppercorns, monosodium glutamate (flavor enhancer), mustard flour, caramel color, onion, xanthan gum, sugar, spices, disodium inosinate and disodium guanylate (flavor enhancers), garlic, cream of tartar, lecithin (to prevent separation), and sulfating agents.

See Appendix B for Answer

Many cultures have valued basil as a sacred plant. In India, a species of basil called *tulasi* is an object of veneration, cultivated in temples and garden shrines. *Tulasi* is said to kill mosquitoes and demons, to cure disease and cleanse the air. In ancient Greece and Persia, sweet basil was associated with mourning and planted on graves. In ancient Rome, basil was associated with fertility, love and sexual stimulation. In China, basil traditionally provided a base for perfume and was planted in gardens to mask the bad odor of fertilizer.

Today the delicious taste and aroma of basil is the signature of Mediterranean cooking. The French call it *l'herbe royale* (the royal plant) for good reason. Tests have shown that the smell of basil has a salutary effect on people's outlook and disposition. It is valued for its ability to relieve intestinal gas and inhibit dysentery. The leaves may be brewed into a tea for these complaints. A relative of mint, basil is easy to grow. It goes beautifully with tomato, fish and meat dishes. SWF

Cilantro is a hardy annual herb (*Coriandrum sativum*) that produces two products—one is the coriander seed, a spice valued in both cooking and medicine; the other is the leaves, known in America by the plant's Spanish name, Cilantro.

Sometimes called Chinese parsley, cilantro actually reached China rather late in history, after a long period of use in Persia and the Mediterranean area. Coriander is mentioned in a 16th-century BC Egyptian medical treatise, and coriander remains have been identified in the tomb of Tutankhamen. The plant is compared to manna in the book of Exodus and Numbers and is also frequently referred to in the Talmud. It was exten-

WATERCRESS SAUCE
Makes 1 1/2 cups

1 bunch watercress, stems removed
1 egg yolk
2 tablespoons lemon juice
1/2 cup extra virgin olive oil
1/2 cup piima cream or creme fraiche (page 84)
sea salt

Place watercress in food processor and pulse until chopped. Add egg yolk and lemon juice and pulse until well blended. Using the attachment that allows you to add liquids drop by drop, add olive oil with motor running. Stir in cultured cream and season to taste.

Variation: Cilantro Sauce

Use *1 large bunch cilantro, stems removed,* instead of watercress.

PESTO
Makes 1 cup

2 cups packed fresh basil leaves,
*   washed and dried*
2-4 cloves garlic, peeled
1/2 teaspoon sea salt
1/4 cup crispy pine nuts (page 514)
1/4 cup good quality grated Parmesan cheese
1/4-1/2 cup extra virgin olive oil

Pesto is normally mixed with pasta, but it is delicious as an accompaniment to fish and meat, or even spread on corn on the cob!

Place basil leaves in food processor. Pulse until well chopped. Add garlic, salt, pine nuts and cheese and blend well. Using attachment for adding liquids drop by drop, and with motor running, add olive oil to form a thick paste. Pesto will keep several days, well sealed, in refrigerator; or it may be frozen.

Variation: Cilantro Pesto

Use *2 cups fresh cilantro leaves* instead of basil.

PESTO SAUCE

Makes 1 1/2 to 2 cups

1 cup pesto (page 144)
1/2 to 1 cup fish, chicken or beef stock
(pages 119-124)

Use fish stock if you are serving this sauce with fish, chicken stock with chicken and beef stock with red meat.

Bring stock to a boil and pour in a thin stream into pesto, whisking constantly, until desired thickness is attained. Keep warm in a glass or ceramic container set in a pan of hot water over a very low flame.

CILANTRO MARINADE

Makes 1/2 cup

1 bunch cilantro, chopped
juice of one lemon
3 garlic cloves, mashed
1/2 cup extra virgin olive oil
1/4 teaspoon pepper

Mix all ingredients together. This is delicious as a marinade for swordfish and eggplant.

sively cultivated in Persia—where it is still used today in many dishes—whence it spread to India and finally to China, where it is used liberally in fish and fowl preparations, as well as in soups. Chinese treatises include cilantro among the five "vegetables of strong odor" that are forbidden to monks. Some people do find that cilantro has a soapy taste but, in general, cilantro is widely accepted and liberally used in a variety of refreshing dishes, especially as it is now readily available in U.S. markets.

Cilantro leaves are rich in calcium, iron, carotenes and vitamin C. It is the seed that is most often mentioned in ancient medical treatises, but recently the leaves have become a source of great interest to holistic practitioners. A Japanese investigator, Yoshiaki Omura, has made the revolutionary discovery that cilantro can mobilize mercury and other toxic metals from the central nervous system if large enough amounts are consumed daily. This makes it very useful to individuals who are attempting to detoxify after the removal of mercury fillings, as detoxification of more peripheral tissues is a relatively straight forward matter; but mercury in the central nervous systems is recalcitrant and can remained lodged there permanently. Cilantro is the first known substance that stimulates the body to remove mercury and other toxic metals from the central nervous system and excrete them via the stool or urine. Dried cilantro does not work, which implies that the active principle is an aromatic substance (that soapy taste?) in the fat-soluble portion of the leaves. The heavy metal detox capabilities of cilantro should also make it of great use in the treatment of depression, Alzheimer's disease, lack of concentration and related disorders. SWF

Once upon a time there was a scientific debate. The debate was between the ideas put forth by Louis Pasteur and the ideas outlined by Antoine Bechamp. The scientific community adopted the ideas of Pasteur and completely rejected the ideas of Bechamp. Because of that rejection, and the growth of dogma attached to the theories of Pasteur, our modern medical science may be digging a deep hole for all of us in our desires to overcome disease.

Medical and biological education today is based upon Pasteur's "germ theory of disease." Pasteur, who had immense political clout with Emperor Napoleon at the time, put forth the theory that germs, or microbial life, may be divided into "invariable" species and families. He proclaimed that each species caused a specific disease. Later, Dr. Robert Koch put forth his famous "postulates" of microbial infections which solidified Pasteur's point of view. Thus, any germ shown to cause a disease is called a pathogen.

At the time of Pasteur, the greatest acknowledged biological scientist in France was Professor Bechamp, a physiologist who had no political clout despite enormous scientific prestige and credentials. Historians have shown that Pasteur plagiarized Bechamp in one important discovery about fermentation. Bechamp's discovery about the nature of microbial life was exactly the opposite of what Pasteur proclaimed and science adopted. Briefly, Bechamp discovered a "symbiotic" relationship between microbes and larger animals. He also declared that all animal and plant cells contain extremely small granules, which are not destroyed even when the organism or cell dies. He called them microzymas and demonstrated that these tiny specks could change form and could result in changing the forms and the activity of other microbes.

RED PEPPER SAUCE
Makes 4 cups

9 large red bell peppers, seeded and quartered
3 cloves garlic, peeled and coarsely chopped
2 tablespoons extra virgin olive oil
3 tablespoons balsamic vinegar
1/3 cup sun dried tomatoes packed in olive oil
sea salt and pepper

Place pepper quarters in an oiled pyrex dish, skin side up. Place in an oven set at 400 degrees. When peppers begin to soften, turn and bake until skin loosens. Transfer to a plate and cover with a plastic bag for 10 minutes before removing skin.

Place skinned pepper pieces in food processor and process until smooth. Add remaining ingredients and process until smooth. Season to taste.

Variation: Creamy Red Pepper Sauce
Stir in *1/2 cup piima cream* or *creme fraiche (page 84).*

Variation: Thin Red Pepper Sauce
Stir in *1/2 to 1 cup warm fish, chicken or beef stock (pages 119-124)* until desired consistency is obtained.

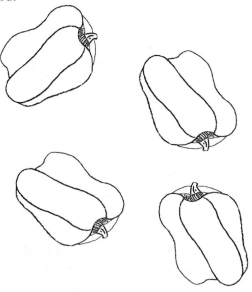

PEANUT SAUCE

Makes 2 cups

6 garlic cloves, peeled and coarsely chopped
2 inches fresh ginger, peeled and chopped
1 large bunch cilantro, chopped
1 tablespoon extra virgin olive oil
1 teaspoon Oriental hot chile oil
3/4 cup freshly ground roasted peanuts or
    homemade peanut butter (page 516)
3/8 cup naturally fermented soy sauce
3 tablespoons rice vinegar
1/2-1 cup warm chicken stock (page 124)
    or whole coconut milk (page 160)

Place garlic, ginger and cilantro in a food processor and pulse until finely chopped. Add all remaining ingredients except stock or coconut milk, pulse until well blended and transfer to a bowl. Gradually blend warm stock or coconut milk into peanut mixture, whisking thoroughly. Keep warm by setting bowl in a pan of hot water over a very low flame.

TERIYAKI SAUCE

Makes 3/4 cup

1 tablespoon freshly grated ginger
3 garlic cloves, mashed
1 tablespoon toasted sesame oil
1 tablespoon rice vinegar
1 tablespoon raw honey
1/2 cup naturally fermented soy sauce

Mix all ingredients together with a whisk.

BARBECUE SAUCE

Makes 1 1/2 cups

3/4 cup teriyaki sauce
3/4 cup naturally sweetened ketchup (page 104)
1/4 cup fermented fish sauce (page 157), optional

Mix all ingredients together with a whisk.

Bechamp declared that Pasteur was wrong, that the nature of germs was not like higher animals. Microbial life is not firmly set into invariable species. Rather, microbial life is "pleomorphic"—capable of changing form and nature.

Despite his elegant presentations, the orthodoxy dominating scientific education ignored Bechamp and moved excitedly into what became the era of the pathogen hunters and "wonder drugs" that killed the pathogens. In its ignorance of the forgotten Bechamp, medical science did not realize that the poisons they called drugs were opposed to nature's "symbiosis" and were perhaps encouraging pleomorphism to generate new and deadlier varieties of infections each generation. Tom Valentine *Search for Health*

The real value of the soybean is that it can be made into soy sauce, the salty elixir that gives Oriental food its unique character. Traditional soy sauce is made by a fermentation process that takes six to eight months to complete. This long and careful procedure creates a mix of phenolic compounds, including a natural form of glutamic acid, that contributes to the unique taste and aroma of traditionally brewed soy sauce. The modern bioreactor method produces a product by rapid hydrolysis, rather than by complete fermentation, in the space of two days and uses the enzyme glutamase as a reactor, so that the final product contains large amounts of the kind of unnatural glutamic acid that is found in MSG. Always buy the more expensive varieties of soy sauce that say "Naturally Brewed" on the label. Tamari, a variety of soy sauce made without wheat, can be used by those with wheat allergies. SWF

At Baylor University, heart surgeon Michael DeBakey conducted a survey of 1,700 patients with such severe atherosclerosis that they had to be hospitalized, and only 20 percent—one out of five—had what is termed high blood serum cholesterol values. What does this indicate? That other factors than elevated cholesterol cause atherosclerosis.

Nicholas Sampsidis sums up the story neatly in *Homogenized*: "Heart disease doesn't start until something first induces cholesterol to come out of its liquid state and to solidify in the artery walls . Cholesterol has been implicated as the guilty party because of its presence at the scene of the crime. Cholesterol is very much like the school boy in a group caught throwing the last snowball after a window is broken. Although the whole group was involved in the crime, only the boy seen throwing the last snowball is blamed. . . cholesterol shares only a remote responsibility for heart disease. . . ." James F. Scheer *Health Freedom News*

Tahini is the paste of ground sesame seeds. Sesame seeds contain a high content of methionine and tryptophan, two amino acids usually lacking in vegetable foods. Sesame oil contains about 41% stable oleic acid and an equal amount of omega-6 linoleic acid, with only trace amounts of omega-3. A small amount of flax seed oil added to tahini will correct this imbalance, and the combination of omega-3 fatty acids in flax oil with sulphur-containing methionine is a synergistic one. The high vitamin E and antioxidant content of sesame seed oil makes it resistant to rancidity. Buy tahini made from hulled seeds as the hulls contain oxalic acid, phytates and enzyme inhibitors—all antinutrients. SWF

ITALIAN ANCHOVY SAUCE
(Bagnat Sauce)
Makes 2 cups

1 bunch Italian flat leaf parsley, coarsely chopped
4 cloves garlic, peeled and finely minced
1 small can anchovy filets, drained and minced
3/4 cup oil-packed, sun dried tomatoes, diced
1 cup extra virgin olive oil
3 tablespoons balsamic vinegar

This is an Italian sauce served with grilled chicken, duck, fish and meat. Don't let the anchovies deter you as their inclusion is essential to the character of this sauce. Do not use the food processor for this recipe. You will get a better texture by mincing all ingredients by hand.

Mix all ingredients except vinegar. The sauce may be kept refrigerated several days. Stir in vinegar just before serving.

TAHINI SAUCE
Makes 2 cups

2 cloves garlic, peeled and coarsely chopped
1 teaspoon sea salt
1/2 cup tahini
1 cup water
1/2 cup fresh lemon juice

This wonderful sauce is delicious with falafel (page 506) or mazalika (page 314). Place garlic in food processor with salt. Blend until minced. Add tahini and blend. Using the attachment that allows you to add liquids drop by drop, add water with the motor running. When completely blended, add lemon juice all at once and blend until smooth. The sauce should be the consistency of heavy cream. If it is too thick, add more water and lemon juice.

CURRY SAUCE

Makes 2 cups

2 tablespoons butter
2 tablespoons extra virgin olive oil
1 cup onion, finely chopped
1 cup yellow pepper, finely chopped
1 tablespoon red or green hot chile pepper, minced
3-4 tablespoons curry powder or curry paste
1 cup fish, chicken or beef stock (pages 119-124)
1 1/2 cups coconut milk or
    7 ounces creamed coconut (See page 160)
1/4 cup fresh lime juice
pinch of sea salt
1/4 teaspoon pepper

Use fish stock if your sauce is for fish, chicken stock for chicken, beef stock for red meat.

Sauté vegetables in butter and oil until tender. Add curry powder or paste and blend in. Add stock, bring to a boil and whisk smooth. Add coconut milk. Let mixture boil gently until reduced to about half. Remove from heat, stir in lime juice and season to taste.

Strain sauce and serve with steamed fish, or with chicken or beef left from making stock.

Demographic indications are that countries whose populace consumes large amounts of coconut have very low incidences of coronary diseases. In one study of two groups of Polynesians, those consuming coconut oil as 89% of their fat intake had lower blood pressure than those whose coconut oil intake was only 7% of fat intake. In Sri Lanka, a major coconut producing and consuming nation (in some areas each adult consumes as much as one coconut per day), the 1978 rate of heart disease was 1 per 100,000 contrasted with a rate of 18 to 187 in countries with no coconut oil consumption. Valerie MacBean *Coconut Cookery*

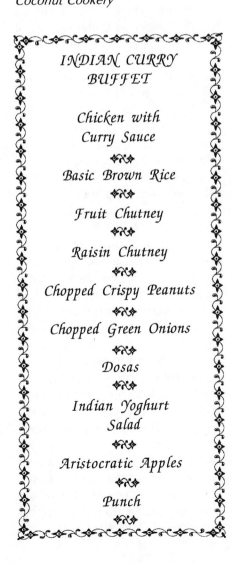

INDIAN CURRY BUFFET

Chicken with Curry Sauce

Basic Brown Rice

Fruit Chutney

Raisin Chutney

Chopped Crispy Peanuts

Chopped Green Onions

Dosas

Indian Yoghurt Salad

Aristocratic Apples

Punch

Speaking of manufacturers reminds me of a talk upon a steamboat which I overheard. . . . It soon transpired that they were drummers—one belonging in Cincinnati, the other in New Orleans. Brisk men, energetic of movement and speech; the dollar their god, how to get it their religion.

"Now as to this article," said Cincinnati, slashing into the ostensible butter and holding forward a slab of it on his knife blade, "it's from our house, look at it—smell of it. . . . Butter, ain't it? Not by a thundering sight—it's oleomargarine. Yes sir, that's what it is—oleomargarine. You can't tell it from butter; by George, an *expert* can't. It's from our house. We supply most of the boats in the West. There's hardly a pound of butter on one of them. We are crawling right along—*jumping* right along is the word. We are going to have that entire trade. Yes, and the hotel trade, too. You are going to see the day, pretty soon, when you won't find an ounce of butter to bless yourself with, in any hotel in the Mississippi and Ohio Valleys, outside of the biggest cities. Why, we are turning out oleomargarine now by the thousands of tons. And we can sell it so dirt cheap that the whole country has got to take it—can't get around it you see. Butter don't stand any show—there ain't any chance for competition. Butter's had its day—and from this out, butter goes to the wall. There's more money in oleomargarine than—why, you can't imagine the business we do. I've stopped in every town, from Cincinnati to Natchez, and I've sent home big orders from every one of them."

. . . . Then New Orleans piped up and said: "Yes, it's a first-rate imitation, that's a certainty; but it ain't the only one around that's first rate. For instance, they make olive oil out of cottonseed oil, nowadays, so that you can't tell them apart."

MARY'S MARVELOUS MIXTURE
Makes 1 cup

1/3 cup coconut oil (see Sources), gently melted
1/3 cup expeller-expressed sesame oil
1/3 cup extra virgin olive oil

Mix ingredients together and store in an airtight glass jar at room temperature. This serves well for light sautéing and can be used as a substitute for butter when preparing kosher meals.

BUTTER SPREAD
Makes 3/4 cup

1/2 cup butter, softened
2 tablespoons expeller-expressed flax oil
2 tablespoons extra virgin olive oil

This is softer than butter and will spread more easily. In a food processor mix softened butter, flax oil and olive oil by pulsing. Place in a small bowl or crock, cover and refrigerate.

CLARIFIED BUTTER
Makes 3/4 cup

1 cup (1/2 pound) butter

Those who are unable to tolerate milk protein in even the smallest amounts will want to clarify their butter, which is the process of removing the small amount of milk protein or casein contained in butter fat. Place butter in a small bowl in an oven set at 200 degrees for 1/2 hour. The butter will melt and foam will rise to the top and form a crust, which should be carefully skimmed off. To remove every trace of milk solids, pour through a strainer lined with cheese cloth. Store in a tightly covered jar in the refrigerator. Use clarified butter for cooking and eating.

LEMON BUTTER SAUCE

Makes 3/4 cup

about 1/2 cup clarified butter, melted (page 150)
juice of 1 lemon, strained

Mix butter and lemon juice. This is excellent with artichokes.

HERB BUTTER

Makes 1 cup

1/8 cup parsley sprigs
1 tablespoon fresh tarragon leaves
1 teaspoon thyme leaves
1 cup (1/2 pound) butter, softened

Place herbs in a strainer and plunge into boiling water for a few seconds. Rinse under cold water and pat or squeeze very dry. Place in food processor and pulse several times. Add butter and pulse until well blended. Chill in a crock or in individual molds.

RED PEPPER BUTTER

Makes 3/4 cup

1/2 red pepper, cut into two pieces
1/2 butter, softened

Place pepper pieces skin side up on an oiled pyrex pan and bake at 400 degrees until skin begins to buckle. Cover pepper pieces with plastic bag for about 10 minutes to loosen skin. Remove skin and place pepper pieces in food processor and blend until smooth. Add butter blend well. Serve with meat or fish.

"Yes, that's so," responded Cincinnati, "and it was a tiptop business for a while. They sent it over and brought it back from France and Italy, with the United States customhouse mark on it to endorse it for genuine and there was no end of cash in it; but France and Italy broke up the game— of course, they naturally would. Cracked on such a rattling import that cottonseed olive oil couldn't stand the rise; had to hang up and quit."

"Oh, it *did*, did it? You wait here a minute." Goes to his stateroom, brings back a couple of long bottles, and takes out the corks—says: "There now, smell them, taste them, examine the bottles, inspect the labels, one of 'm's from Europe, the other's never been out of this country. One's European olive oil, the other's American cottonseed olive oil. Tell 'm apart? 'Course you can't. Nobody can. . . . We turn out the whole thing—clean from the word go—in our factory in New Orleans; labels, bottles, oil, everything. Well, no, not labels: Been buying *them* abroad—get them dirt cheap there. You see, there's just one little wee speck, essence, or whatever it is, in a gallon of cottonseed oil, that gives it a smell, or a flavor, or something—get that out, and you're all right—perfectly easy then to turn the oil into any kind of oil you want to, and there ain't anybody that can detect the true from the false. Well, we know how to get that one little particle out—and we're the only firm that does. And we turn out an olive oil that is just simply perfect—undetectable! We are doing a ripping trade, too—as I could easily show you by my order book for this trip. May be you'll butter everybody's bread pretty soon, but we'll cottonseed his salad for him from the Gulf to Canada, and that's a dead certain thing." Mark Twain *Life on the Mississippi*

The special nutritional factors present in butter as known up to 1942 are without question. It was shown that butter has the following characteristics of superiority over other fats and oleomargarine imitations: (1) The nation's best source of vitamin A; (2) Unit for unit, the vitamin A in butter was three times as effective as the vitamin A in fish liver oils; (3) The natural vitamin D in butter was found 100 times as effective as the common commercial form of D (viosterol); (4) Butter, prescribed by physicians as a remedy for tuberculosis, psoriasis, xerophthalmia, dental caries and in preventing rickets, has been promptly effective; and (5) Butter carries vitamin E in sufficient quantity to prevent deficiency reactions.

Since that time, new and important evidence has accumulated which indicates other nutritional functions supplied by butter. This evidence appears to revolve around the physiological ramifications of the effects of the vitamin E complex. Royal Lee, DDS *Butter, Vitamin E and the "X" Factor of Dr. Price*

AUGUST DINNER

French Bean Salad

❀❀❀❀

Marinated Grilled Swordfish

❀❀❀

Bernaise Sauce

❀❀❀

Onions Chardonnay

❀❀❀❀❀

Berry Sherbert

BERNAISE SAUCE
Makes 1 1/4 cup

2 tablespoons shallots or green onions, finely chopped
1 tablespoon fresh tarragon, finely chopped, or 1 teaspoon dried tarragon
2 tablespoons white wine vinegar
2 tablespoons dry white wine or vermouth
5 egg yolks, at room temperature
1/2 cup butter, preferably raw, cut into pieces
fresh lemon juice
pinch of sea salt
pinch of pepper

Properly made, Bernaise sauce never attains more than a moderate heat, so that all the enzymes in the egg yolks are preserved. So delicious with meats and grilled fish, it is a sauce worth mastering—and not very hard to master at that.

In a small saucepan combine the shallots or onions, tarragon, wine and vinegar. Bring to a boil and reduce to about 1 tablespoon of liquid. Strain into a bowl.

Meanwhile, beat the egg yolks with a whisk. Set the bowl in a pan of hot water over a low flame. Add about half the butter, piece by piece, to the liquid, whisking constantly until melted. Add the egg yolks very slowly, drop by drop or in a very thin stream, whisking constantly. Add the remaining butter and whisk until well amalgamated. Sauce should now be warm and slightly thickened. Remove from heat and add lemon juice, salt and pepper to taste. The sauce may be kept warm in the bowl set in hot water. Whisk occasionally until ready to serve.

BUTTER SAUCE

(Beurre Blanc)
Makes 1/2 cup

6 tablespoons shallots, minced
6 tablespoons dry white wine
2 tablespoons fresh lemon juice
1/2 cup butter, preferably raw, cut into pieces
pinch of sea salt and pepper

This is the classic French sauce for fish. Properly made and not overheated, the butter will retain its enzyme content.

Place shallots, wine and lemon juice in a small pan. Bring to a boil and reduce to about 2 tablespoons. Strain into a small bowl.

Place the bowl in a pan of hot water over a low flame and add the butter piece by piece, whisking thoroughly after each addition. Sauce should become frothy and slightly thick. As soon as butter is amalgamated, remove from heat and season to taste. Serve immediately.

PARSLEY BUTTER SAUCE

Makes about 1 cup

3 tablespoons shallots or green onions, minced
2 tablespoons sherry vinegar
1/4 cup dry white wine
1 cup fish, chicken or beef stock (pages 119-124)
1/2 cup piima cream or creme fraiche (page 84)
3 tablespoons butter, softened
1 tablespoon coarse mustard
2 tablespoons parsley, finely chopped

Combine shallots or green onions, vinegar, wine, stock and cream in a pan, bring to a boil and reduce to about half, or until sauce thickens slightly. Reduce heat and whisk in butter and mustard. Season to taste. Just before serving, stir in the parsley.

. . . the idea of butter, and words like "buttery," "deep-buttered," or "butterball," retain their enticing power in North American language. The reason is partly traditional. The English and the Dutch who emigrated to the States in the seventeenth, eighteenth and nineteenth centuries took the butter habit with them. Foreign travellers commonly noted that Americans ate absolutely everything—porridge, soup, meat, vegetables and puddings—swimming in butter. Margaret Visser *Much Depends on Dinner*

I have referred to the importance of a high-vitamin butter for providing the fat-soluble activators to make possible the utilization of the minerals in the foods. In this connection, it is of interest that butter constitutes the principal source of these essential factors for many primitive groups throughout the world. In the high mountain and plateau district in northern India, and in Tibet, the inhabitants depend largely upon butter made from the milk of the yak and the sheep for these activators. The butter is eaten mixed with roasted cereals, is used in tea and in a porridge made of tea, butter and roasted grains. In Sudan, Egypt, I found considerable traffic in high-vitamin butter which . . . was being exchanged for and used with varieties of millet grown in other districts. . . . Its brilliant orange color testified to the splendid pasture for the dairy animals. The people in Sudan, had exceptionally fine teeth with exceedingly little tooth decay. The most physically perfect people in northern India are probably the Pathans who live on dairy products largely in the form of soured curd, together with wheat and vegetables. The people are very tall and are free of tooth decay. Weston Price, DDS *Nutrition and Physical Degeneration*

In one fascinating experiment
scientists deprived a group of test rats
of taste sensation. Both this group and
a control group were placed on normal rat diets, and in a short time the
taste-deprived rats all died. When the
rats were autopsied, scientists could
find only one cause of death—clinical
malnutrition. The scientists could come
up with only one explanation—that
there are important yet unknown physiological connections between taste
and health. Similarly, hospital patients
fed intravenously or through feeding
tubes that bypass the mouth often
report a nagging hunger for taste.
Though the mechanisms that govern
these phenomena are little understood, this much is certain: To be fully
nourished by food, we must experience it through tasting and chewing.
Marc David *Nourishing Wisdom*

SMOOTH TOMATO SAUCE
Makes 2 cups

2 ripe tomatoes
1 red pepper, seeded and chopped
1 onion, peeled and coarsely chopped
1/2 teaspoon sea salt
1/2 cup beef or chicken stock (pages 122 or 124)
8 tablespoons extra virgin olive oil

Blend tomatoes, pepper and onions in food processor. Place in a pan with remaining ingredients. Bring to
a boil, cover and simmer 3 minutes. Remove top and
cook, stirring constantly, for another 5 minutes or so.

CHUNKY TOMATO SAUCE
Makes 2 cups

2 tablespoons extra virgin olive oil
1/2 cup onion, finely chopped
3 cups fresh tomatoes, peeled, seeded and diced
2 tablespoons balsamic vinegar
2 cloves garlic, mashed
1/2 cup basil, finely chopped
pinch of sea salt
1/4 teaspoon pepper

This sauce is good with grilled tuna, sweetbreads
and many other dishes. To peel tomatoes, see page 70.

Sauté onions in olive oil until tender. Add tomatoes,
vinegar and garlic. Bring to a boil and reduce until liquid
is almost gone. Stir in basil and seasonings. Remove
from heat for about 1/2 hour to allow herb flavor to
amalgamate into the sauce. Reheat before serving.

GRANDPA'S SALSA

Makes 2 cups

1 medium onion, peeled and finely chopped
1 cup green chile peppers, fresh or canned, diced
2 ripe tomatoes, diced
4 tablespoons extra virgin olive oil

Sauté onions in olive oil until soft. Add tomatoes and peppers to onions and cook, stirring frequently, until most of the liquid has evaporated. This is delicious with scrambled eggs.

GREEN ENCHILADA SAUCE

Makes 3 cups

2 onions, chopped
8 fresh tomatillos, husked and finely chopped
3 medium mild green Anaheim chiles,
*   seeded and chopped*
2 small jalapeno chiles, seeded and chopped
2 cloves garlic, peeled and chopped
3 tablespoons extra virgin olive oil
1 3/4 cups chicken stock (page 124)
pinch of sea salt
1 bunch cilantro, chopped

This may be made in large batches and frozen. Be careful when preparing the chiles. It's best to wear rubber gloves when seeding and chopping jalapenos and to avoid touching any part of your face.

In a heavy skillet, sauté onions in olive oil. Add tomatillos and chopped chiles and sauté gently several minutes. Add the stock, garlic and salt and bring to a boil. Simmer about 30 minutes, uncovered, until the sauce has reduced and thickened. Remove from heat and stir in the cilantro. Process in batches in a food processor until smooth. Reheat gently.

In 1957, Dr. Norman Jolliffe, Director of the Nutrition Bureau of the New York Health Department, initiated the Anti-Coronary Club, in which a group of businessmen, ranging in age from 40 to 59 years, were placed on the Prudent Diet. Club members used corn oil and margarine instead of butter, cold breakfast cereals instead of eggs and chicken and fish instead of beef. Anti-Coronary Club members were to be compared with a "matched" group of the same age who ate eggs for breakfast and had meat three times a day. . . .

Nine years later, the results of Dr. Jolliffe's Anti-Coronary Club experiment were published in the *Journal of the American Medical Association*. Those on the Prudent Diet of corn oil, margarine, fish, chicken and cold cereal had an average serum cholesterol of 220, compared to 250 in the meat-and-potatoes control group. However, the study authors were obliged to note that there were eight deaths from heart disease among Dr. Jolliffe's Prudent Diet group, and none among those who ate meat three times a day. *The Oiling of America*

1923 was also the heyday of Prohibition. When booze became illegal here, sugar consumption zoomed. The whole country acted like a gathering of arrested alcoholics spending the evening at AA; they couldn't keep their mitts out of the candy jar. Teetotalers were often the biggest sugar fiends, vowing alcohol would never touch their lips while pouring in the sugar which produces alcohol in tummies instead of bathtubs. William Dufty *Sugar Blues*

Hydrophilic colloids form the substratum of all living protoplasm. They possess the property of readily taking up and giving off the substances essential to cell life. . . . Man's food in the raw state consists largely of hydrophilic colloids. The heat of cooking . . . precipitates the colloids in our diet. This change in colloidal state alters the hydration capacity of our foods so as to interfere with their ability to absorb digestive juices. . . . Uncooked foods contain sufficient hydrophilic colloid to keep this gastric mucosa in excellent condition. On the other hand, man living largely on cooked foods presents a different problem. . . . The use of a hydrophilic colloid [such as gelatin] in the dietetic treatment of gastric complaint is frequently sufficient in itself to rectify what are apparently serious conditions. Gelatin may be used in conjunction with almost any diet. . . . Its colloidal properties aid the digestion of many foods which cause the patient to suffer from "sour stomach" . . . . In children who present problems of growth and development and those who show symptoms of allergy in the bowel, the hydrophilic colloid proves to be of great value. One usually prefers to use it in conjunction with a diet designed for the child's general upbuilding, although the addition of the colloid to the usual diet may be all that is necessary. Francis M. Pottenger, Jr., MD *Hydrophilic Colloid Diet*

RED ENCHILADA SAUCE
Makes 3 cups

4 ounces whole dried New Mexico
*   or Ancho chiles*
1/4 cup extra virgin olive oil
1 medium onion, finely chopped
1 teaspoon ground cumin
2 cups beef or chicken stock (page 122 or 124)
2 cloves garlic, peeled and chopped
2 small cans tomato paste
1 tablespoon red wine vinegar
sea salt

This sauce is far superior—both nutritionally and in terms of taste—to anything you can buy in a can. It can be made in large batches and frozen to have on hand when needed. Use either Ancho or New Mexican chiles—both are available in Mexican or Latin American markets, in specialty stores and in supermarkets in the West. The New Mexican chiles are slightly milder.

Clean the dried chiles by removing the stem and seeds. Be sure to wear rubber gloves for this process and be careful not to touch any part of your face.

Meanwhile, sauté onion in olive oil. Add cumin and cook, stirring constantly, until well amalgamated into the oil. Add stock and chiles, bring to a boil, skim and reduce heat to a simmer. Whisk in garlic, vinegar and tomato paste. Simmer, covered, for about 45 minutes. Pass the sauce through a food mill. (See A Word on Equipment, page 68.) Season to taste.

PINEAPPLE VINEGAR
Makes 2 quarts

skin and core from 1 pineapple
2 quarts filtered water
2 teaspoons dried oregano
1/4 teaspoon red chile flakes
2 tablespoons whey (page 87), optional

This is a tradition of the West Indies and is used to make cortido (page 93). Place all ingredients in a bowl, cover and leave at room temperature about 36 hours. Skim and remove pineapple pieces. Strain vinegar into clean jars and cover tightly. This will keep in a cool place for several months.

PAPAYA PEPPER

seeds from 2 papayas

The papaya seed is rich in enzymes and can be used in place of pepper in any recipe. Place seeds with adhering pulp in warm water and work with hands to remove pulp. Let stand about 10 minutes. The pulp will rise to the surface where it can be skimmed off. Let seeds soak, covered, about 7 hours. Rinse seeds in a strainer and spread on a stainless steel baking pan. Bake at 150 degrees overnight or until completely dry. To use, grind in a pepper mill.

FERMENTED FISH SAUCE
Makes about 2 cups

1 1/2 pounds small fish, including heads, cut up
3 tablespoons sea salt
2 cups filtered water
2 cloves garlic, mashed
2 bay leaves, crumbled
1 teaspoon peppercorns
several pieces lemon rind
1 tablespoon tamarind paste
*   (available in African markets), optional*
2 tablespoons whey (page 87)

Toss fish pieces in salt and place in a wide-mouth, quart-sized mason jar. Press down with a wooden pounder or meat hammer. Mix remaining ingredients and pour over fish. Add additional water to cover fish thoroughly. The top of the liquid should be at least 1 inch below the top of the jar. Cover tightly and leave at room temperature for about 3 days. Transfer to refrigerator for several weeks. Drain liquid through a strainer and store fish sauce in the refrigerator.

Myth: For good health, serum cholesterol should be less than 180 mg/dl.
Truth: The all-cause death rate is higher in individuals with cholesterol levels lower than 180 mg/dl. (*Circulation* 1992 86:3)

Certain things, like Gorgonzola cheese or hoppy ale, don't necessarily surrender their full charms on first taste. With repeated samplings, though, their complex multilayered flavors finally reveal themselves. Fermented fish definitely belongs on the same list. . . probably the most accessible of the many fermented fish seasonings of Southeast Asia is fish sauce. This thin brown liquid is made by packing anchovies or other small fish in salt and allowing them to ferment for three months or more, drawing off the liquid as it seeps out.

While this may seem faintly repulsive, it is actually a part of the European culinary heritage. In classical Rome, one of the most popular condiments was a sauce called *garum*, made in an almost identical fashion, except that the innards of larger fish were added to ferment along with the anchovies. . . . Fish sauce serves much the same function in Southeast Asian cooking as salt does in Western cuisines, and the Vietnamese mode of cooking with it provides the best model for American tastes. It adds a depth of flavor and intensifies the tastes of other ingredients but does not stand out as an ingredient in itself. Once added to stew, condiment or salad, it ceases to taste of fish and instead serves to round out the many other bold flavors that are typical of the region's cuisine. John Willoughby and Chris Schlesinger *The New York Times*

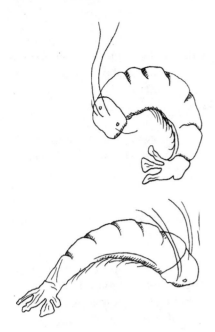

One of the most overlooked elements of traditional diets, especially in Asia and Africa, is the frequent use of shrimp, usually in the form of dried shrimp added to soups, stews and vegetable dishes or as a spicy fermented paste or sauce. The value of shrimp derives from the fact that it is a rich source of vitamin D—shrimp contains at least eight times more vitamin D than liver! Daily use of concentrated shrimp paste ensures the inhabitants of Africa and Asia a healthy daily dose of vitamin D, thereby protecting them from osteoporosis and vitamin-D related ailments, such as multiple sclerosis and colon cancer.

One objection against shrimp consumption is that, as the shrimp is a scavenger, shrimp meat is likely to carry toxins. According to the naturopath Jack Tips, toxins are quickly eliminated from shrimp's tissue, and shrimp protein is particularly easy to digest.

American consumption of shrimp has increased threefold during the last fifteen years. Much of the shrimp consumed in the U.S. is imported from Thailand, Ecuador and Mexico. About half of the shrimp on the American market is farm raised. SWF

SHRIMP BUTTER
Makes about 1 cup

about 2 cups tiny cooked shrimp, drained,
*   reserved from making shrimp stock (page 121)*
1/4 cup butter, softened

Shrimp butter is an excellent thickener for fish sauces and bisques.

Place shrimp in a tea towel and squeeze thoroughly to remove all liquid. Process shrimp in a food processor to form a coarse paste. Add butter and process until well blended. To store, place 2-tablespoon amounts in small crocks and refrigerate, or in small zip-lock bags and freeze.

FERMENTED SHRIMP PASTE
Makes 3 cups

about 3 cups tiny cooked shrimp, drained,
*   reserved from making shrimp stock (page 121)*
6 ounces dried red chile peppers, hot or mild
4 cups water, fish stock (page 119) or
*   shrimp stock (page 121), or a combination*
1 heaping tablespoon sea salt
2 tablespoons whey (page 87)

Remove stems and seeds from peppers. (Use rubber gloves for this procedure.) Boil the chiles in water or stock, uncovered, stirring occasionally until liquid is almost evaporated. Using a slotted spoon, place chiles in a food mill (see A Word on Equipment, page 68) and process to remove skins and produce a purée. Place shrimp in a tea towel and squeeze thoroughly to remove all liquid. Place shrimp, chile purée, salt and whey in a food processor and process until smooth. Place in a quart-sized, wide-mouth mason jar, cover tightly and leave at room temperature about 3 days before transferring to cold storage. Use as a spicy condiment with meat or fish.

COCONUT MILK

Makes 1 1/2 cups

2 coconuts

Using an ice pick, poke two holes in soft spots at the end of the coconuts and allow the coconut water to drain out. Place in a 350 degree oven until the coconuts crack. Use a hammer to split them open. Separate coconut meat from the shell using a sharp knife. Remove dark outer layer and dice white coconut meat into quarter-inch pieces. Place coconut meat in food processor and process until well broken up. Add 1 cup warm water and process until fluffy.

Line a strainer with a kitchen towel and place processed coconut meat in the strainer. Drain coconut milk into a glass container, squeezing out all liquid with the back of a wooden spoon or with your hands. Use immediately or refrigerate and use within 2 days.

You may also use canned whole coconut milk (see page 160), which is one of the few canned products we recommend.

DRIED SWEETENED COCONUT MEAT

Makes 3 cups

coconut meat remaining from making coconut milk
1/4 cup maple syrup

This makes an excellent topping for curry, and it is delicious in oatmeal. We also call for coconut meat in several dessert and cookie recipes. Mix coconut meat with maple syrup, spread on an oiled pan and bake at 150 degrees, turning occasionally, for about 12 hours or until well dried.

Products of the coconut form a dietary staple in many nations, particularly Southeast Asia, the tropical regions of Latin America and East Africa. Marco Polo referred to the coconut as the "Indian nut." Vasco de Gama used the word "coquos" in his *Rotiero* (1498-99) and Pigafetta, the official chronicler of the Magellan expedition to the Philippines, used the Italian form of "coche" (plural "coca") around 1522.

The coconut is relatively low in protein compared to other nuts and seeds. It provides calcium, iron, magnesium, phosphorus, potassium, iodine and many trace minerals. The coconut contains up to 60 percent fat, and this fat is 92 percent saturated. But this is no reason to avoid coconut products. The principle fatty acid in coconut milk, lauric acid, is a medium-chain 12-carbon saturated fatty acid that has potent antiviral, antifungal and antimicrobial properties. *In vitro* it will inactivate the HIV virus as well as the measles virus, herpes simplex virus-1, vesicular stomatitis virus, visna virus and cytomegalovirus. Coconut oil is our best source of lauric acid and is now being used to treat both AIDS and candida because of its antipathogenic effects in the gut. When absorbed, the medium-chain fatty acids in coconut oil give quick energy. Because coconut oil is so highly saturated, it is highly resistant to rancidity.

The medium-chain fatty acids in coconut oil strengthen the immune system. Perhaps this is the reason that Thailand, where coconut holds a prominent place in the national cuisine, has the lowest cancer rate of the fifty countries surveyed by the National Cancer Institute.

Coconut oil is a good substitute for hydrogenated oils. Is this why we hear so much adverse publicity about the coconut? SWF

ABOUT COCONUT PRODUCTS

Coconut oil—and whole coconut products that contain coconut oil—are nature's best source of lauric acid, an essential saturated fatty acid that enhances the immune system and protects us against viruses, yeasts, parasites and other pathogens in the gut. Coconut can be added to the diet in a variety of ways.

Coconut Oil: Use coconut oil in cookie recipes and other baked goods. Coconut oil blended with crispy nuts makes a delicious nut butter (page 516). It can also be used for sautéing, provided it is not subjected to temperatures that are too high. Buy only food-grade coconut oil and avoid any coconut oil that has been hydrogenated. In some parts of the world, coconut oil is extracted from coconuts that have been dried over fires, giving it a smoky odor and taste. The highest quality coconut oil is odorless and tasteless, a white semisolid in cool weather and a creamy-colored oil in hot weather.

Creamed Coconut: Found in the refrigerated section of Asian and Indian markets and in some health food stores, creamed coconut is made of finely ground fresh coconut meat with all of its valuable oil. The hard white blocks melt when added to broth, soups, sauces and curries. This is a wonderful product that imparts a rich texture and true coconut taste to both main dishes and desserts. See Sources for a wholesaler that can provide creamed coconut to your favorite store.

Canned Whole Coconut Milk: A good substitute for creamed coconut, you may make this yourself (page 159) or buy canned whole coconut milk, which can be found in most supermarkets. Look for a brand that contains no additives and be sure to buy *whole*, not *lite*. Add to broth, soups, sauces, curries, smoothies and blender drinks; or use in preparing beans, rice and other grain dishes.

Desiccated Coconut Meat: Unsweetened desiccated coconut meat is available in many health food stores. Use as a topping and in desserts. Finely ground coconut will be easier to digest and will give up its content of lauric acid for assimilation more easily than coarsely shredded coconut. Avoid the coconut meat sold in supermarkets—it is loaded with sugar.

AIDS patients and others with compromised immune system function should consume 20 to 25 grams of lauric acid per day. Approximately 12 grams of lauric acid are contained in 2 tablespoons coconut oil or 3 tablespoons creamed coconut; 10 grams of lauric acid are contained in 1/2 cup canned whole coconut milk or 1/2 cup desiccated coconut meat.

GREAT BEGINNINGS

HORS D'OEUVRES & DIPS

Our recipes for hors d'oeurves and dips derive from a variety of ethnic traditions and feature fresh, unprocessed ingredients, with an emphasis on fish eggs—roe and caviar. Fish eggs are valued by traditional peoples throughout the world for their ability to prevent problems of the thyroid gland, promote fertility, and nourish pregnant women and growing children. Although they come under the category of "gourmet," fish roe can serve as a basis for everyday snacks and lunchtime fare.

If you tolerate milk products, we also recommend our cream cheese-flax spreads (page 165) as a delicious and synergistic combination of omega-3 fatty acids, saturated fats and sulphur-containing proteins.

TARAMOSALATA

(Greek Roe Spread)
Serves 12

1 pound smoked whole cod roe, casing removed (available
    at Middle Eastern markets, often canned or in jars)
1/2 cup piima cream or creme fraiche (page 84)
1 clove garlic, mashed
juice of 1/2 lemon
1/4 teaspoon pepper
1/2 cup extra virgin olive oil

Use this delicious pink cream to spread on toasts, to fill celery, or serve in a crock with whole grain crackers (page 518) or triangle croutons (page 520).

Place roe, cream, garlic, lemon juice and pepper in food processor and process until smooth. Using the attachment for adding oil, add the olive oil drop by drop with the motor running to form a thick, mayonnaise-like emulsion. Chill several hours.

Variation: Budget Roe Spread

Use *1 pound raw fish roe, casing removed*, from any kind of fish, rather than smoked cod roe and add *sea salt* to taste. High-nutrient roe can often be obtained in season at very low cost from a good fish merchant.

SALMON EGG TOASTS

Serves 2-4

2 ounces fresh salmon eggs
2-4 slices whole grain bread
2 tablespoons butter
1 tablespoon fresh dill, chopped

Toast bread and spread liberally with butter. Spread salmon eggs on toast and sprinkle with chopped dill.

ANCHOVY TOASTS

Makes 1 dozen

12 triangle croutons (page 520)
1 cup anchovy paste (page 143)
2 tablespoons salmon roe (optional)

Spread croutons with anchovy paste and decorate each with optional 2 or 3 salmon eggs.

MACKEREL SPREAD

Makes 1 1/2 cups

1 cup pickled mackerel or herring (page 242)
1/2 cup piima cream or creme fraiche (page 84)
juice of 1/2 lemon
sea salt and pepper

Blend mackerel or herring, cultured cream and lemon juice in food processor. Season to taste. Serve with whole grain crackers (page 518) or triangle croutons (page 520). For adventurous eaters!

When it is recognized that in the Sierra the available water is largely that provided to the streams from the melting snows and from rains in the rainy season, it will be realized that these sources of fresh water could not provide the liberal quantity of iodine essential for human growth and development. It was, accordingly, a matter of great interest to discover that these Indians used regularly dried fish eggs from the sea. Commerce in these dried foods is carried on today as it no doubt has been for centuries. When I inquired of them why they used this material, they explained that it was necessary to maintain the fertility of their women. I was informed also that every exchange depot and market carried these dried fish eggs so that they were always available. Another sea product of very great importance, and one which was universally available, was dried kelp. Upon inquiry I learned that the Indians used it so that they would not get "big necks" like the whites. The kelp provided a very rich source of iodine as well as of copper which is very important to them in the utilization of iron for building an exceptionally efficient quality of blood for carrying oxygen liberally at those high altitudes. An important part of their dietary consists today as in the past of potatoes which are gathered and frozen, dried and powdered, and preserved in the powdered form. This powder is used in soups with llama meat and other products. Weston Price, DDS *Nutrition and Physical Degeneration*

There is more simplicity in the man who eats caviar on impulse than in the man who eats grapenuts on principle.
G. K. Chesterton

The hardy folk of the Northern Isles feasted on "made-dishes." They had *strubba*—coagulated milk whipped to consistency of cream. *Klokks* was new milk simmered until clotted and flavored with cinnamon and sugar. *Kirn* mill was a curd of buttermilk with mill-gruel. *Blaund* was whey of *bleddik* or buttermilk. *Hungmill* was cream hung in a bag, like cream cheese. *Klabba* was junket set thick by action of *yearmin* (rennet). *Eusteen* was hot milk reduced by sherry to curd and whey. *Pramm* was cold milk mixed with meal, a dish for bairn or beggar. *Eggaloorie* was salt, eggs and milk boiled. *Da pukkle* was oats, called *bursteen* when ground. *Virpa* was a brew made of corn husks. A very popular dish was *knocket* made of corn, cracked wheat or groats boiled with kale and pork. At Christmas they had *Yule-brunies* or rye cakes. *Ploy-skonn* was a shortbread. The dairy and vegetable products were enhanced with *slott*, fish roe beaten to cream with flour and salt added, or with *stapp*, a mixture of fish heads with liver. Special palates were pleased with *kiossed heeds,* fish heads which had become gamey. At Christmas and at embarking on perilous voyages they had *whipkill*, egg yolks with sugar beaten with cream and enforced with potent spirit. *Orkney and Shetland Miscellany*

Myth: Vitamin B$_{12}$ can be obtained from certain plant sources such as blue-green algae and soy products.

Truth: Vitamin B$_{12}$ is not absorbed from plant sources. Modern soy products increase the body's need for B$_{12}$. (*Soybeans: Chemistry & Technology* Vol 1 1972)

SALMON SPREAD
Makes 2 cups

1 cup cooked fresh salmon
1 small onion, grated
3/4 cup piima cream or creme fraiche (page 84)
juice of 1 lemon
1 tablespoon capers, drained, rinsed
*   and dried with paper towels*
dash cayenne pepper
sea salt and pepper

Blend salmon, onion, cultured cream, lemon juice and capers together in food processor. Season to taste. Spread on whole grain crackers (page 518) or toast.
Variation: Salmon Stuffed Endive Leaves
Place a small spoonful salmon spread in the hollow of *30 endive leaves*. Garnish with *sprigs of fresh dill.*

SHRIMP SPREAD
Makes 1/2 cup

1/2 cup shrimp butter (page 158)
1 tablespoon fresh dill, finely chopped
sea salt

Mix shrimp butter with dill and season to taste. Serve with whole grain crackers (page 518) or round croutons (page 520).

SHRIMP PLATTER
Serves 24

48 large cooked shrimp, shells removed
2 cups fermented shrimp paste (page 158)
*   or shrimp cocktail sauce (page 142)*

Place shrimp paste or cocktail sauce in a bowl in the center of a large round platter. Arrange shrimp around the bowl and serve.

CREAM CHEESE-FLAX SPREAD

Makes 1 cup

1 cup cream cheese (page 87), softened
2 tablespoons expeller-expressed flax oil

Use a food processor to mix cheese with flax oil. Place in a crock or serving bowl. Cover and chill well. Serve with sourdough bread or whole grain crackers (page 518).

Variation: Herbed Cheese Spread
Add *1 tablespoon fresh herbs, finely minced.*

Variation: Pepper Cheese Spread
Add *1 tablespoon cracked pepper.*

Variation: Garlic Cheese Spread
Add *2 garlic cloves, peeled and mashed*

Variation: Smoked Salmon Spread
Pulse *2 ounces smoked salmon* in the food processor. Blend in cream cheese, flax oil, *1 tablespoon fresh dill, chopped* and *1 tablespoon chives, chopped.*

STUFFED ENDIVE LEAVES

Serves 15-30

30 Belgian endive leaves
3/4 cup radish, finely diced
3/4 cup celery, finely diced
2 tablespoons piima cream or creme fraiche
  (page 84)
2 tablespoons homemade cream cheese
  (page 87), softened
1 teaspoon expeller-expressed flax oil
1-2 teaspoons lemon juice
1/4 teaspoon pepper
30 tiny watercress sprigs

Mix cream, cream cheese, flax oil, lemon juice and pepper. Stir in radishes and cucumbers. Chill several hours. Place a spoonful in each endive leaf and garnish with watercress sprigs.

The groups that depend on the blubber animals are the most fortunate, in the hunting way of life, for they never suffer from fat-hunger. This trouble is worst, so far as North America is concerned, among those forest Indians who depend at times on rabbits, the leanest animal in the North, and who develop the extreme fat-hunger known as rabbit-starvation. Rabbit eaters, if they have no fat from another source—beaver, moose, fish—will develop diarrhoea in about a week, with headache, lassitude, a vague discomfort. If there are enough rabbits, the people eat till their stomachs are distended; but no matter how much they eat they feel unsatisfied. Some think a man will die sooner if he eats continually of fat-free meat than if he eats nothing, but this is a belief on which sufficient evidence for a decision has not been gathered in the north. Deaths from rabbit-starvation, or from the eating of other skinny meat, are rare; for everyone understands the principle, and any possible preventive steps are naturally taken. Vilhjalmur Stefansson *The Fat of the Land*

The cows are our friends, they give food, they give strength, they likewise give a good complexion and happiness.
Gautama Buddha

EGGPLANT CAVIAR

Makes about 2 cups

2 medium eggplants
2 tablespoons sea salt
1 medium onion, finely chopped
2-4 cloves garlic, mashed
1/2 cup parsley or cilantro, minced
1/4 cup crispy pine nuts (page 514), optional
2 tablespoons lemon juice
1/4 cup extra virgin olive oil
dash cayenne pepper

Puncture the eggplants in a few spots and bake at 375 degrees for about 1 hour or until skin is wrinkled and eggplant is tender. Let cool. Peel and chop into a fine dice, sprinkle with salt, mix well and leave in a colander about 1 hour. Rinse well with water and squeeze dry in a tea towel. Mix with remaining ingredients. Serve with pita bread, triangle croutons (page 521) or Belgian endive leaves.

Variation: Tangy Eggplant Caviar

Add *2 tablespoons raw wine vinegar, 1 jalapeno pepper, seeded and chopped,* and *2 tablespoons small capers, drained, rinsed and dried with paper towels.*

How many Americans would you guess eat french fries in fast food chain restaurants every year? After all, "billions of burgers sold" surely translates to an equal number of french fry orders consumed. Originally, the delicious fingers of deep-fried potato, which have been blamed on the famed French chefs, were cooked in, horror of horrors, old-fashioned tallow. Over the past several years, the public relations conscious fast food giants were pressured mightily by well-meaning advocacy groups, especially the Center for Science in the Public Interest (CSPI), who obviously knew nothing about *trans* fats, to make their french fries "more healthy." This meant that the famous french fry had to be cooked in "partially hardened vegetable shortening" cooking oil rather than a saturated animal fat. Never mind that a potato deep-fried in . . . lard may be cooked in less time at a higher temperature—thereby leaving less total fat imbedded in the finished, more thoroughly cooked, less soggy, less rancid food product.

According to Dr. Mary Enig, Research Associate in the Lipids Research Group, Department of Chemistry and Biochemistry, University of Maryland, the nations' leading authority on the amounts of *trans* fats in foods, the new fast food french fries are loaded with the molecular misfits, the *trans* fatty acids. The fat in a fast food french fry cooked with partially hydrogenated vegetable shortening can have as high as 46% *trans* fat. Old fashioned tallows had zero percent *trans* fat. This means that almost half the fat in the french fries is now the worst kind for human nutrition! Tom Valentine *Facts on Fats & Oils*

EGGPLANT RELISH

Makes about 5 cups

4 medium eggplants
4 tablespoons sea salt
4 medium tomatoes, peeled, seeded and chopped
1 medium onion, finely minced
1/2 cup parsley, finely chopped
2 tablespoon small capers, drained, rinsed
   and dried with paper towels
2 tablespoons crispy pine nuts (page 514)
1/4 teaspoon ground cumin
dash cayenne pepper
sea salt and pepper
2 cups tahini sauce (page 148)

Puncture the eggplants in a few spots and bake at 375 degrees for about 1 hour or until skin is wrinkled and eggplant is tender. Let cool. Peel and chop into a fine dice, sprinkle with salt, mix well and leave in a colander for about 1 hour. Rinse well with water and squeeze dry in a tea towel.

To peel tomatoes, see page 70. Mix all ingredients and season to taste. Cover and refrigerate at least 1 hour before serving. Serve with whole grain bread, pita chips (page 520) or triangle croutons (page 520).

*FINGER FOOD
BUFFET*

Rosemary Walnuts

*Eggplant Relish
with Pita Chips*

Salmon Egg Toasts

Assorted Canapés

Mushroom Crustades

*Stuffed
Belgian Endive*

Stuffed Grape Leaves

*Herbed Cheese Spread
with Whole Grain
Crackers*

*Red Pepper Quiche
Squares*

Chicken Brochettes

*Hummus with
Vegetable Sticks*

*Carob Dipped
Strawberries*

Macaroons

Punch

It appears that if you want a dental law you can approximate it by saying that the most primitive people usually have the best teeth, but that no people of the past or present are known who had complete freedom from tooth decay unless they were hunting, fishing, pastoral in their way of life and got little or none of their food direct from the vegetable kingdom. You might add that in some cases a highly vegetarian people, while not attaining the 100 percent perfection of meat eaters, do, nevertheless, have very good teeth as compared with ours. Vilhjalmur Stefansson *The Fat of the Land*

Dr. V. G. Heiser in a recent talk to the National Association of Manufacturers told of experiments on 4,000 rats in which half were fed on a natural diet and the other half received the kind of food the average family uses. At the end of two years, the first group was essentially free from disease while the group partaking of human diet was afflicted with a number of diseases including gout, gastric ulcer, arthritis and tuberculosis. Edward Howell, MD *Food Enzymes for Health and Longevity*

The effect of fatty acids on serum cholesterol levels is dependent on the original serum cholesterol levels: high serum cholesterol decreases with most fatty acids including all saturates; low serum cholesterol increases with many of the fatty acids including saturates, monounsaturates and sometimes the polyunsaturates. Mary G. Enig, PhD *Know Your Fats*

MUSHROOM CRUSTADES
Makes 3-4 dozen

1/2 recipe yoghurt dough (page 485)
1/2 cup shallots, minced
1 pound mushrooms, washed, well dried and
  finely chopped
2 tablespoons butter
2 tablespoons extra virgin olive oil
juice of 1/2 lemon
2 egg yolks
1 cup piima cream or creme fraiche (page 84)
sea salt and pepper
dash of nutmeg
2 egg whites
pinch sea salt

Roll out dough thinly and cut into rounds big enough to line miniature muffin tins. Oil miniature muffin tins well and line with dough rounds, removing excess. Bake at 350 degrees about 30 minutes or until dough becomes slightly crusty.

Meanwhile, sauté the shallots and mushrooms in butter and olive oil in a large skillet over a medium-high flame. Add lemon juice and let pan juices evaporate. Process in food processor until smooth. Mix with beaten egg yolks, cream and nutmeg. Season to taste. Beat egg whites with a pinch of salt until stiff and fold into mushroom mixture. Place a spoonful in each pastry cup and bake another 15 minutes at 350 degrees. These may be frozen and reheated.

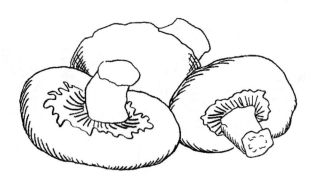

CREAM CHEESE PASTRIES
Makes about 24

1/2 recipe yoghurt dough (page 485)
1 cup cream cheese (page 87), softened
1/2 cup melted butter
1 large or 2 small eggs
sea salt and pepper
1 egg, lightly beaten

Roll out dough and cut into rounds big enough to line miniature muffin tins. Oil miniature muffin tins well and line with dough rounds, removing excess. Mix cream cheese with eggs and melted butter. Season to taste. Place a spoonful in each pastry shell. Bake at 350 degrees for 15 minutes. Brush tops with beaten egg and bake another 10 minutes.

Variation: Poi Pastries
Use *1 cup fermented taro root (page 102)* in place of cream cheese.

CHICKEN BROCHETTES
Serves 6

6 skinless chicken breasts
1 teaspoon ground cardamom
1/2 teaspoon sea salt
1/2 teaspoon pepper
2 cloves garlic, peeled and mashed
1/4 teaspoon cayenne pepper
1/2 cup fresh lemon or lime juice
4 tablespoons clarified butter (page 150)
2 cups peanut sauce (page 147)

Cut chicken into walnut-sized pieces. Marinate chicken pieces in a mixture of the spices and lime or lemon juice in the refrigerator for several hours or overnight. Pat pieces dry with paper towels. Skewer the chicken and brush with butter. Grill under the broiler for about 5 minutes per side or until cooked through. Arrange on a platter and serve with peanut sauce.

It is tempting to wonder . . . what role sugar played in the decline of the Arab Empire. . . the heirs of the Prophet are probably the first conquerors in history to have produced enough sugar to furnish both courts and troops with candy and sugared drinks. An early European observer credits the widespread use of sugar by Arab desert fighters as the reason for their loss of cutting edge. . . . "The Turks and Moors cut off one piece [of sugar] after another and so chew and eat them openly everywhere in the street without shame". . . . After the rise of Islam, sugar became potent political stuff. . . . The same fate that had crippled Arab conquerors was now to afflict their Christian adversaries. En route to wrest the Holy Places from the grip of the Sultan, the Crusaders soon acquired a taste for the sauce of the Saracens. . . . [An] early diplomatic position paper outlines a southern sugar strategy for bringing the wily Saracens to heel. "In the land of the Sultan, sugar grows in great quantities and from it the Sultans draw large incomes and taxes. If the Christians could seize these lands, great injury would be inflicted on the Sultan and at the same time Christendom would be wholly supplied from Cyprus. . . . As regards Christendom, no harm would follow". . . . What followed was seven centuries in which the seven deadly sins flourished across the seven seas, leaving a trail of slavery, genocide and organized crime. British historian Noel Deerr says flatly: "It will be no exaggeration to put the tale and toll of the slave trade at 20 million Africans, of which two-thirds are to be charged against sugar." William Dufty *Sugar Blues*

In many of the [South American] primitive tribes living by the sea we found emphasis on the value of fish eggs and on some animal forms for insuring a high physical development of growing children, particularly of girls, and a high perfection of offspring through a reinforcement of the mother's nutrition. It is also important to note that in several of the primitive tribes studied there has been a consciousness that not only the mothers should have special nutrition but also the father. In this group very great value was placed upon a product obtained from a sea form know locally as the angelote or angel fish, which in classification is between a skate and a shark. . . . [The eggs of the shark] are used as food by all, but the special food product for men is a pair of glands obtained from the male. These glands weigh up to a pound each, when they are dried. They have a recognized value among the natives for treating cases of tuberculosis, especially for controlling lung hemorrhages. The sea foods were used in conjunction with the land plants and fruits raised by means of irrigation in the river valleys. Together these foods provided adequate nutrition for maintaining high physical excellence. Weston Price, DDS *Nutrition and Physical Degeneration*

Myth: Animal fats cause cancer and heart disease.

Truth: Animal fats contain many nutrients that protect against cancer and heart disease; elevated rates of cancer and heart disease are associated with consumption of large amounts of vegetable oils. (*Fed Proc* July 1978 37:2215)

CANAPES

Use thinly sliced sour dough bread (page 490), cut into rounds with a cookie cutter and spread with butter, mayonnaise (page 137) or cream cheese-flax spread (page 165); thinly sliced round croutons (page 520); or small crispy pancakes (page 478). Top canapés with any of the following combinations. Chill well before serving.

Pickled salmon (page 241) with thinly sliced onion rings (use pearl onions) and 2-3 small capers, drained, rinsed and dried with paper towels, on cream cheese-flax spread (page 165)

Salmon eggs with sprinkles of fresh dill on butter

Pickled mackerel or herring (page 242) with sprigs of dill on mayonnaise

Thinly sliced rare beef with a few gratings of pickled daikon radish (page 98), dollop of horseradish or sprinkle of chives

Thinly sliced red radishes on thickly spread butter

Natural peanut butter with sprinkling of finely chopped duck cracklings (page 295), finely chopped crispy peanuts (page 514) or dried sweetened coconut meat (page 159)

Chicken liver paté (page 171) on butter with parsley leaf or sliver of pickled red pepper (page 99)

Black caviar with finely chopped onion on cream cheese-flax spread (page 165) or fermented taro (page 102)

Tomato, peeled, seeded and finely diced mixed with squeeze of lemon juice and finely chopped basil on round croutons (page 520)

Marinated salmon (page 238) on butter

Herbed cream cheese spread (page 165)

Salmon spread (page 164)

Finely diced cooked chicken mixed with finely chopped cashews, green onions and Oriental dressing (page 135)

Crab meat mixed with mayonnaise (page 137)

CHICKEN LIVER PATE

Serves 12-18

3 tablespoons butter
1 pound chicken or duck livers, or a combination
1/2 pound mushrooms, washed, dried
    and coarsely chopped
1 bunch green onions, chopped
2/3 cup dry white wine or vermouth
1 clove garlic, mashed
1/2 teaspoon dry mustard
1/4 teaspoon dried dill
1/4 teaspoon dried rosemary
1 tablespoon lemon juice
1/2 stick butter, softened
sea salt

Melt butter in a heavy skillet. Add livers, onions and mushrooms and cook, stirring occasionally, for about 10 minutes until livers are browned. Add wine, garlic, mustard, lemon juice and herbs. Bring to a boil and cook, uncovered, until the liquid is gone. Allow to cool. Process in a food processor with softened butter. Season to taste. Place in a crock or mold and chill well. Serve with whole grain bread or triangle croutons (page 520).

While glucose [from refined sugar] is being absorbed into the blood, we feel "up." A quick pickup. However, this surge of mortgaged energy is succeeded by the downs, when the bottom drops out of the blood glucose level. We are listless, tired; it requires effort to move or even think until the blood glucose level is brought up again. Our poor brain is vulnerable to suspicion, hallucinations. We can be irritable, all nerves, jumpy. The severity of the crisis on top of crisis depends on the glucose overload. If we continue taking sugar, a new double crisis is always beginning before the old one ends. The accumulative crisis at the end of the day can be a lulu. After years of such days, the end result is damaged adrenals. They are worn out not from overwork but from continued whiplash. Overall production of hormones is low, amounts don't dovetail. This disturbed function, out of balance, is reflected all around the endocrine circuit. The brain may soon have trouble telling the unreal from the real; we're likely to go off half cocked. When stress comes our way, we go to pieces because we no longer have a healthy endocrine system to cope with it. Day-to-day efficiency lags, we're always tired, never seem to get anything done. We've really got the sugar blues. The late endocrinologist John W. Tintera was quite emphatic: "It is quite possible to improve your disposition, increase your efficiency, and change your personality for the better. The way to do it is to avoid cane and beet sugar in all forms and guises." William Dufty *Sugar Blues*

Shoppers err in refusing to buy avocados because of their high fat content. Avocados contain from 5 to 22 percent fat, mostly monounsaturated oleic acid, in a form that is absolutely fresh, with its full complement of lipase and vitamin E. Avocados also contain carotenoids, B-complex and C vitamins and numerous minerals, such as potassium, magnesium, iron, calcium and phosphorus.

The name avocado comes from an Aztec word meaning "testicle tree" because the rounded fruits grow in pairs. There are many varieties. The best from the point of view of flavor and ripening characteristics are the dark-skinned Haas avocados. They should be stored at room temperature (no colder than 55 degrees) until they turn soft. They can then be stored in the refrigerator for a week or so. To prepare, cut in half, remove seed with the point of a knife, peel and slice. Immediately dribble on lemon or lime juice to prevent discoloration. SWF

Fats and oils to be avoided, in addition to partially hydrogenated vegetable fats, include any rancid or overheated fats and oils that contain breakdown products, such as oxidized fatty acids, oxidized sterols, peroxides, acrolein, hydrocarbons and aromatic compounds. These types of abused fats and oils are not safe. They range from immediately toxic to chronically toxic. Free radicals can form in polyunsaturated oils during industrial processing. These can interact with sulfhydryl groups in proteins as well as with unsaturated fatty acids and are very destructive of cell membranes. Mary G. Enig, PhD *Know Your Fats*

AVOCADO DIP
(Guacamole)
Makes 1 1/2 cups

2 ripe avocados
juice of 1 lemon
2 tablespoons cilantro, finely chopped (optional)
pinch of sea salt

Peel avocados, place in a bowl and sprinkle with lemon juice. Mash avocados with a fork—do not use a food processor. Guacamole should be slightly lumpy. Stir in the cilantro. Guacamole should be made just before serving as it will turn dark in an hour or two. Serve with vegetable sticks or baked or fried tortillas (page 519), broken into chips.

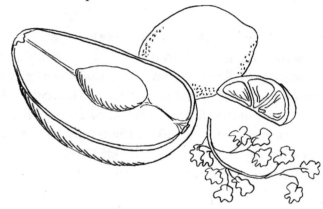

CRAB DIP
Makes about 2 cups

1/2 pound crab meat
1 cup cream cheese (page 87)
1/2 cup piima cream or creme fraiche (page 84)
juice of 1/2 lemon
2 tablespoons dry sherry
dash of cayenne pepper
1/2 teaspoon sea salt
2 tablespoons fresh chives, finely chopped

Place all ingredients except crab in a container set in simmering water. When warmed, blend together with a whisk. Stir in crab and allow to warm through. Serve warm with triangle croutons (page 520).

CUCUMBER YOGHURT DIP

Makes 2 cups

1 large cucumber, peeled, seeded
    and finely chopped
1 teaspoon sea salt
1 cup plain whole yoghurt
2 cloves garlic, crushed
1 tablespoon fresh mint, finely chopped
1 tablespoon fresh parsley, finely chopped
1 tablespoon lemon juice
1/4 teaspoon pepper
pinch of cayenne pepper

Salt chopped cucumber and let stand in a colander about 1 hour. Mix other ingredients together and stir in cucumber.

ROASTED EGGPLANT DIP

(Baba Ganouj)

Makes about 2 cups

3 large eggplants
1 tablespoon sea salt
2 cloves garlic, mashed
juice of 4-5 lemons
1 cup tahini
2 tablespoons extra virgin olive oil
dash of cayenne pepper

Puncture the eggplants in a few spots and bake in a 375 degree oven for about 1 hour or until skin is wrinkled and eggplant is tender. Let cool. Peel and chop into a fine dice, sprinkle with salt, mix well and let sit about an hour in a colander. Rinse well with water and squeeze out juices with a tea towel. Purée eggplant in a food processor. Add remaining ingredients and process until smooth. Place in a bowl and decorate with a sprinkle of cayenne pepper. Serve with pita bread or pita chips (page 521).

When we make chemicals like vitamin C and lactic acid in a laboratory, equal amounts of mirror-image left-handed and right-handed molecules are formed. While these isomers have identical chemical formulas, they don't react equally with other three-dimensional molecules. One isomer will fit and the other will not, just as a left-handed glove will not fit onto a right hand. Life systems are highly specific. Only one mirror image is used and the other has no biological activity. It may even be harmful. Natural lactic acid found in yoghurt and traditionally pickled foods, for example, consists entirely of right-handed molecules. The synthetic is a mixture of equal parts of right-handed and left-handed molecules. When synthetic lactic acid was added to baby formula, a number of babies died. Natural citric acid is a beneficial substance found in many foods, but synthetic citric acid added to manufactured foods can cause adverse reactions. Synthetic ascorbic acid is only half as effective as natural ascorbic acid and amino acids are also useless if not toxic when present in synthetic forms. Only left handed amino acids can be assimilated. SWF

. . . the concept that fat is the best of foods has been universal with mankind in all lands and climates. When Christianity spread northward beyond the Mediterranean, the Biblical phrase "to live on the fat of the land" was readily understood in Greece, Italy and France; in Britain, Sweden and up among the Lapps. In English speech fat food was called rich food, which was the highest praise. The fattest was best among men and gods, in most religions and in all countries. Vilhjalmur Stefansson *The Fat of the Land*

Know Your Ingredients

Name This Product #9

Skim Milk, partially hydrogenated soybean oil, onion, cellulose gel, citric acid, salt, sugar, mono- and diglycerides, hydrolyzed vegetable protein, Romano cheese, sodium hexametaphosphate, monosodium glutamate, cellulose gum, xanthan gum, natural and artificial flavoring, garlic, celery.

See Appendix B for Answer

As a small boy I used to spend my school vacation on a farm where the animals received no food except that which they could find in the pasture and woods. These were not heavy milk producers with enormous udders. The cows were never ill; the need for a veterinarian was negligible. Contrast this with championship milkers with their large udders which are usually afflicted with mastitis and its associated discharge of pus. This unsavory condition usually requires almost continuous use of penicillin to keep the milk flowing. These champions are fed objectionable concentrates and other materials at odds with Enzyme Nutrition. What will you have, less good milk or an abundance of milk incriminated as a cause of heart and artery disease? Edward Howell, MD *Enzyme Nutrition*

ROQUEFORT DIP
Makes 2 cups

1 cup crumbled Roquefort cheese
1/2 cup heavy cream, not ultrapasteurized
1/2 cup piima cream or creme fraiche (page 84)
1 tablespoon expeller-expressed flax oil
1 teaspoon fish sauce (page 157)
1/4 teaspoon pepper

Mix all ingredients together. Serve with raw sugar snap peas or vegetable sticks.

CHEESE DIP
Makes 2 cups

1/4 pound raw cheddar, grated
3 ounces Roquefort cheese, crumbled
1 1/2 cup piima cream or creme fraiche (page 84)
1 tablespoon expeller-expressed flax oil
2 tablespoons chives, chopped
2 tablespoons parsley, finely chopped
1 teaspoon naturally fermented soy sauce
1/4 teaspoon pepper

Mix all ingredients together. Serve with raw vegetable sticks or raw sugar snap peas.

HUMMUS
Makes 2 cups

2 cups basic chickpeas (page 505), cooked
3 cloves garlic, mashed
1/4 cup tahini
1 tablespoon expeller-expressed flax oil
1/2 cup fresh lemon juice
pinch of cayenne pepper

Using a slotted spoon, place cooked chickpeas in a food processor. Add remaining ingredients and process until smooth. The hummus should be creamy and not too thick. Add some of the cooking liquid if it needs thinning. Serve with vegetable sticks and pita chips (page 521).

VEGETABLE SALADS

When we lament the problems of the modern machine age, we sometimes lose sight of the many benefits industrialization confers. One of those blessings is the availability of a variety of fresh vegetables at all seasons of the year. Take advantage of this wonderful state of affairs—as unique in the history of mankind as the ubiquitous availability of junk food.

The key to a good salad is vegetables at the peak of freshness, cut up into small pieces, then dressed with a high enzyme dressing composed of raw ingredients—high quality oils, vinegar, lemon juice, whey, avocado and raw or cultured cream. Chopping or grating vegetables is the first step in the process of thorough digestion, leaving less for the teeth and digestive juices to do, and allowing more surface area of the vegetables to be coated with healthful dressing.

We encourage you to mix vegetables of several colors in your salads. Different colors in vegetables denote the presence of vitamins and minerals in different proportions. A salad that mixes green, white, orange, red and maroon vegetables ensures a full complement of nutrients.

Most vegetables in the salads we present here are raw, but we also include some that are steamed or blanched (cooked in boiling water). Light cooking actually makes the nutrients in some vegetables, such as asparagus and French beans, more available. And raw vegetables are not for everybody, especially those with delicate intestinal tracts. If salads give you problems, turn to soups as a way to consume a variety of fresh vegetables.

For those who tolerate cheese, we submit that the mixture of raw cheese with salad dressing containing flax oil is a synergistic one. According to some researchers, sulphur-containing proteins in cheese combined with omega-3 fatty acids in flax oil make an excellent combination for supporting a host of metabolic processes. Many imported cheeses, such as Roquefort and Parmesan, are made from raw milk. We especially recommend Roquefort cheese, made of sheep milk, as a good source of antimicrobial lauric acid.

Your salad should be a delight to the eye as well as to the taste buds. Take care to make an attractive presentation and use your imagination to create beautiful arrangements on the plate. Don't hesitate to use large plates for your salad course—the way the Europeans do—for a more elegant display. With the right presentation and the right ingredients, even inveterate salad haters will tuck into your offerings of raw vegetables.

The scourge of Asian countries is high rates of cancer of the stomach, oesophagus, pancreas and liver. Asians in their homelands suffer from these virtually untreatable cancers at twice the rate as Westerners. Large quantities of salt is one explanation put forward; another is the use of talc as an additive in rice. The National Cancer Institute studied eating habits in Shandong Province, a region of China with particularly high rates of stomach cancer. They found that those who eat about three ounces a day of garlic, onions, scallions and leeks are only 40 percent as likely to develop stomach cancer as those who eat only one ounce of the allium vegetables daily. SWF

It is a commonly held belief today that we have had a large increase in our fat intake over this century. What we have had, in fact, is a large increase in our intake of fats from vegetable sources, along with a substantial decrease in our fats from animal sources. At the same time, the amount of fat in our diets as a percent of calories has not changed that radically. Fat in the diets of Americans ranges from 30% to 43% of the calories depending on which survey you look at, and even in the 1890's the amount of fat in diets seems to have been this amount. The article on diets in the 1922 *Encyclopaedia Britannica* included information on 339 dietary surveys, of which 238 were done in the US. The highest level of fat intake reported was for American lumbermen at 43.6% of calories, closely followed by Danish physicians at 42.9% of calories. Except for inmates in "insane hospitals" in the US, who averaged 29.9% of the calories as fat, the average American family/adult ranged from 32.4% to 36.5% of calories as fat. Mary G. Enig, PhD *Know Your Fats*

ITALIAN SALAD
Serves 6

1 head romaine lettuce
1 bunch watercress, stems removed
1 red pepper, seeded and cut into a julienne
1 cucumber, peeled, seeded, quartered lengthwise and finely sliced
1 heart of celery with leaves, finely chopped
1 small red onion, finely sliced
1/2 cup small seed sprouts (page 115)
2 carrots, peeled and grated
1 cup red cabbage, finely shredded
1 cup basic chickpeas (page 505), cooked
3/4 cup basic or garlic dressing (page 129)

This is a good, basic salad. Children love it. The secret is to cut everything up small. Remove the outer leaves of the romaine, slice off the end and open up to rinse out any dirt or impurities, while keeping the head intact. Pat dry. Slice across at 1/2-inch intervals. Place romaine in a salad bowl and top with watercress and chopped vegetables in different piles. Finally strew the sprouts and garbanzo beans over the top for an attractive presentation. Bring to the table to show off your creation before tossing with dressing. May be served with grated Parmesan cheese.

Variation: Mexican Salad

Use *Mexican dressing* (page 132) rather than basic or garlic dressing. Omit chickpeas. Top with a *sprinkle of pepitas (page 513)*, or *thin strips of sprouted wheat tortillas, sautéed in olive oil or lard until crisp.*

CAESAR SALAD
Serves 6

2 large heads romaine lettuce
2 ounces freshly grated Parmesan cheese
1/2 cup salad croutons (page 520)
3/4 cup garlic, anchovy or Caesar dressing
(pages 129 and 133)

The secret of this recipe is the quality of the Parmesan cheese. Reggiano is best; Gran Padrino is also very good. For a much better taste than store-bought powdered Parmesan, buy it whole and grate it fresh when needed.

Remove outer leaves of the lettuce, slice off the end and open up to rinse out any dirt or impurities, while keeping the head intact. Pat dry and slice across at 1-inch intervals. Grate cheese using the large-holed side of the grater. Toss romaine and cheese with dressing of your choice. Add the croutons after tossing with the dressing—otherwise they absorb too much oil.

FRENCH STYLE CAESAR SALAD
(Salade D'Auvergne)
Serves 4

1 large head romaine lettuce
1 ounce freshly grated Parmesan cheese
1 cup salad croutons (page 520)
1/4 cup warmed crumpled duck cracklings
(page 295)
1 cup creamy dressing (page 131)

This is the traditional salad of the Auvergne region of France. It resembles a Caesar salad—and, in fact, it almost certainly is the precursor of the Caesar salad—differing in only the type of dressing used. Prepare as Caesar salad in the preceding recipe.

Some researchers believe a higher level of raw food in our diet is very advantageous. In one study, Douglass asked a group of persons with high blood pressure to add as much raw food to their diet as they conveniently could. After six and one-half months, raw food was providing approximately 62% of their daily caloric intake. He reported a statistically significant reduction in both high blood pressure and weight in those consuming much of their food raw. Eighty percent of those persons on the raw food diet also gave up smoking and alcohol spontaneously. Douglass cautioned against trying to consume an exclusively raw food diet, because fruitarians have died from various disease conditions including destruction of the heart muscle and total body edema. Chris Mudd *Cholesterol and Your Health*

Lettuce comes from the plant family that includes daisies and thistles. Romaine lettuce or *Cos* is derived from the word Roman. One of the most popular of numerous varieties of lettuce, it has been grown for thousands of years and was popular during Roman times—so the designation "Caesar salad" for a salad composed of Romaine lettuce is apt. American per capita consumption of lettuce of all types doubled from the 1940's to the 1970's.

Unfortunately, the most popular variety of lettuce—iceberg—is not one that we can recommend. Iceberg lettuce accumulates cadmium, a toxic metal, and rates poorly in nutrient content. But other lettuces provide carotene, B-complex vitamins, potassium, phosphorus and all-important silicon. Oriental medicine uses romaine lettuce in the treatment of alcoholism. SWF

Many thousands of words have been written about the value of raw versus cooked vegetables in the diet. The simplest rules to remember are that man and herbivorous animals must cook their vegetables in order to break down the cellulose (wood) box in which the vegetable cell is stored. Man uses heat; herbivorous animals use fermentation, for which they have separate stomachs. But to man, raw vegetables are also of great value, mainly for bulk and roughage as well as to keep the intestinal content from becoming too dry. The human intestinal tract is so constructed that roughage is needed for rapid elimination of waste products and, equally important, for keeping the muscles strong. It must be remembered, of course, that when the intestinal lining is catarrhal or inflamed, rough textured food often irritates or may even cause bleeding; hence, great discretion must be used with raw vegetables and fruits. Henry Bieler, MD *Food is Your Best Medicine*

Conventional wisdom touts high carbohydrate diets for athletes—pasta, potatoes, breads, fruit juices and carbohydrate-rich "energy" bars. But a new study out of State University of New York raises serious questions about the appropriateness of high-carb, low-fat diets for those who engage in strenuous physical exercise. Subjects ate diets of 15%, 30% and 45% fat respectively. Those on the high fat diets had greater endurance—up to an 11% increase. No adverse changes in blood chemistry were observed in the subjects on the high fat diet, and they did not gain weight. The authors of the study conclude: "The results suggest that a low fat diet may be detrimental to performance and that a

ANY LETTUCE SALAD
Serves 4

1 large head or 2 small heads of any lettuce such as Boston lettuce or red lettuce
1/2 cup walnut dressing (page 130)
2 tablespoons crispy walnuts (page 513), chopped
2 tablespoons freshly grated Parmesan cheese

Wash and dry lettuce. (See Kitchen Tips and Hints, page 70.) Toss with dressing and divide between four plates. Sprinkle on walnuts and cheese.

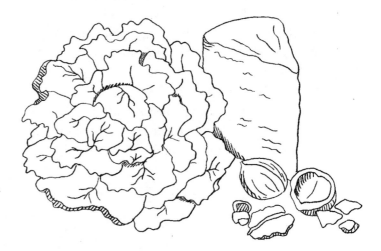

BABY SPINACH SALAD
Serves 4

6 cups baby spinach leaves
1 medium red onion, thinly sliced
1 orange, peeled and sectioned
1/2 cup crumbled Roquefort cheese
3/4 cup crispy pecans (page 513) chopped
2 tablespoons butter
1 tablespoon Rapadura (see page 536)
3/4 cup orange dressing (page 134)

Spinach leaves should be very small and fresh. Remove stems, wash and dry. (See Kitchen Tips and Hints, page 70.) Sauté pecans and Rapadura in butter. Mix all ingredients together, divide between four salad plates and serve.

WATERCRESS SALAD

Serves 4

2 *bunches watercress, stems removed*
2 *heads Belgium endive*
1 *head radicchio or 1/4 head red cabbage,*
   finely shredded
1 *small red onion, thinly sliced*
2 *tablespoons crispy pine nuts (page 514)*
3/4 *cup balsamic dressing (page 130)*
   or blue cheese dressing (page 133)

Wash and dry watercress. (See Kitchen Tips and Hints, page 70.) Remove outer leaves of endive and slice at 1/4-inch intervals. Mix all ingredients with dressing and divide between four plates.

MESCLUN SALAD

Serves 4

6 *cups mesclun greens*
3/4 *cup balsamic or walnut dressing*
   (page 130)
1 *tablespoon crispy pine nuts (page 514)*
1/4 *pound Roquefort cheese (optional)*
8 *round croutons (page 520), optional*

Mesclun is a mixture of tender baby lettuces and herbs, which is becoming widely available in many gourmet and health food stores across the country. It is almost always organic. Mesclun salad can be served at the beginning of the meal, as a side dish to fish or meat, or as a gourmet salad course, with cheese and croutons, coming after the main course and before dessert.

If salad is not prewashed, wash, rinse and dry. (See Kitchen Tips and Hints, page 70.) Mix greens with pine nuts and dressing and divide between four large plates. Garnish each plate with slice of Roquefort cheese and two croutons.

Variation:

Use 3/4 *cup roasted tomato dressing* (page 131) in place of walnut or balsamic dressing. Omit pine nuts.

higher fat diet may result in more energy substrate availability with a lower lactate to pyruvate ratio."

In another recent study, this time in South Africa, trained cyclists on a diet of just seven percent carbohydrate were compared to those who "carb loaded" on a diet of 74% carbohydrates. The low-carb cyclists could pedal almost twice as long as their high-carb opponents

The primary nutrient in animal fats is vitamin A, needed for a host of biological processes including the assimilation of protein and minerals. Strenuous physical exercise depletes vitamin A. Does the current practice of high-carb, low-fat diets explain the prevalence of injury and burnout in modern athletes? *PPNF Health Journal*

Watercress is one of the most delicious of the dark green leafy vegetables, with a peppery, mustard-like flavor. It grows in shallow streams of clear running water. Watercress is rich in essential fatty acids, chlorophyll, carotenoids and many beneficial minerals including iron, sulphur, calcium, iodine and vanadium. Folk medicine values watercress for a variety of ailments including anemia, poor circulation, edema and inflammation. Iodine and vanadium in watercress aid in the formation of red blood corpuscles. Watercress is 20 times richer in vanadium than mother's milk. Raw watercress juice is said to have the property of removing the brown coating that tobacco smoke leaves on the lungs. SWF

Lamb's lettuce, or *mache*, is the queen of salad greens. Every vegetable merchant in France carries *mache*, but it is hard to find in America. If you live in a big city, you can buy *mache* from a wholesaler or restaurant supply merchant. A few specialty markets are now carrying *mache* in smaller plastic containers. It comes with tender green leaves still attached to their dirt plugs so they stay fresh for up to two weeks. Like all dark green vegetables, *mache* is rich in carotenoids, essential fatty acids and minerals. SWF

Belgium endive is a member of the chicory family, bred to produce edible leaves, rather than edible roots. Whiteness of the leaves is achieved by etiolation—that is, dirt is piled up around the plant as it grows upwards to keep the leaves from turning green. With its distinctive crispness and wonderful bitter taste, characteristic of all members of the chicory family, Belgium endive is a versatile vegetable for the gourmet cook. SWF

LAMB'S LETTUCE SALAD
Serves 4

3-4 cups lamb's lettuce leaves
2 heads Belgium endive
1 medium head radicchio, finely shredded
1 tablespoon crispy pine nuts (page 514)
3/4 cup balsamic dressing (page 130)

Remove outer leaves of endive and cut at 1/4-inch intervals. Toss lamb's lettuce, endive, radicchio and pine nuts with dressing. Divide between four plates. If you are serving this as a salad course between the main dish and dessert, you may wish to garnish each plate with a slice of Roquefort cheese and round croutons (page 520).

ENDIVE SALAD
Serves 4

6-8 large heads Belgium endive
l bunch cilantro, chopped
l bunch green onions, finely chopped
1/2 head radicchio, finely shredded (optional)
2 tablespoons parsley, finely chopped
1 tablespoon crispy pine nuts (page 514)
3/4 cup balsamic dressing (page 130)
1/2 cup crumbled Roquefort cheese

Remove outer leaves of endive and discard. Remove several leaves from each head and arrange around the outside of the plates, tapered ends pointing outward. Slice remaining endive at 1/4-inch intervals. Mix vegetables and pine nuts with dressing and mound in the center of the endive leaves. Garnish with cheese. Serve immediately.

Variation: Endive Salad Platter
For parties, arrange endive leaves around outside of a platter. Mound salad in middle and serve crumbled Roquefort cheese on the side.

FENNEL SALAD

Serves 6

6-8 medium fennel bulbs plus leaves
3/4 cup lemon pepper dressing (page 134)
6 ounces good quality Parmesan cheese

Remove outer leaves of fennel, slice very thinly. and cut slices into quarters. Snip 2 tablespoons fennel leaves into a bowl. Mix with the fennel slices and dressing. Arrange on six plates and top each salad with shavings of Parmesan cheese, cut with a cheese slicer.

RADICCHIO AND ORANGE SALAD

Serves 4

3 large heads radicchio, finely shredded
2 oranges, peeled and divided into sections
2 red onions, thinly sliced
about 1/4 cup extra virgin olive oil
3/4 cup orange dressing (page 134)

Place onions on an oiled cookie sheet and brush with olive oil. Bake at 300 degrees for several hours until onions are dried out and browned. Mix radicchio with dressing and divide between four plates. Top with orange wedges and grilled onion slices. Serve at once.

TOMATO-CROUTON SALAD

Serves 4

4 medium ripe tomatoes, peeled, seeded and chopped
sea salt
2 cups salad croutons (page 520)
1/4 cup basil, finely cut up
3/4 cup basic or balsamic dressing (page 129)

To peel tomatoes, see page 70. Toss tomatoes with sea salt and let drain in a colander about 1 hour. Mix all ingredients and serve immediately.

Europeans have used radicchio for years, but this fine vegetable is only now making its way into American cuisine. A member of the chicory family, it is a good source of vitamin C and carotenes; it is also high in calcium. The vegetable is now available year round. Select heads that are firm and fresh looking. Radicchio will keep for up to two weeks in the refrigerator. SWF

Evidence is submitted indicating that a comprehensive test of the capacity of the animal organism to endure on an enzyme-free diet requires exclusion of exogenous enzymes gaining entrance through the agency of airborne bacteria, yeasts and fungi. The efficiency of these unicellular organisms as enzyme producers has been widely demonstrated in industrial processes. There are good grounds for believing that the enzyme-deficient animal organism reluctantly offers a culturing abode to bacteria, yeasts and fungi with the object of confiscating their enzymes. The evidence warrants a strong suspicion that the unnatural appropriateness of enzyme-deficient organisms for exogenous enzymes may invoke bacterial activity of intractable magnitude and engender susceptibility to infections. Due consideration should be accorded these factors in accounting for the widespread incidence of bacterial diseases. Edward Howell, MD *Food Enzymes for Health and Longevity*

Lycopene, a chemical similar to carotene, gives the red tint to tomatoes, watermelon, strawberries, pink grapefruit, paprika, rose hips and palm oil. It has no vitamin A activity but may offer protection against cancer. A Johns Hopkins University study found that pancreatic cancer victims had low levels of lycopene. Those with the least lycopene in their bloodstreams were five times more likely to develop pancreatic cancer than those with the highest levels. SWF

Parenthetically speaking, cooking foods above 118 degrees Fahrenheit destroys digestive enzymes. When this happens, the pancreas, salivary glands, stomach and intestines must all come to the rescue and furnish digestive enzymes. . . to break down all these substances. To do this repeatedly, the body must rob, so to speak, enzymes from the other glands, muscles, nerves and the blood to help in its demanding digestive process. Eventually the glands—and this includes the pancreas—develop deficiencies of enzymes because they have been forced to work harder due to the low level of enzymes found in cooked food. . . . Your chances therefore of not putting a burden on your pancreas are better if you eat as much raw food as possible. William H. Philpott, MD *Victory Over Diabetes*

TOMATO PLATTER

Serves 4-6

4 ripe tomatoes
2 cucumbers, peeled and thinly sliced
1 small red onion, finely sliced
1 head Belgian endive (optional)
2 tablespoons cilantro or basil, chopped
1 ripe avocado
1/2 cup black olives
6 tablespoons extra virgin olive oil
2 tablespoons raw wine vinegar
1 large lemon
cracked pepper to taste
1 cup feta cheese, cut into small pieces

This is a delightful and refreshing first course during the summer months.

Remove the outer leaves of endive, cut off end and separate into leaves. Make a fan of endive leaves at one end of a large, flat platter. Slice tomatoes very thinly and arrange around the outside edge the platter. Strew cucumbers in the center of the tomato ring. Arrange sliced onions over the tomatoes. Strew olives over salad. Dribble the olive oil over all, dribble on vinegar, then squeeze on lemon juice and sprinkle with pepper. Sprinkle on cilantro or basil. Leave the platter at room temperature at least one hour. Just before serving, peel and slice the avocado, brush with a little oil and vinegar in the platter to keep from browning and arrange on the platter. Scatter the feta cheese over the tomatoes and serve.

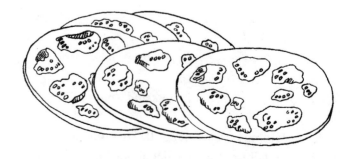

TOMATO CORN SALAD

Serves 4-6

4 ripe tomatoes, peeled, seeded and chopped
3 ears fresh corn, cut off the cob
1 red onion, finely chopped
1 jalapeno pepper, seeded and chopped
1 small bunch basil leaves, chopped
3 tablespoons extra virgin olive oil
1 tablespoon balsamic vinegar
sea salt and pepper
romaine or Boston lettuce leaves

To peel tomatoes, see page 70. Combine tomato, corn, onion, pepper and basil with vinegar and olive oil. Season to taste. Cover salad and refrigerate for several hours. Serve on large lettuce leaves.

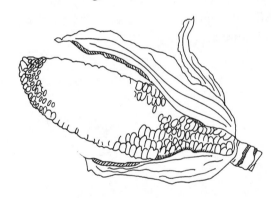

TOMATO CUCUMBER SALAD

Serves 6

3 ripe tomatoes, peeled, seeded and chopped
2 cucumbers, peeled, cut lengthwise into
    quarters, seeded and sliced
1 red pepper, seeded and cut into a julienne
1/2 red onion, thinly sliced
3/4 cup basic or herb dressing (page 129)

To peel tomatoes, see page 70. Mix all ingredients. Chill well before serving.

About 25 years ago, doctors at Michael Reese Hospital in Chicago undertook some rather exhaustive investigations on the enzyme content of the saliva, pancreatic secretions and blood of human subjects including the very old. They found that most of the enzymes became weaker with advancing age. The doctors. . . found in older persons the enzyme lipase was low, with slow fat absorption from the intestine. They speculated that in hardening of the arteries, fat may be absorbed in the unhydrolyzed state. Lipase extracted from the animal pancreas was fed to both young and old subjects. Following use of the enzyme there was definite improvement in the character of fat utilization. There is evidence. . . that indicates that when fats, whether animal or vegetable, are eaten along with their associated enzymes, no harmful effect on the arteries or heart results. No atherosclerosis comes about. All fatty foods contain lipase in their natural state. Cooking or processing removes it. I have found there is no evidence of heart or blood vessel disease among wild animals consuming large quantities of fat. There is no evidence of these afflictions in whole nations of people eating foods containing fat when taken raw. Millions of wild creatures eat animal fats without suffering ill effects from cholesterol. Many different civilizations throughout history used large amounts of raw milk, cream, butter and cheese and maintained a high standard of health, comparatively free from cardiovascular impairment due to cholesterol deposits. Edward Howell, MD *Enzyme Nutrition*

It the 1960's, the Japanese discovered a substance that inhibits cholesterol production. Animal studies revealed that the compound was highly toxic so the Japanese wisely concluded it had no medical use. They sold their discovery to Merck, the American drug company, which received FDA approval for the substance with uncharacteristic speed. The Merck drug is now known as Mevacor and similar products are sold by other companies as Lovastatin, Pravastatin, Fluvastatin and Simvastatin. Side effects include liver damage, reduced libido, slowed reactions, cancer, stroke, intestinal diseases, depression, antisocial behavior, accidents and suicide. Cholesterol-lowering drugs block the body's production of Coenzyme Q10, needed for normal function of the heart. In short, these drugs make people old and grumpy but so pervasive is the anti-cholesterol propaganda that Americans are willing to pay sixty billion dollars for the stuff every year. SWF

Healthy fats and oils are the ones that don't oxidize readily; those fats and oils that are oxidized are either not available for use as energy or for structural purposes because they are in a polymerized unusable form, or they contain toxic components. Naturally occurring fats and oils that have been consumed for thousands of years are invariably found to be the more saturated animal and plant fats. The more readily oxidizable oils have historically been consumed in their original packaging—seeds and plants— and have not contributed to oxidized products. Mary G. Enig, PhD *Know Your Fats*

LATIN AMERICAN TOMATO SALAD
(Chismole)
Serves 4-6

4 large ripe tomatoes, diced
1 medium onion, finely chopped
juice of 2 lemons
1 bunch cilantro, chopped
1 teaspoon dried oregano

This salad comes from Central America and is traditionally served with beans. It makes a synergistic garnish for black bean tostados (page 425) and other South-of-the-Border fare. But this refreshing mixture stands on its own, or goes well with such Yankee food as roast beef and potato salad.

Mix all ingredients. Cover and let stand at least 1 hour before serving.

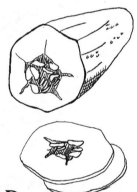

INDIAN SALAD
Serves 4

3 large tomatoes, peeled, seeded and chopped
1 bunch green onions, finely chopped
1 cucumber, peeled, seeded and finely chopped
1 bunch cilantro, chopped
1 tablespoon freshly grated ginger
1 jalapeno pepper, seeded and chopped
juice of 2 lemons

To peel tomatoes, see page 70. Mix all ingredients. Cover and refrigerate for several hours. Serve on lettuce leaves or as an accompaniment to Indian dishes.

INDIAN YOGHURT SALAD

(Raita)
Serves 6

2 cucumbers, peeled, seeded and finely chopped
sea salt
1 red or green pepper, seeded and finely chopped
1 small red onion, peeled and finely chopped
2 cups plain whole yoghurt (page 85)
1/2 teaspoon cumin seeds, toasted in the oven

Place chopped cucumbers in a colander and mix with sea salt. Let stand for an hour or so. Pat cucumbers dry and mix with other ingredients. This is traditionally served with curries and spicy food.

When the sugar in milk, lactose, is turned into lactic acid by bacterial action, it functions as a digestive antiseptic and makes the calcium and phosphorus in milk products more available for absorption and use by the body. When the population of lactic bacteria in the intestine is increased . . . synthesis of vitamin B_6 is improved, which promotes the production of niacin (vitamin B_3) from the amino acid tryptophan. This nutrient enhancement supports the immune system and improves host resistance. William H. Lee, PhD *The Friendly Bacteria*

VARIETY SALAD

Serves 4

4 medium carrots, peeled and grated
1 cucumber, peeled, quartered and finely sliced
1 red pepper, seeded and cut into a julienne
        or 1 large tomato, peeled, seeded and chopped
1/4 head red cabbage, finely shredded
1 teaspoon parsley, finely chopped
3/4 cup basic dressing (page 129)

This is a simple salad that makes an attractive presentation. The different vegetables are arranged in little piles on large plates. Children who are often picky about eating several foods mixed together like this salad because each vegetable is separate. And they like the different colors—white, orange, red and maroon and green.

Mix carrots, cucumber, red cabbage and pepper or tomato separately with a portion of dressing. Put four piles, one of each vegetable, on large plates. Sprinkle with parsley. Serve immediately.

Carotenes are what give orange and yellow vegetables their color. In green vegetables they are masked by the green color of chlorophyll. Animals and humans convert carotenes to vitamin A, but the carotenes themselves have many functions. Beta carotene, the most active of several carotene compounds, has been shown to boost the immune system and to fight against cancer.

We need to get betacarotene from the foods we eat—carrots, squash, sweet potatoes, orange fruits, green leafy vegetables—because synthetic betacarotene has adverse effects when used in human studies. Carotenes are more available in foods that have been chopped, grated, cooked or puréed. Only about 5 percent of carotene is absorbed from eating a raw carrot. Cooking makes 25 percent to 30 percent of carotenes available, and puréeing allows the body to absorb 50 percent. SWF

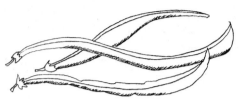

In certain Eastern and European esoteric healing traditions, the body is characterized as cyclically passing through three distinct phases: cleansing, building and sustaining. . . . Different nutritional systems enhance one particular phase more than others, sometimes in dramatic fashion. For example, a raw foods diet steers the body into a cleansing state, causing the breakdown of diseased tissues and the release of stored toxins. If you undertake a raw foods diet while the body is already in a cleansing state, or ready to move into one (for instance in the early spring when we naturally shed excess fatty tissue accumulated in the winter), the diet may have profound effects. Illness and pains may vanish, stores of energy be released and a wonderful clarity of mind appear.

Those who have this experience correctly perceive the healing effect of the diet but often incorrectly conclude that the diet works all the time and for all bodies. . . . What is more, many people who follow a year-round raw foods regimen meet with relative success because they live in hot weather or tropical locations like Hawaii, Florida, or Southern California—environments that naturally support the cleansing process. Try eating raw fruits and vegetables for twelve months in Montana and you will learn firsthand why it does not always work.
Marc David *Nourishing Wisdom*

VARIETY SALAD FOR GROWN-UPS
Serves 6

1/2 pound French beans, ends removed
*   and cut into 1-inch pieces*
2 heads fennel, sliced very thin
2 red peppers, seeded and cut into a julienne
about 1/2 cup extra virgin olive oil
sea salt and pepper
1 cup anchovy paste (page 143)

Plunge beans into boiling water for about 8 minutes or until tender. Pour into a colander and rinse with cold water. Toss each vegetable separately with olive oil and season to taste. Chill well. Arrange a pile of beans, of fennel and of peppers on each of six plates and place a generous spoonful of anchovy paste in the center.

FRENCH BEAN SALAD
Serves 4

1 pound French beans, ends removed
1 medium red onion, finely sliced
2 tomatoes
4 tablespoons crispy pecans (page 513), chopped
3/4 cup basic dressing (page 129)

This elegant and unusual salad features tender French beans or *haricots verts*, not to be confused with string beans. Remove ends from beans and plunge into boiling water. Cook for about 8 minutes until beans are tender. Pour into a colander and rinse with cold water. Let drain and cool.

Slice tomatoes thinly and cut slices in half. Arrange the slices around the outer edge of four plates. Place beans in the center and sprinkle with onions and chopped pecans. Spoon on dressing and serve.

RAINBOW SALAD

Serves 6

2 fennel bulbs
2 heads Belgium endive
1/4 head red cabbage, shredded
2 large carrots, grated
1 red pepper, seeded and cut into thin strips
1 cucumber, peeled, cut lengthwise into quarters
*   and thinly sliced*
1 heart of celery with leaves, finely chopped
1 small red onion, finely sliced
1 bunch cilantro, chopped
1 tablespoon crispy pine nuts (page 514)
3/4 cup balsamic dressing (page 130)
1 avocado, thinly sliced
1 tomato, cut into wedges
1/4 pound Roquefort cheese (optional), crumbled

The basis of this substantial salad is fennel and the secret to its success is to cut the vegetables up very small.

Remove outer leaves from fennel bulbs, slice very finely and cut slices into quarters. Remove outer leaves of endive and slice across at 1/4-inch intervals. Toss fennel, cabbage, Belgium endive, carrots, pepper, cucumber, celery, red onion, cilantro and pine nuts with dressing. Divide between six plates and decorate with thin slices of avocado and tomato. Garnish with crumbled Roquefort cheese.

Most people do not seem to have a large variance of vitamins and minerals over the years. However, the enzyme levels drop significantly in aging; as the body gets weaker and the enzymes get fewer, old age symptoms manifest. At the world famous Michael Reese Hospital in Chicago, researchers found that old people have only one-thirtieth as much enzymes in the saliva as young folks. Also people with high enzyme diets have extensive longevity patterns. For example, people like Georgians, Equadorans, and Hunzas have a diet rich in enzymes and have a high concentration of centenarians. They make extensive use of fermentation—soy, dairy, vegetables and fruits. Also, they utilize sprouting as well as soaking of seeds, which increases the enzyme level up to twenty times, and raw or undercooked food. They also fast seasonally during periods of food scarcity. . . during fasting there is a halt in digestive enzyme production. The enzymes are used to digest the partially digested stored food of fatty tissue, scars, arthritis, tumors, hardening of the arteries, etc. Thu, the enforced fast is another health and longevity promoting benefit. Victoras Kulvinskas *Introduction to Food Enzymes for Health and Longevity*

ASPARAGUS VINAIGRETTE

Serves 4

24 spears medium-sized asparagus
3/4 cup sun dried tomato dressing (page 130)

Wash asparagus and trim green skin off about one inch of the ends. Steam in a vegetable steamer until just tender. Divide between four plates and spoon dressing over.

In order to evaluate the status of food enzymes in normal nutrition and metabolism, [it is important] to learn the condition of health of animals reared under aseptic conditions, given sterile food with the usual sterile vitamin accessories, and allowed to drink only sterile water and breathe only sterile air. Just such an experiment has been in progress at the Laboratories of Bacteriology, University of Notre Dame, for the past 12 years, during which time more than 2,000 germ-free guinea pigs, as well as germ-free chicks, rats, mice, rabbits, cats and insects, were born and reared under rigidly aseptic conditions. . . . Sterility of the intestinal tract during the lifetime of the animal is assured by frequent tests for bacteria. . . [the] sterile animals often grow to unusual size but very few of them are healthy. It is stated their digestive tracts are "delicate" and they apparently lack something which germs could furnish them. . . sterile animals are on the whole a little more susceptible to infectious diseases than animals raised normally, and a great many organic diseases show up in germ-free animals. Edward Howell, MD *Food Enzymes for Health and Longevity*

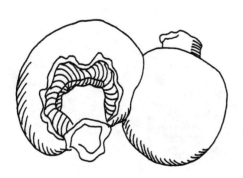

SUMMER SALAD
Serves 6

3/4 cup lemon pepper dressing (page 134)
1 bunch celery, finely chopped
2 cucumbers, peeled, quartered lengthwise
*   and finely chopped*
2 bunches green onions, finely chopped
2 green peppers, seeded and finely chopped
1 bunch radishes, finely chopped
3 tomatoes
1 tablespoon parsley or chives, finely chopped

This salad may be prepared several hours in advance of your meal. The secret to its success is, as always, to cut the vegetables into a fine dice.

Prepare the dressing in a large bowl. Add celery, cucumbers, green onions, peppers and radishes. Toss well with dressing, cover and refrigerate several hours.

Just before serving, slice the tomatoes thinly and cut the slices in half. Arrange the slices around the outer edge of six plates and make a mound of salad in the center of each. Sprinkle with chopped parsley or chives.

MUSHROOM SALAD
Serves 4

12 medium mushrooms
l bunch green onions, finely chopped
l bunch cilantro, chopped
3/4 cup lemon pepper dressing (page 134)

This salad is very rich—three mushrooms per person will suffice. The mushrooms must be very fresh.

Have your dressing ready in a mixing bowl. Remove stems from mushrooms, wash and dry well with paper towels. Slice very thinly. Mix immediately with dressing, green onions and cilantro. Divide between four plates and serve.

GELATIN SALAD MOLD
Serves 6

1 tablespoon gelatin (See Sources)
1/2 cup cold water
1 cup boiling water
1-2 tablespoons raw honey
1/2 teaspoon sea salt
1/4 cup lemon juice
1 cup carrots, grated
1 1/2 cups finely shredded cabbage
1/2 pepper, green or red, seeded and finely sliced

Place cabbage in a strainer and dip into boiling water for 1 minute. Drain well. Mix with carrots and pepper and strew into a 4-cup ring mold. Soften gelatin in cold water. Add boiling water and dissolve thoroughly. Add honey, salt and lemon juice and pour mixture into mold. Chill until firm. To unmold, dip briefly in hot water.

Variation: Gelatin Cabbage and Apple Mold

Omit carrots and pepper. Add *1 1/2 cups chopped apples* and *1/3 cup chopped crispy walnuts (page 513)*.

CARROT-COCONUT MOLD
Serves 6

1 tablespoon gelatin (See Sources)
1/2 cup cold water
1 cup boiling water
1-2 tablespoons raw honey
1/2 teaspoon sea salt
1/4 cup freshly squeezed orange juice
2 cups carrots, grated
1 cup dried unsweetened coconut meat, finely cut
1 teaspoon freshly grated ginger
1/2 cup chopped crispy pecans (page 513).

Mix carrots, coconut, ginger and pecans and strew into a 4-cup ring mold. Soften gelatin in cold water. Add boiling water and dissolve thoroughly. Add honey, salt and orange juice and pour mixture into mold. Chill until firm. To unmold, dip briefly in hot water.

In 490 BC the Greeks defeated the Persians in a battle that was fought in a fennel field. Thus, one of the most famous battles in history was named after a vegetable. A runner raced 26 miles to carry news of the victory to Athens. The word for fennel in Greek is *marathon.*

A member of the anise family, fennel is as common in Mediterranean markets as celery and carrots are in ours. The stalks form a kind of false bulb that has many of the properties of celery. In fact, fennel can be used in place of celery in a variety of recipes. Fennel is a good source of carotenes and is said to help in weight reduction. SWF

Some intriguing experiments were performed on normal people and diabetics . . . at George Washington University Hospital in 1929. The subjects ate almost two ounces of raw starch and then had blood tests for sugar. Eating cooked starch, as is well known, causes the blood sugar of diabetics to skyrocket, unless they use insulin. The diabetics in the study used no insulin, and yet after raw starch ingestion the blood sugar rose only 6 milligrams the first half hour. Then it decreased 9 milligrams after 1 hour and 14 milligrams 2 1/2 hours after ingestion of the raw starch. In some diabetic individuals, the decrease in blood sugar was as much as 35 milligrams. In the normal persons, there was a slight increase followed by a slight decrease in blood sugar in 1 hour. This is convincing evidence that there is a difference between raw and cooked calories. Edward Howell, MD *Enzyme Nutrition*

> No man will be satisfied for any length of time with a nourishment that tastes and smells of nothing, regardless of how rich it is in proteins, vitamins and trace elements.
> *Rudolf Steiner*

Trans fatty acids that are products mainly of partial hydrogenation of vegetable oils were introduced into human foods in the U.S .beginning in 1910, and greatly increased amounts of partially hydrogenated vegetable fat products were added to human diets in the U.S. beginning in the 1950's. Although the *trans* fatty acids were ignored during the early decades of their use, they became a focus of concern for a few researchers beginning in the 1950's, and since 1990 they have been a prominent topic in the biomedical and fats and oils literature as researchers around the world continued to ask hard questions about the problematic effects *trans* fatty acids in the diet have on physiological functions. Many of these researchers have recently published their findings as they gradually unraveled the mechanisms responsible for the adverse effects related to heart disease, cancer, diabetes, immune dysfunction, obesity, low birth-weight and lactation deficits. Mary G. Enig, PhD *Know Your Fats*

DILLED POTATO SALAD
Serves 8

16 small red potatoes
2 red onions, finely chopped
1 bunch fresh dill, snipped
3-4 tablespoons raw wine vinegar
1 1/4 cups creamy mayonnaise dressing
    (page 132)

Wash potatoes but do not peel. Bring a large pot of water to boil. Plunge in the potatoes and cook until still slightly firm. Remove with slotted spoon.

While potatoes are still warm, cut lengthwise into quarters, slice thinly and toss with vinegar. Mix with onions and dill and toss with dressing. Add salt and pepper to taste. (Note: Potatoes require more salt than most vegetables.)

FRENCH POTATO SALAD
Serves 8

16 small red potatoes
2 green peppers, seeded and cut into a julienne
2 red peppers, seeded and cut into a julienne
1 large red onion, chopped
3-4 tablespoons raw red wine vinegar
3/4-1 1/4 cups basic dressing (page 129)

Wash potatoes but do not peel. Bring a large pot of water to the boil. Plunge in the potatoes and cook until still slightly firm. Remove with slotted spoon.

While potatoes are still warm, cut lenghtwise into quarters, slice finely and toss with vinegar. Mix with peppers and onions and toss with dressing. Add salt and pepper to taste. (Note: Potatoes require more salt than most vegetables.)

MAGGIE'S POTATO SALAD

Serves 8

8 yellow potatoes, preferably Yukon gold variety
1 small head celery, finely chopped
1 cucumber, peeled, seeded and finely chopped
1 red onion, finely chopped
1 bunch radishes, finely chopped
2 tablespoons celery seeds
1 1/4 cup creamy mayonnaise dressing (page 132)
1 tomato

In this recipe, celery seeds, rather than mustard and pickles, provide a pleasant tart taste that combines so well with starchy potatoes.

Peel potatoes and cook in boiling water until still slightly firm. (Save potato peels for potassium broth, page 607.) Cut into a 1/2-inch dice. Mix with vegetables, celery seeds and dressing. Season with salt and pepper. Garnish with tomato wedges.

CELERY ROOT SALAD

(Celeriac Roumelade)
Serves 4

1 large celery root
1/4 cup lemon juice
1/2-3/4 cup creamy mayonnaise dressing (page 132)

The French enjoy this salad with cold meats and sausage. It makes a nice accompaniment to cold roast beef.

Bring a pot of filtered water to boil and add lemon juice. Meanwhile, peel the celery root. Use a food processor to grate or make a julienne of the celery root and immediately plunge it into boiling water. After about 10 seconds, pour into a colander and rinse with cold water. Shake or pat dry and mix with dressing. Refrigerate several hours before serving.

These facts suggest clearly that the enzymes present in raw, uncooked food relieve the pancreas and salivary glands of the necessity of enlarging from excess work. The considerable hypertrophy of the pancreas and salivary glands, which has been found to occur in human races living upon large quantities of cooked carbohydrates, indicates the nature of the intrepid but deplorable compensatory measure the organism is forced to adopt and is added proof of the profound influence for good of enzymes naturally supplied in raw foods. That the pancreas and salivary glands of human beings living upon the customary heat-treated enzyme deficient diet are hypertrophied and overworked organs is not difficult to believe. Those races subsisting largely upon heat-treated carbohydrates appear to have the largest pancreatic and salivary glands. Thus, Stisen has shown that the pancreas of Malays of Java has an average weight of 105 grams, while the average weight of the American pancreas is about 20 grams less. And this in spite of the fact that Americans average some 20 or 30 pounds heavier in body weight than Javanese. Stisen observed that other organs are heavier in Occidental than in Malays, excepting the pancreas and salivary glands which alone are heavier in Malays. He attributes the large pancreas and salivary glands of Malays to a diet rich in carbohydrates. Edward Howell, MD *Food Enzymes for Health and Longevity*

We experience the living relationship of macrocosm to microcosm in our tasting.
Rudolf Steiner

The idea that too much animal fat and a high cholesterol is dangerous to your heart and vessels is nothing but a myth. . . . Cholesterol is not a deadly poison, but a substance vital to the cells of all mammals. There are no such things as good or bad cholesterol, but mental stress, physical activity and change of body weight may influence the level of blood cholesterol. A high cholesterol is not dangerous by itself, but may reflect an unhealthy condition, or it may be totally innocent. Uffe Ravnskov, MD, PhD *The Cholesterol Myths*

Glutathione is a tripeptide—a substance composed of three amino acids—containing cysteine, glutamic acid and glycine, which can serve as both a hydrogen acceptor and a hydrogen donor. It acts as an antioxidant and can inactivate cancer-causing agents that may damage cells. It also seems to neutralize rancid, oxidized fats that initiate the artery-clogging process.

Glutathione is found at very high concentrations in the lens of the eye, where it protects the lens from the destructive effects of ultraviolet light. As an antioxidant, glutathione protects against cataracts.

Green leafy vegetables, such as broccoli, parsley and spinach, are rich sources of glutathione—yet another reason to eat your greens. From 30 percent to 60 percent of glutathione is lost during cooking and up to 100 percent in canning. Raw parsley is probably the best source of glutathione as raw spinach has substances that block calcium absorption, and raw broccoli contains goitrogens, substances that block thyroid function. SWF

ORIENTAL CELERY ROOT SALAD
Serves 4

1 medium celery root
2-3 carrots, peeled and grated
1 red pepper, seeded and cut into a julienne
1 bunch green onions, finely chopped
2 tablespoons cilantro, chopped
1 cup Oriental dressing (page 135)

Peel and grate celery root and immediately mix with dressing. Stir in remaining ingredients. Chill well before serving.

TABOULI
(Parsley Salad)
Serves 8

1/2 cup bulgur (page 460)
3 bunches parsley, washed and well dried
2 bunches green onions, finely chopped
3 tomatoes, peeled, seeded and chopped
1/2 cup fresh mint leaves, cut up finely
*   with scissors (optional)*
1/2 cup or more lemon juice
1/2 cup or more extra virgin olive oil

This middle eastern salad makes a wonderful buffet dish. Soak bulgur for about 10 minutes in warm—not hot—water. Pour into a strainer, rinse and squeeze dry with your hands.

To wash and dry parsley and peel tomatoes, see page 70. Chop parsley finely in batches using a food processor. Mix all ingredients. Cover and refrigerate several hours before serving.

SPROUT SALAD
Serves 4

6 cups fresh mung bean sprouts (page 114)
1 bunch green onions, finely chopped
1 tablespoon sesame seeds, toasted in oven
1/2 cup Oriental dressing (page 135)

Steam sprouts for about 1 minute or until just tender. Let cool. Mix all ingredients. Divide between four plates and serve.

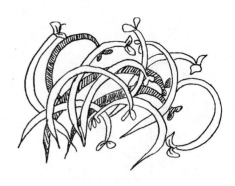

HIGH ENZYME SALAD
Serves 4

1 cup sprouted sunflower seeds (page 115)
4 carrots, peeled and grated
1 cucumber, peeled and finely chopped
1 red pepper, seeded and finely chopped
1 bunch green onions, finely chopped
2 ounces grated raw Cheddar cheese (optional)
3/4 cup basic dressing (page 129)
1 avocado, sliced
radicchio or red lettuce leaves

This salad is a meal in itself. Mix sprouted sunflower seeds, carrots, cucumber, pepper, onions and cheese with dressing. Serve on radicchio or lettuce leaves and garnish with avocado slices.

Organic gardeners, in my opinion, are way ahead of pill-popping users of nutritional supplements—at least synergistically speaking. That's because eating carrots—an excellent source of betacarotene—is probably superior to taking betacarotene alone; eating collard greens—which contain lots of vitamin C—is probably better than taking vitamin C alone (yes, even natural vitamin C); and eating endive—a good source of vitamin E—is probably better than taking natural vitamin E in capsules. And the superiorities of which I speak are not due to nonrelated beneficial characteristics (like the fiber in carrots) of the whole food. Nope. I mean that eating a carrot that contains a fixed amount of the cancer-fighting nutrient betacarotene will probably provide more cancer-fighting betacarotene nutritional benefit than taking the same fixed amount of betacarotene in the purest, most concentrated, most natural betacarotene supplement you can find. Why? Synergy. Jim Duke, PhD
Organic Gardening July/August 1995

CARROT SALAD
Serves 6

12 medium carrots, peeled and grated
1 cup fresh pineapple, drained and chopped
1/2 cup raisins
1/2 cup crispy pecans (page 513), chopped
1 tablespoon parsley (optional), finely chopped
3/4 cup basic dressing (page 129)

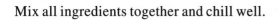

Mix all ingredients together and chill well.

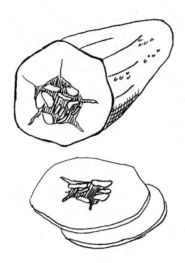

Good quality milk products are very hard to find in American markets these days. Even so-called organic milk products may come from cows kept in barns and given inappropriate feed, such as soybean meal. Biodynamic farmers have come to the rescue by providing milk products from pasture-fed cows, usually in the form of delicious, naturally produced whole milk yoghurt. Several brands of biodynamic yoghurt are available in health food stores and gourmet markets.

The fermentation of milk to make yoghurt renders milk's nutrients more available to adults. Yoghurt aids digestion and prevents constipation. The *lactobacilli*, lactic acid and enzymes that it provides protect against infection-causing bacteria, including salmonella, which causes food poisoning, and *E. coli*, bacteria often responsible for traveler's diarrhea. Some studies now show that yoghurt can protect against colon cancer. SWF

BALSAMIC CARROT SALAD
Serves 10-12

1 pound carrots, peeled and
  processed into a small julienne
1 heart of celery, chopped very fine
2 red peppers, seeded and cut into small slices
2 bunches green onions, chopped
1 bunch cilantro, chopped
1 1/2 cups balsamic dressing (page 130)

This makes an excellent buffet salad. Mix all ingredients well.

JICAMA SALAD
Serves 4

1 large jicama (about 1 1/4 pounds)
seeds from 1 pomegranate
3/4 cup cilantro lime dressing or
  Mexican dressing (page 132)

Peel and grate jicama. Mix immediately with dressing. Chill well. Add pomegranate seeds and serve.

CUCUMBER YOGHURT SALAD
Serves 6

3 cucumbers
1 teaspoon sea salt
3/4 cup plain whole yoghurt (page 85)
2 cloves garlic

Peel cucumbers and slice very thinly using the fine blade in your food processor. Place in a bowl and mix with salt. Cover and refrigerate for several hours.

Place cucumbers in a colander and drain them about 1/2 hour, turning occasionally. You may wish to pat or squeeze cucumbers in a towel to remove remaining moisture. Peel and crush garlic and mix with yoghurt. Add cucumbers to yoghurt mixture and chill well. Serve with pita bread.

COLE SLAW

Serves 6

1 head cabbage, finely shredded
2 carrots, peeled and grated
1 small red onion, finely chopped
1 tablespoon celery seeds
1 cup creamy dressing (page 131)

Mix all ingredients. Chill well before serving.

ORIENTAL COLE SLAW

Serves 6

1 head oriental cabbage, finely shredded
1 bunch green onions, finely chopped
1/2 cup crispy almond slivers (page 515), toasted
4 ounces buckwheat or brown rice pasta, broken
    into 1-inch lengths, cooked and drained
about 4 tablespoons olive oil or lard
1 teaspoon finely grated orange rind
1 cup Oriental dressing (page 135)

This is an excellent salad for a buffet. Pat cooked noodles dry and sauté in olive oil or lard until crisp. Drain well. Mix all ingredients. May be refrigerated several hours before serving.

AVOCADO GRAPEFRUIT SALAD

Serves 4

2 ripe avocados, well chilled, peeled and sliced
2 grapefruit, well chilled, peeled and sectioned
1 head Boston lettuce
2 tablespoons green onions, finely chopped
3/4 cup basic dressing (page 129)
    or Mexican dressing (page 132)

Arrange avocado and grapefruit on Boston lettuce leaves, sprinkle with green onions, spoon on dressing and serve.

It is widely believed that obesity is a disease of civilization and is associated with adverse nutrition in which enzyme undernutrition is implicated. Thus, it can be said that the brain becomes smaller both under the influence of civilization and obesity. The evidence creates strong suspicion that as a person puts on useless fat his brain gets smaller. It is a glorious thought that if you are overweight and take off 20 to 30 pounds through a diet containing 75 percent raw calories, you may add good weight to your brain for more brain power and be in a better mental condition to deal with taxing business and personal problems. Edward Howell, MD *Enzyme Nutrition*

There is not a known remedy that will cure diabetes without a reformation along the lines that caused it . . . . Raw vegetables of all kinds—red cabbage, cauliflower, watercress, Brussels sprouts, okra, cucumbers, onions, etc. A big emphasis needs to be placed on raw foods as they stimulate the pancreas and increase insulin production. Green beans and cucumber juice contain a hormone needed by the cells of the pancreas in order to produce insulin. Jerry Lee Hover, ND *Health Freedom News*

I am frequently asked about the value of a vegetarian diet. I do not advocate it as a way of life. While one cannot live comfortably in our environment without vegetables and fruits, one cannot live entirely on them and still remain in a state of buoyant health. I do, however, advocate a vegetable diet when the patient is "over-proteinized" after eating too much meat over a long period of time. When this happens, I place him on a vegetable diet until his tissues are free of too much stored animal protein. And then I suggest a diet with not too high a percentage of flesh, eggs and dairy products. Henry Bieler, MD *Food is Your Best Medicine*

Personal observations have led many food faddists to conclude that certain food combinations are dangerous. For example, it is commonly said that starch and protein is a bad combination. What these faddists miss seeing is that starch and protein and *toxic bile* form a bad combination. As most diet books are based on personal idiosyncrasies and prejudices, the usual result is an amazing collection of good and bad combinations. Nature, in her wisdom, has never created a food which is entirely protein, starch or sugar. Even meat contains relatively large amounts of starch (as glycogen and muscle sugar). Henry Bieler, MD *Food is Your Best Medicine*

RUSSIAN BEET SALAD
Serves 4

6 medium beets
3 tablespoons raw apple cider vinegar or
*   beet kvass (page 608)*
4 tablespoons extra virgin olive oil
1 tablespoon orange juice
pinch of sea salt
pinch of cayenne pepper
1 teaspoon caraway seeds
pinch of cloves
pinch of cinnamon
1/2 teaspoon finely grated lemon peel
1/2 teaspoon finely grated orange peel
lettuce leaves for garnish

Bake beets at 350 degrees about 1 hour or until tender. Peel and chop finely. Mix remaining ingredients in a bowl, toss with beets and refrigerate several hours. Serve on lettuce leaves.

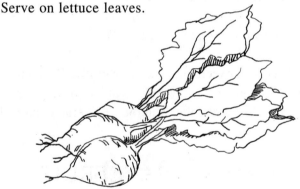

ZUCCHINI SALAD
Serves 4

4 small zucchini
3/4 cup lemon pepper dressing (page 134)
2 teaspoons dried oregano
8 Boston lettuce leaves

Wash zucchini and remove ends. Cut lengthwise into quarters and slice thinly. Mix with dressing and oregano and marinate several hours at room temperature. Serve on Boston lettuce leaves.

SOUPS

The preparation of soup is a neglected art; yet nothing is so satisfying as a bowl of homemade soup. The virtual absence of homemade soup in today's American diet is an unfortunate circumstance—soups form an integral part of every one of the world's great cuisines. For many cultures, soup is a breakfast food. The Japanese begin their day with a bowl of fish broth and rice. French children traditionally consumed leftover soup before they started off to school—the very unhealthy French breakfast of coffee and white bread was adopted on a wide scale only after the Second World War.

To make matters worse, most restaurant soups are not made from scratch, using nourishing broth, but from a "base" of hydrolyzed vegetable protein—which is loaded with neurotoxic MSG and related compounds.

Our soups are all based on homemade broth or stock. They can be divided into two categories. Clear unblended soups featuring meat, vegetables or grains in a meat-based broth; and creamy blended soups. We have already discussed the health-promoting properties of meat broths in the diet; the addition of vegetables, legumes, grain and meat to such a broth, in which all the minerals of meat, bone and marrow are present in easily assimilable form, results in a soup that can serve as a meal in itself.

Blended soups may seem more trouble to make, but a small investment in a handheld blender will enable you to prepare them with ease. The French, who traditionally eat blended soups with the evening meal, have made use of these nifty gadgets for decades. A handheld blender allows you to blend your soup in its own cooking pot. The whole process takes less than a minute or two and leaves no other pans or equipment to clean up.

Most of our blended soups call for the addition of piima cream or *creme fraiche* (page 84) as a final step. It is important to add the cream to your soup in the bowl, and not in the pot, for any heating the cream receives will destroy its valuable enzyme content. Most traditional soup recipes call for the addition of cultured cream in this way—to the slightly cooled soup in the bowl rather than in the pot. Here is another example of folk wisdom serving as a guide to healthy eating. Remember, if you can touch the soup with your finger and not be burned, the enzymes will survive.

Do not hesitate to add cultured cream to your soup for fear of eating too much fat. It supplies not only enzymes but also valuable fat-soluble vitamins. These fat-soluble vitamins are what your body needs to utilize the minerals in the soup. Furthermore, cultured cream imparts a smooth texture and delicious taste, ensuring that your soup will be eaten with relish by young and old.

You may also, in the Russian tradition, add beet kvass (page 608) or cultured whey (pages 86-87) to your soups. If you do not reheat the soup after doing so, beet kvass and whey will, like cultured cream, provide valuable enzymes and lactic acid, along with an agreeable sour taste. Another excellent addition to soup is fish sauce. You can make this yourself (page 157), or buy a Thai or Vietnamese variety (called *nam pla* or *nuoc mam*). These clear brown fermented sauces, made from small whole fish including the head and organs, are rich in iodine and other substances that benefit the thyroid gland. On heating the fishy taste disappears but the nutrients remain. You may add fish sauce to any heated soup instead of salt.

We urge you to make homemade soups a standard of your repertoire. With a judicious choice of ingredients, they provide nourishing, easily assimilated fare for young and old. Soup is the perfect way to get vegetables into those members of your family who normally turn up their noses at green things, or who may have trouble digesting raw salads. Lentil and bean soups, prepared with meat stocks and served with whole grain bread, make a complete meal that's quick to prepare and easy on the budget.

COCONUT CHICKEN SOUP

Serves 4

1 quart chicken stock (page 124)
1 1/2 cups whole coconut milk
*   or 7 ounces creamed coconut (page 160)*
1/4 teaspoon dried chile flakes
1 teaspoon freshly grated ginger
juice of 1 lemon
sea salt or fish sauce (page 157)
several green onions, very finely chopped (optional)
1 tablespoon finely chopped cilantro (optional)

This simple but flavorful soup is a good way to begin a rich meal like Thanksgiving dinner; served in a mug, it is a powerful and comforting remedy for colds and sore throat.

Bring the stock to a boil, skim any foam that rises to the top and add coconut milk or creamed coconut, lemon juice, chile flakes and ginger. Simmer for about 15 minutes. Season to taste with salt or fish sauce. Ladle into soup bowls or mugs and garnish with onions and cilantro.

Variation: Coconut Turkey or Duck Soup
Use *turkey or duck stock (page 125)* instead of chicken stock.

CHICKEN RICE SOUP

Serves 6

2 quarts chicken stock (page 124)
1 cup brown rice
1 cup finely diced chicken meat and/or chicken liver
  and heart (leftover from making stock)
1 1/2 cups finely diced vegetables such as carrot,
  celery, red pepper or string beans
sea salt or fish sauce (page 157) and pepper

Bring stock and rice to a boil and skim off any foam that may rise to the top. Reduce heat and cook, covered, about 1 hour until rice is tender. Add the vegetables, diced meats, season to taste and cook until just tender, about 5 to 10 minutes. Children love this!

LIVER DUMPLING SOUP

(Leberknodel)
Serves 6

1/2 pound beef or calves liver
2 cups whole grain bread crumbs
1 egg, lightly beaten
1/4 cup melted butter
grated rind of 1 lemon
1 tablespoon finely chopped parsley
1 small onion, finely chopped
2 cloves garlic, peeled and mashed
1 teaspoon sea salt
1/2 teaspoon pepper
6 cups beef stock (page 122)

Remove any veins from the liver and place in a food processor. Pulse a few times to grind it. Meanwhile, soak bread crumbs in egg and melted butter. Place bread crumb mixture and all other ingredients, except stock, in processor and process until well mixed. Form into 6 large balls or 12 small ones. Carefully place dumplings in boiling stock, reduce heat and simmer for 10 to 15 minutes. To serve, place one or two dumplings in individual soup bowls and ladle stock over the dumplings.

Know Your Ingredients
Name This Product #10

Enriched wheat flour (wheat flour, niacin, reduced iron, thiamine mononitrate, riboflavin), partially hydrogenated cottonseed oil, dehydrated vegetables (green pea, carrot, green bean), salt, freeze dried chicken, whey, buttermilk, nondairy creamer (corn syrup solids, partially hydrogenated soybean oil, whey, sodium caseinate, sugar, dipotassium phosphate, mono- and diglycerides), butter powder, hydrolyzed vegetable proteins, monosodium glutamate, xanthan gum, onion powder, cheddar cheese powder, chicken fat, natural flavors, soy sauce powder, garlic powder, chicken powder, spices, potassium carbonate, sodium carbonate, sugar, carrot and turmeric oleoresins as color, sodium alginate, disodium guanylate, disodium inosinate, sodium tripolyphosphate, citric acid, tocopherols, sodium citrate and sodium sulfite to preserve freshness. [!]

See Appendix B for Answer

A 1994 study contradicts assertions that vegetarians have lower rates of cancer than the general population. Researchers found that although vegetarian Seventh Day Adventists have the same or slightly lower cancer rates for some sites, for example 91% instead of 100% for breast cancer, the rates for numerous other cancers are much higher than the general US population standard. California Seventh Day Adventists have a much higher percentage of numerous types of cancers, especially cancers of the reproductive tract. For SDA males, these cancers included more brain cancer (149% versus 100%), more malignant melanoma (177%) and more prostate cancer (126%). For SDA females, these cancers included more Hodgkins disease (131%), more brain cancer (118%), more malignant melanomna (171%), more uterine cancer (191%), more cervical cancer (180%) and more ovarian cancer (129%) on average. Beef is often blamed for causing colon cancer but a 1975 study found that physicians who are Seventh Day Adventists (and who presumably do not eat beef) have a significantly higher rate of colon cancer than non-Seventh Day Adventist physicians (who presumably do eat beef). SWF

To me, true health is. . . achieved by following the laws of nature; when you break them, illness results. Health is not something bestowed on you by beneficent nature at birth; it is achieved and maintained only by active participation in well-defined rules of healthful living—rules which you may be disregarding every day. Henry Bieler, MD *Food is Your Best Medicine*

SAFFRON SOUP
Serves 6

6 cups chicken or duck stock (pages 124-125)
1/8 teaspoon saffron threads
1 cup finely chopped spinach
2 green onions, very finely chopped
2 tablespoons lemon juice or whey (pages 86-87)
sea salt or fish sauce (page 157) and pepper

Bring stock to a boil and skim off any foam that may rise to the top. Add saffron and simmer for about 1/2 hour. Add spinach and onions and simmer a few minutes more. Remove from heat, add lemon juice or whey and season to taste. Ladle into heated bowls.

FRENCH ONION SOUP
Serves 6

4-5 red onions
4 tablespoons butter
2 quarts beef stock
1/2 cup cognac
1/2 cup red wine
2 tablespoons arrowroot mixed with
    2 tablespoons water
sea salt or fish sauce (page 157) and pepper

Use your food processor to slice onions very thinly. Melt butter in a large, stainless steel pot. Add the onions and cook on the lowest possible heat, stirring occasionally, for about 2 hours, or until the onions are very soft and slightly caramelized. Raise heat a bit and cook a few minutes longer, stirring constantly. The onions should turn brown but not burn. Add wine, cognac and stock. Bring to a rapid boil and skim off any foam that may rise to the top. Add the arrow root mixture and season to taste. Serve with round croutons (page 520) and a platter of raw cheeses.
Variation: Creamy Onion Soup
Use *1/2 cup armagnac* instead of cognac and serve with *piima cream or creme fraiche* for garnish.

JAPANESE NOODLE SOUP
Serves 6-8

1 1/2 quarts fish stock, clarified
*   (pages 119 and 125) or bonito broth (page 120)*
1/2 cup dry white wine
4 tablespoons naturally fermented soy sauce
1 cup brown rice or buckwheat noodles,
*   broken into one-inch pieces*
1/2 cup chopped dried seaweed (see Sources)
1 cup chopped spinach
2 tablespoons fish sauce (page 157)

Combine stock or broth, wine, soy sauce and seaweed and simmer at least 1 hour. About 10 minutes before serving add noodles, spinach and fish sauce.

MISO SOUP
Serves 6-8

1 1/2 quarts clarified fish stock (pages 119 and 125)
*   or bonito broth (page 120)*
4 tablespoons naturally fermented soy sauce
4 tablespoons naturally fermented miso (See Sources)
1 onion, sliced
1/2 green or Chinese cabbage, coarsely shredded
2 tablespoons fish sauce (page 157), optional

Bring stock or broth to a boil, skim and whisk in miso. Add remaining ingredients and simmer gently until vegetables are soft.

TOFU IN BROTH
Serves 6

1 1/2 quarts fish stock or bonito broth
*   (pages 119-120)*
4 tablespoons naturally fermented soy sauce
12 1/2-inch cubes tofu

Bring stock or broth to a boil, skim and add soy sauce. Place 2 cubes of tofu in each of six individual bowls and ladle stock over. Serve immediately.

Analysis of ancient Chinese texts reveals that the soy bean was originally cultivated for its nitrogen-fixing qualities and not as a food source. This is because soy beans contain potent enzyme inhibitors that cause intestinal problems, cancer and growth retardation. Soy is also high in phytic acid, which blocks the absorption of essential minerals, such as iron, calcium, magnesium and zinc.

It was during the Chou Dynasty (1134-246 BC) that soy beans were first designated as the fifth sacred grain, along with barley, wheat, millet and rice, as the Chinese had learned to ferment soy beans to make them edible. Fermentation of cooked beans to make soy sauce, *miso*, *natto* and *tempeh* removes not only enzyme inhibitors but phytates as well. The process of precipitation to make *tofu* and bean curd removes a portion of the enzyme inhibitors but only small amounts of the phytates.

Miso is thus superior to *tofu* from a nutritional point of view. It is a salty paste—smooth or chunky—with a meat-like flavor. It is used as a seasoning and as a dietary staple in the daily preparation of *miso* soup in Japanese homes. It is rich in omega-3 fatty acids and has a complete protein profile because it is made with grains as well as soy beans.

For optimum nutritional benefit, *miso* and *tofu* should be combined with fish stock. In the Orient, these products are consumed in small amounts as nourishing condiments—not as substitutes for animal foods.

Various phytoestrogens, such as genistein, diadzen and isoflavones, which occur in high quantities in modern cultivars of soybeans, are currently promoted as panaceas for heart disease, cancer and osteoporosis. Analysis shows that they are goitrogens—substances that depress thyroid function. SWF

. . . vegetable oils also cause premature aging in millions of Americans. A plastic surgeon did a study in which he examined the diets of his patients and correlated them with facial skin wrinkling. Those patients eating a high vegetable fat diet had 78% more facial wrinkles and many appeared 20 years older than they were. William Campbell Douglass, MD *Eat Your Cholesterol*

Chinese doctors 2,000 years before Christ rejuvenated aging patients with failing faculties by means of an animal thyroid soup, with the result that patients felt younger, had more energy, and often regained ability to think and remember. Many centuries later, during Queen Victoria's reign, London's most prominent Harley Street doctors took a cue from the Chinese and served elderly and failing patients special sandwiches whose main ingredient was raw animal thyroid gland. Stephen E. Langer, MD *Solved: The Riddle of Illness*

Pickled fish brine or sauce, made from fish heads, organs and bones, is called "ke-tsiap" in the Chinese Amoy dialect. This became the Malay "kechap," a condiment that Dutch traders imported from the Orient. It was a fish sauce similar to the Roman garum. It wasn't until American seamen added tomatoes from Mexico or the Spanish West Indies to the condiment that tomato ketchup was born. The original universal condiment was fish sauce, not tomato sauce! Fish sauce is rich in special substances that nourish the thyroid gland and makes a most nutritious addition to soups and stews. SWF

THAI FISH SOUP
Serves 6-8

1 1/2 quarts Oriental fish stock (page 120)
3/4 pound shelled shrimp
3/4 pound fish, skinned and cut into chunks
1 cup brown rice
2 cloves garlic, peeled and mashed
1 tablespoon freshly grated ginger
grated rind of 1 lemon
5-6 basil or kaffir lime leaves
    (available at Oriental markets), chopped
4 tablespoons fish sauce (page 157)

Bring stock and rice to a boil and skim. Add garlic, ginger, lemon rind, basil or kaffir lime leaves and fish sauce. Simmer at least 1 hour. Add fish and shrimp and simmer about 10 minutes more.

CREOLE FISH SOUP
Serves 6-8

1 1/2 quarts fish stock (page 119)
1/2 cup red wine or brandy
1 pound fish, skinned and cut into chunks
3/4 pound shelled shrimp or crab meat
2 onions, peeled and chopped
3 tablespoons extra virgin olive oil
4 tablespoons tomato paste
3 cloves garlic, peeled and mashed
1/4 teaspoon cayenne pepper
sea salt or fish sauce (page 157) and pepper
several sprigs fresh thyme and rosemary,
    tied together

In a large pot, sauté onions in olive oil. Add tomato paste and stir around. Add fish stock and wine, bring to a boil and skim. Add garlic, cayenne and herbs and simmer about 1/2 hour. Add fish and shrimp or crab and simmer 10 minutes more. Season to taste. Remove thyme and rosemary before serving.

JAPANESE FISH SOUP

Serves 8

1 whole fish, including head, about 3 pounds
2 medium onions, chopped
1 carrot, peeled and chopped
3 tablespoons olive oil or lard
1/2 cup white wine
1 inch fresh ginger, peeled and chopped
3 quarts filtered water
2 zucchini, cut into a fine julienne
1 carrot, peeled and grated
2 bunches green onions, finely chopped
sea salt or fish sauce (page 157)

In a large, stainless steel pot, sauté onions and chopped carrot in lard or olive oil until soft. Add wine and bring to a boil. Add fish, water and ginger. Bring to a boil and skim. Reduce heat, cover and simmer for several hours or overnight. Remove fish and pour remaining stock through a strainer into a clean pot. Remove flesh from fish and return to stock along with grated carrot and zucchini. Season generously with sea salt or fish sauce. Simmer several minutes and serve.

COCONUT FISH SOUP

Serves 6-8

1 1/2 quarts fish stock or bonito broth
    (pages 119-120)
1 1/2 cups coconut milk
    or 7 ounces creamed coconut (page 160)
1 pound fresh fish, cut into small cubes
3 jalapeno chiles, diced
1 tablespoon grated fresh ginger
2-4 tablespoons lime juice
5-6 basil leaves chopped
sea salt or fish sauce (page 157)
chopped cilantro for garnish

Combine stock or broth, coconut milk, fish, chiles, ginger, lime juice and basil and simmer for 10 minutes. Season to taste and garnish with cilantro.

Essential fatty acids are traditionally thought of as being polyunsaturated fatty acids. These are the fatty acids that the body cannot make; they must be obtained in the diet. Most saturated fatty acids can be made in the body; the basic fatty acid that the body makes is palmitic acid, the 16-carbon saturated fatty acid from which other fatty acids such as stearic acid (an 18-carbon saturated fatty acid) and palmitoleic acid (a 16-carbon monounsaturated fatty acid) are made.

However, one saturated fatty acid can only be made by the mammary gland; this is lauric acid, the 12-carbon saturated fatty acid. The body needs lauric acid to make antimicrobial monoglycerides used for fighting pathogenic viruses, bacteria and protozoa. Thus, lauric acid is a conditionally essential saturated fatty acid. Except for human milk and small amounts in bovine and other ruminant milks, the major sources of lauric acid are lauric oils, such as coconut oil and palm kernel oil. Mary G. Enig, PhD
Know Your Fats

Myth: Heart disease in America is caused by consumption of cholesterol and saturated fat from animal products.

Truth: During the period of rapid increase in heart disease (1920-1960), American consumption of animal fats declined but consumption of hydrogenated and industrially processed vegetable oils increased dramatically. (*USDA-HNI*)

In their native state the natives of the Torres Strait Islands have exceedingly little disease. Dr. J. R. Nimmo, the government physician in charge of the supervision of this group, told me in his thirteen years with them he had not seen a single case of malignancy, and had seen only one that he had suspected might be malignancy among the entire four thousand native population. He stated that during this same period he had operated on several dozen malignancies for the white population, which numbers about three hundred. He reported that among the primitive stock other affections requiring surgical interference were rare. The environment of the Torres Strait Islanders provided a very liberal supply of sea foods and fertile islands on which an adequate quantity of tropical plants are readily grown. Toro, bananas, papaya, and plums are all grown abundantly. The sea foods include large and small fish in great abundance, dugong and a great variety of shellfish. These foods have developed for them remarkable physiques with practically complete immunity to dental caries. Wherever they have adopted the white man's foods, however, they suffer the typical expressions of degeneration, such as loss of immunity to dental caries; and in the succeeding generations there is a marked change in facial and dental arch form with marked lowering of resistance to disease. Weston Price, DDS *Nutrition and Physical Degeneration*

An analysis of cholesterol values . . . in 1,700 patients with atherosclerotic disease revealed no definite correlation between serum cholesterol levels and the nature and extent of atherosclerotic disease.
Michael De Bakey, MD
Famous Heart Surgeon

CRAB SOUP
Serves 6

2 quarts fish stock (page 119)
1/4 teaspoon red chile flakes
generous pinch saffron threads
several sprigs fresh thyme, tied together
1 pound fresh lump crab meat
3 ripe tomatoes, peeled, seeded and chopped
3 ears white corn, cut off the cob
sea salt or fish sauce (page 157) and pepper
1/2 cup fresh chives, chopped, for garnish

To peel tomatoes, see page 70. Bring fish stock to a boil and skim. Add red chile flakes, saffron and thyme. Reduce heat and simmer for about 1 hour. Remove the thyme. Add crab, tomatoes and corn. Simmer about 5 minutes until corn is tender. Season to taste. Ladle into heated soup bowls and garnish with chives.

OYSTER CHOWDER
Serves 8

2 onions, finely chopped
1 red pepper, finely chopped
1/2 cup butter
1/2 cup unbleached flour
1 quart fish stock (page 119)
2 cups red potatoes, cut into 1/4-inch dice
2 cups piima cream or creme fraiche (page 84)
2 cups chopped oysters, including liquid
1/2 cup dry sherry (optional)
sea salt and pepper
pinch nutmeg
2 tablespoons parsley, finely chopped

Sauté pepper and onions gently in butter in a large pot. Over medium heat, blend flour with butter and cook, stirring constantly, for several minutes. Add stock and bring to a boil, blending with a wire whisk. Add potatoes and simmer until tender. Add cultured cream, optional sherry and oysters and simmer until just cooked. Season to taste and stir in nutmeg and parsley.

MEXICAN SOUP

Serves 6

2 quarts chicken stock (page 124)
1 cup tomato paste, preferably organic
4 cloves garlic, mashed
1/4-1/2 teaspoon red chile flakes
1/2 cup fresh lime juice
sea salt or fish sauce (page 157) and pepper
strips of corn or sprouted whole wheat tortilla,
    fried until crisp in olive oil or lard,
    for garnish
1 avocado, diced, for garnish
piima cream or creme fraiche (page 84) for garnish

   Bring stock to a boil with tomato paste, garlic and red chile flakes. Simmer about 1/2 hour. Add lime juice and season to taste. Serve with garnishes.

KOREAN SOUP

(Sol Long Tang)
Serves 6

1 1/2 quarts beef stock (page 122)
1/2 pound beef brisket, sliced very thin
1/2 cup brown rice
1/2 cup buckwheat or brown rice noodles,
    broken into pieces
2 tablespoons naturally fermented soy sauce

   Bring stock and rice to a boil and skim. Add brisket and soy sauce and simmer for 1 hour. About 10 minutes before serving add noodles.

   Hawk reported in 1923 on feeding experiments which established the supplementary action of gelatin in connection with a cereal diet. Downey, in the same year, found gelatin to be an efficient supplement for the proteins of whole rye, pearl barley and whole barley. Based on the findings of McCollum, Downey was also led to the conclusion that white wheat bread and whole wheat bread would be increased in nutritive value by the inclusion of gelatin. He accordingly conducted feeding experiments with the addition of 5% of gelatin to white wheat bread (salts and vitamins A and B were added) and found that the food value was improved to such an extent that growth rate of the experimental animals was normal and they were able to reproduce and raise healthy, well-formed young. On the same ration, but without the gelatin, ratio of growth was about half normal and only two scrawny and poorly formed young were raised. . . while rats fed exclusively on chick peas exhibited retarded growth, normal growth resulted on the addition of gelatin. N. R. Gotthoffer *Gelatin in Nutrition and Medicine*

   If there is one dish that is the Korean cuisine's soul food, it is sol long tang, a long-simmered beef broth served with paper-thin slices of beef brisket, rice and noodles. Koreans eat it morning, noon and night. Elaine Louie *The New York Times*

"Eat carrots for vitamin A." Such statements, found in many popular diet and nutrition books, create the impression that the body's requirements for this essential nutrient can be exclusively met with plant foods like carrots, squash, green leafy vegetables and orange colored fruits. The lowfat school of nutrition benefits greatly from the fact that the public has only vague notions about vitamin A; for the family of water-soluble nutrients called carotenes are not true vitamin A, but are more accurately termed provitamin A. True vitamin A, or retinol, is found only in animal products like cod liver oil, liver and other organ meats, butter, cream, fish and fish roe, shell fish and animal fats. This fact is clearly stated in the prestigious *Merck Index*: "Vitamin A is only in animal foods." *Vitamin A Vagary*

Cholesterol is a peculiar molecule. It is often called a lipid or a fat. However, the chemical term for a molecule such as cholesterol is an alcohol, although it doesn't behave like an alcohol. Its numerous carbon and hydrogen atoms are put together in an intricate three dimensional network, impossible to dissolve in water. All living creatures use this indissolvability cleverly, incorporating cholesterol into their cell walls to make cells waterproof. This means that cells of living creatures can regulate their internal environment undisturbed by changes in their surroundings, a mechanism vital for proper function. The fact that cells are waterproof is especially critical for the normal function of nerves and nerve cells. Thus, the highest concentration of cholesterol in the body is found in the brain and other parts of the nervous system. Uffe Ravnskov, MD, PhD *The Cholesterol Myths*

ROE SOUP
Serves 6

about 3/4 pound fish roe (small fish eggs, not large)
2 tablespoons fresh thyme leaves, chopped very fine
2 teaspoons sea salt
2 medium onions or leeks, peeled and chopped
3 large tomatoes, seeded and chopped
1 fennel bulb, chopped
6 tablespoons extra virgin olive oil
1 quart filtered water
3 cloves garlic, peeled and mashed
pinch of saffron threads, soaked in warm water
1 cup brown rice or buckwheat noodles,
    broken into one-inch pieces
2 tablespoons fennel leaves, chopped

Popular in the French city of Nice, this recipe dates back to Roman times. Mash roe with thyme and salt. Meanwhile gently sauté onions or leeks, tomatoes and fennel in olive oil until vegetables are tender. (To peel tomatoes, see page 70.) Add cold water, bring to a boil and skim. Reduce to a simmer and blend in fish roe paste, garlic and soaked saffron. Add noodles and fennel leaves and simmer about 5 minutes or until noodles are tender.

ROMAN EGG SOUP
(Stracciatella)
Serves 6

2 quarts chicken stock (page 124)
4 eggs
4 tablespoons finely powdered Parmesan cheese
sea salt or fish sauce (page 157) and pepper
2 tablespoons very finely chopped parsley

Bring stock to a boil and skim. Meanwhile whisk up the eggs with the cheese. While stock is boiling vigorously, add the egg-cheese mixture in a thin stream, all the while beating the soup with a whisk. Season to taste. Just before serving stir in the finely chopped parsley.

MEDITERRANEAN FISH SOUP

(Cioppino)
Serves 8

1 or 2 onions, finely chopped
1/4 cup extra virgin olive oil
6 ounces tomato paste
1 cup dry white wine or vermouth
1 1/2 quarts fish stock (page 119)
several sprigs fresh thyme
1/2 teaspoon oregano
1/4 teaspoon red chile flakes
pinch saffron threads
3 large garlic cloves, peeled and mashed
2-4 tablespoons fish sauce (page 157)
sea salt and pepper
4 tomatoes, peeled, seeded and chopped
1 pound fresh sea bass, cut into cubes
1 pound fresh crab meat
1 pound fresh scallops
1 pound bay shrimp
16 fresh clams
8 crab claws

Needless to say, all the seafood you use must be very fresh. You can substitute lobster for crab and mussels for clams, etc.

In a large, stainless steel pot, sauté onion gently in olive oil. Stir in tomato paste and add wine, stock, spices and garlic. Bring to a rapid boil and cook vigorously, skimming occasionally, until the stock is reduced to the consistency of thin cream. Remove thyme, add fish sauce and season to taste. Add the seafood and tomatoes and cook gently for about 10 minutes. (To peel tomatoes, see page 70.) Ladle into large heated bowls, making sure everyone has one crab claw and two clams.

Serve with a Caesar salad (page 177) and fresh sourdough whole grain bread with butter.

Since Viti Levu, one of the islands of this group, is one of the larger islands of the Pacific Ocean, I had hoped to find on it a district far enough from the sea to make it necessary for the natives to have lived entirely on land foods. . . . By using a recently opened government road, I was able to get well into the interior of the island by motor vehicle and from this point to proceed father inland on foot with two guides. I was not able, however, to get beyond the piles of sea shells which had been carried into the interior. My guide told me that it had always been essential, as it is today, for the people of the interior to obtain some food from the sea and that even during the times of most bitter warfare, between the inland or hill tribes and the coast tribes, those of the interior would bring down during the night choice plant foods from the mountain areas and place them in caches and return the following night to obtain the sea foods that had been placed in those depositories by the shore tribes. . . . He told me, further, that they require food from the sea at least every three months, even to this day. This was a matter of keen interest and the same time disappointment since one of the purposes of the expedition to the South Seas was to find, if possible, plant or fruits which together, without the use of animal products, were capable of providing all of the requirements of the body for growth and for maintenance of good health and a high state of physical efficiency. . . . No places were found where the native plant foods were not supplemented by sea foods. Weston Price, DDS *Nutrition and Physical Degeneration*

A recent research report has de-demonized, at least a little, one of our most important nutrients—cholesterol. The experts who have been telling us not to eat high-cholesterol foods, such as eggs, butter and T-bone steak (all the good stuff that made America great), are now saying it's okay to eat these foods—*if* you're over 70. The Yale University study reported in the November 2, 1994 issue of the *Journal of the American Medical Association* claims that people over 70 with "high cholesterol" levels do not have any more heart attacks than those whose cholesterol is considered normal or even low. They are no more likely to die of any form of heart disease or from any cause.

Dr. Stephen B. Hulley, of the University of California at San Francisco, said he was "deeply concerned" about the number of elderly people who were taking cholesterol-lowering drugs when "we actually don't know whether you're better off with a high or low [cholesterol], so there is no point in measuring it." William Campbell Douglass, MD *Second Opinion*

Whoever is failing in his whole body and whose veins are withered should often sip the juice of lamb and of the soup in which it was cooked. Also he should eat some of the meat and, when he improves, he can eat even more of the meat if he wants.

St. Hildegard of Bingen

LEFTOVER LEG-OF-LAMB SOUP

Serves 8

1 leftover leg of lamb (page 343)
leftover sauce from leg of lamb
1/4 cup vinegar
3 onions or leeks, peeled and coarsely chopped
3 carrots, peeled and coarsely chopped
1 red or green pepper, seeded and chopped
3 turnips, peeled and chopped
3 zucchini, chopped
4 cloves garlic, peeled and chopped
filtered water
several sprigs fresh thyme, tied together
1/2 teaspoon crushed dried green peppercorns
1/4 teaspoon dried red chile flakes
generous pinch saffron threads
1 cup brown rice
1/2 cup dried currants (optional)
sea salt or fish sauce (page 157) and pepper

This is a good way to stretch a leg of lamb into another meal. Leftover lamb meat, normally unappetizing when served a second time, becomes flavorful and tender when simmered with vegetables and seasonings. While not exactly gourmet fare, this soup always gets eaten to the last spoonful. It should be started in the early morning and allowed to simmer all day. This recipe uses all the vegetables and seasonings of couscous but substitutes brown rice for white-flour semolina.

Place vegetables in a large, stainless steel pot with the lamb, vinegar and leftover sauce. Cover with filtered cold water and bring to a boil. Skim before adding thyme, chile flakes and saffron. Cook gently, covered, about 12 hours or longer. At least 1 hour before serving, remove the lamb and strain the sauce into another large pot. Add rice and optional currants to this broth and simmer an hour or more. Meanwhile discard the cooked vegetables and let the meat cool. Remove the meat from the bone and cut across the grain into small pieces. When the rice is tender, return the meat to the broth and season to taste.

OXTAIL BARLEY SOUP

Serves 8

4 pounds fresh oxtail
filtered water
1/2 cup dry white wine
1/4 cup vinegar
2 onions, peeled and chopped
2 carrots, peeled and chopped
2 celery stalks, chopped
fresh thyme sprigs, tied together
1-2 teaspoons dried green peppercorns, crushed
pinch red pepper flakes
l cup barley, roasted in the oven,
    and soaked at least 7 hours
sea salt or fish sauce (page 157) and pepper
chopped cilantro or finely chopped parsley
    for garnish

Place oxtail in a stainless steel baking pan and bake in a 350 degree oven for about 1 hour or until well browned. Transfer oxtail to a stainless steel pot and pour out grease. Add wine and a little filtered water to the baking pan and deglaze by bringing to a rapid boil, while stirring to loosen any coagulated beef juices in the pan. Pour this liquid into the pot and cover all the oxtail with cold water. Add vinegar, bring to a boil and skim. Add thyme, onions, carrots, celery, red pepper flakes and peppercorns. Simmer, covered, for at least 24 hours.

Remove oxtail and allow to cool. Strain 3 quarts of stock into another pot and add soaked barley. (Reserve any remaining broth for other uses.) Bring to a boil and simmer for about 1 hour or until barley is tender. Meanwhile, pick the meat off the bones and chop finely. When the barley is tender, add chopped meat. Season generously. Ladle into individual bowls and garnish with chopped parsley or cilantro.

Barley is one of the oldest cereal grains, used most frequently in the making of beer but also traditionally made into bread and gruels. It was the main food of the Greeks, who valued barley's ability to give physical strength and mental alertness. Barley water, a thin porridge made of barley, is said to be easy to digest and a tonic to the liver. In Britain it is fed to convalescents. Most barley is available to the consumer in "pearled" form, with the thick outer layer, and hence most of the nutrients, removed. Look for whole barley and be sure to soak it before using it or the results will be difficult to digest. SWF

The recent national meeting of the American Chemical Society reported new studies on the effects of soluble fiber. Barley reduced serum cholesterol levels by as much as 15% in hypercholesterolemic persons in two studies cited by Rosemary K. Newman of Montana State University. She cited three reasons for this effect of barley. First, it contains beta-glucans and other viscous soluble fiber components which reduce absorption of fats and cholesterol. Other soluble fibers, such as those of oat and guar gum, also contain beta-glucans. Also, the fiber tends to bind to bile acids, which are removed from the body rather than recycled, thus requiring the conversion of more cholesterol to bile acids. Finally, barley contains fat-soluble antioxidants related to vitamin E called tocotrienols that reduce cholesterol synthesis in the liver. Newman says, "We have not seen any other grain that carries barley's double whammy"—that is, high beta-glucan levels as well as tocotrienols. James F. Scheer *Health Freedom News*

Little is known of the part potassium plays in the human body, but certainly it must be important as small quantities of it are present in all parts of the body, particularly within the cells. Osmotic balance between the contents of the cells and their surrounding fluids depends greatly upon potassium. When meat is being cooked, a considerable portion of the potassium content passes into the broth. When this is eaten in the form of a soup, bouillon or consomme, it results in a stimulatory effect upon the digestive organism. This is given as one good reason for beginning a meal with a meat broth soup. H. Leon Abrams *Your Body Is Your Best Doctor*

When harvested with dedication and care, the oceans give us a natural sea salt with the most exquisite taste and physiologically vital mineral mix. Today, every common table salt is artificial and pales beside the real sea salt. Out of the richest spectrum of 92 essential minerals found in the ocean, the industrial refined variety retains only two! Debased white table salt deserves all of its bad name and all the misdeeds as charged. Jacques DeLangre *Seasalt's Hidden Powers*

MINESTRONE
Serves 6

2 quarts beef stock (page 122)
1 clove garlic, peeled and mashed
2 cups cooked kidney beans (page 496)
1 cup buckwheat or brown rice pasta,
*   broken in bits*
2 carrots, peeled and chopped
2 tomatoes, peeled, seeded and chopped
1 cup fresh spinach or chard, finely chopped
sea salt or fish sauce (page 157) and pepper
freshly grated Parmesan cheese for garnish

This hearty soup is a meal in itself. As always, the secret is in the richness of the stock.

To peel tomatoes, see page 70. Bring stock to a boil and skim. Add garlic, beans, pasta, carrots, tomatoes and spinach or chard and simmer about 10 minutes. Season to taste and garnish with cheese.

SAUERKRAUT AND BEAN SOUP
Serves 4

3 cups basic small white beans (page 496), cooked
1 quart beef or chicken stock
*   (pages 122 or 124)*
2 cloves garlic, peeled and mashed
pinch red pepper flakes
1 pound spicy chicken or beef sausage,
*   sliced into rounds*
sea salt or fish sauce (page 157) and pepper
2 cups sauerkraut (page 92)

Bring stock to a boil and skim. Add garlic, red pepper and sausage and simmer for 15 minutes or until sausage is cooked. Season to taste. Let cool until the soup can be touched without burning and stir in sauerkraut. Ladle into heated bowls and serve.

PESTO SOUP

Serves 8

2 quarts beef stock (page 122)
1/4 teaspoon saffron threads
1/2 teaspoon pepper
3 carrots, peeled and diced
1 leek, trimmed, washed and diced
2 cups cooked small white beans (page 496)
4 ounces buckwheat or brown rice pasta,
  broken into 1-inch pieces
1 cup green beans, french cut (page 370)
1/2 cup pesto (page 144)
2 tablespoons tomato paste
sea salt or fish sauce (page 157)

Bring stock to a boil, skim and add saffron, pepper, carrots, leeks and cooked beans. Simmer gently until vegetables are soft. Add green beans and pasta and simmer about 10 minutes more. Place pesto and tomato paste in a bowl. Blend with a little of the hot stock and then return this mixture to the soup. Stir until well blended. Season to taste with sea salt or fish sauce and serve.

KISHK SOUP

Serves 6

1 1/2 quarts beef or chicken stock
  (pages 122 or 124)
1 1/2 cups kishk (page 461), broken into small pieces
sea salt or fish sauce (page 157) and pepper

This traditional Middle Eastern winter soup incorporates all the elements found universally in traditional ethnic cuisines—sprouted grains, fermented grains, fermented milk products and meat broths.

Bring stock to a boil and skim. Add kishk and simmer about 1 hour. Season to taste.

An article in the January 1973 issue of the *National Geographic* points out that there are places in the world where people live much longer and remain more vigorous in old age than in most of our modern societies. Dr. Alexander Leaf, MD. . . visited three of the best known of these regions. They were all remote, mountainous, and over a mile high—the Andean village of Vilcabamba in Ecuador—the Land of the Hunzas in Kashmir—and Abakhazia in Russia on the border of the Black Sea. . . . Dr. Leaf commented that his confidence in the importance to health and longevity of low animal fat, low cholesterol, low caloric diet was somewhat shaken by the eating habits of the Caucasus. Dietary study of the habits of 1,000 persons above the age of 80, including more than 100 centenarians, showed that the old people consumed about 1,900 calories daily—considerably more than most people of such advanced age. Seventy to ninety grams of protein were included in the diet— milk being the main source of protein. The daily fat intake was about 40 to 60 grams. Bread provided the major source of carbohydrates. . . . [Dr. Leaf] does not discuss the fact that each of these communities is situated in a valley supplied with water which washes silt from a mountain behind them. He does not recognize that they drink the silted water, they fertilize the crops they eat with the silted water, they eat the flesh and drink the milk of the animals that were raised on this silted water, and they have a constant supply of trace elements throughout their lives that is as good or better than any other place on earth. John A. Myers, MD *Metabolic Aspects of Health*

Calcification of the arteries (ar-teriosclerosis), the joints (degenera-tive arthritis) and the [pineal] gland may be due to the excessive intake of fractionated milk, i.e., skim or lowfat milk. On the advice of physicians, millions of people have switched to lowfat milk under the mistaken belief that avoiding the milk fat will enable them to avoid hardening of the arter-ies. Drinking fractionated milk may cause exactly the opposite effect!

Many other millions are drinking lowfat milk to avoid weight gain. . . . Do you know how a farmer fattens his hogs? *He feeds them skim milk.* Wil-liam Campbell Douglass, MD *The Milk Book*

CREAM OF VEGETABLE SOUP

(Potage Bonne Femme)
Serves 6-8

2 medium onions or leeks, peeled and chopped
2 carrots, peeled and chopped
4 tablespoons butter
3 medium baking potatoes or 6 red potatoes,
    washed and cut up
2 quarts chicken stock (page 124)
    or combination of filtered water and stock
several sprigs fresh thyme, tied together
1/2 teaspoon dried green peppercorns, crushed
4 zucchini, trimmed and sliced
sea salt or fish sauce (page 157) and pepper
piima cream or creme fraiche (page 84)

This basic vegetable soup recipe is a perennial favorite—and it's a great way to get your children to eat zucchini!

Melt butter in a large, stainless steel pot and add onions or leeks and carrots. Cover and cook over lowest possible heat for at least 1/2 hour. The vegetables should soften but not burn. Add potatoes and stock, bring to a rapid boil and skim. Reduce heat and add thyme sprigs and crushed peppercorns. Cover and cook until the potatoes are soft. Add zucchini and cook until they are just tender—about 5 to 10 minutes. Remove the thyme sprigs. Purée the soup with a handheld blender.

If soup is too thick, thin with filtered water. Season to taste. Ladle into heated bowls and garnish with cultured cream. Serve with round croutons (page 520).

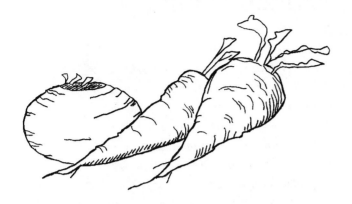

The food engineers seem determined to wipe out the entire dairy industry. . . and maybe the human race. Europeans are now producing margarine cheese. The price differential will be enormously in favor of fake cheese guaranteeing its popularity. It is so much like real cheese that "if a cheese made with vegetable oil was judged together with other cheese, it is doubtful whether anyone would realize that a margarine cheese was among them."

Crest Foods of Ashton, Illinois now produces vegetable fat "sour cream." It is doubly pasteurized and homogenized *at least twice.* William Campbell Douglass, MD *The Milk Book*

WINTER ROOT SOUP

Serves 6-8

3 medium onions, peeled and chopped
2 leeks, washed, trimmed and sliced
4 carrots, peeled and sliced
2 turnips, peeled and sliced
1 rutabaga, peeled and sliced
3 parsnips, peeled and sliced
4 tablespoons butter
1 1/2 quarts chicken stock (page 124)
     or combination of filtered water and stock
several thyme sprigs, tied together
4 cloves garlic, peeled and mashed
pinch cayenne pepper
sea salt or fish sauce (page 157) and pepper
pinch of nutmeg
piima cream or creme fraiche (page 84)

> Soup is a healthy, light, nourishing food, good for all of humanity; it pleases the stomach, stimulates the appetite and prepares the digestion.
>
> J. A. Brillant-Savarin

Melt butter in a large, stainless steel pot and add onions, leeks, carrots, turnips, rutabaga and parsnips. Cover and cook gently about 1/2 hour over low heat, stirring occasionally. Add stock, bring to a boil and skim. Add, garlic, thyme and cayenne. Simmer, covered, for about 1/2 hour until the vegetables are soft.

Remove thyme and purée soup with handheld blender. Season to taste. If soup is too thick, thin with a little water. Ladle into heated bowls and serve with cultured cream.

Feeding tests were conducted to compare the feeding value of the following fats and oils for calves: butterfat, lard, tallow, coconut oil, peanut oil, corn oil, cottonseed oil, and soybean oil. . . . In average daily gain in weight as well as in general wellbeing, the calves fed butterfat excelled those in all other groups; following closely were those receiving lard and tallow. Corn oil, cottonseed oil and soybean oil were the least satisfactory. . . . They appeared unthrifty, listless and emaciated. Some calves in these groups died and others were saved only by changing to whole milk. Weston Price, DDS *Nutrition and Physical Degeneration*

FENNEL SOUP

Serves 6

3 fennel bulbs, trimmed and sliced
2 leeks or medium onions, trimmed and sliced
4 tablespoons butter
1/2 teaspoon ground anise seed
1 teaspoon ground fennel seed
1/2 cup dry white wine (optional)
2 quarts chicken stock (page 124)
*   or combination of filtered water and stock*
3 cloves garlic, peeled and coarsely chopped
1 teaspoon dried green peppercorns, crushed
6 medium red potatoes, cut in quarters
sea salt or fish sauce (page 157) and pepper
3-4 tablespoons snipped fennel leaves
piima cream or creme fraiche (page 84)

Cook fennel and onion gently in butter until tender. Add ground anise and fennel seeds and stir around until amalgamated. Add stock and optional wine. Bring to a boil and skim. Add potatoes, peppercorns and garlic. Cover and simmer until the potatoes are soft, about 1/2 hour.

Purée soup with a handheld blender. If the soup is too thick, thin with a little water. Season to taste and stir in fennel snippings. Ladle into heated bowls and serve with cultured cream.

Raw foods enthusiasts point to scientific evidence which shows that when cooked foods are consumed, the white blood cell count immediately rises, while no such increase occurs when eating raw fruit or vegetables. The white blood cells function as immune system scavengers, removing foreign organisms and any chemical compounds the body considers invasive. The conclusion is drawn that, therefore, cooked foods are bad because the body considers them invasive and toxic, and raw foods are good because they evoke no immune system response. However, one can look at the same results and conclude that the cooked food is stimulating the immune function and causing the increase in white blood cells not because the food itself is toxic, but because a function of cooked food is to "exercise" the immune system in producing white blood cells for real emergencies, somewhat akin to a biological fire drill. Indeed, it is quite natural for the body to use the invasion of low doses of microorganisms or chemical poisons to immunize itself against greater danger. And on one level food *is* a foreign substance that the body must "overcome" through the process of digestion and assimilation. In this sense cooked food can be seen to strengthen the system while raw foods simply do not have the same white-blood-cell-stimulating effect. Marc David *Nourishing Wisdom*

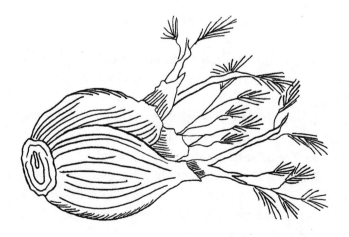

ROMAN LENTIL SOUP

Serves 8

3 medium onions, peeled and sliced or
*   3 leeks, washed, trimmed and sliced*
3 carrots, peeled and sliced
2 tablespoons butter
2 tablespoons extra virgin olive oil
2 quarts beef or chicken stock (pages 122 or 124)
*   or combination of filtered water and stock*
2 cups red or brown lentils, soaked for 7 hours
several sprigs fresh thyme, tied together
1/2 teaspoon dried green peppercorns
1/4 cup fresh lemon juice or whey (pages 86-87)
sea salt or fish sauce (page 157) and pepper
piima cream or creme fraiche (page 84)

In a large, stainless steel pot, cook onions or leeks and carrots gently for about 1/2 hour in butter and olive oil. When the vegetables are soft, add stock and lentils and bring to a boil. The lentils will produce a great deal of foam—be sure to skim this off. Reduce heat and add thyme and crushed peppercorns. Simmer, covered, until the lentils are tender—about 1/2 hour. Remove the thyme.

Purée soup with a handheld blender. Thin with water to desired consistency. Reheat slightly and add lemon juice or whey. Season to taste. Ladle into heated bowls and serve with cultured cream.

Variation: Curried Lentil Soup

Add *2 or more tablespoons curry powder or curry paste* to soup along with thyme and peppercorns.

Variation: Split Pea Soup

Use *2 cups split peas* instead of lentils.

The hearty Roman soldier carried 80 pounds plus his armor and walked 20 miles per day. His fare consisted of coarse bread and porridge of millet or lentils, supplemented with *garum* or *liquamem*, fermented fish sauce. This condiment supplied him with nutrients from the animal kingdom on a daily basis. Made from the heads and organs of fish, it is especially rich in iodine and vitamins A and D and thus contributed to the robust strength of the Roman legions. SWF

The basic foods should be the entire grains such as whole wheat, rye or oats, whole wheat and rye breads, wheat and oat cereals, oatcake, dairy products, including milk and cheese, which should be used liberally, and marine foods. All sea foods are high in minerals and constitute one of the very best foods you could eat. Canned fish such as sardines, tuna or salmon are all excellent; also the fresh fish such as oysters, halibut, haddock, etc. The protein requirement can be provided each day in one egg or a piece of meat equivalent to the bulk of one egg a day. The meals can be amply modified and varied with vegetables, raw and cooked, the best of the cooked vegetables being lentils used as a soup.

There are only a few foods that would give you your fat-soluble vitamins. These are either fish products, including practically all fresh water and salt water foods, milk, cheese and butter made from cows that have been on a rapidly growing green young wheat, either fresh or stored grass, particularly butter made in June. This is much richer than butter made during other seasons of the year. Weston Price, DDS *Letter to His Nieces and Nephews* 1934

I found Junkie dead this morning. She was cold and still and dark red-brown blood showed on her nose and paws.

What had I done? I killed her. For fourteen weeks I fed her "junk" food. She ate white flour products of white bread, saltines, doughnuts, sweet rolls, dinner rolls and cookies. Highly sweetened foods were candies, gum drops, malted milk balls, candy corn, marshmallows, sugar frosted cereals, chocolates and jelly on her bread.

Her death abruptly ended my experiment raising two young white rats. Junkie's food contrasted with Goodie's which were nutritious whole foods. She drank milk, had hard boiled eggs, shells and all, whole wheat bread, butter and peanut butter, oats, popcorn, dry beans and seeds, meat, fish, chicken, liver and a fresh dark green cabbage leaf or a piece of fruit.

I wanted to demonstrate the effects of these two diets so I could show off my rats at fairs, in nutrition classes and at day care centers, for both children and parents. The two rats showed a startling difference.

They began when about a month old, weighing almost the same at 128 and 129 grams. . . . I kept them in separate cages and fed them enough of their different diets so they always had more food than they could eat . . . . Goodie drank milk, but Junkie refused uncarbonated soft drinks so I

CHESTNUT SOUP
Serves 6

2 onions, peeled and chopped
2 carrots, peeled and chopped
4 tablespoons butter
6 cups chicken stock (page 124)
    or combination of filtered water and stock
1/2 cup sherry
1/4 teaspoon cayenne pepper
pinch nutmeg
several sprigs fresh thyme, tied together
13 ounces frozen peeled chestnuts or
    about 4 cups unpeeled fresh chestnuts
sea salt or fish sauce (page 157) and pepper
piima cream or creme fraiche (page 84)

You can make this delicious, sweetly flavored soup very easily with peeled, frozen chestnuts if you can find them. Its still worth doing if you have to start with the unpeeled variety. (See page 381 for preparation of chestnuts.)

Cook carrots and onions gently in butter until soft. Add sherry, stock and chestnuts. Bring to a boil and skim. Add thyme and nutmeg and simmer, covered, for about 15 minutes. Remove thyme.

Purée soup with a handheld blender. Season to taste. Ladle into heated bowls and serve with cultured cream.

WATERCRESS SOUP

Serves 6

2 medium onions, peeled and chopped
3 tablespoons butter
1 1/2 quarts chicken stock (page 124)
4 red potatoes, cut into quarters
2 large bunches watercress leaves, rinsed
sea salt or fish sauce (page 157) and pepper
piima cream or creme fraiche (page 84)

Sauté onions gently in butter until soft. Add stock and potatoes, bring to a boil and skim. Simmer until potatoes are soft, about 1/2 hour. Add watercress and simmer another 5 minutes, no longer.

Purée soup with a handheld blender. Season to taste. Ladle into heated bowls and serve with cultured cream.

ASPARAGUS SOUP

Serves 6

2 medium onions, peeled and chopped
3 tablespoons butter
1 1/2 quarts chicken stock (page 124)
4 red potatoes, washed and cut into quarters
2 bunches tender asparagus, tough ends removed
*   and cut into 1/4-inch pieces*
2 cloves garlic, peeled and coarsely chopped
sea salt or fish sauce (page 157) and pepper
piima cream or creme fraiche (page 84)

Sauté onions gently in butter until tender. Add stock, garlic and potatoes. Bring to a boil and skim. Simmer for about 15 minutes. Add asparagus and simmer another 10 minutes or so until tender. Blend with a handheld blender. Pass the soup through a strainer to remove any strings from the asparagus. Season to taste. Reheat gently, ladle into heated bowls and serve with cultured cream.

stopped offering them. . . when both were about the ages of an eight year old child, Goodie weighed 469.1 grams and Junkie weighted 168.7 grams.

This contrast in weight showed. When I picked up Goodie she felt firm and solid, but Junkie was light and frail. Goodie's fur was full and thick, but Junkie's fur was so thin her skin showed through. . . . . There were contrasts in endurance. I noticed this when I took both out of their cages to let visitors examine them closely. This extra handling had no effect on Goodie, but Junkie tired quickly and curled up for sleep at every chance while Goodie was up and peering out at the excitement.

I had little warning that the end was near for Junkie. She was vigorous, though small and undersized, until the day before yesterday when I saw her lose her balance briefly. . . when she tried to walk she kept falling over . . . . I endeavored to revive her with a little milk, whole wheat bread, peanut butter and a green cabbage leaf . . . . She nibbled on the leaf but I was too late.

It was sobering to wheel a shopping cart later today in a supermarket past shelf after shelf of candies and sweet rolls from which I had selected Junkie's foods. If mothers and teachers could see my little Junkie cold and dead on these foods, they would think twice about letting their children have them, certainly not as a day to day diet.

It could be misleading to look at an undersized active child and think he's doing well. You often hear, "He's the wiry type." Beware. Junkie was active and outwardly healthy up to the day before she collapsed. Ruth Rosevear *PPNF Health Journal*

Modern science has figured out a use for the toxic radioactive wastes being produced by nuclear reactors. Foods can be exposed to radiation and thus be preserved for longer shelf life while at the same time bacteria, fungus, molds and parasites can be controlled. Consequently, rather than having to store deadly radiation in toxic waste sites, the radiation can be used on our food and spread out all over the country. . . . We are concerned with the question of what happens to the nutritional value of irradiated foods. The simple answer is that the nutritional value is ruined because radiation renders the food sterile or dead . . . . Many spices are already being irradiated to control the little bugs that hatch out. . . . We need to oppose irradiation because it kills the life force in our foods, kills the enzymes and maybe even alters molecules into new chemicals. We all know that radiation affects cells resulting in mutations. If new molecules are created or altered by the irradiation process, they will be extremely foreign to the body and present new problems for the immune system. Scientists opposing irradiation of foods are concerned that such new molecules may cause cancer. They are also concerned about alteration of the food's inherent molecular structure making it unable to function as a food in the body. . . scientists employing Kirlian photography, a method to photograph the energetic patterns of a substance, are concerned about the major differences between a fresh strawberry and one that has been irradiated. The fresh strawberry shines with vital energy, radiating out an inch or more in an aura with vibrant patterns. In contrast, the irradiated food has virtually no aura, is flat, dull and the patterns which can be seen are significantly altered. Jack Tips, ND, PhD *The Pro Vita Plan*

MUSHROOM SOUP

Serves 6

2 medium onions, peeled and chopped
3 tablespoons butter
2 pounds fresh mushrooms
4 tablespoons butter
4 tablespoons extra virgin olive oil
1 quart chicken stock (page 124)
1/2 cup dry white wine or sherry
1 piece whole grain bread, broken into pieces
pinch of nutmeg
sea salt or fish sauce (page 157) and pepper
piima cream or creme fraiche (page 84)

Sauté the onions gently in butter until soft. Meanwhile, wash mushrooms and dry well. Cut into quarters. In a heavy, cast-iron skillet, sauté the mushrooms in small batches in a mixture of butter and olive oil. Remove with slotted spoon and drain on paper towels. Add sautéed mushrooms, wine or sherry, bread and chicken stock to onions, bring to a boil and skim. Reduce heat and simmer about 15 minutes. Purée soup with a handheld blender. Add nutmeg and season to taste. Ladle into heated soup bowls and serve with cultured cream.

RED PEPPER SOUP

Serves 6

6 red peppers, seeded and chopped
2 medium onions, peeled and chopped
4 tablespoons extra virgin olive oil
1 1/2 quarts chicken stock (page 124)
1 small bunch fresh basil, cut into small pieces
sea salt or fish sauce (page 157) and pepper
piima cream or creme fraiche (page 84)

Sauté peppers and onions in olive oil. Add stock, bring to a boil and skim. Reduce heat and simmer about 1/2 hour. Pass soup through a food mill. (See A Word on Equipment, page 68.) Return soup to the pot and stir in basil and season to taste. Simmer about 5 minutes, ladle into heated bowls and serve with cultured cream.

GARLIC SOUP

Serves 6

2 medium onions, peeled and chopped
16 cloves garlic, peeled and chopped coarsely
2 stalks celery, chopped
4 tablespoons butter
1 1/2 quarts chicken stock (page 124)
2 medium potatoes, washed and cut up
several sprigs fresh thyme, tied together
1 teaspoon dried green peppercorns, crushed
3 yellow crookneck squash, trimmed and sliced
sea salt or fish sauce (page 157) and pepper
piima cream or creme fraiche (page 84)

To peel garlic, see page 70. Sauté onions, garlic and celery gently in butter until soft. Add chicken stock and potatoes. Bring to a boil and skim. Add thyme and crushed peppercorns. Simmer, covered, until potatoes are tender. Add squash and simmer about 10 minutes more or until squash is tender. Purée soup with a handheld blender. If soup is too thick, thin with a little water. Season to taste. Ladle into heated bowls and serve with cultured cream.

PEA SOUP

Serves 6

2 medium onions, peeled and chopped
3 tablespoons butter
2 pounds freshly shelled or frozen peas
1 1/2 quarts chicken stock (page 124)
1/2 teaspoon dried green peppercorns, crushed
sea salt and pepper
piima cream or creme fraiche (page 84)

This delicious soup can be made in less than 15 minutes and will satisfy the most exacting gourmet. Sauté onions gently in butter until tender. Add peas and stock, bring to a boil and skim. Simmer about 15 minutes. Purée soup with a handheld blender. Season to taste. Ladle into heated bowls and garnish with cultured cream. Good with round croutons (page 520)

Know Your Ingredients
Name This Product #12

Water, mushrooms, modified food starch, cream, corn starch, vegetable oil (corn, cottonseed or partially hydrogenated soybean oil), wheat flour, sugar, salt, whey protein concentrate, potassium chloride, spice extracts, disodium inosinate, disodium guanylate, maltodextrin, dehydrated garlic, mushroom powder, and calcium lactate.

See Appendix B for Answer

In view of beliefs that remain strangely current, it is worth emphasizing that we liked our meat as fat in July as in January. This ought not to surprise Americans (though it usually does), for they know or have heard that fat pork is a staple and relished food of the Negro in the Deep South. Our Negro literature is rich with the praise of opossum fat. Nor did Negroes develop the taste for fats in our southern states; for Carl Akeley brought from tropical Africa such yarns of fat-gorging as have not yet been surpassed from the Arctic. Vilhjalmur Stefansson *The Fat of the Land*

Primary prevention trials which have shown that the lowering of serum cholesterol concentrations in middle-aged subjects by diet, drugs, or both leads to a decrease in coronary heart disease have also reported an increase in deaths due to suicide or violence... published work [describes] a physiological mechanism that might account for this curious finding. One of the functions of serotonin in the central nervous system is the suppression of harmful behavioral impulses. When mouse brain synaptosomal membrane cholesterol is increased there is a pronounced increase in the number of serotonin receptors. Low membrane cholesterol decreases the number of serotonin receptors. Since membrane cholesterol exchanges freely with cholesterol in the surrounding medium, a lowered serum cholesterol concentration may contribute to a decrease in brain serotonin, with poorer suppression of aggressive behavior. Hyman Engelberg, MD *The Lancet*

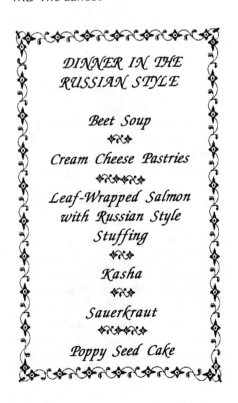

DINNER IN THE RUSSIAN STYLE

Beet Soup

Cream Cheese Pastries

Leaf-Wrapped Salmon with Russian Style Stuffing

Kasha

Sauerkraut

Poppy Seed Cake

TOMATO-DILL SOUP
Serves 6

2 medium onions, peeled and coarsely chopped
3 celery stalks, coarsely chopped
3 tablespoons butter
8 ripe tomatoes, peeled, seeded and chopped
2 cups chicken stock (page 124)
1/2 teaspoon dried green peppercorns, crushed
sea salt or fish sauce (page 157) and pepper
1/4 cup snipped fresh dill
piima cream or creme fraiche (page 84)

To peel tomatoes, see page 70. Sauté onions and celery gently in butter until tender. Add tomatoes and stock, bring to a boil and skim. Add crushed peppercorns. Simmer about 15 minutes.

Purée soup with a handheld blender. Thin soup with a little water, if necessary, and season to taste. Stir in the dill. Simmer gently about 5 minutes, ladle into heated bowls and serve with cultured cream.

BEET SOUP
Serves 6

6 medium beets
4 tablespoons butter
1 quart filtered water
sea salt or fish sauce (page 157) and pepper
2 tablespoons finely chopped chives
piima cream or creme fraiche (page 84)

This easy soup brings out the exquisite sweet flavor of beets. Use water, not stock.

Peel beets, chop coarsely and sauté very gently in butter for 1/2 hour or until tender. Add water, bring to a boil and skim. Simmer about 15 minutes. Purée soup with handheld blender. Season to taste, ladle into heated bowls and serve with cultured cream and chives.

CARROT SOUP

Serves 6

2 medium onions, peeled and chopped
1 pound carrots, peeled and sliced
4 tablespoons butter
2 teaspoons curry powder
1 1/2 quarts chicken stock (page 124)
1/2 teaspoon freshly grated lemon rind
1/2 teaspoon freshly grated ginger
sea salt or fish sauce (page 157) and pepper
piima cream or creme fraiche (page 84)

Sauté onions and carrots very gently in butter about 45 minutes or until tender. Add curry powder and stir around until well amalgamated. Add stock, bring to a boil and skim. Add lemon rind and ginger. Simmer, covered, about 15 minutes. Purée soup with a handheld blender. Season to taste. Ladle into heated bowls and serve with cultured cream.

The traditional medical school teaches that alcoholism is primarily a mental disease, a personality disorder or a weakness from which the person is trying to escape. The medical community fully recognizes that an alcoholic is generally malnourished, but the idea that alcoholism might be caused by lack of nourishment to the brain cells has received very little consideration. Dr. Roger J. Williams, former Director of the Clayton Foundation Biochemical Institute and first elected President of American Chemical Society, claims that it is quite possible that malnutrition develops as a forerunner of alcoholism, and that it is only when malnutrition of the brain cells becomes severe that true alcoholism appears. "Furthermore," he states, "I will herewith positively assert that no one who follows good nutritional practices will ever become an alcoholic." Lynn Sorenson *Health Freedom News*

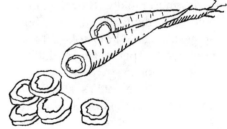

The black hat that butter has worn for the past generation may not be entirely warranted. Nor is the white hat worn by corn oil.

At least this is the indication from research conducted at Oregon Health Sciences University. Although butter does raise blood cholesterol in some individuals, the Oregon scientists found that rats given a diet rich in butterfat showed lower blood pressure than those given corn oil as their sole dietary fat. James F. Scheer *Health Freedom News*

Myth: A lowfat diet will make you "feel better . . . and increase your joy of living."

Truth: Lowfat diets are associated with increased rates of depression, psychological problems, fatigue, violence and suicide. (*Lancet* 3/2/92 v339)

Weston A Price did more than travel and practice dentistry. He also worked daily in his lab, usually testing vitamin A and D content in butter samples sent to him from throughout the country. Vitamin content typically peaked in June when the grass was growing most rapidly. They then declined throughout the summer, but rose again slightly in October. They were at least 50 percent lower during the winter months.

In the late 1920's Dr. Price gathered mortality statistics for heart disease for the entire United States and plotted them on the same graph as vitamin levels in butter. The graphs were a mirror image of each other. In other words, when levels of vitamin A and D were high, deaths from heart disease were low and when levels of vitamin A and D were low, deaths from heart disease were high.

It was after Dr. Price's death, when Americans abandoned butter completely in favor of hydrogenated vegetable oils, that deaths from heart disease soared. Price's neglected study indicates that the answer to this crisis is not, as we've been told, lowfat, but *better* fat. SWF

SQUASH AND SUN DRIED TOMATO SOUP
Serves 6

1 butternut squash
2 medium onions, peeled and chopped
3 tablespoons butter
1 cup sun dried tomatoes, packed in oil
1 quart chicken stock (page 124)
1/4 teaspoon red chile flakes
2 tablespoons finely chopped basil
sea salt or fish sauce (page 157) and pepper
piima cream or creme fraiche (page 84)

Cut squash in half lengthwise and place, cut sides down, in a glass baking pan with about 1/2 inch of water. Bake at 350 degrees until tender, about 1 hour. Meanwhile, sauté onions gently in butter until tender. Add tomatoes, stock and chile flakes. Bring to a boil and skim. Scoop cooked squash out of skin and add to soup. Simmer about 1/2 hour. Purée soup with a handheld blender. Thin with water if necessary. Add basil and season to taste. Simmer gently about 5 minutes, ladle into heated bowls and serve with cultured cream.

BLACK BEAN SOUP

Serves 6

2 medium onions, peeled and coarsely chopped
4 tablespoons extra virgin olive oil
4 cups cooked beans with bean juice (page 496),
    or 4 cups thick leftover bean liquid
1 quart beef or chicken stock (pages 122 or 124)
1/2 cup sherry
4 cloves garlic, peeled and mashed
1 teaspoon ground cumin
1 teaspoon dried oregano
1/4-1/2 teaspoon red chile flakes
1/4 cup fresh lime juice
sea salt or fish sauce (page 157) and pepper
piima cream or creme fraiche (page 84)
chopped cilantro for garnish
finely chopped green onion for garnish

This is a good way to use leftover beans, or the thick bean juice that is left after all the beans have been eaten. Sauté onions gently in olive oil until tender. Add beans or bean liquid, sherry and stock, bring to a boil and skim. Add cumin, oregano, garlic and chile flakes and simmer about 15 minutes. Purée soup with a handheld blender. Reheat and add lime juice. Season to taste. Ladle into heated bowls and serve with cultured cream, cilantro and green onions.

I see too many risks in the Spartan vegetarian diet. Most vegetarians are opposed to eating red meat, but I see no reason why they can't include poultry and fish in their diets, or at least dairy products and eggs. . . . The great peril of the strict vegetarian diet is suppression of the protective and life-giving thyroid function by minimizing the intake of essential vitamins. Stephen E. Langer, MD *Solved: The Riddle of Illness*

Dr. T. W. Gullickson, Professor of Dairy Chemistry, University of Minnesota, proved the nutritional superiority of butterfat over vegetable oils, which are the main ingredients of the vegetable margarines. Gullickson used skim milk and combined it with lard, tallow, coconut oil, corn oil, cottonseed oil or soybean oil in place of the cream and fed it to calves. The vegetable oil substitutes were mixed with skim milk in an attempt to imitate the 3.5 percent butterfat of milk. As often happens in research, they proved something entirely different from their original objective. They had set out to find a cheaper way to raise calves for veal production. What they found was that calves will only grow on God's own natural milk, and when fed vegetable oil substitutes instead of the cream, they sicken and die.

On the corn oil mix three out of eight died within one hundred-seventy days, some as soon as thirty-three days. On cottonseed oil three out of four died within one hundred-twenty-six days. Pick your favorite vegetable oil—the result was the same. The survivors quickly recovered when switched to whole raw milk. If vegetable oil products are so devastating to the health of calves, do you think maybe they are bad for you, too? William Campbell Douglass, MD *The Milk Book*

The peanut is a legume that is particularly rich in protein and fat. It is an excellent source of niacin, pantothenic acid and biotin as well as other B vitamins, vitamin E, iron, calcium and potassium. Peanuts are also rich in tryptophan, an amino acid that promotes a healthy nervous system. As peanuts are often grown as a rotation crop with cotton, a heavily sprayed commodity, it is important to buy only organic peanuts and peanut butter. The carcinogenic mold aflatoxin that sometimes develops in peanuts, especially those grown in moist climates, is virtually neutralized by cooking or soaking. Peanuts should never be eaten raw. Buy freshly ground peanut butter made from roasted organic peanuts, or make your own peanut butter (page 516). SWF

Nuts are a wonderful source of boron, a trace mineral that, for reasons not quite understood, plays an important role in bone health. Postmenopausal women placed on boron supplements had reduced calcium and magnesium losses and increased concentrations of circulating estrogen. One explanation is that boron plays a key role in the production of hormones that regulate bone modeling.

Peanuts are the richest source of boron, followed by almonds and hazelnuts. Apples, pears and tomatoes are also good sources. SWF

PEANUT SOUP
Serves 6

2 medium onions, peeled and chopped
1 Anaheim pepper, seeded and chopped
1 teaspoon freshly grated ginger
3 tablespoons butter
1 cup freshly ground peanut butter
1 1/2 quarts chicken stock (page 124), heated
4 cloves garlic, peeled and coarsely chopped
1/4 cup naturally fermented soy sauce
1/4 cup finely chopped cilantro
piima cream or creme fraiche (page 84)

Sauté onion, pepper and ginger in butter until tender. Add peanut butter. Slowly add heated stock, beating constantly with a whisk. Bring to a simmer, not a boil. Add soy sauce and garlic and simmer about 10 minutes.

Purée soup with a handheld blender. Ladle into heated bowls, garnish with cilantro and serve with cultured cream.

ALMOND SOUP
Serves 6

2 medium onions, peeled and coarsely chopped
3 tablespoons butter
3 cups finely ground crispy almonds (page 515)
1 quart chicken stock (page 124), heated
1/2 teaspoon ground cardamom
sea salt or fish sauce (page 157) and pepper
piima cream or creme fraiche (page 84)

Sauté onions gently in butter until tender. Add almonds and stock, blend together with a whisk and heat gently. Add cardamom and simmer about 15 minutes. Purée soup with a handheld blender. Reheat and season to taste. Ladle into heated bowls and serve with cultured cream; or allow to cool, stir in cream and serve the soup chilled.

SEAFOOD BISQUE

Serves 6

6 cups shrimp stock (page 121)
4 tablespoons tomato paste
1/4 teaspoon saffron threads
1/8 teaspoon cayenne pepper
2 cloves garlic, peeled and mashed
2/3 cup armagnac or dry sherry (optional)
2 tablespoons arrowroot mixed with
    2 tablespoons water
4-6 tablespoons shrimp butter (page 158)
1 cup piima cream or creme fraiche (page 84)
sea salt or fish sauce (page 157) and pepper
2 cups small shrimp, shelled
1 cup crab meat

Bring shrimp stock to a boil and whisk in tomato paste. Add saffron threads, garlic, cayenne pepper and armagnac or dry sherry. Gradually whisk in arrowroot mixture, shrimp butter and cultured cream. Season to taste. Add shrimp and crab and simmer for about 10 minutes.

When animals are placed on skim milk . . . the animals develop very poorly. But when four percent butter fat is fed to similar animals, they develop normally. The vegetable oils now being pushed on the American people by organized medicine and self-styled nutrition experts will not work as a substitute for cream. Skim-milk-fed animals develop testicular atrophy with complete sterility. Male sterility is a major concern in our country today and the skim milk fad may be a major contributing factor. The test animals also developed severe calcification of most large blood vessels, anemia, and high blood pressure. Another characteristic of the syndrome that may be of significance in human medicine is the development of calcium deposits around the bone openings in the spine that provide for the exit of nerves. Sciatica and other nerve compression syndromes may be caused by this nutritional deficiency. Also, a decrease in hearing, leading to complete deafness was consistently found. William Campbell Douglass, MD *The Milk Book*

One of the modern diseases that confounds the medical profession is the syndrome of chemical sensitivities. Desperate patients make radical life style changes to avoid exposure to chemicals that most people find innocuous; and they are pointed to lowfat foods that tend to be full of additives. But one likely cause of chemical sensitivities is a malfunctioning liver that is unable to do its job of detoxification. Two factors in the modern diet must be suspected as major contributors: the disappearance of saturated fats, which are protective of liver function, and high levels of fructose, which impair liver function. SWF

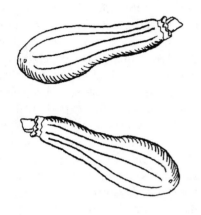

These oils [in margarine and tub spreads] are as refined as the gasoline in your car. In the refinery they are treated with a caustic soda solution which removes the lecithin, an essential nutrient. Then the oil is steam-cleaned under a vacuum at tremendous temperature. This second step should destroy any remaining food value in the oil, but, just in case, the oil is then bleached at a high temperature to remove any color.

The liquid oil is then chemically treated by being bombarded with hydrogen under pressure in the presence of the metal nickel. This "hydrogenation" process is what makes the oil look like real butter. But now it's no longer a "polyunsaturate" which is supposed to be so good for you. The remaining step in the manufacture of plastic butter is to steam-clean it *again* at high temperatures to deodorize it. Then the preservative and color are added, and it is ready for your table.

The liquid part of margarine, which is the second largest component, is usually *re-pasteurized*, that is reheated, skim milk. So the butter substitute on your toast has been steam-cleaned or superheated at least *four times*. William Campbell Douglass, MD *The Milk Book*

DR. CONNELLY'S VEGETABLE SOUP
Serves 4-6

4 cups chicken stock (page 124) or filtered water
4 tablespoons tomato paste
1 cup french beans, cut into 1-inch lengths
1 cup finely chopped celery with leaves
2-3 medium zucchini, quartered lengthwise and thinly sliced
2 tablespoons parsley, finely chopped
1/2 teaspoon paprika
sea salt or fish sauce (page 157) and pepper

This is a tasty version of Bieler broth (page 606), recommended for increased energy and treatment of stress. In particular, zucchini with its high sodium content nourishes the adrenal glands. Thomas Connelly, a chiropractor from Washington D.C., recommends this soup for back pain, ligament problems and other symptoms of depleted adrenal function.

Bring stock or water and tomato paste to a boil, blend with a wire whisk and skim. Reduce heat, add beans, celery and zucchini and simmer until they are just tender and still green, about 10 minutes. Stir in parsley and season to taste.

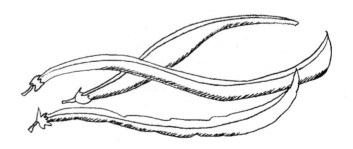

RUSSIAN SHRIMP SOUP

(Chlodnik)
Serves 8

2 cups piima cream or creme fraiche (page 84)
5 cups cultured buttermilk (page 83)
1/2 cup sauerkraut juice (page 92)
4 cloves garlic, crushed
1 teaspoon sea salt
1/2 teaspoon pepper
1 pound cooked, shelled shrimp,
      cut into 1/2-inch slices
2 medium cucumbers, peeled, seeded and diced
3 tablespoons chopped fresh dill
1 teaspoon freshly ground fennel seed,
1 bunch green onion, finely chopped
2 hard boiled eggs, finely chopped,
      for garnish (optional)

Place cultured cream, buttermilk, sauerkraut juice, garlic, salt and pepper in a large glass or stainless steel bowl and blend with a whisk. Stir in the shrimp, cucumbers, dill, fennel and green onions. Cover and refrigerate for several hours or overnight.

To serve, ladle into chilled soup bowls and sprinkle with optional chopped hard boiled egg.

COLD CUCUMBER SOUP

Serves 4

2 medium cucumbers, peeled and sliced
1 cup chicken stock (page 124)
1 cup piima cream or creme fraiche (page 84)
2 cloves garlic, mashed
1 tablespoon lemon juice
1 teaspoon finely chopped mint or dill (optional)
sea salt and pepper

Place cucumbers, stock, cultured cream, garlic and lemon juice in food processor and blend until smooth. Stir in the mint or dill and season to taste. Serve well chilled.

Although needed only in very small quantities, vitamin B_{12} is one of those nutrients that make life worth living. Deficiencies can manifest as the living hell of depression, multiple sclerosis, dementia and psychiatric disorders, such as obsessive-compulsive behavior and manic-depression, not to mention life-threatening anemia, cancer and heart disease. Many cases diagnosed as Alzheimer's are actually the result of inadequate B_{12}.

Early signs of deficiency include fatigue, tingling in the hands and feet, sleep disorders and a tendency to irrational anger.

Usable vitamin B_{12} is found *only* in animal products. It is absorbed through a complex process involving an "intrinsic factor," secreted by the parietal cells in the stomach. Deficiencies are most likely to appear in vegetarians, who do not consume animal products, and in the elderly and those deficient in hydrochloric acid or pancreatic enzymes, who cannot produce or use the intrinsic factor.

B_{12} is rendered unusable by pasteurization, which is why it is so important for vegetarians to use *raw* milk products. Unfortunately, vegetarian groups have opted for soy products, rather than lobby for access to raw milk products *as a religious right.*

Rather than universal testing for serum cholesterol, wouldn't it be better to test all adults for B_{12} status on a regular basis? In the early stages of deficiency, symptoms can be reversed by supplements of the vitamin in a form that is easy to absorb. At later stages of deficiency, the neurological damage is irreversible. SWF

Both Weston Price and Francis Pottenger accurately predicted that western man would develop more and more diseases as he substituted vegetable oils for animal fats, and that reproduction would become increasingly difficult. By some estimates, 25 percent of American couples are now infertile, a condition that may send the population reductionists into paroxysms of glee but that causes untold heartache to millions of individuals. Infertility treatments are problematic, painful and expensive compared to the primitive prescription: more animal fat. *Nasty, Brutish and Short?*

OCTOBER
DINNER

Curried Apple Soup
❀❀❀❀❀
Teriyaki Duck Breasts
❀❀❀
Pineapple Chutney
❀❀❀
Algerian
Wedding Rice
❀❀❀
Brussels Sprouts
❀❀❀❀❀
Baked Pears

CURRIED APPLE SOUP
Serves 6

6 tart apples, peeled and quartered
4 tablespoons butter
2 medium onions, peeled and chopped
1 teaspoon grated fresh ginger
1 teaspoon each dry mustard, turmeric, ground
    cumin and ground coriander
1/4 teaspoon each cloves, cinnamon and cayenne
1 1/2 quarts chicken stock (page 124)
juice of 1 lemon
sea salt
piima cream or creme fraiche (page 84)

Sauté onions in butter until soft. Stir in spices. Combine onion mixture, apples and stock and simmer until apples are soft. Purée soup with a handheld blender. Add lemon juice and season to taste. Ladle into heated bowls and serve with cultured cream.

POTATO LEEK SOUP
(Vichissoise)
Serves 8

3 leeks, peeled, cleaned and chopped
2 tablespoons butter
2 tablespoons extra virgin olive oil
4 potatoes, peeled and chopped
6 cups chicken stock (page 124)
several sprigs thyme, tied together
1 cup piima cream or creme fraiche (page 84)
sea salt and pepper
finely chopped chives for garnish

Sauté leeks until soft in butter and olive oil. Add potatoes and stock, bring to a boil and skim. Add thyme and simmer until all vegetables are soft. Let cool. Remove thyme. Purée soup with a handheld blender. Chill well. Process in food processor in batches with piima cream until frothy. Season to taste. Serve in chilled soup bowls and garnish with chives.

SPICED GAZPACHO

Serves 6

8 tomatoes, peeled, seeded and chopped
5 garlic cloves, peeled and chopped
5 stalks celery, chopped
2 medium red onions, peeled and chopped
5 tablespoons extra virgin olive oil
2 tablespoons lemon juice
1 tablespoon raw wine vinegar
2 1/2 teaspoons paprika
1 1/2 teaspoon ground cumin (optional)
1/4 teaspoon cayenne pepper
1/2 cup cilantro, coarsely chopped
1/2-1 cup filtered water
sea salt and pepper

To peel tomatoes, see page 70. Mix all ingredients except water together. Process in batches in a food processor until not quite smooth. Thin to desired consistency with water. Season to taste. Serve well chilled.

UNBLENDED GAZPACHO

Serves 6

1 1/2 cups lemon pepper dressing (page 134)
2 bunches green onions, finely chopped
2 green peppers, seeded and finely chopped
1 bunch celery, with leaves, finely chopped
3 cucumbers, peeled, seeded and finely chopped
1 bunch radishes, finely chopped
1 quart chicken stock (page 124)
6 tomatoes, peeled, seeded and chopped
1/4 cup finely chopped chives
1 tablespoon finely chopped parsley

The secret of this unusual gazpacho is to chop all the vegetables very small and use a very rich chicken stock. To peel tomatoes, see page 70.

Mix green onions, celery, peppers, cucumbers and radishes with dressing and marinate, refrigerated, for 12 to 24 hours. Stir in stock and tomatoes. Ladle into soup bowls and garnish with chives and parsley.

OUTDOOR
CONCERT PICNIC

Cold Cucumber Soup
✦✦✦✦✦
Spiced Chicken
Breasts
✦✦✦
Pickled Red Peppers
✦✦✦
Tabouli
✦✦✦✦✦
Carob Cookies
✦✦✦
Grapes

We now know that to replace saturated fats with unsaturated fats, while it *may* limit the risk of cardiovascular disease, presents other less well-known dangers. Although scientists are usually little inclined to base their arguments on tradition, they have nonetheless noticed that no peoples have consumed large quantities of polyunsaturated fats over long periods. The remarkable fact is that studies of nonindustrialized peoples lead to the conclusion that the amount of polyunsaturated fats in the diet should be about 4% of the total caloric intake which is really very little—about 1 1/2 soup spoons per day of sunflower oil. . . . On the other hand, the amount of saturated fat consumed varies considerably from one ethnic group to another. Claude Aubert *Dis-Moi Comment Tu Cuisines*

PINK GAZPACHO

Serves 6

NEW WORLD
DINNER

Pink Gazpacho

Crab Cakes with
Red Pepper Sauce

Gourmet Succatash

Strawberry Pecan Tart

6 ripe tomatoes, peeled, seeded and chopped
1 cucumber, peeled and chopped
2 green peppers, seeded and chopped
3 cloves garlic, peeled and chopped
1 cup whole grain bread crumbs
5 tablespoons raw vinegar
5 tablespoons extra virgin olive oil
2 tablespoons tomato paste
2-3 cups filtered water
sea salt and pepper
salad croutons (page 520) for garnish
1 bunch green onion, finely chopped, for garnish
1 cucumber, peeled and finely chopped, for garnish

Many of those biochemists and serious clinicians involved in the latest research on refined sugar have condensed their experience and research into one statement: "Consumption of refined sugar is the most pleasant means of gradual suicide." Only a handful of these researchers and serious clinicians realize that the above statement is only half true. The true part is that refined sugar consumption is gradual suicide. The untrue half is that it is pleasant. Anyone who has experienced the misery of constant tooth or gum problems, the financial ruin of constant illness, the frustration of low energy, the incapacitation of allergies, the pain of arthritis, the crippling effects of a survived heart attack, or the terror of cancer is well aware that no matter how gradual the process there is nothing pleasant about any of these afflictions. The latest research and serious clinical experience demonstrate that consumption of refined sugar is a major factor in all of the above conditions, plus many more. Bruce Pacetti, DDS *PPNF Health Journal*

The combination of ingredients in this soup seems unlikely but this version of gazpacho is truly delicious, a wonderful starter for a summer meal. The accompaniments—croutons, green onions and cucumber—are a must.

To peel tomatoes, see page 70. Mix vegetables, vinegar, oil, bread crumbs and tomato paste in a bowl and let stand about 1 hour. Blend in batches in a food processor, adding water as needed to make a purée. Thin with water to desired consistency. Season to taste. Chill well before serving. Serve with croutons, finely chopped green onion and finely diced cucumber.

RAW MEAT APPETIZERS

When Dr. Weston Price made his pioneering studies of primitive peoples around the world, he was struck by the fact that almost every group he visited ate a certain amount of their animal protein raw. The proportion of raw animal protein in the diet varied considerably. Among some Eskimo groups it verged on 100 percent; natives of the Polynesian islands consumed a good portion of the sea food they caught without cooking it; African tribes valued liver in its raw state as essential to good health and optimum growth and strength. Tribes whose eating habits were largely vegetarian nevertheless ingested raw animal protein in the form of grubs and insects. The principal source of raw animal protein for European communities was unpasteurized milk products.

Today, unfortunately, raw dairy products are largely unavailable in America. We can and should, however, eat raw meat and fish on a regular basis. Almost every world cuisine offers recipes to satisfy what seems to be a universal requirement for raw animal protein—*steak tartare* from France, *carpaccio* from Italy, *kibbeh* from the Middle East and raw, marinated fish dishes from Scandinavia, Hawaii, Latin America and Asia. The collection we offer here attests to the universality of this practice.

Many researchers have recommended that raw meat be included in the diet on a regular basis; but others, citing the problem of intestinal parasites, insist that meat should never be eaten raw. (No wonder most of us are confused about nutrition!) Parasite infection occurs frequently among the Japanese and Koreans, who habitually eat raw fish, so these warnings must be taken seriously. Fortunately, we can eliminate parasites in animal foods without cooking them.

The problem of parasites in beef or lamb is easily solved. Simply freeze the meat for 14 days. According to the United States Department of Agriculture, this will kill off all parasites. Needless to say, you should use only organic meat for your raw meat appetizers. Raw meat dishes should contain the fat as well as the lean, because meat fat contains antimicrobial fatty acids. The problem with fish is trickier as fish loses its firmness and texture when frozen. The solution—found among many ethnic cuisines, especially in hot countries—is to marinate or ferment fish in an acid solution of lemon juice, lime juice or whey. This will effectively kill off all parasites and pathogens and will serve to predigest the fish as well. We do not recommend *sushi*, which contains raw fish that has not been marinated.

If you are not used to eating meat raw but want to take that courageous first step, we suggest you begin with *kibbeh*, a mixture of raw lamb and bulgur (sprouted cracked wheat) from the Middle East. It is simply delicious, a meal in itself, as well as a dish that will please the most exacting gourmet. Then move on to the other recipes offered here, an eclectic sampling of raw meat dishes from around the world.

In the *National Geographic* (1970), William S. Ellis described *kibbeh*, the national dish of Lebanon. It consists basically of raw lamb and crushed wheat. These foods are pounded together for about an hour in a large stone mortar, then kneaded, seasoned, and eaten raw—*kibbeh niebh*. The enzymes cathepsin and lipase of the lamb and the protease, amylase and lipase of wheat, being liberated from their bondage by pulverization, cooperate to achieve predigestion and inactivation of enzyme inhibitors during the hour the food is being pulverized. Thereafter, the predigestion continues both before and after the food is eaten, until the stomach acidity becomes very strong. People who eat this Lebanese dish save their own enzymes. Edward Howell, MD *Enzyme Nutrition*

Pyridoxine or B_6 deficiencies are widespread in America, partly because our traditional source of this heat-sensitive vitamin—raw milk—is no longer sold commercially. It requires some courage to consume the best source of B_6—raw liver. This leaves raw cheese, meat and fish as the only sure sources of B_6 available to most Americans. When B_6 is lacking, the pathways for use of vitamins B_1 and B_2 may be less effective, leading to widespread symptoms of B vitamin deficiencies. Deficiencies of B_6 have been linked with diabetes, heart disease, nervous disorders, carpel tunnel syndrome, PMS, morning sickness, toxemia of pregnancy, kidney failure, alcoholism, asthma, sickle cell anemia and cancer. B_6 supplements have been shown to be highly effective in preventing blindness in diabetics. Americans would be wise to include raw meat or fish on a frequent basis to avoid these debilitating conditions. SWF

RAW LAMB APPETIZER
(Kibbeh)
Serves 6-12

1 pound ground lamb, frozen 14 days and thawed
1 cup bulgur (page 460)
1/4 cup pickled red pepper (page 99), processed to a paste in food processor (optional)
1 small onion, very finely chopped
sea salt and pepper
1 tablespoon extra virgin olive oil
1 small onion, finely sliced
1-2 lemons, cut into wedges

Soak bulgur in warm water for 10 minutes. Pour into a strainer, rinse and squeeze out moisture. Mix with lamb, optional red pepper paste and onion. Add salt and pepper to taste. Form into a mound or loaf on a plate and brush with olive oil. Garnish with onion slices and lemon wedges. Serve with pita bread as an appetizer or on lettuce leaves as a first course.

SPICY RAW LAMB APPETIZER
(Spicy Kibbeh)
Serves 6-12

1 pound ground lamb, frozen 14 days and thawed
1 1/2 cup bulgur (page 460)
1 small onion, finely minced
2 tablespoons lemon juice
1 teaspoon each ground allspice and cinnamon
generous pinch nutmeg
1/4 teaspoon cayenne pepper
sea salt and pepper
1/4 cup crispy pine nuts (page 514)
extra virgin olive oil
2 small onions, thinly sliced
1-2 lemons, cut into wedges

Soak bulgur in warm water for 10 minutes. Pour into a strainer, rinse and squeeze out moisture. Mix with lamb, lemon juice, spices and onion. Season to taste. Form into a mound or loaf on a plate and brush with olive oil. Garnish with pine nuts, onion slices and lemon wedges. Serve with pita bread as an appetizer or on lettuce leaves as a first course.

LAMB AND CRACKED WHEAT APPETIZER

(Keuftah)
Serves 6

1/2 pound ground lamb,
    frozen 14 days and thawed
1 1/2 cups bulgur (page 460)
1 onion, minced
pinch cayenne pepper
1 tablespoon extra virgin olive oil
1 tablespoon lemon juice
2 tablespoons green pepper, minced
2 tablespoons green onions, minced
1/4 cup parsley, finely chopped
1 tablespoon fresh mint or basil, minced
sea salt and pepper
2 tablespoons extra virgin olive oil
1-2 lemons, cut into wedges

Keuftah differs from *kibbeh* in that it contains a higher proportion of bulgur (cracked wheat). Soak bulgur in warm water for 10 minutes. Pour into a strainer, rinse and squeeze out moisture. Mix with lamb, lemon juice, olive oil, spices, pepper, onion and herbs. Season to taste. Form a mound on a platter, brush with olive oil and decorate with lemon wedges. Serve with pita bread as an appetizer or on lettuce leaves as a first course.

Variation: Meatball Appetizer
Form into balls and sauté in *4 tablespoons olive oil or lard*. Serve with tahini sauce (page 148).

There is a close relationship between silica and aluminum in Alzheimer's brain lesions, as the two substances bind together to form aluminosilicates. High levels of silica in drinking water in the form of silicic acid do seem to protect against the adverse effects of aluminum ingestion, and silicic acid ingestion increases urinary aluminum excretion Melvyn R. Werbach, MD *The Natural Activist* Citizens for Health

Among the many items of information of great interest furnished by Dr. Romig [when I visited the Eskimos] were facts that fitted well into the modern picture of association of modern degenerative processes with modernization. He stated that in his thirty-six years of contact with these people he had never seen a case of malignant disease among the truly primitive Eskimos and Indians, although it frequently occurs when they become modernized. He found, similarly, that the acute surgical problems requiring operation on internal organs, such as the gall bladder, kidney, stomach and appendix, do not tend to occur among the primitives but are very common problems among the modernized Eskimos and Indians. Growing out of his experience in which he had seen large numbers of the modernized Eskimos and Indians attacked with tuberculosis, which tended to be progressive and ultimately fatal as long as the patients stayed under modernized living conditions, he now sends them back when possible to primitive conditions and to a primitive diet, under which the death rate is very much lower than under modernized conditions. Indeed, he reported that a great majority of the afflicted recover under the primitive type of nutrition. Weston Price, DDS *Nutrition and Physical Degeneration*

Animal feeding experiments show that many changes besides bone growth take place when cooked foods are used. One extensive study, involving 900 cats over a period of 10 years, was done by F. M. Pottenger, Jr., M. D. Cats receiving raw meat and raw milk reproduced normally from one generation to the next. All kittens showed the same good bone structure, were able to nurse, were resistant to infections and parasites, and behaved in a predictable manner. From generation to generation they maintained regular broad faces with adequate nasal cavities, broad dental arches, and regular dentition with firm, pink membranes, and no evidence of infection.

Cats receiving cooked meat presented quite a different picture. Abortion was about 25 percent in the first generation and 70 percent in the second generation. Deliveries were difficult, many cats dying in labor. Mortality rates of the kittens were high, frequently due to the failure of the mother to lactate, or the kittens being too frail to nurse. The kittens did not have the homogeneity of those cats fed on raw foods. Instead, each kitten was different in skeletal pattern.

In the second generation the kittens had irregularities in the skull and longer, narrower faces; the teeth did not erupt at the regular time; and diseases of the gums developed. By the third generation the bones were very fine with scarcely enough structure to hold the skull together. The teeth were smaller and more irregular. Some mothers steadily declined in health, dying from some obscure tissue exhaustion about three months after delivery.

The cooked-meat-fed cats were irritable, the females dangerous to handle, and the males more docile, often to the point of being unaggressive. Sex interest was slack or per-

RAW BEEF, FRENCH STYLE

(Steak Tartare)
Serves 20, as an appetizer

*1 pound ground sirloin or filet, frozen
    14 days and thawed*
1 medium onion, finely minced
1/4 cup parsley, finely chopped
3 tablespoons Dijon-type mustard
2 egg yolks
sea salt, pepper and cayenne pepper
2 hard boiled eggs, finely chopped
1 red onion, finely chopped
*1 cup small capers, drained, rinsed and
    dried with paper towels*
sourdough bread or round croutons (page 520)
1/2 cup butter, softened

Mix beef with egg yolks, onion and parsley and season to taste. Form into a mound on a platter. Surround meat with bread or croutons. Serve with chopped egg, chopped onion, capers and butter.

RAW BEEF, ITALIAN STYLE

(Carpaccio)
Serves 6

*2 pounds filet of beef, frozen 14 days, partially
    thawed and sliced very thin*
4-6 tablespoons extra virgin olive oil
*1 tablespoon dried pink
    or green peppercorns, crushed*
2 cups egg mustard sauce (page 143)

Arrange meat slices on individual plates leaving the center of the plate empty, cover with plastic wrap and place in freezer for about 1 hour or until meat is very cold. To serve, sprinkle with olive oil and peppercorns. Place a ramekin of sauce in the middle of each plate. Serve with round croutons (page 520).

RAW BEEF, MEXICAN STYLE
Serves 4

1/2 pound ground sirloin, frozen for
    14 days and thawed
1/2 cup lime juice
1 small tomato, peeled, seeded and finely chopped
1 small onion, finely chopped
4 small green chiles, seeded and finely chopped
sea salt

To peel tomatoes, see page 70. Mix beef with lime juice and marinate, covered, in the refrigerator for about 4 hours. Mix with remaining ingredients, season to taste and refrigerate another 2 hours. Serve with baked or fried sprouted whole wheat tortillas (page 519).

RAW BEEF, VIETNAMESE STYLE
Serves 4

1 pound sirloin roast, frozen 14 days, partially
    thawed and sliced very thin
1 tablespoon extra virgin olive oil
3 tablespoons fresh lime juice
1 small onion, thinly sliced
1 jalapeno pepper, seeded and thinly sliced
1 bunch green onions, finely chopped
1/2 cup crispy peanuts (page 514), finely chopped
1/2 cup dried onion flakes, sautéed in olive oil
    and drained on paper towels
1 bunch cilantro, chopped
2 limes, cut into wedges

Mix olive oil with lime juice, sliced onion and jalapeno pepper and brush on meat slices. Marinate meat in refrigerator for several hours.

Shake off excess marinade and vegetable slices from meat and arrange on a platter or individual plates. Sprinkle green onions, peanuts, fried onion flakes and cilantro over meat. Garnish with lime wedges.

verted; and skin lesions, allergies and intestinal parasites become progressively worse from one generation to the next. Pneumonia, diarrhea, osteomyelitis, arthritis and many other degenerative conditions familiar in human medicine were observed. The kittens of the third generation were so degenerated that none lived beyond the sixth month, thus terminating the strain.

At autopsy the cooked-meat-fed females frequently were found to have ovarian atrophy and uterine congestion, and the males showed failure in the development of active sperm. Organs showed signs of degenerative disease. Bones were longer but smaller in diameter and had less calcium. In the third generation some had bones as soft as rubber—a true condition of osteogenesis. Emory W. Thurston, PhD *Nutrition for Tots to Teens*

As with men, insufficient intake of certain nutrients can often make women less prone to become pregnant. Much research reveals that subnormal intake of vitamin B_6 (pyridoxine) can diminish the chances of conception . . . . Sometimes birth control pills diminish the amount of available vitamin B_6 so that women who discontinue this oral contraceptive often cannot conceive until a year after cessation. Then, in one study, 98 percent of them taking vitamin B_6 regularly resumed normal menstruation and became pregnant within four months. A painful complication that often comes with deficiency of vitamin B_6 is premenstrual syndrome, which could also serve to indicate why certain women are unable to conceive. James F. Scheer *Health Freedom News*

It is possible to starve to death eating lean meat. I'm not making this up. The ancient tribes of the West knew this and would not eat female bison in the spring because nursing and pregnant bison cows burned off their fat reserves during the winter months, leaving few calories in their flesh that might help the natives to digest the pure protein of the meat. Explorers like Randolph Marcy discovered this truth the hard way. Members of his 1856 expedition to Wyoming continued to weaken and lose weight even though they consumed six pounds of horse and mule meat a day. The problem: the horses and mules were so starved that their meat had no fat. Eugene Linden *Forbes FYI*

Many people have reported the disappearance of numerous symptoms and increased vitality within days of adding raw meat, fish or milk to the diet. Observers of Eskimos report that when these people suffer from heart disease, diabetes and other problems associated with their adopted Western diet, they invariably experience complete cure when they returned to their native diet containing large amounts of raw meat and fish.

How much in the way of raw animal products should the diet include? The answer varies with the individual. Some will thrive on a diet in which almost all meat and fish is raw; others find that cooked meats are easier to digest. For most of us, a combination of both raw and cooked animal foods gives the best long-term results. SWF

RAW BEEF, KOREAN STYLE
Serves 4-6

1 pound well marbled flank or skirt steak,
*   frozen for 14 days and partially thawed*
1 cup naturally fermented soy sauce
1/4 cup rice vinegar
1 teaspoon grated ginger
4 cloves garlic, mashed
1 teaspoon raw honey
3 tablespoons toasted sesame oil
1 bunch green onions, chopped
2 tablespoons toasted sesame seeds
dash of cayenne pepper

Cut the flank steak on the bias at 1/8-inch intervals. Cut these strips into a julienne, and chop with a cleaver. Mix remaining ingredients and marinate beef in this mixture, refrigerated, for several hours. Serve with basic brown rice (page 466) and kimchi (page 94).

RAW BEEF, THAI STYLE
(Laab Isaan)
Serves 4

1/2 pound beef brisket, frozen 14 days, partially
*   thawed and sliced very thin*
2 tablespoons lemon juice
2 tablespoons fish sauce (page 157)
1 teaspoon red chile powder
1 jalapeno pepper, seeded and thinly sliced
2 green onions, sliced very thin
1/3 cup each cilantro and mint leaves, chopped
1 head Romaine lettuce, outer leaves removed

Process meat slices briefly in food processor to a consistency somewhat coarser than hamburger. Mix lemon juice, fish sauce, cayenne pepper, green onion, chopped cilantro and chopped mint. Mix well with the meat and marinate, covered, for several hours. Serve mounded on a platter, garnished with sprigs of mint and cilantro and surrounded with lettuce leaves.

CORNED BEEF

Makes 2 pounds

1 2-pound beef brisket,
    frozen 14 days and thawed
1/2 cup whey (page 87)
1 cup filtered water
2 tablespoons sea salt
1 tablespoon mustard seeds
4-5 bay leaves, crumbled
1 tablespoon juniper berries, crushed
1 teaspoon red pepper flakes

Mix seasonings and rub into both sides of brisket. Place in a bowl that just contains it. Mix whey with water and pour over brisket. Cover and marinate at room temperature for about 2 days, turning frequently. Transfer to refrigerator. Use for sandwiches or corned beef hash (page 398).

MARINATED FISH IN COCONUT CREAM

Serves 4

1 pound whitefish, cut into 1/2-inch cubes
1 teaspoon sea salt
1/2 cup lime juice
1 tablespoon whey (page 87)
3/4 cup coconut milk (page 160)
1 bunch scallions, chopped
1 tomato, peeled, seeded and chopped (optional)
1 clove garlic, crushed (optional)
Boston lettuce leaves
1 tablespoon sesame seeds, toasted

To peel tomatoes, see page 70. Mix salt with lime juice and whey. Toss with fish and marinate at least 4 hours in the refrigerator. Drain the fish. Add coconut milk, scallions and optional tomato and garlic. Serve on Boston lettuce leaves and garnish with sesame seeds.

One of the outstanding changes which I have found takes place in the primitive races at their point of contact with our modern civilization is a decrease in the ease and efficiency of the birth process. When I visited the Six Nation Reservation at Brantford, Ontario, I was told by the physician in charge that a change of this kind had occurred during the period of his administration, which had covered twenty-eight years, and that the hospital was now used largely to care for young Indian women during abnormal childbirth. . . . In Alaska, Dr Romig told me that in his thirty-six years among the Eskimos he had never been able to arrive in time to see a normal birth by a primitive Eskimo woman. But conditions have changed materially with the new generation of Eskimo girls, born after their parents began to use foods of modern civilization. Many of them are carried to his hospital after they had been in labor for several days. Weston Price, DDS *Nutrition and Physical Degeneration*

Cod liver oil is an excellent source of vitamins A and D. Cod liver oil also contains DHA, a fatty acid essential to the development of the brain and nervous system. Adequate DHA in the mother's diet is necessary for the proper development of the retina in the infant she carries. DHA in mother's milk helps prevent learning disabilities and vision problems. Cod liver oil and foods like liver and egg yolk supply this essential nutrient to the developing fetus, to nursing infants and to growing children. Saturated fats help the body put the DHA in the tissues where it belongs. This explains why Weston Price got such miraculous results when he gave high-vitamin butter and cod liver oil together for the treatment of caries and many other diseases. SWF

In Japan the food is meager, blood cholesterol is low and the risk of getting a heart attack is much smaller than in any other country. Given these facts you will most probably say that in Japan atherosclerosis must be rare.

The condition of the arteries of American and Japanese people was studied in the fifties by Professors Ira Gore and A. E. Hirst at Harvard Medical School and Professor Yahei Koseki from Sapporo, Japan. At that time US people on average had a blood cholesterol of 220 whereas Japanese had about 170.

The aorta, the main artery of the body, from 659 Americans and 260 Japanese people were studied after death. Meticulously all signs of atherosclerosis were recorded and graded. As expected, atherosclerosis increased from age 40 upwards, both in Americans and in Japanese. Now to the surprising fact.

When degree of atherosclerosis was compared in each age group there was hardly any difference between American and Japanese people. Between age forty and sixty, Americans were a little more arteriosclerotic than Japanese; between sixty and eighty there was practically no difference, and above eighty Japanese were a little more arteriosclerotic than Americans.

A similar study was conducted by Dr. J. A. Resch from Minneapolis and Dr. S. N. Okabe and K. Kimoto from Kyushu, Japan. They studied the arteries of the brain in 1408 Japanese and in more than 5000 American people and found that in all age groups Japanese people were more arteriosclerotic than were Americans.

The conclusion from these studies is of course that the level of cholesterol in the blood has little importance for the development of atherosclerosis, if any at all. Uffe Ravnskov, MD, PhD *The Cholesterol Myths*

MARINATED SALMON
(Gravlox)
Serves 10-12

2-3 pounds fresh salmon, center cut, cleaned, scaled, with skin left on, cut into 2 filets
1/4 cup sea salt
1/4 cup Rapadura (see page 536)
2 tablespoons green peppercorns, crushed
1/4 cup whey (page 87)
2 large bunches fresh dill, snipped

This gourmet delicacy is so easy to make yourself—why pay dozens of dollars per pound to purchase it from a delicatessen?

Using pliers, remove any small bones in the filets. Rinse well and pat dry. Mix Rapadura, peppercorns and salt together and rub thoroughly into the flesh side of both filets. Sprinkle with whey and cover both filets with dill. Place the filets flesh side together and wrap well in plastic wrap. Wrap all in aluminum foil. Place between two cookie sheets and set a heavy weight, such as a brick, on top. Refrigerate at least 2 days and as long as 6 days, turning every 12 hours or so.

To serve, remove foil and plastic wrap. Slice thinly on the diagonal. Serve as an hors d'oeuvre with sour dough bread or round croutons (page 520) and fresh chives or finely chopped onion; or on individual plates with a similar garnish and lemon wedges.

Variations:

Use *snapper or bass* instead of salmon and substitute *parsley, chervil or chives* for dill.

RAW TUNA SALAD

Serves 4

3/4 pound fresh tuna, cut into a 1/4-inch dice
1/4 cup lime juice
2 tablespoons whey (page 87), optional
1 small red pepper, cut into quarters
1/3 cup celery, diced
2 tablespoons red onion or scallions, finely diced
2 tablespoons small capers, rinsed,
    well drained and dried with paper towels
1 tablespoon fresh chives, chopped
1 tablespoon parsley, finely chopped
1 teaspoon fresh thyme leaves
1 tablespoon fresh basil, minced
1 tablespoon fresh lemon juice
3 tablespoon extra virgin olive oil
sea salt and pepper
Boston lettuce leaves

Mix tuna with lime juice and optional whey, cover and marinate in refrigerator for 12 to 36 hours.

Place pepper pieces skin side up in an oiled pyrex dish and bake at 450 degrees about 10 minutes. Turn pepper pieces over and bake another 10 minutes or so until skins are browned and begin to buckle. Remove pepper pieces to a plate and cover with a plastic bag. Let cool about 10 minutes and carefully remove skin. Cut into a fine dice.

Lift tuna out of marinade with slotted spoon and mix with vegetables and herbs. Mix lemon juice with olive oil and toss with tuna mixture. Refrigerate, covered, for at least 1 hour. Serve on Boston lettuce leaves.

Health of the primitive Eskimo is stated by a number of qualified observers to be surpassed by no other race of people on this earth and equalled by few if any. . . .The Eskimos showed no ketosis, having a remarkable power to oxidize fats completely, as evidenced by the small amount of acetone bodies excreted in the urine during fasting. It is well known that in most human subjects ketosis appears when the material metabolized is restricted to protein and fat. . . . It is not unlikely that freedom of the Eskimo from ketosis is related to ingestion of lipase with the food, causing better metabolism of fat than is the case with persons subsisting on the conventional heat-treated diet. . . . Garber lived a number of years among Eskimos in northern Alaska and had occasion to observe their habits. Quotation: "Fish are put into a hole and covered with grass and earth and the mass is allowed to ferment and decay. I learned, to my utter astonishment, they would eat those rotten poisonous foods and thrive on them. Lest the reader might think that the cooking process would destroy the poisons in their vitiated foods, I wish to say that in only a few instances did they cook their food. The usual customary method was to devour it raw." Edward Howell, MD *Food Enzymes for Health and Longevity*

The food of these Eskimos in their native state includes caribou, ground nuts which are gathered by mice and stored in caches, kelp which is gathered in season and stored for winter use, berries including cranberries which are preserved by freezing, blossoms of flowers preserved in seal oil, sorrel grass preserved in seal oil, and quantities of frozen fish. Another important food factor consists of the organs of the large animals of the sea, including certain layers of the skin of one of the species of whale, which has been found to be very high in vitamin C. Weston Price, DDS *Nutrition and Physical Degeneration*

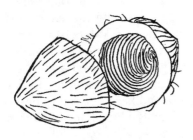

As we have seen, the practice of eating autolyzed (predigested) meat and fish has been reported by a number of authorities as being common among diverse groups of Eskimos scattered over the northern regions and not related to each other. These groups are willing to overlook the objectionable odor because experience has taught them that the partially digested food gives them more endurance. Other groups of people around the world have likewise shared in finding unique values in partially digested protein food, such as aged cheese and hung, aged meat, In other words, autolyzed food, which has already been broken down into peptones and proteoses, uses less of our personal enzymes. This is what produces the feeling of well-being and surplus energy. Edward Howell, MD *Enzyme Nutrition*

RAW SALMON SALAD
Serves 4

*1 pound fresh salmon, skinned and cut into a
    1/2-inch dice*
1 small red onion, finely diced
2 teaspoons sea salt
dash tabasco sauce
1 cup fresh lime juice
2 tablespoons whey (page 87), optional
3 medium tomatoes, peeled, seeded and diced
1 bunch cilantro, chopped
Boston lettuce leaves
1 lime, cut into wedges

To peel tomatoes, see page 70. Mix lime juice with optional whey, onion, salt and tabasco sauce and toss with salmon pieces. Cover and marinate in the refrigerator for at least 7 hours, and up to 24 hours, stirring occasionally. Remove from marinade with a slotted spoon and mix with tomatoes and cilantro. Serve on Boston lettuce leaves and garnish with lime wedges.

LATIN AMERICAN RAW FISH SALAD
(Ceviche)
Serves 4-6

1 pound sea bass, white fish filets or mackerel
1/2 cup lime juice
2 tablespoons whey (page 87), optional
2 medium tomatoes, peeled, seeded and diced
1 small red onion, finely chopped
1/4 cup extra virgin olive oil
2 small green chiles, seeded and finely chopped
sea salt
2 tablespoons cilantro, finely chopped
2 avocados, cut into wedges
1 lemon, cut into wedges

To peel tomatoes, see page 70. Cut fish into 1/2-inch cubes. Mix with lime juice and optional whey in a bowl and marinate in the refrigerator for 12 to 36 hours, stirring occasionally, until fish becomes opaque or "cooked." Remove from marinade with a slotted spoon. Mix with tomatoes, onion, peppers, olive oil, cilantro and marinate another hour. Season to taste. Serve with avocado and lemon wedges.

Variation:

Use *1 pound fresh shrimp* or *1 pound fresh oysters* instead of fish.

PICKLED SALMON

Makes 1 quart

1 pound salmon, skinned and
*   cut into 1/2-inch pieces*
1 cup water
1/8 cup whey (page 87)
1 tablespoon raw honey
1 tablespoon sea salt
1 cup pearl onions, peeled or
*   2 small onions, coarsely chopped*
1 lemon, thinly sliced
1 tablespoon mustard seeds
1 teaspoon cracked pepper
2 bay leaves
1 bunch fresh dill, snipped

Mix water with whey, honey, and salt until salt and honey dissolve. Stir in lemon, onions, seasonings and fish. Place all in a quart-sized, wide-mouth mason jar. Add more water if necessary to completely cover the fish. The top of the liquid should be at least 1 inch below the top of the jar. Cover tightly. Keep at room temperature for 24 hours before removing to refrigerator where the salmon will keep for several weeks.

To serve as an appetizer, arranges pieces of fish, onions and lemon in a bowl and serve with toothpicks. To serve as a first course, arrange on individual plates and garnish with tiny new potatoes, steamed and then tossed in a little of the marinade.

Myth: Lowfat diets prevent breast cancer.

Truth: A recent study found that women on very lowfat diets (less than 20%) had the same rate of breast cancer as women who consumed large amounts of fat. (*NEJM* 2/8/96)

Dr. Crewe reported on the remarkable effects seen in such a great variety of diseases, that raw milk may be supplying some hormonal elements to the patient. He repeatedly saw marked improvement in patients with toxic thyroid disease, a hormonal malady. Dr. Crewe was especially enthusiastic about raw milk in the treatment of disease of the prostate gland. . . . Although Dr. Crewe's experiments were on the feeding of raw milk for disease, the key is not milk but raw. The same results might be obtained, as Crewe implies, by eating fresh raw meat. He relates the story of the explorer Stefansson, who traveled the frozen Arctic with his colleagues living on fish, seal, polar bear, and caribou—nothing else for nine months. Most of this was eaten raw; and, although undergoing the severest of hardships, they were never sick. On the return journey, they discovered a cache of civilized food, including flour, preserved fruits and vegetables, and salted, cooked meat. Against Stefansson's advice, the men ate this preserved food for several days. They quickly developed diarrhea, loose teeth, and sore mouths. Stefansson immediately placed them on raw caribou tongue, and in a few days they were well. William Campbell Douglass, MD *The Milk Book*

Herring and mackerel are two of the most abundant fish in the oceans. They thrive in waters that are rich in minerals from upwellings deep below the surface. Herring and mackerel form a staple of many ethnic cuisines, particularly in Holland and Scandinavia where they are usually consumed pickled or smoked. Both are high in protein, fat-soluble vitamins and omega-3 fatty acids. Herring is exceptionally rich in zinc, containing 110 milligrams per four-ounce serving, almost ten times as much as the food next richest in zinc, sesame seeds. SWF

The greatest concentration of zinc in our body is in our eyes . . . .The eyes alone use one-third as much oxygen as the heart, need ten to twenty times as much vitamin C as the joint capsules involved in the movement of our extremities, and require more zinc (our intelligence chemical) than any other organ system in the body. *PPNF Health Journal*

Pottenger proved there is a yet undiscovered deficiency disease, similar to Vitamin C deficiency (scurvy), that can be cured by giving an endocrine product *that contains no Vitamin C.* Raw milk has this unknown nutrient and pasteurized milk does not. Stefansson, a famous arctic explorer, demonstrated that a supposedly adequate intake of vitamin C in the form of tomato juice did not prevent scurvy in an Arctic Sea captain but just a few days on raw meat cured him completely. As shown by Pottenger, raw milk, if it had been available, would have accomplished the same thing. William Campbell Douglass, MD *The Milk Book*

PICKLED HERRING OR MACKEREL

1 1/2 pounds herring or mackerel
2 teaspoons sea salt
1 cup filtered water
1/8 cup whey (page 87)
1 medium onion, peeled and coarsely chopped
1 teaspoon cracked pepper
1 teaspoon coriander seeds
2 bay leaves
1/4 teaspoon dried chile flakes

Scale, wash, skin and filet the fish (or have your fish merchant do this for you) and cut into small pieces. Mix with onions and spices and place in a quart-sized, wide-mouth mason jar. Mix salt, water and whey and pour over fish. Add more water if necessary to bring liquid to the top of the fish. The top of the liquid should be at least 1 inch below the top of the jar. Cover tightly. Leave at room temperature for 24 hours before transferring to refrigerator where it will keep for several weeks.

MUSTARD HERRING
Serves 6-8

2 pounds herring filets
1-2 cups raw vinegar
2 tablespoons Dijon-type mustard
1 teaspoon sea salt
4 tablespoons rice syrup or maple syrup
1/2 cup expeller-expressed sesame oil
1 cup chopped fresh dill

Wash the herring filets. Cover with vinegar and let stand 1 hour or more at room temperature until filets turn white. Pour off the vinegar. Mix mustard, salt and rice syrup or maple syrup. Slowly add the oil to the mustard mixture, stirring constantly with a fork. If sauce is too thick, thin with a little water. Stir in the dill. Spread the filets in a glass dish and cover with sauce. Cover the dish and marinate for 2 days in the refrigerator. Serve with sourdough bread.

GOURMET APPETIZERS

A simple salad, a hearty soup, or a small serving of raw meat or fish—these serve best as starters for most evening meals. But sometimes the occasion calls for something grander. We offer this assortment of gourmet appetizers for your dinner parties and holiday feasts. Most feature nourishing traditional foods high in fat-soluble vitamins, such as sea food and organ meats. Start with the freshest and highest quality ingredients you can find and do pay attention to the presentation of your appetizers on the plate. The combination of good-tasting nutritious food, attractively served, is sure to please your guests.

CORIANDER PRAWNS

Serves 4

12 large fresh prawns
4 tablespoons coriander seeds
1 tablespoon grated lemon peel
1 tablespoon cracked pepper
1 teaspoon sea salt
4 tablespoons extra virgin olive oil or lard
1 1/2 cups cilantro sauce or cilantro pesto (page 144)
cilantro sprigs for garnish

Peel the prawns carefully, leaving the tail intact. Using a mini grinder, grind the coriander seeds briefly until they are cracked. Mix cracked coriander seeds with lemon peel, pepper and salt. Press the mixture into the prawns, coating them completely. In a heavy skillet, sauté the prawns in olive oil or lard, a few at a time, until golden and cooked through. Spoon several tablespoons of cilantro sauce into each plate. Place three prawns on each plate and garnish with coriander sprigs.

Here in the land of the Three Musketeers, the Gascony region of southwest France, goose and duck fat are slathered on bread instead of butter, the people snack on fried duck skin and eat twice as much *foie gras* as other Frenchmen, and fifty times as much as Americans.

It was no surprise when Dr. Serge Renaud, in a 10-year epidemiological study that included surveys of eating habits, concluded that Gascons eat a diet higher in saturated fat than any other group of people in the industrialized world.... But scientists crinkled a collective brow over Dr. Renaud's related findings about this region, which produces much of the world's *foie gras*, the fattened livers of ducks and geese. "The *foie gras* eaters of the Gers and Lot Departments in Southwest France have the lowest rate of death from cardiovascular disease in the country," he said. . . . The basic Gascon in his blue beret would not be surprised. Standing in his barnyard Mr. Saint-Pe listened to Dr. Renaud's findings as though he were being told the obvious. "The people in my family live to be ninety years old," he said. "We cook everything in duck fat. We have *foie gras* on Sunday. Everybody knows this is the long-life diet." Elisabeth Rosenthal *New York Times*

Atherosclerosis isn't the only disease the polyunsaturated oils can give you. Cancer can be induced in experimental animals with corn oil. Hypertension will occur in rats and chickens by feeding unsaturated oils whereas animal fats (lard, milk, butter) do not cause high blood pressure. Amyloidosis, a disease of protein degeneration, can also be induced by polyunsaturates. William Campbell Douglass, MD *The Milk Book*

DUCK AND CHICKEN LIVER MOUSSE
Serves 8-10

1 1/2 pounds fresh duck livers
1 1/2 pounds fresh chicken livers
2 tablespoons butter
2 tablespoons extra virgin olive oil
1/2 cup dry white wine or cognac
1 cup beef or duck stock (pages 122 or 125)
2 eggs
1 cup piima cream or creme fraiche (page 84)
sea salt and pepper
1-2 tablespoons truffle,
    very finely chopped (optional)
1 cup clarified beef or duck stock, cooled
    (page 125)

Sauté livers in butter and olive oil until they turn brown. Pour in cognac or wine and 1 cup stock. Boil down until all liquid has almost completely evaporated. Let cool. Process half the livers with 1 egg and 1/2 cup cultured cream in food processor; repeat with other half. Transfer liver mixture to a bowl. Season generously and stir in optional truffles.

Line an oiled 1-quart loaf pan with oiled parchment paper. Pour mousse into pan—it should be about two-thirds full. Spread top smooth. Cover with a piece of parchment paper (see Sources) and cover tightly with aluminum foil. Place in a pan of hot water and bake at 350 degrees for about 45 minutes. Let cool. Remove foil and top layer of parchment paper. Pour stock over, cover and chill well.

To serve, remove from loaf pan and slice. Serve with round or triangle croutons (page 520) or whole grain sourdough bread and thin slices of pickled cucumber (page 97).

Note: If duck livers are not available, you may use *3 pounds chicken livers*, but the taste will not be as good.

DUCK TERRINE

Serves 10-12

1 5-pound domestic duck or 2 smaller wild ducks
livers from the duck(s)
1/4 pound calf's liver
3/4 pound ground veal
1 small onion, finely chopped
1 teaspoon canned green peppercorns, drained,
    rinsed and dried with paper towels
1/2 teaspoon ground allspice
1 teaspoon dried rosemary
1 teaspoon sea salt
1/2 teaspoon pepper
1/4 cup dry white wine
grated rind and juice of 1 orange
about 1 cup clarified beef stock (page 125),
    at room temperature

Terrines of all sorts form an important part of European cuisine. Here is an unusual recipe that does not contain pork. To prepare it you will need a rectangular or oval glazed 1-quart casserole or "terrine," with a board cut to fit just inside the rim.

Remove skin and fat from the duck and cut away the duck meat. (Use skin and fat to make duck cracklings, page 295, and the carcass to make duck stock, page 125.) Cut duck meat and liver into small pieces and mix with the onion and seasonings. Process the mixture in batches in a food processor. Stir in the wine, orange juice and orange rind.

Generously oil the terrine and fill with the duck mixture. Wrap the board in parchment paper (see Sources) and set over the duck mixture. Weight the board down crosswise with a brick so the brick pushes down the board but is not in danger of falling into the terrine. Set in a pan of hot water and bake at 350 degrees for 1 1/2 hours. Refrigerate until cold. Pour the stock over the terrine and return it to the refrigerator.

To serve, slice the terrine and its layer of aspic (jelled meat stock) into 1-inch slices. Arrange on individual plates and garnish with triangle croutons (page 520) and finely sliced pickled cucumber (page 97).

An arty salad of radicchio and arugula, balsamic vinegar dressing made with canola oil, followed by lean meat and more vegetables—you might think this is some kind of designer reducing diet, served up to the denizens of weight-loss spas. Guess again. This, according to a well-known food writer, is the incarnation of the cave man diet! Amazing how Dr. Price's research has been turned on its end to promote the industry agenda—canola oil and lean soy-fed beef. To find out how the cave man was likely to eat, let's turn to an account by John Lame Deer, a full-blooded Sioux born eighty years ago on the Rosebud Reservation in South Dakota. "We always had plenty of food for everybody, squaw bread, beef, the kind of dried meat we called *papa*, and *wasna*, or pemmican which was meat pounded together with berries and kidney fat. . . *wasna* kept a man going for a whole day." He fondly remembers gorging himself on fat ducks. As for vegetables, "In the old days we used to eat the guts of the buffalo, making a contest of it, two fellows getting hold of a long piece of intestines from opposite ends, starting chewing toward the middle, seeing who can get there first; that's eating. Those buffalo guts, full of half-fermented, half-digested grass and herbs, you didn't need any pills and vitamins when you swallowed those." The foods that made the cave man healthy and strong were guts and grease, not canola oil and lean meat. SWF

On the twenty-second of July, we met several strangers, whom we joined in pursuit of the caribou, which were at this time so plentiful that we got everyday a sufficient number for our support, and indeed too frequently killed several merely for the tongues, marrow and fat. *The Journeys of Samuel Hearne* 1768

The Samburu tribe of northern Kenya continues to baffle the cholesterol-fat alarmists. They drink nothing but milk for three days and then eat nothing but meat for one day. The sequence may vary, but in general, there are three milk days to one meat day. Pasteurization is unknown to them. The milk is cultured, similar to yoghurt. They eat *four hundred grams* of fat per day. The average American, with his hardened arteries, eats a meager *eighty grams* of fat per day. The Samburu warrior, by tribal tradition, is bound from age fourteen to an *exclusive diet* of milk and meat for twenty years. No vegetable products are eaten except for some tree bark tea. The Samburu's cousins to the south, the Masai, drink an average of seven quarts of very rich milk per day. Their diet is 60% saturated fat. When you consider that the average warrior weighs only one hundred thirty-five pounds, that's a *lot* of milk.

Mann and co-workers studied these tribes exhaustively. They found remarkably little heart disease, consistently normal blood pressure, no obesity, and a complete absence of rheumatoid arthritis, degenerative arthritis, and gout. What about cholesterol? The average African child had a cholesterol value of 138. The average American child, 202. With increase in age, the native cholesterol values went *down* and the American values went *up*. Beyond the age of fifty-five, the mean cholesterol value of the African natives was 122. The American mean cholesterol for men was 234. William Campbell Douglass, MD *The Milk Book*

BREADED BRAIN APPETIZER
Serves 8

2 pounds fresh organic calves brain
    (See note on brains, page 310)
3 tablespoons naturally fermented soy sauce
1 medium onion, peeled and sliced
1 cup red wine
1 tablespoon green peppercorns, crushed
2 cups unbleached flour
1 teaspoon pepper
3 eggs lightly beaten
2 cups whole grain bread crumbs
2 teaspoons fine herbs
1/2 teaspoon salt
2 tablespoons or more butter
2 tablespoons or more extra virgin olive oil
round croutons (page 520) for garnish
pickled cucumbers (page 97) for garnish
lime wedges for garnish

Marinate brains in mixture of soy sauce, wine, onions and pepper for several hours in the refrigerator. Mix flour with pepper and bread crumbs with fine herbs and salt. Carefully life the brains out of the marinade and pat dry. Dredge first in flour, then in egg, then in bread crumb mixture. Sauté in butter and olive oil until golden and crispy on both sides. Arrange on individual plates with round croutons, thinly sliced pickles and lime wedges.

MARINATED SALMON PLATE
Serves 8

24 slices marinated salmon (page 238)
24 round croutons (page 520)
1/2 cup pickled daikon radish (page 98)
parsley sprigs

Arrange 4 slices marinated salmon and 4 croutons on each plate. Garnish each plate with a teaspoon of daikon radish and parsley sprigs.

BRESAOLA AND MELON
Serves 4

4-6 ounces thinly sliced bresaola (air cured beef),
  available in Italian markets
1 ripe cantaloupe
cracked pepper
edible flowers for garnish (optional)

Slice melon, remove rind and seeds and arrange artistically on four plates with slices of bresaola. Sprinkle with cracked pepper and garnish with optional edible flowers.

COLD POACHED TROUT WITH MAYONNAISE
Serves 6

6 small whole trout, cleaned
2-3 cups fish stock (page 119)
1 cup herbed or Creole mayonnaise
  (pages 138 and 139)
parsley sprigs for garnish

Place trout in a buttered pyrex dish. Bring stock to a boil and pour over fish. Bake at 350 degrees for about 15 minutes or until fish is tender.

Carefully remove fish and chill well. To serve, remove skin but leave head and tail intact. Arrange on individual plates with parsley sprigs and a ramekin of homemade mayonnaise.

Bresaola is one of several air cured or fermented meats found throughout the Mediterranean region. It can be purchased at Italian delicatessens. Similar fermented meats include pemmican of the North American Indians (made from venison, buffalo or fish, bear fat or buffalo fat, maple syrup and berries), air dried mutton from the Faeroe Islands (valued by the natives for its strengthening properties) and cured dry sausages from France. SWF

The available evidence indicates that Orientals on a high-carbohydrate cooked diet, essentially rice, display a pancreas approximately 50 per cent relatively heavier than that of Americans. The salivary glands of Orientals are also larger. Organ weight studies on experimental animals show that when a group of rats. . . is placed upon a heat-treated, high-carbohydrate diet and sacrificed after a period of feeding, the average weight of the pancreas and salivary glands shows a marked increase over a similar control group of animals on a mixed diet. This indicates that the pancreas and salivary glands are forced to undergo considerable hypertrophy to furnish the additional enzymes required. . . . . It is a singular circumstance that whereas cattle and sheep, ingesting a full quota of food enzymes, consummate the digestion of a comparatively high-carbohydrate raw diet with only a small pancreas and without help from the salivary glands, human beings on a heat-treated mixed diet, lacking food enzymes, require a large pancreas and active salivary glands to digest a smaller amount of carbohydrate. And, furthermore, a high-carbohydrate, heat-treated diet engenders still greater enlargement of the pancreas and salivary glands in humans and animals. Edward Howell, MD *Food Enzymes for Health and Longevity*

In nature fatty acids assume what is called the *cis* form. These *cis* fatty acids are naturally curved and biochemically suited for human nutrition because of the curvature of their shape and how electrons form around them. A *trans* fatty acid has the curve straightened out by placing a hydrogen atom (hydrogenation) in the wrong place—especially the wrong place for use by human metabolism. The *trans* molecule simply doesn't fit in—it's the wrong shape and, even more importantly, it has the wrong electrochemistry. However, and this is the dangerous part, *trans* fats do get taken up in the human metabolism and become part of the various functions required by fat in the human body, especially the making of cell membranes. Tom Valentine *Facts on Fats & Oils*

The only hope of keeping up a low-carbohydrate diet and achieving the desired success is to replace the missing carbohydrates with fat. Man cannot live on protein alone. In Central American states, feeding political opponents with lean meat was an elegant way of getting rid of them without resorting to stronger measures. After a few months diarrhoea develops and death soon follows. Stefansson reported something similar in Canadian Eskimos if they had to live on lean caribou meat for longer periods of time and were unable to catch fish. Wolfgang Lutz *Dismantling a Myth: The Role of Fat and Carbohydrates in our Diet*

FISH TERRINE WITH WATERCRESS SAUCE
Serves 8-10

1 1/2 pound filet of sole or flounder
3/4 pound salmon
1/2 cup dry white wine or vermouth
1/4 cup tarragon vinegar
1 small onion, finely chopped
several sprigs fresh tarragon
1 cup piima cream or creme fraiche (page 84)
1 stick butter, melted
1 egg
2 egg whites
sea salt and pepper
2 cups watercress sauce (page 144)

Cut the filets and the salmon into small pieces, keeping the two fish separate. Place wine, vinegar, onion and tarragon in a saucepan and bring to a boil. Boil vigorously until reduced to about 3 tablespoons. Strain liquid and stir in the butter and the cream.

Butter a 1-quart terrine. Place half the white fish in the food processor along with 1/3 of the liquid and 1 egg white. Process until smooth. Season generously to taste. Pour into the terrine and level with a knife. Process the salmon with another 1/3 of the liquid and the whole egg. Season generously to taste. Pour this over the first layer. Finally, process the remaining filets with the remaining liquid, 1 egg white and seasonings and pour this into the terrine. Cover with a piece of waxed paper, or buttered parchment paper (see Sources), and a lid. Set in a pan of hot water and bake at 350 degrees for 50 minutes. Chill well before serving.

To serve, ladle several spoonfuls of sauce onto individual plates and place a slice of terrine on top of the sauce.

Variation:

Use *4 cups thin red pepper sauce (page 146)* in place of watercress sauce.

SALMON MOUSSE WITH CREAMY DILL SAUCE

Serves 12-18

1 tablespoon plus 2 teaspoons gelatin (See Sources)
1/2 cup cold water
1 cup boiling water
4 cups cooked salmon, flaked
2 tablespoons grated onion
1 cup mayonnaise (page 137)
2 tablespoons lemon juice
1/2 teaspoon tabasco sauce
1/2 teaspoon paprika
1 teaspoon sea salt
2 tablespoon small capers, rinsed, drained,
    dried with paper towels and chopped
2 tablespoons snipped dill
1 cup piima cream or creme fraiche (page 84)
about 1 tablespoon extra virgin olive oil
1 egg white, unbeaten
2 cups creamy dill sauce (page 142)

Soften gelatin in cold water, add boiling water and stir until well mixed. Add mayonnaise, lemon juice, onion, tabasco sauce, paprika, salt and dill. Mix well and chill to obtain a consistency of unbeaten egg white. Stir in the salmon, capers and cultured cream. Brush a 3-quart mold or individual molds with olive oil and then with unbeaten egg white. Pour in mousse and chill well.

To serve, dip mold or molds briefly into hot water and invert onto a plate. Serve with creamy dill sauce.

In the treatment of feverish and acute infectious diseases, it is evident that gelatin plays a double role. In the first place, the nutritive qualities of gelatin, its ready absorption and colloidal properties, make it ideally suited for inclusion in the diet both during the height of the fever and during convalescence. Bayley emphasized this factor from a nurse's viewpoint, observing that gelatin acts as a base for the preparation of many dainty, pleasing dishes which appeal to the patient with poor appetite, thus providing much needed nourishment. N. R. Gotthoffer *Gelatin in Nutrition and Medicine*

Scientists say they have the first direct evidence that viruses can mutate and become deadly because of nutritional deficiencies in the hosts they infect. In their experiments, researchers found that a human virus normally harmless to mice mutated and became a heart-damaging agent in mice suffering from a nutritional deficiency. Once changed, they said, the virus was also able to infect and damage the hearts of nutritionally well-balanced mice.

This is the first time that a nutritional deficiency in a host has been shown to alter viruses to make them permanently more virulent, the scientists said in a report published in today's issue of the journal *Nature Medicine.* Warren E. Leary *NY Times News Service*

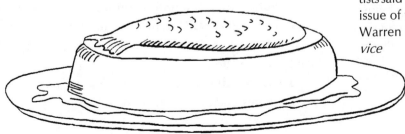

Strict vegetarian women who breast-feed their infants may be subjecting them to possible long-term brain damage.

So indicate the findings of a research team made up of scientists from the University of Cincinnati, Harvard School of Public Health, Vanderbilt and Brandeis Universities.

Often, these women eat sea vegetables, tempeh, miso and tamari that theoretically contain adequate amounts of vitamin B_{12}, believing that they fully supply the body's required vitamin B_{12}. However, . . .tests reveal that individuals who ingested such products showed no increase in vitamin B_{12} blood levels.

A similar study by Dutch biochemists demonstrated that ingested seaweed products did not correct vitamin B_{12} deficiencies in infants. Neither did spirulina, a micro algae. And the researchers are still trying to understand why not.

Blood levels of vitamin B_{12} in adult vegetarians were also found deficient by both research groups. Half the subjects tested were low in this vitamin and one-quarter of them were extremely low.

The Dutch researchers learned that infants of many vegetarian women have abnormal red blood cells, delayed motor skills and slow growth, compared with control group babies.

Best sources of vitamin B_{12}? Liver, sardines, mackerel, herring, salmon, lamb, Swiss cheese, eggs, haddock, beef, blue cheese, halibut, scallops, cottage cheese, chicken and milk. James F. Scheer *Health Freedom News*

SALMON QUENELLES WITH DILL SAUCE
Serves 6-8

1 1/2 pounds skinless salmon
1 1/2 tablespoons softened butter
5 slices whole grain bread, crusts removed, processed into crumbs
2/3 cup heavy cream
1 large egg, lightly beaten
2 tablespoons fresh lemon juice
1 teaspoon sea salt
1 teaspoon pepper
3 cups fish stock (page 119)
1 cup piima cream or creme fraiche (page 84)
1 tablespoon shrimp butter (page 158), optional
1 tablespoon fresh dill, chopped

Quenelles are cylindrical concoctions of fish mousse, poached in stock and served with a sauce. They take time to make but are greatly appreciated by gourmets.

In a food processor, purée salmon until smooth. Add the butter and purée until incorporated. Meanwhile, soak the bread crumbs in cream for several minutes. Add soaked bread crumbs to food processor, along with egg, salt, pepper and lemon juice. Process until well blended.

Bring stock to a boil, then reduce to a simmer. Shape fish mixture into cylinders using about 2 tablespoons of the mixture each. Place carefully in simmering stock and poach about 6-8 minutes. Remove with a slotted spoon to paper towels and keep warm in the oven while making sauce.

Strain the stock into another saucepan and bring to a rapid boil. Add the cultured cream and optional shrimp butter to thicken. Boil vigorously until reduced and thickened to desired consistency. Stir in the dill and check for seasonings.

To serve, divide the quenelles among individual serving plates and spoon sauce over.

Variation: Use *whitefish* instead of salmon. Omit dill.

CRAB CAKES WITH RED PEPPER SAUCE

Makes 8 patties

2 cups crab meat
2 small onions, finely minced
3 eggs, lightly beaten
2 tablespoons Dijon-type mustard
1/4-1/2 teaspoon cayenne pepper
1 cup whole grain bread crumbs
1 bunch cilantro, chopped
1 teaspoon grated lemon rind
sea salt and pepper to taste
3 tablespoons or more butter
3 tablespoons or more extra virgin olive oil
2 cups red pepper sauce (page 146)
cilantro sprigs for garnish

Combine eggs with onions, bread crumbs and seasonings. Mix in crab and form into cakes. Sauté until golden, a few at a time, in butter and olive oil. To serve, spread a few spoonfuls of sauce on individual plates. Place one or two crab cakes on top. Garnish with cilantro sprigs.

There are certain characteristics of the various dietaries of the primitive races which are universally present when that dietary program is associated with a high immunity to disease and freedom from deformities. In general, these are the foods that provide adequate sources of bodybuilding and body-repairing material. The use by primitives of foods relatively low in calories has resulted in forcing them to eat large quantities of these foods . . . . The primitives have obtained, often with great difficulty, foods that are scarce but rich in certain elements. In these rare foods were elements which the body requires in small quantities, including minerals such as iodine, copper, manganese and special vitamins. In connection with the vitamins it should be kept in mind that our knowledge of these unique organic catalysts is limited. The medical profession and the public at large think of vitamin D as consisting of just one chemical factor, whereas investigations are revealing continually new and additional factors. A recent review describes in considerable detail eight distinct factors in vitamin D and refers to information indicating that there may be at least twelve. Clearly, it is not possible to undertake to provide an adequate nutrition simply by reinforcing the diet with a few synthetic products which are known to represent certain of these nutritional factors. By the mass of the people at large, as well as by members of the medical profession, activated ergosterol is considered to include all that is necessary to supply the vitamin D group of activators to human nutrition. Weston Price, DDS *Nutrition and Physical Degeneration*

There's another phony milk you should know about. It's called UHT milk. The dairy industry is producing this one in an attempt to regain business lost to filled milk and other junk beverages. UHT stands for ultra high temperature. What it means is that milk has been heated to such a high temperature that it is sterilized, just like surgical instruments. It can be shipped in unrefrigerated trucks—a tremendous savings to the dairymen. It will sit on a shelf, unrefrigerated, for months without spoiling. The reason it won't spoil is because no self-respecting bug will eat it. Bugs are smart. They like fresh food with nutrient value, not steam-cleaned pseudo food. William Campbell Douglass MD *The Milk Book*

It is evident from published studies of the *trans* fatty acids that a number of earlier researchers had questioned the biological safety of the *trans* fatty acids viz a viz their relationship to both cancer and heart disease. In fact, Ancel Keys had originally claimed that the partially hydrogenated vegetable oils with their *trans* fatty acids were the culprits in heart disease. This was in 1958, and the edible oil industry was very swift in their squelching of that information; they shifted the emphasis to "saturated" fat and started the unwarranted attack on meat and dairy fats. It has taken 30 years for research to get back on track. Now research is being reported on adverse effects from *trans* fatty acids related to heart disease, diabetes, cancer, low birth weight, obesity, and immune dysfunction. Mary G. Enig, PhD *Know Your Fats*

CRAB CREPES
Serves 8

16 buckwheat crepes (page 480)
2 tablespoons butter
1 cup shallots, finely chopped
1/4 cup dry white wine
1 cup fish stock (page 119)
1 cup piima cream or creme fraiche (page 84)
juice of 1/2 lemon
sea salt and pepper
1 tablespoon arrowroot mixed with
    1 tablespoon water
1 pound fresh mushrooms, washed, well dried,
    sliced and sautéed in butter and olive oil
2 pounds fresh crab meat

Sauté shallots in butter until soft. Add wine and stock and bring to a boil. Add cream and boil until sauce has reduced to about one half. Add lemon juice and seasonings to taste. Spoonful by spoonful, add the arrowroot mixture until desired thickness is obtained. Stir in mushrooms and crab meat and simmer until warmed through. Using a slotted spoon, place a spoonful or two in each crepe and roll up. Place two filled crepes each on heated plates and spoon a little of the remaining sauce over. Serve immediately.

Variation: Shrimp Crepes
Use *2 pounds bay shrimp* in place of crab meat. Omit mushrooms.

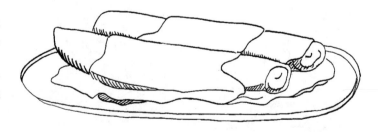

NEW POTATOES WITH CAVIAR

Serves 6

12 medium new potatoes
melted butter
1 cup piima cream or creme fraiche (page 84)
1/2 teaspoon sea salt
4 ounces black caviar

Brush potatoes with butter and bake at 400 degrees for about 45 minutes or until soft. Cut tops off of potatoes and carefully scoop out the flesh. Mash potato flesh with piima cream and sea salt and carefully stuff the potatoes skins with this mixture. Keep warm in oven until ready to serve.

To serve, place two potatoes on each plate and a generous spoonful of caviar on top of each.

STUFFED GRAPE LEAVES

(Dolmas)
Serves 8

3 dozen grape leaves, home pickled (page 101)
    or store bought, preserved in brine
3 large onions, finely chopped
4 tablespoons extra virgin olive oil
2 cups basic brown rice (page 466)
1 cup fresh dill, chopped
1/2 cup fresh parsley, chopped
1 bunch green onions, chopped
3 tablespoons crispy pine nuts (page 514)
juice and grated rind of 2 lemons
sea salt and pepper

Rinse grape leaves and spread on paper towels to drain. Sauté onions in olive oil until soft. Remove from heat and stir in remaining ingredients. Place the grape leaves on a board, shiny sides down, and put 1-2 tablespoons of rice mixture in the center of each leaf. Fold the sides of the leaves to the center, then roll them up tightly, starting from the stem end. Serve with lemon wedges and yoghurt sauce (page 143).

Myth: Vegetarianism is healthier than meat eating.
Truth: The annual all-cause death rate of vegetarian men is slightly more than that of nonvegetarian men (.93% vs .89%); the annual death rate of vegetarian women is significantly more than that of nonvegetarian women (.86% vs .54%) (*PPNF Journal* 1998 22:4:30)

Pasteurization began in 1895, and thus began the unfortunate habit of not worrying about cleanliness in the dairy because, with the heating of milk, cleanliness was no longer considered necessary. The bacteria in the milk would simply be boiled, killing the germs, and then the milk could be sold in this adulterated form. It has been sold that way ever since; and, because of pasteurization, tuberculosis was not completely eliminated from cows in the United States until 1942. If the United States Public Health Service and the American Medical Association had done the responsible thing and backed the various medical milk commissions' efforts to keep milk clean, tuberculosis could have been eliminated from American cows many decades sooner.

Dr. Henry Coit, the father of certified milk, recognized clearly that top quality milk depended upon getting the milk fresh from the cow and not heating it as is done in the pasteurization process. He recognized that the best way to present the best and most nutritious product to the public was to deliver it as made by nature from a completely clean environment. William Campbell Douglass, MD *The Milk Book*

Up to the present, vitamin E has been considered a tocopherol, and its function analyzed as nothing more than a physiological antioxidant. It now appears evident that the real vitamin E is that factor in the E complex that is being protected from oxidation by the tocopherol group; and that the same mistake has been made in attributing E activity to tocopherols as in the case of the promotion of pure viosterol as vitamin D, ascorbic acid as vitamin C, niacin as the antipellagra vitamin, pyridoxine as B_6, or folic acid as the antipernicious anemia fraction of liver. In each case the isolation of one factor as the "vitamin" in question has embarrassed the discoverer, in his assumption that he had discovered the "pot of gold" at the rainbow's end, by the attribution of vitamin activity to some synthetic or pure crystalline component of a natural complex. No reasonable student of nutrition can today deny the axiom that all vitamins are complexes and cannot exert their normal physiological effect other than as

ROASTED VEGETABLE PLATTER
Serves 8

8 thick-skinned red peppers
12 Japanese eggplants
about 3/4 cup extra virgin olive oil
3 cloves garlic, finely chopped
1/4 teaspoon cracked pepper
edible flowers or cilantro sprigs for garnish
round croutons (page 520)

Seed the peppers and cut into quarters. Place skin side up in an oiled pyrex dish and bake at 450 degrees about 10 minutes. Turn pepper pieces over and bake another 10 minutes or so until skins are browned and begin to buckle. Remove pepper pieces to a platter and cover with a plastic bag. Let cool about 10 minutes and remove skins.

Meanwhile, wash and peel eggplants. Slice lengthwise and salt the slices. Let stand about 1 hour, rinse and pat dry. Place eggplant slices on well oiled cookie sheets and brush top side with oil. Broil under the grill until lightly browned, turn, brush with olive oil and brown remaining side, being careful not to burn. Mix the chopped garlic with a little olive oil and brush cooked eggplant slices with the mixture.

Both the peppers and the eggplant may be made ahead of time and kept covered at room temperature for several hours. To serve, arrange four slices of pepper and several slices of eggplant on individual plates. Sprinkle with cracked pepper. Garnish with edible flowers or cilantro sprigs and serve with round croutons.

STUFFED MUSHROOMS

Serves 4

8 large or 12 medium mushrooms
1 1/2 cups whole grain bread crumbs
2 bunches green onions, chopped
1/2 cup freshly grated Parmesan cheese
sea salt and pepper
2-3 cloves garlic, crushed
2 tablespoons butter
2 tablespoons extra virgin olive oil

Remove stems from mushrooms. Wash both stems and caps and dry well. Chop stems and sauté with green onions in butter and olive oil. Add bread crumbs, garlic and cheese and mix thoroughly. Season to taste. Stuff each mushroom cap with a spoonful of the bread crumb mixture. Place in a pyrex pan with a little water and bake at 350 degrees for about 1/2 hour.

SPINACH FETA PASTRIES

Serves 8-10

3 cups cooked chopped spinach, squeezed dry
1 large onion, finely chopped
1/2 cup crispy pine nuts (page 514)
sea salt and pepper
pinch of nutmeg
2 cups feta cheese, crumbled
1 recipe yoghurt dough (page 485)
unbleached white flour

Mix spinach with onion, pine nuts, and nutmeg. Season to taste. Form dough into 1-inch balls and coat balls in flour. Roll into rounds. Place a tablespoon of spinach filling on each and top with 2 teaspoons of crumbled cheese. Fold edges up to form a three-sided pastry, leaving a small hole in the middle for air to escape. Place on well-greased pans and brush with butter. Bake at 350 degrees for about 20 minutes or until golden.

the complete complex, as found in natural foods.

The true vitamin E is found in the chromatin material of the germinal tissues of plant and animal and in young plants that are in a state of rapid growth. It seems to be a phospholipid carrying a special fatty acid in combination that has heretofore traveled under the cognomen of vitamin F. (Vitamin F was first discovered as a part of the wheat germ oil vitamin complex; at least the term vitamin F was first used to designate the essential fatty acid fraction.)

The fact that an unsaturated fatty acid as vitamin F is a part of the E complex, probably in molecular combination, explains the close relationship between the two vitamins in their synergistic support of cell division in reproduction, in maintenance of epithelium (where cell division is also predominant), and in kidney and liver metabolism, both epithelial activities. It explains the fact that both are factors in calcium metabolism, vitamin E deficiency resulting in bone resorption just as vitamin F deficiency results in less calcium available to bone.

Tocopherol administration in excess also results in bone-calcium loss, just as is caused by a deficiency of vitamin E. So again we have more evidence that tocopherol is NOT the vitamin E, but rather a protector that can in excess reduce the availability of traces of the real vitamin. Royal Lee, DDS *Butter, Vitamin E and the "X" Factor of Dr. Price*

University of Kentucky researchers evaluating 18 elements in the brains of 10 Alzheimer's disease patients, compared to 18 age-matched controls, found increased mercury/selenium and mercury/zinc ratios in microsomal and nuclear fractions in the brains. Most significant was the increase in mercury in Alzheimer's disease bulk brain samples, especially in the cerebral cortex, compared to controls. Alzheimer's patients also had elevation of mercury in the nucleus basilis of Meynert, which is the major cholinergic projection to the cerebral cortex and is severely degenerated in Alzheimer's disease patients. The elevated mercury/selenium and mercury/zinc ratios are of importance because selenium and zinc are used to protect against mercury toxicity. The release of mercury from dental amalgams is the main means of human exposure to inorganic mercury and vapor in the general population. There has been shown a direct correlation between the amount of inorganic mercury in the brain and the number of surfaces in Alzheimer's fillings. Mercury from dental amalgam is passed rapidly and directly into body tissue and accumulates in patient bodies with time. This author feels that no exposure to mercury vapor can be considered harmless, since it has no known toxic threshold. Dental amalgams cannot be excluded as a primary potential source of Alzheimer's disease. G. Bjorklund *PPNF Health Journal*

ROOT VEGETABLE TIMBALE WITH RED PEPPER SAUCE

Serves 8

1 pound carrots, peeled and coarsely chopped
1 pound rutabagas, peeled and coarsely chopped
1 pound parsnips, peeled and coarsely chopped
3 tablespoons softened butter
3 tablespoons piima cream or
   creme fraiche (page 84)
6 eggs, lightly beaten
sea salt and pepper
pinch of nutmeg
2 cups red pepper sauce (page 146)
8 tablespoons pesto (page 144), optional

Cook carrots, rutabagas and parsnips in water until just tender—they shouldn't absorb too much water. Let cool and drain well on paper towels. Process in food processor with butter, cream, eggs and nutmeg. Season to taste. Brush 8 individual conical timbale molds with melted butter and fill about three-fourths full with the vegetable mixture. Place in pan of hot water and bake at 350 degrees for about 45 minutes or until well set.

To serve, dip each mold briefly in hot water and invert on individual plates. Spoon red pepper sauce around the timbale and garnish each plate with a spoonful or two of pesto.

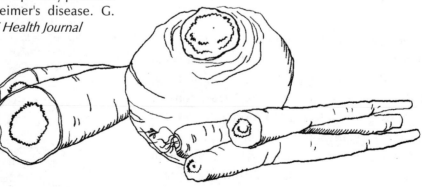

THE MAIN
COURSE

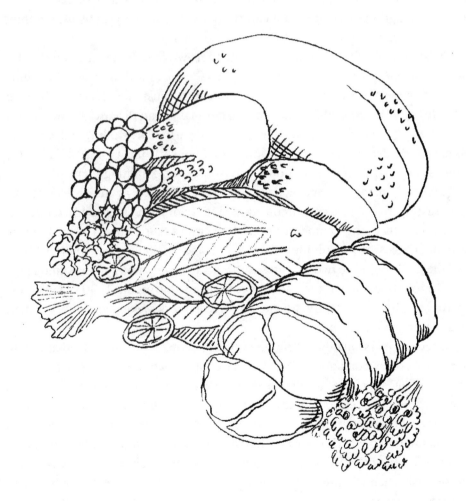

FISH

For most Americans, fish is a restaurant food; few know how to prepare it at home, and the average American child doesn't like it. This is a lamentable state of affairs, especially as nowadays fresh fish is so readily available in our markets.

Fish is *the* health food, *par excellence* (except, of course, for those who are allergic to it). When Dr. Weston Price traveled throughout the world, studying traditional peoples on native diets, he discovered that those who ate seafoods had the best health, as revealed by their freedom from caries, width of palate and general state of well-being. Fish eaters had thicker bones and better skeletal structure than groups that ate red meat. (Largely vegetarian groups placed third in all categories Dr. Price used to determine good health.)

Consumption of fish promotes excellent growth and bone structure; it also protects from the degenerative diseases so prevalent in this modern age. In a study conducted in the Netherlands, researchers found that just one serving of fish per week substantially reduced the incidence of coronary heart disease. All ocean fish are excellent sources of macro and trace minerals, particularly iodine and zinc. Our soils may be depleted of certain trace minerals, but every one we need exists in the boundless oceans; seafood is our only sure source for obtaining them all.

Mackerel, anchovies and herring are especially rich in mineral nutrients. Deep-sea oily fish, such as salmon, tuna and swordfish, are good sources of omega-3 and other long-chain fatty acids. Most important, fish and all seafood are excellent sources of fat-soluble vitamins—A and D. Remember that Dr. Price found the intake of these two essential nutrients to be *ten* times greater among the isolated groups he studied than among Americans during the 1930's. Today the disparity is almost certainly greater, as Westerners have cut back on their consumption of animal fats.

In recent years, many people have been persuaded to give up fish due to reports of mercury contamination. Mercury contamination *is* a danger when one eats fish from shoreline waters near industrial areas or from contaminated freshwaters. For this reason, we advise you to avoid freshwater fish unless you are sure of their origin, especially cat fish, carp and other scavengers, and to avoid overconsumption of shell fish. Shoreline feeders, such as sole and flounder, may be contaminated with PBC's. You needn't be concerned about mercury levels in deep-sea fish, such as salmon, tuna and swordfish, or from sole or flounder that come from relatively clean waters, such as those of the North Atlantic. Small amounts of mercury occur naturally in these fish, and they contain substances that bind with mercury to take it out of the body. Farm-raised fish are best avoided. Their fatty acid profile will not be as good as that of wild fish, and they are usually given inappropriate feed, such as soy pellets containing pesticide residues. Farm-raised salmon are actually given a die to make their flesh pink!

If you have not cultivated the art of preparing fish but wish to begin, we advise you to start with simple preparations, such as sautéed filet of sole or grilled salmon, tuna or swordfish. These take little time to prepare and are most readily accepted by children and inveterate fish avoiders. They can be served plain or with any number of accompaniments listed in the sauces and condiments chapter (page 136). We allow unbleached white flour in small amounts for browning and breading.

From these simple recipes you can graduate to our parchment paper and leaf-wrapped recipes. Many traditional societies prepare fish by wrapping it in leaves and steaming it in the coals of a fire. This method best preserves nutrients and protects the fish from possible carcinogens.

Classic gourmet recipes call for poaching fish in stock, then reducing the stock to make a flavorful sauce. Butter or cream, or both, are then added. These gelatin-rich sauces are easy to digest and just loaded with minerals (from concentrated stock) and fat-soluble vitamins (from cream and butter). Poached fish may be kept warm in a heated oven, covered with a piece of parchment or waxed paper, for up to one-half hour while the sauce is reduced and thickened by boiling and while you eat your first course. (See About Stock-Based Sauces, page 126.)

Fish must be fresh to be good. Look carefully at the eyes and gills of the fish you buy—the eyes should be clear, not glazed, and the gills should be red. Always ask your fish merchant when his fish came in. If the fish has been sitting in his display case more than a day, don't buy it.

A good habit to initiate in your household is to serve fish at least once a week; and we hope that the variety of recipes presented in this chapter, culled from many different cuisines, will make this easy for you to accomplish. You may want to prepare a special dessert for the same evening meal if your children need coaxing. No fish, no dessert, is a good rule. Serve fish the day you buy it to ensure that it is fresh.

Cayenne pepper is the powder produced from dried chile peppers. The so-called chile or cayenne peppers contain almost twice as much capsaicin as red peppers and thus have a much stronger, burning flavor. Cayenne pepper acts as a stimulant to the appetite, as a digestive aid and as an antibacterial agent. It is probably the high magnesium content of chile peppers that makes this universal spice so useful in treating cardiovascular problems. It is said that a spoonful of cayenne pepper is the best emergency treatment for a heart attack. However, in excess cayenne pepper may do harm to the mucous membranes and provoke ulcers and kidney problems.

Use cayenne pepper in moderate amounts with eggs, fish, meat and bland foods like grains and pulses. SWF

TUESDAY NIGHT
DINNER

Variety Salad
❦❦❦❦

Baked Whitefish
❦❦❦

Tomato Pepper Relish
❦❦❦

Sugar Snap Peas
❦❦❦❦❦

Gingerbread

BAKED WHITEFISH
Serves 4

*1 1/2 pounds filet of whitefish such as
    sole, whiting or turbot*
juice of 1 lemon
1 tablespoon fish sauce (page 157), optional
pinch of cayenne pepper
1 tablespoon snipped fresh herbs
1/2 teaspoon sea salt
about 1 tablespoon butter

Place fish in a buttered baking dish. Sprinkle with lemon juice, cayenne, fish sauce, herbs and salt. Dot with butter. Cover baking dish with foil (but don't let foil touch the fish) and bake at 300 degrees for about 15 minutes.

BAKED SALMON
Serves 4

1 1/2 pounds wild salmon filet
1/2 lemon
2 tablespoons melted butter
1 tablespoon unbleached flour
1/4 teaspoon paprika
1/2 teaspoon sea salt

Set salmon, skin side down, in a buttered pyrex baking dish. Squeeze on lemon juice, then brush generously with butter. Sprinkle on flour and spread with your fingers to make a thin, even coat. Sprinkle on paprika and sea salt. Bake at 350 degrees for 10 to 15 minutes or until salmon is almost, but not quite, cooked through. Place under broiler for about 1 minute until flour coating becomes browned.

Serve plain or with any one of a number of condiments and sauces, including butter sauce (page 153), pesto sauce (page 145) or thin red pepper sauce (page 146).

SAUTEED FILET OF SOLE

(Filets of Sole Meuniere)
Serves 6

1 1/2 pounds fresh filet of sole
2/3 cup unbleached flour
1/2 teaspoon pepper
1/2 teaspoon sea salt
about 1/2 cup clarified butter (page 150)
about 1/2 cup extra virgin olive oil

This is the classic and simple recipe for sautéed fish. Purists will object that we include recipes for pan-fried fish. Poached fish is probably preferable from a nutritional point of view; but some individuals, especially children, need an extra incentive to eat sea food, and a crisp, golden exterior is the best one we know of.

Wipe filets thoroughly and trim off any ends that are very thin in comparison to the rest of the filet. You may wish to cut the filets in half, crosswise. Dredge well in the flour mixed with sea salt and pepper.

In a cast-iron skillet, heat about 1/8 cup each clarified butter and olive oil until they foam. Sauté the fish filets until golden brown, a few at a time, over a moderately high flame, starting with the flatter side. Sauté about 3 to 5 minutes per side, depending on the thickness of the fish. Transfer to a heated platter and keep warm in the oven while you prepare the other filets. You will need to replenish butter and oil between batches.

Serve with lemon wedges, tartar sauce (page 141), red pepper butter (page 151) or Creole mayonnaise (page 139).

Communication is very difficult among many of the remote islands off the Irish Coast. It would be difficult to find more complete isolation. . . . We tried to get to the islands of Taransay and Scarpa on the west coast of the Isle of Harris but were unable to obtain transportation, since the trip can be made only in special, seaworthy crafts, which will undertake the passage only at certain phases of the tide and at certain directions of the winds. On one of these islands, we were told, the growing boys and girls had exceedingly high immunity to tooth decay. Their isolation was so great that a young woman of about twenty years of age who came to the Isle of Harris from Taransay Island had never seen milk. . . . There are no dairy animals on that island. Their nutrition is provided by their oat products and fish and by a very limited amount of vegetable foods. Lobsters and flat fish are a very important part of their foods. Fruits are practically unknown, yet the physiques of these people are remarkably fine. Weston Price, DDS *Nutrition and Physical Degeneration*

If you just can't do without your coffee, you may have to do without some of the calcium in your bones, as various studies reveal. The more coffee you take in, the more calcium goes out. In one study, adult volunteers drank about four cups of coffee . . . . Three hours later, they passed more calcium in their urine than individuals not drinking coffee. James F. Scheer *Health Freedom News*

The Watusi is a very interesting tribe living on the east of Lake Kivu, one of the headwaters of the West Nile in Ruanda which is a Belgian Protectorate. They are tall and athletic. . . . They have magnificent physiques. Many stand over six feet without shoes. Several of the tribes neighboring Ethiopia are agriculturists and grow corn, beans, millet, sweet potatoes, bananas, kafir corn and other grains as their chief articles of food. Physically they are not as well built as either the tribes using dairy products liberally or those using fish from the freshwater lakes and streams. They have been dominated because they possess less courage and resourcefulness. The government of Kenya has for several years sponsored an athletic contest among the various tribes, the test being one of strength for which they use a tug-of-war. One particular tribe has carried off the trophy repeatedly. This tribe resides on the east coast of Lake Victoria and lives very largely on fish. The members are powerful athletes and wonderful swimmers. Weston Price, DDS *Nutrition and Physical Degeneration*

Consider now that it is the goal of the National Cholesterol Education Program to lower the intake of animal fat of all Americans to about ten per cent of their caloric intake. Almost fifteen percent of the Tecumseh participants already ate that little animal fat, and yet it was impossible to see a difference between the cholesterol of those who ate that little and of those who ate much more. Does it make sense to recommend this drastic reduction of animal fat intake if the cholesterol of those who already eat that little is just as high as the cholesterol of the others? Uffe Ravnskov, MD, PhD *The Cholesterol Myths*

BREADED WHITEFISH
Serves 6

1 1/2 pounds thick filets of whitefish, such as
*   turbot or whiting*
2/3 cup unbleached flour
1/2 teaspoon pepper
1 teaspoon sea salt
3 eggs, lightly beaten
1 cup whole grain bread crumbs
1/4 teaspoon grated lemon peel
about 1/2 cup clarified butter (page 150)
about 1/2 cup extra virgin olive oil

Cut filets into pieces of approximately equal size. Mix sea salt and pepper with flour on a plate. Mix bread crumbs with lemon peel in a bowl. Dredge each piece of fish first in the flour mixture, next in egg and lastly in the flour mixture. Sauté in batches in equal parts of butter and oil. Remove to a heated platter and keep warm while preparing the remaining pieces. You will need to replenish butter and oil after each batch.

Serve with lemon wedges, tartar sauce (page 141) or ginger carrots (page 95).

GRILLED SWORDFISH
Serves 6

1 1/2 pounds swordfish
3/4 cup cilantro marinade (page 145)

Brush both sides of swordfish with the marinade and let stand, covered, in refrigerator for several hours. Grill under broiler or on barbecue for 5 to 10 minutes per side, depending on thickness of fish. Be careful not to let the fish burn. Serve with Bernaise sauce (page 152);

Variation: Grilled Tuna
Use *1 1/2 pounds tuna* instead of swordfish. Serve with chunky tomato sauce (page 154).

TROUT WITH ALMONDS

Serves 6

6 fresh whole wild trout
2 cups corn meal
1/2 teaspoon pepper
1 teaspoon sea salt
about 1/2 cup clarified butter (page 150)
about 1/2 cup extra virgin olive oil
1 cup crispy almond slivers (page 515)

Use trout that comes from unpolluted water. Clean well but do not remove heads. Pat dry. Dredge well in mixture of salt, pepper and cornmeal. Sauté fish, one or two at a time, in equal amounts of butter and olive oil over a medium-high flame, using a heavy skillet . They will need 5 to 10 minutes on a side, depending on thickness. Remove to a heated platter and keep warm in the oven while preparing remaining trout.

Pour out used oil and butter. Add 2 tablespoons each clarified butter and oil. Sauté almonds until golden and pour over fish.

The purpose of these studies has included the obtaining of data which will throw light also on the etiology of deformities of the dental arches and face, including irregularity of position of the teeth [crowded, crooked teeth]. A marked variation of the incidence of irregularities was found in the different [African] tribes. This variation could be directly associated with the nutrition rather than with the tribal pattern. The lowest percentage of irregularity occurred in the tribes living very largely on dairy products and marine life. For example, among the Masai living on milk, blood and meat only 3.4 percent had irregularities. Among the Kikuyu and Wakamba 18.2 and 18.9 percent respectively, had irregularities. These people were largely agriculturists living primarily on vegetable foods. In the native Arab school at Omdurman, among the pupils living almost entirely according to the native customs of selection and preparation of foods, 6.4 percent had irregularities, while in the native school at modernized Khartoum, 70 percent had irregularities. Weston Price, DDS *Nutrition and Physical Degeneration*

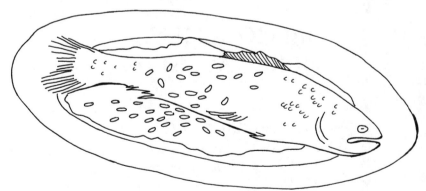

To preserve health is a moral and religious duty, for health is the basis for all social virtues. We can no longer be useful when not well.
Samuel Johnson

The biggest reason for the art of hydrogenation is firmly stated by Mr. Eckey in this book—hydrogenation provides an amazing shelf life and savings for consumers. John Tobe remarked that "you save yourself a couple of pennies by buying a hydrogenated product, and will probably pay the doctor or the druggist or the hospital thousands of dollars through the years for the lousy few pennies these great benefactors of mankind, the processors, have saved you. They should be given citations and medals for their great work for humanity. You saved pennies but gained ill health." Tom Valentine *Facts on Fats & Oils*

DINNER IN THE
ORIENTAL STYLE

Oriental Celery
Root Salad
❀❀ ❀❀

Salmon Filet,
Oriental Style
❀❀

Basic Brown Rice
❀❀

Asparagus with
Sesame Seeds
❀❀❀❀

Plum Sherbert

RED SNAPPER, MEXICAN STYLE
Serves 4

4 red snapper filets
2 tablespoons lime juice
3 tablespoons extra virgin olive oil
1 medium onion, thinly sliced
2 ripe tomatoes, peeled, seeded and chopped
1 bunch cilantro, chopped
1 teaspoon fresh chile pepper, diced
2 cloves garlic, peeled and mashed
pinch cinnamon
sea salt or fish sauce (page 157)

To peel tomatoes, see page 70. Rub filets with lime juice, cover and refrigerate for several hours.

Dry the filets with paper towels. In a cast iron skillet, sauté the filets briefly in olive oil on both sides. Transfer to an oiled pyrex baking dish. Add more olive oil to the skillet. Sauté the onion until soft. Add remaining ingredients and simmer for about 30 minutes or more until most of the liquid is absorbed. Season to taste with sea salt or fish sauce. Strew the sauce over fish and bake at 350 degrees until tender, about 25 minutes. Serve with Mexican rice casserole (page 471).

SALMON FILET, ORIENTAL STYLE
Serves 6

2 pounds wild salmon filet
4 tablespoons sesame seeds
2 tablespoons rice vinegar
3 tablespoons naturally fermented soy sauce
2 tablespoons fish sauce (page 157), optional
2 tablespoons toasted sesame oil
1 tablespoon grated ginger
1 bunch finely chopped green onions
3 cloves garlic, minced
3 tablespoons fresh chives (optional)
grated rind of 1 lemon

Place salmon filet skin side down in an oiled pyrex baking dish. Combine all other ingredients and pour over fish. Cover pan with foil (but don't let foil touch the fish) and bake at 350 degrees about 15 minutes or until fish is just barely cooked through.

Slice the salmon into servings, transfer to individual plates and spoon sauce over each slice. Serve with buckwheat or brown rice pasta, or basic brown rice (page 466).

SWORDFISH STEAKS, ORIENTAL STYLE
Serves 6

2 pounds swordfish steak, about 1-inch thick
2 tablespoons extra virgin olive oil
sea salt and pepper
3 cloves garlic, peeled
1/4 cup fresh ginger, peeled and coarsely chopped
2 tablespoons Dijon-type mustard
1/4 cup naturally fermented soy sauce
2 tablespoons fish sauce (page 157), optional
1 tablespoon raw honey
1/2 cup rice vinegar
1 tablespoon toasted sesame oil
1/3 cup extra virgin olive oil
1 bunch green onions, chopped
3 tablespoons sesame seeds, toasted in oven

Brush swordfish steaks with olive oil and sprinkle with salt and pepper. Grill about 5 minutes to a side, or until cooked through, on a barbecue or under a broiler. Transfer to a heated platter and keep warm until ready to serve. Meanwhile, place garlic, ginger, mustard, optional fish sauce and soy sauce in food processor and process until blended. Add honey and vinegar and process again. With motor running, add the sesame and olive oils gradually so that sauce emulsifies and thickens.

Place swordfish servings on warmed plates. Spoon sauce over and garnish with green onions and sesame seeds. This dish goes well with spinach, chard, Chinese peas or steamed Chinese cabbage.

A splendid illustration of the primitive Maori instinct or wisdom regarding the value of sea foods was shown in an experience we had while making examinations in a native school on the east coast of the North Islands. I was impressed with the fact that the children in the school gave very little evidence of having active dental caries. I asked the teacher what the children brought from their homes to eat at their midday lunch. . . . I was told that they brought no lunch but that when school was dismissed at noon the children rushed for the beach where, while part of the group prepared bonfires, the others stripped and dived into the sea and brought up a large species of lobster. The lobsters were promptly roasted on the coals and devoured with great relish. Weston Price, DDS *Nutrition and Physical Degeneration*

Since the seafoods are, as a group, so valuable a source of the fat-soluble activators, they have been found to be efficient throughout the world not only for controlling tooth decay but for producing a human stock of high vitality. Unfortunately, the cost of transportation in the fresh state often constitutes a factor limiting distribution. Many of the primitive races preserved the food value, including vitamins, very efficiently by drying the fish. While our modern system of canning prevents decomposition, it does not efficiently preserve some of the fat-soluble activators, particularly vitamin A. Weston Price, DDS *Nutrition and Physical Degeneration*

While many of the primitive races studied have continued to thrive on the same soil through thousand of years, our American human stock has declined rapidly within a few centuries and in some localities within a few decades. In the regions in which degeneration has taken place the animal stock has also declined. A decadent individual cannot regenerate himself, although he can reduce the progressive decadence in the next generation, or can vastly improve that generation, by using the demonstrated wisdom of the primitive races. No era in the long journey of mankind reveals in the skeletal remains such a terrible degeneration of teeth and bones as this brief modern period records. Must Nature reject our vaunted culture and call back the more obedient primitives? The alternative seems to be a complete readjustment in accordance with the controlling forces of Nature. Weston Price, DDS *Nutrition and Physical Degeneration*

After an excellent meal, body and spirit experience a very special sense of well-being. Physically, the face lights up, while the brain refreshes itself; the facial line reddens, the eyes shine, and a gentle warmth permeates all the limbs. Psychologically, the spirit becomes more alert, fantasy more lively. . . . In addition, one frequently finds united around the same tables all factors which make society possible: love, friendship, business, speculation, power, protection, ambition, intrigue—that is why a feast brings fruits of all kinds.
J. A. Brillant-Savarin

FISH WITH CURRY SAUCE
Serves 4

2 *pounds firm-fleshed fish, such as halibut or swordfish*
6 *tablespoons extra virgin olive oil or lard*
2 *medium onions, very thinly sliced*
1/4 *cup fresh chile peppers, chopped*
2 *tablespoons curry powder or curry paste*
1 1/2 *cups coconut milk or 7 ounces creamed coconut (page 160)*
1 *cup fish stock (page 119)*
1 *tablespoon freshly grated ginger*
2 *tablespoons fresh lime juice*
5-6 *basil leaves or kaffir lime leaves (available at Oriental markets), chopped*
sea salt or fish sauce (157)

Remove skin and bone from fish steaks and cut into cubes. Dry well and sauté in batches in a cast-iron skillet in about 3 tablespoons olive oil or lard. Remove to a heated platter, cover with parchment paper (see Sources) and keep warm in the oven while preparing remaining fish and sauce.

To prepare the sauce, add remaining olive oil or lard to the skillet. Sauté onions and chile peppers until soft. Stir in the curry powder or paste until well amalgamated. Add coconut milk and fish stock, bring to a boil and skim. Add ginger, lime juice and basil or kaffir lime leaves. Boil vigorously, stirring frequently until the sauce reduces and thickens slightly. Season to taste. Return fish to the skillet and simmer for about 5 minutes or until fish is tender. Do not overcook. Transfer to a heated bowl and serve immediately. Serve with basic brown rice (page 466), raisin chutney (page 108), chopped crispy peanuts (page 514) and chopped green onions.

FISH CAKES

Makes 8 patties

1 1/2 pounds whitefish
1/2 pound fresh fish roe (optional)
2 eggs, lightly beaten
2 small onions, finely minced
1 cup whole grain bread crumbs
2 tablespoons Dijon-type mustard
1/4-1/2 teaspoon cayenne pepper
1 bunch cilantro, chopped (optional)
1 teaspoon grated lemon rind
sea salt or fish sauce (page 157) and pepper
about 1/2 cup clarified butter (page 150)
about 1/2 cup extra virgin olive oil

This is a delicious way to eat inexpensive, coarsely grained fish. If your fish merchant can supply you with roe from cod, whitefish, etc., don't hesitate to add this highly nutritious ingredient.

Place fish in a pan with filtered water and simmer gently until fish is tender. Remove with a slotted spoon, place in a bowl and break up with a fork. Meanwhile, place optional fish roe in its casing in a pan with water and a little vinegar or lemon juice and simmer for about 10 minutes. Rinse in a colander and remove roe from casing. Add to flaked fish and mix thoroughly.

Combine eggs with onions, bread crumbs, mustard, cayenne pepper, cilantro and lemon rind. Season to taste. Add to fish and mix well. Form into cakes. Sauté until golden, a few at a time, in butter and olive oil. Serve with parsley butter sauce (page 153), Creole mayonnaise (page 139) or red pepper sauce (page 146).

Cholesterol is an antioxidant and free radical scavenger which protects cell membranes. It is liberally disbursed in cell walls, protecting vital phospholipids from free radical damage. Cholesterol also acts as a precursor to the many steroid hormones and vitamin D. Vitamin D is normally produced in the skin by exposure of cholesterol to ultraviolet radiation from sunlight. Ultraviolet light is a form of ionizing radiation, which produces free radicals in living tissues.

Total cholesterol (reflected by blood cholesterol) is determined primarily by cholesterol synthesis in response to ongoing oxidative stress from free radicals, not primarily by dietary cholesterol intake. Serum cholesterol levels are indicators of free radical damage and, therefore, correlate with the risk of atherosclerosis. Cholesterol is synthesized in the body as needed and with epidemic free radical diseases, blood cholesterol levels increase with age. . . . Dietary restriction of cholesterol and medications to reduce blood cholesterol have been counterproductive in the treatment of atherosclerosis because the antioxidant role of cholesterol has not been recognized. Unoxidized cholesterol is widely dispersed in cell membranes as a protective factor against atherosclerosis, cancer and other free radical induced diseases. E. M. Cranton, MD and J. P. Frackelton, MD *Journal of Holistic Medicine*

The Zutphen Study. . . was a study of the eating habits of inhabitants of one village in the Netherlands. In this study, the researchers found that even one serving of sea fish each week substantially reduced the incidence of CHD in the individuals who ate the fish. Two interesting points were made in this study. First, for those men who ate the fish, it did not matter how old they were, what their blood pressure or blood cholesterol level was, or, incredibly, how much they smoked. It also made no difference how active they were. Secondly, the men who ate the fish not only had a lowered risk of heart disease, but they consumed significantly more animal protein, cholesterol and alcohol and significantly less carbohydrate than the men who didn't eat fish and who suffered higher mortality rates. The men who had a lower risk of heart disease ate the very foods we are continually told not to eat, and they ate significantly less of the foods we are advised to eat! The authors noted one other very astounding relationship. Those men who consume the most calories had the lowest blood cholesterol levels and those who consumed the least calories had the highest cholesterol levels. Chris Mudd *Cholesterol and Your Health*

Although it is possible to change blood cholesterol a little in laboratory experiments and clinical trials by dieting, it is impossible to find any relationship between the makeup of the diet and the blood cholesterol in individuals who are not participating in a medical experiment. In other words, individuals who live as usual and eat their food without listening to doctors or dieticians show no connection between what they eat and the level of their blood cholesterol. Uffe Ravnskov, MD, PhD *The Cholesterol Myths*

FISH FILETS IN PARCHMENT PAPER
Serves 6

2 pounds filet of sole, turbot or whiting
2 medium onions, very thinly sliced
1 cup piima cream or creme fraiche (page 84)
2 tablespoons fish sauce (page 157), optional
1 bunch cilantro, chopped

Cut six pieces of aluminum foil and line them with six pieces of parchment paper (see Sources) of slightly smaller size. Place a portion of fish on each. Top with onions, a teaspoon of optional fish sauce and a dollop of cultured cream. Fold foil, with parchment paper, together at center, then at ends. Bake in a 350-degree oven or on the barbecue for about 20 minutes. To serve, place "packages" on individual plates. Open and sprinkle with cilantro. The foil and parchment paper will serve as bowls for the fish and its creamy sauce.

TROUT IN PARCHMENT PAPER
Serves 4

4 whole wild trout, skin on
8 shallots, peeled and finely chopped
3 tablespoons butter
1 cup dry white wine
1 tablespoon fresh herbs such as thyme,
  tarragon or rosemary
sea salt or fish sauce (page 157) and pepper

Wash trout well and pat dry. Cut six pieces of aluminum foil and line them with six pieces of parchment paper (see Sources) of slightly smaller size. Place a trout on each one. Sauté shallots in butter, add wine and boil down until liquid is reduced to only a few tablespoons. Let cool. Stir in herbs and season to taste. Spoon a little sauce over each fish. Fold foil, with parchment paper, together at center, then at ends. Bake in a 350-degree oven, or on the barbecue, for about 30 minutes.

POACHED SALMON

Serves 20-30

1 whole wild salmon, cleaned,
*   with head, tail and skin*
cheesecloth and string
1/2 cup vinegar
3 bay leaves,
1 teaspoon juniper berries
1 lemon, sliced
1 teaspoon dried green peppercorns
1 1/4 cups green gelatin mayonnaise (page 140)
2 cucumbers

This is a great buffet dish and not very difficult to make. If you do not have a fish poaching pan, just use a turkey roaster with a rack.

Remove the fins from the salmon. Wrap in cheesecloth and tie with string, leaving little handles of cheesecloth at each end. This will help you remove the fish without breaking it. Place in the pan on a rack and cover with boiling filtered water. Add vinegar, bay leaves, juniper berries, lemon slices and peppercorns. Simmer—do not boil—until just tender. A good rule is to cook 10 minutes per inch of thickness at the thickest part of the salmon. (Use a ruler and measure across the back.)

Lift fish out with cheesecloth handles and place on a large platter. Remove cheesecloth. Remove skin but leave head and tail. Turn over carefully and remove skin from other side. Remove any liquid and debris from platter with paper towels. Cover and refrigerate.

When fish is cool, spread with green gelatin mayonnaise and decorate with cucumber slices to resemble scales. Serve with a choice of sauces such as egg mustard sauce (page 143), Bernaise sauce (page 152), creamy dill sauce (page 142), red pepper sauce (page 146) or watercress sauce (page 144).

NEW YEAR'S EVE
BUFFET DINNER

Poached Salmon with
Egg Mustard Sauce

Steak Tartare

Balsamic Carrot Salad

Asparagus Vinaigrette

Spinach Feta
Pastries

Suet Pudding with
Brandy Butter

The results of Pottenger's cat experiments are often misinterpreted. They do not mean that humans should eat only raw foods—humans are not cats. Part of the diet was cooked in all the healthy groups Price studied. (Milk products, however, were almost always consumed raw.) Pottenger's findings must be seen in the context of the Price research and can be interpreted as follows: When the human diet produces "facial deformities"— the progressive narrowing of the face and crowding of the teeth—extinction will occur if that diet is followed for several generations. The implications for western civilization—obsessed as it is with refined, highly sweetened convenience foods and lowfat items—is profound. *Ancient Dietary Wisdom for Tomorrow's Children*

What could be better for us than protein? And everyone knows vegetables are good for us. Thus, "hydrolyzed vegetable protein" sounds safe and even wholesome. However, this is the chemical method of producing monosodium glutamate. A mixture of hydrolyzed proteins contains the salts of other proteins as well, and monosodium glutamate may comprise as much as 20% of hydrolyzed vegetable protein (the usual range is 12-20%). The flavor enhancement produced by this mixture is almost entirely dependent on MSG. Few people are aware that products containing hydrolyzed vegetable protein frequently are advertised as "all natural." While MSG must be specifically listed on food labels, hydrolyzed vegetable protein, which contains MSG, may be designated simply as "natural flavorings." George R. Schwartz, MD *In Bad Taste: The MSG Syndrome*

Thinking is as biologic as is digestion, and brain embryonic defects are as biologic as are club feet. Since both are readily produced by lowered parental reproductive capacity, and since Nature in her large-scale human demonstration reveals that this is chiefly the result of inadequate nutrition of the parents and too frequent or too prolonged child bearing, the way back in indicated. Like the successful primitive racial stocks, we, too, can make, as a first requisite, provision for adequate nutrition both for generation and growth and can make provision for the regulation of the overloads. We, like the successful primitives, can establish programs of instruction for growing youth and acquaint it with nature's requirements long before emergencies and stresses arise. Weston Price, DDS *Nutrition and Physical Degeneration*

LEAF-WRAPPED SALMON
Serves 8

2 wild salmon filets, equal in size,
about 1 1/2 pounds each, skin removed
3 heads butter lettuce or other soft-leaf lettuce
1-2 cups stuffing (see below)

Prepare lettuce leaves by dipping whole heads into boiling filtered water about 10 seconds. Remove immediately. Drain, remove leaves and spread out on kitchen towels. Meanwhile, prepare stuffing.

Butter an oblong pyrex dish and line it with one layer of overlapping lettuce leaves. Place one filet with skinned side up on the lettuce. Spread filet with stuffing and set other filet on top, skin side up. Fold lettuce leaves up to cover sides and a portion of the top of the fish. Cover top with one layer of overlapping leaves and tuck under. Bake about 45 minutes at 350 degrees. To serve, cut fish with lettuce wrapping crosswise into slices about 1-inch thick.

Lemon Almond Stuffing:
1 cup whole grain bread crumbs
1 cup crispy almonds (page 515)
1 cup fresh parsley sprigs
1 tablespoon fresh tarragon or thyme leaves
1 tablespoon freshly grated lemon rind
1/4 cup fresh lemon juice
1/2 stick softened butter
pinch cayenne
sea salt and pepper

Place bread crumbs, almonds and parsley in food processor and pulse until coarsely chopped. Add herbs, lemon rind, lemon juice and butter. Process until well mixed. Add cayenne and season to taste.

Cilantro Coconut Stuffing

1 bunch fresh cilantro
1/3 cup fresh mint leaves
1 cup dried unsweetened coconut (see page 160)
1/3 cup lemon juice
8 cloves garlic, peeled
8 small hot or 4 medium mild fresh green chiles
1 tablespoon grated fresh ginger
sea salt and pepper

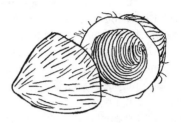

Place all ingredients except salt and pepper in food processor and process into a thick paste. Season to taste.

Russian Style Stuffing:

3 small bunches sorrel leaves or
   1 large bunch spinach
4 tablespoons butter
1/2 pound fresh mushrooms, washed and
   dried with paper towels
2 tablespoons butter
2 tablespoons olive oil
1 bunch green onions, finely chopped
1 tablespoon dried dill or 2 tablespoons fresh dill
1 cup basic brown rice (page 466)
sea salt and pepper

Wash and chop spinach or sorrel. In a heavy skillet, sauté in 4 tablespoons butter until soft. Set aside. Meanwhile chop mushrooms. Sauté with the onions in butter and olive oil until well browned. Mix sautéed mushroom mixture with dill, spinach and rice. Season to taste.

Variation: Individual Leaf Wrapped Salmon:

Use *8 salmon steaks*. Cut each in half at the spine bone, creating 16 pieces, and remove skin and bones. Place a spoonful of stuffing on one piece and another piece on top to form a "sandwich." Wrap each portion with *2 or 3 blanched lettuce leaves*. Place in a buttered pyrex dish and bake about 20 minutes.

Studies of African tribes have shown that intakes of enormous amounts of animal fat not necessarily raises blood cholesterol; on the contrary it may be very low. Samburu people, for instance, eat about a pound of meat and drink almost two gallons of raw milk each day during most of the year. Milk from the African Zebu cattle is much fatter than cow's milk, which means that the Samburus consume more than twice the amount of animal fat than the average American, and yet their cholesterol is much lower, about 170 mg/dl.

According to the view of the Masai people in Kenya, vegetables and fibers are food for cows. They themselves drink half a gallon of Zebu milk each day and their parties are sheer orgies of meat. On such occasions several pounds of meat per person is not unusual. In spite of that the cholesterol of the Masai tribesmen is among the lowest ever measured in the world, about fifty percent of the value of the average American.

Shepherds in Somalia eat almost nothing but milk from their camels. About a gallon and a half a day is normal, which amounts to almost one pound of butter fat, because camel's milk is much fatter than cow's milk. But although more than sixty percent of their energy consumption comes from animal fat, their mean cholesterol is only about 150 mg/dl, far lower than in most Western people. Uffe Ravnskov, MD, PhD *The Cholesterol Myths*

One of the earliest warnings about the rising tide of sugar in our diet came from that 1942 AMA report: "The consumption of sugar and of other relatively pure carbohydrates has become so great during recent years that it presents a serious obstacle to the improved nutrition of the general public." In the strongest terms possible, the report called for "all practical means to be taken to limit consumption of sugar in any form" in which significant nutrients are not present. . . . It was a call unheeded. From the end of wartime rationing to the present, the food industry has known no limit, beyond the technical, in using sugar to cheaply enhance the appeal of its processed and fabricated foods. In these last 40 years industry has more than doubled the sugar it adds to our diet. But protests are no longer heard—the watchdogs of the public's welfare appear to have been pacified.

In the mid 1970's the blue-ribbon FASEB (Federation of American Societies for Experimental Biology), on contract to the FDA, wholeheartedly recommended the agency again approve sugar as a food additive, saying that with the possible exception of dental caries sucrose presents *no* risk to human health. Joseph D. Beasley, MD and Jerry J. Swift, MA *The Kellogg Report*

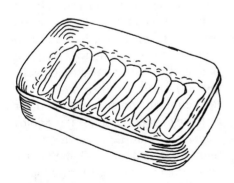

FILETS OF SOLE WITH CREAM SAUCE

(Filets de Sole Bonne Femme)
Serves 4

8 to 12 very fresh filets of sole (3 per person for small Dover sole, 2 per person for larger grey sole)
4 cups fish stock (page 119)
1 onion, finely chopped
sea salt and pepper
1 tablespoon shrimp butter (page 158), optional
1 cup piima cream or creme fraiche (page 84)
finely chopped parsley for garnish

Butter an oblong pyrex dish and strew the onions evenly on the bottom. Lay the sole pieces on the onions, being careful that they overlap as little as possible. Bring the stock to a boil and pour over the filets. Immediately transfer to a 300-degree oven.

Let the filets poach until just tender, from 5 to 15 minutes depending on the thickness of the filets. Carefully lift the filets onto a heated platter, cover with a piece of parchment paper (see Sources), and keep warm in the oven while you are making the sauce. The filets will keep for 1/2 hour or more if properly covered without losing taste or moisture.

Strain the stock into a large skillet and bring to a rapid boil. Whisk in the cream and optional shrimp butter. Continue boiling, skimming the froth occasionally, until the sauce has reduced to the consistency of thick cream. This will take from 10 to 15 minutes. As soon as the sauce reduces to the desired thickness, turn down to simmer. If the sauce gets too thick, thin with a little filtered water or with the juices exuded by the filets on their heated platter. Season to taste. (Salt may not be necessary.)

To serve, transfer the filets to heated plates and pat around with paper towels to mop up any juices. Pour the sauce over the filets and sprinkle on parsley. Serve with lightly steamed small red potatoes or baby vegetables. Basic brown rice (page 466) is also an excellent accompaniment for this dish.

Variation: Filets of Sole with Portuguese Sauce

In addition to the basic ingredients, you will need *two ripe tomatoes*, peeled, seeded and chopped. (To peel tomatoes, see page 70.) Strew them in the pyrex pan with the onions. When you transfer the stock to a frying pan for reduction, do not strain out the onions and the tomatoes. Let them reduce with the sauce. Don't forget the chopped parsley—it looks so pretty with the tomatoes.

Variation: Filets of Sole with Vegetables

Prepare the basic recipe. When the sauce has reduced to the desired thickness, stir in a julienne of vegetables made in the following manner:

Peel *1 small carrot* and cut into thin strips, approximately 1/8 inch by 1/8 inch by 1 inch long; cut the skin off *1 zucchini* and cut this skin into similar strips. (Save the pulp for soups.) Remove the end and leaves from *1 leek* and slit lengthwise half way through. Rinse clean under the tap. Cut rounds about 1/8 inch thick. (The rounds will open and separate when cooked, forming julienne strips.)

Bring a pan of salted filtered water to a boil. Put the carrots in a strainer, hold down in the boiling water for about 1 minute, then rinse with cold water. Strew onto a plate lined with several thicknesses of paper towels and pat dry. Repeat the process with the zucchini strips and the leeks. Mix vegetables together and add to sauce.

Variation: Filets of Sole with Pink Grapefruit Sauce

This is an easy variation with a beautiful presentation, yet worthy of the most elegant dinner party. Prepare the basic recipe, adding *1/2 cup fresh grapefruit juice* to the sauce.

Prepare individual plates with the following garnishes alternating around the outer edge of the plate: *sections of pink grapefruit, steamed Chinese peas,* and spoonfuls of *fresh tomato, peeled, seeded and finely chopped.* (To peel tomato, see page 70.) Place filets in center of plate, pour sauce over and sprinkle on a small amount of *finely chopped parsley.*

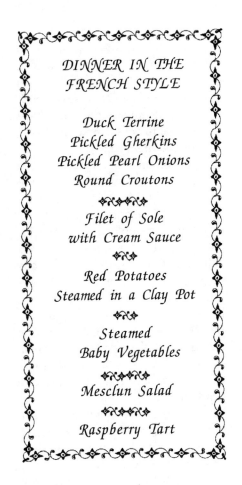

DINNER IN THE FRENCH STYLE

Duck Terrine
Pickled Gherkins
Pickled Pearl Onions
Round Croutons

❀❀❀❀

Filet of Sole
with Cream Sauce

❀❀❀

Red Potatoes
Steamed in a Clay Pot

❀❀❀

Steamed
Baby Vegetables

❀❀❀❀❀

Mesclun Salad

❀❀❀❀❀

Raspberry Tart

Organ weight studies have shown over and over again that poor nutrition profoundly disturbs the weight of most of the endocrine glands (such as the pituitary, thyroid and pancreas) as well as many organs. Obesity is accompanied by profound changes in endocrine and organ weights. Obesity *per se* is only the visible aspect of hidden and far more serious pathological conditions. In Dr. Marshall's mice, the liver became greatly enlarged, while the heart, kidneys, and pancreas also became enlarged. There is strong evidence recorded in the periodical literature that heavy use of refined sugar causes pituitary lesions and perhaps brain lesions. Edward Howell, MD *Enzyme Nutrition*

No wonder there is so much chronic and metabolic disease in America today. In order to deal with all the pollutions and stresses of modern living, healthy bodies must have strong, healthy cells. The key to strong, healthy cells lies first in the cell membrane. Human cell membranes are made of a remarkable combination of fatty acids and proteins—with fatty acids the dominant material. When this man-made molecule of fatty acid, called the *trans* fatty acid, gets into cell membrane construction our cells cannot function optimumly—we cannot ward off viruses as well; the vital biochemical exchanges going on between the interior and exterior of our cells can be fouled up; and our cellular oxidation cannot be as robust as nature intended. Additionally, this degeneration of the cell membrane is cumulative as we continue to eat these *trans* fats every day—it doesn't improve over time, or simply vanish, it slowly gets worse and worse. And the rottenest thing about this entire story is that this molecular misfit, the *trans* fatty acid, is generally hyped by colorful and clever advertising to be "good for you." How in the world did this happen? How did a man-made molecule of very bad fat become a major part of everyday nutrition and get a reputation for being good? Encouraged by our mass media, we took ourselves off butter and stopped cooking with lard and bought margarines and vegetable shortening because we were told it was the "healthy thing to do." And it's not true. It's the opposite—and the money power behind the promotional campaign knew it! They had to know it. Tom Valentine
Facts on Fats & Oils

SALMON WITH BUTTER SAUCE
Serves 6

2 pounds filet of wild salmon
4 cups fish stock (page 119)
several sprigs fresh tarragon
1/2 cup butter, softened
1 tablespoon fresh tarragon leaves, snipped
1 teaspoon vinegar

Butter a small oblong pyrex dish and set the filet, skin side down, in the dish. Strew with tarragon sprigs. Bring the stock to a boil and pour over the filet. If the liquid does not entirely cover the fish, add filtered water. Set in a 325-degree oven and poach until just tender, from 10 to 15 minutes depending on the thickness of the filet. You can check for doneness with a fork. Be careful not to overcook. Remove from the oven when the inside is still a little rare. Set the filet on a heated platter, cover with a piece of parchment paper (see Sources), and keep in a heated oven while you prepare the sauce.

Pour stock into a heavy skillet and boil vigorously until it reduces to about 1 cup. Allow to cool slightly. Pour cooled stock into a bowl set in barely simmering water. Using a wire whisk, add the butter to the stock, 1 tablespoon at a time, beating vigorously with each addition. Stir in vinegar and tarragon snippings. Do not let the sauce boil. When all the butter has been amalgamated, check for seasoning. Salt will probably be unnecessary. Divide the filet into servings and place on individual plates. Spoon a little sauce over each and serve immediately.

SALMON WITH SUN-DRIED TOMATO SAUCE

Serves 4

1 filet of wild salmon, about 1 1/3 pounds
2 cups fish stock (page 119)
3 tablespoons butter
8 shallots, finely chopped
4 tablespoons sun dried tomato bits (see Sources)
sea salt or fish sauce (page 157) and pepper

Butter a small oblong pyrex dish and set the filet, skin side down, in the dish. Bring stock to a boil and pour over the filet. If the liquid does not entirely cover the fish, add filtered water. Set in a 325-degree oven and poach until just tender, from 10 to 15 minutes depending on the thickness of the filet. You can check for doneness with a fork. Be careful not to overcook. Remove from the oven when the inside is still a little rare. Set the salmon on a heated platter, cover with a piece of parchment paper (see Sources), and keep in a heated oven while you are preparing the sauce.

While the salmon is cooking, sauté shallots a few minutes in butter, add the tomato bits and cook a few minutes more. After the fish has poached, strain stock into the shallot mixture, bring to a rapid boil and reduce the stock, skimming occasionally, until you have about a cup of liquid plus vegetables. Season to taste.

To serve, portion the fish and lift off the skin. Divide among four heated plates and spoon on the sauce.

FRIDAY NIGHT DINNER

Mushroom Salad

Salmon with Sun Dried Tomato Sauce

Rosemary Potatoes

Green Beans

Flourless Carrot Cake

Two recent studies have confirmed what Weston Price discovered over 60 years ago—that seafood makes a vital contribution to good health. A study conducted in Britain found that middle-aged men, who had already suffered a heart attack, cut their death rate by one-third by adding oily fish like salmon, tuna, mackerel and sardines to their diet. In the study of 2,033 men under age seventy, researchers told one group of men to eat fish high in omega-3 oils at least twice a week; another group was told to cut down on high-fat foods; another to eat more fiber; and a fourth was given no dietary advice. After two years the odds of dying of heart disease dropped by 29 percent among the fish eaters compared with the other men in the study. In Japan, a series of studies has shown that those who consumed lots of seafood were much less likely to die of strokes. Residents of fishing villages who eat about nine ounces of seafood daily have a 25 to 40 percent lower risk of stroke than farmers who eat only three ounces of fish a day. SWF

Dr. Clive McCay. . . found in his longtime experiments at Cornell University that "animals fed very modest amounts of natural foods lived in excellent health until equal in age to people over a hundred years old. They died without getting cancer. Animals fed a high-fuel diet [high in refined fats, starches, sugars and highly refined foods] lived a normal or shortened span of life and had the usual diseases of old age such as cancer." Dean Conrad *The Great American Tragedy*

Don't forget that your body needs some high-quality saturated fat in your diet. The antifat craze that has swept America for the past 30 years is responsible for a lot of harm—a lot of misinformation. Here's another example: Researchers with the Department of Agriculture's Human Nutrition Research Center at Tufts University have learned that people who cut back on fat to the tune of eating only fish and vegetables appear to open themselves up to more infection. The lowfat diet, which called for eating fish every day, "significantly reduced the infection fighting power of certain white blood cells." This does not mean you can't eat fish every day if you want to, it means you need to eat some quality fat with it. Tom Valentine *Search for Health*

SALMON WITH SORREL SAUCE
Serves 6

2 pounds filet of wild salmon
4 cups fish stock (page 119)
1 cup piima cream or creme fraiche (page 84)
1 tablespoon shrimp butter (page 158), optional
about 4 packed cups fresh sorrel leaves
3 tablespoons butter
sea salt and pepper

Butter an oblong pyrex dish and set the filet, skin side down, in the dish. Bring the stock to a boil and pour over the filet. If the liquid does not entirely cover the fish, add filtered water. Set in a 325-degree oven and poach until just tender, from 10 to 15 minutes depending on the thickness of the filet. You can check for doneness with a fork. Be careful not to overcook. Remove from the oven when the inside is still a little rare. Set the filet on a heated platter, cover with a piece of parchment paper (see Sources) and keep in a heated oven while you prepare the sauce.

Meanwhile, wash the sorrel leaves, shake dry and chop coarsely. Sauté in butter until completely wilted. Set aside.

Pour poaching stock into a heavy skillet and bring to a rapid boil. Add cream and optional shrimp butter and boil vigorously, until sauce has thickened and reduced to about 1 cup. Stir in the sorrel and season to taste. Divide the filet into six servings and place on individual plates. Spoon a portion of sauce over each and serve immediately.

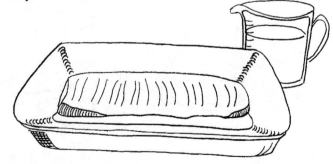

SALMON WITH FENNEL

Serves 6

6 wild salmon steaks
4 cups fish stock (page 119)
1 fennel bulb, coarsely chopped
1/2 cup dry white wine
1 tablespoon fennel seeds
1 teaspoon dried green peppercorns
1 cup piima cream or creme fraiche (page 84)
1 tablespoon gelatin (see Sources), optional
1/4 cup butter, softened
18 small sprigs fennel leaves
1 tomato, peeled, seeded and finely chopped
sea salt and pepper
6 teaspoons salmon eggs (optional)

Remove bone and skin from steaks. They will form two pieces. Roll up each piece and tie with string, forming two small "medallions" per person. Set in a buttered pyrex dish, just large enough to hold the medallions, and strew on the chopped fennel. Bring stock to a boil and pour over medallions. Add a little filtered water if stock does not cover the fish. Bake about 8 minutes at 350 degrees or until just cooked. Strain stock into a heavy saucepan, cover medallions with parchment paper (see Sources), and keep warm in the oven while you prepare the sauce. (Discard the fennel.)

Strain the stock into a heavy skillet, bring to a rapid boil, skim and reduce by half. Add wine, fennel seeds, peppercorns, optional gelatin and cream and reduce to about 1 cup or until sauce has thickened. Strain into a bowl and beat in butter with a whisk, 1 tablespoon at a time. Season to taste. Set bowl in simmering water to keep warm.

Decorate plates with alternating fennel sprigs and spoonfuls of tomato around the outside edge. (To peel tomatoes, see page 70.) Remove strings from medallions and set two in the middle of each plate. Spoon sauce over each and decorate with salmon eggs.

For decades we've had dinned in our ears by research foundations and associations that we should follow a lowfat, high-polyunsaturated diet to prevent heart disease.

Then we learned that excess vegetable oils increase the need for vitamin E, bring on premature aging and cause facial skin to wrinkle far before it normally would.

Now the results of research by Gabriel Fernandes, associate professor of medicine in the division of Clinical Immunology at the University of Texas Health Center (San Antonio), point an accusing finger at this dietary change as a probable cause of the near epidemic proportions of malignant melanoma, a deadly skin cancer.

Experiments by Fernandes with mice on calorie-controlled diet with various amounts of polyunsaturated and saturated fats show that heavy emphasis on polyunsaturated fats could indeed be the culprit.

Mice on a diet of 20 percent polyunsaturated fat proved to be far more susceptible to transplanted melanoma and to the spread of it to their lungs than mice on a diet of 20 percent saturated fats. James F. Scheer *Health Freedom News*

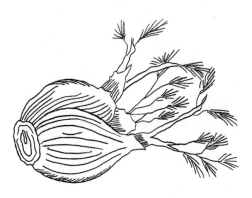

In all of these experiments, immature animals were found to be much more vulnerable to the toxic effects of MSG than were older animals. This was true in all animal species tested.

Yet, food manufacturers continue to add tons of this excitotoxin additive to foods of all kinds, including baby foods. Even the government's public health watchdog agency, the Food and Drug Administration, refused to take action. Dr. Olney, one of the leading researchers in this area, felt compelled to do something to protect unsuspecting mothers and their infants from this danger. First, he informed the FDA of the real danger to human infants and encouraged them to take action. But they refused. His only recourse was to go public with what he knew to be true—that MSG was a dangerous compound that should not be added to infant foods. It was only after his testimony before a Congressional committee that the food manufacturers agreed to remove MSG from baby foods. But did they really?

Instead of adding pure MSG, they added a substance known as hydrolyzed vegetable protein that contains three known excitotoxins and has added MSG. . . this substance is even more dangerous than MSG. They continued this practice for seven more years, and there is evidence that excitotoxins are still added to baby foods today. Usually these are in the form of caseinate, [factory-made] beef or chicken broth, or flavoring. Russell L. Blaylock, MD *Excitotoxins: The Taste That Kills*

CREOLE CRAWFISH CASSEROLE

(Etouffée)
Serves 6

24 crawfish tails with shells, fresh or frozen
4 tablespoons olive oil
2 large onions, chopped
2 ripe plum tomatoes, seeded and chopped
1 green pepper, seeded and chopped
4 cloves garlic, peeled and mashed
1/2 cup butter
1/2 cup unbleached white flour
1 quart crawfish stock (page 121)
2-3 tablespoons shrimp butter (page 158)
1/2 teaspoon dried thyme
1/4 teaspoon cayenne pepper
sea salt

Remove crawfish tails and use the shells to make crawfish stock, reserving crawfish tail meat in the refrigerator.

Sauté onion and green pepper in olive oil until soft. Add tomato, raise heat and sauté, stirring constantly, until liquid has evaporated. Remove pan from heat and stir in garlic.

Melt butter in a heavy pot. Stir in flour and cook over medium heat, stirring constantly with a wooden spoon, for about 5 minutes or until flour turns light brown. Slowly add crawfish stock, stirring constantly with a whisk. Whisk in shrimp butter and cook over a medium flame, stirring constantly, until sauce thickens. Add sautéed vegetables, cayenne pepper and thyme and season to taste. Add crawfish and simmer over low heat until crawfish are cooked through, stirring frequently. Serve in soup bowls with basic brown rice (page 466) or coconut rice (page 467).

Variation: Creole Shrimp Casserole

Use *about 3 dozen large shrimp* in place of crawfish and *shrimp stock (page 121)*, in place of crawfish stock.

Variation:

Add *1 pound spicy sausage, sliced.*

POULTRY

As Americans have cut back on red meat, chicken has played an increasingly important role in the nation's diet. Although chicken is a perfectly good source of animal protein, frequent chicken consumption requires a cautionary note. First of all, we must be careful of the source of chickens we buy. Battery-raised chickens are subjected to crowded living conditions and often substandard feed; they require frequent doses of antibiotics and growth hormones to reach adulthood. Many develop cancers and these cancerous chickens are not necessarily discarded. According to researcher Virginia Livingston Wheeler, these cancers can be transmitted to humans. We advise you to find a source of organic, cage-free or pasture-fed chicken, which is becoming more available directly from farmers and in our markets and is worth the additional price.

Secondly, we warn you against eating chicken—even pasture-fed chicken—to excess. Any food eaten to the exclusion of others can lead to allergies, food addictions and adverse reactions. This is true of meats as well as vegetables, dairy products and grains. It is best to eat a variety of fowl—chicken, turkey, Cornish game hens and domesticated duck—and to vary your source of animal protein between poultry, fish, game and red meat.

The collection presented here includes recipes for baked, roasted, grilled and stewed chicken. Chicken meat left over from making stock can be used in the recipes found on pages 288-289.

Most of our recipes call for the use of chicken stock in the sauce. Chicken stock provides a concentrated source of minerals and hydrophilic colloids that make your entire meal more digestible.

Don't neglect to eat the skin and the dark meat as well as the white. The skin provides valuable fat-soluble vitamins and antimicrobial fatty acids, while the dark meat contains more minerals than the white. And speaking of dark meat, do take advantage of domestic farm-raised duck now becoming more available in our markets. We suggest cutting ducks into pieces before preparing them, rather than cooking them whole. One duck will yield four generous servings; the carcass makes a rich stock for sauces and soups; the excess skin, when rendered of its fat, makes delicious cracklings for salads and is an excellent substitute for bacon; and the fat itself can be used in many ways. Duck fat is highly prized in France for cooking potatoes; and in Scandinavia where it is spread like butter on dark bread to make delicious sandwiches. It is high in stable oleic acid and rich in fat-soluble vitamins.

ROAST CHICKEN
Serves 6

1 roasting chicken, about 4 pounds
1 medium onion, peeled and thinly sliced
2 whole heads garlic (optional)
3 tablespoons melted butter
sea salt and pepper
several sprigs fresh thyme, oregano or tarragon
1/2 cup dry white wine or vermouth
4 cups chicken stock (page 124)
1 tablespoon gelatin (see Sources), optional

Strew onion slices in a stainless steel roasting pan. Cut optional heads of garlic in half and place, cut side down, in pan. Stuff fresh herbs into the cavity of the chicken and place on a rack in the roasting pan, underside up. Brush with melted butter and sprinkle with sea salt and pepper. Bake at 375 degrees for 1 hour. To turn chicken, insert a wooden spoon into the cavity. Lift chicken and rotate so that top side is up. Brush with more butter and oil, season with salt and pepper and return to oven. Bake another hour. Remove chicken to a carving board and cut into individual pieces. Reserve chicken pieces and garlic in a warm oven while making sauce. (Serve garlic heads to garlic lovers. Softened, individual cloves can be picked out with a fork. They are delicious.)

Remove rack from baking pan. You may pour off the fat if you wish, but it is not necessary. Pour in wine and bring to a boil, stirring to loosen onion slices. Add stock and optional gelatin and reduce to about half by vigorous boiling. Strain sauce into a small saucepan and keep warm over a low flame.

SUNDAY DINNER

Cream of Vegetable Soup with Round Croutons

❀❀❀

Roast Chicken

❀❀❀

Cottage Potatoes

❀❀❀

Pickled Beets

❀❀❀

Applesauce

A series of feeding experiments on rats showed differences in the nutritive value of common fats. The rats which received butterfat grew better than the rats fed vegetable oils, were better in appearance, and had better reproductive capacity. Apparently butterfat contains a substance not present in the other fats tested, which is essential for growth and health of young animals. This difference is not due to vitamins A, D or E but to a difference in the chemical constitution of the fats. These findings are significant to the knowledge of nutrition because they indicate additional reasons why milk fat has superior value for human diets. Weston Price, DDS *Nutrition and Physical Degeneration*

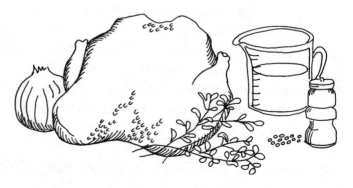

BASIC BAKED CHICKEN
Serves 6

1 frying chicken, cut into pieces
2 tablespoons Dijon-type mustard
2 tablespoons melted butter
1 tablespoon dried tarragon
1/2 cup dry white wine
2 cups chicken stock (page 124)
1 tablespoon gelatin (see Sources), optional
sea salt and pepper

Place chicken pieces skin side up in a stainless steel roasting pan. Mix mustard, butter and tarragon and brush on chicken. Bake for about 2 hours at 350 degrees or until pieces are golden. Remove to a heated platter and keep warm in the oven while making sauce. Add wine, stock and optional gelatin to the baking pan and boil vigorously, stirring to loosen any accumulated drippings, until sauce reduces and thickens. Season to taste and serve.

Variation: Chicken with Cream Sauce
Strew *several sprigs fresh tarragon* over chicken in the pan. (Omit dried tarragon.) Add *1 cup piima cream or creme fraiche (page 84)* to the stock and wine when you are reducing the sauce. Strain sauce into a small pan and add *2 tablespoons fresh tarragon leaves, chopped.*

Variation: Chicken with Red Pepper Sauce
Place *3 red peppers, cored, seeded and coarsely chopped in pan with chicken pieces.* After chicken has cooked, sauté peppers in the fat in the roasting pan. Add wine and stock and reduce. Pass the sauce through a food mill (see A Word on Equipment, page 68) and into a saucepan. Reheat gently and season to taste.

Variation: Chicken with Peanut Sauce
Prepare chicken according to master recipe, omitting mustard. When sauce has reduced, remove from heat and gradually add *1 1/2 cups peanut sauce (page 147)*, using a wire whisk. Transfer sauce to a container set in hot water. Do not let the sauce boil or it will burn.

Actually, the digestive mechanism of man is adapted to a mixed meat and vegetable diet. Human teeth consist of three types: canines or piercing teeth of the meat-eating animals, the incisors of plant-eating animals, and the molars or grinders of grain-and-nut-eating animals. With respect to structure, human teeth are conclusive proof that the human body is adapted to a mixed animal and plant diet. Man has specific digestive ferments for meat proteins and other special digestive juices for carbohydrates. His stomach and intestinal tract is equipped to handle both. Man is naturally adapted to a mixed diet of animal and plant foods. H. Leon Abrams *Your Body Is Your Best Doctor*

Know Your Ingredients
Name This Product #13

Water, corn syrup, partially hydrogenated soybean oil, mono- and diglycerides, soy protein, sodium stearoyl lactylate, dipotassium phosphate, polysorbate 60, sodium acid pyrophosphate, salt, artificial flavor, colored with betacarotene.

See Appendix B for Answer

It was the Miss America Pageant and, after viewing it, I actually fell to prayer for the return of the American Beauty. This Pageant became for me a tragic testimonial to the physical degeneration that has occurred in the modern civilized world, especially during the last 40 years of advanced technology.

Deaf Smith County, Texas has sponsored an inordinate number of attractive pageant winners. It is not coincidence but the result of the water supply, which is higher in zinc, iodine and magnesium, all of which contribute to the much denser and better proportioned bone structure of the men and women living there. It has become famous as an area without a toothache. What do teeth have to do with beauty? Decayed teeth, like crowded ones and under developed bones, also detract from our attractiveness.

Because of impoverished soils, poor water supplies, overprocessed foods and inadequate diets, that begin unwittingly as "high-tech" baby formulas instead of human breast milk, we are seeing a rapid decline in beauty, intelligence and grace. The evidence is found in these pageants, lower SAT scores and in the growing consensus of distrust, inhumanity and immorality between men. Beauty is more than skin deep. The so-called "civilized" world is turning mean and ugly to the very bone. R. M. Dell'Orfano *PPNF Health Journal*

MOROCCAN STYLE CHICKEN
Serves 6

1 frying chicken cut into pieces
1/4 cup naturally fermented soy sauce
1/4 cup dry white wine
2 tablespoons honey
juice of 2 lemons
grated rind of 2 lemons or 3 tablespoons
    preserved lemon peel (page 109)
1 clove garlic, peeled and mashed
1 teaspoon curry powder
1/4 teaspoon ground ginger
1/2 teaspoon each dried oregano, thyme and
    crushed green peppercorns
3 tablespoons melted butter
2 cups chicken stock (page 124)
8 dried apricot halves, coarsely chopped
    and soaked in warm filtered water

Mix soy sauce, wine, honey, lemon juice, lemon rind and all spices together. Marinate chicken pieces in this mixture in the refrigerator for several hours or overnight. Remove pieces, pat dry and set skin side up in a stainless steel baking pan, reserving marinade. Brush with butter, season with sea salt and pepper and bake at 375 degrees for about 2 hours. Reduce heat if chicken begins to burn. Remove chicken to heated platter while making sauce.

Pour chicken stock into the pan, bring to a boil and stir well. Add marinade and drained apricot pieces. Let sauce reduce by about one-half. Check seasoning and pour over chicken pieces.

SIMPLE CHICKEN BREASTS
Serves 6

6 chicken breasts, with skin on
juice of two lemons
3 tablespoons extra virgin olive oil

Trim chicken breasts and pound lightly with the small prong side of a meat hammer. Marinate several hours in lemon juice. Brush a heavy-bottomed skillet with olive oil and allow it to heat up. Pat chicken pieces dry. Cook over moderate heat on both sides, two or three at a time, for about 7 minutes to a side. Transfer to a heated platter and keep warm in the oven. Serve plain or with an accompaniment such as cilantro pesto (page 144), corn relish (page 100), chismole (page 184), curry sauce (page 149), or red enchilada sauce (page 156); or serve cold with Creole mayonnaise (page 139).

Variation: Mexican Chicken Breasts

Use *juice of 4 limes* in place of lemons. Add *1/2 teaspoon oregano* and *1/4 teaspoon chile flakes* to marinade. May be grilled or barbecued.

SPICED CHICKEN BREASTS

Serves 6

6 chicken breasts, with skin on
4 tablespoons extra virgin olive oil
1 teaspoon turmeric
1 teaspoon cinnamon
1 teaspoon ground cumin
1 teaspoon paprika
1 teaspoon curry powder
1/2 teaspoon dried chile flakes
3 cloves garlic, peeled and mashed
1/2 teaspoon sea salt

Trim chicken breasts and pound lightly with the small prong side of a meat hammer. Mix spices and garlic with oil and brush onto chicken pieces. Marinate chicken breasts in refrigerator several hours or overnight. Brush a heavy skillet with olive oil and allow it to heat up. Pat chicken breasts dry and cook over medium-high flame, two or three at a time, for about 7 minutes per side. Transfer to a heated platter and keep warm in the oven. To serve, slice across the grain and arrange slices on individual plates. Dribble marinade over chicken. Serve with Algerian wedding rice (page 472).

Know Your Ingredients
Name This Product # 14

Tomatoes with tomato puree, cooked macaroni product, tomatoes, tomato puree, dry curd cottage cheese, onions, beef, mushrooms, low-moisture part-skim mozzarella cheese, corn syrup, modified cornstarch, garlic, tomato paste, enriched wheat flour, Parmesan cheese, salt, spices, Romano cheese (made from cow's milk), hydrolyzed vegetable protein and autolyzed yeast extract, corn oil, sugar, xanthan gum, dehydrated onions, erythorbic acid, caramel coloring, dried beef stock, natural flavorings.

See Appendix B for Answer

Inquiry into the dietary history of patients diagnosed as schizophrenic reveals the diet of their choice is rich in sweets, candy, cakes, coffee, caffeinated beverages and foods prepared with sugar. These foods, which stimulate the adrenals, should be eliminated or severely restricted. A. Cott *Orthomolecular Approach to the Treatment of Learning Disabilities*

The teenage suicide rate has doubled since 1968, largely because mothers demonstrate their love by keeping the refrigerators stocked with sugary soda drinks and feed them cereals for breakfast and spaghetti for dinner. Their grandparents bring them candy and ice cream. Why do we insist upon rotting the brains of a whole generation of children, turning them into scholastic failures, delinquents, dropouts and welfare recipients? Why do we drive more and more of them to suicide by feeding them ever more processed foods? I'll tell you why: Many people are getting rich at their expense. We look askance at African tribes when they cut faces and rub dyes into the wounds and when they circumcise women. That's child's play compared to what we do to our children. In our society, it's perfectly all right to maim and kill—so long as we do it in a socially acceptable way. H. L. Newbold, MD *Type A Type B Weight Loss Book*

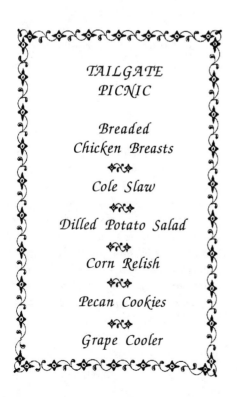

TAILGATE PICNIC

Breaded Chicken Breasts

❦❦❦

Cole Slaw

❦❦❦

Dilled Potato Salad

❦❦❦

Corn Relish

❦❦❦

Pecan Cookies

❦❦❦

Grape Cooler

CHICKEN WITH SWEET AND SOUR SAUCE
Serves 8

8 chicken breasts, with skin on
1 cup fresh orange juice
1 cup fresh lemon juice
1 cup vinegar
2 tablespoons fresh ginger, peeled and minced
2 tablespoons fresh garlic, peeled and minced
1/2 teaspoon red chile pepper flakes
3 tablespoons extra virgin olive oil
2 cups chicken stock (page 124)

Trim chicken breasts and pound lightly with the small prong side of a meat hammer. Combine remaining ingredients except olive oil and chicken stock in a saucepan and bring to a boil. Reduce heat and simmer for several minutes. Allow to cool and stir in olive oil. Marinate the chicken breasts in this mixture for several hours or overnight. Remove from marinade and broil about 7 minutes per side. Keep warm on a heated platter in the oven while making sauce.

Place marinade and stock in a saucepan and boil vigorously until sauce is reduced by half. To serve, slice the chicken breasts across the grain, arrange on individual plates and spoon sauce over. Serve with steamed cabbage (page 376), sautéed red peppers (page 395) and sautéed mushroom slices (page 389).

BREADED CHICKEN BREASTS
Serves 4-6

8 skinless chicken breasts
1 1/2 cups unbleached flour
1 teaspoon pepper
4 eggs, beaten
2 cups whole grain bread crumbs
1/2 cup grated Parmesan cheese
about 4 tablespoons butter
about 4 tablespoons extra virgin olive oil

This is a delicious substitute for fried chicken. It makes an excellent picnic dish. Leftover breaded chicken breasts can be warmed and sent to school in children's lunch boxes.

Trim chicken breasts and pound lightly with the small prong side of a meat hammer. Mix flour and pepper together on a plate; have beaten eggs ready in a bowl; mix bread crumbs and Parmesan cheese in another bowl. Using tongs dip each piece first in the flour mixture, then in the beaten egg, then in the bread crumb mixture. Sauté a few at a time in butter and olive oil about 7 minutes per side, being careful not to burn. Transfer to a heated platter and keep warm in the oven until ready to serve. Serve with lemon wedges, ginger carrots (page 95) or pineapple chutney (page 106).

SESAME BUFFALO WINGS
Serves 8

24 chicken wings, separated at the joints
1/2 cup soy sauce
1/2 cup rice vinegar
2 tablespoons honey
juice of 2 lemons
grated rind of 2 lemons
1 clove garlic, peeled and mashed
1 teaspoon curry powder
1/4 teaspoon ground ginger
1/2 teaspoon dried oregano
1/2 teaspoon dried thyme
1/2 teaspoon dried green peppercorns, crushed
3 tablespoons melted butter
1/4 cup sesame seeds

Mix soy sauce, vinegar, honey, lemon juice, lemon rind and all seasonings. Marinate buffalo wings in the mixture several hours or overnight. Remove from mixture and pat dry. Place in a stainless steel baking pan, brush with butter, sprinkle with sesame seeds and bake at 350 degrees about 1 1/4 hours. May be served with the marinade, gently heated, as a dip.

[There are many reports] about the excellent track record of glucosamine in the treatment of osteoarthritis. Now evidence is strong that another of these complex sugar molecules, chondroitin sulfate, has the ability to attack the osteoarthritic joints from a different biochemical pathway. . . . Chondroitin is found in many different tissues and, as you would expect, is highly concentrated in the "gristle" and cartilage around joints. You can get a lot of chondroitin by eating the gristle around your chicken bones. Apparently, much of this animal chondroitin is absorbed from the intestinal tract. The chondroitin works synergistically with glucosamine and blocks certain enzymes that "eat" cartilage. Chondroitin, like its partner glucosamine. . . is really a food substance. William Campbell Douglass, MD *Second Opinion*

CHILD'S
BIRTHDAY PARTY

Sesame
Buffalo Wings

Carrot Salad

Apple Slices
in Orange Juice

Crispy Cashews

Buttered Popcorn

Spice Layer Cake

Raspberry Drink

Other than the fact that margarine may kill you, what else is wrong with it? An English institution for boys ran a nutritional experiment in 1938. A group of boys were fed one and three-fourths ounces of New Zealand "grass-fed butter." Another group was fed margarine. The margarine proved "worthless for growth," but the butter group grew an extra .38 inches during the experimental period. The investigators had previously done a similar test on rats. They concluded, "There is something in butter that isn't in margarine and it works on boys the same as on rats." William Campbell Douglass, MD *The Milk Book*

Michael DeBakey, the world renowned heart surgeon from Houston who has devoted extensive research into the cholesterol-coronary disease theory, states that out of every ten people in the United States who have atherosclerotic heart disease that only three or four of these ten have high cholesterol levels; this is approximately the identical rate of elevated cholesterol found in the general population. His comment: "If you say cholesterol is the cause, how do you explain the other 60 percent to 70 percent with heart disease who don't have a high cholesterol?" De Bakey made an analysis of cholesterol levels from usual hospital laboratory analyses of 1,700 patients with atherosclerotic disease and found that there was no positive or definitive relationship or correlation between serum cholesterol levels and the extent or nature of atherosclerotic disease. H. Leon Abrams *Vegetarianism: An Anthropological/ Nutritional Evaluation*

CHICKEN STIR-FRY STEW
Serves 4-6

1 pound chicken breasts cut into small pieces
juice of 2 lemons
about 1/2 cup extra virgin olive oil or lard
1 cup crispy peanuts (page 514)
1 bunch green onions, sliced on an angle
2 large carrots, peeled and cut into a julienne
1 red bell pepper, seeded and cut into a julienne
1 cup broccoli, cut into flowerets
2 cloves garlic, finely chopped
1 teaspoon freshly grated ginger
1 tablespoon Rapadura (see page 536)
1/4 teaspoon red pepper flakes
2 tablespoons naturally fermented soy sauce
1/8 cup rice vinegar
2-3 cups chicken stock (page 124)
2 tablespoons arrowroot
    mixed with 2 tablespoons filtered water

This a delicious, low-cost family dish—always a favorite. Marinate chicken pieces several hours in lemon juice. Remove and pat dry with paper towels. Mix chicken stock with vinegar, soy sauce, pepper flakes, ginger, Rapadura and garlic and set aside. In a heavy skillet or wok, sauté chicken in batches in olive oil or lard until cooked through. Using a slotted spoon, transfer chicken to a bowl and reserve. Add more oil or lard and sauté peanuts a minute or two. Remove with slotted spoon. Add more oil or lard and sauté onions, carrots and pepper about 2 minutes. Add sauce mixture to vegetables and bring to a boil. Return chicken and peanuts to the pan and mix well. Add arrowroot mixture and simmer a minute or so until sauce thickens. Add broccoli and simmer until tender. Serve with basic brown rice (page 466).

CHICKEN CURRY

Serves 6

meat from 2 cooked chickens, cut up
  (reserved from making stock, page 124)
about 3 tablespoons clarified butter (page 150)
2 medium onions, finely chopped
2 tablespoons turmeric
1 tablespoon ground fenugreek seeds
1 teaspoon ground cumin
1/4 teaspoon cayenne pepper
1/2 teaspoon ground cloves
1 teaspoon ground coriander
1 teaspoon ground cardamom
2-3 cups chicken stock (page 124)
juice of 1-2 lemons
2 cloves garlic, peeled and mashed
1 cup piima cream, creme fraiche (page 84),
  1 can whole coconut milk or
  7 ounces creamed coconut (see page 160)
sea salt

Sauté onions until soft in clarified butter. Add spices and sauté, stirring, for several minutes. Add chicken stock and lemon juice and bring to a boil. Stir in garlic, chicken and cream. Simmer, uncovered, for about 15 minutes, stirring frequently, until sauce is reduced and thickened. Stir in chicken and season to taste. Serve with traditional curry garnishes such as chopped green onions, chopped crispy peanuts (page 514), dried sweetened coconut meat (page 159), raisin chutney (page 108) and fruit chutney (page 106).

Obtaining adequate fat was a great challenge for the Australian Aborigine, living in a hot, dry climate. They were close observers of nature and knew just when certain animals were at their fattest. For example, kangaroos were fat when the fern leaf wattle was in flower; possums when the apple tree was in bloom. Other signs indicated when the carpet snake, kangaroo rat, mussels, oysters, turtles and eels were fat and at their best. Except in times of drought or famine, the Aborigine rejected kangaroos that were too lean—they were not worth carrying back to camp. During periods of abundance "animals were slaughtered ruthlessly, and only the best and fattest parts of the killed game were eaten." Favorite foods were fat from the intestines of marsupials and from emus. Highly saturated kidney fat from the possum was often eaten raw. The dugong, a large seagoing mammal, was another source of fat available to natives on the coasts.

Other sources of fat included eggs—from both birds and reptiles—and a great variety of insects. Chief among them was the witchety grub, or moth larva, found in rotting trunks of trees. These succulent treats—often over six inches long—were eaten both raw and cooked. Fat content of the dried grub is as high as 67 percent of calories. The green tree ant was another source of valuable fat, with a fat-to-protein ration of about twelve to one. Another important seasonal food in some parts of the country was the begong moth. The moths were knocked off rock walls on which they gathered in large numbers, or smoked out of caves or crevices. They were roasted on the spot or ground up for future use. Moth abdomens are the size of a small peanut and are rich in fat. *Nasty, Brutish and Short?*

Because table salt comes from the same batch as vacuum-refined industrial salt, it is treated with caustic soda or lime to remove all traces of magnesium salts. These vital magnesium salts are not taken out because they keep the salt from flowing out of the dispenser spout, it is because they bring in more profits on the chemical market. Yet these magnesium salts are a very necessary part of the food salt and fill important biological and therapeutic roles. Further, to prevent any moisture from being reabsorbed, salt refiners now add alumino-silicate of sodium or yellow prussiate of soda as desiccants plus different bleaches to the final salt formula. But since table salt, chemically treated in this way, will no longer combine with human body fluid, it invariably causes severe problems of edema (water retention) and several other health disturbances. The fear of salt that we witness today and the virtual ban on consuming products with a high sodium content is a matter of serious concern to biologists. Salt-free diets can cause salt starvation, which is a stark reality of our modern world, but it is actually a starvation of macro- and trace minerals, a biological deficiency that refined sodium chloride alone cannot correct. Jacques DeLangre *Seasalt's Hidden Powers*

Myth: A vegetarian diet will protect you against atherosclerosis.
Truth: The International Atherosclerosis Project found that vegetarians had just as much atherosclerosis as meat eaters. (*Lab Invest* 1986 18:465)

CHICKEN WITH WALNUTS
(Fesenjan)
Serves 6-8

meat from 2 cooked chickens, cut up
    (reserved from making stock, page 124)
2 cups crispy walnuts (page 513)
2-3 cups chicken stock (page 124)
2-4 tablespoons Rapadura (see page 536)
12 ounces concentrated pomegranate juice,
    or 1/3 cup pomegranate "molasses"
    (available at Middle Eastern markets)
sea salt and pepper

This delicious recipe comes from Persia. Place walnuts in food processor and grind to a paste. Mix with stock, concentrated pomegranate juice and Rapadura. (Note: Use the larger amount of stock if using pomegranate "molasses.") Heat up slowly and simmer for about 1/2 hour. Season to taste. Add chicken meat to sauce and simmer about 5 minutes or until chicken is warmed through. Serve with basic brown rice (page 466).

CHICKEN SUPREME
Serves 6

meat from 2 cooked chickens, cut up
    (reserved from making stock, page 124)
1 pound fresh mushrooms, washed, dried
    and sliced
4 tablespoons shallots, chopped
2 tablespoons butter
2 tablespoons extra virgin olive oil
1/2 cup dry white wine
2 cups chicken stock (page 124)
1 cup piima cream or creme fraiche (page 84)
1 tablespoon gelatin (see Sources), optional
sea salt and pepper

In a heavy skillet, sauté mushrooms in two or three batches until golden. Reserve. Add more butter and olive oil and sauté shallots until soft. Add wine, stock and optional gelatin, bring to a boil and cook, uncovered, until stock has reduced to about one-third. Add cream and reduce further. Stir in chicken meat and mushrooms and simmer about 5 minutes. Season to taste. Serve with basic brown rice (page 466) or as a filling in buckwheat crepes (page 480).

CHICKEN GUMBO
Serves 8

meat from 2 cooked chickens, cut up
(reserved from making stock, page 124)
2 tablespoons butter
2 tablespoons extra virgin olive oil
2 large onions, chopped
1 red pepper, seeded and chopped
1 green pepper, seeded and chopped
1/2 cup tomato paste
2-4 cups chicken stock (page 124)
2 cloves garlic, crushed
1 teaspoon dried basil
1 teaspoon dried oregano
1 teaspoon green peppercorns, crushed
2-3 tomatoes, peeled, seeded and chopped
sea salt
1 tablespoon filé powder (available in gourmet markets and specialty shops)

To peel tomatoes, see page 70. Sauté onions and peppers in butter and olive oil until soft. Add tomato paste and chicken broth and bring to a boil. Skim, reduce to a simmer, and add chicken meat and seasonings. Simmer about 1 hour, uncovered, stirring occasionally. About 10 minutes before serving, stir in tomatoes and season to taste. Remove from heat and stir in filé powder. Serve with basic brown rice (page 466) or wild rice (page 474).

The penalties for using a synthetic, imitation, chemically embalmed substitute for butter seem to be quite drastic. Some appear to be: (1) Sexual castration for the growing child, in more or less degree, with oversized females fatter and taller than the boys. (Remember, meat animals are castrated for the purpose of making them fat.) (2) Loss of ability to maintain calcified structure, such as teeth and bones. Dental caries, pyorrhea, arthritis, etc., would be logical end results that would inevitably follow, especially in view of the added influence of other refined and devitalized foods. Dr. Price's experience in curing arthritis, dental diseases and lowered resistance with good butter directly bears out this conclusion. (3) Evidence is accumulating to show that multiple sclerosis is a result of deficiencies in which vitamin E complex (as found in butter) is vitally involved. Further, vitamin E is now found to be a remedy for the disorders of menopause, showing how these deficiency diseases follow their victim through life. Royal Lee, DDS *Butter, Vitamin E and the "X" Factor of Dr. Price*

Gumbo soups are often flavored and thickened with filé powder (pronounced "fee-lay"), which is mucilage obtained from the dried and powdered leaves and pith of the sassafras tree. The Choctaw Indians of Louisiana are responsible for introducing filé powder to the French of New Orleans. The leaves were gathered in the Fall, dried in the sun and pounded in a wooden mortar. To prevent the powder from becoming stringy, it should be added to soups and stews after removing them from the stove. Filé powder may also be placed on the table in a salt shaker and added according to preference. SWF

Your body makes saturated fats, and your body makes cholesterol—about 2000 mg per day. In general, cholesterol that the average American absorbs from food amounts to about 100 mg per day. So, in theory, even reducing animal foods to zero will result in a mere 5% decrease in the total amount of cholesterol available to the blood and tissues. In practice, such a diet is likely to deprive the body of the substrates it needs to manufacture enough of this vital substance. *The Oiling of America*

If the best current knowledge were employed, enough food to feed the four billion people could be grown in the southern half of Sudan! It is only the Western bias, the idea spread throughout the world that one must eat white grain and drink soda pop to be "civilized," that is responsible for the suffering of the millions of starving people in the world. It is a myth that there is not enough to go around, that there is no way the Earth can support its exploding population. The truth is that most of the world's food resources are controlled by a handful of greedy men, who deny people the right to grow food for themselves but try to sell them Western-produced junk instead. [Some experts] estimate that if all the arable land on earth were used properly and sowed with foods for human consumption, the Earth could support 60 billion people—almost fifteen times our current population! But it is true that there is no way we can feed the world population on Whoppers and Cheez-Wiz, let alone nourish it. Paul Stitt *Fighting the Food Giants*

CHICKEN STEW

Serves 8-10

2 whole chickens, cut into pieces
2 cups red or white wine
3 tablespoons butter
3 tablespoons extra virgin olive oil
about 2 cups unbleached flour
2 teaspoons each sea salt and pepper
3 tablespoons butter
4 cups chicken stock (page 124)
several sprigs fresh thyme, tied together
2-3 small pieces lemon peel
1 teaspoon dried green peppercorns, crushed
10-15 small red potatoes
1 pound fresh mushrooms
2 pounds medium boiling onions
4 tablespoons butter
4 tablespoons extra virgin olive oil
2 tablespoons parsley, finely chopped

Mix chicken pieces with wine and marinate in the refrigerator for 4 to 12 hours. Dry pieces well with paper towels, reserving marinade. Make a mixture of flour, salt and pepper. Melt butter and oil in a large, flameproof casserole. Dredge chicken pieces in flour mixture and brown on both sides in butter and oil over medium heat, a few at a time, reserving on a plate. Pour out browning fat and melt 3 tablespoons butter in the casserole. Add about 3/4 cup of the flour mixture and cook, stirring constantly, for several minutes or until flour becomes lightly browned. Add wine marinade and chicken stock to casserole, blending well using a wire whisk. Bring to a boil and skim. Add thyme, peppercorns, lemon peel and chicken pieces to the pot, cover and bake at 325 degrees for about 2 hours. One hour before serving, add potatoes to the casserole.

Meanwhile, wash the mushrooms, dry well and sauté them, whole or sliced, in 2 tablespoons each of butter and olive oil. Peel the onions and sauté them gently in the remaining butter and olive oil for about 20 minutes. Just before serving, add mushrooms and onions to the casserole and stir in chopped parsley.

CORNISH GAME HENS WITH GRAPES

Serves 4

2 Cornish game hens, split lengthwise
2 tablespoons extra virgin olive oil
2 tablespoons melted butter
sea salt and pepper
1/2 cup dry white wine or vermouth
2 cups chicken stock (page 124)
2 cups fresh grapes, red or green
2 tablespoons arrowroot mixed with
    2 tablespoons filtered water

Place game hen halves, skin side up, in a stainless steel baking pan. Brush with a mixture of butter and oil and season with salt and pepper. Bake at 375 degrees for about 1 1/2 hours. Remove to a heated platter and keep warm in the oven while making sauce.

Pour wine or vermouth into the pan and bring to a boil, stirring with a wooden spoon to scrape up any accumulated juices in the pan. Add chicken stock, bring to a rapid boil, skim and let the sauce reduce for about 10 minutes until it thickens. Add the grapes and simmer about 5 minutes more. Spoonful by spoonful, add arrowroot mixture until desired thickness is obtained. Transfer game hens to individual plates and pour sauce over.

Cholesterol is . . . the central structure in the steroid group that includes the female and male hormones, the contraceptive pill, cortisone, vitamin D, and the steroid drugs that some athletes and older movie stars take. Cholesterol, despite all the bad press it has received, is a vital material in the human organism. It is part of the bile acids that digest fats, a major component of brain and nerve tissue, and a forerunner of many hormones, particularly the sex hormones. Cholesterol is found widely in animal foods (eggs, dairy products, poultry, shellfish), and our bodies manufacture significant amounts of it every day. "Without it the skin would dry up, the brain would not function, and there would be no vital hormones of sex and adrenal."

In the Big Fat Controversy, some researchers have reported statistical correlations between blood cholesterol levels and heart disease. Despite an enormous effort, however, scientists have not been able to establish, among normal healthy people on a good diet, understandable links between the cholesterol in one's food, the cholesterol in one's blood, and heart attacks or strokes. To the degree there are relationships—as there are among myriad factors and events in the body—no one knows what is causing what. Joseph D. Beasley, MD and Jerry J. Swift, MA *The Kellogg Report*

The Medical Research Council of Great Britain in 1968 did a study in which the fate of patients put on a low-saturated fat diet after a heart attack was determined and compared to patients on a high-saturated fat diet. They concluded that the unsaturated fat diet had no effect on the ultimate course of the patients. The number of second heart attacks and deaths were the same in both groups. Two other studies, one done in Oslo, Norway and one in England, came to the same conclusion. William Campbell Douglass, MD *The Milk Book*

—How much, sir? asked the old woman.

—A quart, Stephen said.

He watched her pour into the measure and thence into the jug rich white milk. . . . Old and secret she had entered from a morning world, maybe a messenger. She praised the goodness of the milk, pouring it out. Crouching by a patient cow at daybreak in the lush field, a witch on her toadstool, her wrinkled fingers quick at the squirting dugs. . . .

—It is indeed, ma'am, Buck Mulligan said, pouring milk into their cups.

—Taste it, sir, she said.

He drank at her bidding.

—If we could only live on good food like that, he said to her somewhat loudly, we wouldn't have the country full of rotten teeth and rotten guts. Living in a bogswamp, eating cheap food and the streets paved with dust, horsedung and consumptives' spits.

—Are you a medical student, sir? the old woman asked.

—I am, ma'am, Buck Mulligan answered.

James Joyce *Ulysses*

CORNISH GAME HENS, INDIAN STYLE

Serves 4

2 Cornish game hens, split lengthwise
1/2 cup plain yoghurt
1 teaspoon ground cumin
1 teaspoon turmeric
1 teaspoon ground fenugreek seeds
1 tablespoon lemon juice
2 cloves garlic, peeled and mashed
1/2 teaspoon freshly grated ginger
1/2 teaspoon paprika
1/2 teaspoon salt
1 tablespoon extra virgin olive oil
2 tablespoons crispy almond slivers (page 515)

Combine yoghurt, cumin, turmeric, fenugreek seeds, lemon juice, garlic, ginger, paprika, oil and salt in a large bowl. Brush on game hens and marinate in refrigerator for 4 to 6 hours. Place game hen halves, skin side up, in a stainless steel baking dish, spoon on any remaining marinade and bake at 375 degrees for about 1 1/4 hours. Sprinkle almonds on and bake another 15 minutes.

TURKEY WITH CHESTNUT STUFFING

Serves 12-18

1 16-20 pound turkey
8 cups whole grain bread crumbs
2 teaspoons rubbed sage
2 teaspoons dried thyme
1 teaspoon sea salt
1 teaspoon pepper
4 medium onions, peeled and chopped
1 bunch celery, chopped
1/2 cup butter
2 cups chestnuts, coarsely chopped (see page 381)
large needle and thick thread
2 onions, peeled and sliced
1 cup unbleached flour
4-6 cups turkey stock (page 125)
cooked giblets, finely chopped (optional)

Remove neck and giblets from turkey and use for making stock (page 125). Sauté onions and celery in butter in a large skillet until softened. Mix with bread crumbs, seasonings and chopped chestnuts. The stuffing may be made ahead of time, but you should wait until you are ready to cook to stuff the turkey.

Stuff the neck cavity loosely and sew skin flaps to the body of the turkey with a large needle and thick thread. Stuff the main cavity loosely and fasten with skewers or merely bring the legs through a slit cut just behind the tail. Strew sliced onions in a large roasting pan. Set a rack over the onions and set turkey on the rack. Rub skin with salt and pepper and bake at 350 degrees for about 5 hours, basting frequently.

Remove the turkey to a carving board. Sprinkle flour in the drippings and cook over a medium flame about 5 minutes, stirring constantly. Add stock and blend with a whisk. Bring to a boil and cook several minutes, stirring occasionally. Strain gravy into a saucepan and allow to simmer for 1/2 hour or so until it reduces and thickens. Stir in optional giblets. If gravy gets too thick, thin with a little water.

THANKSGIVING DINNER

Coconut Turkey Soup

Turkey with Chestnut Stuffing

Onion Cranberry Compote

Sweet Potato Casserole

Celery Root Potato Purée

Peas

Sauerkraut

Pear Cranberry Pie

Pumpkin Pie

Apple Cider

The first happy lesson gleaned from a study of traditional diets is that healthy food can and should taste good; that we can put butter on our porridge and cook in lard, that it's OK to consume whole milk, fatty meats, liver and onions, shrimp and lobster, even insects, if you like them; that heavenly sauces made from bone broth and cream confer more benefits than pills and powders and ersatz low-fat concoctions, the stepchildren of technology, pawned off as health foods.

Wisely used, technology can take the drudgery out of cooking, and help us bring properly grown and prepared foods to the marketplace. Wrongly used, technology produces breads that are soft and sweet rather than sour and chewy; coca-cola rather than cottage-industry lacto-fermented soft drinks; bouillon cubes rather than homemade broth; sugar-embalmed ketchup with infinite shelf life rather than enzyme-rich condiments and pickles preserved to last a few months in a way that adds nutrients, instead of taking them away.

The second lesson is that healthy eating is good for the ecology. The building blocks of a healthy diet are pesticide-free foods raised on mineral-rich soil, and healthy animals that live free to manure the paddocks of thousands of farms, rather than suffer in factories, confined to misery and disease. The road to health starts with a willingness to pay a good price for such food, thus rewarding the farmer who preserves the land through wise farming practices, rather than the agribusiness that mines the soil for quick profits. *Nasty, Brutish and Short?*

TURKEY STIR-FRY STEW
Serves 4-6

1 1/2 pounds raw turkey, cut into small pieces
about 6 tablespoons extra virgin olive oil or lard
2 bunch green onions, sliced on an angle
1 green or red bell pepper, seeded and
*   cut into a julienne*
1 cup chopped pineapple, drained
1 small can water chestnuts, drained and sliced
2 cloves garlic, finely chopped
1 teaspoon grated ginger
1/2 teaspoon red pepper flakes
2 tablespoon naturally fermented soy sauce
1 tablespoon Rapadura (see page 536)
1/8 cup rice vinegar
2-3 cups chicken or turkey stock (pages 124-125)
2 tablespoons arrowroot
*   mixed with 2 tablespoon filtered water*

Mix stock with garlic, ginger, pepper flakes, soy sauce, Rapadura, and vinegar and set aside. Pat turkey pieces dry. In a heavy skillet or wok, sauté turkey in batches in 3 tablespoons olive oil or lard until cooked through. Using a slotted spoon, transfer to a heated bowl. Add remaining olive oil or lard and sauté onions and pepper about 2 minutes. Add sauce mixture and bring to a boil. Add cooked turkey, pineapple and water chestnuts to pan and mix well. Add arrowroot mixture and simmer a minute or so until sauce thickens. Serve with basic brown rice (page 466).

PREPARATION OF WHOLE DUCK
Serves 8

2 whole ducks
juice of 4 lemons

Whole ducks are worth doing if you are willing to take a little time in preparation. Two ducks will yield 8 good servings. The carcasses and wings make a rich duck stock (page 125), and meat picked from the carcasses will be sufficient to make a meal of burritos or enchiladas (page 426). The livers make a delicious mousse (page 244) and the fat can be rendered and used for frying potatoes (page 397). The crispy pieces of fat produced by rendering are delicious on salads.

Using a very sharp, flexible fish filleting knife, trim off neck fat and skin, the tail, and fat at the back of the cavity. Remove the wings and then the leg plus the thigh. Carefully remove the wishbone in the front of the carcass. Make a slit along the backbone, cut down along the rib cage and remove the breasts on both sides. Trim all the fat and skin off the carcass. Repeat the process with the second duck.

Trim excess fat off the four breasts and four thigh-leg pieces and marinate for several hours in fresh lemon juice; or marinate only the duck breasts and make preserved duck with legs and thighs (page 298). Proceed with the following recipes or any of your own invention.

DUCK FAT AND CRACKLINGS

To render duck fat and make cracklings, cut pieces of fat and skin into small chunks and place in a heavy-bottomed pan. Cook about 3/4 hour over medium heat until all fat has been rendered and skin pieces turn golden brown. Remove cracklings with a slotted spoon to paper towels. Strain fat into a jar, cover tightly and store in the refrigerator. Cracklings are delicious French style Caesar salad (page 177). They should be stored in the refrigerator but heated gently before use.

The record indicates that the incidence of tooth decay has increased as humans have increased the refined plant carbohydrate of their diet and lowered their intake of animal protein. During the paleolithic period, humans were largely meat eaters and consumed most of their plant foods as they found them; however, as long as humans used whole grains, the incidence of tooth decay remained low. For example, skeletal remains from Middle Age Denmark show about 6 percent of the total teeth with caries while other populations of Northern Europe approach a cavity rate of approximately 10 percent. As consumption of meat has decreased, and the consumption of grain foods and other carbohydrates (sugar and white flour) has formed a significant percentage of the diet, tooth decay has increased to epidemic proportions. H. Leon Abrams *Vegetarianism: An Anthropological/Nutritional Evaluation*

It would be extraordinary if sugar and white flour, known to wreak havoc on the teeth, did not also have profound repercussions elsewhere in the body. Coronary disease has heretofore been regarded as a "complication" of diabetes. Both coronary disease and diabetes have a common cause: White sugar and white flour. William Dufty *Sugar Blues*

It is not true. . . that the absolute length of life has lengthened. Actually, fewer persons alive at 70 today survive until 90 than 40 years ago. The lengthened life span of today is due to saving the lives of more babies and children. Edward Howell, MD *Food Enzymes for Health and Longevity*

The current medical theory is that a high-cholesterol diet causes high serum cholesterol which causes the atherosclerotic process. Although this theory appears to be correct, it isn't. . . . In the 1970's I started looking at patients' cholesterol levels and saw many which didn't fit the theory. Many who were big cholesterol eaters and had a good lipid profile and many who were not cholesterol eaters who had a poor lipid profile. I knew then that something was wrong with the dietary cholesterol theory. . . . I knew the real answer to the atherosclerotic process would be found by finding the cause of the initial injury to the intimal cells. I knew that all the theories of that injury had no scientific bases. In the early 1980's I suspected the oxidant free radical was the culprit. Finally in early 1987 I found the proof in the study of the exposure of guinea pigs to kerosene fumes. The liver increases the production of cholesterol in response to the injury to the intimal cells by oxidant free radicals. The cholesterol goes to the site of injury and itself becomes oxidized in an attempt to protect the cells. Roy W. Dowdell, MD *Health Freedom News*

DUCK WITH GREEN PEPPER SAUCE

Serves 8

*4 duck breasts and 4 thigh-leg pieces,
    marinated in lemon juice (see page 295)*
3 cups beef or duck stock (page 122 or 125)
1/2 cup dry white wine or vermouth
*1 small can green peppercorns, drained,
    rinsed well and patted dry*
1 cup piima cream or creme fraiche (page 84)
sea salt and pepper

Dry duck pieces with paper towels. Using a sharp knife, score the fat on the breasts and thighs. Cut the meat away from the underside of the thigh bone, open up and remove the thigh bone—this will facilitate browning. In a heavy-bottomed skillet, sauté the breasts, two at a time, about 5 minutes per side. (Start by sautéing on the skin side, and the duck pieces will produce their own fat.) Remove to a heated platter. Pour out fat and sauté the legs in the same manner. Pour out fat and add wine to the pan. Bring to a boil. Add stock and peppercorns and reduce to a simmer. Return the thigh pieces to the pan and simmer, uncovered, about 15 minutes. (Keep breast pieces in a warm oven—they should be medium rare or rare.) Remove leg pieces to heated platter, add cream to stock, bring liquid to a rapid boil and reduce to about 1 cup. Season to taste.

To serve, slice the breasts thinly and distribute to individual serving plates. Cut the leg from the thigh and place a leg or a thigh on each plate. Pour sauce over and serve immediately.

Variation: Duck Breasts with Green Pepper Sauce
Prepare recipe using *8 duck breasts*. Omit thighs.

DUCK WITH PLUM SAUCE

Serves 8

4 duck breasts and 4 thigh-leg pieces,
marinated in lemon juice (see page 295)
3 cups beef or duck stock (page 122 or 125)
1/2 cup dry white wine
1 teaspoon freshly grated ginger
2 tablespoons naturally sweetened plum jam
2 tablespoons arrowroot mixed with
2 tablespoons filtered water
sea salt and pepper

Dry duck pieces with paper towels. Using a sharp knife, score the fat on the breasts and thighs. Cut the meat away from the underside of the thigh bone, remove bone and open up a bit—this will facilitate browning. In a heavy-bottomed skillet, sauté the breasts, two at a time, about 5 minutes per side. (Start by sautéing on the skin side, and the duck pieces will produce their own fat.) Remove to a heated platter. Pour out fat and sauté the legs in the same manner. Pour out fat and add wine and stock to the pan. Bring to a boil, add ginger and jam and reduce to a simmer. Return the thigh pieces to the pan and simmer, uncovered, about 15 minutes. (Keep breast pieces in a warm oven—they should be medium rare or rare.) Remove leg pieces to heated platter, bring liquid to a rapid boil and reduce to about 2 cups. Spoonful by spoonful, add arrowroot mixture until desired thickness is obtained. Season to taste.

To serve, slice the breasts thinly and distribute to individual serving plates. Cut the leg from the thigh and place a leg or a thigh on each plate. Pour sauce over and serve immediately.

Variation: Duck Breast with Plum Sauce

Prepare recipe with *8 duck breasts*. Omit thighs.

That which is produced by Yin originates in the five flavors; the five organs which regulate the functions of the body are injured by the five flavors. Thus, if acidity exceeds the other flavors, then the liver will be caused to produce an excess of saliva and the force of the spleen will be cut short. If salt exceeds among the flavors, the great bones become weary, the muscles and the flesh become deficient, and the mind becomes despondent. If sweetness exceeds the other flavors, the breath of the heart will be asthmatic and full, the appearance will be slack and the force of the kidneys will be unbalanced. If among the flavors bitterness exceeds the others, then the atmosphere of the spleen becomes dry and the atmosphere of the stomach becomes dense. If the pungent flavor exceeds the others, the muscles and the pulse become slack and the spirit will be injured.

Therefore, if people pay attention to the five flavors and mix them well, their bones will remain straight, their muscles will remain tender and young, their breath and blood will circulate freely, their pores will be fine in texture, and, consequently, their breath and bones will be filled with the essence of life. *The Yellow Emperor's Classic of Internal Medicine*

A high-cholesterol diet is not the cause of atherosclerosis. In 50 men with a fourfold increase in dietary cholesterol, two-thirds failed to show an increase in serum cholesterol. Seven patients in another study, while consuming large amounts of beef fat and vitamin and mineral supplements, showed a decrease in average cholesterol levels. Roy W. Dowdell, MD *Health Freedom News*

Now researchers have designed rations for maneuvers and battlefield for U.S. Army infantry men that almost guarantee to undermine their health, morale and weaken them for actual combat. Their rations contain nutritional Trojan Horses: junk foods and nonfoods.

The army used to offer C-rations for eating on the battlefield. Then in 1980 they came out with Meals Ready to Eat (MRE), combat rations with 3,600 calories and, according to the surgeon general, the military daily allowance of minerals and synthetic vitamins.

Now the U.S. Army's Natick Research Development and Engineering Center has "improved" these rations by offering more of the food that GI's ate at home, along with more choices on entrees.

These dietary delights include white bread, pound cake, M&M's, Tootsie Rolls, one-inch tall bottles of Tabasco sauce and drink mixes such as Kool-Aid and even pizza crusts baked with refined sugar to keep them from growing stale. The bread is wrapped in a small packet of preservative that absorbs oxygen and moisture.

That's not all. Coming up in the next few years are battlefield burritos, hamburgers and even hot dogs with buns. The hot dogs are smaller than the nitrate and nitrite-loaded kind sold in your supermarket, but—and get this—they taste "just like ballpark franks"—although they're lower in cholesterol and sodium.

Goody! Goody! Perhaps this "Eat for Defeat" diet should be shared with the Soviet Union! James F. Scheer *Health Freedom News*

TERIYAKI DUCK BREASTS
Serves 4

4 duck breasts
3/4 cup teriyaki sauce (page 147)

Trim excess fat off the duck breasts, score the fat and marinate for several hours in teriyaki sauce.

Pat dry with paper towels and sauté in a heavy skillet, two at a time, about 5 minutes per side, starting with the skin side down. Keep warm on a heated platter in the oven while doing the second batch. To serve, slice thinly across the grain, arrange on individual plates and dribble marinade over.

PRESERVED DUCK LEGS
(Confit de Canard)
Serves 6-8

2-4 duck thighs
2-4 duck legs (see page 295)
juice of 2 lemons
3 tablespoons coarse sea salt
6 cloves garlic, peeled and mashed
1 tablespoon dried thyme
2-3 cups rendered duck fat (page 295)
clarified butter (page 150) or lard (optional)

You should be able to stuff the legs and thighs into one quart-sized, wide-mouth mason jar. Mix lemon juice, sea salt, garlic and thyme together and rub this marinade thoroughly into duck pieces. Place in a bowl, cover and marinate in refrigerator for 24 hours. Stuff duck pieces into the jar. Melt fat and pour into jar. The duck pieces should be completely covered—if lacking sufficient duck fat, add melted clarified butter or lard. Cover tightly and store in refrigerator for 2 to 4 weeks.

To serve, place jar in pan of hot water and allow fat to melt. Remove duck pieces and pat dry. (Reserve fat for another batch of preserved duck legs or use it to sauté potatoes.) Sauté duck pieces gently in a heavy skillet, about 10 minutes per side.

ORGAN MEATS

Almost all traditional cultures prize organ meats for their ability to build reserves of strength and vitality. Organ meats are extremely rich in fat-soluble vitamins A and D, as well as essential fatty acids, important very-long-chain superunsaturated fatty acids and the whole gamut of macro and trace minerals. Wild animals eat the organs of their kill first, thus showing a wisdom superior to our own. The first solid food that native African mothers give to their babies is raw liver, which they thoughtfully chew for them. Folk wisdom throughout the world, including Europe, values brains as a food for babies and growing children.

American cookbooks of a century ago contained plenty of recipes for organ meats, and any authentic cookbook for ethnic cuisine—French, Italian, Greek, Middle Eastern or English—will feature several recipes for liver, kidney, heart, sweetbreads and brains. What a pity these delicious and nutritious foods have disappeared from our tables.

Many of our grandparents will remember the days when liver was served once a week. Establishment nutritionists now recommend we discontinue this healthful practice in order to avoid cholesterol! Others have stopped eating liver fearing toxic substances, which can accumulate in the livers of all animals. As the function of the liver is to remove toxic substances from the blood, this is a legitimate concern. For this reason, it is best to buy organic liver now becoming increasingly available in supermarkets and health food stores. Even organic liver may contain some toxic substances, but its nutritive value outweighs the dangers of any toxins it contains. Not only does liver provide copper, zinc, iron and vitamins A and D in abundance, but it is also a rich source of antioxidants—substances that help your own liver remove toxic substances from the body.

If you are not used to eating organ meats but wish to reinstate this healthful practice, start with sweetbreads (part of the thymus gland of the young calf), which do not have a strong flavor—breaded sweetbreads taste just like chicken. You can then graduate to liver, kidney, heart and brains, all of which have stronger flavors or more exotic textures. These meats all benefit from strongly flavored sauces featuring onions, wine, balsamic vinegar and that magic elixir—homemade beef or chicken stock.

If you cannot get your family to eat organ meats when served as such, there are plenty of ways to add them to their food without their knowledge. All ground meat dishes can be made with a combination of ground heart and ground muscle meat. Poached brains can be chopped up and added to any ground meat dish, as can grated raw liver. A spoonful or two of grated liver added to brown rice as it cooks results in a flavorful casserole that is a complete meal. (See page 467.) You can serve rice this way, without any other meat dish, and know that your family's requirements for high-quality animal products are being met.

Until recent years, it has been common knowledge among the superintendents of large zoos of America and Europe that members of the cat family did not reproduce efficiently in captivity, unless the mothers had been born in the jungle. Formerly, this made it necessary to replenish lions, tigers, leopards and other felines from wild stock as fast as the cages were emptied by death . . . . The story is told of a trip to Africa made by a wild animal specialist from the London zoo for the purpose of obtaining additional lions and studying this problem. While in the lion country, he observed the lion kill a zebra. The lion proceeded then to tear open the abdomen of the zebra and eat the entrails at the right flank. This took him directly to the liver. After spending some time selecting different internal organs, the lion backed away and turned and pawed dirt over the carcass which he abandoned to the jackals. The scientist hurried to the carcass and drove away the jackals to study the dead zebra to note what tissues had been taken. This gave him the clue which, when put into practice, has entirely changed the history of the reproduction of the cat family in captivity. The addition of the organs to the foods of the captive animals born in the jungle supplied them with foods needed to make reproduction possible. Their young, too, could reproduce efficiently. As I studied this matter with the director of a large lion colony, he listed in detail the organs and tissues that were particularly selected by animals in the wilds and also those that were provided for animals reproducing in captivity. Weston Price, DDS *Nutrition and Physical Degeneration*

PREPARATION OF SWEETBREADS

Sweetbreads need careful advance preparation before they can be cooked up for a final dish. Allow one pair of sweetbreads for two to four people, depending on appetites. They must be very fresh. Wash the sweetbreads, cover with cold filtered water to which you have added a little vinegar and soak for about 2 hours, changing the water once or twice. This extracts the blood and helps remove any impurities. Remove, rinse and place in a saucepan. Cover with filtered water or chicken stock (page 124), add 1 teaspoon of salt, bring to a boil and simmer for about 15 minutes. Remove from poaching liquid (which can be reserved for another use) and allow to cool. Using a sharp knife, carefully remove all loose tissue, skin, fat and membranes. Place on a plate or platter, cover with parchment paper (see Sources) and place a weighted flat plate or cookie sheet on top. Let the sweetbreads flatten in the refrigerator for several hours or overnight.

BREADED SWEETBREADS
Serves 6

2 pair prepared sweetbreads
1 cup unbleached flour
1/2 teaspoon pepper
1/2 teaspoon sea salt
3 eggs, lightly beaten
1 cup whole grain bread crumbs
1/2 teaspoon fine herbs
3 tablespoons butter
3 tablespoons extra virgin olive oil

Mix salt and pepper with flour and fine herbs with bread crumbs. Slice sweetbreads at 3/8-inch intervals on the bias. Dredge first in the flour mixture, then in eggs, then in the bread crumb mixture. Sauté a few at a time in butter and olive oil. Keep warm in the oven while completing the remaining sweetbreads. Serve with ginger carrots (page 95) or raisin chutney (page 108).

SWEETBREADS IN TOMATO SAUCE

Serves 6

2 pair prepared sweetbreads
1 cup unbleached flour
1/2 teaspoon sea salt
1/2 teaspoon pepper
3 tablespoons butter
3 tablespoons extra virgin olive oil
2 cups chunky tomato sauce (page 154)

Mix flour with salt and pepper. Pat sweetbreads dry and dredge in flour. Sauté in a mixture of butter and olive oil. Serve with tomato sauce.

SWEETBREADS WITH MUSHROOMS AND CREAM

Serves 6

2 pair prepared sweetbreads
3 tablespoons butter
3 tablespoons extra virgin olive oil
1 pound fresh mushrooms, washed
  well dried and sliced
1 cup dry white wine
2 cups beef or chicken stock (page 122 or 124)
1 tablespoon gelatin (see Sources), optional
1 cup piima cream or creme fraiche (page 84)
sea salt and pepper

Slice sweetbreads at 3/8-inch intervals on the bias. In a heavy skillet, sauté sweetbread slices in batches in 2 tablespoons each butter and olive oil until golden. Transfer to a heated platter and keep warm in the oven. Add the remaining butter and oil and sauté the mushrooms. Strew over the sweetbreads. Pour out the browning fat and add wine to the pan. Bring to a boil, stirring with a wooden spoon. Add stock and optional gelatin, bring to a boil and reduce to about half. Add cream and simmer until sauce thickens further. Season to taste. Pour sauce over sweetbreads and serve.

SATURDAY
NIGHT DINNER

Watercress Salad

Breaded Sweetbreads

Ginger Carrots

Steamed Green Cabbage

Berry Pie

Of all the dishes cooked by the Indians, a *beeatee*, as it is called in their language, is certainly the most delicious that can be prepared from caribou only, without any other ingredient. It is a kind of haggis, made with the blood, a good quantity of fat shred small, some of the tenderest of the flesh, together with the heart and lungs cut, or more commonly torn into small shivers; all of which is put into the stomach and toasted by being suspended before the fire on a string. . . . it is certainly a most delicious morsel, even without pepper, salt or any other seasoning. *The Journeys of Samuel Hearne* 1768

Studies of Professor Fred Hale of Texas A. and M. College reveal he produces blind pigs at will by depriving healthy mothers of natural vitamin A before and after mating. Then, by placing these blind pigs on a complete ration and mating them, these blind mothers farrow healthy pigs with good eyes. It is believed that much of the poor eyesight suffered by human beings today could be prevented by eating foods that provide complete nutrition for the whole body including the eyes. R. Dean Conrad *The Great American Tragedy*

Sherman, who has made many important contributions to our knowledge of vitamin A, has shown in a recent communication that an amount of vitamin A sufficient to support normal growth and maintain every appearance of good health in animals may still be insufficient to meet the added nutritive demands of successful reproduction and lactation. With the failure to reproduce successfully, there usually appears in early adult life an increased susceptibility to infection, and particularly a tendency to lung disease at an age corresponding to that at which pulmonary tuberculosis so often develops in young men and women. He states, further, that vitamin A must be supplied in liberal proportions not only during the growth period but during the adult period as well if a good condition of nutrition and a high degree of health and vigor are to be maintained.

Hughes, Aubel and Lienhardt have shown that a lack of vitamin A in the diets of pigs has resulted in extreme incoordination and spasms. They also emphasize that gilts bred prior to the onset of the nervous symptoms either aborted or farrowed dead pigs. Hart and Gilbert have shown that the symptoms most commonly seen in cattle having a vitamin A deficiency are the birth of dead or weak calves, with or without eye lesions. They report also a condition of newborn calves which simulates white scours and the development of eye lesions in immature animals.

Hughes has shown that swine did not reproduce when fed barley and salt but did so when cod liver oil was added to this food. Sure has shown that a lack of vitamin A pro-

SWEETBREADS ON TOAST
Serves 6

2 pairs prepared sweetbreads (page 300)
3 tablespoons butter
3 tablespoons extra virgin olive oil
1 cup shallots, chopped
1/2 cup red wine
1 1/2 cup beef stock (page 122)
1 teaspoon green peppercorns, crushed
2 tablespoons arrowroot mixed with
    2 tablespoons filtered water
sea salt and pepper
6 large round croutons (page 520)

Slice the sweetbreads at 3/8 inch intervals on the bias. Sauté, a few slices at a time, in 2 tablespoons each of butter and olive oil. Remove to a heated platter and keep warm in the oven. Pour off browning oil, add remaining butter and oil and sauté shallots until golden. Add wine and bring to a boil, stirring with a wooden spoon to scrape up any accumulated juices. Add crushed peppercorns and stock, bring to a boil and reduce to about half. Spoonful by spoonful, add arrowroot mixture until desired thickness is obtained. Season to taste.

To serve, place one crouton on each plate, place sweetbreads on the crouton and spoon sauce over.

SWEETBREADS WITH PEARL ONIONS
Serves 6

2 pair prepared sweetbreads (page 300)
3 tablespoons butter
3 tablespoons extra virgin olive oil
1/2 cup balsamic vinegar
2 cups beef stock (page 122)
2 tablespoons arrowroot mixed with
    2 tablespoons filtered water
2 pounds pearl onions, peeled
    and sautéed in butter

Slice the sweetbreads at 3/8-inch intervals on the bias. Sauté, a few slices at a time, in butter and olive oil. Remove to a heated platter and keep warm in the oven. Pour off browning oil, add balsamic vinegar and bring to a boil, stirring with a wooden spoon to scrape up any accumulated juices. Add stock, bring to a boil and reduce to about half. Spoonful by spoonful, add arrowroot mixture until desired thickness is obtained. Return sweetbreads to the sauce and stir in pearl onions. Simmer a minute or so before serving.

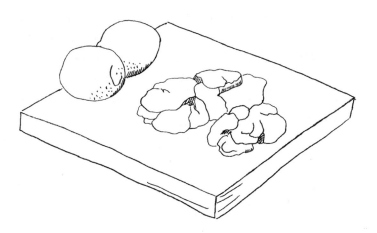

PREPARATION OF KIDNEYS

Most kidneys are sold with their layer of fat and the thin filament surrounding the kidneys peeled off. There may be a button or knob of fat on the underside of the kidneys; retain this if possible—it is a very nourishing fat, highly prized by primitive peoples.

Both whole and sliced kidneys should be marinated in lemon juice for several hours before they are cooked. Remove from lemon juice and dry well with paper towels before browning. Whole kidneys should be cooked until they are just pink inside.

Both lamb and veal kidneys can be used in the following recipes. They should be very fresh with no unpleasant odor—check with your nose.

duces in females a disturbance in oestrus and ovulation, resulting in sterility. Further, he states that resorption of the fetus may be produced by lack of vitamin A, even on a diet containing an abundance of vitamin E, which is called the antisterility vitamin.

One of the most important contributions in this field has been made by Professor Fred Hale. He has shown that many physical deformities are readily produced by curtailing the amount of vitamin A in the ration of pigs. He produced fifty-nine pigs that were born blind, every pig in each of six litters, where the mothers were deprived of vitamin A for several months before mating and for thirty days thereafter. In pigs, the eyeballs are formed in the first thirty days. He found, as have several others, that depriving pigs of vitamin A for a sufficient period produced severe nerve involvements, including paralysis and spasms, so that the animals could not rise to their feet. He reported that one of these vitamin A-deficient pigs that had previously farrowed a litter of ten pigs, all born without eyeballs, was given a single dose of cod liver oil two week before mating. She farrowed fourteen pigs that showed various combinations of eye defects, some had no eyes, some had one eye, and some had one large eye and one small eye, but all were blind. . . . One important result of Professor Hale's investigations has been the production of pigs with normal eyes, born to parents both of whom had no eyeballs due to lack of vitamin A in their mother's diet. The problem clearly was not heredity. Weston Price, DDS *Nutrition and Physical Degeneration*

Many investigators have presented important data dealing with the role of vitamin A in prenatal as well as postnatal growth processes. It is known that the eye is one of the early tissues to develop injury from the absence of vitamin A, hence the original name for this vitamin was the xerophthalmic vitamin. . . . Edward Mellanby has presented important new data dealing with vitamin A deficiency and deafness. He states, in an abstract of a paper read before the Biochemical Society, in London in November 1937, the following: In previous publications I have shown that a prominent lesion caused by vitamin A deficiency in young animals, especially when accompanied by a high-cereal intake, is degeneration of the central and peripheral nervous systems. In the peripheral system it is the afferent nerves which are principally affected, including the eighth nerve . . . . It has now been possible to show that vitamin A deficiency produced in young dogs degenerative changes in the ganglia, nerves and organs of both hearing and balance inside the temporal bone. All degrees of degeneration have been produced, from slight degeneration to complete disappearance of the hearing nerve. . . . The serious effects of deficiency in vitamin A on pregnant rats have been investigated and reported by Mason as follows: Abnormalities are described in the pregnancies of rats maintained on diets deficient in vitamin A in varying degrees. Prolongation of the gestation period up to 26 days in severe cases and a long and difficult labor, which might last 2 days and often resulted in death of both mother and young, were characteristic. Weston Price, DDS *Nutrition and Physical Degeneration*

GRILLED KIDNEYS WITH HAZELNUT BUTTER SAUCE
Serves 4

1 pound kidneys, cut into walnut-sized pieces and
*   marinated several hours in lemon juice*
2 tablespoons melted butter
3 tablespoons crispy hazelnuts (page 514)
1/2 stick butter
1 tablespoon finely chopped chives

Remove kidney pieces from lemon juice and dry well. Thread on buttered skewers and baste with melted butter. Grill under the broiler about 5 minutes per side. Meanwhile, chop hazelnuts and sauté in butter until lightly browned. Stir in chives. Divide kidneys among individual plates and spoon sauce over.

KIDNEYS IN WINE SAUCE
Serves 4-6

2 pounds kidneys, cut into walnut-sized pieces
*   and marinated in lemon juice*
3 tablespoons butter
3 tablespoons extra virgin olive oil
1/2 cup shallots, finely chopped
2 cups beef stock (page 122)
1/2 cup red wine
2 tablespoons arrowroot mixed with
*   2 tablespoons filtered water*
sea salt and pepper

Remove kidney pieces from lemon juice and dry well. In a heavy skillet, sauté in batches in 2 tablespoons each butter and olive oil over a medium flame until browned all over. Keep in a warm oven while making sauce. Pour out browning fat and add remaining butter and oil to the pan. Sauté shallots gently until soft. Add stock and wine, bring to a rapid boil and reduce to about half. Add arrowroot mixture a spoonful at a time until desired thickness is obtained. Season to taste. Serve kidney pieces whole, with the sauce poured over; or slice the kidneys and warm the slices very briefly in the sauce.

KIDNEYS IN MUSHROOM SAUCE

Serves 4-6

*2 pounds kidneys, cut into walnut-sized pieces
    and marinated in lemon juice*
3 tablespoons butter
3 tablespoons extra virgin olive oil
*1/2 pound fresh mushrooms, washed,
    well dried and sliced*
1/2 cup red wine
2 cups homemade beef stock (page 122)
1 cup piima cream or creme fraiche (page 84)
1 tablespoon fish sauce (page 157), optional
2 teaspoons Dijon-type mustard
2 tablespoons softened butter

Remove kidney pieces from lemon juice and dry well. In a heavy skillet, sauté in 2 tablespoons each butter and olive oil over medium-high heat until browned all over. Do not overcook—they should be pink inside. Transfer to a heated platter and keep warm in the oven while making the sauce.

Pour out browning fat. Add remaining butter and oil to the pan and sauté the mushrooms over medium-high heat until browned. Transfer to a bowl and keep warm in the oven.

Pour out browning fat and pour wine and beef stock into the pan, bring to a boil and reduce to about half. Add the cream and optional fish sauce and reduce further. Meanwhile, blend the mustard and softened butter together with a fork.

When sauce has reduced to desired thickness, reduce to simmer and whisk in mustard mixture. Slice kidneys and add to the sauce along with their juice and the mushrooms. Heat briefly and serve immediately.

Americans are being saturated with anti-cholesterol propaganda. If you watch very much television, you're probably one of the millions of Americans who now has a terminal case of cholesterol phobia. The propaganda is relentless and is often designed to produce fear and loathing of this worst of all food contaminants. You never hear the food propagandists bragging about their product being fluoride free or aluminum free, two of our truly serious food-additive problems. But cholesterol, an essential nutrient not proven to be harmful in any quantity, is constantly pilloried as a menace to your health. If you don't use corn oil, Fleishmann's margarine and Egg Beaters, you're going straight to atherosclerosis hell with stroke, heart attack and premature aging—and so are your kids. William Campbell Douglass, MD *Eat Your Cholesterol*

The numbers game is the biggest weapon used by the anticholesterol centurions to frighten the populace into a diet fit only for a zebra. These commanders have decreed that the magic number is 200 (mg. per deciliter) for blood cholesterol, and the lower the reading the better. But recent exhaustive studies have shown that 250 is a level not associated with any increase in cardiovascular disease. Furthermore, the "lower-the-better" rule is not only bad science but very dangerous advice. Extremely low cholesterol readings, those in the lower 10% of the population, have an increased mortality from all causes. "From all causes" means accidents, cancer, strokes, lung or kidney disease, etc. William Campbell Douglass, MD *Eat Your Cholesterol*

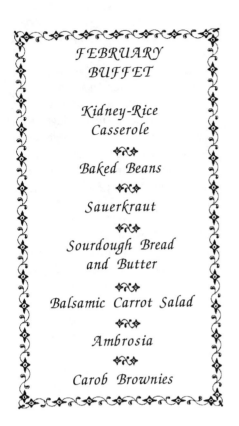

FEBRUARY
BUFFET

Kidney-Rice
Casserole

❦❦❦

Baked Beans

❦❦❦

Sauerkraut

❦❦❦

Sourdough Bread
and Butter

❦❦❦

Balsamic Carrot Salad

❦❦❦

Ambrosia

❦❦❦

Carob Brownies

KIDNEY-RICE CASSEROLE
Serves 12

3 pounds kidneys
1/2 teaspoon sea salt
1/2 teaspoon pepper
juice of 4 lemons
2 medium onions
6 tablespoons butter
6 tablespoons extra virgin olive oil
1/2 cup red wine
2 cups beef stock (page 122)
2 cloves garlic, peeled and mashed
3 cups brown rice
2 medium onions
6 cups chicken stock (page 124) or combination
*   of chicken stock and filtered water*
1/2 teaspoon sea salt
1/4 teaspoon pepper
1 cup raisins
1 cup crispy pecans (page 513), chopped
2 bunches green onion, finely chopped

Cut kidneys into small pieces and marinate for several hours in mixture of lemon juice, salt and pepper. Meanwhile, prepare rice. Sauté onion in 3 tablespoons each butter and olive oil. Add rice and stir around until milky. Add chicken stock, salt, pepper and raisins and bring to a rapid boil until the liquid reduced to the level of the rice. Cover and place on lowest heat. Cook without removing top for at least 2 hours.

Drain kidneys and pat dry. Sauté onion in remaining butter and olive oil until golden. Remove with a slotted spoon and reserve. Sauté kidneys in batches until well browned. Reserve. Pour out cooking fat, add wine, beef stock and garlic to pan and bring to a boil. Return onions and kidneys to pan. Boil, uncovered, until liquid has reduced and thickened to the consistency of thick cream.

To serve, press rice into a ring mold and turn onto a large round platter. Place kidneys with sauce in the center and garnish with pecans and chopped onions.

There are two absolutely essential fatty acids—omega-6 linoleic acid and omega-3 alpha-linolenic acid—and there are several other conditionally essential fatty acids. The former cannot be made by man and must be provided in the diet. . . . Fatty acids range from 3 to 24 carbons in length; the two major essential fatty acids are both 18 carbons long.

Essential fatty acids are needed by each animal, humans included, for proper nutrition and health. However, the essential fatty-acid status of individuals cannot always be predicted with ease, in part because the range of levels of *trans* fatty acids in people's diets has complicated the situation . . . the minimum amount of the essential fatty acid linoleic acid thought to be required in the diet is 2-3% of calories; the minimum amount of the essential fatty acid alpha-linolenic acid currently thought to be required in the diet is approximately 0.5-1.5% of calo-

PREPARATION OF LIVER

Buy liver that is organic and very fresh. The butcher should remove the surrounding filament; otherwise, the edges will curl when it is cooked. Liver should be sliced about 1/4-inch to 3/8-inch thick. All liver recipes will be greatly improved if the liver slices are first soaked in lemon juice for several hours. This draws out impurities and gives a nicer texture.

LIVER AND ONIONS
Serves 4

1 1/2 pounds sliced liver
juice of 2-3 lemons
1 cup unbleached flour
1/2 teaspoon sea salt
1/2 teaspoon pepper
4 tablespoons clarified butter (page 150) or lard
4 cups onions, finely sliced
2 tablespoons butter
2 tablespoons extra virgin olive oil

Marinate liver slices in lemon juice for several hours. Pat slices dry and dredge in a mixture of flour, salt and pepper. In a heavy skillet and over a high flame, sauté the slices, two at a time, in clarified butter or lard. Transfer to a heated platter and keep warm in the oven. Meanwhile, in a separate pan, sauté the onions in butter and olive oil over medium heat for about 1/2 hour or until golden brown. Strew over liver and serve.

Variation: Liver and Mushrooms
Instead of onions, sauté *1 pound of fresh mushrooms, washed, patted dry, and sliced.*

ries. Balance between the two fatty acids is important. Unfortunately, currently some American are getting up to 20% of calories as linoleic acid and almost none as alpha-linolenic acid.

The conditionally essential fatty acids include gamma-linolenic acid (GLA), arachidonic acid (AA), eicosapentaenoic acid (EPA) and docasahexaenoic acid (DHA). These conditionally essential fatty acids are 18, 20 and 22 carbons long. All four of these fatty acids can be made by cells in the body, but there are a number of interfering food substances or illnesses or genetic inadequacies that make these latter fatty acids become dietary essentials for some people. These interfering conditions include consumption of *trans* fatty acids, overconsumption of omega-6 linoleic acid from commercial vegetable oils, zinc deficiency, alcohol consumption and various vitamin deficiencies. People whose ancestors were largely meat eating often cannot make these conditionally essential fatty acids and must obtain them from dietary sources. Sources of EPA and DHA include organ meats, egg yolks from properly raised chickens, fish eggs and fish oils. Sources of AA include butter, tallows and organ meats. Sources of GLA are evening primrose oil, borage oil and black current oil. Mary G. Enig, PhD *Know Your Fats*

Since the organs, particularly the livers of animals, are storage depots of the vitamins, an important source of some of the fat-soluble activators can be provided by extracting the fat of the livers and shipping it as liver oils. Modern methods of processing have greatly improved the quality of these oils. Weston Price, DDS *Nutrition and Physical Degeneration*

George Bernard Shaw seems to have come into vegetarianism mainly because it was one of the trendy things to do among the English intellectuals he admired and envied. He had been drawn to the original Fabians . . . and through their interest in diet reform to Henry S. Salt, author of the book that had revolutionized Gandhi's ideas. . . . While Shaw did not remove the image of peculiarity from the public view of the vegetarianism, he did a tremendous amount to convince the public that it was an eminently healthy regime. . . . However, Mr. Shaw was forced to remind his correspondents "that vegetarianism does not mean living wholly on vegetables." Shaw ate cheese, butter, honey, eggs and on occasions cod liver oil. He also had to take extracts of liver for anemia, which began to affect him seriously in 1938, when he was 82. This is a common ailment with vegetarians who do not eat many eggs and is due to deficiency in vitamin B_{12}. . . . This vitamin is only found in animal foods, liver, kidneys and clams being rich sources, and, unfortunately, cannot yet be synthesized in the laboratory.

However, journalists found out the situation [that George Bernard Shaw took liver extract for anemia] and naturally considered it a good story that the Grand Old Man of vegetarianism was "cheating" on his diet. Alexander Woolcott spread the story in America and there was an immediate outbreak of fury in the American Vegetarian Party that their idol should have taken liver extract. Symon Gould of the Party wrote letters to Shaw in such a fierce vein that one can only imagine that he would have preferred the playwright to die unsullied than to go on living a useful life with the help of animal food. Shaw finally wrote a long, open letter to Gould in 1948 telling him bluntly not to exaggerate

BREADED LIVER
Serves 4

1 1/2 pounds liver, sliced 1/2-inch thick
juice of 2-3 lemons
1 cup unbleached flour
1/2 teaspoon sea salt
1/2 teaspoon pepper
2 tablespoons butter
2 tablespoons olive oil
3 tablespoons Dijon-type mustard
1 tablespoon shallots, finely chopped
1 tablespoon parsley, finely chopped
1 clove garlic, peeled and mashed
2 cups whole grain bread crumbs
4 tablespoons melted butter

This recipes requires that the liver be more thickly sliced than usual as it undergoes two cookings, once in the pan and once under the broiler. Marinate liver slices in lemon juice for several hours. Pat slices dry and dredge in a mixture of flour, salt and pepper. In a heavy skillet and over a high flame, sauté the slices, two at a time, in butter and olive oil. Sauté until liver becomes just slightly stiffened but not cooked through.

Make a mixture of the mustard, herbs and garlic and brush it well on the liver slices. Dredge in bread crumbs. Arrange slices on an oiled broiler pan. Dribble half the butter over. Broil for a minute or so until well browned. Turn, dribble over remaining butter and broil the second side in the same manner.

LIVER WITH BALSAMIC VINEGAR SAUCE
Serves 4

1 1/2 pounds sliced liver
juice of 2-3 lemons
1 cup unbleached flour
1/2 teaspoon sea salt
1/2 teaspoon pepper
4 medium onions, thinly sliced

2 tablespoons butter
2 tablespoons extra virgin olive oil
4 tablespoons clarified butter (page 150) or lard
4 tablespoons balsamic vinegar
4 cups beef stock (page 122)
2 tablespoons arrowroot mixed with
*   2 tablespoons filtered water*

Marinate liver slices in lemon juice for several hours. Using a heavy skillet, sauté the onions in butter over medium heat about 1/2 hour or until golden. Remove with a slotted spoon and keep warm in the oven. Pat liver slices dry and dredge in a mixture of flour, salt and pepper. In a heavy skillet and over a high flame, sauté the slices, two at a time, in clarified butter or lard. Transfer to a heated platter and keep warm in the oven. Pour out browning fat. Add vinegar and stock to the pan, bring to a boil and reduce to about half. A spoonful at a time, add the arrowroot mixture until desired thickness is obtained. Divide liver between individual serving plates, top with a spoonful of the onions and pour sauce over.

HEART KEBOBS

(Antichuchos)
Serves 4

1 beef heart
1 cup extra virgin olive oil
1 cup raw vinegar
1/4 teaspoon powdered cumin
1 1/2 teaspoons sea salt
3/4 teaspoon pepper
1/2 teaspoon paprika
1 teaspoon annatto seeds
*   (available in Latin American markets)*
1 tablespoon garlic, finely chopped

Remove any hard parts from the heart and cut into 1-inch cubes. Combine remaining ingredients and marinate heart cubes in the mixture for about 24 hours in the refrigerator. Place cubes on skewers and cook about 7 minutes to a side on the barbecue or under the grill.

the benefits of vegetarianism and to keep the moral and religious claims for the diet in some sensible proportion. He also made the point, which is unfortunately still valid—that a strict vegetarian diet without dairy foods can cost a lot of money to keep up because of the need for nuts and similar rather expensive sources of protein to replace the animal protein: "What you have to rub in," wrote Shaw testily, "is that it is never cheap to live otherwise than as everybody else does, and that the so-called simple life is beyond the means of the poor." Terence McLaughlin *A Diet of Tripe*

In the Anglo-Egyptian Sudan, there are several tribes living along the Nile. . . . There are wonderful hunters and warriors among them. These tribes use milk, blood and meat from cattle and large quantities of animal life from the Nile River. Some of the tribes are very tall, particularly the Neurs. The women are often six feet or over and the men seven feet, some of them reaching seven and a half feet in height. I was particularly interested in their food habits both because of their high immunity to dental caries, which approximated one hundred percent, and because of their physical development. I learned that they have a belief, which to them is their religion; namely, that every man and woman has a soul, which resides in the liver, and that a man's character and physical growth depend upon how well he feeds that soul by eating the livers of animals. The liver is so sacred that it may not be touched by human hands. It is accordingly always handled with their spear or saber, or with specially prepared forked sticks. It is eaten both raw and cooked. Weston Price, DDS *Nutrition and Physical Degeneration*

Cows frequently partake in the bizarre habit of eating their colleagues' afterbirth after calving, and I was particularly intrigued to watch my own home-reared cows, free of Bovine Spongiform Encephalopathy (BSE), positively relishing the delicacies of afterbirth tissues derived from a group of pedigree cows that I purchased into my farm in 1989. As the majority of these imported cows went on to develop BSE, it is interesting that BSE has not surfaced in my home-reared cows, despite their overzealous exposure to the allegedly "infectious" blood and lymph found in the afterbirths of the BSE cows. Other farmers sharing the same experience, report the same outcome.

Another anecdote hails form the farming community of Shetland, who boast of the fact that the island folk are free of Creutzfeldt-Jakob disease, despite their ancient custom of eating potted sheep's brain. Interestingly, scrapie disease has been rife in the sheep flock on Shetland for centuries. Mark Purdey *Animal Pharm*

Defects due to deficiencies in vitamin A in the diet of dairy animals . . . have been reported upon by Meigs and Converse as follows: In 1932 we reported from Beltsville that farm rations frequently fed to calves may be dangerously low in vitamin A . . . . Of six calves born to these cows, two were dead, one was unable to stand and died shortly after birth, and three were both weak and blind. Weston Price, DDS *Nutrition and Physical Degeneration*

PREPARATION OF BRAINS

Brains are highly valued in many ethnic cultures. Europeans formerly added a little chopped brain to baby food to give their children good memories. But today we hear dire warnings that brain consumption may cause a rare, insidious degeneration of the brain tissues called Creutzfeldt-Jakob disease (CJD). The theory is that this disease can be transmitted to humans from cattle that are infected with Bovine Spongiform Encephalopathy (BSE) due to feeding cattle animal parts in their feedlot rations. However, the evidence indicates that the true cause of CJD is mineral deficiencies combined with the toxic effects of organophosphate insecticides. In any event, BSE has not occurred in U.S. herds and there is no reason to eschew brains, a particularly nutrient-dense traditional food.

Brains have much the same texture as sweetbreads but they are more delicate. Like all organ meats, brains must be very fresh. Wash the brains, cover with cold filtered water to which you have added a little vinegar and soak for about 2 hours, changing the water once or twice. This extracts the blood and helps remove any impurities. Remove, rinse and place in a saucepan. Cover with water or chicken stock (page 124), add 1 teaspoon of salt and juice of 1/2 lemon, bring to a boil and simmer for about 15 minutes. Remove from poaching liquid and allow to cool. Using a sharp knife, carefully remove all loose tissue, skin, fat and membranes. You may now place on a plate or platter, cover with parchment paper (see Sources) and place a weighted flat plate or cookie sheet on top. Let the brains flatten in the refrigerator for several hours or overnight.

SAUTEED BRAINS
Serves 6

1 1/2 pounds prepared calves brains (see above)
3 tablespoons lemon juice
2 tablespoons extra virgin olive oil
1/2 teaspoon sea salt
1/2 teaspoon pepper

1 cup unbleached flour
3 tablespoons butter
3 tablespoons extra virgin olive oil

Cut the brains into 1-inch slices. Whisk the lemon juice, olive oil, salt and pepper together. Marinate brains in the mixture for an hour or so. Remove from marinade, pat dry and dredge in flour. In a heavy skillet, sauté the slices a few at a time in butter and olive oil. Transfer to a heated platter and keep warm in the oven until ready to serve. Serve with chunky tomato sauce (page 154) or a lacto-fermented condiment, such as pickled cucumbers (page 97) or pickled beets (page 98).

BRAINS IN WINE SAUCE
Serves 6

1 1/2 pounds prepared calves brains (page 310)
3 tablespoons butter
3 tablespoons extra virgin olive oil
1/2 pound fresh mushrooms, washed,
    well dried and sliced
1/2 cup shallots, finely chopped
1 cup red wine
2 cups beef stock (page 122)
2 tablespoons arrowroot mixed with
    2 tablespoons filtered water
6 round or triangle croutons (page 520)

Slice the brains into 3/8-inch slices and set aside. In a heavy skillet, sauté the mushrooms until browned in 2 tablespoons each butter and olive oil. Remove with a slotted spoon and set aside. Add remaining butter and oil to the pan and sauté the shallots. Pour in wine and stock, bring to a rapid boil and skim. Allow sauce to reduce to about half. Spoonful by spoonful, add the arrowroot mixture until desired thickness is obtained. Strain the sauce into a saucepan. Add the brain slices and mushrooms and simmer briefly until they are warmed through.

To serve, place a crouton on each plate, carefully place brain slices on top and spoon sauce over.

In the case of BSE where no viral cause has been identified, it is illogical to assume that one animal has to eat another in order to catch the same disease. Initially, the direction of any epidemiological research program should follow elementary logic and investigate the most likely assumption that the various different species of mammal suffering from the same disease have all been exposed to the same causal factor in the environment. But it seems that nobody has investigated this route. Sheep did not cannibalize each other to catch scrapie, nor did wild deer in the Rocky Mountains cannibalize each other to catch their BSE-equivalent disease, chronic wasting disease. . . .

One of the most relevant long standing observations on Creutzfeldt-Jakob disease epidemiology is that people who are occupationally involved with pets and farm animals are at greater risk of developing CJD. . . . During the 1980's and early 1990's, cattle and cats (the species of animals that have developed BSE) were exclusively treated with systematically acting types of organophosphate (OP) insecticide which were designed to penetrate the entire physiological system of the animal, transforming the bloodstream into a toxic medium so as to kill off any unwanted parasites present. . . . Systemic OP's are recognized as exerting their toxic effect by entering the central nervous system and deforming the molecular shape of various nerve proteins. . . .

OP's are known to generate a highly reactive type of free radical in the tissues that they intoxicate. And it is this free radical legacy of OP poisoning which is capable of instigating a chain reaction of lethal attack on nerve membranes and proteins in the central nerves of susceptible individuals. Mark Purdey *Animal Pharm*

That [the Indians] had knowledge of the use of different organs and tissues of the animals for providing a defense against certain of the affections of the body, which we speak of as degenerative diseases, was surprising. When I asked an old Indian, through an interpreter, why the Indians did not get scurvy, he replied promptly that that was a white man's disease. I asked whether it was possible for the Indians to get scurvy. He replied that it was, but said that the Indians know how to prevent it and the white man does not. When asked why he did not tell the white man how, his reply was that the white man knew too much to ask the Indian anything. I then asked him if he would tell me. He said he would if the chief said he might. He went to see the chief and returned in about an hour, saying that the chief said he could tell me because I was a friend of the Indians and had come to tell the Indians not to eat the food in the white man's store. He took me by the hand and led me to a log where we both sat down. He then described how when the Indian kills a moose he opens it up and at the back of the moose just above the kidney there are what he described as two small balls in the fat. These he said the Indian would take and cut up into as many pieces as there were little and big Indians in the family and each one would eat his piece. They would eat also the wall of the second stomach. By eating these parts of the animal the Indians would keep free from scurvy, which is due to the lack of vitamin C. The Indians were getting vitamin C from the adrenal glands and organs. Modern science has very recently discovered that the adrenal glands are the richest source of vitamin C in all animal or plant tissues. Weston Price, DDS *Nutrition and Physical Degeneration*

BRAIN OMELET
Serves 4

*1/3-1/2 cup prepared calves brains (page 310),
    finely chopped*
4 eggs
1/2 cup parsley, finely chopped
1 small onion, finely chopped
sea salt and pepper
2 tablespoons butter
1 tablespoon olive oil

Whisk eggs and stir in brains, parsley and onions. Season to taste. Melt butter and olive oil in a large, well-seasoned skillet. When butter froths, pour in egg mixture. Cook several minutes until omelet sets, then fold in half. Slide onto a heated platter and serve.

SAUTEED CHICKEN LIVERS
Serves 4

1 pound fresh chicken livers
1 cup unbleached flour
1/2 teaspoon sea salt
1/2 teaspoon pepper
2 tablespoons butter
2 tablespoons extra virgin olive oil
1/4 cup dry white wine
1 cup chicken stock (page 124)
1 tablespoon gelatin (see Sources), optional
pinch of powdered sage

Carefully remove veins from chicken livers and slice. Dredge in a mixture of flour, salt and pepper. In a heavy skillet, sauté slices, a few at a time, in butter and olive oil until golden. Remove and keep warm in oven. Pour out browning fat and add wine, stock, optional gelatin and sage to the pan. Bring to a rapid boil, skim and reduce to about half. Lower heat and return livers to the sauce to warm through. Serve with basic brown rice (page 466) or triangle croutons (page 520).

CHICKEN LIVERS WITH HAZELNUTS

Serves 4

1 pound fresh chicken livers
1 cup unbleached flour
1/2 teaspoon sea salt
1/2 teaspoon pepper
4 tablespoons butter
2 tablespoons olive oil
2/3 cup crispy hazelnuts (page 514), chopped
1 bunch green onions, minced
4 cloves garlic, minced
2 cups chicken stock (page 124)
1 tablespoon gelatin (see Sources), optional

Carefully remove veins from chicken livers and slice each one into about 3 slices. Dredge in a mixture of flour, salt and pepper. In a heavy skillet, sauté the slices, a few at a time, in 2 tablespoons butter and olive oil until golden. Remove and keep warm in oven. Pour out browning fat and add remaining butter. Sauté hazelnuts until golden. Add scallions and sauté briefly. Add chicken stock, garlic and optional gelatin. Bring to a rapid boil and reduce until sauce thickens. Lower heat to a simmer. Return livers to the sauce to warm through. Serve with basic brown rice (page 466) or triangle croutons (page 520).

Acute and chronic pesticide exposure, such as to cholinesterase inhibitors used on citrus fruits, will overdrive the neurotransmitter acetylcholine, which is responsible for relaying the nervous impulses across the nerve channel junctions to the muscles, glands, behavioral centers, etc. Such a poisoning incident will put the heart muscle into varying degrees of overdrive, culminating in a paralysis scenario at worst. . . . Could not the residues of these and other pollutants detectable in most types of our daily foodstuffs and water supplies be insidiously accountable for a slice of the increased rate of coronary disease surfacing in the Western world?

In a major rice growing area of the Philippines, Dr. Loevinsohn from Imperial College, London, found that the onset of a massive epidemic of stroke and heart disease corresponded with the advent of the green agrarian revolution in 1970, when pesticide use rose by nearly 250% in the area. Dr. Loevinsohn believes that the full scale of deaths, largely confined to the farmworker sector of the population and to the month of August which is the height of the spray season, has been hidden by the local doctors who misattributed these cardiac deaths to deaths of natural degeneration.

Just how many millions of other cardiac deaths from twentieth-century toxic exposure have been misappropriated and scapegoated on to saturated fat? Mark Purdey *Heart Rot, the Amish and Homeostasis*

Food without fat is like life without love.
Modern Proverb

The British like kidneys in their meat pies. Peruvians enjoy *anticuchos*—marinated, grilled beef heart. Sicilians on the streets of Palermo can grab a quick spleen sandwich, Italians in general—and Egyptians—are partial to liver, while the Japanese go in for intestines. Chinese restaurants in New York serve pigs' ears. But in the US, where it is also known euphemistically as "variety meat," most offal is exported or processed into sausage and lunch meat or it ends up as pet food. Peter Gumbul *The Wall Street Journal*

Leopold Bloom ate with relish the inner organs of beasts and fowls. He liked thick giblet soup, nutty gizzards, a stuffed roast heart, liver slices fried with crustcrumbs, fried hencod's roes. Most of all he liked grilled mutton kidneys. . . James Joyce *Ulysses*

Know Your Ingredients
Name This Product #15

Salt, hydrolyzed vegetable protein, sugar, monosodium glutamate, dehydrated onion, maltodextrin, dextrin (with beef extract and partially hydrogenated soybean oil), caramel color, autolyzed yeast, corn oil, dry malt syrup, disodium inosinate, disodium guanylate, natural flavoring, not more that 2% silicon dioxide added as an anti-caking agent.

See Appendix B for Answer

MAZALIKA
(Variety Meat Medley)
Serves 8

1 pound beef heart
1 pound veal or lamb kidneys
1 pound sweetbreads
1 pound brains
juice of 4 lemons
1 teaspoon sea salt
1 teaspoon pepper
3 medium onions, finely chopped
6 tablespoons butter
6 tablespoons extra virgin olive oil
1 cup red wine
2 cups beef stock (page 122)
1 tablespoon gelatin (see Sources), optional
2 cloves garlic, peeled and mashed

This wonderful dish from Egypt is testimony to the importance of organ meats in ethnic cuisines.

Cut all organ meats into a small dice. (None need be prepared in advance.) Marinate heart and kidneys together for several hours in juice of 2 lemons plus 1/2 teaspoon each salt and pepper; marinate sweetbreads and brains together for several hours in juice of 2 lemons and remaining salt and pepper. Drain all meats and pat dry.

Sauté onions in 2 tablespoons each butter and olive oil until soft. Reserve. Sauté heart and kidneys in remaining butter and oil in batches until well browned. Reserve. Pour out browning fat and add wine, stock and garlic to pan and boil, uncovered, about 10 minutes. Reduce to simmer. Add heart and kidneys to pan and simmer, uncovered, for about 15 minutes. Add onions, brains and sweetbreads and simmer, uncovered, for another 5 minutes or so, or until most of liquid has evaporated. Serve with basic brown rice (page 466)
Variation:

Continue boiling until liquid is almost completely gone. Serve with pita bread, tahini sauce (page 148), very thin slices of tomato and shredded romaine lettuce dressed with a little lemon juice.

SIMPLE SHAD ROE

Serves 4-6

1 shad roe (2 lobes)
1/2 teaspoon sea salt
2 tablespoons vinegar
4 tablespoons butter
1 teaspoon paprika
sea salt and pepper
1 lemon, cut into wedges

Place roe in a pan and cover with a mixture of filtered water, salt and vinegar. Bring to a boil, reduce heat and simmer about 10 minutes. Place roe in a colander and rinse with cold water. Using a sharp knife, peel off as much of the membrane as you can and cut out the vein.

Place roe in a baking dish and sprinkle with paprika. Season to taste. Pour melted butter over. Broil until golden, turn and broil other side. Serve with lemon wedges.

SHAD ROE WITH WINE SAUCE

Serves 4-6

1 shad roe (2 lobes) prepared as in preceding
    recipe, omitting paprika
2 tablespoons butter
1 cup shallots, finely minced
1 cup white wine
2 cups fish or chicken stock (page 119 or 124)
2 tablespoons arrowroot mixed with
    2 tablespoons filtered water
1 cup spinach or kale, finely chopped
sea salt and pepper
juice of 1 lemon

I have presumed in this discussion that the primitive races are able to provide us with valuable information. In the first place, the primitive peoples have carried out programs that will produce physically excellent babies. This they have achieved by a system of carefully planned nutritional programs for mothers-to-be. Those groups of primitive racial stocks, who live by the sea and have access to animal life from the sea, have depended largely upon certain types of animal life and animal products. Specifically, the Eskimos, the people of the South Sea Islands, the residents of the islands north of Australia, the Gaelics in the Outer Hebrides, and the coastal Peruvian Indians have depended upon these products for their reinforcement. Fish eggs have been used as part of the program in all of these groups. The cattle tribes of Africa, the Swiss in isolated high Alpine valleys, and the tribes living in the higher altitudes of Asia, including northern India, have depended upon a very high quality of dairy products. Among the primitive Masai in certain districts of Africa, the girls were required to wait for marriage until the time of the year when the cows were on the rapidly growing young grass and to use the milk from these cows for a certain number of months before they could be married. In several agricultural tribes in Africa, the girls were fed on special foods for six months before marriage. Weston Price, DDS *Nutrition and Physical Degeneration*

A return to traditional foods is a way of taking power away from the multinationals and giving it back to the artisan. The kind of food processing that makes food more nutritious is the same kind of food processing that the farmer or the farming community can do *in situ*—sour milk and grain products, aged cheeses, pickles, sausages, broth and beverages. All the boxed, bottled and frozen products in modern supermarkets—the cheerios, crackers, cookies, egg-beaters, margarines, diet sodas and TV dinners—have made fortunes for a few and impoverished the rest of us. The way we eat determines not only how healthy we will be, but what kind of economy we have—the kind where a few people make millions and millions of dollars or the kind where millions of people make a decent living.

Technology propels us headlong into the future, but there will be no future unless that technology is tamed to the service of wise ancestral foodways. *Nasty, Brutish and Short?*

SOUTHERN-STYLE BREAKFAST

Sliced Peaches in Cream

✦✧✦✧✦

Scrambled Eggs

✦✧✦

Roe Cakes

✦✧✦

Grits

✦✧✦

Raisin Muffins with Apricot Butter

✦✧✦

Herb Tea

While preparing roe, sauté shallots in butter until soft. Add wine and stock, bring to a boil and skim. Boil vigorously until sauce reduces and thickens. Spoonful by spoonful, add arrowroot mixture until desired consistency is obtained. Stir in greens and simmer until wilted. Add lemon juice and season to taste. Slice roe, divide between individual plates and spoon sauce over.

ROE CAKES
Makes 8 patties

1 shad roe (2 lobes) or
* 3/4 pound roe from other fish*
1/2 teaspoon sea salt
2 tablespoons vinegar
1 medium onion, finely chopped
2 tablespoons butter
1 1/2 cup whole grain bread crumbs
2 eggs, lightly beaten
sea salt and pepper
1/2 teaspoon paprika
1 teaspoon dried thyme
2 tablespoons butter
2 tablespoons extra virgin olive oil

This recipe is for those who know they should eat fish eggs but don't like the taste. There is no fishy taste in these delicious patties. They may be frozen and then sautéed after thawing.

Place roe in a pan and cover with a mixture of filtered water, salt and vinegar. Bring to a boil, reduce heat and simmer about 15 minutes. Remove roe to a colander and rinse with cold water. Using a sharp knife, remove roe from casing and place roe eggs in a bowl. Meanwhile, sauté onion in butter until soft. Add onions, bread crumbs, eggs and seasonings to roe and mix well with hands. Form into patties. Sauté until golden in butter and olive oil. Serve with a pickled condiment such as daikon radish (page 98) or ginger carrots (page 95); or serve for breakfast with scrambled eggs.

GAME

Game is not usually considered a health food but it should be. The meat of game animals like deer, caribou, buffalo and elk, and of game birds like wild duck, goose, pheasant and quail is particularly rich in minerals and many other valuable nutrients.

One common misconception is that the fat from game animals is lower in saturated fat than fat from domesticated animals. Ruminant animals—whether domestic ruminants, such as cattle, goats and sheep, or wild ruminants, such as deer, caribou, buffalo and elk—contain special bacteria and protozoa in their intestinal tracts that do a very efficient job of turning largely unsaturated fats and carbohydrates from plant foods into saturated and monounsaturated fats. The amount of saturated fat in various ruminant animals varies only slightly, whether they consume grains or wild grasses. Buffalo fat is actually more saturated than beef fat! Only about 4% of the adipose fat of all ruminants is polyunsaturated. There may be slightly more omega-3 fatty acids in wild game compared to domestic beef, but the difference is too small to be of significance.

Another misconception is that game meat is lean and that primitive peoples therefore had a lowfat diet. Actually, the hunter-gatherer hunted animals selectively. He preferred older male animals because they had an accumulated slab of fat along the back which, in larger animals, could weigh as much as 40 or 50 pounds. He also consumed the marrow, which is rich in monounsaturated fats, and used the highly saturated cavity fat to make pemmican and similar preparations. (If you are a hunter, you should save this fat and use it in cooking.) Small animals like beaver were also a very rich source of fat for hunter-gatherers.

It is true, however, that most game meat is not marbled like beef and lamb and may, therefore, be very tough. This difficulty can be overcome with proper preparation and cooking. Game should "hang" or be aged for as long as possible in a cool, dry place to allow cathepsin, an enzyme naturally present in meat, to begin breaking down muscle fibers; and in most cases, game meat should be marinated for at least several hours, and as long as 48 hours, before it is cooked. If you take care in the preliminaries, your final dish will be flavorful and tender. You may also add cream or other fat to the sauce, to compensate for the leanness of the meat.

If you are lucky enough to have a hunter in your family, or if you have access to fresh game through a meat wholesaler or your local butcher, do take advantage of your good fortune and serve healthful game to your family as often as possible.

A note to hunters: If it is possible to save the organ meats of your deer, elk, etc., by all means do so. (They must be chilled down quickly.) The liver and kidneys may be prepared according to the recipes in our chapter on organ meats. Antlers and feet, cut up and added to your stock pot, will give you a very rich broth.

Myth: The "cave-man diet" was low in fat.

Truth: Throughout the world, primitive peoples sought out and consumed fat from fish and shellfish, water fowl, sea mammals, land birds, insects, reptiles, rodents, bears, dogs, pigs, cattle, sheep, goats, game, eggs, nuts and milk products. (Abrams, *Food & Evolution* 1987)

Whoever eats of this meat [venison] frequently is cleansed of slime and filth. Whoever is plagued by precancerosis (vicht) should eat often from its liver and it will devour the vicht in him.

St. Hildegard of Bingen

VENISON MEDALLIONS IN TANGY SAUCE

Serves 6

12 venison pieces from the loin or back leg, about 2-3 inches by 1-1 1/2 inches
grated rind of 2 lemons
juice of two lemons
1 teaspoon dried green peppercorns, crushed
1 teaspoon dried thyme
2 tablespoons butter
2 tablespoons extra virgin olive oil
1/4 cup red wine or balsamic vinegar
1 cup red wine
2 tablespoons naturally sweetened blackberry or plum jam
2 cups beef or venison stock (pages 122-123)
1 tablespoon gelatin (see Sources), optional
sea salt and pepper

Make a mixture of the lemon rind, lemon juice, peppercorns and thyme. Pound the venison pieces lightly with the small prong side of a meat hammer and marinate in the mixture for several hours at room temperature or overnight in the refrigerator.

Pat the pieces very dry with paper towels. In a heavy skillet, brown the medallions quickly in butter and olive oil, a few at a time, about 4 or 5 minutes per side. (The meat should be rare.) Transfer medallions to a heated platter and keep warm in the oven while making sauce.

Pour off the browning fat and add wine and vinegar to the pan. Bring to a boil, stirring with a wooden spoon to scrape up any accumulated juices in the pan. Add stock, optional gelatin and jam, bring to a boil and skim. Let sauce reduce until it thickens. Season to taste.

Serve with any chestnut preparation (page 381) or with sautéed Asian pears (page 540).

VENISON WITH GINGER SAUCE

Serves 6

12 venison pieces from the loin or back leg,
about 2-3 inches by 1-1 1/2 inches
juice of 3 limes
2 bunches cilantro, chopped
1 tablespoon freshly grated ginger
1 teaspoon dried green peppercorns, crushed
2 tablespoons butter
2 tablespoons extra virgin olive oil
1/2 dry white wine
3 cups beef or venison stock (pages 122-123)
1 tablespoon gelatin (see Sources), optional
2 tablespoons naturally sweetened plum jam
1 tablespoon freshly grated ginger
sea salt and pepper
cilantro sprigs

Make a mixture of lime juice, grated ginger, cilantro and peppercorns. Pound the venison pieces lightly with the small prong side of a meat hammer and marinate in the mixture for several hours at room temperature or overnight in the refrigerator.

Pat the pieces very dry with paper towels. In a heavy skillet, brown the medallions very quickly in butter and olive oil, a few at a time, about 4 or 5 minutes per side. (The meat should be rare.) Transfer medallions to a heated platter and keep warm in the oven while making sauce.

Pour off the browning fat and add wine and stock. Bring to a boil, stirring with a wooden spoon to scrape off any accumulated juices in the pan. Add ginger, optional gelatin and jam, bring to a boil and skim. Let sauce reduce until it thickens. Season to taste. To serve, place two pieces of venison on each plate, spoon sauce over and decorate with cilantro sprigs.

Serve with basic brown rice (page 466) or buckwheat or brown rice noodles.

The Eskimos, like the Homeric Greeks, prefer the flesh of older animals to that of calves, yearlings and two-year olds. . . . Homer is quoted to the effect that the Greeks preferred the meat of bulls five years old. It is approximately so with those northern forest Indians with whom I have hunted, and probably with all caribou-eaters. . . . Dr. R. M Anderson, who was naturalist and second in command of our 1908-1912 expedition, says: "The largest slab of back fat which I have seen taken from a caribou on the Arctic coast was from a bull killed near Langton Bay early in September, the fat weighing 39 pounds. A large bull killed by Mr. Stefansson on Dease River in October . . . must have weighed at least fifty pounds." Vilhjalmur Stefansson *The Fat of the Land*

For centuries, uninformed and unskilled physicians would continue to relegate signs of sugar blues—the simple remedy for which they overlooked—to bewitchment. Three centuries of medical mischief would produce a veritable babel of Greek and Latin symptoma: Schizophrenia, paranoia, catatonia, dementia praecox, neuroses, psychoses, psychoneuroses, chronic urticaria, neurodermatitis, cephalalgia, hemicrania, paroxysmal tachycardia—all as scarifying as the devil himself. The wise people who understood what sugar blues were all about—the midwives, village herbalists and healers—had been driven underground. . . . Physicians and priests condemned natural healers at home as witches and consigned them to damnation. William Dufty *Sugar Blues*

In the summer of 1933, [we made] contact with large bands of Indians who had come out of the Pelly mountain country to exchange their furs at the last outpost of the Hudson Bay Company... they have remained as nomadic wandering tribes following the moose and caribou herds in the necessary search to obtain foods.

The rigorous winters reach seventy degrees below zero. This precludes the possibility of maintaining dairy animals or growing seed cereals or fruits. The diet of these Indians is almost entirely limited to the wild animals of the chase. This made a study of them exceedingly important. The wisdom of these people regarding Nature's laws and their skill in adapting themselves to the rigorous climate and very limited variety of foods, and these often very hard to obtain, have developed a skill in the art of living comfortably with rugged Nature that has been approached by few other tribes in the world. The sense of honor among these tribes is so strong that practically all cabins, temporarily unoccupied due to the absence of the Indians on their hunting trip, were entirely unprotected by locks; and the valuables belonging to the Indians were left in plain sight .... The condition of the teeth, and the shape of the dental arches and the facial form, were superb. Indeed, in several groups examined not a single tooth was found that had ever been attacked by tooth decay. . . . Careful inquiry regarding the presence of arthritis was made in the more isolated groups. We neither saw nor heard of a case in the isolated groups. However, at the point of contact with the foods of modern civilization many cases were found including ten bed-ridden cripples in a series of about twenty Indian homes. Some other affections made their appearance here, particu-

VENISON STROGANOFF

Serves 6

12 venison pieces from the loin or back leg,
*   about 2-3 inches by 1-1 1/2 inches*
juice of 3 lemons
1 teaspoon green peppercorns, crushed
2 tablespoons butter
2 tablespoons extra virgin olive oil
1 cup red wine
3 cups beef or venison stock (pages 122-123)
2 tablespoons tomato paste
1 teaspoon paprika
1 cup piima cream or creme fraiche (page 84)
sea salt and pepper

Make a mixture of lemon juice and peppercorns. Pound the venison pieces lightly with the small prong side of a meat hammer and brush with the lemon juice mixture. Marinate in for several hours at room temperature or overnight in the refrigerator.

Pat the pieces very dry with paper towels. In a heavy skillet, cook the medallions very quickly in the butter and olive oil, a few at a time, about 4 or 5 minutes per side. (The meat should be rare.) Transfer medallions to a heated platter and keep warm in the oven while making sauce.

Pour off the browning fat and add wine and stock. Bring to a boil, stirring with a wooden spoon to scrape off any accumulated juices in the pan. Add tomato paste, paprika and cream, bring to a boil and skim. Let sauce reduce until it thickens. Season to taste. To serve, place two pieces of venison on each plate and spoon sauce over.

VENISON STEW

Serves 6

3 pounds venison, cut into 1-inch cubes
2 cups red wine
2 tablespoons butter
2 tablespoons extra virgin olive oil
4 cups beef or venison stock (pages 122-123)
several sprigs fresh thyme, tied together
2 cloves garlic, peeled and mashed
8 juniper berries
1/2 teaspoon dried green peppercorns, crushed
several small pieces lemon rind
1 rutabaga, peeled and cut into 1/2 inch cubes
1 pound pearl onions, peeled and
*   sautéed in butter*
1 cup spinach or kale, chopped
2 tablespoons arrowroot mixed with
*   2 tablespoons filtered water*
sea salt and pepper

Marinate venison cubes in wine for several hours at room temperature or overnight in the refrigerator. Remove meat and dry well with paper towels, reserving marinade.

In a heavy flameproof casserole, brown the venison cubes, a few at a time, in butter and olive oil. Transfer with a slotted spoon to a plate. Pour out browning fat and pour wine marinade into the pan. Bring to a boil, stirring with a wooden spoon to scrape up any accumulated juices. Add stock, bring to a boil and skim. Add thyme, garlic, juniper berries, peppercorns and lemon rind. Return meat to casserole, cover and bake in the oven at 350 degrees for several hours. About 45 minutes before serving, add the rutabaga.

When rutabaga is tender, transfer casserole to the stove. Spoonful by spoonful, add the arrowroot mixture to the stew while it simmers, until sauce reaches desired thickness. Season to taste. Add the onions and kale and simmer a few minutes more.

larly tuberculosis which was taking a very severe toll of the children who had been born at this center. . . . The suffering from tooth decay was tragic. There were no dentists, no doctors available within hundreds of miles to relieve suffering.

The physiques of the Indians of the far north who are still living in their isolated locations and in accordance with their accumulated wisdom were superb. There were practically no irregular teeth including no impacted third molars, as evidenced by the fact that all individuals old enough to have the molars erupted had them standing in position and functioning normally for mastication. . . . Where the Indians were using the white man's food tooth decay was very severe. . . . In the new generation, after meeting the white civilization and using his foods, many developed crooked teeth, so-called, with deformed dental arches. Weston Price, DDS *Nutrition and Physical Degeneration*

The [Pima] Indians are especially fond of squirrels or any game. The old folks say that the reason the tribe is dying is because they are compelled to eat beef and flour instead of fish, game, acorns, buckeyes, wild bulbs and tubers, shell fish and seaweed, salt from the ocean and sugar from the pine tree.

Grace Hudson

It is significant that while these important factors are just coming to light in our modernized civilization, the evidence clearly indicates that several so-called primitive races have been conscious of the need for safeguarding motherhood from reproductive overloads, which would reduce the capacity for efficient reproduction. For example, G. T. Gaden in his book *Among the Ibos of Nigeria* states: It is not only a matter of disgrace but an actual abomination, for an Ibo woman to bear children at shorter intervals than about three years. . . . The idea of a fixed minimum period between births is based on several sound principles. The belief prevails strongly that it is necessary for this interval to elapse in order to ensure the mother being able to recuperate her strength completely and thus be in a thoroughly fit condition to bear another child. Should a second child be born within the prescribed period the theory is held that it must inevitably be weak and sickly, and its chances jeopardized.

Similarly, the Indians of Peru, Ecuador and Columbia have been familiar with the necessity of preventing pregnancy overload of the mother. Whiffen in his book *North-West Amazona* states: The numbers (of pregnant women) are remarkable in view of the fact that husbands abstain from any intercourse with their wives, not only during pregnancy but also throughout the period of lactation—far more prolonged with them than with Europeans. The result is that two and a half years between each child is the minimum difference of age, and in the majority of cases it is even greater.

It may also be important to note that the Amazon Indians have been conscious of the fact that these matters are related to the nutrition of both

VENISON CHOPS

Serves 6

6 venison chops
2 cups red wine
1 teaspoon grated orange peel
1 teaspoon dried thyme
2 tablespoons butter
2 tablespoons extra virgin olive oil
2 cups beef or venison stock (pages 122-123)
juice of 1 orange
2 tablespoons arrowroot mixed with
*   2 tablespoons filtered water*
sea salt and pepper

Marinate the chops in a mixture of the wine, orange peel and thyme for several hours at room temperature or overnight in the refrigerator. Dry cutlets well and reserve marinade.

In a heavy skillet, brown the chops, two at a time, in butter and olive oil, about 5 minutes per side. Transfer to a plate while browning the remaining chops. Pour off browning fat and pour marinade into the pan. Bring to a boil, stirring with a wooden spoon to scrape up any accumulated juices in the pan. Add stock and orange juice, bring to a boil and skim.

Add the chops to the liquid, reduce heat, cover and cook about 1 hour. (If chops are from a young deer, and very tender, this step will not be necessary. They can be eaten medium rare.) Remove to a heated platter and keep warm in oven while finishing sauce. Bring sauce to a rapid boil and reduce to about half. Add the arrowroot mixture, spoonful by spoonful, until desired thickness is obtained. Season to taste and serve.

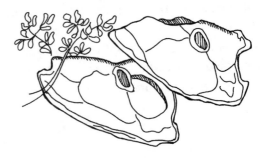

WILD DUCK STEW

Serves 6-10

4 wild ducks
2 cups dry white wine or vermouth
4 tablespoons duck fat (page 295)
2 medium onions, peeled and finely chopped
2 carrots, peeled and finely chopped
1 red pepper, seeded and chopped
1/4 cup red wine
3-4 cups duck stock (page 125)
several sprigs fresh thyme, tied together
1/2 teaspoon dried green peppercorns, crushed
2 tablespoons arrowroot mixed with
    2 tablespoon filtered water
1 pound pearl onions, sautéed in butter
sea salt and pepper

Cut the ducks into parts. (See page 295.) Use the carcass, including the feet and heads, to make duck stock (page 125). Marinate the wing, leg, thigh and breast pieces in wine for several hours at room temperature or overnight in the refrigerator.

Dry pieces well with paper towels. Prick skin all over with a sharp needle—this will allow fat to drain out during the browning process. Place duck pieces skin side up in a stainless steel baking dish and brown in a 400 degree oven for about 1/2 hour until skin becomes golden. Meanwhile, sauté onions, carrots and pepper gently in a heavy flameproof casserole in duck fat. Add wine marinade, stock and red wine. Bring to a boil, skim and reduce liquid to about half. Add the duck pieces, thyme and seasonings. Cover and bake at 300 degrees for several hours.

Remove from oven and set casserole over a low flame. Add the arrowroot mixture, spoonful by spoonful, until desired thickness is obtained. Season to taste. Add the onions and serve.

parents. Whiffen states that: These Indians share the belief of many peoples of the lower cultures that the food eaten by the parents—to some degree of both parents—will have a definite influence upon the birth, appearance or character of the child.

This problem of the consciousness among primitives of the need for spacing children has been emphasized by George Brown in his studies among Melanesians and Polynesians in which he reports relative to the native on one of the Solomon Islands as follows: After the birth of a child the husband was not supposed to cohabit with his wife until the child could walk. If a child was weak or sickly, the people would say, speaking of the parents, "Ah, well, they have only themselves to blame." Weston Price, DDS *Nutrition and Physical Degeneration*

The newcomers to 16th-century Ireland brought with them not merely their farming methods and their money but also their prejudices and their tastes. The consumption of blood, in a jellified form or mixed with butter, oats or salt, was an aspect of Gaelic cuisine that particularly repelled English observers. They were appalled, too, by the willingness of the native population to devour animal entrails and to eat carrion and horse meat, by their partiality for warm milk straight from the cow, adorned with straw and worse, by their habit of eating rancid butter, by their unhopped ale and by their preference for oatcakes and gruels rather than good wheaten bread. S. J. Connolly *The Oxford Companion to Irish History*

The flesh of bear hath a good relish, very savory and inclining nearest to that of Pork. The Fat of this Creature is least apt to rise in the Stomach of any other. The Men for the most part chose it rather than Venison. . . . And now, for the good of mankind, and for the better Peopling an Infant colony, which has no want but that of Inhabitants, I will venture to publish a Secret of Importance, which our Indian . . . disclosed to me. I asked him the reason why few or none of his Country women were barren? To which curious Question he answered with a Broad grin upon his Face, they had an infallible SECRET for that. Upon my being importunate to know what the secret might be, he informed me that, if any Indian woman did not prove with child at a decent time after Marriage, the Husband, to save his Reputation with the women, forthwith entered into a Bear-dyet for Six Weeks, which in that time makes him so vigorous that he grows exceedingly impertinent to his poor wife and 'tis great odds but he makes her a Mother in Nine Months. Col. William Byrd II, 1728

In a short time a great number of people came to the spot. . . . They stood around the lions and talked about them. . . . Pooran Singh himself appeared . . . his melliferous Indian smile shone in the midst of his thick black beard, he stuttered with delight when he spoke. He was anxious to procure for himself the fat of the lions, that with his people is held in high esteem as a medicine—from the pantomime by which he expressed himself to me, I believe against rheumatism and impotence. Isak Dinesen *Out of Africa*

DUCK STEW WITH DRIED CHERRIES
Serves 6-10

3 wild ducks
2 cups red wine
4 cups duck stock (page 125)
several sprigs fresh thyme, tied together
1/2 teaspoon dried green peppercorns, crushed
several small pieces orange rind
8 ounces dried cherries
2 tablespoons arrowroot mixed with
*   2 tablespoons filtered water*
sea salt and pepper

Cut the ducks into parts. (See page 295.) Use the carcass, including the feet and the heads, to make duck stock (page 125). Marinate the wing, leg, thigh and breast pieces in wine for several hours at room temperature or overnight in the refrigerator.

Dry pieces well with paper towels. Prick skin all over with a sharp needle—this will allow fat to drain out during the browning process. Place duck pieces skin side up in a stainless steel baking dish and brown in a 400-degree oven for about 1/2 hour until skin becomes golden. Remove duck pieces to a flameproof casserole. Pour duck fat out of baking pan and pour in wine marinade. Bring to a boil, stirring with a wooden spoon to scrape up any accumulated juices in the pan. Add stock, bring to a boil and skim. Boil vigorously until liquid has reduced by about half. Add the thyme, peppercorns, orange rind and cherries. Pour sauce over duck pieces, cover casserole and bake at 300 degrees for several hours.

Remove from oven and set casserole over a low flame. Add the arrowroot mixture, spoonful by spoonful, until desired thickness is obtained. Season to taste.

DUCK CURRY

Serves 8-12

3 wild ducks
3 tablespoons duck fat (page 295)
2 large onions, peeled and finely chopped
2 cups finely chopped celery
4-5 tablespoons curry powder or curry paste
1 teaspoon ground cardamom
1 teaspoon fennel seeds
1 teaspoon fenugreek seeds
1/4 teaspoon cayenne pepper
4 cups duck stock (page 125)
1 tablespoon freshly grated ginger
4 cloves garlic, peeled and mashed
1 cup piima cream or creme fraiche (page 84)
sea salt and pepper

Remove the skin and excess fat from the ducks and make duck stock from the whole birds, including the feet and heads (page 125). (Make cracklings from the excess fat and skin, page 295.) Remove the meat from the ducks, chop coarsely and reserve in the refrigerator. Strain stock into a bowl, refrigerate until it congeals and remove fat. (Save fat for other uses.)

In a heavy skillet, sauté onions and celery in duck fat until soft. Add curry powder or paste and other seasonings and cook about 5 minutes, stirring constantly. Add stock, bring to a boil and stir with a whisk to remove any lumps. Add garlic, ginger and cream. Boil vigorously until sauce reduces to about half. Season to taste. Stir in reserved duck meat and simmer until heated through.

Serve with basic brown rice (page 466) and traditional curry accompaniments such as fruit chutney (page 106), raisins, dried sweetened coconut meat (page 159), chopped crispy cashews (page 515) and chopped scallions. You may also serve with duck cracklings (page 295).

Under optimal conditions, humans convert carotenes to vitamin A in the upper intestinal tract by the action of bile salts and fat-splitting enzymes. But the transformation of carotenes to retinol is rarely optimal. Diabetics and those with poor thyroid function—a group that includes at least half the adult U.S. population—cannot make the conversion at all. Children make the conversion very poorly and infants not at all—they must obtain their precious stores of vitamin A from animal fats—yet the lowfat diet is often recommended for children. Strenuous physical exercise, excessive consumption of alcohol, excessive consumption of iron (especially from "fortified" white flour and breakfast cereals), use of a number of popular drugs, excessive consumption of polyunsaturated fatty acids, zinc deficiency and even cold weather can hinder the conversion of carotenes to vitamin A. So does the lowfat diet. Carotenes are converted by the action of bile salts, and very little bile reaches the intestine when a meal is low in fat. The epicure who puts butter on his vegetables and adds cream to his soups and stews is wiser than he knows. Butterfat stimulates the secretion of bile needed to convert carotenes from vegetables into vitamin A and at the same time supplies very easily absorbed true vitamin A. Polyunsaturated oils also stimulate the secretion of bile salts but can cause rapid destruction of carotene unless antioxidants are present. *Vitamin A Vagary*

Anchorage. . . has an excellent government hospital, which probably has been built around the life of one man whom many people told us was the most beloved man in all Alaska. He is Dr. Josef Romig, a surgeon of great skill and with an experience among the Eskimos and Indians, both the primitive and modernized, extending over thirty-six years. . . . He took me, for example, to several typically modernized Indian homes in the city. In one, the grandmother, who had come from the northern shore of Cook Inlet to visit her daughter, was sixty-three years of age and was entirely free from tooth decay and had lost only one of her teeth. Her son, who had accompanied her, was twenty-four years of age. He had only one tooth that had ever been attacked by tooth decay. Their diet had been principally moose and deer meat, fresh and dried fish, a few vegetables and at times some cranberries. Recently, the son had been obtaining some modern foods. Her daughter, twenty-nine years of age, had married a white man and had had eight children. She and they were living on modern foods entirely. Twenty-one of her thirty-two teeth had been wrecked by dental caries. Their diet consisted largely of white bread, syrup and potatoes. Her children whom we examined ranged from five to twelve years of age, and in that family 37 percent of all teeth have already been attacked by dental decay. . . not only was dental caries rampant, but that there were marked deformity of the dental arches and irregularity of teeth in the cases of the children. Weston Price, DDS *Nutrition and Physical Degeneration*

DUCK WITH OLIVES

Serves 8-12

3 wild ducks
3 tablespoons duck fat (page 295)
2 small onions, peeled and finely chopped
2 carrots, peeled and diced
3 cups duck stock (page 125)
1 teaspoon fresh or dried tarragon leaves
1/2 teaspoon dried green peppercorns, crushed
juice of 1 lemon
1 cup piima cream or creme fraiche (page 84)
1 1/2 cups sliced green olives
sea salt and pepper

Remove the skin and excess fat from the ducks and make duck stock from the whole birds, including the feet and heads (page 125). (Make cracklings from the excess fat and skin, page 295.) Remove the meat from the ducks, chop coarsely and reserve in refrigerator. Strain stock into a bowl, refrigerate until it congeals and remove fat. (Save fat for other uses.)

In a heavy skillet sauté onions and carrot in duck fat until soft. Add stock, bring to a rapid boil and skim. Add tarragon and peppercorns. Boil vigorously until stock is reduced to about 1 cup. Remove from heat and stir in lemon juice, cream, olives and duck meat. Season to taste. Transfer to a casserole and warm in a 200-degree oven for about 15 minutes. Serve on triangle or round croutons (page 520).

PHEASANT WITH ORANGE SAUCE

Serves 4

2 pheasant, cut into quarters
2 cups dry white wine
grated rind from 2 oranges
4 tablespoons melted butter
sea salt and pepper
3 cups chicken, turkey or duck stock
    (pages 124-125)
juice from 2 oranges
2 tablespoons arrowroot mixed with
    2 tablespoons filtered water

Marinate pheasant pieces, turning occasionally, in a mixture of white wine and orange rind for several hours at room temperature or overnight in the refrigerator. Pat dry with paper towels and reserve marinade. Place pheasant pieces, skin side up, in a stainless steel roasting pan. Brush with melted butter and sprinkle with salt and pepper. Bake at 400 degrees for about 1 hour or until pieces are golden. Transfer pheasant pieces to a flame-proof casserole. Add wine marinade to the roasting pan and bring to a rapid boil, stirring with a wooden spoon to scrape up any accumulated juices. Add stock and orange juice, bring to a boil and skim. Allow liquid to reduce slightly. Pour over pheasant pieces, cover casserole and bake at 300 degrees for at least 2 hours.

Remove pheasant pieces to a heated platter and keep warm in the oven. Strain the sauce into a saucepan and bring to a boil. Add the arrowroot, spoonful by spoonful, until desired thickness is obtained. Season to taste and serve.

> *HUNTERS' FEAST*
>
> *New Potatoes with Caviar*
>
> *Pheasant with Orange Sauce*
>
> *Fruit Chutney*
>
> *Steamed Spinach*
>
> *Any Lettuce Salad*
>
> *Pecan Tart*

Teeth superior on average to those of the presidents of our largest toothpaste companies are found in the world today and have existed during past ages among people who violate every precept of current dentifrice advertising. . . . The best teeth and the healthiest mouths were found among people who never drank milk since they ceased to be suckling babes, and who never in their lives tasted or tested any of the other things which we usually recommend for sound teeth. . . . They never took any pains to cleanse their teeth or mouths. They did not visit their dentist twice a year or even once in a lifetime. . . so far as an extensive correspondence with authorities has yet been able to show, a complete absence of tooth decay from entire populations has never existed in the past and does not exist now, except where meat is either exclusively or heavily predominant an the diet. Vilhjalmur Stefansson *The Fat of the Land*

> Every moving thing that liveth shall be meat for you; even as the green herb have I given you all things.
>
> *Gen 9:3*

The San Diego Indians of Southern California changed their home sites with the supply of native foods. They fished from the ocean, hunted the plentiful game on the mountains, and gathered acorns, seeds and wild greens when in season. They collected wild onion and sage for seasoning. Their staple meal was acorn mush, eaten from a common pot. The acorns were prepared by grinding on basaltic stones, leaching in sand, or pounding with rocks, which introduced much abrasive material to wear down the tooth enamel but at the same time prevented cavities. The acorn mush, supplemented with wild game, seafood and greens, supplied them with all the necessary nutrients. They kept rabbits, quail and other game birds in holes and baskets, and prepared dishes with the whole animals. Early explorers and missionaries of the San Diego area reported that the local Indians were strong, hardy and seldom ill. But later studies indicate that when the Indians were deprived of their natural foods by living on reservations and eating modern foods, most of them suffered a sharp decrease in general health and within a single generation became susceptible to eye diseases, a high tooth decay rate, bowed legs and tuberculosis. "Nutrition: The Appetite of Man" PPNF

TERIYAKI QUAIL
Serves 6

12 quail, ribs removed and torso opened out
2 cups teriyaki sauce (page 147)

Marinate quail several hours or overnight in teriyaki sauce. Grill under broiler about 10 minutes per side or cook on the barbecue. Eat with fingers—this is the only way to eat quail!

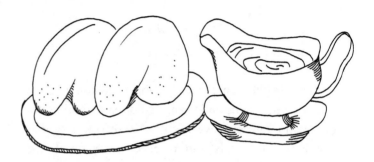

QUAIL MASALA
Serves 6

12 quail, ribs removed and torso opened out
1 cup yoghurt
1 medium onion, peeled and finely chopped
3 cloves garlic, peeled and crushed
1 teaspoon grated fresh ginger
1 teaspoon ground cumin
1/2 teaspoon turmeric
1/2 teaspoon ground cardamom
1/4 teaspoon ground cloves
1/4 teaspoon cinnamon
1/4 teaspoon cayenne pepper
1 teaspoon sea salt
1 bunch cilantro, chopped

Mix yoghurt and remaining ingredients together. Marinate quail in yoghurt mixture several hours or overnight. Grill under broiler about 10 minutes per side or cook on the barbecue. Eat them with your fingers—no knives or forks allowed.

BEEF & LAMB

Politically Correct Nutrition has singled out red meat—beef and lamb—as a major contributing factor, or even the main cause, of our two greatest plagues—cancer and heart disease. Consumption of these meats has dropped in recent years, but the incidence of both heart disease and cancer continue to climb.

What light can the practices of traditional societies shed on the question of red meat? Surveys of ethnic diets show that red meat in the form of beef, sheep and goat is the second most preferred source of animal protein and fat in nonindustrialized societies, second only to chicken (flesh and eggs) and more popular, or at least more available, than foods from the sea. These societies rarely suffer from cancer and heart disease. This fact alone should be enough to allay any fears about red meat.

The dangers inherent in red meat are due, we believe, to modern methods of raising cattle. Most commercially available red meat comes from animals that have been raised in huge feedlots on grains laden with pesticides—or worse on soy feed which is too high in protein and therefore toxic to their livers—injected with steroids to make their meat tender and treated with antibiotics to stave off infections that inevitably result from poor diet and crowded conditions.

Fortunately, organically raised, pasture-fed beef is now becoming more available. Cattle and sheep should spend most of their life on the open range. However, it is entirely appropriate for these animals to be fattened on grain during their last few weeks. Such practices imitate natural processes, as ruminant animals get fat on seeds and grains in their natural habitat during summer and fall. Grain feeding is an ancient practice that ensures that red meat contains ample amounts of fat. It should, however, be carried out in healthy, uncrowded conditions.

If you eat red meat, we urge you to make every effort to obtain meat that has been raised mostly on pasture. Many markets in our larger cities now sell organically raised or pasture-fed beef, and with a little searching a wholesale supply can always be found. Many farmers will sell sides or quarters directly to consumers. If you have freezer space, this is the most economical way to buy good quality beef and veal. (Be sure to specify, when buying sides of meat directly from a farmer, that the meat be hung and allowed to age, like commercial meat, before it is packaged for your freezer. Otherwise it will be very tough.) Both domestic and imported lamb is, for the most part, pasture fed and can be purchased from regular supermarkets.

When you purchase directly from the farm, you have the additional advantage of being able to obtain organ meats, bones and hooves. Traditional societies do not let these valuable parts go to waste. The organ meats, extremely rich in fat-soluble vitamins, are relished as delicacies in primitive societies; and the bones and hooves are used to make nutritious stocks that provide abundant minerals in a form that is particularly easy to assimilate.

Red meat is an excellent source of both macro and trace minerals, particularly zinc and magnesium. In meat, these minerals exist in a form that is much easier for the body to break down and utilize than the minerals in grains and pulses. Red meats are rich in vitamin B_{12}, so important for a healthy nervous system and blood; and in carnitine, which is essential for healthy functioning of the heart. Beef and lamb fat contain fat-soluble vitamins and small amounts of essential fatty acids, especially if these animals have been allowed to graze on green grass. These fat-soluble vitamins are what your body needs to utilize the minerals in all foods. In animal studies, beef fat has a cholesterol-lowering effect. Lamb and beef fat are rich in conjugated linoleic acid, which has strong anticancer effects; and both lamb and beef fat contain palmitoleic acid, which protects us from viruses and other pathogens.

Our recipes for tender portions of beef and lamb—filet and rib cuts of beef, leg of lamb and lamb chops—call for these cuts to be eaten rare, with most of their enzyme content still intact. Tougher cuts can be braised in stock to make flavorful stews. In braising, the temperature of the meat does not exceed 212 degrees so denaturing of proteins is minimized. The enzyme content is destroyed, but any minerals and amino acids that come out of the meat will be contained in the sauce. Many ethnic recipes call for marinating tougher cuts for 24 to 48 hours in wine, yoghurt or buttermilk. This process tenderizes and predigests the meat.

We do not recommend deep frying of red meats or any cooking methods that raise the internal temperature above 212 degrees. Research indicates that meats subjected to high heats are harder to digest and may even foster the growth of pathogens and viruses in the colon. Here is yet another reason to consume meats with sauce or broth containing gelatin and, hence, hydrophilic colloids to facilitate protein digestion.

We hate to be spoilsports but we must caution you against too frequent consumption of barbecued meats. Meat and meat fat that come in contact with open flames synthesize certain highly carcinogenic hydrocarbons. Meat that has been cooked in a pan or in liquid contains very few hydrocarbons in comparison with meat that has been barbecued. Your body can deal with these hydrocarbons if it is healthy and not overloaded. We urge you to eat barbecued meats only occasionally and, when you do, be sure to eat them with one or more cruciferous vegetables, such as cabbage, broccoli or Brussels sprouts. Even better, serve barbecued meats with lacto-fermented vegetables or relishes. The combination is synergistic, not only in terms of flavor but also because the vegetables with their lactic-acid-producing bacteria and high enzyme content will help neutralize carcinogens in the intestinal tract.

PEPPER STEAK

Serves 4

4 small beef tenderloin steaks, cut at least 1-inch
   thick, or 2 rib eye or T-bone steaks
1 tablespoon dried green peppercorns, crushed
juice of one lemon
1 teaspoon olive oil
2 tablespoons butter
4 shallots or 1 bunch green onions,
   finely chopped
1/2 cup red wine
2 cups beef stock (page 122)
1 tablespoon gelatin (see Sources), optional
sea salt and pepper

Crush the peppercorns and mix them with lemon juice. Rub into the steaks and marinate at room temperature for several hours.

Brush a cast-iron skillet with olive oil. Pat the steaks dry, leaving as much pepper adhering to the steaks as possible. Heat the pan and cook steaks in two batches over medium-high flame about 5 minutes to a side or until medium rare. Transfer to a heated platter and keep warm in the oven while making sauce.

Pour out any grease from the pan. Add butter and gently sauté the shallots or green onions. Add wine and bring to a rapid boil. Add stock and optional gelatin and skim. Boil rapidly, until sauce is reduced to about 2/3 cup. Season to taste. Transfer steaks to individual plates and spoon a little sauce over each.

The Masai are tall and strong . . . . For their food throughout the centuries they have depended very largely on milk, meat and blood, reinforced with vegetables and fruits. In the Masai tribe, a study of 2,516 teeth in eighty-eight individuals distributed through several widely separated manyatas showed only four individuals with caries. These had a total of ten carious teeth, or only 0.4 percent of the teeth attacked by tooth decay. In contrast with the Masai, the Kikuyu tribe are characterized by being primarily an agricultural people. Their chief articles of diet are sweet potatoes, corn, beans, and some bananas, millet, and Kafir corn, a variety of Indian millet. The women use special diets during gestation and lactation . . . .The Kikuyus are not as tall as the Masai and physically they are much less rugged. . . . A study of 1,041 teeth in thirty-three individuals showed fifty-seven teeth with caries or 5.5 percent. There were 36.4 percent of the individuals affected. Weston Price, DDS *Nutrition and Physical Degeneration*

There is no society in the world that is entirely vegetarian. The Hindus of India come closest. Dr. H. Leon Abrams reports on India, " . . . the greater percentage of the population, who subsist almost entirely on vegetable foods, suffer from kwashiorkor, other forms of malnutrition, and have the shortest life span in the world." William Campbell Douglass, MD *The Milk Book*

No culture in the history of mankind has been based on a one hundred percent vegetarian diet, and although one can theoretically, in the light of contemporary nutritional scientific knowledge, obtain all the nutrients needed to provide good health, the technology to insure such has not been developed and such a vegetarian diet is extremely risky. H. Leon Abrams *Vegetarianism: An Anthropological/Nutritional Evaluation*

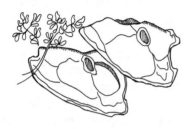

A tragic illustration of what a strict vegetarian, no-cholesterol diet may do to you is the case of famous basket ball star, Bill Walton. Walton was a fanatic about what he considered to be good nutrition. No animal food—dairy or otherwise—passed his lips. He developed severe osteoporosis and consequent foot and ankle fractures from the constant jumping on hard wood floors required of his sport. A brilliant career was finished. Walton, learning from his mistake, became a spokesman for the meat industry. William Campbell Douglass, MD *Eat Your Cholesterol*

Besides containing heat units in the proportion of nine to four as compared to candy, natural fat furnishes normal heat and energy as intended by nature; whereas sugars do so by upsetting the body's chemistry. H. Leon Abrams *Your Body Is Your Best Doctor*

QUICK STEAK
Serves 3-4

1 1/2-2 pounds steak such as rib eye or T-bone
1-2 tablespoons cracked pepper
1 tablespoon butter
1 tablespoon extra virgin olive oil
2-4 tablespoons fish sauce (page 157)
1 cup piima cream or creme fraiche (page 84)
sea salt

Sprinkle steaks with pepper and press in. Melt butter and olive oil in a heavy skillet. Sauté steaks a few minutes on a side, until rare or medium rare. Transfer to a heated platter and keep warm in the oven while making sauce.

Pour out browning fat. Add fish sauce and cream to the pan and bring to a boil, scraping up any accumulated juices with a wooden spoon. Skim sauce and simmer for several minutes until sauce thickens. Season to taste. Transfer to a heated sauce boat and serve with the steaks.

RIB ROAST
Serves 6-8

a 3-rib standing roast, about 5 pounds
sea salt and pepper
a meat thermometer

Set roast in a baking pan on a rack and rub fat with salt and pepper. Insert meat thermometer into center of the roast. Place in a 400 degree oven. Reduce heat to 350 degrees and bake for 15-20 minutes per pound or until thermometer indicates meat is rare or medium rare.

This is delicious with Yorkshire pudding (page 481), onion compote (page 389) or any fermented relish or vegetable.

FILET OF BEEF
WITH RED WINE SAUCE

Serves 8

3 pounds filet of beef, trimmed of fat and tied
a meat thermometer
2 quarts beef stock (page 122)
2 cups red wine
2 tablespoons gelatin (see Sources), optional
sea salt

This is an elegant party dish. The sauce may be prepared in advance and reheated.

The beef should be at room temperature. Insert the thermometer and place the meat on a rack in a baking pan. Place in an oven set at 450 degrees. Reduce heat to 350 and bake for about 1 hour or until the meat is cooked rare or medium rare.

Meanwhile, bring the stock to a rolling boil and add wine and optional gelatin. Boil, uncovered, until the sauce is reduced to about 1 cup, skimming frequently—this may take as long as 1 hour. The sauce should be thickened and shiny, about the consistency of maple syrup. If the sauce gets too thick, thin with a little water. Taste before you season—but you may not need salt.

Slice beef thinly and arrange on individual plates. Spoon sauce over and serve immediately.

If it were not for beef, the United States could produce perhaps 25% of the small grain it does. . . . The factors that would limit our production is winter kill and tillering.

First, winter kill happens when small grains, such as wheat or oats, get into what is called the joint stage. Grain planted in the fall sprouts and grows fairly rapidly. Once it sends up the stem that the grain head grows on, and it makes the first joint in that stem, if it gets about 10 degrees Fahrenheit it will kill the plant.

To prevent this from happening, cattlemen and wheat farmers graze small grains with cattle. Without cattle grazing, the wheat, all wheat planted as well as oats, would have to be planted in the spring. Usually, moisture conditions remain too wet for this to work well.

Without beef you can kiss goodbye probably to 50% of the earth's population.

Another misconception is water supposedly taken up by cattle. Water weighs approximately eight pounds per gallon. A one thousand-pound steer, if 100% water, would be 125 gallons of water. Where is the rest of the thousands of gallons of water? If handled properly, the waste water from cattle is a very valuable resource. It removes nitrate nitrogens and ammoniacal nitrogens and returns them to the soil. Nitrate nitrogens make forage, and ammoniacal nitrogens make seeds and flowers. Farmers pay big money for these in bag form to apply to the land. Charles Hallmark *Health Freedom News*

One of the most nutty, stereotype fallacies . . . is the vegetarian claim that crop husbandry is less chemically and energy intensive than livestock farming. Whilst this is true in consideration of the intensive grain-fed livestock units, the traditional mixed farming unit raises livestock for meat and milk off extensively managed, low-input grassland systems; and each acre of well-managed grassland can produce four harvests a season of high-protein forage utilizing its all-inclusive clover plants as a green manure for fixing free atmospheric nitrogen into the soil. Whereas, an arable cropping system will only yield one or two crops per season and will largely remain reliant on the inputs of artificial fertilizer for its nitrogen source; one ton of which requires ten tons of crude oil in the manufacturing process. . . . Well-managed grassland is rarely sprayed with pesticide/fungicide/herbicide, not even on the most chemically orientated of farms. Yet virtually all vegetable and arable systems receive an average of ten chemical sprayings annually through from the initial seed stage to the final storage of the produce. Vegetables are so heavily sprayed that the more perceptive elements of the medical establishment have actually linked the victims of a mystery, novel neurological syndrome to the fact that they are all vegetarians in common. One team led by Dr. David Ratner from the Central Emek Hospital, Afula, in Israel, bloodtested several isolated cases of those suffering from this syndrome and found that various organophosphate pesticide residues intensively present in their vegetarian diet were responsible. Once the victims were convinced that they should return to a diet including meat and milk products, their symptoms and abnormal blood enzyme levels normalized rapidly. Mark Purdey *The Nutcracker Suite*

STUFFED FLANK STEAK
Serves 4

1 flank steak
sea salt and pepper
1/2 head bok choy
1 small onion, finely chopped
1 slice whole grain bread, crumbled
2 tablespoons raisins
2 tablespoons butter
2 tablespoons extra virgin olive oil
3/4 cup unbleached flour
1/2 teaspoon pepper
1/2 cup red wine
2 cups beef stock (page 122)

When you buy the flank steak, have the butcher pass it through the tenderizer one time. Spread out flank steak and rub with pepper and salt. Cut 4 lengths of string and set aside.

To make stuffing, cut the leaves off the fleshy part of the bok choy stalks. Chop the leaves coarsely and set aside. Chop the stalks and sauté with onions in olive oil and butter until soft. Add bread slice, crumbled, and raisins and sauté about 5 minutes more. Spread stuffing on flank steak. Roll up steak, tie with string and dredge in flour mixed with pepper.

In a heavy skillet, brown the flank steak on all sides in butter and olive oil. Remove and pour out fat. Add wine and stock to pan, bring to a boil and skim. Reduce to a simmer, return flank steak to pan and simmer, covered, for 2 hours or until meat is tender.

Transfer flank steak roll to a heated platter and keep warm in oven while making sauce. Bring sauce to a boil and let it boil uncovered, skimming frequently, until sauce has reduced by about one half and has thickened slightly. Stir in chopped bok choy leaves and let simmer a minute or so.

To serve, slice crosswise and place slices on individual plates. Spoon sauce over.

Variation:

Use *celery* instead of bok choy stalks for stuffing and add *2 cups chopped spinach or chard* to sauce instead of bok choy leaves.

KOREAN BEEF

Serves 4

1 flank steak
1/2 cup naturally fermented soy sauce
2 tablespoons toasted sesame oil
1 bunch green onions, finely chopped
6 cloves garlic, peeled and mashed
2 tablespoons sesame seeds
1/4 teaspoon cayenne pepper
pinch stevia powder

Using a very sharp and heavy knife, slice the flank steak as thinly as possible across the grain and on the diagonal. (This will be easier if the meat is partially frozen.) Mix other ingredients and marinate beef in the mixture, refrigerated, for several hours or overnight.

Fold or "ribbon" the strips and stick them on skewers, making four to six brochettes. Cook on barbecue or under grill, about 5 to 7 minutes per side. Meat should still be rare or medium rare inside. This is delicious with kimchi (page 94) or any of the fermented vegetables, especially ginger carrots (page 95). The lactic-acid-producing bacteria in the fermented vegetables are the perfect antidote to carcinogens which may have formed in the meat if it has been barbecued.

KOREAN BEEF
DINNER

Tuna Tartare

Korean Beef

Basic Brown Rice

Chinese Peas

Kimchi

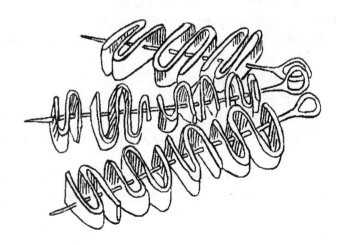

For 12 years Russian researchers have been observing 180 men and women living in and around the town of Dageston and ranging in age from 90 to 100 years. The men and women living in town were heavier in weight and had more disease of blood vessels than the people living in the nearby mountains. All of the people studied ate some meat, but the town dwellers ate more carbohydrate food than the mountain folk, whose diet was mainly dairy products and vegetable foods. Modern nutrition condemns butter as a source of cholesterol, but these Russians managed to reach ages past 90 while eating butter freely. . . . In another study, Metchnikoff studied communities of Bulgarians who ate mainly raw dairy food—and lived past 100. Are we to close our eyes to this evidence? Perhaps there is a difference between the milk and butter of these simple people and ours. In fact, more than 90 percent of the enzymes in milk are destroyed by pasteurization. Chemists have identified 35 separate enzymes in raw milk, with lipase one of the chief enzyme actors. How much longer are we to ignore the value of food enzymes? Edward Howell, MD *Enzyme Nutrition*

Fats have more than twice as many calories as carbohydrates, foods such as sugar, wheat, potatoes and fruits. Conventional wisdom says that reducing fats in the diet is essential for people who want to lose weight.

That *sounds* logical doesn't it? *But it's not true.* In real life, eating fats helps you lose weight—but only if you make a deep cut in the carbohydrates you eat. Fats have more calories, but fats satisfy your hunger four or five times as much as carbohydrates. That's one of several reasons why eating fats helps people lose weight. H. L. Newbold, MD *Type A Type B Weight Loss Book*

BEEF BOURGIGNON
Serves 6-8

3 pounds stew beef, cut into 2-inch pieces
2 cups red wine
4 cups beef stock (page 122)
6 tablespoons butter
3 tablespoons extra virgin olive oil
1/2 cup unbleached flour
several small slivers orange peel
several sprigs fresh thyme, tied together
1/2 teaspoon dried green peppercorns, crushed
1 pound fresh mushrooms
2 pounds medium boiling onions
sea salt and pepper

Marinate beef in wine for several hours or overnight. Remove and dry very well with paper towels. (This is important. If beef is too wet, it will not brown.)

Melt 3 tablespoons each butter and oil in a heavy, flameproof casserole. Brown the meat cubes in small batches, transferring with a slotted spoon to a plate when done. When all are browned, pour out cooking fat. Add remaining 3 tablespoons butter to the casserole, let it melt and add flour. Cook the flour in the butter, stirring constantly, for several minutes. Add wine from the marinade and stock. Bring to a boil, stirring up scrapings from the bottom of the pan and blend well with a wire whisk. Return meat and juices that have accumulated in the plate. Add thyme, crushed peppercorns and orange peel.

Transfer casserole to a 300-degree oven and cook 3 or 4 hours or until meat is tender. Meanwhile, brown the mushrooms, either whole or sliced (page 389). Peel the onions and sauté them gently in butter and oil for about 20 minutes.

When meat is tender, remove from oven. Season to taste. Remove thyme. Stir in onions and mushrooms and serve.

ALL-DAY BEEF STEW

Serves 6-8

3 pounds stew beef, cut into 1-inch pieces
1 cup red wine
3-4 cups beef stock (page 122)
4 tomatoes, peeled, seeded and chopped
   or 1 can tomatoes
4 tablespoons tomato paste
6 whole cloves
1/2 teaspoon black peppercorns
several sprigs fresh thyme, tied together
2 cloves garlic, peeled and crushed
2-3 small pieces orange peel
8 small red potatoes
1 pound carrots, peeled and cut into sticks
sea salt and pepper

This recipe and the two following are ideal for working mothers. The ingredients can be assembled in about fifteen minutes in the morning—or even the night before. The family will come home to wonderful smells permeating the house and a delicious dinner waiting.

To peel tomatoes, see page 70. Marinate meat in red wine overnight. Place all ingredients except for potatoes and carrots in a flameproof casserole and cook gently in a 250-degree oven for about 12 hours. (You may also use a crock pot set at medium temperature.) Add carrots and potatoes during the last hour. Season to taste.

What dietary changes have caused Americans to suffer more cancer and heart disease since the turn of the century? It is true that we consume more beef—79 pounds per person per year versus 54 in 1909, a 46 percent increase—but poultry consumption has increased a whopping 280 percent, from 18 pounds per person per year to 70. Consumption of vegetable oils, including those that have been hydrogenated, has increased 437 percent, from 11 pounds per person per year to 59; while consumption of butter, lard and tallow has plummeted from 30 pounds per person per year to just under 10. Whole milk consumption has declined by almost 50 percent, while lowfat milk consumption has doubled. Consumption of eggs, fresh fruits (excluding citrus), fresh vegetables, fresh potatoes and grain products has declined; but consumption of sugar and other sweeteners has almost doubled. Why, then, do today's politically correct dietary gurus continue to blame beef consumption for our ills? Is it because it is the one wholesome food that has shown an increase over the past ninety years? SWF

THURSDAY NIGHT DINNER

Italian Salad

All-Day Beef Stew

Pickled Beets

Natural Yeast Bread with Butter

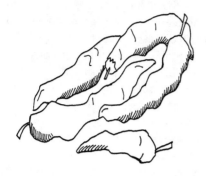

Under the stress of the industrial depression, the family dietary of the children we studied was very deficient. They were brought to a mission where we fed them one reinforced meal at noon for six days a week . . . . It is important to note that the home nutrition, which had been responsible for the tooth decay, was exceedingly low in body building and repairing material while temporarily satisfying the appetite. It usually consisted of highly sweetened strong coffee and white bread, vegetable fat, pancakes made of white flour and eaten with syrup, and doughnuts fried in vegetable fat. . . . The nutrition provided these children in this one meal included the following foods. About four ounces of tomato juice or orange juice and a teaspoonful of a mixture of equal parts of a very high-vitamin natural cod liver oil and an especially high-vitamin butter was given at the beginning of the meal. They then received a bowl containing approximately a pint of very rich vegetable and meat stew made largely from bone marrow and fine cuts of tender meat. The meat was usually broiled separately to retain its juice and then chopped very fine and added to the bone marrow meat soup, which always contained finely chopped veg-

ALL-DAY SPICY STEW
Serves 6-8

3 pounds beef, cut into 1-inch cubes
juice of 2 lemons
4 tomatoes, peeled, seeded and chopped
  or 1 can tomatoes
2 tablespoons tomato paste
2 medium onions, chopped
3 cups beef stock (page 122)
1/4 teaspoon ground coriander
2 cloves garlic, peeled and chopped
1/2 teaspoon dried green peppercorns, crushed
1/2 teaspoon ground allspice
2 teaspoons chili powder
1/4 teaspoon cayenne pepper
sea salt

To peel tomatoes, see page 70. Marinate beef overnight in lemon juice. Place all ingredients except salt in an flameproof casserole or crock pot and and cook gently in a 250-degree oven for about 12 hours. (You may also use a crock pot set at medium temperature.) Season to taste. Serve with Mexican rice (page 470) or corn tortillas.

BEEF STEW
WITH CHILES
Serves 6-8

3 pounds beef cut into 1-inch cubes
juice of 2 lemons
2-3 cups beef stock (page 122)
2 onions, chopped
1 cup green chiles (mild or hot), chopped
2 cloves garlic, peeled and mashed
2 teaspoons oregano
1 1/2 teaspoon ground cumin
2 tablespoons fish sauce (page 157)
2 tablespoons arrowroot powder
  mixed with 2 tablespoons filtered water
sea salt

Marinate beef overnight in lemon juice. Place all ingredients, except arrowroot mixture and salt, in a flameproof casserole and cook gently in a 250-degree oven for about 12 hours. (You may also use a crock pot set at medium temperature.) Remove casserole to the stove over a low flame. Spoonful by spoonful, add arrowroot mixture until desired thickness is obtained. Season to taste. Serve with barley casserole (page 463).

BEEF STIR-FRY STEW
Serves 6

1 pound stewing beef, cut into small pieces
juice of 2 oranges
6 tablespoons extra virgin olive oil or lard
1 cup crispy almond slivers (page 515)
1 bunch green onions, sliced on an angle
2 large carrots, peeled and cut into a julienne
1 red bell pepper, seeded and cut into a julienne
1 cup broccoli cut into flowerets
2 cloves garlic, finely chopped
1 teaspoon grated ginger
grated rind of 2 oranges
1 tablespoon Rapadura (see page 536)
1/4 teaspoon red pepper flakes
4 tablespoons naturally fermented soy sauce
1/8 cup rice vinegar
2-3 cups beef stock (page 122)
3 tablespoons arrowroot
*   mixed with 3 tablespoons filtered water*

Marinate beef in orange juice for several hours. Remove beef and pat pieces dry with paper towels. Mix stock with vinegar, soy sauce, pepper flakes, grated orange rind, ginger, Rapadura and garlic and set aside. In a heavy skillet or wok, brown beef in half the olive oil or lard in small batches. Using a slotted spoon, transfer beef to a bowl and reserve. Add more oil or lard and sauté almonds a minute or two. Remove with slotted spoon. Add more oil or lard and sauté onions, carrots and pepper about 2 minutes. Add sauce mixture and bring to a boil. Return beef and almonds to pan and mix well. Add arrowroot mixture and simmer a minute or so until sauce thickens. Add broccoli and simmer until tender.

etables and plenty of very yellow carrots; for the next course they had cooked fruit, with very little sweetening, and rolls make from freshly ground whole wheat, which were spread with the high-vitamin butter. The wheat for the rolls was ground fresh every day in a motor driven coffee mill. Each child was also given two glasses of fresh whole milk. The menu was varied from day to day by substituting for the meat stew, fish chowder or organs of animals. . . . Clinically this program completely controlled the dental caries of each member of the group . . . . Several incidents of special interest occurred. Two different teachers came to me to inquire what had been done to make a particular child change from one of the poorest in the class in capacity to learn to one of the best. Dental caries is only one of the many expressions of our modern deficient nutrition. Weston Price, DDS
Nutrition and Physical Degeneration

It has long been assumed that beef and eggs should be restricted in the diet because eggs and beef contain high levels of cholesterol.

The American Heart Association has recommended that cholesterol intake be reduced to 300 milligrams per day. The most current recommendations, however, call for dietary cholesterol levels to be reduced to even less than 300 milligrams per day, especially if one's blood cholesterol level is above 200 mg/dl.

To discover beef fat's effect on blood cholesterol levels, Reiser, a researcher, compared beef fat, coconut oil (another very saturated fat) and safflower oil (an unsaturated oil thought to be very desirable to one's health). It was found that when beef fat was added to the diet, blood cholesterol levels rose no more than when safflower oil was added.

Another researcher, according to Reiser, found that as beef fat was added to the diets of students with blood cholesterol levels of 140mg/dl, no increase in blood cholesterol could be measured. But in students with a blood cholesterol level of 190-195 mg/dl, beef fat consumption increased blood cholesterol levels to 210 mg/dl.

In another experiment, O'Brien tested the effect of red meat, fish, poultry, and three eggs daily on the blood cholesterol levels of test subjects. He found no difference in blood cholesterol levels in the test subjects regardless of which of the above foods they ate.

In one part of the trial, egg consumption increased blood cholesterol levels. However, in another part of the same trial eggs had no effect on blood cholesterol levels.

Another researcher compared beef tallow to corn oil in rats. He found liver fat (usually considered bad

TRADITIONAL POT ROAST
Serves 6-8

3 pounds rump roast, chuck roast
*   or other cut suitable for pot roast*
1 quart buttermilk (page 83)
2 tablespoons butter
2 tablespoons extra virgin olive oil
1 cup red wine
2 cups beef stock (page 122)
several sprigs thyme, tied together
1/2 teaspoon green peppercorns, crushed
1 dozen small red potatoes
1 pound carrots, peeled and cut into sticks
2 tablespoons arrowroot
*   mixed with 2 tablespoons filtered water*
sea salt and pepper

In the German-speaking areas of Europe, housewives marinated beef or game several days in buttermilk before cooking it. The results are extremely tender and flavorful.

Using a needle or skewer, stick the meat all over. Place in a bowl or glass loaf pan just large enough to contain the meat and pour buttermilk over it. Allow to marinate in the refrigerator, turning occasionally, for several days.

Remove from buttermilk and dry off meat with paper towels. In a heavy, flameproof casserole, brown on all sides in butter and olive oil. Remove meat from casserole and pour out browning fat. Add wine, stock, thyme and peppercorns, bring to a boil and skim. Return pot roast to casserole and bake at 300 degrees, covered, for several hours or until tender. One hour before serving add potatoes and carrots.

Remove meat and vegetables to a platter and bring sauce to a boil on the stove. Spoonful by spoonful, add arrowroot mixture until desired thickness is obtained. Season to taste.

POT ROAST WITH CHILES

Serves 6-8

3 pounds rump roast, chuck roast
 or other cut suitable for pot roast
1-2 cups red wine
2 tablespoons butter
2 tablespoons extra virgin olive oil
2 cups beef stock (page 122)
2 ounces dried red chiles (hot or mild)
8 cloves garlic, peeled and chopped
3 tablespoons red wine vinegar
2 tablespoons tomato paste
1/4 teaspoon cinnamon
1/2 teaspoon dried green peppercorns, crushed
1/2 teaspoon dried oregano
several sprigs fresh thyme, tied together
sea salt and pepper

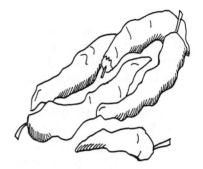

Marinate meat in red wine for several hours or overnight. Remove from wine and dry off well with paper towels. In a heavy, flameproof casserole, brown the meat on all sides in butter and olive oil. Transfer meat to a plate and pour out browning fat.

Remove stems and seeds from chiles. (Use rubber gloves for this.) Add all ingredients (except salt and pepper) to the casserole, bring to a boil, skim and return the roast to the pot. Bake in a 300-degree oven for several hours or until meat is tender.

Remove roast to a heated platter and keep warm in the oven. Run the sauce through a food mill. (See A Word on Equipment, page 68.) Return sauce to the casserole and reheat. If it is too thin, boil down for a bit; if too thick, add a little water. Season to taste. To serve, slice the beef and ladle sauce over each slice. Serve with Mexican rice (page 470).

for health) was lower in the rats which were fed beef tallow compared to those which received corn oil.

Another recent investigator found that as men on a lowfat, low-cholesterol diet increased their stearic acid consumption, blood cholesterol levels dipped by 14%. . . .

According to this researcher, many scientific reports over the years have indicated that stearic acid does not raise blood cholesterol in man, "but the idea has not been widely accepted." Stearic acid is the major component of beef fat.

Many reports can be found indicating that egg consumption in a normal diet has no effect on long term blood cholesterol levels. In addition, egg consumption has never been shown to increase death rates in persons initially free of coronary heart disease. Some of the studies showing egg consumption to have no appreciable effect on blood cholesterol levels were with men who already suffered from cardiovascular disease.

In addition, it has now been discovered that eggs contain substantially less cholesterol than once thought (220mg/egg rather that the 300 mgs they were believed to have.) Chris Mudd *Cholesterol and Your Health*

The Congressional Record pointed out that Frederick Stare, professor of nutrition at Harvard, has accepted research funds from various food manufacturers. The Congressional Record said that food processing companies pay him a large personal salary for consulting with their boards of directors. Dr. Stare was at that time on the board of directors of food companies that put sugar in their canned beans. Which is Dr. Stare going to advocate, red meat or his company's sugar-laced canned beans? How do you think he will advise congressional committees asking his advice? H. L. Newbold, MD *Type A Type B Weight Loss Book*

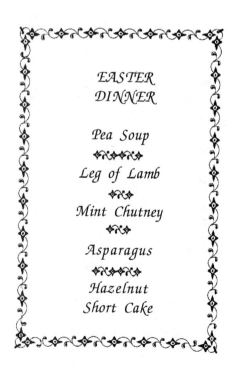

EASTER DINNER

Pea Soup

❊❊❊❊❊

Leg of Lamb

❊❊❊

Mint Chutney

❊❊❊

Asparagus

❊❊❊❊❊

Hazelnut Short Cake

SIMPLE LAMB CHOPS
Serves 4

8 lamb rib chops, about 1/2-inch thick
1 cup unbleached flour
1 teaspoon salt
1 teaspoon pepper

Dredge lamb chops in a mixture of flour, salt and pepper. Place on a broiler pan and bake at 400 degrees for about 20 minutes, turning once.

LAMB CHOPS WITH SAUCE
Serves 4

8 lamb chops
about 1 tablespoon cracked pepper
1/2 cup dry red wine
2 to 3 cups beef or lamb stock (page 122 or 123)
1 tablespoon gelatin (see Sources), optional
sea salt

You will need a very well-seasoned, cast-iron skillet for this recipe. Season the lamb chops with cracked pepper. Place the skillet over a moderately high fire. When it is hot, set four lamb chops in the pan. (No fat is required. The lamb chops will render their own fat, enough to keep the chops from sticking.) Cook about 5 minutes to a side, or until they are rare or medium rare. Keep in a warm oven while you are cooking the second batch and preparing the sauce.

Pour the grease out of the pan and add red wine, stock and optional gelatin. Bring sauce to a rapid boil, stirring with a wooden spoon to scrape up any accumulated juices. Boil vigorously until the sauce reduces to about 3/4 cup, skimming occasionally. The sauce should be the consistency of maple syrup. Season to taste.

Place the lamb chops on heated plates, with their accompanying vegetables, and spoon on the sauce. This is excellent with rosemary potatoes (page 397).

LEG OF LAMB

Serves 6

1 small leg of lamb
3 tablespoons butter
3 tablespoons Dijon-type mustard, smooth or grainy
1 onion, peeled and sliced
3 cloves garlic, peeled
several sprigs fresh thyme, rosemary or tarragon
a meat thermometer
12 new potatoes
1/2 cup dry white wine or vermouth
3-4 cups beef or lamb stock (page 122 or 123)
1 tablespoon gelatin (see Sources), optional
sea salt

Peel the garlic cloves but leave them whole. Place garlic and onion in a stainless steel roasting pan. Set the leg of lamb, fat side up, on a rack in the pan. Melt butter with mustard, mix thoroughly and brush on the lamb. Place sprigs of herbs on top and insert the meat thermometer. Set in an oven preheated to 450 degrees and reduce heat immediately to 350 degrees. Cook until the thermometer registers rare or medium rare, about 15 minutes to the pound. One-half hour before the roast finishes, strew the potatoes around the roast on the rack.

Remove the roast, set on a heated platter and keep warm in the oven while finishing the potatoes and making the sauce. Remove the rack. Cut potatoes in half and place cut side down in the drippings. Bake another 15 minutes or so until the potatoes are soft. Transfer them to the heated platter. Pour wine, stock and optional gelatin into the pan and bring to a rapid boil, stirring with a wooden spoon to scrape up any accumulated juices. Boil until the sauce reduces to about 1 cup, skimming occasionally. Season to taste.

Use leftovers to make leftover leg of lamb soup (page 208).

Variation: Leg of Lamb with Apricot Sauce

Using scissors, snip *1/2 cup dried unsulphured apricots* into strips. Soak in *1/2 cup red wine* for several hours. Add this to the sauce, omitting white wine. Serve with winter root medley (page 393).

From the strictly nutritional point of view, the macrobiotic diet has been reported to result in kwashiorkor (extreme protein deficiency) among strict adherents. A group of researchers at the University of Michigan made a study of babies who were maintained on the Zen macrobiotic diets and not only found that they were suffering from malnutrition but further warned that mothers should not restrict their babies entirely to the macrobiotic diet. The Zen macrobiotic diet includes a special infant formula called Kokoh and the American Academy of Pediatrics Committee on Nutrition reported that infants fed on this baby formula from birth usually are underweight within a few months and below average in their total body length. Additional research and clinical observation found that babies who eat no animal protein fail to grow at a normal rate; this study found that infants on "vegan" diets, except for early breast feeding, did not grow nor develop as normally as babies on diets containing animal products or vegetarian diets supplemented with cow's milk. The American Academy of Pediatrics Committee on Nutrition stated that perhaps the most harmful diet for growing children is the Zen macrobiotic diet and reported that the results of such diet can be scurvy, anemia, hypoproteinemia, hypocalcemia, emaciation and even death. H. Leon Abrams *Vegetarianism: An Anthropological/Nutritional Evaluation*

Currently the American Heart Association's recommendations call for a diet of no more than 2000 calories per day of which no more than 30 percent should be fat, with only 10 percent as saturated fat. We analyzed the 1896 *Boston Cook Book* menus for calories, fat, protein and carbohydrates. . . .

The *Boston Cook Book* menus suggest that the typical city-dwelling American at the turn of the century consumed about 2900 calories per day, with about 40 percent of these calories as fat and 20 percent of calories as protein. (Farm families probably consumed even greater numbers of calories.) The ratio of saturated fat to unsaturated was at least one to one. This rich diet of cream, butter, eggs, meats, vegetables, grains and fruit produced a generation of healthy, hearty, intelligent Americans, in spite of the fact that they consumed substantial amounts of sugar and white flour. Abundant dietary dairy fats contributed to strong bones, keen minds and healthy immune systems. The "prudent" low-calorie, lowfat diet of the American Heart Association is hardly a prescription for good health, even if sugar and white flour are absent. Traditional diets, including the traditional American diet, were hearty and rich, and provided nutritious protective factors for strong bodies, freedom from degenerative disease and clear minds well into old age. *Americans Now and Then*

STUFFED LEG OF LAMB
Serves 6-8

1 leg of lamb, boned removed and butterfly cut
3 tablespoons butter
1 medium onion, peeled and finely chopped
1 cup crispy pecans (page 513), chopped
6 cloves garlic, peeled and minced
1 cup cooked spinach, well drained and chopped
1/2 cup mint leaves, chopped
grated rind of 2 oranges
1 teaspoon dried thyme
1/4 teaspoon sea salt
1/4 teaspoon pepper
1/4 teaspoon cinnamon
1 egg, lightly beaten
2 tablespoons Dijon-type mustard
2 tablespoons butter, melted
1 medium onion, peeled and sliced
1 cup dry white wine or vermouth
3-4 cups beef or lamb stock (page 122 or 123)
1 tablespoon gelatin (see Sources), optional
juice of two oranges
sea salt

Open out the roast. Cut several lengths of string and have them ready. To prepare stuffing, sauté onion in butter. Add pecans, spinach, mint, garlic, orange rind, thyme, and cinnamon and blend well. Season to taste with salt and pepper. Allow to cool a minute and stir in the egg. Spread mixture on the roast, roll up and tie well at intervals. Slice the second onion and spread it in a stainless steel roasting pan. Place the roast on a rack in the pan. Blend mustard with melted butter and brush on the roast. Bake about 1 1/2 to 2 hours at 350 degrees. Remove roast to a heated platter and keep warm in the oven while you make the sauce.

Remove rack from pan. Add wine, stock, optional gelatin and orange juice to the pan and bring to a boil, stirring with a wooden spoon to scrape up any accumulated juices. Boil until the sauce reduces and thickens, skimming occasionally. Season to taste. Strain into a small saucepan and keep warm until lamb is served.

RACK OF LAMB

Serves 4

1 rack of lamb
1 slice whole grain bread
2 tablespoons butter, softened
1 tablespoon parsley, finely chopped
1/2 teaspoon sea salt
2 cloves garlic, peeled
1 medium onion, peeled and sliced
1/2 cup dry white wine or vermouth
3-4 cups beef or lamb stock (page 122 or 123)
1 tablespoon gelatin (see Sources), optional
sea salt and pepper

In the food processor, process the bread into bread crumbs. Add butter, sea salt and parsley and blend well. Spread this mixture on the top side of the rack of lamb. Place garlic cloves and sliced onion in a stainless steel roasting pan. Set the lamb on a rack in the pan and bake at 400 degrees for about 45 minutes. The lamb should be rare to medium rare. Remove lamb to a heated platter and keep warm in the oven while making the sauce. Remove rack from the roasting pan. Add wine, stock and optional gelatin and bring to a boil, stirring with a wooden spoon to scrape up any accumulated juices. Boil vigorously until sauce reduces and thickens, stirring occasionally. Strain into a saucepan and keep warm on low heat. Season to taste. To serve, cut the rack of lamb between the ribs. Place two chops on each plate and spoon sauce over.

LAMB RIBLETS

Serves 4

8 lamb riblets
1/2 cup naturally fermented soy sauce
2 tablespoons raw honey

Marinate riblets in a mixture of soy sauce and honey for several hours or overnight. Place in a baking pan and bake at 375 degrees for about 30-40 minutes or until nicely browned. This is great substitute for bacon.

When cooking is done well and with care, the good smells all go together to contribute not only to the pleasure of the meal but also to its thorough digestion. The good smells coming from the kitchen activate the secretion of saliva and digestive juices. The stimulation of the taste buds by delicious tastes has the same beneficial effect.

A meal well presented by the harmony of its forms and colors, evocative of a work of art, is not a simple esthetic exercise; it is also an aid to digestion as the sight of an appetizing dish stimulates the digestive juices, just as does its good smell and taste. Claude Aubert *Dis-Moi Comment Tu Cuisines*

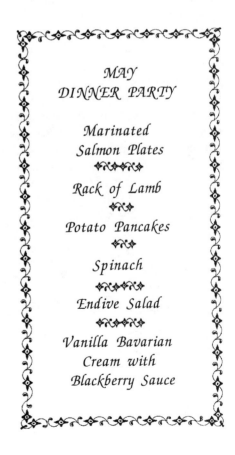

MAY
DINNER PARTY

Marinated
Salmon Plates

Rack of Lamb

Potato Pancakes

Spinach

Endive Salad

Vanilla Bavarian
Cream with
Blackberry Sauce

The experts on the Senate Select Committee claim that countries with a high animal fat intake have higher rates of colon and breast cancer. This is simply not true. In fact, the opposite appears more likely.

Take Finland and the Netherlands for example. Their per capita daily animal fat consumption is the same. But the Dutch consume four times as much vegetable fat as the Finns, and they have twice the rate of colon and breast cancer. Many other examples could be cited.

Enig and co-workers at the University of Maryland did a statistical analysis of the same USDA data relied on by the Senate Committee. They found a "*strong significant positive correlation with. . .vegetable fat and an essentially strong negative correlation. . .* with animal fat to total cancer deaths (and) breast and colon cancer incidence."

In plain language, you are more likely to get cancer from vegetable fat, such as margarine, than you are from animal fat, such as butter. "Negative correlation" means that despite what the experts said, butter and other animal fats may be protective from cancer! William Campbell Douglass, MD *The Milk Book*

BUTTERFLY LEG OF LAMB
Serves 6-8

1 leg of lamb, bone removed and butterfly cut
1/2 cup fresh lemon juice
1/2 cup naturally fermented soy sauce

Score the lamb fat if it is very thick. Marinate lamb at room temperature several hours or all day in soy sauce and lemon juice. Broil or barbecue about 15-20 minutes per side, until the lamb is medium rare. To serve, slice thinly across the grain and serve with heated marinade.

LAMB SHANKS
Serves 4

4 lamb shanks
1 cup red wine
2 tablespoons butter
2 tablespoons extra virgin olive oil
3 tablespoons vinegar
2 cups beef or lamb stock (page 122 or 123)
2 tablespoons tomato paste
1/2 teaspoon dried oregano
1/2 teaspoon ground cumin
1/4 teaspoon cayenne pepper
3 cloves garlic, peeled and mashed
several sprigs thyme, tied together
sea salt and pepper

Marinate lamb shanks in wine for several hours or overnight. Remove from marinade and pat dry. In a heavy, flameproof casserole, brown the meat on all sides in butter and olive oil. Pour out browning fat. Add tomato paste, marinating wine and stock, bring to a boil and skim. Add seasonings, except salt and pepper. Bake in a 300-degree oven for several hours or until lamb shanks are tender. Remove lamb shanks to heated platter. Remove thyme. Bring sauce to a rapid boil, skimming occasionally, until it has reduced to about one-half and thickened. Season to taste.

LAMB STEW
Serves 6-8

1 leg of lamb, cut into 2-inch pieces
1 cup red wine
3 tablespoons butter
3 tablespoons extra virgin olive oil
3-4 cups beef or lamb stock (page 122 or 123)
several sprigs fresh thyme, tied together
1/2 teaspoon green peppercorns, crushed
1/2 teaspoon whole cloves
several small pieces orange peel
4 cloves garlic, peeled and crushed
2 tablespoons tomato paste
2 tablespoons arrowroot mixed
*   with 2 tablespoons filtered water*
sea salt and pepper
1 pound turnips, scrubbed
*   and quartered lengthwise*
1 pound carrots, peeled and cut into sticks
1 pound small boiling onions, peeled
*   and sautéed in butter*
1/2 pound Chinese or sugar snap peas,
*   ends removed*
sea salt and pepper

Marinate lamb in wine for several hours or overnight. Remove from wine and dry off well with paper towels. (This is very important. If the meat is too damp, it will not brown.) In a heavy, flameproof casserole, brown the meat in batches in butter and olive oil, removing to a plate. Pour out browning oil and add stock, wine used in the marinade and tomato paste. Bring to a boil and skim. Add peppercorns, cloves, orange peel and garlic. Return meat to casserole along with the lamb bone, if you have it, cover and bake at 300 degrees for several hours or until meat is tender.

One-half hour before serving, add turnips and carrots to the casserole. Just before serving, add arrowroot mixture, spoonful by spoonful, until desired thickness of sauce is obtained. Remove bone and thyme. Season to taste. Add sautéed onions. Steam peas in a vegetable steamer for about 1 minute and add to stew.

Carnitine is an unusual amino acid that is biosynthesized in the liver of humans and is found highest in muscle and organ meats in the human diet. [The most abundant source of carnitine is lamb.] Carnitine is not found in vegetable sources. In human metabolism, it is utilized as a material which transfers fatty acids across the membranes of the mitochondria . . . where they can be used as a source of fuel to generate energy. In the absence of proper carnitine levels within the cell, the fatty acids are poorly metabolized and can build up within the cell or the surrounding medium, thereby leading to elevated blood fat and triglyceride levels. Carnitine has been found to have an important regulatory effect upon fat metabolism in heart and skeletal muscles. The administration of carnitine in tissue culture has been shown to stimulate fat metabolism and encourage the clearance of triglycerides and fatty acids.

Carnitine. . . is manufactured in the body from the amino acids lysine and methionine but again not at levels adequate to meet the needs of all individuals, particularly if they are on a low lysine or methionine diet. . . . The spermatozoa from lysine-depleted animals became infertile due to potential carnitine insufficiency. This is the first tissue to show deficiencies in animals that have been deprived of carnitine or lysine. . . . There seem to be genetic limitations on the ability of some individuals to synthesize carnitine from lysine or methionine, and therefore in these individuals carnitine may be an essential nutrient. Jeffrey Bland, PhD *Octacosanol, Carnitine and Other "Accessory" Nutrients*

Animal foods containing saturated fat and cholesterol provide vital nutrients necessary for growth, energy and protection from degenerative disease. Animal fats, like sex, are necessary for reproduction. Humans are drawn to both by powerful instincts. Suppression of natural appetites leads to weird nocturnal habits, fantasies, fetishes, bingeing and splurging.

Animal fats are nutritious, satisfying and they taste good. "Whatever is the cause of heart disease," said the eminent biochemist Michael Gurr in a recent article, "it is not primarily the consumption of saturated fats." And yet the high priests of the lipid hypothesis continue to lay their curse on the fairest of culinary pleasures—butter and Bernaise, whipped cream, soufflés and omelets, full-bodied cheeses, juicy steaks and pork sausage. *The Oiling of America*

Zinc is critical for brain function. It is absorbed from the blood supply into the outer cortical areas of the brain where memory, language, reason and insight are controlled. The eyes are equally dependent on zinc. In fact, one of the highest concentrations of zinc is in the eyes. High concentrations are also found in the prostate gland and the seminal fluid. Zinc plays a part in hundreds of enzymes including those that break down alcohol and help digest carbohydrates. Zinc is also required in the synthesis of insulin and in DNA, the master substance of life.

The best sources of zinc are oysters and red meat. Brewer's yeast, whole grains and pumpkin seeds will also supply this vital mineral if properly prepared to neutralize zinc-blocking phytic acid. Soy foods will block zinc unless they undergo a long period of fermentation. SWF

INDIAN-STYLE LAMB STEW
Serves 4-6

2 pounds lamb, cut into 3/4-inch pieces
1 cup yoghurt
seeds of 5 cardamom pods
1 teaspoon cumin seeds
1 teaspoon coriander seeds
4 tablespoons clarified butter (page 150)
1 medium onion, finely chopped
2-3 cups beef or lamb stock (page 122 or 123)
2 cloves garlic, peeled and mashed
1/2 teaspoon saffron threads
*   soaked in 2 tablespoons water*
1 tablespoon freshly grated ginger
3 tablespoons green chile peppers, chopped
*   (hot or mild)*
1/4 teaspoon ground turmeric
juice of 3 limes or 2 lemons
2 tablespoons arrowroot mixed with
*   2 tablespoons filtered water*
1/4 cup cilantro, chopped
1 cup crispy almond slivers (page 515)

Marinate the lamb in yoghurt in the refrigerator for 12 to 24 hours.

Spread the cardamom, cumin and coriander seeds on a plate and bake at 350 degrees for 10 to 15 minutes until browned. Heat clarified butter in a flameproof casserole and sauté the onions with the seeds. Add lamb, marinade and stock. Bring to a boil and skim. Add soaked saffron threads, garlic, ginger, chile peppers, turmeric and lemon or lime juice. Cover the pot and simmer over low flame for about 1 1/2 hours, stirring occasionally. Add arrowroot mixture, a spoonful at a time, until desired thickness is obtained. Just before serving, stir in cilantro and almonds. Serve with basic brown rice (page 466) and fruit chutney (page 106).

MOROCCAN-STYLE LAMB STEW

Serves 4-6

3 pounds lamb cut into 2-inch chunks
6 cloves garlic, peeled and mashed
1/2 cup extra virgin olive oil
4 teaspoons ground cumin
1 tablespoon freshly grated ginger
1 teaspoon sea salt
1 teaspoon ground turmeric
1 teaspoon paprika
1 teaspoon ground cinnamon
2 teaspoons dried green peppercorns, crushed
2-4 cups beef or lamb stock (page 122 or 123)
1/4 teaspoon saffron threads
2 tablespoons arrowroot combined with
*   2 tablespoons filtered water*
15 black olives (optional)
1/2 cup chopped preserved lemons (page 109) or
*   grated rind of one lemon*
1 cup pitted prunes or dried apricots, chopped
1/4 cup chopped cilantro for garnish

Make a mixture of garlic, olive oil, cumin, ginger, salt, turmeric, paprika, cinnamon and pepper. Marinate lamb pieces in marinade for several hours or overnight.

Place marinated lamb and marinade in a heavy, flameproof casserole along with stock. Bring to a boil and skim. Reduce heat to a simmer and add saffron. Cover casserole and bake at 300 degrees for about 2 hours or until meat is tender. Stir in olives, lemons or lemon peel and prunes or apricots and simmer another 1/2 hour. Transfer casserole to medium flame on stove. Spoonful by spoonful, add the arrowroot mixture until desired thickness is obtained. Ladle into bowls and garnish with cilantro. Serve with bulgur casserole (page 462) or wheat berry casserole (page 463).

Roger J. Williams, PhD. . . . believes that, since adults of widely different ethnic stock can physically thrive, without any cardiovascular symptom formation, on a high-fat, high-cholesterol, high-caloric diet, "the evidence points strongly (contrary to popular medical thinking) toward the conclusion that the nutritional micro-environment of the body cells—involving minerals, amino acids, vitamins—is crucial, and that the amount of fat or cholesterol consumed is relatively inconsequential." William H. Philpott, MD *Victory Over Diabetes*

Candida albicans resides in the lower bowel of the intestinal tract and consumes simple sugars and produces alcohol as one of its by-products. While the yeast cells live off sugar and carbohydrates, the HIV virus lives off proteins that are not completely broken down in the stomach into their constituent amino acids. For harder to digest proteins, like "glutens" in certain grains like wheat and "casein" in most dairy products and other proteins like eggs and meat cooked at high temperatures, the efficiency of protein digestion could drop to 60% or less. The higher the temperature the meat is cooked, the more coagulated the protein becomes and the harder it is for the digestive juices, like hydrochloric acid and pancreatic enzymes, to break down the proteins into simple amino acids. If 40% of the protein you ate passed into the colon undigested, the HIV virus could have a field day reproducing itself. Mark Konlee *Health Freedom News*

About the time we began exporting cokes and fast foods to the Soviet Union, we imported from the Russkies a book brimming over with secrets of long life. You judge who got the better deal.

Dr. G. Z. Pitskhelauri, famous Russian gerontologist, based his book *The Long Living of Soviet Georgia* on underlying reasons for the super longevity of residents of Georgia, supposedly the home of more 100-year-olds (and older) than any other area of the world. . . . Startling is the word for their typical diet, which contains two main items that are almost taboo in this country: fatty meats and whole milk products, as well as native sauces, herbs, various vegetable greens and a moderate amount of natural wines (nonsulphured). James F. Scheer *Health Freedom News*

On average, Finnish people have the highest cholesterol in the world. According to the diet-heart idea's proponents, this is due to the fat-rich Finnish food. The answer is not that simple, however. This was demonstrated by Dr. Rolf Kroneld who compared inhabitants of the village of Inio near Turku with those of North Karelia and in southwest Finland.

Apparently a health campaign had struck Inio. There the consumption of margarine was twice as great and the consumption of butter only half as what it was in the other places. Also, the people of Inio preferred skimmed over more fat milk; the residents in the other places did not. But the highest cholesterol values were found in Inio. The average value for male Inio inhabitants was 283, in the two other places it was 239 and 243 mg/dl. Regarding women, the difference was still greater. Uffe Ravnskov, MD, PhD *The Cholesterol Myths*

VEAL CHOPS
Serves 4

4 pasture-fed veal chops
juice of one lemon
1/2 teaspoon dried thyme
2 tablespoons butter
2 tablespoons extra virgin olive oil
1/2 cup dry white wine or vermouth
2 cups beef stock (page 122)

Marinate chops for several hours in lemon juice mixed with thyme. Dry thoroughly and brown in a heavy skillet, two at a time, on both sides in the butter and oil. Pour out browning oil and pour in the wine and stock. Bring to a rapid boil, stirring to scrape up any accumulated juices in the pan. Skim sauce and return the chops to the pan. Reduce heat to a simmer, cover and cook about 1/2 hour or until chops are tender. Remove chops to a heated platter and keep warm in the oven. Bring the liquid to a rapid boil, skimming occasionally, until sauce reduces and thickens.

VEAL SCALLOPINI
Serves 6

1 1/2 pounds pasture-fed veal scallopini
juice of 2 lemons
1 cup unbleached flour
1 teaspoon pepper
3 tablespoons butter
3 tablespoons extra virgin olive oil
1/2 cup cognac or dry white wine
2 cups beef stock (page 122)
1 cup piima cream or creme fraiche (page 84)

Trim the veal of any fat or gristle and pound on both sides with the small prong side of a meat hammer. Marinate in lemon juice for several hours. Remove from marinade and dry meat very well with paper towels. (This is important. If the meat is too damp, it will not brown.) Dredge pieces well in mixture of flour and pepper. Using a heavy skillet, brown scallopini in batches in butter and olive oil, transferring to a heated platter when done. Keep veal warm in the oven while making sauce. Pour out cooking oil and add cognac or wine to the pan. Bring to a rapid boil, add the stock and optional cream and let the liquid boil down, skimming occasionally, until you have about 1/2 cup. Season to taste. Pour sauce over veal and serve.

VEAL BIRDS
Serves 6

2 pounds pasture-fed veal scallopini
1 cup basic brown rice (page 466)
1/2 cup dried apricots, chopped
grated rind of two lemons
1 bunch scallions, finely chopped
1/4 teaspoon sea salt
3 tablespoons butter
3 tablespoons extra virgin olive oil
1 cup unbleached flour
1 teaspoon pepper
1/2 cup dry white wine
2-4 cups beef stock (page 122)
1 tablespoon gelatin (see Sources), optional
juice of two lemons

Soak apricot pieces in hot water for about 1 hour. Strain and mix them with rice, lemon rind, scallions and salt. Trim the veal of any fat or gristle and pound on both sides with the small prong side of a meat hammer. Place a spoonful of stuffing on each piece of veal, roll up and tie securely with string. Dry the birds with paper towel.

Dredge the veal birds in mixture of flour and pepper. In a heavy, flameproof casserole, brown the birds in batches in butter and olive oil, transferring to a plate for succeeding batches. Pour out browning oil and add wine to the pan. Bring to a rapid boil and add stock, optional gelatin and lemon juice. Skim the sauce, return veal birds to the pan, cover and set in a 300-degree oven for about 2 hours. When birds are tender, transfer to a heated platter. Bring the sauce to boil on the stove and reduce until it has thickened, skimming occasionally. Transfer the birds to individual plates and spoon sauce over them.

Taurine is an amino acid that is essential for the functioning of the heart muscle and the retina of the eye. Most of the taurine in your body is concentrated in your heart and eye; there is 100 to 400 times more taurine in these vital organs than in the bloodstream. Until recently, most nutritionists assumed that taurine (a nonessential amino acid) does not have to be absorbed from food, because it can be manufactured within the body through a chemical process involving the essential amino acids methionine and cysteine.

However, recent studies have shown that humans may have a critical nutritional need for dietary taurine. Scientists at the UCLA Medical Center in Los Angeles have found that lack of taurine in the diet leads to low blood taurine levels and retinal dysfunction. It was also found that a degenerative disease of the heart muscle in animals leading to heart failure can be completely reversed by the simple addition of taurine to their diet. Kurt W. Donsbach *Health Freedom News*

[For good vision] the first trait is adopting good habits of nutrition. Although the eyes and brain represent only 2% of our body weight, they require 25% of our nutritional intake. The eyes alone use one-third as much oxygen as the heart, need ten to twenty times as much vitamin C as the joint capsules involved in the movement of our extremities, and require more zinc (our intelligence chemical) that any other organ system in the body. Claude A. Valenti *PPNF Health Journal*

In deficiency of vitamin B_{12}, slow and insidious brain, spinal cord, red and white blood cells abnormalities occur, some not reversible. Malabsorption, defective delivery, dietary absence or interference, bacterial overgrowth or parasites, such as tapeworms, are all important causes of deficiency. . . . B_{12} seems to be synthesized only by microorganisms, wherever they are found in nature: on germs growing in the soil, sewerage and intestines. The main source appears to be the intestine of animals who chew their cud, thus the only real sources of B_{12} are essentially those of animal origin: liver, eggs, meat, milk and cheese. . . . Vegetarians, particularly vegans, may experience a deficiency with insidious neurological damage occurring before it is noticed. This need to gain B_{12} from animal sources may explain why chimpanzees go on a rampage of killing and devouring other animals, as noted by the famous Jane Goodall. The very best form of cobalamin [B_{12}] is only found in animal products. . . . Perhaps all the needs for vitamin B_{12} are not yet fully understood. It is also required for repairing and maintaining the spinal cord and, perhaps, other parts of the brain, such as the myelin sheath. Kenneth Seaton
Health Freedom News

Whatever causes coronary heart disease, it is not primarily a high intake of saturated fat.
Michael Gurr, PhD
Renowned Lipid Chemist

VEAL STEW
Serves 6

2 pounds pasture-fed veal stew meat
juice of two lemons
3 tablespoons butter
3 tablespoons extra virgin olive oil
1/2 cup white wine
4 cups beef stock (page 122)
several small slices lemon rind
1/2 teaspoon green peppercorns, crushed
several sprigs fresh thyme, tied together
12 small red potatoes
1 pound carrots, peeled and cut into sticks
2 tablespoons arrowroot powder
*   mixed with 2 tablespoons filtered water*
sea salt and pepper
1/2 pound mushrooms
1/4 pound Chinese or sugar snap peas,
*   ends removed*

Marinate the veal pieces in lemon juice for several hours. Dry thoroughly with paper towels. (This step is very important. If the meat is too damp, it will not brown.) In a heavy, flameproof casserole, brown the meat in batches in the butter and olive oil. Transfer batches to a plate. Pour out browning oil and add the wine and stock. Bring to a rapid boil and skim. Add lemon peel, thyme and pepper. Add veal and any juices accumulated in the plate. Cover and cook for about 2 hours in a 300 degree oven. One hour before serving add potatoes and carrots.

Meanwhile, wash, dry and sauté the mushrooms, either sliced, quartered or whole (page 389).

When meat and vegetables are tender, transfer the casserole to the stove and bring to a boil. Add arrowroot mixture, spoonful by spoonful, until desired thickness is obtained. Season to taste. Just before serving, steam the peas in a vegetable steamer for 1 minute and add to the casserole with the mushrooms.

VEAL POT ROAST

Serves 6

2-3 pounds pasture-fed veal roast
juice of three lemons
2 tablespoons butter
2 tablespoons extra virgin olive oil
1 cup unbleached flour
1 teaspoon sea salt
1 teaspoon pepper
3 tablespoons butter
1/2 cup white wine
3 cups beef stock (page 122)
several small slices lemon rind
1/2 teaspoon green peppercorns, crushed
several sprigs fresh thyme, tied together
1 cup piima cream or creme fraiche (page 84)

Tap the roast lightly all over with a meat hammer and rub lemon juice into the tissues. Place in a bowl with remaining lemon juice and marinate for several hours at room temperature, turning frequently. Dry roast thoroughly with paper towels. (This step is very important. If the meat is too damp, it will not brown.) Mix flour with salt and pepper. In a heavy, flameproof casserole, melt butter and olive oil. Dredge roast in the flour mixture and brown on all sides in butter and olive oil over medium-high heat. Set roast aside.

Pour out browning fat and add butter. Mix remaining flour with butter and cook over medium heat, stirring constantly, until flour has browned. Add wine and stock, bring to a boil and skim. Return roast to casserole along with thyme, peppercorns and lemon peel. Transfer to a 300-degree oven and cook for about 2 hours.

To serve, remove thyme and transfer roast to a heated platter. Add cultured cream to sauce and boil vigorously until sauce has reduced and thickened. Slice the roast, arrange on individual plates and spoon sauce over.

The practice of breeding and feeding domestic animals is not to be disdained, providing these animals are naturally and humanely raised. For thousands of years, domesticated animals have supplied mankind with the kinds of fats that give him energy and help his body work more efficiently. The domestication of animals was a great step forward in man's evolution, because these animals ensured a steady supply of quality meat and fat and freed him from the risks and uncertainties of a hunter-gatherer existence so that his energies could be directed to mental and spiritual growth. Mary G. Enig, PhD *PPNF Health Journal*

Saturated fatty acids have recently been shown to be necessary for the proper utilization of essential fatty acids and for efficient modeling of the bones. Consumption of saturated fatty acids also results in lowering of Lp(a) in the blood. Elevated levels of Lp(a) are a marker for heart disease. The textbooks tell us that saturated fats protect the liver from alcohol ingestion. Mary G. Enig, PhD *PPNF Health Journal*

Whenever eating meat—chops, steaks, roast, etc.—one would be wise to eat part of the fat, as it is essential to good health. Too often we turn up our noses at the fat and thus waste the part that is of prime importance for balanced nutrition. H. Leon Abrams *Your Body Is Your Best Doctor*

To distinguish the "strict" vegetarian diet from the easier regime allowing dairy products, it became the custom to call the strict dieters *vegans* and the others *lacto-vegetarians.* . . vegans run a serious risk of deficiency diseases owing to the difficulties of providing, with a vegetable diet, all the essential materials that the human body cannot synthesize for itself. Vitamin B_{12} is one of these, and vegans often get anemia. . . . Other materials are the essential amino acids, some of which are not included in very large amounts in the vegetable proteins in nuts and pulses; and vegans can suffer from a kind of kwashiorkor arising not from a gross shortage of protein but from a lack of some of the essential building-blocks for it. Terence McLaughlin *A Diet of Tripe*

Cutting out cholesterol to avoid heart attacks increases the risk of dying by violent means, according to a study published Friday in the *British Medical Journal.* . . researchers. . . found a low-cholesterol diet appeared to make people more aggressive. They said that in 1980 U.S. average mortality rate from motor vehicle accidents, murders and suicides among middle-aged white males was 62 per 100,000 people, as against 107 per 100,000 among people trying to cut their cholesterol level. Attempts to cut cholesterol, the researchers said, "do not have a robust favorable effect on overall survival." *Reuters Wire Service*

VEAL MARROW BONES

(Osso Bucco)
Serves 6

6 1-inch slices pasture-fed veal shanks
2 tablespoons butter
2 tablespoons extra virgin olive oil
1 large onion, coarsely chopped
2 carrots, peeled and coarsely chopped
1/2 cup dry white wine or vermouth
3-4 cups beef stock (page 122)
1 tablespoon gelatin (see Sources), optional
4 tomatoes, peeled, seeded and chopped
    or 1 large can tomatoes
2 cloves garlic, peeled and mashed
several sprigs thyme, tied together
1/2 teaspoon dried green peppercorns, crushed
sea salt and pepper

Tie the pieces of veal shank around the perimeter with string so that they hold together during cooking. Dry well with paper towels. In a heavy, flameproof casserole, sauté the onions and carrots until soft in butter and olive oil. Remove with a slotted spoon. In the same casserole, brown the shanks two at a time, transferring to a plate. Pour out browning oil. Add wine, stock and optional gelatin, bring to a boil and skim. Add tomatoes, garlic, and seasonings. (To peel tomatoes, see page 70.) Return veal and sautéed carrots and onions to the casserole, cover and bake at 300 degrees for several hours or until tender.

Remove veal to a platter, remove thyme and reduce the sauce by boiling, skimming occasionally. Spoon over the shanks and serve. This is excellent with polenta (page 487) or basic brown rice (page 466).

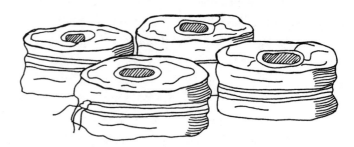

GROUND MEATS

Ground meats are fine, as long as they are freshly ground and the meat is of good quality. The beauty of ground meat dishes is that almost any type of meat can be used in their preparation. For variety you can use buffalo meat in recipes that traditionally call for beef or lamb. If you have hunters in your family, you can even use ground venison or other game in any of these recipes, but they will require the addition of some lamb, beef or venison fat. You may also add a small amount of ground heart meat, which is especially rich in Co $Q_{10.}$

If you prefer not to eat red meat, ground chicken or turkey can always be substituted but be careful—as their fat contains high amounts of polyunsaturates, ground turkey and chicken spoil more quickly than red meats. The results will also probably be more dry than the same dish prepared with red meat.

Always buy "regular" full-fat ground meat but avoid cooking hamburgers and sausage on the barbecue, where flames can come in contact with the fat and form cancer-causing substances. Cook hamburgers and similar meats in a heavy, cast-iron skillet to minimize carcinogen formation in the final product.

Our readers may have noticed that we do not have a chapter on pasta in our book; simply because pasta, even and especially whole grain pasta, is difficult to digest due to the fact that pasta flour, in general, has not been soaked, fermented or sprouted. Nevertheless, nobody expects today's mothers to raise children without preparing spaghetti for them once in a while. For this reason, we have included two spaghetti sauce recipes, one of which can be made without tomato products. Serve these with Oriental pasta made from brown rice or buckwheat flour, which is more nutritious and easier to digest than pasta made from whole wheat or white flour.

HAMBURGERS
Serves 6

2 pounds ground beef or buffalo, including the fat
1/2 pound ground heart (optional)

Form meat into six patties about 1-inch thick. Heat a heavy, cast-iron skillet over a medium flame. When skillet is hot, add three patties. Cook about 7 or 8 minutes per side—hamburgers should be medium rare. Keep warm in oven while preparing the second batch.

Serve with whole grain hamburger buns (commercially available spelt buns are recommended), ketchup (page 104), mayonnaise (page 137), pickled cucumber slices (page 97), corn relish (page 100) and thinly sliced onions.

*FOURTH OF
JULY DINNER*

Hamburgers
❦❦❦
Mayonnaise
❦❦❦
Corn Relish
❦❦❦
*Pickled Cucumber
Slices*
❦❦❦
*Sliced Tomato
and Red Onion*
❦❦❦❦
Three Bean Salad
❦❦❦❦
Corn on the Cob
❦❦❦❦
Ginger Ale
❦❦❦❦
Stars and Stripes Cake

John Ott, of time-lapse photography fame. . . tested three young athletes who ate hamburgers, with all the trimmings, that were prepared in a fast-food restaurant. The first group of the hamburgers were cooked in the restaurant's microwave oven while another was prepared conventionally in an iron frying pan. This latter group and even the raw hamburgers held in hand resulted in strong muscle test results, while the same athletes tested muscularly weak with the microwave cooked food. Ott also reported most food prepared in these appliances and especially meat was less tasty. This opinion seems to be shared by most who use this form of cooking. George Meinig, DDS "Nutritionally Speaking" *Ojai Valley News*

SPICY MEAT LOAF
Serves 8

2 pounds ground beef or other red meat
1/2 pound ground heart (optional)
1 medium onion, peeled and finely chopped
1 carrot, peeled and finely chopped
1 stalk celery, finely chopped
4 tablespoons butter
1/4 teaspoon dried chile flakes
1 teaspoon dried thyme
1 teaspoon cracked pepper
1 teaspoon sea salt
1 1/2 cups whole grain bread crumbs
1 cup cream
1 egg
1 tablespoon fish sauce (page 157), optional
4 tablespoons tomato paste or
    naturally sweetened ketchup (page 104)

Sauté onions, carrots and celery in butter until soft. Add chile flakes, thyme, pepper and salt and stir around. Meanwhile, soak bread crumbs in cream.

Have a 9-inch by 13-inch pyrex pan ready. Using your hands, mix meat with sautéed vegetables, soaked bread, egg and optional fish sauce. Form into a loaf and set in the pan. Ice with ketchup or tomato paste. Add about 1 cup water to the pan. Bake at 350 degrees for about 1 1/2 hours. Serve with ketchup (page 104), sauerkraut (page 92) or ginger carrots (page 95).

Leftovers are great on sandwiches!

SPAGHETTI SAUCE

Serves 8

2 pounds ground beef or other red meat
2 onions, peeled and finely chopped
1 green pepper, seeded and finely chopped
3 tomatoes, peeled, seeded and chopped or 1 can
    tomatoes, drained and coarsely chopped
1 small can tomato paste
1 cup beef stock (page 122)
1/2 cup red wine
1/2 pound chicken livers
2 tablespoons butter
1 teaspoon each dried thyme, rosemary,
    oregano and sage
sea salt and pepper

To peel tomatoes, see page 70. Sauté meat in a large pot until it becomes crumbly and all the pink is gone. You may pour out the melted fat, but it is not necessary. Meanwhile, sauté the chicken livers in butter until cooked through. Cut into a fine dice. Add chopped livers and remaining ingredients to the beef, blend well, season to taste and simmer, covered, for about 1/2 hour. Serve with buckwheat or brown rice noodles.

TOMATO-FREE SPAGHETTI SAUCE

Serves 8

2 pounds ground beef or other red meat
2 medium onions, peeled and finely chopped
3 cups beef stock (page 122)
1 cup red wine
2 tablespoons fresh rosemary leaves, chopped,
    or 1 tablespoon dried rosemary
sea salt and pepper

Sauté ground meat in a heavy skillet until crumbly. Add onions, stock, wine and rosemary. Bring to a boil and cook, uncovered, for 15 to 30 minutes until liquid has reduced to a thick sauce. Season to taste. Serve with buckwheat or brown rice noodles.

If you're buying extra-lean ground beef to lessen your intake of fat and cholesterol and think that the extra cost is worthwhile, think again! That's the finding of nutritionists Kenneth Prusa and Karla Hughes, at the University of Missouri at Columbia, who conducted an experiment to decide this very issue.

These researchers broiled hamburgers made from 100 grams of three grades of ground beef: regular, lean and extra lean. And what did they find? That the broiling process almost leveled out the cholesterol and fat content of the hamburger. The remaining fat content varies by just five percent, despite a threefold difference in the raw meat. (Regular hamburger has 28.5 percent fat content, compared with extra-lean meat's 9 percent.)

However, other surprising things happened during broiling. The higher-fat hamburger lost mainly fat and cholesterol, while leaner patties lost moisture. Is it logical that regular hamburger would cook down appreciably more in weight than lean and extra-lean? Actually, it cooked down only four percent more than the others. Hughes stated that lean and extra-lean hamburger may not be worth the premium price compared with the regular grinds.

Then came the crusher to leaner grinds. A trained panel of hamburger tasters voted in favor of regular grinds because they were juicier and more tender! James F. Scheer *Health Freedom News*

Most people are prone to think that eating fat makes fat; however, fat does not make fat in the body. A healthy body must have fat to carry on its vital processes. Carbohydrates—the grains, bread, starches, and sugar—are the foods that make fat—and it is these foods that must be curtailed for the person who has great difficulty with obesity. People who wish to lose weight should give up grains, sugar and starches until their desired weight is attained, then they should eat grains and starches only moderately. H. Leon Abrams *Your Body Is Your Best Doctor*

SPICY STUFFED CABBAGE
Serves 6

1 large cabbage
1 pound ground red meat or turkey
2 tablespoons olive oil
2 medium onions, peeled and finely chopped
2 cups basic brown rice (page 466)
1/2 cup raisins
1/4 cup fresh dill, chopped
2 cloves garlic, peeled and mashed
2 teaspoons ground cumin
1/2 teaspoon cinnamon
1/8 teaspoon ground cloves
sea salt and pepper
1/4 cup crispy pine nuts (page 514)
1 egg, lightly beaten
4 cups beef or chicken stock (page 122 or 124)
2 tomatoes, peeled, seeded and coarsely chopped
2 tablespoons arrowroot mixed with
*   2 tablespoons filtered water*

To peel tomatoes, see page 70. Remove core from the cabbage and set, cored side down, in a large pot containing about 2 inches of water. Cover and steam about 15 minutes. Remove wilted outer leaves and steam a bit longer, if necessary, to soften inner leaves. Strew leaves on a tea towel to drain and set aside.

In a heavy skillet, brown meat in olive oil until crumbly. Add onion, rice, raisins, pine nuts, herbs and spices. Season to taste. Let cool slightly and stir in the egg. Place a spoonful of stuffing on each cabbage leaf, fold in sides and roll up. Arrange in several layers in a flameproof casserole and cover with stock and tomato pieces. Bring to a boil and transfer to the oven. Bake at 300 degrees about 1 hour.

Use tongs to remove cabbage rolls to a platter and keep warm in the oven. Return the casserole and its liquid to the stove. Bring to a boil and cook vigorously about 15 minutes, skimming occasionally, until stock has reduced. Add arrowroot mixture, spoonful by spoonful, until desired thickness is obtained. To serve, place two or three cabbage rolls on each plate and spoon on sauce.

STUFFED CABBAGE, ORIENTAL STYLE

Serves 6

1 large cabbage
2 pounds ground turkey
2 tablespoons extra virgin olive oil
1 cup basic brown rice (page 466)
2 bunches green onions, finely chopped
2 tablespoons toasted sesame oil
1 tablespoon freshly grated ginger
2 tablespoons naturally fermented soy sauce
1/4 teaspoon red chile flakes
1 bunch cilantro, minced
sea salt and pepper
4 cups chicken or turkey stock (page 124 or 125)
2 tablespoons arrowroot mixed with
2 tablespoons filtered water

Remove the core from cabbage and set, core side down, in a large pot containing about 2 inches of water. Cover and steam about 15 minutes. Remove wilted outer leaves and steam a bit longer, if necessary, to soften inner leaves. Strew leaves on a tea towel to drain and set aside.

In a heavy skillet, brown turkey in olive oil until crumbly. Stir in green onions, rice, green onions, sesame sauce, ginger, soy sauce, red chile flakes and cilantro. Season to taste. Place a spoonful of stuffing in each cabbage leaf, fold in sides and roll up. Arrange in several layers in a flameproof casserole and cover with stock. Bring to a boil and transfer to the oven. Bake at 300 degrees about 1 hour.

Use tongs to remove cabbage rolls to a platter and keep warm in the oven. Return the casserole and its liquid to the stove. Bring to a boil and cook vigorously about 15 minutes, stirring occasionally, until stock has reduced. Add arrowroot mixture, spoonful by spoonful, until desired thickness is obtained.

To serve, ladle sauce onto individual plates and place two or three cabbage rolls on top.

Babies fed a strict vegetarian diet. . . do not grow at a normal rate. They get shortchanged on B_{12}, folic acid, zinc, calories, proteins, calcium and riboflavin (B_2). Even a *breast-fed* baby may become malnourished if the mother has been a true vegetarian for a number of years. William Campbell Douglass, MD *The Milk Book*

The propaganda blitz has been so awesome that even the *New England Journal of Medicine*. . . has abandoned science and swallowed the killer-cholesterol line. "The optimal intake of cholesterol," they editorialize, "is probably zero, meaning the avoidance of animal products."

After making this wrong-headed and unscientific statement, they temporize by admitting that "sound data are needed," "The lack of more direct human evidence remains frustrating," "In the absence of fully satisfactory data. . . a reasonable policy would seem to admit uncertainty. . ." and "we must hedge our bets." There is a certain wistfulness to this editorial as if they were saying, "Would someone please prove that our dietary recommendations have some scientific justification?" William Campbell Douglass, MD *Eat Your Cholesterol*

Rat colonies maintained during their whole lives on conventional human-style diets, or even on diets supplemented artificially with minerals and vitamins, develop many pathological conditions not seen in rats during the abbreviated course of vitamin assaying. It is difficult to avoid the inference that the appearance of disease in long-term, vitamin-supplemented diet experiments presages the need of the organism for all food constituents, including food enzymes, if optimal health and longevity are to be attained. Edward Howell, MD *Food Enzymes for Health and Longevity*

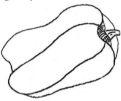

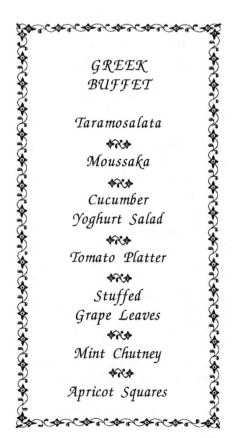

GREEK BUFFET

Taramosalata

❖❖❖

Moussaka

❖❖❖

Cucumber Yoghurt Salad

❖❖❖

Tomato Platter

❖❖❖

Stuffed Grape Leaves

❖❖❖

Mint Chutney

❖❖❖

Apricot Squares

STUFFED PEPPERS
Serves 6

6 green peppers
1 pound ground beef or other red meat
1/4 pound ground heart (optional)
2 tablespoons olive oil
1 medium onion, peeled and finely chopped
1 small can tomato paste
1 cup beef stock (page 122)
1/2 teaspoon each thyme, rosemary and oregano, fresh or dried
2 cups basic brown rice (page 466)
1/4 cup crispy pine nuts (page 514)
sea salt and pepper
1 cup grated Parmesan or Cheddar cheese

Carefully remove stems from peppers, slice in half lengthwise and remove seeds. In a heavy skillet, brown meat in olive oil until crumbly. Add onion, tomato paste, stock and herbs. Bring to a boil and cook until liquid has reduced by about one half. Stir in rice and pine nuts and season to taste. Set the pepper halves in a buttered pyrex dish, fill each with stuffing and top with cheese. Bake for about 1 hour at 350 degrees.

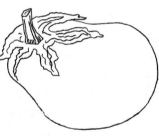

MOUSSAKA
(Eggplant Casserole)
Serves 12-18

8-10 large eggplants
about 1 cup extra virgin olive oil
4 pounds ground lamb
3 medium onions, minced
8 ripe tomatoes, peeled, seeded and coarsely chopped or 2 cans tomatoes, drained and coarsely chopped
1 cup beef or lamb stock (page 122 or 123)
1 teaspoon cinnamon
sea salt and pepper
2 cups grated Cheddar or Parmesan cheese

Moussaka makes a wonderful buffet dish, and it is a welcome and healthier alternative to lasagna. You will need a rectangular pan that is at least 2 inches deep—a stainless steel baking pan will do nicely. Do not make the mistake of skimping on the eggplant—that is what gives this dish its distinctive character.

Cut ends off eggplants and peel. Cut into 3/8-inch lengthwise slices. Salt and set aside, covered with a towel, for about 1 hour. Rinse slices well, dry off, and place on cookie sheets brushed with olive oil. Generously brush top sides with olive oil and grill under broiler until lightly browned. Meanwhile, cook the lamb in a large pan until crumbly. To peel tomatoes, see page 70. Add onions, tomatoes, stock, and cinnamon. Season to taste. Bring to boil, skim and simmer, uncovered, until most of the liquid has evaporated.

Oil the baking pan. Arrange a layer of eggplant on the bottom, then a thin layer of the meat. Repeat for at least two more layers to give at least three layers of eggplant—but four is better. Sprinkle cheese on top. Bake at 350 degrees for 1 hour.

LAMB MEATBALLS
Serves 6

2 pounds ground lamb
1 medium onion, finely diced
2 tablespoons olive oil
1 tablespoon dried rosemary or thyme
2 eggs
2 cups whole grain bread crumbs
1 cup cream
1 teaspoon sea salt
1 teaspoon pepper
1 1/2 cups unbleached flour
about 1/2 cup olive oil
1 cup red wine
2-3 cups beef or lamb stock (page 122 or 123)
3-4 ripe tomatoes, peeled, seeded and chopped or
    1 can tomatoes, drained and chopped
2 cups spinach, chard, kale or beet greens, chopped

A lowfat, low-cholesterol diet seems reasonable. Increased amounts of cholesterol and saturated fats in the diet will cause, on the average, an increase in the blood cholesterol level. The higher the levels of cholesterol in an individual, the greater his chances are of developing heart disease and of having a heart attack. Therefore, it seems obvious that a lowfat, low-cholesterol diet, with or without medicine, will cause a decrease in both heart disease mortality and in total mortality.

There is a problem with this simple deduction, however, that the medical community has chosen to overlook. The above supposition is incorrect. There is very little scientific evidence to directly indicate that reducing cholesterol and saturated fat in the diet will prolong an individual's life.

For years the medical profession has chosen to ignore scientific evidence from numerous studies that indicate such a diet may not increase an individual's life span and reduce total mortality. Now the medical community may be ready to back off a bit and at least partially replace the cholesterol theory with the idea that genetics may be the primary culprit in CHD [coronary heart disease]. The problem here is, obviously, that no one has control over his genetic makeup.

I would like to ask a simple question here. If genetics is a primary cause of CHD, why was there such a great increase in deaths from coronary heart disease between the mid 1920's and 1968? Did our genes change in a matter of just a few decades? Chris Mudd *Cholesterol and Your Health*

The American Heart Association . . . has gone way out on a limb concerning fat and cholesterol in our diet. They have recommended a shift to less milk, eggs, meat. . . to a diet containing more margarine, fish, and vegetable oils. They are *committed*. They must continue to support their completely untenable and nutritionally disastrous position or admit that they have made a terrible mistake. The American Heart Association, the principle promoter of the fat-cholesterol theory of atherosclerosis, is now going after the children and recommending low-cholesterol diets for *3-year-olds*. But the American Academy of Pediatrics is striking back. They point out that cholesterol is vital in growing children for the formation of bile salts, hormones and nerve tissue. *There is no population of children that has been raised on such a radical diet.* Yet the American Heart Association assures America's mothers that "there appear to be no demonstrated major hazards involved" if the kids follow the AHA's radical diet plan. But they go on to admit that ". . . several epidemiologic studies. . . have failed to observe significant correlations among dietary fat, serum cholesterol concentrations and coronary heart disease rates." William Campbell Douglass, MD *The Milk Book*

In one study by Pearce and Dayton that the AHA did *not* mention, it was found that eighty-year-olds on a low-cholesterol, high-unsaturated fat diet caused a twofold increase in *cancer*. . . . But the AHA is recommending a drastic increase to *20% unsaturated fat.* William Campbell Douglass, MD *The Milk Book*

To peel tomatoes, see page 70. Sauté onion and rosemary in 2 tablespoons olive oil until soft. Meanwhile, soak bread crumbs in cream. Mix onion mixture, eggs, bread crumbs, sea salt and pepper with ground lamb. Form into 1-inch balls. Dredge in flour and sauté a few at a time in olive oil. Pour out browning oil and add red wine to the pan. Bring to a boil, scraping up coagulated juices in the pan with a wooden spoon. Add stock and tomatoes and reduce by boiling until sauce thickens, skimming occasionally. Add meatballs and chopped greens to sauce and simmer for about 15 minutes or until meatballs are cooked through. Serve with basic brown rice (page 466) or buckwheat or brown rice noodles.

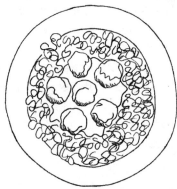

CHICKEN PATTIES

Makes 8-10 patties

2 pounds ground chicken
2 cups whole grain bread crumbs
1 cup cream
3/4 cup cooked spinach, chopped and well drained
1 medium onion, peeled and finely chopped
1/2 red pepper, finely chopped
2 eggs
1/4 teaspoon cayenne pepper
1 teaspoon sea salt
1/2 teaspoon dried thyme
4 tablespoons butter
4 tablespoons extra virgin olive oil

Soak bread crumbs in cream. Mix chicken with bread crumb mixture, spinach, onion, pepper, eggs and seasonings and form into patties. Sauté about 7 minutes per side in butter and olive oil, or until cooked through.

SPICY LAMB PASTRIES

(Samosas)

Makes 20-24

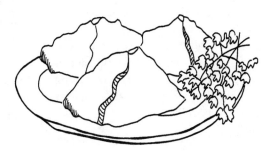

1 recipe basic yoghurt dough (page 485)
2 pounds ground lamb
2 medium onions, peeled and finely chopped
2 tablespoons olive oil
2 cups basic brown rice (page 466)
1/2 cup crispy pine nuts (page 514)
1/2 teaspoon cinnamon
1/4 teaspoon cayenne pepper
3/4 teaspoon sea salt
1/4 teaspoon pepper
1 bunch cilantro, chopped
grated rind of 2 lemons
about 1/2 cup melted butter

In a heavy skillet, cook the lamb until crumbly. Remove with a slotted spoon. Mix onions, pine nuts, rice, seasonings, cilantro and lemon rind with the cooked lamb. Form yoghurt dough into 1 1/2-inch balls and roll out on a well-floured pastry cloth to form 6-inch rounds. Place about 1/4 cup of lamb mixture on each. Fold edges up and pinch together to form a three sided pastry, leaving a small hole in the middle for air to escape. Place on well-greased pans and brush with butter. Bake at 350 degrees for about 40 minutes or until golden. Serve with yoghurt sauce (page 143) or ginger carrots (page 95).

If you have a few spoonfuls of meat stuffing left over, use to make a sausage omelet (page 439).

The most dramatic failure to prove the cholesterol connection came when the Multiple Risk Factor Intervention Trial (MRFIT) collapsed in 1982. This long-term study was meant to provide conclusive answers about the causes of heart disease. Five to six thousand men would be "put under intensive treatment. . . not only for reduction of cholesterol, by diet or drugs, but also for reduction of smoking and high blood pressure." The experimental group would then be compared to a control group who had received "usual care" from their own doctors. The results were resoundingly inconclusive. The difference in heart attack rates between the two groups was statistically insignificant. . . . Most importantly "the cholesterol question. . . remains unresolved after two decades of controversy. . . . The benefits of cholesterol reduction—and cholesterol's causal role in heart disease—remain uncertain." Joseph D. Beasley, MD and Jerry J. Swift, MA *The Kellogg Report*

TURKEY BREAKFAST SAUSAGE

Serves 6

1 pound ground turkey
1 small onion, peeled and finely chopped
1/4 teaspoon each cumin, marjoram, pepper, nutmeg
*   oregano, cayenne pepper, and ginger*
1/2 teaspoon each dried basil, thyme, sage

> Whatever the father of illness,
> the mother is wrong food.
> *Chinese Proverb*

Myth: Children benefit from a lowfat diet.

Truth: Children on lowfat diets suffer from growth problems, failure to thrive and learning disabilities. (*Food Chem News* 10/3/94)

No two soils have exactly the same history, topography and climate, and soil-mineral differences may occur within the same fence lines. Albrecht [the soil specialist] visited a famous Hereford farm in Missouri and found an entire beef herd seriously afflicted with diseases that doctoring seemed unable to cure. On another farm nearby he found a similar herd in practically perfect health. Oddly, the herd on the second farm was started by animals born and brought up on the first farm. The health difference was a soil difference. The first man had been operating for fifty years on the same farm and had not maintained soil minerals. The second man, a newcomer, had taken sound advice and built up his soils. "Are We Starving to Death?" *The Saturday Evening Post* 1945

Man has been eating meat and fat for thousands of years, but hardening of the arteries is a new disease. My father, practicing medicine in Georgia fifty years ago, rarely saw a heart attack. Heart attacks have only become common since the advent of homogenized pasteurized milk, oleomargarine, and the increased consumption of polyunsaturated vegetable oils. William Campbell Douglass, MD *The Milk Book*

2 teaspoons sea salt
2 tablespoons whole grain bread crumbs
1 egg, lightly beaten
2 tablespoons butter

Mix all ingredients and chill well. Form into patties and sauté in butter.

To store in the freezer, form into patties and store in an air tight plastic container, using parchment paper to line the container and separate the patties. (See Sources.)

SPICY LAMB SAUSAGE

Makes about 20 small patties

2 1/4 pounds ground lamb
1/2 cup sun dried tomato bits (see Sources)
1 medium onion, peeled and finely chopped
1/2 red bell pepper, finely chopped
4 tablespoons extra virgin olive oil
2 tablespoons tomato paste
2 cloves garlic, peeled and mashed
1/4 cup crispy pine nuts (page 514)
1/2 cup fresh cilantro, chopped
1 tablespoon fresh mint, chopped
1/2 teaspoon ground allspice
1 teaspoon cayenne pepper
1 teaspoon cumin
1 teaspoon ground coriander
2-3 teaspoons sea salt
1 teaspoon cracked pepper
1/4 cup fresh lemon juice
2 eggs, lightly beaten

Sauté onions, peppers and tomato bits in olive oil until soft. Mix all ingredients together and form into patties. Sauté about 7 minutes on a side in a well-seasoned, cast-iron skillet

A CATALOG of VEGETABLES

A CATALOG
of VEGETABLES

The American love affair with fast food is almost incomprehensible considering the great variety of fresh vegetables now available year round in every American town. Relatively few take advantage of this cornucopia. Most Americans eat vegetables rarely, and when they do their choices are confined to a few favorites—carrots, peas, tomatoes and potatoes. Yet fresh vegetables can be the highlight of every meal. Few of them require much time to prepare, and most need very little time to cook. Furthermore, almost every vegetable that has been studied has been found to contain substances that benefit the heart and blood or counteract the formation of tumors. Fresh vegetables, eaten with the right fats on a daily basis, are one of our best protections against coronary heart disease and cancer.

Steaming is the best way to cook most vegetables. This preserves most vitamins and minerals and a good many enzymes as well, if the process is not allowed to continue too long. Light sautéing in butter, olive oil or coconut oil is also an acceptable cooking method. Some research indicates that cooking foods in fats and oils actually makes nutrients more available. Other methods include blanching in boiling filtered water and, for root vegetables, cooking in a clay pot.

While we recommend the inclusion of much raw food in the diet, some vegetables are best eaten cooked. For example, cabbage, broccoli, Brussels sprouts and kale contain chemicals that block the production of thyroid hormone (known medically as goitrogens). Beet greens, spinach and chard contain oxalic acid that blocks calcium and iron absorption and irritates the mouth and intestinal tract. Raw potatoes contain substances called hemagglutinins that disrupt the proper function of red blood cells. Cooking destroys or neutralizes these harmful substances (as does the fermentation process). Spinach and cabbage are popular salad foods but should be eaten raw only occasionally.

It may sound like heresy, but we do not recommend saving vegetable cooking water. Adelle Davis was the first popular nutrition writer to suggest reusing cooking water, on the premise that vitamins and minerals lost from vegetables during cooking end up in the water. This may well be true, but unfortunately a lot of other things end up in the water as well—pesticides and nitrites from commercially grown produce along with many of the harmful compounds listed above, particularly oxalic acid. The solution is to steam lightly and not very long. Most of the vitamins and minerals will remain in the vegetables where they belong, and the small loss will be compensated by the fact that light cooking makes the nutrients in vegetables more readily available and assimilated.

There are several broad categories of vegetables. First are the dark green, leafy vegetables, such as spinach, chard and beet greens. These contain abundant vitamins and minerals, particularly B vitamins, calcium and trace minerals, and should be included in the diet on a regular basis—at least once or twice a week. A second category is the cruciferous vegetables—cabbage, chard, Brussels sprouts, cauliflower and broccoli—which contain natural chemicals shown to block the formation of tumors in the digestive tract. Other categories are tubers (potatoes and sweet potatoes), root vegetables (carrots, turnips, parsnips and beets), the squash family (including zucchini), the lily family (onions, leeks and garlic) and the nightshade family (tomatoes, eggplant and peppers).

While all vegetables contain good things, we must once again caution that our choice of vegetables must take into account individual food sensitivities. Vegetables from the nightshade family may cause arthritis and painful joints in sensitive individuals. The cruciferous vegetables have been in the spotlight recently, but they are not for everybody—their high sulphur content may cause problems for some. Vegetables from the onion family tend to stimulate the glands and should therefore be avoided by those suffering from fatigue or weak adrenal function. Almost any vegetable can cause adverse and allergic reactions if eaten to excess—that is why variety is so important.

The most important piece of equipment you will need for vegetable preparation is a two-part, stainless steel steamer—like a double boiler with holes in the bottom of the upper pan. A wooden cutting board, a heavy stainless steel or cast-iron frying pan and a collection of sharp knives complete the list of items necessary for successful vegetable preparation. A clay pot is also useful—potatoes are delicious cooked this way.

Frozen vegetables are acceptable on occasion, but most of the vegetables you eat should be fresh and, if possible, organically or biodynamically grown. All commercial vegetables should be washed in water with a little Clorox bleach, hydrogen peroxide or Dr. Bronner's Sal Suds (see Kitchen Tips and Hints, page 69), and then thoroughly rinsed to remove chemical residues.

Dark green, leafy vegetables tend to concentrate nitrites when commercially grown with high-nitrogen fertilizer. In the intestinal tract these nitrates may be transformed into potent carcinogens. Nitrates also tend to form in cooked vegetables during storage; for this reason we caution you against eating reheated vegetables, particularly green vegetables.

Don't hesitate to put butter on your steamed vegetables. The fat-soluble vitamins and the Price Factor in butter are just what your body needs to fully utilize minerals in plant foods. Season vegetables lightly after cooking with sea salt.

The artichoke is of Arabic origin—called *al-kharshuf* in the Middle East—which comes to us by way of Italy. Like all members of the thistle family, artichokes concentrate iodine when it is in the soil. Research indicates that the artichoke can benefit the intestinal tract and the heart; it has been shown to reduce blood clotting time and to neutralize certain toxic substances. Studies in Japan and Switzerland show that artichokes can lower blood cholesterol. In fact, a constituent of artichoke called cynarin has been formulated into a cholesterol-lowering drug. Folk wisdom values the artichoke as a stimulant to the bile. Artichokes are in season in the spring. Choose artichokes that seem heavy for their size and whose leaves are more or less free from dark streaks. SWF

Asparagus is an Italian vegetable that dates from the Renaissance. Much prized in Europe, asparagus dishes are featured in fine restaurants during the peak season—May and June. One restaurant in Germany lists 209 separate asparagus dishes on its menu!

Asparagus is a good source of rutin, a substance that prevents small blood vessels from breaking. Medieval medicine valued asparagus for the treatment of heart palpitations and as a diuretic. Asparagus is high in carotenoids, B Complex, vitamin C and vitamin E as well as potassium, iodine and zinc.

Asparagus must be fresh to be good. Check the tips to see that the little buds are distinct; if the tips have gone mushy, the asparagus is not worth buying. SWF

ARTICHOKES

Cut the stems off the artichokes and place with leaves up in a vegetable steamer or in a large pot containing about 1 inch of filtered water. Steam, covered, until tender, about 1/2 hour. Remove with tongs and place artichokes, leaves down, in a colander to drain. Remove the outermost leaves and serve warm or cold with basic dressing (page 129), herbed mayonnaise (page 138) or lemon butter sauce (page 151).

Stuffed Artichokes
Serves 4

4 artichokes
1/2 cup extra virgin olive oil
  or 1/2 cup melted butter
4 cloves garlic, peeled and mashed
2 cups whole grain bread
sea salt and pepper

Steam artichokes in a vegetable steamer as described above until just barely tender. Mix olive oil with garlic and bread crumbs and season to taste. Pull artichoke leaves open a bit and use scissors to snip points off leaves. Press stuffing down between leaves. Return to steamer for another 5 to 10 minutes. These are messy to eat but delicious.

ASPARAGUS

Trim off the tough ends and rinse well. If asparagus is of large diameter, you may want to pare off about an inch of green from the ends. Place in a vegetable steamer and steam about 5 minutes until stalks turn bright green and can be pierced easily with a fork. Don't overcook! Transfer to a heated serving dish, place a generous pat of butter on top and finish with a squeeze of lemon juice. May be kept warm in the oven for about 1/2 hour.

Asparagus with Sesame Seeds
Serves 6

2 1/2 pounds asparagus, trimmed
2 tablespoons extra virgin olive oil or melted butter
2 tablespoons shallots, minced
2 tablespoons sesame seeds, lightly toasted
juice of 1 lemon
sea salt

Place oil and asparagus in a glass baking dish and toss so that the asparagus is completely coated with oil. Bake at 400 degrees for about 8 minutes, shaking the dish every two minutes or so. Sprinkle on the shallots and sesame seeds and bake, with one or two shakes, for 1 minute more. Transfer to heated serving bowl and squeeze on lemon juice. Season to taste.

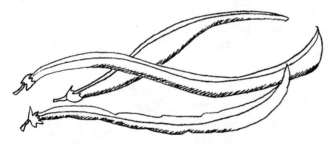

BEANS, FRENCH

These slender, tender beans are new in American markets and still too expensive for everyday dinner fare; but they are worth buying for special meals, as they make a beautiful addition to the plate. Best time to buy is late summer, when they are in season locally and have not been shipped long distances.

Snip off both ends. French beans can be steamed in a vegetable steamer, but better results are obtained from blanching. Bring a pot of salted filtered water to boil. Plunge in beans and cook rapidly for about 8 minutes, until they are tender. Pour beans into a colander and rinse with cold water. This will bring out an intense green color. Transfer to a heated serving dish and top with a generous pat of butter. Place in a warm oven to restore heat—they may be kept there for up to 1/2 hour before serving.

Strawberries lead the list of the thirteen most contaminated fruits and vegetables sold in American supermarkets. According to a 1993 Environmental Working Group study, on some farms strawberries are sprayed with 500 pounds of pesticides per acre. Red and green bell peppers come next, which are high in neurotoxic residues. Other highly contaminated foods include spinach, cherries, peaches, Mexican cantaloupe, celery, apples, apricots, green beans, Chilean grapes and cucumbers.

Fruits and vegetables from foreign countries are subject to even less stringent regulations than domestic varieties. Imported bananas, for example, often are treated with benomyl (linked to birth defects) and chlorpyrifos (a neurotoxin).

Among grains, rice and oats were found to be the most contaminated.

The solution? Buy organic, especially when it comes to the popular fruits and vegetables listed above. Even better, buy biodynamic, which is an all-natural farming technique developed by Rudolf Steiner, the multifaceted Austrian mystic and philosopher. In the U.S., biodynamic standards are higher than organic standards. Biodynamic crops are nourished with naturally composted manure from cows allowed to graze freely.

Many varieties of commercial fruits rot before they ripen—a sign of nutrient deficiencies. Fruits and vegetables from properly nourished soil, on the other hand, have good ripening and keeping qualities. They may cost a bit more, but the long-term benefits include personal good health and an economy in which the wealth is spread among thousands of independent farmers, rather than concentrated in the hands of a few multinational corporations. SWF

BEANS, GREEN

Green beans and French beans are a variety of legume; and, hence, the relative of peas, peanuts, lentils and the many varieties of dried beans. Their pods are edible because of selective breeding to make them flavorful at an early or immature stage of growth. Like their cousins, the dried beans, they are high in calcium, potassium and B-complex vitamins. They have a higher carotenoid content than the dried variety and are often more digestible. String beans were particularly recommended by the late physician Henry Bieler as a treatment for the pancreas and salivary glands because they are rich in alkaline-ash minerals. SWF

In movies with war themes, it is frequently the Marines who come to the rescue; in disease, it is just as frequently fresh and cooked vegetables which do the same thing. There is usually no need to rely on drugs. It must be remembered that all drugs are chemicals; the same chemicals in organic form are found in vegetables and other foodstuffs. Henry Bieler, MD *Food Is Your Best Medicine*

In the 1880's the great majority of Americans ate at home: three family meals a day, homemade, from whole foods.

In the 1980's the great majority of Americans do *not* eat three family meals a day at home, meals are *not* normally homemade and the whole foods are *not* chosen to any great extent. Joseph D. Beasley, MD and Jerry J. Swift, MA *The Kellogg Report*

In France our green or string beans are called *mange tous* and are considered inferior to the French beans or *haricots verts*. It is true that green beans are rather tough and unappetizing eaten whole. They are more tender when "French cut," which is quite easy with a food processor.

Cut each end from the bean with a knife, being careful to pull down at the same time so as to remove any strings. Break or cut the beans to fit sideways into your food processor. Fit the processor with the regular slicing blade and place the beans in sideways. When processed the result will be beautifully French-cut beans.

Place beans in a vegetable steamer and steam about 8 minutes until they have turned bright green and are just tender. Transfer to a heated bowl and toss with a generous pat of butter. May be kept in a warm oven for up to 1/2 hour before serving.

Green Beans with Almonds
Serves 6

1 1/2 pounds string beans, French cut
4 tablespoons butter
2/3 cup crispy almond slivers (page 515)

Steam beans as described above. Melt the butter in a frying pan, raise heat, add almonds and cook, stirring, until lightly browned. Be careful the almonds do not burn. Toss with the beans and keep warm in the oven until ready to serve.

Green Beans with Onions
Serves 6

1 1/2 pounds string beans, French cut
4 tablespoons butter
1/2 cup dehydrated onions

Steam the beans as described above. Meanwhile, melt butter in a frying pan, add onions and sauté, stirring, until lightly browned. Be careful the onions do not burn. Toss with beans and keep warm in the oven until ready to serve.

Stir Fry Green Beans with Cashews
Serves 6

2 pounds string beans, French cut
1 cup crispy cashews (page 515), chopped
4 tablespoons extra virgin olive oil or lard
1 teaspoon freshly grated ginger
1/4 cup naturally fermented soy sauce
1 cup filtered water, orange juice
*   or chicken stock (page 124)*
2 tablespoons arrowroot mixed with
*   2 tablespoons filtered water*
1 teaspoon raw honey
2 teaspoons toasted sesame oil
2 cloves garlic, peeled and mashed (optional)
1/2 teaspoon dried rosemary

Combine ginger, soy sauce, water or stock, honey, sesame oil, garlic and rosemary. Mix thoroughly with a wire whisk. Heat the oil or lard in a skillet or wok. Stir fry the beans until just tender, about 5 minutes. Add cashews and the sauce mixture and bring to a boil. Add the arrowroot mixture and simmer until sauce thickens and all the beans are well coated.

Go ahead and eat those veggies! They help prevent lung cancer, but it isn't just the betacarotene in them that protects you.

This is the finding of Loic Le Marchand, whose group recently finished a study at the Cancer Research Center of Hawaii in Honolulu, reported in the *Journal of the National Cancer Institute.*

Over and above beta carotene, not-so-well-known vegetable constituents, such as lutein, lycopene and indoles, could be virtually anonymous soldiers who battle to protect our lungs.

Le Marchand and associates discovered that crucifers, such a broccoli and cabbage, other green vegetables and tomatoes, reduce the risk of lung cancer as much as beta carotene-rich vegetables. Cabbage and broccoli have previously been linked with reducing the risk of colon cancer but not necessarily with lung cancer.

Indoles and related substances in vegetables have prevented various tumor formations in animals. In his human study, Le Marchand found that while a diet high in beta carotene reduced risk of lung cancer by three times in females and by two times in males, a diet of many different vegetables reduced the risk by seven times in females and by three times in males. Variety may be the spice of life, or, in the case of vegetables, it could be life itself. James F. Scheer *Health Freedom News*

BEAN SPROUTS

The bean from which the bean sprout grows is the mung bean, a small green bean used extensively in Asia. Mung bean sprouts are excellent sources of carotenoids, B complex and vitamin C plus phosphorus, potassium, calcium and iron. Bean sprouts are exceptionally high in enzymes, and these magic substances will survive a very brief steaming. SWF

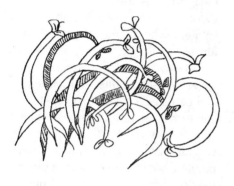

Among the many minerals contained in the beet one must cite first of all iron and copper, important trace minerals, and also calcium, phosphorus, potassium and sodium. Under certain types of agriculture, the amount of sugar in the red beet can be more than 5 percent. These natural sugars and the minerals that the beet contains are in balanced proportions and make of the beet an especially precious food. Beets help re-establish numerous functions of the body and a diet based on beets has an incontestable curative effect. Beets are permitted to diabetics and are used in cancer therapies. Because of its dark red color, the beet has for a long time been considered a blood restorative and a food that strengthens the entire organism. The beet should appear often on our tables. Annelies Schoneck *Des Crudités Toute L'Année*

Bean sprouts must be very fresh. Check that the little leaf is not shriveled, and cook them the day you buy them. Rinse in a colander and place in a vegetable steamer. Steam about one minute, or until just tender. Transfer to a heated serving bowl and toss with a little naturally fermented soy sauce.

Stir-Fry Bean Sprouts
Serves 6

4 cups bean sprouts
1 red pepper, seeded and cut into strips
3 carrots, peeled and cut into a julienne
1/4 pound Chinese peas, ends removed
4 tablespoons extra virgin olive oil or lard
1 teaspoon freshly grated ginger
1/4 cup naturally fermented soy sauce
1 cup water or chicken stock (page 124)
1 tablespoon arrowroot mixed with
    1 tablespoon filtered water
2 tablespoons toasted sesame seeds

Mix soy sauce, ginger and water or stock together and set aside. Heat olive oil or lard in a frying pan or wok. Stir-fry carrots a minute or two, add peppers and cook a minute more. Add Chinese peas and stir-fry another minute. Add liquid mixture to vegetables and bring to a boil. Add arrowroot mixture along with sprouts and sesame seeds and cook a minute more, stirring constantly, until sauce thickens and vegetables become coated. Serve immediately.

Bean Sprout Curry
Serves 4

1 bunch green onions, finely chopped
2 stalks celery, finely chopped
1/4 green pepper, finely chopped
1 apple, peeled and chopped
4 tablespoons butter

1 1/2 cups chicken stock (page 124)
2 tablespoons arrowroot mixed with
* 2 tablespoons filtered water*
1 tablespoon curry powder
pinch cayenne pepper
1/2 cup currants
3-4 cups bean sprouts
finely chopped crispy peanuts (page 514)
* for garnish*
finely chopped chives for garnish

Melt butter in a large, heavy skillet. Sauté onion, celery, pepper and apple about 1 minute. Add stock, currants, seasonings and arrowroot mixture. Sauté, stirring, until liquid begins to thicken. Add sprouts, mix well and cook until just tender, about 1 minute. Serve with basic brown rice (page 466) and garnish with peanuts and chives.

BEETS

Remove leaves, wash, and place in a heavy pan. Meanwhile, cut stems off the beets. There are two ways of cooking them. One is to cover with water and boil until tender. The other is to bake in a 250 degree oven for 2 hours or so or until tender. The later method is preferable from the nutritional point of view, but it takes longer. Peel the cooked beets, slice them and transfer to a heated serving bowl. Meanwhile, cover the greens and simmer on lowest heat. (Do not add water as the moisture adhering to the leaves is sufficient to steam them.) As soon as greens are wilted, remove to a strainer or colander. Press out the juice, chop the leaves coarsely and mix with sliced beets. Toss with a pat of butter or with a little butter that has been melted with one mashed clove of garlic and a squeeze of lemon juice.

Beets were developed by German gardeners in the Middle Ages. Long valued as a blood tonic, they are rich in calcium, iron, magnesium and phosphorus, as well as carotene, B complex and vitamin C.

Beets are so concentrated, nutritionally speaking, that many natural vitamins are derived from them. Dr. Bruce West recommends eating a few spoonfuls of beets per day—either raw, fermented or cooked—as a sure method of ingesting adequate vitamins and minerals on a regular basis and as a way of detoxifying the body as well. Beets and their tops contain special substances that protect the liver and stimulate the flow of bile. Beets and beet juice have been used successfully in cancer therapies.

Beet tops contain the same nutrients as the root with the added bonus of an exceptionally high carotenoid content. Always buy beets untrimmed as the leaves are a good indication of freshness, and make a habit of eating beet roots with their tops. The combination is excellent, nutritionally speaking, and the sweet beets are a good complement to their bitter greens. SWF

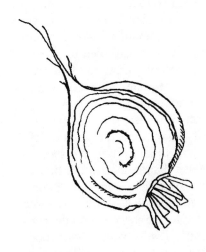

BROCCOLI

Broccoli tops the list of common vegetables for nutrient content. It is high in carotenoids and vitamin C and contains B complex, calcium, phosphorus and potassium as well. New research reveals that broccoli is rich in chromium, a mineral that protects against diabetes. It contains some protein and is a good source of fiber. Like all vegetables of the crucifer family, broccoli is rich in indoles, a potent anticancer substance, as well as such antioxidant and anticancer agents as quercitin and glutathione. Not surprisingly, many studies show that broccoli is the preferred vegetable among those with lower rates of all kinds of cancer. Organic broccoli is now almost universally available—it is, of course, superior in taste and nutrient content to broccoli grown with high-nitrate fertilizers. SWF

The more defective this individual biochemical makeup is, by inheritance, enzyme deficiency, malnutrition, harbored infection or otherwise, the more likely the person is to develop maladaptive, allergic-like symptoms on exposure to food and environmental contacts. Our peculiar cultural preferences for eating only a few types of food, for example, or our heavy consumption of refined carbohydrates. . . add materially to a developing state of nutritional deficiency with a corresponding multiple symptom production in our body tissue systems. Likewise, our nation's propensity to consume nutritionally deficient junk foods further increases the defective tissue states in the human body. These defective states undermine an individual's ability to handle without symptom formation the contacts he has with toxins, pollens, foods or chemical fumes. William H. Philpott, MD *Victory Over Diabetes*

Broccoli not only ranks number one in nutrient content, it is also the easiest vegetable of all to prepare. Cut into flowerets and steam about 5 minutes or until broccoli has turned bright green and is just tender. Transfer to a heated serving dish, top with a generous pat of butter and keep warm in the oven.

Broccoli Timbales
Serves 6

1 large bunch broccoli
4 tablespoons butter, softened
4 tablespoons piima cream or
    creme fraiche (page 84)
4 eggs, lightly beaten
1 small onion, very finely chopped
1/2 teaspoon sea salt
1/4 teaspoon pepper

Steam broccoli according to the master recipe. Place in food processor and pulse a few times until well chopped. Add butter, cream, eggs and onion and blend well. Season to taste. Pour into six well-buttered conical timbale molds. Place in a pan of hot water and bake at 350 degrees for 20 minutes. Loosen timbales with a knife and turn onto a warmed platter or individual plates.

BRUSSELS SPROUTS

Cut tough ends off the sprouts and remove loose outer leaves. Make a little cross in the end. This will help the sprouts cook more evenly. Steam for 5 to 10 minutes until just tender—do not overcook! Transfer to a heated serving dish and top with a pat of butter. An alternate method is to cut the sprouts lengthwise into quarters, steam them about 1 minute and then sauté in a mixture of butter and olive oil.

BUTTERNUT SQUASH

Cut squash in half, remove seeds and set cut side down in a buttered glass baking pan with about 1/2 inch of water. Bake at 350 degrees until tender, about 1 hour. Meanwhile, melt equal parts of butter and raw honey together in a pitcher set in hot water. (Don't let the mixture surpass 118 degrees or the valuable amylase enzymes in the honey will be destroyed.) To serve, place cut side of squash up and pour a little honey-butter mixture into each cavity.

Butternut Squash Purée with Pecans
Serves 6

3 butternut squash
3 eggs, lightly beaten
1/4 teaspoon nutmeg
sea salt and pepper
2 tablespoons butter
3/4 cup crispy pecans (page 513), chopped

Cook the squash as described above, scoop out into a food processor and blend until smooth. Add eggs and nutmeg and season to taste. Transfer purée to an ovenproof serving dish. Melt the butter and pour over the purée. Sprinkle on pecans. Bake at 350 degrees for about 30 minutes.

First planted in America by Thomas Jefferson, Brussels sprouts are a flavorful winter vegetable that can be ruined by overcooking. They contain a similar vitamin profile to other members of the cruciferous family; namely, carotenoids and vitamin C along with the minerals phosphorus and calcium. Like cabbage and broccoli, Brussels sprouts contain a host of anticancer substances.

To remove insects from Brussels sprouts, cauliflower, artichokes, etc., soak thirty minutes in water to which 2 tablespoons of salt and vinegar have been added. Rinse well and proceed with cooking. SWF

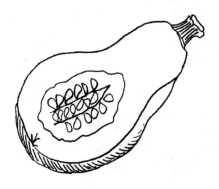

Why did the McGovern Committee ignore the scientific literature incriminating vegetable fats in atherosclerosis? Extensive studies with monkeys fed vegetable oils proved beyond a doubt that peanut oil. . . and other vegetable fats cause severe hardening of the arteries. With the current fixation on cholesterol in the nutritional establishment, it is important to note that on peanut oil the serum cholesterol remained low. The peanut oil may kill you, but you can die with a normal cholesterol. William Campbell Douglass, MD *The Milk Book*

Among vegetables, there's no question that the cabbage family gets the prize. It is rich in vitamin C, in protective indoles and in fiber and contains, as well, lesser quantities of other protective substances. Broccoli and Brussels sprouts are the richest in cancer-inhibiting elements. A study done with two groups of volunteers confirmed the effectiveness of these crucifers. The first group ate what might be called a normal diet, while the second was given a diet rich in vegetables from the cabbage family, notably Brussels sprouts. Both groups ingested carcinogenic substances. The group eating a diet rich in crucifers eliminated these substances more quickly than the other group. Other vegetables rich in anticancer substances are the pumpkin and squash family. . . rich in vitamin C, carotene, and fiber, and carrots. Most other vegetables also help protect us from carcinogens. According to some studies, beets have specific anticancer properties. Claude Aubert *Dis-Moi Comment Tu Cuisines*

Unhappily, anxiety-ridden Americans, following the warning voices of televised drug commercials and newspaper ads, consider health something that can be purchased in a bottle at the drugstore; they forget, or never knew, that health can be found only by obeying the clear-cut laws of nature. Henry Bieler, MD *Food Is Your Best Medicine*

CABBAGE, GREEN

Cooked cabbage is delicious if prepared properly. The secret is to shred the cabbage very finely and to cook until just tender.

Remove outer leaves and shred cabbage with a sharp knife, or by cutting into quarters and feeding it through the food processor fitted with a fine slicing disk. Rinse cabbage with filtered water and place in a heavy skillet. Do not shake water off—water adhering to cabbage will be sufficient to cook it. Top cabbage with a little salt, plenty of pepper and several generous pats of butter. Turn on heat and lower when cabbage starts to steam. Cook about 5 minutes, covered, or until cabbage is just wilted.

CABBAGE, RED

Red cabbage may be prepared as green cabbage, but it takes a little longer to cook. It has a stronger flavor than green cabbage and is therefore more appetizing when dressed up according to the following recipes.

Red Cabbage, Dutch Style
Serves 6

1 medium red cabbage, shredded
1 bay leaf
1/2 teaspoon cloves
1/2 teaspoon sea salt
1 teaspoon raw honey
1/4 teaspoon cinnamon
1 cup water
2 apples, peeled and quartered
2 tablespoons butter
1 tablespoon raw wine vinegar

Rinse cabbage with filtered water and place in a heavy pan. In a small pan, mix bay leaf, cloves, salt, honey and cinnamon with water and bring to a boil. Pour over the cabbage and cook gently about 20 minutes. Add the apple and cook another 10 minutes. Remove cabbage with a slotted spoon to a heated serving dish and toss with the butter and vinegar.

Red Cabbage with Orange
Serves 6

1 medium red cabbage
1 small onion, peeled and chopped
grated rind of two oranges
juice of two oranges, strained
1 teaspoon sea salt
1 clove garlic, peeled and finely chopped
1 tablespoon raw honey
3 tablespoons whey (page 87)
  or raw wine vinegar
4 tablespoons butter

Shred cabbage. Combine onion, orange rind, orange juice, garlic, salt, honey and whey or vinegar. Pour over the cabbage and toss well. Marinate overnight, tossing occasionally.

Melt butter in a large saucepan or frying pan. Add cabbage mixture and bring to a simmer. Reduce heat, cover and cook gently for about 1 hour, uncovered, until cabbage is tender and liquid has evaporated.

Since ancient times, cabbage has been a source of vitamin C during the winter months for peoples living in northern climes, from the Orient to the New World. Cabbage is a good source of fiber as well as of carotenoids, B complex, vitamin C, potassium, magnesium and calcium.

Raw cabbage has more vitamin C than cooked but cannot be recommended on a daily basis because of the presence of goitrogens, substances that block the formation of thyroid hormone. This in turn makes it difficult for the liver to convert the plant form of vitamin A (carotene or carotenoids) into the animal form, which it needs for thousands of biochemical processes.

On the plus side, cabbage is rich in substances that block the formation and spread of tumors. Folk medicine values the cabbage for the stomach; Irish girls traditionally drank cabbage water for the complexion. Recent research has shown the juice of cabbage to be highly therapeutic for ulcers. SWF

Latest research on this subject indicates that sodium intake contributes less to hypertension than the ratio of sodium to potassium. In other words, it may be possible to prevent high blood pressure by adding more potassium to the diet rather than necessarily lessening the dietary sodium. . . [researchers] suggest that people take an extra helping of a potassium rich food—for instance, a banana, some fresh broccoli, an avocado, Brussels sprouts, cauliflower, potatoes with skins, cantaloupe, dates, prunes and raisins. James F. Scheer *Health Freedom News*

CARROTS

A native of Afghanistan and a relative of celery, parsnips, caraway, cilantro, cumin and dill, the carrot is a most useful, versatile, nutritious and popular vegetable, revered not only as an accompaniment to other dishes but as a base ingredient for soups, stocks and stews. In hotels in the town of Vichy, France, carrots are eaten daily as part of a cure for overloaded digestion; and many cultures have valued them as an aphrodisiac. Research has shown that three raw carrots, eaten daily, lower blood cholesterol; and that a single carrot per day cuts the risk of lung cancer among smokers in half. Carrots are rich sources of carotenoids, B vitamins, phosphorus, calcium and all important iodine. SWF

Many people hate carrots because their only experience of this staple vegetable has been carrots boiled to death in water. A much more satisfactory way to prepare carrots is to sauté them in butter. Don't be afraid to peel carrots. Unlike potatoes, which have nutrients concentrated just under the skin, the vitamins and minerals of carrots are more evenly distributed.

Peel carrots and cut into sticks about 3 inches long and 1/4 inch in width, or cut them into a large julienne using the julienne blade of a food processor. Sauté in butter about 20 minutes until golden but still slightly firm.

Carrots Vichy
Serves 4

1 pound carrots
filtered water
4 tablespoons butter
2 tablespoons honey
sea salt

Peel carrots and slice into rounds. Cover with filtered water and bring to a boil. Add butter and honey. Boil uncovered, skimming frequently, until liquid is reduced to almost nothing and carrots are well coated. You may want to add a tablespoon or two more of butter at the end. Season to taste.

Roasted Carrot Purée
Serves 4-6

2 pounds carrots, peeled and cut into 1-inch pieces
1/4 cup extra virgin olive oil
3/4 cup piima cream or creme fraiche (page 84)
1/2 teaspoon sea salt

Toss carrots with olive oil and strew in a baking pan. Bake at 400 degrees about 1 hour or until carrots become well browned and tender. Watch carefully that they do not burn. Transfer to a food processor and process with cultured cream and salt.

WEDNESDAY
NIGHT DINNER

Avocado
Grapefruit Salad
❀❀❀❀❀

Veal Chops
❀❀❀

Potato Quarters
❀❀❀

Carrots Vichy
❀❀❀

Pickled Beets

Carrot Curry

Serves 6-8

1 pound carrots, peeled and cut into sticks
2 tablespoons butter
2 tablespoons extra virgin olive oil
1 teaspoons mustard seeds
2 teaspoons ground cumin
2 teaspoons ground coriander
2 teaspoons turmeric
1 teaspoon fenugreek seeds
1 teaspoon dried dill
pinch cayenne pepper
2 medium onions, sliced
2 red bell peppers, cut into a julienne
3-4 cups chicken stock (page 124)
grated rind of 1 orange
1 tablespoon freshly grated ginger
2 tablespoons arrowroot mixed with
    2 tablespoons water
2 cups spinach leaves, chopped
sea salt
2 cups crispy cashews (page 515), chopped

Melt butter and olive oil in a large pot. Sauté spices for several minutes, stirring constantly. Add onion and sauté until soft. Add peppers and carrots and sauté a few minutes more. Add stock, ginger and orange rind and bring to a boil. Reduce to simmer and stir in cashews. Simmer, uncovered, until liquid is partially evaporated and carrots and peppers are soft. Spoonful by spoonful, add arrowroot mixture until desired thickness is obtained. Season to taste. Stir in spinach and simmer another minute more. Serve with basic brown rice (page 466) and fruit chutney (page 106) or raisin chutney (page 108).

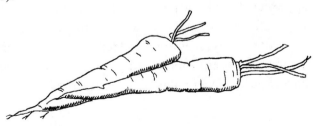

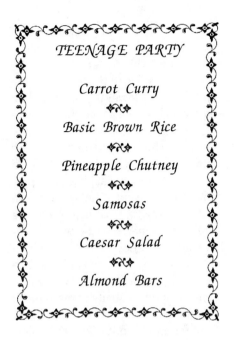

TEENAGE PARTY

Carrot Curry
❀❀❀
Basic Brown Rice
❀❀❀
Pineapple Chutney
❀❀❀
Samosas
❀❀❀
Caesar Salad
❀❀❀
Almond Bars

A sharp profile of how we Americans die, and what disables us in life, shows that chronic degenerative diseases are the enemy we all face. Heart attacks and heart disease, cancer, strokes, high blood pressure, diabetes, arthritic conditions, obesity, mental illnesses, addiction—and a host of other chronic conditions [including] cirrhosis, kidney disease, back pain, chronic bronchitis, multiple sclerosis, migraine, ulcers, phlebitis, chronic impotence, asthma, allergies, lupus erythematosus, cataracts, ileitis and colitis, diverticulitis and diverticulosis, chronic constipation, gastritis, insomnia, anxiety, depression and chronic fatigue.

The superb accomplishments of modern medicine in managing accidents, infections and surgery will be of little help curing any of these. Before the "diseases of civilization" medicine is almost as powerless as we are. Joseph D. Beasley, MD and Jerry R. Swift, MA *The Kellogg Report*

Mark Twain once called the cauliflower a "cabbage with a college education." This does not speak very highly for college educations, as the cauliflower is lower in nutrients than its cousin broccoli. Nevertheless, cauliflower is a staple winter vegetable and not to be despised for its fiber and mineral content. It is also high in biotin, a B vitamin that plays an important role in the body's fat production. Studies in Norway indicate that the cauliflower may give better protection against cancer of the colon than its cousins broccoli and cabbage. The new purple varieties now seen in some markets actually contain more carotenoids than white cauliflower. You needn't be put off by the color, they taste fine. SWF

The cooked vegetables are better since raw vegetables are usually too bulky to allow very much mineral to be obtained from them. Some of the best of the cooked vegetables are cauliflower, brussels sprouts, asparagus tips and celery. Weston Price, DDS *Letter to His Nieces and Nephews* 1934

Chard is a member of the beet family, selectively bred for its leaves rather than its root. Although chard is often referred to as Swiss chard, the champions of this versatile vegetable are the French who add it to soups, stuffings, patés and pancakes. Like all dark green leafy vegetables, chard is rich in iron, calcium, magnesium, vitamin C and carotenoids. Chard should always be eaten cooked as it contains oxalic acid that may irritate the mouth and intestinal tract. These are neutralized during cooking. Chard grown with high-nitrate commercial fertilizers may also be high in nitrates. Avoid buying chard that is not organically grown. SWF

CAULIFLOWER

Separate cauliflower into flowerets. Steam about 10 minutes or until just tender. Transfer to a heated bowl and toss with a generous pat of butter, pepper, sea salt and a few grindings of nutmeg.

Breaded Cauliflower
Serves 6

1 head cauliflower
6 tablespoons melted butter
2 cups whole grain bread crumbs
4 tablespoons Parmesan cheese, finely powdered
sea salt and pepper

Steam cauliflower flowerets until not quite tender. Drain, pat dry and toss well with melted butter. Mix bread crumbs with cheese and season to taste. Dip each floweret into bread crumb mixture. Place flat side down in a buttered, glass baking dish. Bake at 350 degrees for about 15 minutes or until golden brown.

CHARD

Chard is one of many nutritious greens available year round. It is more bitter than spinach but less expensive.

Remove stalks from leaves and tear into pieces. Wash well in filtered water but do not shake off water. Place in a covered, heavy pan over a medium flame. When chard begins to simmer, reduce heat and simmer until just wilted. Using a slotted spoon, transfer to a serving dish. Use the back of the spoon to squeeze out any excess liquid, and pour this off. Cut up coarsely, toss with butter and season to taste with sea salt and pepper.

Alternately, sauté chopped red onion in a generous amount of butter. Chop chard coarsely, add to onions, cover and steam a minute or so until wilted.

CHESTNUTS

To cook chestnuts, sauté frozen or freshly peeled chestnuts in a little butter. Season to taste with sea salt, pepper and a little freshly grated nutmeg. (To peel chestnuts, see sidebar.)

Chestnut Purée
Serves 6

6 1/2 ounces (1 package) frozen chestnuts
    or 2 cups freshly peeled chestnuts
1 cup beef or chicken stock (page 122 or 124)
1/2 cup piima cream or creme fraiche (page 84)
sea salt and pepper

Cook chestnuts, uncovered, in stock until tender. Remove with a slotted spoon to food processor and process along with enough stock to achieve desired consistency. Blend in cream and season to taste. Transfer to a heated serving dish and keep warm in oven.

Chestnut-Stuffed Zucchini
Serves 6

2 cups chestnut purée
6 medium zucchini
sea salt

Trim ends off the zucchini and plunge into boiling salted, filtered water. Cook about 8 minutes or until just tender. Remove to a colander and rinse with water. Cut the zucchini lengthwise and scoop out center, leaving about 1/4 inch of outer flesh. Sprinkle insides with sea salt and place on paper towels, cut side down, for about 15 minutes to drain. Wipe insides with paper towel and fill with purée. Arrange in a buttered, glass baking dish and bake at 250 degrees for about 1/2 hour.

Highly prized in Europe, the chestnut is a vegetable almost completely absent from American tables. This may be because a blight destroyed America's vast chestnut forests in the early 1900's.

As the flesh is soft at maturity, chestnuts are consumed as vegetables. The chestnut has the lowest fat content of any edible nut and, conversely, a high carbohydrate content—hence the characteristic sweetness of the chestnut. They contain some protein and are rich in B vitamins, calcium, iron, phosphorus and potassium. Like the fruit of all trees whose roots extend far into the ground, chestnuts are a good source of trace minerals.

Chestnuts are in season in the fall. Select firm nuts with shiny skins.

To peel chestnuts, cut an X with a sharp knife on the flat side and roast or boil them for 10 to 15 minutes before removing the skin. Peeling chestnuts for purées, soups or stuffings is a chore; but fortunately peeled, frozen chestnuts are now available. Asian markets also carry peeled, dried chestnuts. These take all the work out of serving chestnuts and should set the stage for a comeback of this delicious vegetable. SWF

CORN

Were it not for corn, archeologists say, the Spaniards would have been mightily disappointed when they arrived in the Americas. . . .

Corn was what made the great civilizations of Central and South America possible. . . .

Christopher Columbus first sampled corn in Cuba. . . declaring it "most tasty boiled, roasted, or ground into flour." When he returned to Spain, he took along a few specimen Indians, some handfuls of gold dust, and a packet of corn kernels. These first seeds may not have made a big impression on Ferdinand and Isabella, but they quickly proved their value. Within a few years the Spaniards had introduced maize around the Mediterranean. By the mid 16th century corn was so familiar in the Southern European diet that it formed the basis of such national dishes as Italian *polenta* and the Romanian staple *mamaliga* (a sort of cornmeal mush). Corn also traveled to the Philippines and the rest of Asia; by 1560 it was a fixture in Chinese cooking, in everything from porridge to stir-fry. Portuguese traders, who used corn as slaveship stores, carried the grain to Africa. It was an instant success there: corn grew more rapidly than other grains and it needed very little cultivation . . . . But its advent in Africa was not an unmixed blessing. It produced something of a population boom, which may in turn have fed the slave trade. . . . And it led to a serious imbalance in the African diet. By the late 18th century many Africans ate almost nothing but corn and suffered from vitamin deficiency as a result. Africans today are still afflicted by pellagra or "mealie disease," a sickness related to malnutrition from over-reliance on corn. Mary Talbot *Newsweek*

Shuck and wash corn. Place sidewise in a frying pan with about 1/2 inch filtered water. Cover and steam lightly for 5-10 minutes or until corn is just tender. Don't let corn get mushy—it should still have some crunch. Serve with butter, herb butter (page 151) or pesto (page 144).

An alternate method is to leave the husks on corn and bake at 350 degrees until the green husks turn the color of straw. Remove and eat immediately.

You may also place the ears, husks on, in the coals of a barbecue, turning from time to time until corn is tender.

Corn off the Cob, Mexican Style
Serves 6

6 ears corn, cut off the cob
1 red pepper, seeded and chopped
1 green pepper, seeded and chopped
1 bunch green onions, chopped
4 tablespoons butter
sea salt
cracked pepper

Sauté peppers and onions gently in butter. Add corn, cover and cook, stirring occasionally, for 5-10 minutes or until corn is just tender. Season with sea salt to taste and lots of cracked pepper.

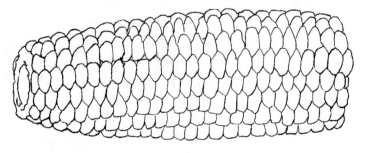

Corn off the Cob, Indian Style
Serves 6

6 ears of corn, cut off the cob
2 teaspoons mustard seed
1/2 teaspoon fenugreek seeds
1/4 teaspoon red pepper flakes
1 teaspoon freshly grated ginger
6 tablespoons butter
2 medium onions, peeled and chopped
1/2 teaspoon turmeric
2-4 jalapeno peppers, seeded and chopped
2 cloves garlic, peeled and minced
2 cups plain yoghurt
sea salt
1/4 cup cilantro, chopped

Sauté mustard seeds, fenugreek seeds, red pepper flakes and ginger in butter. Add onion and jalapeno peppers and sauté until tender. Add turmeric and stir around. Add corn and garlic and mix well. Simmer gently until corn is just tender. Stir in yoghurt and season to taste. Garnish with chopped cilantro.

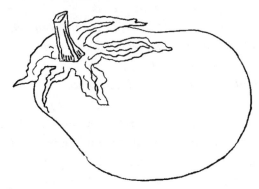

EGGPLANT

Eggplant contains a bitter juice that must be removed by salting. Peel the eggplant and cut into 1/2-inch cubes. Place in a bowl and toss with a generous spoonful of fine sea salt. Let stand, covered, about 1 hour. Rinse in a colander and pat cubes dry with paper towels or a tea towel. Use prepared eggplant cubes in the following recipes.

The evidence points to MSG sensitivity of epidemic proportions among the general population. But for most people the symptoms are vague: depression, headache, mild nausea, pressure around the eyes, tingling of the face, behavioral disturbances in children and mood swings, accentuating those already present in adolescents and also in adults. . . . Recently, we have witnessed important changes in personal habits. Families eat together less often. When they do sit down to a family meal, it often consists of convenience foods, such as fried chicken, frozen dinners, canned soups, vegetables in sauces and prepared salad mixes, all of which usually contain MSG. When you further consider that monosodium glutamate is an ingredient of seasoning salts, bouillon, hydrolyzed vegetable protein, meat tenderizers, most prepared spaghetti sauces, most sausages, some bacons and even such ethnic foods as gefilte fish and matzo balls, it becomes quite evident that the level of MSG in any family meal may be quite high. . . . MSG is a standard ingredient in most canned soups, soy sauces, bouillon cubes, soup stocks and frozen dinners. It is difficult to avoid even in the finest of restaurants. . . even the cigarette smoker may get additional MSG since tobacco leaves have been cured with MSG for smell and flavor enhancement. George R. Schwartz, MD *In Bad Taste: The MSG Syndrome*

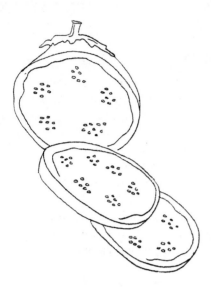

Although the eggplant is associated with Mediterranean cooking, its original home is tropical Asia. Primitive forms in this part of the world were very small and were invariably eaten pickled. The European name for eggplant—*aubergine*—is derived rather circuitously from the Sanskrit *vatin-ganah* which means "antiwind vegetable."

Until the potato reached Europe from the New World, the eggplant was the principle starchy vegetable prepared in numerous ways, including fried like potatoes.

Eggplant contains carotenoids, B complex, particularly folic acid, vitamin C, potassium, phosphorus and calcium. It contains some protein and is a good source of fiber. Eggplant contains compounds called scopoletin and scoparone that block convulsions. African folk medicine values the eggplant to relieve nervous excitement and to counteract epilepsy. It is also taken as a natural contraceptive. In Korea, dried eggplant is used to treat a variety of illnesses, including measles, alcoholism and stomach cancer. SWF

Broiled Eggplant Slices
Serves 6

2 large eggplants
sea salt
1 cup cilantro marinade (page 145)

Peel eggplants and slice lengthwise about 3/8-inch thick. Sprinkle with salt and let stand 1 hour. Rinse and pat dry. Place on a well-oiled cookie sheet and brush half the marinade on top of slices. Broil until golden, turn, brush other side with remaining marinade and broil again.

Ratatouille
Serves 8

2 large eggplants
1 zucchini, cut lengthwise and thinly sliced
1 green pepper, seeded and cut into strips
2 onions, peeled and sliced
4 tomatoes, peeled, seeded and chopped
4 cloves garlic, peeled and mashed
1 teaspoon dried thyme
about 3/4 cup extra virgin olive oil

There are two secrets to a good ratatouille: One is to sauté all the vegetables separately; the second is to bake your casserole in a shallow open pan so that most of the liquid evaporates. Peel and cube eggplant and prepare according to master recipe (page 383). Sauté eggplant cubes in batches in several tablespoons olive oil. Remove with a slotted spoon to an oiled rectangular pyrex baking dish. Sauté zucchini, pepper, onions and tomatoes in succession, adding more olive oil as necessary and removing to casserole. (To peel tomatoes, see page 70.) Add mashed garlic and thyme to casserole. Mix well and bake, uncovered, at 350 degrees for at least 1 hour. Ratatouille often tastes better reheated the next day.

Eggplant Curry
Serves 6

2 large eggplants
2 medium onions, peeled and chopped
1 teaspoon fenugreek seeds
1 tablespoon ground coriander
1 tablespoon ground cumin
1 teaspoon turmeric
1/4 teaspoon cayenne pepper
1 teaspoon freshly grated ginger
4 tomatoes, peeled, seeded and chopped
1/4 cup cilantro, chopped
about 1/2 cup extra virgin olive oil

To peel tomatoes, see page 70. Peel and cube eggplant and prepare according to the master recipe (page 383). Sauté eggplant cubes in batches in olive oil and transfer to a rectangular pyrex baking dish. Sauté the onions and spices in olive oil until onions are tender. Add remaining ingredients to onions except chopped cilantro. Simmer a few minutes, stirring, until well mixed. Add to casserole and mix well. Bake, uncovered, at 350 degrees about 1 hour. Garnish with chopped cilantro.

JERUSALEM ARTICHOKES

Peel tubers and plunge into boiling filtered water. Cook for about 15 minutes, adding some fresh lemon juice to the cooking water during the last 5 minutes. Drain in a colander. They may now be sliced and sautéed in butter and olive oil, or mashed with butter, freshly grated ginger, salt and pepper.

An alternate method is to place washed but unpeeled tubers in a clay pot. Add about 1/2 cup of filtered water to the pot, cover and bake at 200 degrees for about 6 hours, or until very tender. (They will turn quite black.) To serve, peel and mash with butter, salt and pepper.

Jerusalem artichokes or "sunchokes" are actually the root or tuber of a type of sunflower native to North America. They resemble ginger root, and their flavor has been compared to water chestnuts. They provide carotenes, B vitamins, potassium, calcium and magnesium and are an excellent source of iron.

European culinary writers at first greeted the sunchoke with enthusiasm but soon discovered that the vegetable—so easy to grow and store—had a drawback. They "cause a filthy, loathsome, stinking wind within the body," said the Englishman John Goodyer in 1617. The tuber can cause flatulence because about 50 percent of its dry weight is made up of inulin, a long-chain starch composed of fructose molecules. The human digestive system lacks enzymes to break down inulin into absorbable sugars.

Fortunately, inulin dissolves in hot water, so the vegetable must be eaten well cooked rather than raw. Lemon juice added to the cooking water will prevent the iron-rich flesh from turning black. The Indians of North America also roasted the Jerusalem artichokes in pits for as long as 48 hours, during which the flesh turns brown and jellylike and a sweet, distinctive flavor develops—a sign that the hard-to-decompose inulin has broken down into simple sugars. A long period of cold storage will also cause most of the inulin to be converted into fructose. Raw or slightly cooked Jerusalem artichokes have been recommended for diabetics because most of the starch is unavailable. Unfortunately, when undercooked these tubers can cause severe intestinal distress. But diabetics can still enjoy properly prepared Jerusalem artichokes by mixing them with plenty of butter or cream, so that absorption of simple sugars into the bloodstream occurs gradually. SWF

KALE

Kale is one of several dark green leafy vegetables of the cabbage family, related to collards and mustard greens. All of these greens provide calcium, iron and carotenoids in abundance, as well as many anticancer factors. Kale and related greens should always be eaten cooked—but not overcooked—so that the oxalic acid they contain is neutralized. Make an effort to buy organically grown kale. Dark green, leafy vegetables grown in nitrogen fertilized soils tend to concentrate nitrites, compounds that are transformed into carcinogenic nitrates and nitrosamines in the intestine. SWF

Remove stems, wash well in filtered water, tear into pieces and place in a large covered pot. Place over a medium flame. When kale begins to simmer, reduce heat. Simmer about 8 minutes until leaves are wilted. Transfer to a strainer or colander and squeeze out liquid. Chop coarsely, place in a heated serving dish and toss with a generous pat of butter.

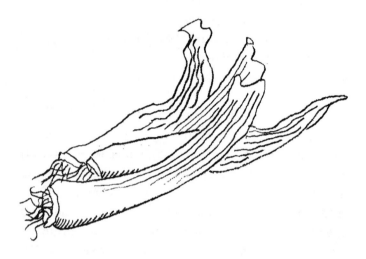

LEEKS

Leeks were once the staple vegetable of Europe. Unfortunately, this fine root fell from favor in the 17th century, along with onions and garlic and any food that would "taint the breath." In recent years, leeks have made something of a comeback. They can always be used in place of onions although they have a slightly more pungent flavor than their bulbous cousins. Leeks are good sources of carotenoids, B complex and vitamin C and are considered salutary for the liver.

Buy leeks that have not been trimmed as the leaves are your indication of freshness. Both the white part and the green should be used.

Leeks are often gritty, and it is important to clean them well. To clean leaks, cut off end, remove outer leaf and slit lengthwise into the center. Open up and clean all layers under running water. SWF

Braised Leeks
Serves 6

6 medium leeks
2 cups beef stock (page 122)
1 cup grated Gruyere cheese

Trim ends off leeks and split lengthwise. Rinse well and set in a pyrex pan. Bring beef stock to a boil and pour over leeks. Bake at 350 degrees for about 1/2 hour or until stock has reduced and leeks are tender. Sprinkle on cheese and melt under broiler for a few minutes. Serve immediately.

Vegetable Leek Medley
Serves 6

2 medium leeks
2 zucchini
2 carrots
1 red pepper
4 tablespoons butter
sea salt and pepper

The secret of this attractive dish is proper preparation—the vegetables should be cut into small and uniform pieces. Cutting can be done in advance, and the dish prepared just before your meal.

Clean leeks, slice crosswise at 1/4-inch intervals and set side. Cut ends off zucchini and make thick peelings of the skin. Cut the skin into a fine julienne and set aside. (Use the inner part for soups.) Peel the carrots and cut into a fine julienne. Seed the pepper and cut into thin, 1-inch strips.

Sauté carrots and leeks in butter. When they are just tender, add the pepper and cook about 1 minute. Finally, add zucchini and sauté another minute. Season to taste.

LIMA BEANS

Plunge freshly hulled or frozen lima beans in boiling filtered water and cook about 8 minutes or until tender. Drain in a colander and transfer to a heated serving dish. Toss with butter and season to taste with sea salt and pepper. You may want to first melt the butter and add to it one or two mashed garlic cloves.

Every new concept developed in medical science points the way to a new area awaiting further exploration. Discarding both the use of drugs and the germ theory of disease opened the way for me to explore new methods of eliminating the stagnating waste products from the body. Briefly stated my position is: improper foods cause disease; proper foods cure disease. In upholding this theses, I have been in disagreement, at times sharp, with organized orthodox medicine. Henry Bieler, MD *Food Is Your Best Medicine*

Lima beans are one of the few beans that are eaten both dried, as a legume, and fresh, as a vegetable. They grow well in hot climates.

Lima beans contain B complex vitamins, iron, potassium and phosphorus and a fair amount of protein. They contain more starch and less fat than most beans.

If you grow your own lima beans, you will be able to enjoy them freshly hulled. Avoid the hulled lima beans that sometimes appear in supermarkets and gourmet shops—these are usually dosed with preservatives. If you do not have a garden, your best bet is frozen lima beans, only slightly inferior, nutritionally speaking, to freshly hulled beans. SWF

Dr. William A. Albrecht, the famous soil specialist, reminds us that plants will make a lot of growth, just as you and I will, even when certain wanted minerals are missing. But the plants themselves will be different. Thus, cabbage is one thing if grown on one kind of soil, another if grown on another kind of soil. There are more minerals in it, or less, depending on the minerals in the soil; and, apparently, more or less proteins and vitamins in it. The same is true of carrots, beets, peas, oranges, apples, potatoes, sweet corn or any other plant product we use as food. The calcium concentration of a lettuce leaf can be varied twofold and spinach threefold, according to the calcium in the soil . . . the same mineral variations occur in grasses and other plants eaten by domestic animals; and what they eat, in turn, affects their products which we eat. Our beefsteaks, pork chops, lamb roasts and omelets can be mineral-shy if the cows, hogs, lambs and chickens were shortchanged on their minerals. "Are We Starving To Death?" *The Saturday Evening Post 1945*

Simple Succatash
Serves 6

2 cups shelled lima beans
6 ears corn, cut off the cob
4 tablespoons butter
1/2 cup piima cream or creme fraiche (page 84)
1/2 cup chicken stock (page 124)
sea salt and pepper

Succatash comes from the Narragansett Indian word "misick-quatash," meaning "ear of corn." Indian succatash consisted of beans, corn kernels, dog meat and bear grease. The succatash that finds its way to American tables has a slightly different list of ingredients.

Sauté corn in butter until just tender. Add lima beans, cream and stock. Bring to a boil and skim. Simmer, uncovered, until the liquid has reduced and beans are tender. Season to taste. Succatash should be soupy, not too thick, and it is served in bowls.

Gourmet Succatash
Serves 8-12

2 cups shelled lima beans
6 ears of corn, cut off the cob
2 cups french beans, cut into 1-inch pieces
4 tablespoons butter
1 bunch green onions, chopped
1 red pepper, chopped
1 cup piima cream or creme fraiche (page 84)
1 cup chicken stock (page 124)
sea salt and pepper

Sauté onion and pepper in butter. Add remaining ingredients, bring to a boil and skim. Simmer, uncovered, for about 10 minutes or until beans are tender. Season to taste and ladle into heated serving bowls.

MUSHROOMS

Mushrooms must be very fresh or they are not worth cooking. Remove stems, wash well and, most importantly, dry well. They can now be sautéed in olive oil and butter either whole, quartered or in slices. To sauté whole, melt butter and olive oil until it froths. Place mushrooms top side down in pan. When this side is golden, turn to other side. Sauté another minute and transfer to heated platter or serving dish. Sauté sliced or quartered mushrooms in small batches or they will not brown.

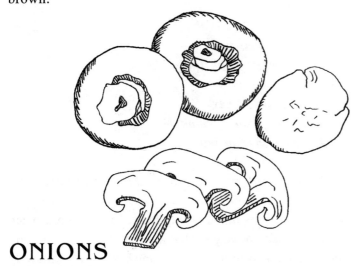

Mushrooms belong to the fungus family, one of the most primitive of all plant groups. Actually, the mushroom is the fruit of the fungus, which grows underground. Mushrooms contain over 90 percent water and thus act as sponges, absorbing the flavors of other foods with which they are cooked. They contain protein, phosphorus, potassium, calcium, iron and B complex vitamins, particularly biotin. Mushrooms are also rich in selenium, necessary for a healthy heart and circulatory system. Certain varieties of mushroom have long been valued for their medicinal properties in the Orient, and in recent years the Japanese have done some interesting research in this area. A substance called adenosine has been isolated from the tree-ear mushroom; it has potent blood thinning and anticoagulating properties. Just a small amount of black tree-ear mushroom can have a profound effect on reducing blood stickiness, clots and plaque buildup. Other commercially available mushrooms that seem to have these positive effects on the blood include the shiitake, enoki and oyster mushrooms. These mushrooms may also have anticancer properties. Other commercially grown mushrooms seem to be devoid of specific pharmacological effects, but they are still valuable in the diet for their trace mineral and B vitamin profile. SWF

ONIONS

This versatile vegetable is usually used in conjunction with other vegetables, but it also performs well on its own.

Onion Compote
Serves 6

6 large onions, peeled and thinly sliced
4 tablespoons butter
2 tablespoons extra virgin olive oil

In a heavy skillet, cook onion in butter and olive oil on low heat for 1 hour or more, stirring occasionally. Onions will turn light brown and develop a caramel taste. This is delicious with rib roast (page 332).

The onion species—a subset of the lily family—is ubiquitous, and no cuisine has developed that does not use the onion or one of its many cousins. They may have first been cultivated in Asia or India, but wild onions are native in many localities including North America. The Great Lakes Indians called them *She-kheony*, and it is from this Indian word that the city of Chicago derives its name. Onions are valued for their distinct flavor, which enhances the flavors of other ingredients in any dish; and they are a particularly good marriage with bland, starchy foods, such as legumes or potatoes.

Onions contain carotenoids, B complex vitamins—including all-important B_6—and vitamin C, calcium, magnesium, potassium and sulphur compounds. They are universally valued for their medicinal properties, which include improvement of kidney function and antibacterial qualities. According to some researchers, half a cup of raw onions per day is an excellent means of protecting the blood from a tendency to coagulate and clot. Onions also have been shown to lower elevated blood sugar levels in test animals. Pasteur was the first to recognize that onions have strong antibacterial powers; onions are also helpful in breaking up mucus in the throat, lungs and nasal passages. Finally, recent research indicates that

Onions Chardonnay
Serves 4

6 medium or 4 large onions,
*   peeled and very thinly sliced*
1 cup dry Chardonnay wine

Place onions and wine in a pan. Bring to a boil, reduce and simmer, stirring occasionally, until most of the liquid has evaporated. This is a nice accompaniment to fish.

Baked Onions with Pecans
Serves 8

4 large onions, peeled
1 cup chicken stock (page 124)
3 tablespoons butter
1 tablespoon honey
1 teaspoon grated lemon rind
1/4 teaspoon paprika
sea salt
1/2 cup crispy pecans (page 513), finely chopped

Cut onions in half along the equator and place cut side up in a buttered glass baking dish. Mix stock, butter, honey, lemon rind, and paprika and heat gently until well blended. Season to taste. Pour over onions. Bake, covered, for about 50 minutes at 350 degrees, basting occasionally, until onions are just tender. Remove cover, sprinkle with pecans and bake another 10 or 15 minutes until lightly browned.

Stuffed Onions
Serves 8

4 large onions
2 tablespoons extra virgin olive oil
1 1/2 cups whole grain bread crumbs or
    basic brown rice (page 466)
1/4 cup crispy pine nuts (page 514)
1 teaspoon dried oregano
1/4 cup Parmesan cheese, grated
2 teaspoons parsley, finely chopped
1 egg, lightly beaten
sea salt and pepper

Cut onions in half along the equator and remove the inner part of the onion, leaving a shell two or three layers thick. Make a small slice on the bottom of each onion shell so that it will stand upright. Place shells in a buttered glass oven dish.

Chop the onion taken from the centers and sauté in olive oil until tender. Add rice or bread crumbs, pine nuts, oregano, cheese and parsley and mix well. Remove from heat, stir in the egg and season to taste. Fill the onion shells with the stuffing. Add a little water to the baking pan and bake at 300 degrees for 1 hour.

Glazed Pearl Onions
Serves 6

30 pearl onions, peeled
1 tablespoon butter
1 tablespoon extra virgin olive oil
1 teaspoon honey
1/2 cup filtered water or beef stock (page 122)
1/2 cup red wine vinegar (optional)
pinch of sea salt

onions, with their concentrated sulphur compounds, can be useful in treating cancer in some people. Onions also concentrate germanium when it is found in the soil. Germanium acts as an oxygen transporter and has been useful in cancer therapy.

On the other hand, certain yogic diets prohibit the onion because it is said to "increase body heat and the appetites." This may be because the onion acts as a stimulant to the adrenal glands. Those with weak adrenal glands should eat of the onion family sparingly as should individuals sensitive to sulphur-containing foods.

To peel small onions, remove ends and plunge briefly into boiling water. Skins will then come off easily. SWF

One of your greatest difficulties will be to provide the children and yourselves with sufficient of the fat-soluble activators and vitamins. We, being mammals, have bodies prepared to get these from milk and its butter-fat, which is not in skimmed milk. There is not much left for the children when the cream has been taken from the milk for the parents' coffee. Where possible, have June butter stored for winter use. Cod-liver oil can be given in moderate doses without injury and to great advantage. Seldom, however, should the child be given more than one teaspoonful a day for extended periods, because of toxic effects that often develop. It is better to take the cod-liver oil with the meal rather than before or after, as it aids in the utilization of the minerals in the food. Weston Price, DDS *Letter to His Nieces and Nephews* 1934

Scattered across the earth are people of vastly different races, cultures, body types, and belief systems. They live near mountains, oceans, rivers, deserts, tundra, tropics, forests and flatlands. Some have only fish and a few varieties of plants available to eat; some, an assortment of tropical fruits and vegetables; some have only yak milk, meat and a little grain; while others have enough fertile land and resources to raise crops, herd animals, and mass-produce every imaginable variety of food.

Is it sensible for any one people to tell another about the "true" ways to eat? Can a tribesman from West Africa whose staple food is cassava root tell an Eskimo he is wrong because his staple food is fish? Or can the Japanese tell the Mexicans of the absurdity of eating dairy, corn, hot peppers and food fried in lard, staple products completely unknown to native Japan? Marc David *Nourishing Wisdom*

The cranberry grows wild in marshy places in New England and as far south as North Carolina. First called "fen berries" by the settlers, they were soon incorporated into their diets. Eventually the name changed to "craneberry" or "cranberry" because the slender stems of the fruit curve like the neck of a crane.

As early as 1860, medical science recognized the value of cranberries or their juice for the treatment of urinary tract infections and other kidney problems. Cranberries raise the level of acid in the urine and act as an antibiotic. SWF

To peel small onions, see sidebar, page 391. Mix honey with stock or water and heat until honey is dissolved. Place onions, butter, oil, honey mixture and salt in a skillet large enough to accommodate the onions in one layer. Add the vinegar if you want a sour taste. Bring mixture to a boil, cover and cook a few minutes until the onions begin to soften. Remove lid from pan and continue cooking, stirring frequently, until liquid has evaporated and the onions become coated with glaze.

Onion-Cranberry Compote
Makes 4 cups

2/3 cup yellow raisins
2/3 cup dark raisins
1 1/2 cups hot filtered water
2 pounds small white onions, peeled
4 tablespoons butter
3/4 cup white wine vinegar
1 cup dry white wine
3 cloves garlic, peeled and minced
1/2 teaspoon dried thyme
1 teaspoon sea salt
1 2/3 cups fresh cranberries

This is an excellent substitute for sugary cranberry relish at Thanksgiving. To peel small onions, see sidebar, page 391.

Soak raisins in water for 10 minutes. Meanwhile, in a large saucepan, sauté onions in butter until well coated. Add wine and vinegar and boil down for several minutes. Add raisins with soaking liquid and remaining ingredients except cranberries. Liquid should just cover the onions—if not, add a little water. Simmer, covered, for about 1 hour, stirring occasionally. Remove cover, add cranberries and simmer uncovered for 15 to 30 minutes until liquid has thickened. Let cool. May be made up to 3 days in advance and stored in the refrigerator. Serve at room temperature.

PARSNIPS

The parsnip is a much maligned vegetable. When boiled in water, they are not very appetizing; but sautéed in butter they have a delicious taste and a nice texture. Remove ends, peel and cut into strips. Sauté in butter until golden and just tender.

Parsnip Purée
Serves 6-8

1 1/2 pounds parsnips, peeled and
*   cut into 1-inch pieces*
2 potatoes, baked (page 396)
1/2 cup piima cream or creme fraiche (page 84)
4 tablespoons butter, softened
1 teaspoon freshly grated ginger (optional)
pinch nutmeg
sea salt and pepper

Cook parsnips in boiling, salted water until tender, about 20 minutes. Drain and purée in a food processor along with scooped out potato flesh. (Save the skins for potato skins, page 524.) Add cream, butter and optional ginger and process until well blended. Season to taste. Transfer purée to a heated serving dish and keep warm in the oven.

Winter Root Medley
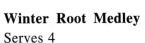
Serves 4

4 parsnips, peeled and cut into sticks
4 turnips, peeled and cut into quarters
1 rutabaga, peeled and cut into chunks
3 tablespoons butter
3 tablespoons extra virgin olive oil

In a heavy skillet, sauté vegetables in butter and olive oil until tender and golden brown.

The parsnip was more popular in medieval times than it is today. Several centuries ago parsnips gave way to carrots at human tables and developed a reputation as an animal food. The Italians believe that pigs raised for *prochutto*—raw ham—give a more flavorful product if raised on parsnips. In Russia the word for parsnip is *pasternak*, a common last name and the moniker of one of Russia's most beloved writers, Boris Pasternak. The parsnip is sweeter than the carrot, especially if left in the ground until after the first frost. It contains carotenoids and vitamin C, calcium and potassium. The parsnip is rich in fiber. Medieval doctors prescribed the parsnip for toothache, stomachache, impotence and dysentery. Modern researchers have not yet turned their attention to the parsnip. Who knows but that they wouldn't confirm these pharmacological properties of this flavorful and underrated vegetable. SWF

Community Supported Agriculture (CSA) is a community-based organization of growers and consumers. The consumer households live independently but agree to provide direct, up-front support for the local growers who produce their food. . . the primary need is not for the farm to be supported by the community, but rather for the community to support itself through farming. This is an essential of existence, not a matter of convenience. . . . Some things are typical for all community-supported farms. In all of them there is a strong dedication to quality; most of them are organic or biodynamic farms, most of them show great diversification, most are integrated farm organisms having their own livestock and thus their own source of manure. Trauger Groh and Steven McFadden *Farms of Tomorrow Revisited*

PEAS

Peas belong to the legume family; and the common garden green pea is a staple in many cuisines, usually eaten dried. But nothing can match fresh green peas for sweetness and flavor. Unfortunately, few of us have time to shell fresh peas. Frozen peas are an acceptable alternative for soups and stews; and the Chinese pea or sugar snap pea brings all the flavor of fresh peas to your table without putting you to the trouble of shelling them.

Fresh peas provide carotenoids, B complex, vitamin C and vitamin E, as well as copper, iron, phosphorus and potassium. Studies have shown that peas can help prevent cancer in animals and that they act to lower blood cholesterol. A survey of diets in England and Wales indicates that peas may ward off appendicitis.

The surprising thing about peas is the fact that they contain antifertility agents. According to Indian scientist Dr. S. N. Sanyal, the population of Tibet has remained stable over the last 200 years because the pea forms a staple of the Tibetan diet. Dr. Sanyal isolated an antifertility compound in peas called m-xylohydroquinone which, when given to women in synthesized form, cut down the rate of conception by 50 to 60 percent. Unfortunately, the results are not as predictable as for other contraceptives and so this derivative of the pea has not been developed for the commercial market. Now that adverse side effects of the pill and other contraceptive methods are becoming known, it is time to renew research into the natural antifertility agents found in the pea. SWF

Use freshly shelled peas or frozen peas. Plunge into boiling salted, filtered water for a few minutes, until just tender. Drain in a colander. Transfer to a heated serving dish, toss with butter and keep warm in the oven.

PEAS, CHINESE OR SUGAR SNAP

These are the delight of every serious cook. They take very little time to prepare, and they add an elegant touch of bright green to the plate. Remove ends and strings and place in a vegetable steamer. Do not cook until just before serving your main course. Steam about 1 minute—no more—or until peas turn bright green. Arrange artistically on plates or transfer to a heated serving dish. This is one of the few vegetables that is not enhanced by butter; they are naturally buttery and can be eaten plain.

Stir-Fry Chinese Peas with Sesame Seeds
Serves 6

1 pound Chinese peas, ends and strings removed
3 tablespoons extra virgin olive oil or lard
1 bunch green onions, cut into 1-inch pieces
2 tablespoons crispy pine nuts (page 514)
2 tablespoons sesame seeds, toasted in oven
1 tablespoon toasted sesame oil
sea salt and pepper

Stir fry onions and Chinese peas in olive oil or lard for about 3 minutes. Add pine nuts and sesame seeds and cook another minute. Remove from heat and stir in the toasted sesame oil. Season to taste.

PEPPERS

Remove stems and seeds and cut into strips or chunks. Sauté quickly in olive oil until tender. If you are using peppers of different colors, sauté them separately and mix together at the end.

Peppers and Onions
Serves 4

2 medium onions, peeled and thinly sliced
2 red peppers, seeded and sliced into strips
2 tablespoons butter
2 tablespoons extra virgin olive oil
1/2 teaspoon dried fine herbs
2 cloves garlic, peeled and crushed
1/2 cup finely shredded basil leaves
sea salt and pepper

Sauté onions and peppers gently in butter and olive oil for about 45 minutes until soft. Add herbs, crushed garlic and basil and cook another few minutes, stirring constantly. The consistency should be like marmalade. Season to taste. Serve as a side dish or as an appetizer on triangle croutons (page 520).

Peppers with Almonds
Serves 6

3 red peppers, seeded and cut into strips
2 green peppers, seeded and cut into strips
3 tablespoons extra virgin olive oil
3/4 cup crispy almond slivers (page 515)
1/2 cup raisins
1 teaspoon honey
1/4 cup red wine vinegar
sea salt and pepper

Sauté peppers in olive oil until tender. Meanwhile, dissolve honey in vinegar over a low flame. Add raisins and vinegar-honey mixture to peppers and boil down until most of liquid is evaporated. Stir in almonds and season to taste. Serve hot or at room temperature.

The pepper is one of those foods that came from the New World, but which is associated with many ethnic cuisines in Europe and Asia—the typical cuisines of India, Thailand, China, Hungary, Italy and Spain are almost inconceivable without the pepper.

Peppers can be divided into two main categories: sweet peppers, which are eaten as a vegetable; and chile peppers or hot peppers, which are used as flavorings and spices. Both are members of the capsicum family, a subset of the nightshade category of plants. Thus, the pepper is the cousin of eggplant, tomato and potato.

Peppers are rich in vitamin C and carotenoids and contain potassium and calcium. Red peppers are richer in these vitamins than green ones. The inner ribs of peppers are good sources of bioflavonoids, substances that protect blood capillaries from breakage.

Chile peppers are a good source of magnesium—the hotter the peppers the more magnesium they contain. Chile peppers have numerous medicinal properties, most notably the ability to loosen phlegm. Consumption of chile peppers in moderate amounts is an effective remedy for chronic bronchitis and emphysema. Compounds found in chile peppers act as decongestants and also help dissolve blood clots. Extracts of pepper have been used to treat toothache and conjunctivitis. Like so many other vegetables, peppers have been shown to lower blood cholesterol. SWF

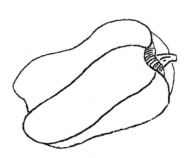

POTATOES

The potato ranks first among the many vegetables that came from the New World. European cuisine is unthinkable without the potato. Yet the potato had difficulty winning acceptance. Starving German peasants at Kolberg could only be persuaded to eat potatoes at gunpoint; Antoine Parmentier succeeded in kindling an interest in the French by presenting a bouquet of potato flowers to Marie Antoinette; the English offered subsidies to grow potatoes. Only in Ireland did the potato catch on quickly. Since it grew underground, it was a crop that could survive the devastations of military skirmishes, all too frequent on the soil of poor Ireland at the time.

Potatoes provide vitamin C and B complex as well as potassium, calcium and iron. Most of the nutrients are just under the skin, so don't peel them. The skin itself is full of fiber and can be retained in many potato preparations.

In spite of the potato's popularity, there has been little research on its pharmacological effects. Eating potatoes was formerly recommended by doctors in America for purifying the blood and curing indigestion. Potatoes contain chlorogenic acid, a chemical that prevents cell mutations leading to cancer. In some individuals potatoes raise blood sugar levels quickly, so potatoes may not be a good choice for some diabetics. Yet the maverick physician Henry Bieler recommended potatoes as the most digestible carbohydrate food.

Nothing can match the versatility of the potato, and potatoes in their simplest form can be as satisfying as the most complicated dish. To bake, wash potatoes and cut a bit off each end. Bake in a preheated 350 degree oven for 1 to 1 1/2 hours or until tender. If you brush the skins with oil, they will get crispy. Serve with butter or cultured cream.

To cook red potatoes, wash well, dry and put them in a clay pot. Cover, set in a cold oven and turn on to 250 degrees. The potatoes will cook in 2 to 3 hours depending on their size. (They will cook faster if you raise the heat but the flavor will be less intense.) May be served plain or tossed with a little butter. Tiny red potatoes may be cooked in a clay pot for about 1/2 hour and then sautéed whole in butter.

Stuffed Potatoes
Serves 6

6 medium baking potatoes
4 tablespoons butter
1/2 cup piima cream or creme fraiche (page 84)
1 red onion, finely chopped
1/2 cup Parmesan or raw Cheddar cheese, grated
2-3 tablespoons basil leaves, chopped (optional)
sea salt and pepper

Bake potatoes as described above. Cut butter into pats and place in a large bowl. When potatoes are done, cut lengthwise and scoop out soft potato flesh into the bowl with the butter. Mash with a potato masher. Mix in cultured cream, cheese, optional basil and onions. Season to taste. Spoon the potato mixture back into the shells and return them to a 150-degree oven to keep warm. If potatoes are not reheated to a high temperature, the enzymes in the cream will be preserved.

Rosemary Potatoes
Serves 6

2 pounds small red potatoes
6 tablespoons clarified butter (page 150)
      or duck fat (page 295)
1 teaspoon dried rosemary
1/2 teaspoon sea salt

Cook potatoes until just tender in a clay pot (page 396). Place in a pyrex pan with butter or duck fat, rosemary and salt. Bake at 400 degrees, shaking pan frequently, until golden brown.

Cottage Potatoes
Serves 6

6 large baking potatoes
4 tablespoons butter
4 tablespoons extra virgin olive oil
sea salt

These are a nice alternative to deep-fried potatoes. Wash potatoes but do not peel. Cut into 1/4-inch slices. Melt butter and oil together. Brush two stainless steel cookie sheets with the oil mixture. Place slices on cookie sheets and brush top sides with remaining oil mixture. Sprinkle with a little sea salt. Bake in a 350 degree oven for about 45 minutes or until golden brown. Check the potatoes frequently for burning. If they are cooking unevenly, remove potatoes as they become done to a heated platter and keep warm.

Sautéed Potatoes with Onions
Serves 4

4 medium onions, peeled and thinly sliced
8 red potatoes
about 6 tablespoons clarified butter (page 150)
      or duck fat (page 295)
sea salt and pepper

Potatoes should be stored in a cool dark place but not in a refrigerator, as extreme cold will cause their starch to turn to sugar. Potatoes will sprout if kept in the light too long—avoid eating these sprouts, as they contain poisonous alkaloids. However, there's nothing harmful about eating a potato that has small sprouts after they have been trimmed off. It is important to buy organic potatoes. Most commercial potatoes have been treated with sprout inhibitors that have mutagenic effects. SWF

You will probably be as surprised as I was to find practically nothing in a search of the literature on the effect of fried foods on the digestion. The one article on the subject refutes the old medical prejudice against fried foods.

Boggess and Ivy did their frying experiment with potatoes. They concluded that pan-fried potatoes were more easily digested than French fried potatoes boiled in grease.

Dr. Frank Howard Richardson, commenting on the prejudice against frying, said, "There is a widely held belief, cherished by physicians and laity alike, to the effect that fried foods are harmful in general and that they are particularly harmful for children. An analysis. . . clearly demonstrates that it is not documented with scientific proof or with any proof at all for that matter. Rather, it is merely a repetition and reiteration in many different forms of this unproved unscientific prejudice."

Food that is pan-fried in butter . . . is no worse than any other cooked food. In fact, Boggess in his experiment found that fried potatoes were more digestible than boiled potatoes. William Campbell Douglass, MD *The Milk Book*

A question arises at this point as to the efficiency of the human body in removing all the minerals from the ingested foods. Extensive laboratory determinations have shown that most people cannot absorb more than half of the calcium and phosphorus from the foods eaten. The amounts utilized depend directly on the presence of other substances, particularly fat-soluble vitamins. It is at this point, probably, that the greatest breakdown in our modern diet takes place; namely, in the ingestion and utilization of adequate amounts of the special activating substances, including the vitamins [A and D] needed for rendering the minerals in the food available to the human system. Weston Price, DDS *Nutrition and Physical Degeneration*

Know Your Ingredients
Name This Product #18

Potatoes, cottonseed oil, sour cream and onion seasoning, salt. Sour cream and onion seasoning contains: dehydrated whey, dextrose, partially hydrogenated soybean oil, salt, dehydrated sour cream, onion and nonfat dry milk, monosodium glutamate, modified food starch, lactose, sodium caseinate, sugar, dehydrated parsley, garlic powder, citric acid, sodium citrate and imitation flavor.

See Appendix B for Answer

There are two secrets to this recipe. One is to parboil the potatoes first, before they are sliced and sautéed; the other is to cook the onions separately.

Plunge potatoes into boiling water and cook about 10 minutes until just barely tender. Remove with a slotted spoon. Slice into 1/4-inch slices or cut into quarters. Sauté in batches in about 4 tablespoons butter or duck fat in a large frying pan. Meanwhile, sauté the onions in remaining butter or duck fat in a separate frying pan. When both onions and potatoes are golden, transfer to a heated serving dish and mix together. Season to taste.

Hash Brown Potatoes
Serves 4

4 medium potatoes, washed but not peeled
filtered water
1/2 cup whey (page 87)
2 tablespoons sea salt
3 tablespoons butter
3 tablespoons extra virgin olive oil
sea salt and pepper

These have a wonderful sour taste. Use the food processor to cut potatoes into a small julienne. Place in a bowl with water, whey and salt. Press potatoes down so that they are entirely covered with water, cover bowl and soak overnight. Pour out water, skim off top layer of potatoes (which will have turned brown), place potatoes in a tea towel and wring out thoroughly. Melt butter and olive oil in a large, heavy skillet. Place half the potatoes in the pan and press down firmly. Sprinkle with salt and pepper, cover pan and cook over medium heat about 5 minutes. Turn potatoes and cook, covered, another 5 or so minutes or until potatoes are well browned. Repeat with second batch.

Variation: Corned Beef Hash

Mix *1 cup finely chopped corned beef (page 237), 1 medium onion, finely chopped, and 1 red pepper, seeded and cut into a julienne* with potatoes after they have been squeezed dry and sauté according to recipe for hash browns.

Potatoes Anna
Serves 4

4 medium potatoes
4 tablespoons clarified butter (page 150)
1/2 teaspoon dried thyme
1/2 teaspoon dried rosemary
sea salt and pepper

Potatoes Anna is a traditional French dish, a sort of potato cake that is crisp on the outside and soft in the center. It's the kind of dish that draws raves from dinner guests, and it is not difficult to prepare successfully if the details are adhered to. You will need a 10-inch heavy, nonstick-type skillet with sloping sides, such as an omelette pan. The "cake" also needs to be weighted on top. A 10-inch french tart pan bottom serves this purpose well. It should be buttered, placed on top of the potatoes and weighted down with a several cans.

Wash the potatoes but do not peel. Slice very thinly into a bowl of iced water. Put about 1/3 of the clarified butter in the pan and coat the bottom. Dry the potato slices well and arrange them in a swirling pattern to make one layer in the pan. Dribble butter on this layer and a sprinkle of the herbs, salt and pepper. Repeat process for two more layers. Don't be tempted to make a fourth layer if you have slices left over. The results will not be as good if the potato "cake" is too thick.

Place the tart pan bottom on top of the potatoes and weight it down. Cook the potatoes over medium heat for about 30 minutes or until bottom is golden. Check to see if anything is sticking and slide the potatoes onto a large plate. Place the pan over the potatoes, hold on to the plate and turn quickly. Reweight the "cake" and cook another 10 to 15 minutes more. Cut into wedges to serve.

Nowhere has technology been so misused as in its application to food processing and preservation, and the most egregious example of this misuse has to be the practice of using toxic nuclear wastes to irradiate our food. Irradiation-induced changes include the formation of free radicals, alterations and cross-linking of nucleotides in DNA and RNA, the enhancement of lipid peroxidation and formation of benz-pyrene quinone, formation of formaldehyde and formic acid from sucrose and the conversion of nitrate to mutagenic nitrite. When water is irradiated billions of extremely reactive free radicals are formed. Kirlian photography, a method of photographing the energetic patterns of a substance, shows that fresh fruits and vegetables shine with light radiating out an inch or more in an aura with vibrant patterns. In contrast, irradiated food has virtually no light halo and has significantly altered patterns.

Children fed irradiated wheat developed extra chromosomes in their white blood cells; and animals fed irradiated pork or bacon demonstrated decreased growth, decreased survival of progeny and increased cancer. Yet irradiation is being promoted as a safe way to preserve our foods. Most spices are irradiated and the process is now approved for use on meats.

Irradiation may indeed kill pathogenic bacteria, but it leaves behind their toxic by-products. Thus, irradiated food may cause food poisoning, even though it tests clean. Irradiated seeds will not sprout and so can be stored under conditions that may encourage fungus and mold. Widespread use of irradiation will not bring improved safety but rather a decline in food sanitation standards. SWF

The absence or presence of additives alone does not determine the quality of food. The fundamental secret of quality production is to handle the plants and animals so that they attain their highest performance by their own nature. In each creation, there is an inner harmony of substances and forces that is typical and healthy. It is not the presence of certain substances in certain amounts that makes a vegetable or grain healthy; rather, it is the harmonious relationship between the substances and the forces.

To a large extent, modern agricultural methods have drastically affected this harmony. As research has shown, between 1896 and 1932 many crops exhibited a strong rise in the content of potash while their magnesium content declined. Meanwhile, other research shows that the silica content in cultivated plants has tended to decline while the potash content has been rising.

The results of this change to a less harmonious balance showed up in Eastern Europe, where for hundreds of years people thatched their roofs with rye straw. Those roofs typically lasted for fifteen years. But after the rye crops were treated with synthetic nitrogen, and the natural harmony of substances and forces had been altered, the roofs fashioned from the resulting straw began to rot after just three to five years. Though perhaps not so obvious, similar changes have occurred in the bread grain that is a staple of our diet. . . . Some observers believe the high phosphorous content in many processed foods . . . is a major factor in problems of hyperactive children, and other observers believe that the reduced silica content has led to a dulling of our senses. Trauger Groh and Steven McFadden *Farms of Tomorrow Revisited*

Potatoes Gratin
Serves 4-6

3 large baking potatoes, washed but not peeled
2 cups beef stock (page 122)
1 cup piima cream or creme fraiche (page 84)
1 teaspoon butter
sea salt and pepper
1 clove garlic, peeled and minced

While Americans think that potatoes "au gratin" means potatoes in casserole with cheese, the dish is traditionally made only with milk or stock and *creme fraiche*.

Slice potatoes into the stock and bring to a boil. Cook, stirring almost constantly, for about 10 minutes. Meanwhile, butter a 9-inch by 9-inch glass oblong pan and sprinkle bottom with sea salt, pepper and minced garlic. Remove the potato slices with a slotted spoon and arrange them randomly in the casserole. Bring the cream to a boil, pour into the stock and boil the two together for a minute. Pour over potatoes. Bake at 350 degrees about 1 hour more until the liquid has evaporated and the top has turned golden. You may reduce heat to 250 degrees and cook another hour or so if the casserole seems too liquid.

Potato Quarters
Serves 4

4 large potatoes, washed but not peeled,
*   cut into 1/4-inch cubes*
1/4 cup melted butter
1/4 cup extra virgin olive oil
1 teaspoon sea salt
1/2 teaspoon pepper

Toss potato cubes in butter, olive oil, salt and pepper. Place in a well-oiled stainless steel baking pan. Bake at 450 degrees until bottoms are crisp, then turn occasionally until desired crispness is obtained. Serve with a meat dish or as a snack. May be eaten plain or with cultured cream (page 84), yoghurt (page 85) or naturally sweetened ketchup (page 104).

Potato and Celery Root Purée
Serves 8 to 10

6 baked potatoes (page 396)
3 celery roots, peeled and cut up
2 cloves garlic, peeled and mashed
pinch nutmeg
sea salt and pepper
1/2 cup butter
1/2 to 1 cup piima cream or creme fraiche (page 84)

This beats plain old mashed potatoes any day. Cover the celery root pieces with cold water, bring to a boil and cook until very tender, about 30 minutes. Cut up the butter and place in the bottom of a large bowl. Scoop out potato flesh into the bowl. (Save the skins for potato skins, page 524.) Add the celery root and garlic, and mash all together. Add the cream to obtain desired consistency. If you want your purée really smooth, you may now mix with a handheld beater. Season to taste. Transfer to a buttered ovenproof dish and keep warm in the oven.

Potato Pancakes
Serves 6

6 baking potatoes, washed but not peeled
1 tablespoon sea salt
3-4 tablespoons whey (page 87) or lemon juice
2 medium onions, grated
2 eggs, lightly beaten
3/4 cup spelt or unbleached white flour
sea salt and pepper
3 tablespoons butter
3 tablespoons extra virgin olive oil

Grate potatoes in a food processor. Cover with water and stir in salt and whey or lemon juice. Cover and leave at room temperature about 7 hours. Meanwhile, mix grated onions with eggs and flour and season to taste. Rinse the potatoes in a colander, squeeze dry with a tea towel and stir into batter. Use a 1/4-cup measure to scoop batter for pancakes. Sauté on both sides in a mixture of butter and olive oil.

Myth: To avoid heart disease, we should use margarine instead of butter.
Truth: Margarine eaters have twice the rate of heart disease as butter eaters. (*Nutrition Week* 3/22/91 21:12)

If a woman could see the sparks of light going forth from her fingertips when she is cooking and the substance of light that goes into the food she handles, she would be amazed to see how much of herself she charges into the meals that she prepares for her family and friends.

It is one of the most important and least understood activities of life, that the radiation and feeling that go into the preparation of food affect everyone who partakes of it, and this activity should be unhurried, peaceful and happy. It would be better that an individual did not eat at all than to eat food that has been prepared under a feeling of anger, resentment, depression or any outward pressure, because the substance of the lifestream performing the service flows into that food and is eaten and actually becomes part of the energy of the receiver. That is why the advanced spiritual teachers of the East never eat food prepared by anyone other than their own chelas. Conversely, if the one preparing the food is the only one in the household who is spiritually advanced and an active charge of happiness, purity and peace pours forth into the food from him, this pours forth into the other members and blesses them. I might say that there are more ways than one of allowing the Spirit of God to enter the flesh of man. Maha Chohan *Electrons* AMTF, PO Box 466, Mount Shasta, CA 96067

SPAGHETTI SQUASH

The body probably needs both animal and vegetable fats to maintain sound health. A study conducted among boys of Ruanda, Africa, a vegetarian population by necessity, found that carotene absorption by children was dependent upon the amount of fat in the diet, not the amount of carotene eaten. It was also established that a lowfat intake results in poor absorption of both carotenoids and preformed vitamin A. When small amounts of [animal] fat were added to their vegetarian diet, improvement in the absorption of carotene resulted and vitamin A levels increased. H. Leon Abrams *Vegetarianism: An Anthropological/Nutritional Evaluation*

Even though calcium is present in spinach, children cannot utilize it. Data have been published showing that children absorb very little of the calcium or phosphorus in spinach before six years of age. Adult individuals vary in the efficiency with which they absorb minerals and other chemicals essential for mineral utilization. It is possible to starve for minerals that are abundant in the foods eaten because they cannot be utilized without an adequate quantity of the fat-soluble activators. Weston Price, DDS *Nutrition and Physical Degeneration*

This unusual vegetable is a good substitute for pasta. Cut in half lengthwise, remove seeds and place cut sides down in a baking pan filled with about 1/2 inch of water. Bake at 350 degrees for about 1 hour or until tender. Let cool slightly and remove the "strands" bit by bit with a fork. Garnish with butter and a little Parmesan cheese or any one of a number of sauces, such as pesto (page 144) or tomato sauce (page 154). The strands may also be formed into patties and sautéed in butter.

Spaghetti Squash Casserole
Serves 4

1 large spaghetti squash, prepared as above
2 medium onions, chopped
4 tablespoons extra virgin olive oil
2 ripe tomatoes, peeled, seeded and chopped
2 cloves garlic, peeled and chopped
1/2 teaspoon dried thyme
2 tablespoons fresh basil leaves, cut up
sea salt and pepper
1/4 cup parsley, chopped
1 cup whole grain bread crumbs
1/2 cup freshly grated Parmesan cheese
2 tablespoons melted butter

To peel tomatoes, see page 70. Sauté onion in olive oil until soft. Add tomato, garlic, thyme and basil and cook gently until most of the liquid is absorbed. Mix with spaghetti squash, season to taste and pour into a well-buttered pyrex dish. Mix parsley, bread crumbs and Parmesan cheese and spread on top. Drizzle with melted butter. Bake, uncovered, at 350 degrees for about 1/2 hour or until most of the liquid is absorbed.

SPINACH

In general, one bunch of spinach or one bag will serve three persons. Cut stems off leaves and wash well in filtered water—even if prewashed, the leaves should be rinsed so that they are moist. Place in a large pot. Do not add more water to the pot as the water adhering to the leaves will be sufficient to steam the spinach. Cover pot and place over a medium flame. When spinach begins to simmer, reduce heat. Cook several minutes or until leaves are just wilted. Using a slotted spoon, transfer to a heated serving bowl. Press with the back of the spoon to squeeze out any liquid and pour out. Make a few cuts through the spinach and top with a generous pat of butter.

Mary Jo's Spinach
Serves 6

2 *bunches fresh spinach*
3 *tablespoons butter*
1 *clove garlic, peeled and mashed*
1 *tablespoon crispy pine nuts (page 514)*
1 *tablespoon sun dried tomato flakes (see Sources),*
   optional

Steam spinach as described above. Melt butter with garlic, pine nuts and optional tomato flakes. Pour over spinach and mix slightly.

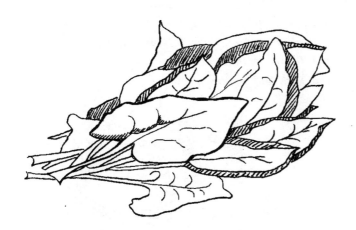

Spinach is the queen of the dark green leafy vegetables, the least bitter and most tender. The first record we have of spinach occurs in the year 647, when the king of Nepal sent a gift of spinach to the emperor of China. It was introduced into England in the middle of the 1500's.

Spinach is exceptionally high in carotenoids and vitamin C. It contains calcium and iron but scientists now believe that the form of iron, contained in spinach is one that is not easily absorbed. Spinach also contains oxalic acid that can prevent calcium absorption. Oxalic acid is neutralized during cooking; so while cooked spinach can be eaten regularly, spinach salads should be eaten only on occasion.

Both the chlorophyll and carotenoids found so abundantly in spinach are potent cancer blockers. Japanese studies also indicate that spinach lowers blood cholesterol in laboratory animals. New research indicates that spinach is effective in preventing macular degeneration of the eye, possibly due to high amounts of glutathione in spinach.

Spinach is now available at almost any time of the year. Many times you can buy it prewashed in sealed plastic bags. Do take advantage of the wonderful things that the modern age has made available to one and all and eat spinach regularly. SWF

Despite proof to the contrary, many doctors still cling to the germ theory of disease and to the necessity of drugs to combat germs. They point out that smallpox, diphtheria, typhoid fever and pneumonia have been conquered. That is true; no one can quarrel with them on that score. But such major chronic disorders as cancer, heart disease, diabetes, arteriosclerosis, nephrosis and hepatitis have increased eightfold. Scientific medicine, while suppressing deadly infectious diseases by the use of modern drugs, antibiotics and immunizations, has not been able to reduce the killing power of another equally frightening set of diseases.

Instead of blindly following Pasteur (as so many medical men have done) I asked myself: Is invasion of the tissues from without—by bacteria and viruses—the only way by which human tissues are injured? Can disease come from other means? Shouldn't man's constitutional and environmental conditions also be considered? Hasn't the time come to expand our notions of illness and treatment beyond Pasteur's bacterial infection theory? Can it be possible that germs are merely a concomitant of disease, present in all of us but able to multiply in a sick individual because of disturbed function?

In seeking answers to these questions, I left Pasteur and his tiny organisms and went off on another road . . . . I came to the conclusion that germs do not initiate a diseased state of the body but appear later after a person becomes ill. Henry Bieler, MD
Food Is Your Best Medicine

Spinach Stuffed Mushrooms
Serves 8

1 cup cooked spinach (page 403)
8 large mushrooms
1 bunch green onions, finely chopped
2 tablespoons butter
2 tablespoons extra virgin olive oil
1/4 teaspoon nutmeg
sea salt and pepper

Chop cooked spinach, place in a strainer and press out liquid. Meanwhile, wash mushrooms and remove stems. Chop stems finely and sauté with onions in butter and olive oil until tender. Add the spinach and cook another minute or so, mixing well, until all moisture is evaporated. Add nutmeg and season to taste. Fill the hollow of each mushroom with a spoonful of stuffing and place in a buttered glass pan. They may be prepared in advance to this point. To cook, add 1/4 inch water to the pan, place in a 350-degree oven and bake for about 20 minutes. This is a delicious and elegant accompaniment to beef.

Spinach Timbales
Serves 6

2 large bunches spinach
4 tablespoons butter, softened
4 tablespoons piima cream
*   or creme fraiche (page 84)*
4 eggs, lightly beaten
1 medium onion, very finely chopped
1/4 teaspoon nutmeg
sea salt and pepper

Steam spinach as described in basic recipe (page 403). Squeeze liquid out thoroughly and place in food processor. Pulse a few times until well chopped. Combine with other ingredients and season to taste. Pour into six conical timbale molds that have been well buttered or oiled. Place in a pan of hot water and bake at 350 degrees for 20 minutes. Loosen timbales with a knife and turn them onto a warmed platter or individual plates.

SWEET POTATOES

Prick whole sweet potatoes in a few places with a knife. Bake at 350 degrees for about 1 1/2 hours or until soft. Cut open and mash the flesh with butter and salt.

Sweet Potato Dollars
Serves 4

3-4 sweet potatoes
3 tablespoons melted butter
3 tablespoons extra virgin olive oil
sea salt

Peel potatoes and slice crosswise at 1/4-inch intervals into "dollars." Brush two cookie sheets with mixture of butter and olive oil. Arrange the dollars in one layer and brush with the remaining butter and oil. Season lightly with sea salt. Bake about 45 minutes at 350 degrees.

There's probably no vegetable with a higher betacarotene content than the sweet potato. This is the betacarotene that protects us against cancer, colds, infections and other diseases. The carotene content of sweet potatoes actually increases as the vegetable is stored throughout the winter. But remember that our bodies can only convert carotene to vitamin A in the presence of bile salts. That's why it's so important to eat sweet potatoes with butter, egg yolks or cream. These fats stimulate the secretion of bile and help the body to convert carotenes to all-important vitamin A. These wonderful fats also make sweet potatoes taste delicious.

The sweet potato is a good source of iron, potassium, niacin and vitamin C. It contains fiber and is very rich in vitamin B_6, a vitamin that is highly protective against heart disease. Last but not least, the sweet potato is rich in magnesium, another nutrient that protects against heart disease. SWF

It is very wise, when one eats grilled fish or meats, to eat them with whole grains or vegetables, as these provide natural antidotes to carcinogenic substances formed during grilling. Claude Aubert *Dis-Moi Comment Tu Cuisines*

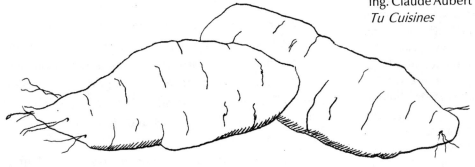

Know Your Ingredients
Name This Product # 19

Peas, water, carrots, partially hydrogenated soybean oil, margarine (liquid corn oil, partially hydrogenated corn oil, water, salt, whey, mono- and diglycerides lecithin, artificially flavored and colored [carotene], vitamin A Palmitate and vitamin D added), maltodextrin, modified food starch, powdered sweet cream (cream cheese [sweet cream, nonfat dry milk, cheese culture], whey, sugar, modified food starch, citric acid, sodium citrate), salt, sugar, natural flavor, hydroxylated lecithin, disodium phosphate, onion powder, garlic powder, xanthan gum, spices.

See Appendix B for Answer

Can anyone imagine Italian or Greek cooking without the tomato? And yet the tomato is another newcomer to European cuisine, an import from the New World. When the tomato was first introduced to European tables, and before it became common fare, it was called the "love apple" and was reputed to be an aphrodisiac. This reputation faded after tomatoes became available to the masses. In America the tomato was long held in suspicion and considered poisonous by the Puritans—perhaps out of fear of its aphrodisiac qualities. As this apprehension faded, the tomato became our most popular garden vegetable.

Sweet Potato Purée
Serves 6

4 large sweet potatoes
grated rind of two lemons
juice of two lemons
1/2 cup butter, softened
2 egg yolks
1/2 teaspoon sea salt

Tart lemon peel is a great foil for the sweetness of sweet potatoes. Boil potatoes in water until tender. Hold potatoes with a pot holder and peel potatoes while they are still hot. Place them in the bowl, mash and mix with butter, lemon rind, lemon juice, egg yolks and sea salt. Transfer mixture to a buttered ovenproof casserole and bake in a 350-degree oven for about 1/2 hour.

Sweet Potato Pancakes
Serves 4-6

2 medium sweet potatoes, peeled and grated
1 large potato, unpeeled, washed and grated
2 tablespoons whey (page 87) or lemon juice
1 tablespoon sea salt
1 medium onion, minced
1 small carrot, grated
3 eggs, lightly beaten
4 tablespoons spelt or unbleached white flour
pinch of nutmeg
sea salt and pepper
3 tablespoons butter
3 tablespoons extra virgin olive oil

Soak grated potato in water plus whey or lemon juice and salt for several hours or overnight. Drain and squeeze dry in a tea towel. Mix eggs with flour and nutmeg and season to taste. Stir in grated vegetables. Use a 1/3-cup measure to scoop out batter. Sauté until golden on both sides in butter and olive oil.

Variation:

Add 1/4 cup finely chopped cilantro to batter. Omit nutmeg.

TOMATOES

Tomatoes are often served boiled or stewed—a particularly nasty way to ruin a tomato. But they are very nice baked.

Baked Tomatoes
Serves 4

8 firm plum tomatoes
2 tablespoons extra virgin olive oil
2 tablespoons Rapadura (see page 536)

Brush tomatoes with olive oil and set in an oiled pie plate. Bake at a very low temperature (200 degrees) for at least 4 hours. Sprinkle on Rapadura, raise heat to 300 degrees and bake another 20 or 30 minutes. The tomatoes will become browned and slightly caramelized. These are delicious with red meats.

Stuffed Tomatoes
Serves 6

3 large tomatoes
sea salt and pepper
2 slices whole grain bread
2 tablespoons butter, softened
2 tablespoons Parmesan cheese, grated
1/2 teaspoon fine herbs

Slice tomatoes in half around the equator, remove seeds and place cut side up in a buttered baking dish. Sprinkle with a little sea salt and pepper. Process bread in a food processor to make fine crumbs. Add butter, cheese and herbs and pulse a few times until well blended. Spread a spoonful of stuffing over each tomato half. Bake at 350 degrees for about 30 minutes.

Tomatoes are well known for their vitamin C content. They also contain carotenoids, B complex, potassium, magnesium, phosphorus and calcium. Unfortunately, many tomatoes are picked green and then treated with ethylene gas, which causes them to turn red without really ripening. These tomatoes have the flavor and texture of cardboard and are nutritionally inferior. Canned tomatoes, picked at the peak of ripeness, surpass most store-bought tomatoes in nutritional qualities. Organic canned tomato products, with no salt added, are now sold in many stores. Even better, fresh organically grown and vine-ripened tomatoes are now becoming more available. Hydroponically grown tomatoes, while perfect in appearance, lack both nutrients and flavor.

To bring store-bought tomatoes to the peak of ripeness, place them upside down in a sunny windowsill. When ripened they will keep about a week refrigerated.

As for the therapeutic benefits of the tomato, they are high in a carotenoid called lycopene that seems to be of great value in protecting us from cancer. Other studies have shown them to be helpful in preventing appendicitis.

On the down side, some individuals are allergic to tomatoes. This is probably due to the fact that many people consume tomatoes in the form of tomato sauces and other tomato products to the exclusion of other vegetables. The solution to this problem is to eat a variety of vegetables, and keep the tomato in its proper place—as one of a great many vegetables that should be eaten on a regular basis but not to excess. SWF

TURNIPS

Turnips and related vegetables like rutabagas do not test high in vitamins but are very rich sources of potent cancer-fighting substances called glucosinolates.

Turnips probably originated in Russia or Scandinavia. They were a staple food in American and European diets until recent times because of their keeping qualities—they could be stored over the winter in root cellars, ready to be cooked up and mashed as a purée or added to soups and stews. This inexpensive cancer-fighter deserves a comeback. They are delicious puréed and can be added to roasting pans, soups and stews. SWF

Squash is another vegetable that hails from the New World. The Massachusetts Indians called it *askut-asquash*. Squash is a member of the gourd family and a relative of cucumbers and melons. The numerous varieties can be divided into two main categories: summer squash has soft skin and includes zucchini and crook necked or yellow squash; winter squash has a harder rind and includes butternut and spaghetti squash.

Both types provide carotenoids and vitamin C plus potassium, calcium and fiber. Winter squash is a better bet nutritionally, but summer squash is more versatile from the cook's point of view.

The American Indians valued the seeds of both squash and pumpkin for various ailments, but the pulp also has pharmacological properties, notably anticancer carotenoids. Winter squash and other deep orange vegetables are especially effective in preventing lung cancer. SWF

This European favorite, and its cousin the rutabaga, is rarely seen on American tables—and yet it was a staple in the early American farmers' diet, usually mashed up with plenty of butter and cream. The following recipes do justice to this neglected vegetable.

Turnip Purée
Serves 6

3 pounds turnips
2-3 baked potatoes
3/4 cup piima cream or creme fraiche (page 84)
1 teaspoon dried thyme
sea salt and pepper

Peel turnips and cook in salted filtered water for about 45 minutes or until tender. Scoop flesh out of potatoes and add to turnips. (Reserve skins for potato skins, page 524.) Mix in the cream, thyme and seasonings to taste. Transfer to an buttered ovenproof casserole and reheat at about 200 degrees.

Variation: Rutabaga Purée
Use *3 pounds rutabagas* instead of turnips.

Glazed Turnips
Serves 6

2 pounds turnips, peeled and quartered
4 tablespoons butter
1 cup beef stock (page 122)
1 teaspoon gelatin (see Sources), optional
1 tablespoon parsley, finely minced

Plunge turnips into boiling salted, filtered water for 3 to 5 minutes. Drain and pat dry. Sauté in butter until lightly browned. Add stock and optional gelatin and boil down until turnips are coated and liquid has almost completely evaporated. Sprinkle with parsley and serve.

YELLOW SQUASH

If you want your children to hate squash, just serve it to them boiled. Nothing could be slimier or more unappetizing. Instead, slice it lengthwise and sauté the slices in butter and olive oil. Finish with sea salt, pepper and a squeeze of lemon juice.

Yellow Squash Medley
Serves 4

4 small yellow squash
sea salt
1 medium onion, thinly sliced
2 medium tomatoes, peeled, seeded and chopped
2 tablespoons crispy pine nuts (page 514)
1 tablespoon finely chopped parsley
4 tablespoons extra virgin olive oil

To peel tomatoes, see page 70. Remove ends from squash and use food processor to cut them into a julienne. Sprinkle with sea salt and let sit about 1 hour. Rinse well and squeeze dry with a tea towel. Sauté onion in olive oil until golden. Add squash and tomatoes and sauté a few minutes more, over medium-high heat, stirring constantly. Stir in pine nuts and parsley.

Yellow Squash Supreme
Serves 4

4 large yellow squash
about 3 tablespoons extra virgin olive oil
3/4 cup grated Parmesan cheese
about 1 tablespoon cracked pepper

Wash squash, remove ends and slice lengthwise at 1/4-inch intervals. Brush a cookie sheet with olive oil and arrange the slices in one layer. Brush top side with olive oil and broil under broiler until slices become lightly browned. Turn over, brush again with olive oil and sprinkle on cheese and plenty of cracked pepper. Just before serving, place under broiler for a few minutes or until golden.

Many people who are sensitive to the effects of MSG have reported that they could eat the additive with impunity when younger but noticed increasing activity with age. With decreasing ability to shop for fresh foods, particularly in winter, older people often must rely more on processed, canned, dried and prepackaged food. With the current level of MSG addition to such foods (either as MSG or as hydrolyzed vegetable protein), this ensures a steady MSG diet, which is a factor in edema and depression. . . . Other symptoms associated with MSG sensitivity include dizziness and balance difficulties, common problems of the elderly. In larger concentrations, MSG is a potent nerve toxin; and it has been theorized that chronic long-term ingestion may be involved with Alzheimer's disease and Parkinson's disease, as well as other nerve cell degenerative diseases, such as amyotrophic lateral sclerosis (Lou Gehrig's disease). . . some women of childbearing age who are sensitive to MSG also associate this substance with worsening of premenstrual syndrome symptoms. PMS affects many women in various degrees and generally includes swelling, mood changes, depression, irritability and general malaise. The reported cases clearly suggest that individual testing is necessary to show which cases of PMS are worsened or possibly even initiated by the use of monosodium glutamate. George R. Schwartz, MD *In Bad Taste: The MSG Syndrome*

Zucchini, a member of the squash family, is a bland vegetable, especially rich in sodium. And since sodium, of all the alkaline elements of the body, is the most important, it follows that zucchini is a most healthful vegetable. The liver is the storehouse of sodium, an element necessary to maintain the acid-base equilibrium of the body. Without this acid-base balance, good health is impossible to maintain. The simple, bland zucchini, used as both food and medicine, is an ideal way to restore a sodium-exhausted liver. Henry Bieler, MD *Food Is Your Best Medicine*

Germs, viruses and other microorganisms are usually present, but merely as scavengers that feed on toxic wastes. While we must thank Louis Pasteur for annihilating the belief that disease was caused by demons and evil, substituting in its place the germ theory, we must not forget that Bechamp, who was a contemporary of Pasteur, strongly maintained that the chemical background on which the germ fed was of equal importance. Man had to choose between the two causes of disease: either the toxic background, due to faulty living and eating habits, was responsible for disease; or a mysterious microorganism, hiding in dark corners, pounced upon the innocent and unsuspecting victim. The cure, according to this latter theory, depended upon the destruction of these microbes. Henry Bieler, MD *Food Is Your Best Medicine*

ZUCCHINI

Like all members of the squash family, zucchini is ruined by boiling. Even steaming gives results that are too watery. Instead, slice lengthwise and sauté slices in butter and olive oil. Finish with a squeeze of lemon juice and sea salt and pepper to taste.

Sautéed Zucchini
Serves 4

6 medium zucchini, washed and trimmed
2 teaspoons sea salt
4 tablespoons butter

Pass zucchini through the small julienne slicer of your food processor. Mix with sea salt and let stand 1 hour. Rinse with filtered water in a colander and squeeze dry in a tea towel. Let butter melt slowly in a heavy skillet. Raise heat and sauté zucchini for about 1 minute.

Zucchini with Tomatoes
Serves 4

2 medium zucchini
2 medium onions, peeled and chopped
2 medium tomatoes, peeled, seeded and chopped
1-2 cloves garlic, peeled and mashed
1/2 teaspoon dried thyme
4 tablespoons butter
4 tablespoons extra virgin olive oil
1/2 teaspoon pepper

To peel tomatoes, see page 70. Cut ends off zucchini, cut into quarters lengthwise and slice thinly. Mix with sea salt and let stand about 1 hour. Rinse in a colander and pat dry. Sauté zucchini in butter and olive oil in batches over medium-high heat until golden. Set aside. Sauté onion in butter and oil until tender. Add tomato, raise heat and sauté a few minutes until liquid is almost all absorbed. Add zucchini, garlic, thyme and pepper. Sauté about 1 minute more until flavors are amalgamated. Don't let zucchini overcook!

Zucchini Cakes
Makes 12-14

4 cups grated zucchini, washed, trimmed and grated
1 tablespoon sea salt
4 eggs, lightly beaten
1 small onion, finely chopped
2 cups whole grain bread crumbs
sea salt and pepper
1/4 teaspoon cayenne pepper
1/2 cup Parmesan cheese
4 tablespoons butter
4 tablespoons extra virgin olive oil

Mix zucchini with salt and let stand 1/2 hour. Rinse well with filtered water and squeeze dry in a tea towel. Mix with eggs, onion, bread crumbs, cheese and cayenne pepper and season to taste. Form into cakes and sauté a few at a time in butter and olive oil.

Stuffed Zucchini
Serves 8

8 small zucchini or 4 large zucchini
2 medium onions, finely minced
3/4 cup crispy almonds (page 515),
*   ground to a powder*
3/4 cup piima cream or creme fraiche (page 84)
1 cup whole grain bread crumbs
3/4 cup grated Swiss or Parmesan cheese
2 eggs
1/4 teaspoon powdered cloves
sea salt and pepper

Remove ends of the zucchini and cook in boiling salted, filtered water about 8 to 10 minutes, depending on the size of the zucchini, or until flesh just becomes tender. Remove to a colander and rinse with cold water. Slice in half lengthwise and scoop out the flesh, reserving it in a bowl. Salt the inside of the zucchini shells and turn over to drain on paper towels. Meanwhile, sauté onion in olive oil. Chop zucchini flesh, squeeze out water and add to the onion. Cook a few minutes more.

Dr. Denham Harman, an authority on free radical chemistry and physiology, has stated that a reduction in these harmful reactions through dietary changes and/or the addition of protective elements in the diet would have a drastic effect. "This approach offers the prospect of an increase in the average life expectancy to beyond 85 years and a significant increase in the number of people who will live to well beyond 100 years."

Modern medicine, using a chemical approach, has failed to achieve this. The mean life span has remained virtually constant at 70 years since the mid 1950's. This life expectancy may well decrease in the future if we continue to be seduced by the false nutritional propaganda of the vegetable oil producers.

Harman studied the effect of various fats and oils on mice. He found that rats fed lard lived 9.2% longer than rats fed a polyunsaturate. In humans that translates to almost *7 years off your life* if you have been suckered into television nutrition and American Heart Association anticholesterol propaganda.

If unsaturated oil and lard are pushed to 20% of the total diet (well within the range of human consumption), the life span of the rats consuming the unsaturated oil was 17% less than those fed lard. Assuming a 70-year life span of man, this translates to almost *12 years less life* for the oil consumer as compared to lard users. William Campbell Douglass, MD *The Milk Book*

Before the advent of agriculture, our ancestors obtained nutrients from several thousand different types of plants. Even a century ago, the variety of food available to Americans was many times greater than today. Now, only 30 crops account for at least 95 percent of everything humanity eats, and just three—rice, corn and wheat—represent 80 percent of our food.

Modern agriculture goes against the grain of nature by discouraging diversity, concentrating instead on only a few plant varieties: ones selected for their suitability to mechanized harvesting and transport (tomatoes that survive crash tests), plus their cosmetic qualities. These traits usually have an inverse correlation to nutrient content.

Methods of farming greatly affect the nutritional value of plants. Studies show that organic produce can have several times the total nutrient content of chemically grown vegetables. Healthy soil is the key, but topsoil is being depleted several times faster than it can be replenished. John MacArthur *Life, Liberty and the Pursuit of Wellness*

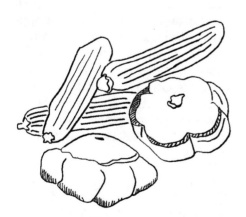

Beat the eggs and cream together. Stir in the onion and zucchini mixture, the almonds, about half the bread crumbs, half the cheese and the powdered cloves. Season to taste. If mixture is too runny, add more bread crumbs. Arrange zucchini shells in a buttered casserole and fill with the stuffing. Sprinkle remaining bread crumbs and cheese on top. You may prepare ahead of time to this point. Bake at 350 degrees for about 1/2 hour or until tops are golden.

BABY VEGETABLES

Baby vegetables are becoming increasingly available in our markets. Unfortunately, they often come from long distances and have therefore been treated with undesirable preservatives. They are rarely grown organically. However, if you can find locally grown baby vegetables, do use them for an appealing presentation. It is usually unnecessary to trim or peel them. Wash well and steam lightly or sauté in a little butter and olive oil.

VEGETABLE PUREE PANCAKES

Makes 4 pancakes

1 cup leftover vegetable purée, such as parsnip purée (page 393), potato and celery root purée (page 401) or sweet potato purée (page 406)
1 small onion, peeled and finely chopped
1 egg, lightly beaten
1/4 cup freshly ground spelt or unbleached white flour
sea salt and pepper
2 tablespoons butter
2 tablespoons extra virgin olive oil

Mix leftover purée with chopped onion, egg, and flour and season to taste. Melt butter and olive oil in a heavy skillet. Drop purée mixture in by spoonfuls and sauté pancakes until golden. Turn and sauté other side until golden. Remove to a heated platter and keep warm until ready to serve.

LUNCHEON & SUPPER FOODS

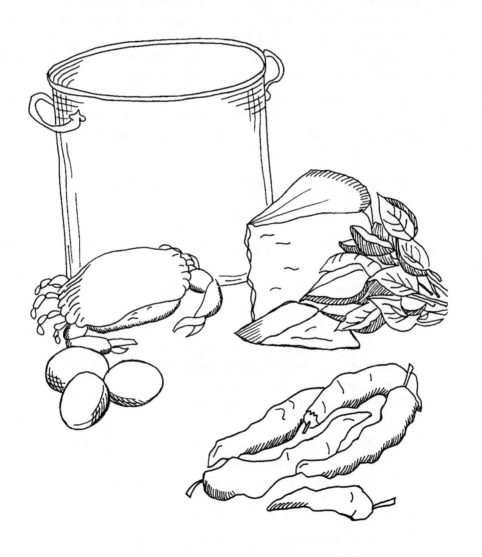

MEAT SALADS

Our luncheon and supper recipes are based on whole, natural foods, especially favoring animal products high in fat-soluble vitamins such as fish, organ meats and eggs, and a variety of vegetables to supply a wide range of vitamins, minerals and anticarcinogenic agents. Dressings, sauces and condiments feature extra virgin olive oil with its full complement of lipase and antioxidants, as well as lacto-fermented dairy and vegetable products.

Many of our meat salads fall in the category of designer fare and are suitable for the most elegant occasions. Others may be quickly assembled for family lunches. If you make chicken, turkey or duck stock regularly, you will have plenty of tender meat for the variety of meat salads presented here.

When you buy canned tuna be sure to read labels. Many brands contain hydrolyzed protein, a source of neurotoxic chemicals. Health food stores and gourmet shops may carry canned tuna that is free of additives.

CURRIED CHICKEN SALAD
Serves 6

meat from 1 whole chicken, used to prepare stock
    (page 124)
1 red pepper, diced
1 bunch green onions, finely chopped
3-4 celery stalks, diced
1/2 cup crispy almond slivers (page 515), toasted
2 cups curried mayonnaise (page 139)
2 tomatoes, sliced, for garnish
1 avocado, peeled and sliced, for garnish

Cut chicken up finely across the grain. Mix with chopped vegetables and toasted almond slivers. Mix well with curried mayonnaise. Serve with tomato slices and avocado wedges for garnish.

Variation: Curried Duck or Turkey Salad
Use *duck or turkey meat* in place of chicken.

ORIENTAL CHICKEN SALAD

Serves 6

meat from 1 whole chicken,
    used to prepare stock (page 124)
1 red pepper, seeded and cut into a julienne
1 can water chestnuts, drained and sliced
1 bunch green onions, chopped
2 tablespoons toasted sesame seeds
1 cup Oriental dressing (page 135)
4 ounces buckwheat or brown rice noodles,
    broken into 1-inch bits, cooked and drained
6 tablespoons extra virgin olive oil or lard
romaine leaves for garnish

Cut chicken up coarsely and mix with vegetables. Toss with dressing and sesame seeds. Refrigerate an hour or so before serving. Meanwhile, sauté noodle pieces in olive oil or lard until crisp and drain on paper towels. Serve chicken salad on romaine leaves and garnish with sautéed noodles.

Variation: Oriental Duck or Turkey Salad

Use *duck or turkey meat* in place of chicken.

CURRIED CHICKEN PLATTER

Serves 12-15

meat from two chickens,
    used to prepare stock (page 124)
4 cups spiced mayonnaise (page 138)
10 cups rainbow rice salad (page 473)
cilantro sprigs for garnish

This is a delicious combination and an attractive presentation for luncheons. You will need a large, flat oval platter. Shape the rice salad into a ring around the outside edge of the platter. Separate the chicken breasts into several pieces but do not cut up any of the other chicken meat. Place in the center of the ring. Spoon a little spiced mayonnaise over the chicken to cover it and garnish with cilantro leaves. Serve with the remaining mayonnaise on the side.

The Anasazi Indians, builders of the famous cliff dwellings in Mesa Verde, Colorado, flourished from 650 to 1300 A.D. and then died out "mysteriously." In the early days of their civilization they had plenty of game, but archeologists find very few animal bones in the trash heaps during the final century or so. Late human skeletal remains show bone deformities, rickets, rampant tooth decay and arthritis in individuals as young as 20 years old. The Anasazi ate corn, beans, pine nuts, yucca, herbs and berries. Their diet contained complete protein, essential fatty acids, minerals and vitamins including lots of carotene. Their lifestyle gave them abundant exposure to sunlight. But in the final years, the Anasazi lacked animal products, particularly vitamins A and D. They died out and so will we if we eliminate animals fats from the diet. SWF

LADIES BUFFET LUNCHEON

Curried Chicken Platter

❖❖❖

Spinach Feta Pastries

❖❖❖

Broiled Eggplant Slices

❖❖❖

Fruit Chutney

❖❖❖

Lemon Tart

❖❖❖

Ginger

You're having a picnic at the beach or in the park; the typical American family arrives. The kids explode out of the station wagon before Dad has turned off the ignition. Mother starts unloading the car and informing Papa where to put the blanket. Before the soft drink cooler is sprung open, Mother attacks the air, sand, and greenery with lethal insecticide spray. Massive retaliation against the insect world that had beleaguered them on the last country jaunt. Mother has forgotten, if she ever knew, that just as spilled sugar in our kitchens attracts ants and insects, so does sugar in our bloodstreams attract mosquitoes, microbes and parasites.

One of the great joys of being sugarfree is to be able to lie on the beach or loll in the mountains without being bothered by mosquitoes or other creatures. Once off sugar for a year or so, try it and see if it isn't true for you, too. If you take along a guest who's still addicted to sugar, lie side by side. See who the mosquitoes go for and who is left alone.

After all, its no accident that the first cases of mosquito-borne yellow fever—in the Western Hemisphere—occurred in the sugar island of Barbados in 1647. In the beginning it was called *nova pestis*. Yellow fever spread from one sugar center to another: Guadalupe, St. Kitts, Jamaica, Brazil, British Guinea, Spain, Portugal, New Orleans, and finally Cuba, where the U.S. Army mounted a massive campaign at the turn of the twentieth century to make our sugar colony of Cuba safe from the mosquito. William Dufty *Sugar Blues*

ORIENTAL CHICKEN PLATTER
Serves 8

meat from 1 whole chicken
used to prepare stock (page 124)
4 ounces brown rice or buckwheat noodles,
broken into 1-inch bits, cooked and
drained
6 tablespoons extra virgin olive oil or lard
3 tablespoons expeller-expressed peanut oil
2 teaspoons toasted sesame oil
1/4 pound snow peas, lightly steamed and cut into
quarters on an angle
1 red pepper, seeded and cut into a julienne
1 bunch scallions, chopped
2 cups bean sprouts, lightly steamed
1/4 cup ginger carrots (page 95)
1 can baby corn, drained and rinsed
cilantro sprigs for garnish
2 cups peanut sauce (page 147)

Cut up chicken meat coarsely. Meanwhile, sauté noodles in olive oil or lard until crisp and drain on paper towels. Toss chicken with noodles and the sesame and peanut oils. Mix in snow peas, pepper and scallions. Place in a mound on a platter. Make a border with the bean sprouts, ginger carrots and baby corn. Garnish with cilantro leaves. Serve with peanut sauce.

SIMPLE TUNA SALAD
Serves 4

1 large can water-packed tuna, drained
1/4 red pepper, diced
1 celery stalk, diced
4 green onions, chopped
1/2 cup mayonnaise (page 137) or
sour cream sauce (page 140)

Flake tuna with a fork and mix all ingredients together thoroughly. Serve in sandwiches or garnished with avocado and tomato wedges.

TUNA TAHINI SALAD

Serves 6-8

2 large cans water-packed tuna, drained
1/4 teaspoon cayenne pepper
2 cups tahini sauce (page 148)
4 medium onions, thinly sliced
4 tablespoons melted butter
1/3 cup crispy pine nuts (page 514)
cilantro sprigs for garnish
pita bread

Flake tuna with a fork and mix with cayenne pepper and 1 cup sauce. Meanwhile, strew the onions on an oiled cookie sheet, brush with butter and bake at 375 degrees until crispy. Mound the tuna on a platter. Scatter onions and pine nuts on top. Garnish with cilantro and serve with pita bread or whole grain crackers (page 518) and remaining sauce.

FRESH TUNA SALAD

(Salade Nicoise)

Serves 6

6 portions fresh tuna steak, about 4 ounces each
2 tablespoons extra virgin olive oil
sea salt and pepper
6 cups baby salad greens or curly lettuce
6 small ripe tomatoes, cup into wedges
6 small red potatoes, cooked in a clay pot
    (page 396)
1 pound cooked french beans (page 369)
2 dozen small black olives
2 cups herb dressing, made with finely chopped
    parsley (page 129)

Brush tuna steaks with olive oil and season with sea salt and pepper. Using a heavy skillet, sauté rapidly, two at a time, for about 4 minutes per side. Set aside.

Divide salad greens between 6 large plates. Garnish with tomatoes, potatoes, beans and olives. Place tuna steaks on top of greens and pour dressing over. Serve with sourdough bread or pizza toasts (page 524).

Dental researchers have proven that the teeth are subject to the same metabolic processes that affect other organs of the body. The entire body is one.

By adapting a technique originally developed to study movement of fluid within organs like the liver and kidneys, two researchers from the Loma Linda School of Dentistry have found that subtle changes in the internal activity of the teeth, *caused by sugar*, can be an early sign of later decay. . . .

Resistance to tooth decay involves the health of the entire body. Complex physiological processes are involved in maintaining and protecting the health of the teeth. The two researchers found that:

—A high-sugar diet can slow the rate of transport of hormonal chemicals by as much as two-thirds even in one week.

—Teeth with sluggish internal activity have a high incidence of decay.

—A hormone released by the hypothalamus stimulates the release by the salivary or parotid gland of a second hormone. This second hormone increases the rate of fluid flow in the teeth.

—A high sugar diet upsets the hormonal balance and reduces the flow in the internal system. This weakens the tooth and makes it more susceptible to decay.

—Healthy teeth are normally invulnerable to the microbes that are always present in the mouth.

Who wants to get rid of friendly germs in the mouth except those crazy people selling mouthwash? William Dufty *Sugar Blues*

Current research on omega-3 fatty acids has brought new appreciation for one of the most delicious fish that our oceans and rivers provide—salmon. Salmon is a wonderful source of 18-carbon omega-3 linolenic acid, which helps protect us against heart disease, high blood pressure, strokes, cancer, arthritis, psoriasis, asthma and autoimmune disorders. Salmon also provides some of the longer chain omega-3 fatty acids, like EPA and DHA, so necessary for proper function of the brain and eyes. Experts advise that adequate EPA and DHA in the diet of pregnant women and growing children will prevent learning difficulties and visual problems by fostering optimum development of the nervous system.

Salmon is also an excellent source of vitamin D—containing more than butter, shrimp or liver. It also supplies moderate amounts of the other fat-soluble vitamins, A and E, as well as iron, iodine and the B vitamins. Raw salmon is a good source of vitamin B_6, which is easily destroyed during cooking.

Buy salmon in season when ocean and river fish are available. These are naturally pink to dark red—the darker the better. Sockeye salmon from the West Coast is a beautiful deep color, indicating that the fish have been feeding on tiny shrimp and other algae-eating organisms and are therefore rich in nutrients, including the Price Factor or Activator X. Farm-raised salmon are fed inappropriate feed like soy meal and are given a chemical to make their flesh pink—otherwise they would be a pale cream color! SWF

SALMON WITH MIXED GREENS
Serves 4

1 1/2 pounds fresh salmon filet
2 tablespoons extra virgin olive oil
lemon juice
sea salt and pepper
2 tablespoons unbleached flour
1/2 teaspoon paprika
6 cups baby lettuces or mixed greens, such as
    watercress or lamb's lettuce
3/4 cup basic dressing (page 129)
1 red pepper, seeded, cut into a julienne and
    sautéed in olive oil
1 pound brown mushrooms, washed, dried very
    well, sliced and sautéed in butter
    and olive oil

Brush salmon with olive oil. Squeeze on lemon juice and rub in salt and pepper. Sprinkle on flour and paprika. Bake at 350 degrees for about 10 minutes. Place under broiler for another 2 minutes until just lightly browned. Meanwhile, mix greens with dressing and divide between four plates. Make a mound of peppers and mushrooms on each plate, place a portion of salmon on each mound of greens and pour pan juices over. Serve immediately.

CRAB SALAD

Serves 6

1 pound fresh crab meat, broken up
1 cup mayonnaise (page 137)
1 tablespoon green peppercorn mustard
   (available at gourmet shops)
12 asparagus spears, lightly steamed
2 tomatoes, cut into wedges
2 grapefruit, sections removed
6 small leaves romaine lettuce

Mix mustard with mayonnaise. Stir in crab meat and mix well. Divide among individual plates and garnish with asparagus spears, tomato wedges, grapefruit sections and lettuce leaf.

SWORDFISH SALAD

Serves 4

1 pound swordfish
1/2 cup naturally fermented soy sauce
2 teaspoons freshly grated ginger
2 bunches watercress, stems removed
4 ounces buckwheat or brown rice noodles,
   broken into 1-inch bits, cooked and
   drained
6 tablespoons extra virgin olive oil or lard
1 cup Oriental dressing (page 135)

Marinate swordfish in soy sauce and grated ginger for several hours in refrigerator. Dry well with paper towels. Broil 3-4 minutes to a side until just cooked through. Meanwhile, sauté noodles in olive oil or lard until crisp and drain on paper towels. Place a mound of watercress on each plate. Place a portion of swordfish on top. Pour dressing over and sprinkle with noodles.

Extensive laboratory determinations have shown that most people cannot absorb more than half of the calcium and phosphorus from the foods eaten. The amounts utilized depend directly on the presence of other substances, particularly fat-soluble vitamins. It is at this point probably that the greatest breakdown in our modern diet takes place; namely, in the ingestion and utilization of adequate amounts of the special activating substances, including the [fat-soluble] vitamins needed for rendering the minerals in the food available to the human system. Weston Price, DDS *Nutrition and Physical Degeneration*

"How is it that. . . the spiritual impulse, especially the inner path of development, is so little effective in the isolated person," asked a student of Rudolf Steiner, founder of the Anthroposophical movement and father of biodynamic farming. "How is it that, despite theoretical insight and the will to action, the successful undertaking of the spiritual impulses is so weak?"

"That is a problem of nutrition," Steiner replied. "Nutrition today does not give man the strength to manifest the spiritual in the physical. The bridge from thinking to willing and acting cannot be built anymore." SWF

Sir Robert McCarrison, M.D., England, found his clinical animals became desexed when fed on highly refined and processed foods. Dr. Clive McCay of Cornell University got similar results with his clinical animals. All animals fed on natural foods retained vitality. Sterility is on the increase among our people. Is the eating of our highly refined and processed foods affecting our people as it does the clinical animals? R. Dean Conrad *The Great American Tragedy*

SHRIMP AND PAPAYA SALAD

Serves 4

1 pound baby shrimp
3-4 stalks celery, finely diced
1 bunch green onions, finely diced
2 ripe papayas
1 cup creamy dressing (page 131)

Peel the papayas, cut in half and remove seeds. (Use seeds to make papaya pepper, page 157). Place hollow side up on individual plates. Mix shrimp with celery and dressing and spoon into papaya halves.

SCALLOP SALAD

Serves 4

1/2 pound sea scallops, rinsed, dried with
*   paper towels and quartered*
juice of 1 lemon
sea salt and pepper
2 tablespoons butter
2 tablespoons extra virgin olive oil
6 cups baby greens
1/2 cup basic dressing (page 129)
1 1/2 cups red pepper sauce (page 146)

Sauté the scallops quickly in butter and olive oil until opaque. Remove with a slotted spoon and toss with lemon juice and sea salt and pepper to taste. Toss the greens with the dressing. Place a portion of the red pepper sauce on each plate, make a mound of salad on top and arrange scallops on dressed greens.

MUSSEL SALAD
Serves 4

2 dozen live mussels
1 cup pickled red peppers (page 99), thinly sliced
2 bunches green onions, chopped
3/4 cup garlic or herb dressing (page 129)

When purchasing mussels, confirm that they are still alive by checking that they are slightly open and can be pushed closed. Place in a pot in about 1 inch of water and steam about 5 minutes until they open. To remove mussels from shells, use a knife to cut away the sinew. Open them lengthwise and remove the brown tongue with hairs attached. Slice each mussel into 3 or 4 pieces. Mix all ingredients together and chill an hour or so before serving. Serve with whole grain bread and butter.

ORIENTAL TUNA SALAD
Serves 4

1 1/2 pounds fresh tuna, cut about 1-inch thick
sea salt and pepper
1 tablespoon olive oil
1-2 heads red or romaine lettuce
1 red pepper, seeded and cut into thin slices
1/3 cup pickled ginger (page 100), drained
1 1/4 cup Oriental dressing (page 135)

Rub sea salt and pepper into tuna. In a heavy skillet, sauté tuna in olive oil over a medium-high flame, about 5 minutes per side until just cooked through. Break up lettuce and toss with pepper, ginger and Oriental dressing. Divide salad between four large plates and place a serving of tuna on top of each. Serve immediately.

As human beings, we are profoundly connected with our world. The elements of this planet are incorporated into the very structure of our bodies, the fluidity of our minds. We are an outgrowth of the earth: interactive beings animated by the amazing molecular dance taking place within and without us.

We need the earth mineral, magnesium, to activate more than 300 different enzymes that conduct the metabolic processes of life. Magnesium is also required by each of our trillions of cells to construct microtubules, the tiny passageways that distribute nutrients within a cell. We get magnesium from the plants we eat. Plants used those same magnesium atoms to capture solar electrons, materializing the energy of the sun to create our food. Plants get magnesium from the earth, thanks to the bacteria in healthy topsoil. . . .

It would be foolish to think that we could ever function without the elements of our world that shape and sustain us. Without an adequate supply of these essential nutrients, our very humanity disintegrates. Our brains would be dead if it weren't for the dynamic interplay of sodium and potassium ions across the membranes of our brain cells. These earth metals create waves of biological lightning that illuminate our nine billion miles of nerve fibers, allowing our inner galaxy of neurons to fully network.

Nutrients from the earth nourish our innate propensity toward wellness. Balances may shift, but harmony and health are the hallmarks of our existence. When all the elements are present, we are in touch with our true nature and can experience our birthright of health and vitality. John MacArthur *Life, Liberty, and the Pursuit of Wellness*

SWEETBREAD SALAD
Serves 6

"There is extensive scientific literature concerning the hazardous effects of direct microwave radiation of living systems. . . . It is astonishing therefore to realize how little effort has been taken to replace this detrimental technique of microwave cooking with technology more in accordance with nature. . . . Of all the natural substances—which are polar—the oxygen of water molecules reacts most sensitively. This is how microwave cooking heat is generated—friction from this violence in water molecules. Structures of molecules are torn apart, molecules are forcefully deformed, called structural isomerism, and thus become impaired in quality. This is contrary to conventional heating of food where heat transfers convectionally from without to within. Cooking by microwaves begins within the cells and molecules where water is present and where the energy is transformed into frictional heat." Dr. Hans Hertel quoted in *Search for Health*

2 pounds prepared veal sweetbreads (see page 300)
1 cup unbleached flour
sea salt and pepper
3 tablespoons butter
3 tablespoons extra virgin olive oil
1 pound fresh asparagus, lightly steamed
6 cups baby lettuces or mixed greens, such as watercress or lamb's lettuce
2 ripe tomatoes, peeled, seeded and finely chopped
1 head Belgian endive, leaves separated
2 cups creamy dressing (page 131)

To peel tomatoes, see page 70. Slice sweetbreads at 3/8-inch intervals. Dredge in a mixture of flour, salt and pepper and sauté in butter and olive oil. Mound greens in the center of individual serving plates and decorate edges with asparagus, chopped tomato and endive leaves. Place slices of warm, sautéed sweetbreads over greens and spoon dressing over.

DELUXE FRENCH BEAN SALAD
Serves 6

1 1/2 pounds cooked French beans, (page 369) cut into 1-inch lengths
3 heads Belgian endive, leaves separated
2 ripe tomatoes, peeled, seeded and finely chopped
12 triangle croutons (page 520)
6 slices duck and chicken liver mousse (page 244)
1 cup basic dressing (page 129) or walnut dressing (page 130)

To peel tomatoes, see page 70. Arrange endive leaves around the edges of individual plates. Place a small amount of tomato on each leaf. Cut each triangle crouton in half, spread with mousse and arrange around the outside edge of the place, alternating with the endive leaves. Mix the beans with basic dressing or walnut dressing and mound in the center of each plate.

ORIENTAL RED MEAT SALAD

Serves 6

1 1/2 pounds beef flank steak
1/2 cup lemon juice
6 tablespoons naturally fermented soy sauce
2 tablespoons extra virgin olive oil
  or expeller-expressed peanut oil
1 tablespoon toasted sesame oil
1 teaspoon freshly grated ginger
pinch of red pepper flakes
2 tablespoons toasted sesame seeds
1/2 pound snow peas, steamed lightly and cut into
  quarters at an angle
1 pound bean sprouts, lightly steamed
1 red pepper, seeded and cut into a julienne

Using a sharp knife, score the flank steak across the grain on both sides. Broil 3 or 4 minutes to a side or until meat is medium rare. Transfer to a cutting board and let stand for 10 minutes. Meanwhile, mix lemon juice, soy sauce, olive oil or peanut oil, sesame oil, ginger and red pepper flakes together. Cut the meat across the grain on an angle into very thin slices and cut these slices into a julienne. Marinate in the soy sauce mixture for several hours in refrigerator. Just before serving, toss with sesame seeds and vegetables.

In early June, Indian Harchand Singh collapsed in the middle of a busy London intersection. He cracked his skull, but even worse he awoke in the hospital to the news that he had suffered a serious heart attack. His cholesterol was normal and he ate a strict vegetarian diet. He was 38 years old.

This is not an unusual story for south Asians, most of whom are vegetarians. The south Asians of India, Pakistan and Bangladesh have a 40 percent higher rate of heart disease than the British, who eat a great deal of every conceivable type of animal meat and fat. In Singapore, the rate of heart disease is *400 percent* higher than the local Chinese—who eat a lot of pork. William Campbell Douglass, MD *Second Opinion*

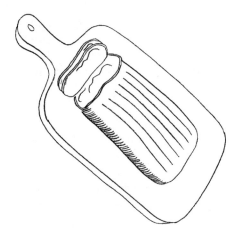

. . . . The same violent friction and athermic deformations that can occur in our bodies when we are subjected to radar or microwaves happens to the molecules in the food cooked in a microwave oven. In fact, when anyone microwaves food the oven exerts a power input of about 1000 watts or more. This radiation results in destruction and deformation of molecules of food and in the formation of new compounds (called radiolytic compounds) unknown to man and nature. Today's established science and technology argues forcefully that microwaved food, and irradiated foods, do not have any significantly high "radiolytic compounds" than do broiled, baked or other conventionally cooked foods—but microwaving does produce more of these critters. Curiously, neither established science nor our ever protective government has conducted any tests of the effects of eating the various kinds of cooked foods on the blood of eaters. Dr. Hans Hertel did test it, and the indication is clear that something is amiss and larger studies should be funded. Tom Valentine *Search for Health*

The research of Weston Price is either misinterpreted—raw foodists, anti-grain enthusiasts and even vegetarians have claimed his work as their own—or it is ignored. In a country where the entire orthodox health establishment condemns saturated fat and cholesterol from animal sources, and where vending machines have become a fixture in our schools, who wants to hear about a peripatetic dentist who warned about the dangers of sugar and white flour, who thought kids should take cod liver oil and who believed that butter was the number one health food? *Ancient Dietary Wisdom for Tomorrow's Children*

DUCK BREAST SALAD WITH HAZELNUTS
Serves 4

2 duck breasts
1/4 cup lemon juice
1/4 cup extra virgin olive oil
6 cups baby lettuce or spinach
1 cup basic dressing (page 129)
1 tablespoon hazelnut oil (see Sources)
1/2 cup crispy hazelnuts (page 514), chopped

Trim excess fat off the duck breasts and score in a diamond pattern. Marinate several hours in mixture of lemon juice and olive oil. Pat dry and cook in a heavy skillet, several minutes to a side until medium rare. Transfer to a board and let stand 10 minutes. Slice thinly across the grain. Blend hazelnut oil with dressing and toss with salad and hazelnuts. Mound in the center of individual plates and place duck slices on top. Serve with round croutons (page 520).

SOUTH of the BORDER

South-of-the-Border foods—tostados, fajitas, enchiladas, quesadillas, tacos, chile, empanadas—can be made with nutritious ingredients and deserve a place in your repertoire. They are especially popular with children and offer a delicious alternative to the array of junk foods with which they are constantly tempted. As they tend to be rather heavy, they should always be served with a high-enzyme condiment, such as cortido (page 93), salsa (page 103) or avocado and, of course, piima cream or *creme fraiche* (page 84). Cultured cream provides vital fat-soluble vitamins to the largely vegetarian corn and bean combination of typical Mexican food. Enchiladas, empanadas and burritos may be made ahead of time and frozen. Sprouted whole wheat tortillas for these recipes are widely available in health food stores and gourmet markets. (See Sources.) For corn tortillas, look for those that have been traditionally made with lime water and contain few or no additives.

BLACK BEAN TOSTADOS

Serves 8

4 cups black beans
2 tablespoons whey (page 87)
1 teaspoon sea salt
4 cloves garlic, peeled and crushed
12 sprouted whole wheat tortillas
about 1/2 cup extra virgin olive oil or lard
2 cups grated raw Monterey Jack cheese
3 cups cortido (page 93)
4 cups chismole (page 184)
2 cups guacamole (page 172)

The combination of black beans on crispy tortillas with cortido (lacto-fermented spicy cabbage), chismole (tomatoes and cilantro) and guacamole is surprisingly synergistic. If you object to frying the tortillas, simply warm them briefly in a skillet and brush with butter for a "soft" tostado.

Soak the beans in filtered water, whey and salt for 7 to 24 hours. Drain and rinse. Place in a large pot, cover with water and bring to a boil. Skim off scum before adding garlic. Cover and cook at least 4 hours. Meanwhile, fry the tortillas in a heavy skillet, one at a time, in several tablespoons olive oil or lard over medium-high flame, adding more oil or lard as needed. Drain on paper towels and keep warm in the oven. To serve, place a tortilla on each plate and spoon on the beans, using a slotted spoon. Sprinkle with cheese and serve with garnishes and remaining half tortilla per person.

CHICKEN ENCHILADAS
Makes 18 enchiladas

A nourishing diet brings more benefits than energy and endurance . . . . Grades of a million New York City public elementary and junior high school students were tested before and after school lunches were improved. Soaring scores surprised school officials and researchers, too.

Average test grades of students in 803 schools rose by 16 percent within four years after the school lunch program was improved . . . in 1980 came the change. The New York City Board of Education reduced the sugar content of foods and banned two artificial food colorings in school lunches. Later that year, achievement test scores rose from the 51st to the 57th percentile nationwide.

Pleasantly surprised at this jump, the New York City public school officials outlawed foods with artificial coloring and flavorings. Again, test scores rose—this time to the 61st percentile.

Once more school officials acted, banning BHT and BHA, two common preservatives, from school lunches and substituting milk for carbonated beverages and candy. This time test scores rose to the 64th percentile.

Not only are school children benefiting. So are the schools because of tremendous cost-savings brought about by the better noonday nutrition. Fewer special education teachers are now needed to offer individual instruction to children with reading problems, say the researchers. James F. Scheer *Health Freedom News*

meat from 2 whole chickens,
*   used to make chicken stock (page 124)*
2 medium onions, finely chopped
2-4 small green peppers, hot or mild, seeded and
*   finely chopped*
2 carrots, peeled and grated
1 cup sprouted small seeds, such as
*   sesame or onion seeds (page 115)*
1/2 teaspoon cayenne pepper
2 teaspoons oregano
1 tablespoon ground cumin
18 corn tortillas
about 1/2 cup extra virgin olive oil or lard
2 cups grated raw Monterey Jack cheese
8 cups green or red enchilada sauce
*   (pages 155-156)*
sliced avocados for garnish
creme fraiche or piima cream (page 84) for garnish
salsa for garnish (page 103)

Finely dice chicken and mix with onion, pepper, carrot, sprouts and spices. Stir in 1 cup enchilada sauce. Meanwhile, fry tortillas very briefly in several tablespoons olive oil or lard so that they are softened, not crisp, adding more oil or lard as necessary. Pat dry. Place about 2 tablespoons of chicken mixture in the center of each tortilla and roll up. Place in an oiled pyrex dish. (May be covered and frozen at this point.)

To serve, cover and heat in 325-degree oven until steaming. Serve with red or green enchilada sauce, grated raw cheese, avocados, cultured cream and salsa.

Variation: Turkey or Duck Enchiladas

Use *turkey or duck meat* instead of chicken.

Variation: Chicken Burritos

Use *sprouted whole wheat tortillas* in place of corn. Heat briefly in a heavy skillet and brush with melted butter before filling with chicken mixture. Fold in sides before rolling up and brush outside with butter. May be individually wrapped in aluminum foil and frozen. Remove foil before heating.

SWORDFISH ENCHILADAS

Makes 12 enchiladas

1 pound swordfish
2 tablespoons extra virgin olive oil
1 bunch green onions, chopped
4 cups green enchilada sauce (page 155)
12 corn tortillas
about 1/2 cup extra virgin olive oil or lard
1 cup grated raw Monterey Jack cheese
1 bunch green onions, finely chopped, for garnish
chopped cilantro for garnish
creme fraiche or piima cream for garnish
(page 84)

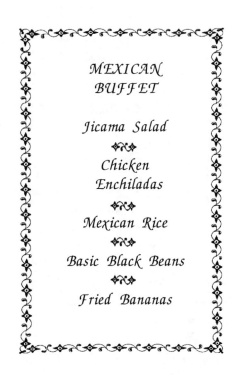

MEXICAN BUFFET

Jicama Salad

❧❧❧

Chicken Enchiladas

❧❧❧

Mexican Rice

❧❧❧

Basic Black Beans

❧❧❧

Fried Bananas

Brush swordfish with olive oil. Heat a well-seasoned cast-iron skillet over medium-high flame. Sauté the swordfish for about 7 minutes per side until cooked through. Allow to cool and flake with a fork. Mix 1 cup sauce and chopped green onions with the fish. Meanwhile, fry tortillas very briefly in several tablespoons olive oil or lard so that they are softened, not crisp, adding more oil or lard as necessary. Pat dry. Place about 2 tablespoons of fish mixture in the center of each tortilla and roll up. Place in an oiled pyrex dish. (May be covered and frozen at this point.)

To serve, cover and heat in 325-degree oven until steaming. Serve with remaining sauce, raw cheese, green onions, cilantro and cultured cream.

Variation: Tuna Enchiladas

Use fresh tuna instead of swordfish.

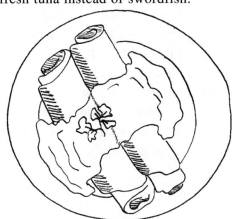

Since the seafoods are, as a group, so valuable a source of the fat-soluble activators, they have been found to be efficient throughout the world not only for controlling tooth decay but for producing a human stock of high vitality. Unfortunately, the cost of transportation in the fresh state often constitutes a factor limiting distribution. Many of the primitive races preserved the food value, including vitamins, very efficiently by drying the fish. While our modern system of canning prevents decomposition, it does not efficiently preserve some of the fat-soluble activators, particularly vitamin A. Weston Price, DDS *Nutrition and Physical Degeneration*

The food industry argues that American *trans* consumption is a low six to eight grams per person per day, not enough to contribute to today's epidemic of chronic disease. Total per capita consumption of margarine and shortening hovers around 40 grams per person per day. If these products contain 30 percent *trans* (many shortenings contain more) then average consumption is about 12 grams per person per day. In reality, consumption figures can be dramatically higher. A 1989 *Washington Post* article documented the diet of a teenage girl who ate 12 donuts and 24 cookies over a three-day period. Total *trans* worked out to at least 30 grams per day. Fat in snack chips, which teenagers consume in abundance, may contain up to 48 percent *trans* which translates into 45.6 grams of *trans* fat in a small ten-ounce bag of snack chips—which a hungry teenager can gobble up in a few minutes. High school "human development" classes do not teach teenagers that altered fats in their snack foods may severely compromise their ability to have normal sex, conceive and give birth to healthy babies. *The Oiling of America*

OFFAL BURRITOS

Makes about 18 burritos

3 pounds brisket of beef or game
2 pounds sweetbreads or brains or combination
(See note on brains, page 310)
2 cups beef stock (page 122)
1 small can tomato paste
2 onions finely chopped
1/4-1/2 teaspoon cayenne pepper
1 tablespoon oregano
1 tablespoon cumin
4 cloves garlic, peeled and mashed
about 18 sprouted whole wheat tortillas
about 1/2 cup melted butter
about 3 cups red enchilada sauce (page 156)
for garnish
cortido (page 93) for garnish
sliced avocados for garnish
piima cream or creme fraiche for garnish
(page 84)

They're not awful—they're good! This is a good way to get organ meats into your children without them knowing it. In this recipe, brains or sweetbreads need no special preparation. Place all ingredients (except garnishes, tortillas and butter) into a large pot. Bring to a boil, cover and place in a 300-degree oven overnight or all day until meat is falling apart. Remove top for last hour or so of cooking so sauce thickens.

Remove meat and brains or sweetbreads and chop finely. Add sauce from the pan to moisten but the mixture should not be runny. Meanwhile, heat tortillas briefly in a heavy skillet and brush one side with melted butter. Place about 1/2 cup of the meat mixture in the center of each buttered side. Fold in sides before rolling up and brush outside with butter. May be individually wrapped in aluminum foil and frozen. (Remove foil before heating.) Heat at 325 degrees in an oiled pyrex dish until steaming. Serve with choice of garnishes.

CHICKEN TOSTADOS

Serves 6

meat from 1 whole chicken,
    used to make stock (page 124)
2 medium onions, chopped
1 red pepper, seeded and diced
1 green pepper, seeded and diced
2-4 jalapeno peppers, seeded and diced
3 tablespoons extra virgin olive oil or lard
1/2 cup tomato paste
1 cup chicken stock (page 124)
1 teaspoon dried oregano
1 teaspoon cumin
1/2 teaspoon red chile flakes
1 teaspoon sea salt
1 clove garlic, peeled and mashed
6 sprouted whole wheat tortillas
6 tablespoons extra virgin olive oil or lard
1 head romaine lettuce, finely shredded
3 cups chismole (page 184)
2 cups cortido (page 93)
grated raw Monterey Jack cheese for garnish
piima cream or creme fraiche for garnish
    (page 84)
avocado slices for garnish

Know Your Ingredients
Name This Product #22

Reconstituted nonfat dry milk, flour, water, chicken, green chiles, modified food starch, soybean oil, salt, chicken fat, chicken broth replacer (maltodextrin, salt, monosodium glutamate, chicken broth, hydrolyzed plant protein, disodium inosinate, disodium guanylate, autolyzed yeast extract), soy protein concentrate, dehydrated onions, jalapenos, whey, flavorings, sodium tripolyphosphate, spices, baking powder, cellulose gum.

See Appendix B for Answer

Sauté onions and peppers in 3 tablespoons olive oil or lard until soft. Add tomato paste, stock, oregano, cumin, red chile flakes, salt and garlic. Cut up chicken meat and stir in. Check seasonings. Simmer for 15 minutes or so until most of the liquid has evaporated. Meanwhile, sauté tortillas in olive oil or lard until crisp. Drain on paper towels and keep warm in oven.

To serve, place a tortilla on each plate. Spoon chicken mixture on tortillas and serve with bowls of shredded lettuce, chismole, avocado, cheese, cultured cream and cortido.

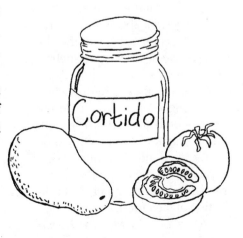

The relation of brain function to soil fertility is demonstrated in many sources of information. These include a percentage of grade school pupils in classes for mentally retarded and backward children. I have found the proportion in several districts to be above thirty percent and progressively increasing in several states. In the group of southern states using the same examination, passing from grade schools to high schools, the data show a marked superiority in the proportion of children for the Panhandle area. The area is underlain with caliche subsoil, which consists of calcium pebbles cemented together with calcium carbonate. . . . I have shown that the milk and cream produced from wheat pasture in that area are very high in vitamin A and Activator X. Many of the children are excellent. The average well above normal. The roots of the wheat plants in this district have been shown to penetrate down six feet, well into the subsoil. The district includes Hereford, which has been highly publicized for its low incidence of dental caries. The cattle raised in that area are very superior, both for beef and for reproduction. The people can be also if they are as wise as the buffalo and cattle in the selection of their food. Weston Price, DDS *Nutrition and Physical Degeneration*

BLACK BEAN BURRITOS
Makes about 12 burritos

3 cups basic black beans (page 496), cooked
3 cups basic brown rice (page 466)
1 medium onion, finely chopped
2-4 small green chiles, hot or mild, seeded
    and finely chopped
1/4 teaspoon cayenne pepper
1 teaspoon oregano
2 teaspoons ground cumin
about 12 sprouted whole wheat tortillas
about 1/2 cup melted butter
3 cups red enchilada sauce (page 156) for garnish
cortido (page 93) for garnish
sliced avocados for garnish
piima cream or creme fraiche for garnish
    (page 84)

Mix beans, rice, onions, chiles and seasonings. Meanwhile, heat tortillas briefly in a heavy skillet and brush one side with melted butter. Place about 1/2 cup of the bean mixture in the center of each buttered side. Fold in sides before rolling up and brush outside with butter. May be individually wrapped in aluminum foil and frozen. (Remove foil before heating.) Heat at 325 degrees in an oiled pyrex dish until steaming. Serve with choice of garnishes.

QUESADILLAS
Makes 1 dozen

12 sprouted whole wheat tortillas
about 3/4 cup extra virgin olive oil or lard
about 2 pounds grated raw Monterey Jack cheese
2 small jars green chile peppers, chopped
quacamole for garnish (page 172)
salsa for garnish (page 103)

Heat about 2 tablespoons olive oil or lard in a heavy skillet. Place one tortilla in the pan and about 1/3 cup cheese on one half, along with a sprinkling of chile peppers. Fold other half of tortilla over. Fry about 3 minutes until golden brown, turn and fry the other side for about 3 minutes. Cheese should be just melted and the exterior should be crisp. Repeat for other tortillas, adding more oil or lard as necessary. If your skillet is large enough you can do two at a time. Serve with quacamole and salsa.

CHICKEN TACOS
Makes about 1 dozen

Cooked meat from 1 chicken, reserved from
    making stock (page 124)
2 onions, peeled and chopped
2 green peppers, peeled and chopped
2 cups red enchilada sauce (page 156)
1 dozen corn tortillas
about 1/2 cup extra virgin olive oil or lard
grated raw Monterey Jack cheese for garnish
cortido for garnish (page 93)

Sauté onions and peppers in olive oil until tender and transfer to a bowl. Break chicken into small pieces. Mix chicken and red enchilada sauce with sautéed peppers and onions.

Heat several tablespoons olive oil or lard in a large heavy skillet. Add a tortilla and sauté briefly on one side. Turn over and place a spoonful of chicken mixture just off center. Fold tortilla over and sauté on both sides until crisp. Transfer to a platter lined with paper towels to drain. Repeat with other tortillas, adding more olive oil or lard as necessary—you can have several tacos going at the same time in a large pan. Serve with grated cheese and cortido.

Variation: Beef Tacos

Use *1 1/2 pounds ground beef, sautéed in 2 tablespoons olive oil until crumbly*, not chicken.

Variation: Green Tacos

Use *green enchilada sauce (page 155)*, not red.

The basic materials of food processing are the refined carbohydrates (mainly white flour and sugar) and processed oils. Given these three basics, processors can produce almost anything. The food industry has taken to sugar and hydrogenated fats not merely because of their taste appeal but because they are the cheapest constituents available for the manufacture of packaged foods. "One company can't sell a tomato, for example, for much more than another company. But process it into ketchup, add spices and a fraction of a cent of flavor, and bottle it; call it barbecue sauce; advertise it; tout its brand name; and higher and higher profits can be made because the product seems unique." We might begrudge the industry these manipulated profits if, in return, the purchaser got nutrients they need from the food product. Unfortunately, they don't. The profits are made at the consumers' twofold expense—in purchasing power and in nutrients needed. Joseph D. Beasley, MD and Jerry J. Swift, MA *The Kellogg Report*

As Yudkin observed, for some adolescents the proportion of calories obtained from sweeteners may go as high as 50 percent. This means that youngsters who are at the peak of their growth period have to meet *all* their elevated nutrient needs with only half their diet. It is not surprising that obesity, hyperactivity, concentration problems, and behavior disorders have been spreading among students. Joseph D. Beasley, MD and Jerry J. Swift, MA *The Kellogg Report*

Know Your Ingredients
Name This Product #23

Skim milk, sugar, sodium caseinate, corn oil, cocoa, artificial flavors, magnesium sulfate, cellulose gel, salt, carboxmethyl cellulose, disodium phosphate, potassium citrate, sodium ascorbate, calcium carrageenan, ferric orthophosphate, vitamin E acetate, zinc sulfate, niacinamide, calcium pantothenate, copper sulfate, vitamin A palmitate, pyridoxine hydrochloride, thiamine hydrochloride, riboflavin, folic acid, biotin potassium iodide, vitamin B12, vitamin D.

See Appendix B for Answer

FAJITAS

Serves 4-6

2 pounds beef, lamb or chicken breast cut into
strips, about 1/4-inch to 1/2-inch thick
6 tablespoons extra virgin olive oil
1/2 cup lemon or lime juice
1/4 cup pineapple juice (optional)
4 garlic cloves, peeled and mashed
1/2 teaspoon chile powder
1 teaspoon dried oregano
1/2 teaspoon dried thyme
1 red pepper, seeded and cut into strips
1 green pepper, seeded and cut into strips
2 medium onions, thinly sliced
about 1/2 cup extra virgin olive oil or lard
12 sprouted whole wheat tortillas
6 tablespoons melted butter
chismole (page 184) for garnish
guacamole (page 172) for garnish
piima cream or creme fraiche for garnish
(page 84)

Make a mixture of olive oil, lemon or lime juice, pineapple juice and spices and mix well with the meat. Marinate for several hours. Remove with a slotted spoon to paper towels and pat dry. Meanwhile, mix vegetables in marinade. Using a heavy skillet, sauté the meat, a batch at a time, in several tablespoons olive oil or lard, adding more oil or lard as necessary. Use a slotted spoon to transfer batches to a heated platter and keep warm in the oven while completing preparations. Sauté vegetables in batches in additional olive oil or lard and strew over meat. Meanwhile, heat tortillas briefly in a heavy cast-iron skillet and brush with melted butter. Serve meat mixture with tortillas and garnishes.

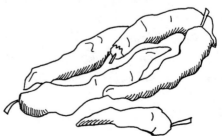

RED MEAT CHILE

Serves 8-12

3 pounds coarsely ground beef or lamb
4 tablespoons extra virgin olive oil or lard
1/4 cup red wine
2 cups beef stock (page 122)
2 onions, finely chopped
2-4 small green chiles, hot or mild,
*   seeded and chopped*
2 cans tomatoes, briefly chopped
*   in food processor*
3 cloves garlic, peeled and mashed
1 tablespoons ground cumin
2 tablespoons dried oregano
2 tablespoons dried basil
1/4-1/2 teaspoon red chile flakes
4 cups basic black or
*   kidney beans (page 496), cooked*
tortilla chips for garnish (page 519)
chopped green onions for garnish
piima cream or creme fraiche for garnish
*   (page 84)*
avocado slices for garnish
chopped cilantro for garnish.

Brown meat until crumbly in a little olive oil or lard in a heavy pot. Add remaining ingredients except garnishes and simmer about 1 hour. Serve with garnishes.

When a woman stays at home and cooks with good judgement and understanding, peace and happiness result. She thus controls the family's health and destiny, also her husband's mood, disposition and feeling, and assures the futures of her children
Jacques DeLangre

When a woman stays at home and cooks with good judgement and understanding, she watches with satisfaction as her children grow up capable and strong and her husband maintains the good health and disposition that allow him to succeed in his work. She also maintains her own good health into middle age, the period of her life when, her family duties accomplished, she can plunge vigorously into meaningful work and community service in order to to bring peace and happiness to the world, while her husband, retired with satisfaction from a successful career, supports her endeavors and cooks with good judgement for her.
Sally Fallon

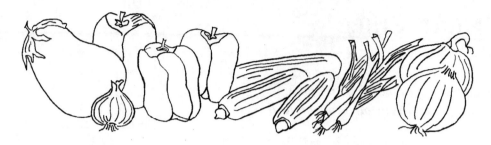

We tried a starvation experiment with male rabbits, which are naturally great breeders. When we fed certain pens of rabbits a mineral-deficient hay in their diet, we reduced the males in a few weeks to the point where they wouldn't look at a woman rabbit. Other rabbits, kept on a similar but mineral-rich diet with hay from treated soil, were regular wolves. By reversing the diets, the wolves became woman shy, and the tame cats became wolves. Lambs fed mineral-rich hay from treated soil made nearly three times as much gain in weight in a given time as other lambs from the same flock fed the same amount of hay from mineral-poor soil. Elephants in Burma and Ceylon, when fed on sugar cane, a mineral-poor diet, quickly become unable to do the heavy timber moving required of them. A properly mineral-rich diet predisposes a man to health and normal functioning. And the healthier we are, the better we resist diseases that ought to lay us low. "Are We starving to Death?" *The Saturday Evening Post* 1945

VEGETABLE CHILE
Serves 8

1 eggplant, peeled, cut into 1/2-inch cubes, salted and drained in a colander for 1 hour
2 zucchini, diced, salted and drained in a colander for 1 hour
about 1/2 cup extra virgin olive oil
2 onions, chopped
1 red pepper, seeded and diced
1 yellow or green pepper, seeded or diced
1 cup chicken stock (page 124)
1 can tomatoes, chopped briefly in food processor
1 small bunch basil leaves, cut up
2 tablespoons chile powder
3 cloves garlic, peeled and mashed
1 tablespoon ground cumin
1 tablespoon oregano
2 cups basic black beans (page 496), cooked
2 cups corn kernels, fresh or frozen
chopped green onions for garnish
grated raw Monterey Jack cheese for garnish
chopped cilantro for garnish
*piima cream or creme fraiche for garnish
    (page 84)*

Rinse eggplant and pat dry. Sauté in batches in several tablespoons olive oil and transfer, using a slotted spoon, to a large casserole, adding more oil as necessary. Rinse zucchini and pat dry. Sauté in batches in olive oil and transfer, using a slotted spoon, to casserole. Sauté peppers and onions in batches and transfer to casserole. Add stock, tomatoes and seasonings to the pot, bring to a boil, skim and simmer for 1 hour. Add beans and corn kernels and simmer another 1/2 hour. Serve with garnishes.

MARIA'S EMPANADAS

Makes about 2 dozen

2 pounds ground beef or turkey
1 cup cooked organ meats, finely chopped (optional)
6 tablespoons olive oil
1 teaspoon cumin seeds
1 medium white onion, chopped
2 bunches green onions, chopped
2 red or green peppers, seeded and finely chopped
4-5 cloves garlic, peeled and mashed
3 carrots, peeled and grated
2 tablespoons finely chopped parsley
1/4 cup chopped cilantro
1 cup cooked peas
1 cup cooked corn
1 1/2 cups basic brown rice (page 466)
sea salt and pepper
2 recipes yoghurt dough (page 485)
unbleached white flour

Sauté beef or turkey in 3 tablespoons olive oil until cooked through, allowing some of it to become well browned. Add 1/2 teaspoon cumin seeds and season to taste. In a separate skillet, sauté onions and peppers in olive oil. Add carrots, garlic, 1/2 teaspoon cumin and salt to taste and sauté a bit more. In a large bowl mix cooked meats, vegetable mixture, peas, corn, rice, parsley and cilantro. Season to taste.

Make a 1-inch ball of dough and roll into a round of about 6 inches, using unbleached white flour to prevent sticking. Place a scant 1/2 cup of filling off center, fold pastry in half and pinch edges together. Repeat until all of dough or filling is used. Bake at 350 degrees until lightly browned. The pastries may be individually wrapped in foil and frozen. Remove foil before reheating.

One will immediately ask about vegetarians. On close examination it will be found that vegetarians omit meat from their diet but include milk, cheese, dairy products, and eggs—all animal protein. Milk is a form of modified blood, more specifically it may be termed white blood. The white of an egg, which is better for the body when cooked, is 100 percent protein. It is necessary for a vegetarian to eat a relatively large amount of food in order to meet his basic needs because plant foods, due to their high cellulose content, are not easily assimilated and necessitate more work in chewing, flow of digestive juices, and intestinal movement. As far as the human body is concerned, vegetable protein is a poor substitute for animal protein. H. Leon Abrams *Your Body Is Your Best Doctor*

Our ancestors knew nothing about vitamins, and they did fine. They didn't know about food additives, artificial coloring and flavoring, and, above all, about pasteurized, homogenized or skim milk. Medical researchers from other countries have attributed the high degree of heart disease and cancer in the U.S. to our high consumption of milk—pasteurized, of course, and in recent years homogenized or skim. This, along with our national addiction to Coca-cola, ice cream, donuts, pizza and candy bars, gives us one of the highest rates of degenerative diseases in the world. For all these and other such popular favorites as powdered fruit drinks, sugarcoated cereals, hot dogs, potato chips, are susceptibility foods—foods, that is, which nibble away at rather than build up, the body's immune system to disease. Bruce Pacetti, DDS *PPNF Health Journal*

EGGS

Shunned for several decades by orthodox practitioners as a high-cholesterol food wrongly believed to cause coronary heart disease, the egg is making the comeback it deserves. Eggs have provided mankind with high-quality protein and fat-soluble vitamins for millennia. Properly produced eggs are rich in just about every nutrient we have yet discovered, especially fat-soluble vitamins A and D. Eggs also provide sulphur-containing proteins, necessary for the integrity of cell membranes. They are an excellent a source of special long-chain fatty acids called EPA and DHA, which play a vital role in the development of the nervous system in the infant and the maintenance of mental acuity in the adult—no wonder Asians value eggs as a brain food. Egg yolk is the most concentrated source known of choline, a B vitamin found in lecithin that is necessary for keeping the cholesterol moving in the blood stream.

It pays to buy the best quality eggs you can find—eggs from chickens fed flax or fish meal or, better yet, pasture fed so they can eat bugs and worms. Their nutritional qualities are far superior to those of battery-raised eggs and even many so-called "free range" eggs. In particular, they contain a better fatty acid profile, one in which the omega-3 and omega-6 fatty acids exist in an almost one-to-one ratio; but in eggs from chickens fed only grains, the omega-6 content can be as much as 19 times greater than all important unsaturated omega-3. Other very-long-chain and highly unsaturated fatty acids—necessary for the development of the brain—are found in properly produced eggs but are almost wholly absent in most commercial eggs. Eggs from pasture-fed chickens will become more available with consumer demand.

When broken into a bowl, the egg should have a dark yellow yolk that stands up in a round hemisphere. The white should have two clearly defined sections— a more viscous part surrounding the yolk and a thinner area on the perimeter.

Never eat powdered eggs, a source of harmful oxidized cholesterol.

What about recent publicity regarding salmonella infections from eggs? The blame for such problems lies squarely on crowded production methods that require extensive use of antibiotics in feed. Eggs from pasture-fed hens pose no danger provided they have been properly refrigerated.

It's fine to eat raw yolks of fresh eggs, but raw egg whites should be consumed only on occasion. Raw egg whites contain a substance called avidin, which interferes with the absorption of biotin, a B vitamin; they also contain trypsin inhibitors, which interfere with protein digestion. These antinutrients are neutralized by light cooking.

FRIED EGG
Serves 1

1 egg
1 tablespoon butter

Some advocates of politically correct nutrition warn against eating fried eggs as if they were a veritable poison. However, many children—and adults as well—find a poached or boiled egg unpalatable but will eat an egg that has been fried or scrambled. There is absolutely nothing harmful in frying an egg gently in butter.

Melt butter in a heavy skillet over a medium flame and crack the egg into the pan. Cover with a lid and cook gently for several minutes until the white becomes firm and the yolk somewhat thickened. Serve with hash browns (page 398), corned beef hash (page 398), roe cakes (page 316) or turkey sausage (page 363).

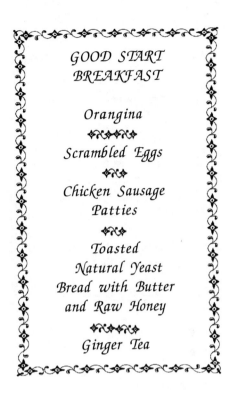

GOOD START
BREAKFAST

Orangina

Scrambled Eggs

*Chicken Sausage
Patties*

*Toasted
Natural Yeast
Bread with Butter
and Raw Honey*

Ginger Tea

SCRAMBLED EGG
Serves 1

1 fresh egg
1 egg yollk (optional)
1 tablespoon cream
pinch sea salt
2 teaspoons butter

For results that have a more pleasant texture and superior taste, add cream rather than milk to eggs for scrambling. The extra yolk makes a super scramble!

Beat egg, optional yolk, cream and salt thoroughly with a wire whisk. Melt butter in a heavy skillet. Add beaten egg mixture and stir constantly with a wooden spoon until egg is scrambled. Serve immediately with hash browns (page 398), corned beef hash (page 398), roe cakes (page 316) or turkey sausage (page 363).

Government sponsored health education programs have carried the lowfat propaganda into our public schools. "My mother is killing me—making me eat two eggs and bacon and toast with butter for breakfast," said an eighth grade boy after taking a health course in a public school near Albany, New York. Future parents are being told that the foods they need to have healthy babies contain cholesterol and saturated fats and will cause heart disease. Programs like these help boost the sales of breakfast cereals and skim milk and can be credited with high rates of injuries on the athletic field, eating disorders, depression, fatigue, infertility and other health problems as the years roll by. SWF

However, the Spirit expressly says that in latter times some will turn away from the faith, addicting themselves to seducing spirits, and to teachings of demons; teaching lies in hypocrisy; burning up their own conscience; hindering marriage; abstaining from foods which God created to be consumed with thankfulness by the faithful, and recognizers of the truth.

Tim 4:1-3

While the fat fighters have been pushing skim milk and peanut oil, Dr. Alan Howard, Cambridge University, England, has discovered that whole milk actually protects against abnormally high cholesterol. Feeding two quarts of whole milk a day to volunteers caused a drop in cholesterol. Butter caused an increase in cholesterol. (That doesn't mean that butter is bad for you. There is *absolutely no proof* that a temporary rise in cholesterol is harmful.) Dr. George Mann, Vanderbilt University School of Medicine, concurs with Dr. Howard. He found that four quarts of whole milk per day will lower the blood cholesterol level by twenty-five percent. Cambridge's Howard concluded, "... all this business that saturated fats in milk are bad for you is nonsense." William Campbell Douglass, MD *The Milk Book*

POACHED EGG
Serves 1

1-2 eggs

This is a good way to test the quality of your eggs. Gently crack 1-2 eggs into a pan of simmering water. If the whites hold together and do not come off in flaky bits, the protein is of good quality and the egg is very fresh. Simmer for about 5 minutes and remove with a slotted spoon.

MEXICAN EGGS
(Heuvos Rancheros)
Serves 4

4 fresh eggs, scrambled or fried
4 corn tortillas
2 tablespoons extra virgin olive oil or lard
2 cups Grandpa's salsa (page 155)

Fry tortillas in olive oil or lard until crisp. Pat dry with paper towels. Place tortillas on individual plates that have been warmed in the oven. Place fried or scrambled egg on each and top with salsa.

DEVILED EGGS
Makes 12

6 medium eggs
1/2 cup piima cream or creme fraiche (page 84)
1/2 teaspoon sea salt
1/4 teaspoon cayenne pepper

Place eggs in a pan of cold water and bring to a boil. Reduce heat to a simmer and cook for 15 minutes. Remove with a slotted spoon and chill in refrigerator. Slice lengthwise and remove yolks carefully. Place yolks, cultured cream, salt and cayenne pepper in a food processor and process until smooth. Carefully return the yolk mixture to the hollow of the egg whites.

PLAIN OMELET

Serves 2-4

4 fresh eggs, at room temperature
3 tablespoons water
dash of tabasco sauce
pinch sea salt
2 tablespoons butter

Crack eggs into a bowl, add water, tabasco and salt and blend with a wire whisk. (Do not whisk too long or the omelet will be tough.) Melt butter in a well-seasoned cast-iron skillet. When foam subsides, add egg mixture. Tip pan to allow egg to cover the entire pan. Cook several minutes over medium heat until underside is lightly browned. Lift up one side with a spatula and fold omelet in half. Reduce heat and cook another half minute or so—this will allow the egg on the inside to cook. Slide omelet onto a heated platter and serve.

Variation: Onion, Pepper and Cheese Omelet

Sauté *1 small onion, thinly sliced* and *1/2 red pepper, cut into strips* in *2 tablespoons butter* until tender. Strew this evenly over the egg mixture as it begins to cook, along with *2 tablespoons grated Parmesan cheese.*

Variation: Herb Omelet

Scatter *1 tablespoon parsley, finely chopped, 1 tablespoon chives, finely chopped* and *1 tablespoon thyme or other garden herb, finely chopped* over the omelet as it begins to cook.

Variation: Mushroom Omelet

Sauté *1/2 pound fresh mushrooms, washed, well dried and thinly sliced* in *2 tablespoons each of butter and olive oil.* Scatter over the omelet as it begins to cook.

Variation: Sausage Omelet

Sauté *1/2 cup turkey sausage mixture (page 363)* in *2 tablespoons butter* until crumbly and scatter over the omelet as it begins to cook. You may also use *1/2 cup leftover samosa filling (page 363)* or *empanada filling (page 435).*

When you sit down to eat a meal it should be a time for pleasure and warmth, family and friends. Food should be enjoyed. Even more importantly, it should also be nourishment that meets all your body's needs. Nothing is more important for the good life than your food supply. In these times our food supply is plentiful, but it lacks quality nourishment.

Chickens and eggs are near the top of the list of staple foods for our modern society. Problem is, most of the eggs and chickens available today are a far cry from the high-quality natural nourishment they used to be—in fact, we consider today's mass-produced eggs and chickens such poor-quality food that we have not consumed a supermarket chicken or egg since we can't remember when. It is precisely because of mass production and chemicalized techniques that the chickens and eggs provided for mainstream America are not fit for human consumption.

Let's start with the egg. The egg from the chicken is considered to be the "most complete" protein source in a single food. In fact, the amino acid complex in eggs is so well proportioned that eggs are used as the reference point for judging the quality of protein in other foods. A good quality egg is particularly high in methionine, an amino acid largely missing from the source of the "staff of life"—grains. Good quality eggs are an excellent source of carotene and vitamin A, thiamin (vitamin B1) and niacin. Eggs are also one of the few viable sources of vitamin D. As for minerals, eggs are an outstanding source of "heme" iron, a most absorbable form, plus calcium and phosphorus and trace minerals. As the ads have stated so well—it's an "incredible, edible egg."

Eggs have been an important part of man's nutrition for a long, long time. Tom Valentine *Search for Health*

Patients with severe burns are often force-fed huge quantities of whole eggs and egg concentrates as a source of protein to rebuild large areas of lost skin. During this egg therapy, however, there is no significant increase in their serum cholesterol. In one study, volunteers fed 18 eggs per day actually showed reduced levels of cholesterol. Perhaps it is because when you are full of eggs you do not have room for sugar and junk foods—the real culprits in the cholesterol scenario. Eggs are one of the healthiest foods on the planet. They provide protein of the highest quality plus all known vitamins and minerals (except vitamin C). David W. Rowland *Health Naturally*

PARMESAN CUSTARD
Serves 6

4 egg yolks
1 1/2 cup whipping cream
1 cups freshly grated Parmesan cheese
pinch of cayenne pepper

Beat yolks. Stir in cream, cheese and cayenne. Pour into individual ramekins and place in a pan of hot water. Bake at 350 degrees for 45 minutes. This makes a hearty first course during the winter months.

EGGPLANT KIKU
Serves 4-8

2 large eggplants, about 2 pounds total, peeled
      and cut into 1/2-inch squares
about 1 tablespoon sea salt
2 medium onions, peeled and thinly sliced
about 4 tablespoons extra virgin olive oil
6 eggs
2 cloves garlic, peeled and crushed
juice of 1 lemon
1/2 teaspoon sea salt
1/4 teaspoon pepper
1/4 teaspoon saffron threads, dissolved in
      1 tablespoon hot water

Kiku is a Persian or Arabic dish that has many variations. It came to Spain during the Moorish invasions where it took the form of the Spanish tortilla or Spanish omelet, with potatoes as a filling.

Mix eggplant cubes with sea salt and leave in a colander to drain for about 1 hour. Rinse well and pat dry. Using a heavy skillet, sauté in batches in olive oil until soft. Transfer to a bowl with a slotted spoon and mash up with a potato masher. Sauté the onions until golden and add to the eggplant. Beat eggs with salt, pepper, lemon juice and saffron. Stir in the eggplant and onions. Pour into a well-oiled 9-inch by 13-inch pyrex pan and bake about 30 minutes at 375 degrees or until top is browned. Cut into squares or diamonds and serve.

Variation: Zucchini Kiku

Omit the eggplant and use *3 medium zucchini, cut into a julienne*, using the julienne slicer of your food processor. Salt and drain in a colander for 1/2 hour. Rinse and squeeze dry in a paper towel. Sauté about 1 minute in olive oil. Proceed with recipe. You may wish to sprinkle the top of the kiku with 1 *cup grated Cheddar or Monterey Jack cheese.*

Variation: Spinach Kiku

Omit eggplant and use *2 cups cooked chopped spinach, squeezed dry* mixed with *1 bunch chopped cilantro, 1 tablespoon chopped dill* and *2 tablespoons chopped chives.* Mix with the sautéed onions and proceed with recipe. Omit saffron and use *1/2 teaspoon ground fenugreek* and *1/2 teaspoon ground cumin.*

The prestigious *New England Journal of Medicine* had a report on eggs and cholesterol. A group of New Guinea natives, whose diet is exceedingly low in cholesterol, were fed eggs to measure the cholesterol-raising effect of eggs. They figured the serum cholesterol levels would be blown off the charts. The eggs had no significant effect on the blood cholesterol.

Another study done by the American Cancer Society revealed that non-egg users had a higher death rate from heart attacks and strokes than egg users. This was a very large (and so convincing) study involving over 800,000 people. William Campbell Douglass, MD *The Milk Book*

SPANISH OMELET

Serves 4

3 red potatoes, thinly sliced
1 medium onion, peeled and thinly sliced
about 4 tablespoons extra virgin olive oil
6 eggs
1/2 teaspoon thyme
sea salt and pepper

Sauté the potatoes in olive oil in a cast-iron skillet until golden. Transfer to a bowl with a slotted spoon. Sauté the onions. Meanwhile, beat the eggs with seasonings. Return potatoes to the pan, combine with onions, flatten to make an even layer and pour the egg mixture over the potatoes. Cook about 5 minutes over medium heat, lifting edges occasionally so uncooked top part can run under. Finish by placing under broiler for a minute or two. Cut into wedges and serve.

With all the publicity about eggs and cholesterol causing heart disease, the food industry quickly responded in making a preparation that looked and tasted like eggs. . . one such product was called EGG BEATERS. An experiment was conducted at the Burnsides Research Laboratory, University of Illinois, by Meena Kasmau Navidi and Fred A. Kummerow in which one group of lactating rats was fed exclusively on fresh shell eggs and another on EGG BEATERS. The rats on fresh shell eggs thrived, were perfectly healthy, and grew normally. Those on EGG BEATERS did not grow normally, were stunted, and all died long before reaching maturity. H. Leon Abrams *Vegetarianism: An Anthropological/Nutritional Evaluation*

Recently health authorities have repeatedly issued warnings about the potential health risk of eating raw or insufficiently cooked eggs. The argument is that *Salmonella* (a human pathogen and naturally occurring organism of the gastrointestinal tract of chickens) is showing up in eggs more frequently than ever before and is therefore causing more human infections. Such an explanation falls short of the real truth. Overuse or abuse of antibiotics is the real cause—a problem perpetuated even by those who pretend to provide a solution. . . .

The truth of the matter is that:
—Salmonella organisms have *always* been in eggs. To reduce their numbers, egg producers now refrigerate their product as soon after collection as possible. . . .
—Not everyone who eats uncooked eggs gets a *Salmonella* infection, even when the eggs contain *Salmonella.*
—The body has a series of natural mechanisms that readily resist *Salmonella* and other intestinal pathogens when properly supported, but which are suppressed by antibiotics.
—The facts that have been reported in recent years concerning how to kill *Salmonella* and other pathogens without antibiotics are credible. Doctors . . . tell us they have yet to encounter an organism that requires a prescription antibiotic to knock it out. In fact, prescription antibiotics tend to hinder the effectiveness of the natural mechanisms. Thus, unless the infection is potentially lethal, antibiotics are more of a hindrance than a help when the doctor is trying to manage the organism using natural means (such as adjusting the body pH upward, eliminating sweets and re-establishing the growth of friendly bacteria in the small intestine). Sam Queen, MA *Health Realities*

VEGETABLE FRITATA

Serves 4

*1 cup broccoli flowerets, steamed until tender
    and broken into small pieces*
1 red pepper, seeded and cut into a julienne
1 medium onion, peeled and finely chopped
2 tablespoons butter
2 tablespoons extra virgin olive oil
6 eggs
1/3 cup piima cream or creme fraiche (page 84)
1 teaspoon finely grated lemon rind
pinch dried oregano
pinch dried rosemary
sea salt and pepper
1 cup grated Monterey Jack cheese

In a cast-iron skillet, sauté the pepper and onion in 1 tablespoon each of butter and olive oil until soft. Remove with a slotted spoon. Beat eggs with cream and seasonings. Stir in broccoli, peppers and onion. Melt the remaining butter and olive oil in the pan and pour in egg mixture. Cook over medium heat about 5 minutes until underside is golden. Sprinkle cheese on top and place under the broiler for a few minutes until the fritata puffs and browns. Cut into wedges and serve.

Variation: Leek Fritata

Omit broccoli, red pepper and onions and use *4 leeks, well rinsed, dried, sliced* and sautéed in butter and olive oil.

Variation: Zucchini Fritata

Omit broccoli, red pepper and onion and use *3 medium zucchini, cut into a julienne,* using the julienne slicer of a food processor. Salt and drain in a colander for 1/2 hour. Rinse and squeeze dry with a paper towel. Sauté about 1 minute in butter and olive oil. Proceed with recipe.

THIN HERB FRITATAS

Makes 6

3 eggs
1 tablespoon each chives and basil leaves, chopped
1 teaspoon fresh thyme leaves
1 teaspoon parsley, finely chopped
2 tablespoons freshly grated Parmesan cheese
2 tablespoons piima cream or creme fraiche
     (page 84)
sea salt and pepper
about 2 tablespoons extra virgin olive oil

These delicious "egg pancakes" may be eaten as is or in sandwiches. Mix eggs with herbs, cheese, cream and seasonings. Heat a small, cast-iron skillet and brush with olive oil. Pour 1/4 cup egg mixture into the pan and tilt the pan to spread the mixture. When the fritata has set, flip over to brown the other side. Transfer to a heated platter and keep warm in the oven while preparing the remaining fritatas.

EMBER DAY TART

Serves 4-6

1 recipe flaky pie crust (page 557)
     or 1/2 recipe yoghurt dough (page 485)
2 large onions, chopped
2 tablespoons butter
4 eggs
2 tablespoons whole grain bread crumbs
1/2 teaspoon saffron threads
     dissolved in 1 tablespoon warm water
1/2 teaspoon sea salt
pinch nutmeg
2 tablespoons currants

This recipe for a meatless holiday is based on one taken from a 1390 Middle English cookbook. Line a pie pan with pastry. Meanwhile, sauté onions in butter until soft. Beat eggs and stir in onions, bread crumbs, seasonings and currants. Pour into pie shell and bake at 350 degrees for 30 to 40 minutes.

An unpublished study carried out at the University of California at Berkeley proves the folk wisdom of the Orient—that eggs are a brain food. Researchers studied men in their eighty's, dividing them into two groups: Those who were senile and required constant care, and those who had all their faculties intact and were able to care for themselves. All men were given dietary surveys. Researchers found only one difference between the dietary habits of those who required care and those who were mentally alert—the latter group ate at least one egg per day.

Scientists engaged in a recent study of breast milk components carried out in China discovered that pregnant and nursing mothers routinely ate up to 12 eggs per day. This is the explanation for the fact that their milk had high levels of DHA, a fatty acid found in egg yolks that is necessary for optimal mental development of the infant. SWF

The public has not been well served by the recommendation that the long-standing custom of having one or two eggs for breakfast be discontinued and not more than two or three eggs per week be eaten—or worse, that the recently marketed "chemical egg" concoctions be substituted for the real thing! Eggs are a valuable food, providing excellent protein, vitamins and minerals. The cholesterol in them is balanced with sufficient lecithin to keep the cholesterol circulating in the blood and prevent it from depositing in the arteries. This is another instance showing the balance in whole, natural foods. Emory W. Thurston, PhD *Nutrition for Tots to Teens*

In Framingham, Massachusetts, the more saturated fat one ate, the more cholesterol one ate, the more calories one ate, the lower people's serum cholesterol. . . we found that the people who ate the most cholesterol, ate the most saturated fat, ate the most calories weighed the least and were the most physically active.

William Castelli, Director
The Framingham Study

For 15 years, an 88-year-old Denver man has been consuming 24 soft-boiled eggs a day. This particular story made it to the *New England Journal of Medicine* because a researcher from the University of Colorado wondered how this compulsive cholesterol cuisine might be affecting the man's health. To his surprise, the scientist found that despite a cholesterol intake close to 6,000 milligrams a day—well above the recommended maximum of 300 milligrams per day—the man had normal blood cholesterol and showed no signs of heart disease . . . . Over the past 13 years, though, there's been a growing body of evidence that it might be something in our food that is causing . . . blood vessel damage. The suspected ingredient is a modified form of cholesterol called oxidized cholesterol. This is not the kind you find in eggs or other fresh foods. Oxidized cholesterol forms when cholesterol reacts with oxygen. This usually occurs when high-cholesterol foods are dried, such as in powdered eggs. Oxidized cholesterol also can be found in small amounts in powdered dairy products such as milk, cheese or butter. One soon-to-be-released study found significant amounts in fast food french fries that had been cooked in animal fat. Edward Blonz *PPNF Health Journal*

EGGPLANT TORTA
Serves 8

6 medium eggplants, peeled and sliced lengthwise
about 2 tablespoons sea salt
about 1/2 cup extra virgin olive oil
2 cups chunky tomato sauce (page 154)
1 cup freshly grated Parmesan cheese
1 cup freshly grated Monterey Jack cheese
3 large eggs, beaten

Salt the eggplant slices, cover and leave at room temperature for 1 hour. Rinse eggplant slices and dry well. Brush both sides with olive oil, place on baking sheets and bake at 375 for about 15 minutes or until lightly browned and soft. Line the bottom and sides of an oiled 9-inch springform pan with eggplant slices. Spread 1/3 of sauce over eggplant and sprinkle with 1/3 of the cheeses. Make another layer of eggplant, cutting edges so it fits neatly, followed by layer of sauce and cheese. Make a final layer of eggplant, sauce and remaining Monterey Jack cheese. Poke holes in the torta and pour the eggs over the top so that they soak in evenly. Sprinkle top with remaining Parmesan. Bake on a baking sheet at 350 degrees for about 1/2 hour. Let cool and run a knife around the inside of the pan before releasing spring. Cut into wedges with a serrated knife. May be served with additional tomato sauce.

RED PEPPER QUICHE

Serves 4-8

1 recipe flaky pie crust (page 557)
    or 1/2 recipe yoghurt dough (page 485)
2 red peppers, seeded and cut into a julienne
1 medium onion, finely sliced
2 tablespoons extra virgin olive oil
3 egg yolks
1/2 cup creme fraiche or piima cream (page 84)
sea salt and pepper
1 cup freshly grated Parmesan or
    Monterey Jack cheese

Roll out dough and line a 10-inch, French-style tart pan with a removable bottom. Half bake the crust at 325 degrees for about 15 to 30 minutes (longer for yoghurt dough). Meanwhile, sauté peppers and onion in olive oil until soft. Beat yolks with cream, seasonings and half of the cheese. Strew the peppers over the crust and pour the egg mixture over. Top with remaining cheese and bake at 350 degrees for about 1/2 hour.

Variation: Mushroom Quiche

Substitute *1 pound fresh mushrooms, washed, well dried and sliced* for the peppers. Sauté in a mixture of *2 tablespoons each of butter and olive oil* and proceed with recipe.

Variation: Zucchini Quiche

Omit peppers and use *2 medium zucchini, cut into a julienne*, using the julienne slicer of your food processor. Mix with *about 1 tablespoon salt* and drain in a colander for 1/2 hour. Rinse and squeeze dry in a dish towel. Strew zucchini over crust and proceed with recipe.

Since eggs have the highest amount of cholesterol per unit weight of all common foods (liver and brains have more), people began to fear them. Once called nature's most perfect food by nutritionists, eggs fell into disfavor and their consumption began to plummet after 1950. The average number of eggs consumed in the U.S. per person per year dropped from a high of 389 in 1950 . . . to only 234 in 1989. Americans are eating many fewer eggs today than at the turn of the century. . . . Thousands of egg farmers have gone out of business over the last 30 years because of the false dietary cholesterol scare. And millions of Americans have given up or substantially reduced their consumption of one of the best and most economical foods available for no good scientific or common sense reasons. Russell L. Smith, PhD *Health Freedom News*

When I was chief physician at Hotel Dieu Hospital, Paris, some 3,500 patients passed through my hands during a year. Before my term expired I tried the experiment of giving one-half of the patients that were then present no medicines at all; the rest, the usual medical treatment. The former were given, instead, only what is known as "Food and Home Remedies," and, to my unbounded surprise, they all got well—not a single death; while among those receiving medical treatment the customary number of deaths occurred. A second trial yielded a like result, and I was converted. Ever since I have given but little medicine to my patients.
Dr. F. Magendie

By far the most efficient plant food that I have found for producing the high-vitamin content in milk is rapidly growing young wheat and rye grass. Oat and barley grass are also excellent. In my clinical work, small additions of this high-vitamin butter [from cows feeding on growing grass] to otherwise satisfactory diets regularly checks tooth decay when active and at the same time improves vitality and general health. . . . Similarly the value of eggs for providing fat-soluble vitamins depends directly upon the food eaten by the fowl. The fertility of the eggs also is a direct measure of the vitamin content, including vitamin E. Weston Price, DDS *Nutrition and Physical Degeneration*

A number of studies reveal that the elimination of eggs from the diet does not lower the risk of coronary heart disease. One study, conducted by Cuyler Hammond and Lawrence Garfinkel of the American Cancer Society, involved 804,409 individuals who had no previous history of coronary heart disease. They were divided into two groups. One group was made up of those who ate five or more eggs each week in addition to eggs used in preparing other foods. The second group ate no eggs or less than four per week. The death rate from heart attacks and strokes was higher in the second group. H. Leon Abrams *Vegetarianism: An Anthropological/Nutritional Evaluation*

CHEESE SOUFFLE
Serves 6

6 eggs, separated, at room temperature
6 tablespoons butter
6 tablespoons unbleached flour
1 cup good quality cream, not ultrapasteurized
*   mixed with 1 cup water, warmed*
1 cup grated Swiss cheese
1 cup grated Parmesan cheese
sea salt and pepper

Melt butter in a heavy saucepan. Add flour and stir with a wooden spoon for several minutes until flour turns light brown. Gradually add warm cream and water mixture, beating with a wire whisk until the mixture thickens. Remove from heat and stir in the egg yolks, one at a time, and then the cheese. Season to taste. Place egg whites in a very clean glass or stainless steel bowl, add a pinch of sea salt and beat until stiff. Gently fold egg yolk mixture into egg whites and pour into a buttered, 2-quart soufflé dish. Place in a preheated 400-degree oven, lower heat to 350 degrees and bake for 40 to 45 minutes. Serve immediately.

WELSH RAREBIT
Serves 3-4

1 tablespoon butter
2 1/2 cups raw Cheddar cheese, grated
1/4 teaspoon sea salt
1/4 teaspoon dry mustard
dash of cayenne pepper
1 teaspoon fish sauce (page 157)
1/2-3/4 cup heavy cream
2 egg yolks

Melt butter in a container set in simmering water. Add the cheese and stir until melted. Stir in salt, mustard, cayenne pepper and fish sauce. Slowly add the cream, stirring constantly, and stir until the mixture is hot. Remove the container from water and beat in egg yolks. To serve, ladle onto triangle croutons (page 520).

SANDWICH SUGGESTIONS

As sandwiches are a fixture on the American food scene, we should make every attempt to prepare them with nutritious ingredients. Fundamental to this effort is avoidance of the usual sandwich ingredients—preserved meats, condiments containing sugar and polyunsaturated oils, processed cheeses and unsuitable breads.

It is, in fact, modern bread that makes the sandwich possible and palatable. Old style, sourdough, slow-rise breads are too dense and hard for sandwich lovers; it was the advent of baker's yeast that allowed bakers to produce softly spongy and uniform bread for sandwiches. Baker's yeast produces a quick rise in bread in a very short period of time so that phytates in whole grains are not properly neutralized. Thus, both commercial whole grain and refined flour sandwich breads present health risks, especially when so many dough conditioners and preservatives are added, as is the custom.

However, there are compromise breads available that will serve for sandwiches. They are, unfortunately, all made with baker's yeast; but the grains are first allowed to sprout or sour. Look for sourdough or sprouted grain sandwich breads, preferably made with a variety of grains, in the freezer compartment of your health food store, or use our yeasted buttermilk bread (page 493) Pita bread has the opposite profile—it is not made with yeast; but, unfortunately, the dough is not allowed to sour. It should be avoided by those with grain allergies. It would be a shame, however, to prohibit pita bread altogether, as it makes such a great pocket for sandwich fillings.

Make an effort, then, to obtain nutritious bread and use it to produce sandwiches featuring fresh meats, marinated fish, nut butters, raw cheeses, sprouts, fresh and fermented vegetables, avocado, fresh butter, homemade mayonnaise and other spreads with a high-enzyme content.

Sandwiches in lunch boxes may be accompanied by fresh fruit, homemade cookies, crispy nuts (pages 513-516), trail mix (page 517), raw vegetables and a thermos of homemade ginger ale (page 586), apple cider (page 587) or other refreshing lacto-fermented beverage. Samosas (page 363), empanadas (page 435) and breaded chicken breasts (page 284) also make nice lunch-box fare.

It seems that our contemporaries have little time to prepare nice meals—frozen foods, canned foods, fast foods have invaded our supermarkets and our restaurants.

We misunderstand our ancestors when we think that they could spend hours and hours preparing their meals. The old cook books may give this impression but these books were for the upper classes that could afford to hire cooks. Among the peasants, the women worked in the fields and there remained little time in the evenings to prepare dinner. At noon, the men often ate in the fields. For lunch they needed foods that were easily prepared—they needed "fast food"—and for dinner they ate one course meals, invariably something simple.

Many fermented foods can be eaten without any preparation—bread, cheese, sausage, lacto-fermented vegetables, olives, anchovies, fish and soy sauces, and many others.

After all, we didn't have to wait for the Americans to invent the cheese sandwich—a fermented fast food that is delicious as well as nutritious as long as the bread and the cheese are of good quality (increasingly rare these days because the fermentation process has been industrialized and therefore denatured).

The Russians also invented fast food—long before the Americans. When Turgenov's hunter arrives without warning at the peasant's cottage, he is invariable offered rye bread, cheese, pickled cucumbers and kvass—three fermented foods and one fermented drink always ready to be served to the passing guest. Claude Aubert *Les Aliments Fermentés Traditionnels*

NUT BUTTER SANDWICHES

Use peanut, cashew or almond butter (page 516) with naturally sweetened jam, apricot butter (page 110) or raw honey.

TUNA SANDWICHES

Use simple tuna salad (page 416) or tuna tahini salad (page 417). Spread bread with mayonnaise (page 137) or mashed avocado and fill with choice of small seed sprouts (page 115), thinly sliced tomato and lettuce.

TURKEY OR CHICKEN SANDWICHES

Used leftover turkey or chicken or buy a whole turkey breast and bake in the oven. Slice thinly. Spread bread with butter, mayonnaise (page 137) or Creole mayonnaise (page 139). Fill with choice of thinly sliced tomato, small seed sprouts (page 115), lettuce, thinly sliced red onions or sliced avocado.

CHICKEN SALAD SANDWICH

Spread bread with curried mayonnaise (page 139) and fill with curried chicken salad (page 414).

REUBEN SANDWICH

This delicious sandwich is composed of four fermented foods—five if you use cultured butter. Spread sourdough bread with butter and fill with thinly sliced corned beef (page 237), thinly sliced Swiss cheese and sauerkraut (page 92). Sauté sandwich lightly on both sides in a small amount of butter or extra virgin olive oil until lightly browned and the interior is slightly warmed.

ROAST BEEF SANDWICHES

Use thinly sliced roast beef with choice of thinly sliced red onions, small seed sprouts (page 115), avocado or lettuce. Spread bread with butter, Creole mayonnaise (page 139), horseradish sauce (page 142) or mustard.

VEGETABLE SANDWICHES

Spread bread thickly with butter and fill with thinly sliced radishes, thinly sliced red onion, thinly sliced cucumber or a combination. Cucumber also goes well with homemade cream cheese (page 87).

RAW CHEESE SANDWICHES

Spread bread with butter or mayonnaise (page 137). Fill with thinly sliced raw cheese. Raw Cheddar cheese goes nicely with raisin chutney (page 108). Raw Monterey Jack cheese goes well with cortido (page 93).

HERB FRITATA SANDWICH

Spread bread with butter or mayonnaise (page 137) and fill with thin herb fritatas (page 443).

MARINATED FISH SANDWICHES

Place sliced marinated salmon (page 238), drained and flaked pickled salmon (page 241) or mackerel (page 242) on toasted bread spread with homemade cream cheese (page 87), butter, mayonnaise (page 137), Creole mayonnaise (page 139) or cream cheese-flax spread (page 165). A small amount of pickled vegetable, such as sauerkraut (page 92) or daikon radish (page 98), may be added as fill.

MEAT LOAF SANDWICH

Spread bread with mayonnaise (page 137) or homemade ketchup (page 104) and fill with sliced spicy meat loaf (page 356) and thinly shredded romaine lettuce.

Know Your Ingredients
Name This Product #25

Enriched flour (wheat flour, malted barley flour, iron, niacin, thiamine mononitrate, riboflavin), water, wheat bran, honey, high fructose corn syrup, soya bran, canola oil and/or soybean oil, rolled oats, rye flakes. Contains 2% or less of each of the following: molasses, raisin juice, crushed wheat, yeast, wheat gluten, salt, cultured whey, calcium sulfate, dough conditioners (may contain one or more of the following: calcium and sodium stearoyl, lactylate, ethoxylated mono- and diglycerides, monocalcium phosphate, calcium carbonate), mono- and diglycerides, yeast nutrient (ammonium sulfate). "No artificial preservatives added."

See Appendix B for Answer

A few decades ago, the late Gena Larson, nutritionist at Helix High School in La Mesa, California, shifted school lunches from junk foods to whole grain breads and rolls, raw certified milk and to fresh fruits and vegetables.

School marks shot up dramatically, and sports records that had stood for years were broken by athletes. Additionally, sports injuries declined sharply with far fewer broken bones than ever before. James F. Scheer *Health Freedom News*

"Doctor, is my baby all right?" is the first question of almost every woman when her child is born. I myself have heard the question thousands of times. If every mother's greatest wish is to have a truly healthy baby, why (in most cases) does she take such poor care of herself before the baby is born? And why does she feed her child from infancy to adulthood so improperly that illness inevitably results?

This century has been called "The Century of the Child" because of the tremendous interest in the physical and psychological growth of children. But as we look around us, where are these radiantly healthy children? Certainly their parents are anxious to rear healthy youngsters. Some eight thousand books on child care have been published in the last twenty-five years. Why then are the offices of the country's thousands of pediatricians and general practitioners filled with runny-nosed, tired, allergic, feverish, rundown, anemic, bespectacled, acne-ridden, too thin or obese children? The answer is simple:

(1) The mother's body was no fit environment for the child because her system was filled with waste products from improper food, drug residues, coffee acids, the poisons of cigarettes and alcohol.

(2) The growing child is improperly fed, spends too much time watching television, is driven everywhere instead of walking and devotes too little time to exercising in fresh air. Henry Bieler, MD *Food Is Your Best Medicine*

PITA BREAD SANDWICHES

Fill whole wheat pita bread with any of the following combinations:

Falafel (page 506), tahini sauce (page 148) and thinly sliced cucumber and tomato.

Mazalika (page 314), tahini sauce (page 148) and thinly sliced cucumber and tomato.

Curried chicken salad (page 414).

Grated raw cheese, shredded lettuce and salsa (page 103).

Sliced chicken or turkey, mayonnaise (page 137) or tahini sauce (page 148), shredded lettuce and thinly sliced tomato.

Simple tuna salad (page 416), mayonnaise (page 137), avocado, thinly sliced tomato and small seed sprouts (page 115).

Oriental red meat salad (page 423).

ROLL UPS

Use sprouted whole wheat tortillas and roll up with any of the following combinations:

Cream cheese flax-spread (page 165), marinated salmon (page 238), dill sprigs and thinly sliced onion.

Creole mayonnaise (page 139), thinly sliced chicken or turkey, small seed sprouts (page 115) and thinly sliced tomato.

Mexican chicken breasts (page 283), sliced across the grain, guacamole (page 172) and chismole (page 184).

Thinly sliced roast beef, egg mustard sauce (page 143) and thinly sliced onion.

GRAINS & LEGUMES

WHOLE GRAINS

The well-meaning advice of many nutritionists, to consume whole grains as our ancestors did and not refined flours and polished rice, is misleading and often harmful in its consequences; for while our ancestors ate whole grains, they did not consume them as presented in our modern cookbooks in the form of quick-rise breads, granolas and other hastily prepared casseroles and concoctions. Our ancestors, and virtually all preindustrialized peoples, soaked or fermented their grains before making them into porridge, breads, cakes and casseroles. A quick review of grain recipes from around the world will prove our point: In India rice and lentils are fermented for at least two days before they are prepared as *idli* and *dosas*; in Africa the natives soak coarsely ground corn overnight before adding it to soups and stews, and they ferment corn or millet for several days to produce a sour porridge called *ogi*; a similar dish made from oats was traditional among the Welsh; in some Oriental and Latin American countries rice receives a long fermentation before it is prepared; Ethiopians make their distinctive *injera* bread by fermenting a grain called teff for several days; Mexican corn cakes, called *pozol*, are fermented for several days and for as long as two weeks in banana leaves; before the introduction of commercial brewers yeast, Europeans made slow-rise breads from fermented starters; in America the pioneers were famous for their sourdough breads, pancakes and biscuits; and throughout Europe grains were soaked overnight, and for as long as several days, in water or soured milk before they were cooked and served as porridge or gruel. (Many of our senior citizens may remember that in earlier times the instructions on the oatmeal box called for an overnight soaking.)

This is not the place to speculate on that mysterious instructive spirit that taught our ancestors to soak and ferment their grains before eating them; the important thing to realize is that these practices accord very well with what modern science has discovered about grains. All grains contain phytic acid (an organic acid in which phosphorus is bound) in the outer layer or bran. Untreated phytic acid can combine with calcium, magnesium, copper, iron and especially zinc in the intestinal tract and block their absorption. This is why a diet high in unfermented whole grains may lead to serious mineral deficiencies and bone loss. The modern misguided practice of consuming large amounts of unprocessed bran often improves colon transit time at first but may lead to irritable bowel syndrome and, in the long term, many other adverse effects. Soaking allows enzymes, *lactobacilli* and other helpful organisms to break down and neutralize phytic acid. As little as seven hours of soaking in warm acidulated water will neutralize a large portion of phytic acid in grains. The simple practice of soaking cracked or rolled cereal grains overnight will vastly improve their nutritional benefits.

Soaking in warm water also neutralizes enzyme inhibitors, present in all seeds, and encourages the production of numerous beneficial enzymes. The action of these enzymes also increases the amounts of many vitamins, especially B vitamins.

Scientists have learned that the proteins in grains, especially gluten, are very difficult to digest. A diet high in unfermented whole grains, particularly high-gluten grains like wheat, puts an enormous strain on the whole digestive mechanism. When this mechanism breaks down with age or overuse, the results take the form of allergies, celiac disease, mental illness, chronic indigestion and *candida albicans* overgrowth. Recent research links gluten intolerance with multiple sclerosis. During the process of soaking and fermenting, gluten and other difficult-to-digest proteins are partially broken down into simpler components that are more readily available for absorption.

Animals that nourish themselves primarily on grain and other plant matter have as many as four stomachs. Their intestines are longer as is the entire digestion transit time. Man, on the other hand, has but one stomach and a much shorter intestine compared to herbivorous animals. These features of his anatomy allow him to pass animal products before they putrefy in the gut but make him less well adapted to a diet high in grains—unless, of course, he lets the friendly bacteria of the microscopic world do some of his digesting for him in a container, just as these same *lactobacilli* do their work in the first and second stomachs of the herbivores.

Grains fall into two general categories. Those containing gluten, such as oats, rye, barley and especially wheat, should not be consumed unless they have been soaked or fermented; buckwheat, rice and millet do not contain gluten and are, on the whole, more easily digested. Whole rice and whole millet contain lower amounts of phytates than other grains so it is not absolutely necessary to soak them. However, they should be gently steamed for at least two hours in a high-mineral, gelatinous broth. This will neutralize some of the phytates they do contain and provide additional minerals to compensate for those that are still bound; while the gelatin in the broth will greatly facilitate digestion. We do not recommend the pressure cooker for grains because it cooks them too quickly.

We use several grains that are new to the Western vocabulary. One is spelt, an ancient grain of the wheat family praised by the medieval sage St. Hildegard as being particularly suited to the sick and those of a weak constitution. It contains gluten and gives excellent results for sourdough bread. Some studies indicate that spelt gluten breaks down easily during fermentation, making it more digestible than modern varieties of wheat. In most cases, spelt can be substituted for modern wheat varieties in whole grain breads and pastries. Another ancient nonhybrid variety of wheat is kamut, which dates back to early Egyptian times. Some people who are allergic to modern varieties of wheat report better results when they use kamut or spelt instead.

Teff is a grain from northern Africa, invariably fermented before being made into bread. Quinoa comes from the South American Andes and was first described in Western literature by Dr. Weston Price. He noted that women in the Andes valued quinoa for its ability to stimulate breast milk. Not technically a grain, but the fruit of the Chenopodium family, it has superior nutritional properties. All quinoa products should be soaked—Andean Indians recognize that the antinutrients in quinoa are neutralized in this way. Amaranth is another newly discovered grain, also from South America, that can be used in many of the following recipes. Buckwheat, another neglected grain, is valuable for its high content of cancer-preventing nitrilosides. Like quinoa, buckwheat is not technically a grain but the seed of an herb, a relative of rhubarb.

Our readers will notice that our recipes for breakfast cereals are all porridges that have been soaked overnight before they are cooked. If you buy grains that have been rolled or cracked, they should be in packages and not taken from bins, where they have a tendency to go rancid. Even better, buy organic or biodynamic whole grains and roll or crack them yourself using a roller or grain grinder. (See Sources.) You may also add a little ground flax seed to start your day with a ration of omega-3 fatty acids. (Flax seed is low in phytic acid and does not require soaking if it is eaten in small amounts.) These porridges marry very well with butter or cream, whose fat-soluble activators provide the necessary catalyst for mineral absorption. Those with milk allergies can usually tolerate a little cream on their breakfast cereal or can eat them with butter—a delicious combination. We do not recommend soy milk, which contains many antinutrients.

Nor do we recommend granola, a popular "health" food made from grains subjected only to dry heat and therefore extremely indigestible. Granola, like all processed breakfast cereals, should have no place on our cupboard shelves. Boxed breakfast cereals are made by the extrusion process, in which little flakes and shapes are formed at high temperatures and pressures. Extrusion processing destroys many valuable nutrients in grains, causes fragile oils to become rancid and renders certain proteins toxic. For a new generation of hardy children, we must return to the breakfast cereals of our ancestors—soaked gruels and porridges.

A word about corn: Traditional recipes call for soaking corn or corn flour in lime water. This releases nicotinamide (vitamin B_3), which otherwise remains bound up in the grain. Soaking also improves the amino acid quality of proteins in the germ. If you use corn products often, the simple precaution of soaking corn flour in lime water will help avoid the vitamin B_3 deficiency disease pellagra with its cruel symptoms of sore skin, fatigue and mental disorders. To make lime water, place about *1 inch pickling lime* (see Sources) in a 2-quart jar. Fill jar with filtered water, shake well, cover tightly and let stand overnight. The powder will settle and the resultant clear liquid is lime water. Store in a cool place (it's not necessary to refrigerate) and use for soaking cornmeal by pouring out carefully. You may also use commercial *masa* flour which is cornmeal that has been prepared by soaking corn kernels in lime water before grinding. However, like all whole grain flours, cornmeal quickly goes rancid and develops a bitter taste, so it's best to grind your own corn. (For corn mills and whole corn kernels, see Sources.)

BREAKFAST PORRIDGE

Serves 4

1 cup oats, rolled or cracked
1 cup warm filtered water plus 2 tablespoons whey,
    yoghurt, kefir or buttermilk (pages 83-87)
1/2 teaspoon sea salt
1 cup filtered water
1 tablespoon flax seeds (optional)

For highest benefits and best assimilation, porridge should be soaked overnight or even longer. Once soaked, oatmeal cooks up in less than 5 minutes—truly a fast *food*. (Note: Those with severe milk allergies can use *lemon juice or vinegar* in place of whey, yoghurt, kefir or buttermilk.)

Mix oats with warm water mixture, cover and leave in a warm place for at least 7 hours and as long as 24 hours. Bring an additional 1 cup of water to a boil with sea salt. Add soaked oats, reduce heat, cover and simmer several minutes. Meanwhile, grind optional flax seeds in a mini grinder. Remove from heat, stir in optional flax seeds and let stand for a few minutes. Serve with plenty of butter or cream and a natural sweetener like Rapadura, date sugar, maple syrup, maple sugar or raw honey. You may also wish to add apricot butter (page 110), chopped crispy nuts (pages 513-516) or dried sweetened coconut meat (page 159).

Variation: Kamut or Spelt Porridge
Use *1 cup rolled or coarsely ground kamut or spelt* instead of oats.

Variation: Rye Porridge
Use *1 cup rolled or coarsely ground rye* instead of oats. Rye may need extra soaking time and more water for complete hydration.

Variation: Teff Porridge
Use *1 cup whole teff.* May be soaked overnight but 24 hours is better. Delicious as a breakfast cereal.

Variation: Amaranth Porridge
Use *1 cup amaranth.* Prepare as teff porridge.

Variation: Grits
Use *1 cup coarsely ground corn* and *1 cup limewater* (see page 454) in place of filtered water.

The basic foods of these [isolated Gaelic] islanders are fish and oat products with a little barley. Oat grain is the one cereal which develops fairly readily, and it provides the porridge and oatcakes which in many homes are eaten in some form regularly with each meal. The fishing about the Outer Hebrides is specially favorable; and small seafoods, including lobsters, crabs, oysters and clams, are abundant. An important and highly relished article of diet has been baked cod's head stuffed with chopped cod's liver and oatmeal. . . [in the ports the] hardy fisherwomen often toil from six in the morning to ten at night. [We saw] fisher people with teeth of unusual perfection. . . . It would be difficult to find examples of womanhood combining a higher degree of physical perfection and more exalted ideals than these weather-hardened toilers. Theirs is a land of frequent gales, often sleet ridden or enshrouded in penetrating cold fogs. Life is full of meaning for characters that are developed to accept as everyday routine raging seas and piercing blizzards representing the accumulated fury of the treacherous North Atlantic. One marvels at their gentleness, refinement and sweetness of character. Weston Price, DDS *Nutrition and Physical Degeneration*

Samuel Johnson defined oats as "a grain used in England to feed horses and in Scotland to feed the populace." It has been observed that in these two regions oats have produced magnificent examples of both species. Folklore values oats as contributing to strength, endurance, energy, beauty and perceptiveness.

Although first discovered growing wild in barley fields in Russia, northern Africa and the Near East, oats thrive in colder climates of Scotland, Ireland and England. They were planted in Massachusetts in the 1600's and served as porridge for the growing nation. Oats are rich in B vitamins and in calcium, iron, magnesium, phosphorus and potassium. They contain more oil than most grains. Oats are low in gluten but contain more phytates than almost any other grain. Thus, it is very important to soak oats before preparation. The phytates are contained in the bran of the oat and can have a chelating or detoxifying effect. This is why the oat bran fad gave beneficial results at first; but frequent ingestion of unsoaked oat bran can lead to mineral losses, allergies and irritation of the intestinal tract.

In Scotland it was the custom to prepare oatmeal in large batches and pour the cooked cereal into a drawer in the kitchen hutch or dresser! Squares of congealed oatmeal could then be cut out as needed and reheated by adding a little water. This process allowed the oatmeal to ferment a second time.

Avoid buying rolled or cracked (steel cut) oats from bins as they may be rancid. Buy them in packages or, better yet, coarse grind whole oats in a grain grinder or "roll your own" with a grain roller. (See Sources.) SWF

IRISH OATMEAL
Serves 4-6

1 cup whole oats
2 cups warm filtered water
4 tablespoons whey, yoghurt, kefir or buttermilk
(pages 83-87)
1 teaspoon sea salt
1 1/2 cups filtered water

Place oats on a baking sheet and bake at 350 degrees until they turn light brown. Process roasted oats to a medium grind in a home grinder. (The resultant meal should be part flour, part small bits.) Soak from 7 to 24 hours in a warm place in 2 cups warm water plus whey, yoghurt, kefir or buttermilk. (Note: Those with severe milk allergies can use *lemon juice or vinegar* in place of whey, yoghurt, kefir or buttermilk.) The fine flour particles will rise to the top and may be lifted off carefully with a spoon.

Bring additional 1 1/2 cups water and sea salt to a boil, add soaked oatmeal and cook over very low heat, stirring frequently, for about 10 minutes.

MISO PORRIDGE
Serves 4

1 cup oats, rolled or cracked
2 cups filtered water
2 tablespoons naturally fermented light miso
(see Sources)

In the evening, cook oatmeal in water for 5-10 minutes or until all water is absorbed. Allow to cool and mix in miso. Cover and leave the mixture at room temperature overnight. In the morning, reheat gently without bringing to a boil.

MUESLI

Serves 4

1 cup rolled oats
1/4 cup crispy almond slivers (page 515)
1/4 cup dried sweetened coconut meat (page 159)
*   or commercial dried unsweetened coconut*
1/2 teaspoon cinnamon
1 1/2 cups warm filtered water
*   plus 2 tablespoons whey, yoghurt,*
*   kefir or buttermilk (pages 83-87)*
1/2 teaspoon salt
1 cup filtered water
1/4 cup raisins
1 tablespoon flax seeds (optional)

Mix oats with almonds, cinnamon and coconut. Combine oat mixture with warm water mixture, cover and soak at room temperature for at least 7 hours and as long as 24 hours. (Note: Those with severe milk allergies can use *lemon juice or vinegar* in place of whey, yoghurt, kefir or buttermilk.) Bring an additional 1 cup of water to boil with sea salt. Add soaked oats and raisins, reduce heat, cover and simmer several minutes. Meanwhile, grind optional flax seeds in a mini grinder. Remove cereal from heat and stir in flax meal. Serve with butter or cream and a natural sweetener like Rapadura, date sugar, maple syrup, maple sugar or raw honey.

FRIED MUSH

Makes 3 patties

1 1/2 cups leftover breakfast porridge or grits
*   (page 455)*
1 egg, lightly beaten
2 tablespoons butter or lard

This makes an excellent and economical after-school snack. Mix porridge with egg. Sauté by spoonfuls in butter or lard until golden and the edges are crispy. Serve with maple syrup, sorghum syrup or honey.

In the history of food, gruel and porridge came before bread. For cereals unsuitable to bread making, such as oats, corn or millet, this remains the principle way of consuming these grains. In northern Europe, oat and rye porridges were daily fare. "Porridge is the mother of us all" is a Russian proverb. Millet and buckwheat porridge were eaten in warmer regions. They were very popular in Germany as well as in eastern Europe and in France. The Gaules were great consumers of millet porridge.

The term "gruel" and "porridge" covers preparations of differing consistencies, from rather liquid gruels that are drunk to *polenta*, which you can cut with a knife. In what measure were these preparations fermented? . . . . *Braga*, one of the most ancient sour gruels that we know of, is prepared with a thick porridge of cooked millet that is then diluted and fermented. Of a rather liquid consistency, it is drunk rather than eaten. Like other sour gruels of central and eastern Europe—*kiesiel, gieslitz, zu, braga*—can be compared to certain "beers" made from grains in Africa and South America—it is impossible to draw a precise line between these gruels and traditional beers. These are true liquid meals, like that of the Babylonians called "drinkable bread" and have played an important role in almost all civilizations. In Brittany *l'ar yod kierc'h*—oat porridge—was formerly eaten after one night of fermentation. This overnight fermentation gives this traditional dish its characteristic taste, slightly acid, that one seeks in vain in modern porridges . . . . But who still eats oatmeal—even in Brittany? Claude Aubert *Les Aliments Fermentés Traditionnels*

The poisons and medicines attack the evil influences. The five grains act as nourishment; the five fruits from the trees serve to augment; the five domestic animals provide additional benefit; the five vegetables serve to complete the nourishment. Their flavors, tastes and smells unite and conform to each other in order to supply the beneficial essence of life. Each of these five flavors—pungent, sour, sweet, bitter, and salt—provides a certain advantage and benefit. Their effect is either dispersing or binding and gathering, retarding or accelerating, strengthening or softening. *The Yellow Emperor's Classic of Internal Medicine*

Flax is an ancient plant found in northern climes whose seed oil is the richest known source of triple unsaturated omega-3 fatty acids. Before the advent of large commercial oil presses, flax "beaters" in European and Russian villages pressed oil out of flax seeds and sold it from door to door on a weekly basis, much as dairy products and eggs were also sold. Without knowing why, northern European peoples valued flax oil as a folk remedy. Flax oil has been used in natural programs for the treatment of heart disease, cancer, diabetes, PMS, arthritis and inflammatory and fibroid conditions. It can be added to the diet in small amounts but should not be consumed in excess.

Flax is also an excellent source of mucilage and fiber. Flax is the richest known source of lignans, substances that have antiviral, antifungal, antibacterial and anticancer properties. It is also rich in silica, needed for healthy skin, hair and ligaments as well as for flexible bones. Flax seeds are low in phytic acid and therefore do not require soaking if they are consumed in small amounts. SWF

FIVE GRAIN CEREAL MIX
Makes 10 cups

2 cups wheat or spelt
2 cups millet
2 cups short grain rice
2 cups barley or oats
2 cups split peas or lentils

This combination of grains conforms to the five grains recommended in the *Yellow Emperor's Classic of Internal Medicine*.

Mix together and grind coarsely. Store in refrigerator.

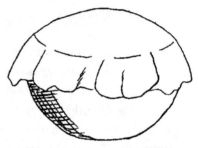

FIVE GRAIN PORRIDGE
Serves 4

1 cup five grain cereal mix
1 cup warm filtered water plus 2 tablespoons whey, yoghurt, kefir or buttermilk (pages 83-87)
1/2 teaspoon salt
1 cup filtered water
1-2 egg yolks

Combine five grain mix with warm water mixture, cover and leave in a warm place for at least 7 hours and as long as 24 hours. (Note: Those with severe milk allergies can use *lemon juice or vinegar* in place of whey, kefir, yoghurt or buttermilk.) Bring an additional 1 cup of water to a boil with sea salt. Add soaked cereal, reduce heat, cover and simmer several minutes. Remove from heat, let cool slightly and stir in the egg yolks. Serve with butter or cream and a natural sweetener, such as Rapadura, date sugar, maple syrup or raw honey.

AFRICAN MILLET PORRIDGE
(Ogi)

4 cups millet
filtered water
1/4 cup whey (page 87)

This is a recipe for the brave, the adventurous and the curious. Place millet in a large bowl. Cover with water. Place a clean towel over the bowl and leave in a warm place for 24 hours. Pour off water and process until smooth, in batches, in a food processor. Place ground millet in a bowl and mix with a generous amount of water. Strain through a strainer into another large bowl or pitcher, discarding the coarse bran slurry left in the strainer. Mix whey with strained liquid, cover and leave in a warm place for 24 to 72 hours.

This thick liquid may now be cooked as porridge. Place 1 cup in a small pan and bring to a boil, stirring constantly with a wooden spoon. Cook, stirring, for several minutes. The resultant porridge will be very sour and may be eaten with a natural sweetener and butter or cream. Store the remaining ogi in the refrigerator until ready to prepare.

The *ogi* may be also be reduced to a very sour paste, called *agidi*, by the following method: Line a large strainer with a linen towel and pour the *ogi* into the strainer. Tie up ends of the cloth to make a sack and tie this sack to wooden spoon suspended over a pitcher or bowl. Let the *ogi* drain, just as you would drain cream cheese (see page 87). Store the strained *agidi* in the refrigerator in an airtight container. To prepare as porridge, bring *1 cup water* to a boil with *1/2 teaspoon salt*. Stir in *1/2 cup agidi* and simmer, covered, several minutes. Eat as you would porridge, with a natural sweetener and butter or cream.

Variation: Welsh Oat Porridge (Llymru)

Use *oats* instead of millet. May be soaked in *buttermilk* instead of water.

Acid porridges prepared from cereals are still eaten . . . in different parts of the world, particularly in the developing countries, where they may represent the basic diet. *Ogi* (Nigeria), *Uji* (Kenya) and *Koko* (Ghana) are examples of these porridges prepared by the fermentation of maize, sorghum, millet or cassava followed by wet-milling, wet-sieving and boiling . . . . Ogi porridge has a smooth texture similar to a hot blancmange and a sour taste reminiscent of yogurt . . . . Ogi is consumed as a porridge (*pap*), with about 8% solids, or a gel-like product (*agidi*) by a very large number of Nigerians. Pap is by far the most important traditional food for weaning infants and the major breakfast cereal of adults. Infants 9 months old are introduced to ogi by feeding once per day as a supplement to breast milk. Keith H. Steinkraus, ed. p189 *Handbook of Indigenous Fermented Foods*, Courtesy Marcel Dekker, Inc.

Millet is the chief cereal grain for millions of people, particularly those living on the poor dry lands of India, Africa, China and Russia. Millet was important in Europe during the Middle Ages before corn and potatoes were know there, but it is of minor importance in Europe today. It is used to make a fermented porridge in Africa and a fermented beer in several parts of the world. As millet lacks gluten, it cannot be used to make leavened bread but it is suitable in diets for those allergic to gluten. It is also relatively low in phytic acid compared to other grains. Millet is very high in silica, which helps keep bones flexible as we age. Millet does contain a goitrogen in the hull or bran, so should be avoided by those with thyroid problems; or, if consumed in large amounts, the bran should be discarded (as it is in African recipes). SWF

That healthy plants are essential to animal life and that animal excrement acts as a soil rejuvenator is widely recognized, but that possible harm is done to human life when disturbances or deficiencies occur in any phase of the biological cycle is not widely recognized.

Modern man has gleaned his fields to fill his larder, but his system of sanitary engineering has destroyed most of the soil rejuvenating, organic materials. No longer does man return to the soil those materials taken from the soil. Instead he pours them into the ocean and loses them to his civilization. Harsh mineral fertilizers, which destroy soil bacteria and earthworms, are being substituted for the organic compost of the past to the long-range detriment of the soil at one end of the biological cycle and of human life at the other. Francis M. Pottenger, Jr., MD *Pottenger's Cats*

Know Your Ingredients
Name This Product #26

Corn, whole wheat, sugar, rolled oats, brown sugar, rice, partially hydrogenated sunflower oil, malted barley, salt, corn syrup, whey, malt syrup, honey, artificial flavor, and annatto extract (for color). BHT added to packaging material to preserve freshness.

See Appendix B for Answer

MILLET CASSEROLE
Serves 6-8

2 cups whole millet
4 cups warm filtered water plus 4 tablespoons whey,
*   yoghurt, kefir or buttermilk (pages 83-87)*
1 teaspoon sea salt
2-4 tablespoons butter

Place millet and warm water mixture in a flameproof pot and leave in a warm place for at least 7 hours. (Note: Those with severe milk allergies can use *lemon juice or vinegar* in place of whey, yoghurt, kefir or buttermilk.) Bring to a boil, skim, reduce heat, stir in salt and butter and cover tightly. Without removing lid, cook over lowest possible heat for about 45 minutes.

MILLET CAKES
Makes about 8

4 cups cooked millet
4 eggs
1/2 cup bulgur flour (page 461) or
*   unbleached white flour*
1/4 teaspoon cayenne pepper
1 teaspoon salt
1/2 teaspoon pepper
1 medium onion, finely chopped
1 bunch cilantro, chopped
3/4 cup grated Parmesan cheese (optional)
3 tablespoons butter
3 tablespoons extra virgin olive oil

Blend eggs with flour and seasonings and fold in millet, onion, cilantro and optional cheese. Form into patties and sauté in a mixture of butter and olive oil.

BULGUR
Makes 4 cups

3 cups soft wheat berries
filtered water

Bulgur or cracked wheat is a staple of Middle Eastern cuisine, used in tabouli, kibbeh, soups and casseroles. It is traditionally made from sprouted grain for a product infinitely more delicious and digestible than today's store-bought cracked wheat.

Sprout the berries in two jars according to instructions (page 114). Drain well, spread on a cookie sheet and set in a warm oven, no more than 150 degrees, overnight or until the berries are well dried. Grind coarsely in a grain grinder. Store the bulgur in an airtight container in your refrigerator. As the bulgur has been sprouted, it does not require a long soaking before cooking.

BULGUR FLOUR
(Sprouted Wheat Flour)
Makes about 6 cups

4 cups bulgur

Grind the bulgur into a fine flour. Store in an airtight container in the refrigerator or freezer. Sprouted wheat flour may be used in cookie and cake recipes where soaking gives less than satisfactory results.

KISHK
Makes 1 quart

4 cups cracked wheat or bulgur
4 cups yoghurt (page 85)

This fermented dish comes from the Middle East. It is traditionally added to soups but can also be eaten with milk or cream as a cold breakfast cereal. In fact, it is the only cold breakfast cereal that we can recommend.

Mix ingredients together in a bowl. Cover and soak at room temperature for 24 hours in a dark place. Spread as thinly as possible on oiled cookie sheets and bake overnight at 150 degrees or until kishk has dried. Place in batches in food processor and pulse until coarsely crumbled. Do not overprocess. Store in airtight containers in the refrigerator.

Sprouting accomplishes a veritable predigestion of grains. Phytic acid, which blocks the absorption of calcium and magnesium, is largely decomposed. So are certain sugars which cause intestinal gas. Part of the starch is transformed into sugars and numerous enzymes that aid digestion are produced. Claude Aubert *Dis-Moi Comment Tu Cuisines*

An example of this product differentiation and cost cutting in action is the process used for making cereals which are shaped like little O's, crowns, moons and the like. The machine used for making shaped cereals, called an extruder, is a huge pump with a die at one end. . . . The slurry goes into the extruder, is heated to a very high temperature and pushed through the die at high pressure. A spinning blade slices off each little crown or elephant, which is carried on a stream of hot air past nozzles which spray a coating of oil and sugar on each piece to seal off the cereal from the ravages of milk and give it crunch. This extrusion process. . . destroys much of the nutrient content of the ingredients, even the chemical vitamins. . . . The amino acid lysine, a crucial nutrient, is especially ravaged by extrusion. Yet the only changes made in the dozens of variables in the extrusion process are those which will cut costs. . . regardless of how these changes will alter the nutritive value of the product. Paul Stitt *Fighting the Food Giants.*

Four sets of rats were given special diets. One group received plain whole wheat, water, vitamins and minerals. Another group received Puffed Wheat, water and the same nutrient solution. A third set was given water and white sugar, and a fourth given nothing but water and the chemical nutrients. The rats which received the whole wheat lived over a year on the diet. The rats who got nothing but water and vitamins lived for about eight weeks, and the animals on a white sugar and water diet lived for a month. But [the company's] own laboratory study showed that rats given vitamins, water and all the Puffed Wheat they wanted died in two weeks. It wasn't a matter of the rats dying of malnutrition; results like these suggested that there was something actually toxic about the Puffed Wheat itself. Proteins are very similar to certain toxins in molecular structure, and the puffing process of putting the grain under 1500 pounds per square inch of pressure and then releasing it may produce chemical changes which turn a nutritious grain into a poisonous substance. . . . I was shocked, so I showed the report to Dr. Clark, who shared my concern. His predecessor, Dr. Graham, had published the report and begged the company not to continue producing Puffed Wheat because of its poisonous effect on animals. Dr. Clark . . . went right to the president. . . . " I know people should throw it on brides and grooms at weddings," [the president] cracked, "but if they insist on sticking it in their mouths, can I help it? Besides, we made $9 million on the stuff last year." Paul Stitt *Fighting the Food Giants*

KISHK GRANOLA
Makes 6 cups

4 cups kishk (page 461)
1 cup crispy pecans, almonds or cashews
    (pages 513 and 515), chopped
1 cup dried sweetened coconut meat (page 159)
1 cup dried fruit, such as raisins or unsulphured
    apricots, cut into small pieces
1/2 cup Rapadura (see page 536)

This cereal will actually keep well for several weeks at room temperature and is a good provision to take when one is traveling and wants to avoid hotel breakfasts.

Mix all ingredients together. Store in zip-lock bags or airtight containers in refrigerator. Eat like granola with milk or cream.

BULGUR CASSEROLE
(Fraykee)
Serves 4

1 cup bulgur (page 460)
2 cups cold filtered water
pinch of cinnamon
1/2 teaspoon sea salt
1/4 cup butter, softened
1/4 cup crispy pine nuts (page 514)

This delicious grain preparation comes from Arabia. Heat a heavy, cast-iron skillet, add the sprouted and cracked bulgur and stir around a few minutes until it is toasted. Place toasted bulgur, water, cinnamon and salt in a pot, bring to a boil, reduce heat, cover and cook for 30 minutes. Remove from heat and allow to sit 5 minutes before removing lid. Turn into a bowl or casserole, toss with butter and top with pine nuts.

WHEAT BERRY CASSEROLE

Serves 4

2 cups soft wheat berries, sprouted
3 cups beef or chicken stock (page 122 or 124)
1 teaspoon sea salt
1/2 teaspoon dried thyme
1/2 teaspoon dried rosemary
1/2 teaspoon dried green peppercorns, crushed

(Sprout wheat berries according to directions on page 114.) Place 2 cups sprouted berries in a flameproof casserole with stock and salt. Bring to a boil and skim. Add thyme, rosemary and peppercorns and boil vigorously until liquid has reduced to the level of the wheat. Transfer to a 250-degree oven and bake for about 4 hours or until berries are tender.

Variation: Barley Casserole

Use *1 cup whole barley, sprouted* instead of wheat berries

CRACKED WHEAT SALAD

Serves 6

3 cups bulgur (page 460)
1 cup fresh lemon juice
2 cups warm water
1 green pepper, minced
1 red pepper, minced
2 bunches green onions, chopped
3/4 cup extra virgin olive oil
sea salt and pepper
fresh pineapple rings, for garnish
orange slices, for garnish
1/2 cup crispy peanuts (page 514), chopped

Soak bulgur in lemon juice and water for 1/2 hour. Squeeze dry with hands and transfer to a bowl. Combine with peppers, onions and olive oil and season to taste. Garnish with pineapple rings, orange slices and peanuts.

Wheat comes to us from Turkey and southern Russia. Over 200 varieties have been described, of which only three account for 90 percent of all the wheat grown in the world today. Winter wheat is planted in the fall and harvested in the following June or July. Spring wheat is planted after the frosts are over and harvested in late summer. For cooking purposes it is sufficient to know that wheat can be classified as either hard or soft. Hard wheat is higher in protein, particularly gluten, a protein unique to wheat and to a lesser extent rye, barley and oats. Gluten imparts elasticity and strength to flours. It entraps carbon dioxide during the leavening process resulting in the unique rising characteristic of wheat flour doughs. Bread makers prefer hard winter wheat. Durum wheats are also hard wheats, but they are typically planted in the spring. They are used for spaghetti, macaroni and noodles. Soft wheats are lower in protein. They are used for flour that is not yeasted but processed into baked goods, such as pastries, cookies and crackers.

Whole wheat grown in fertile soil will be rich in B vitamins, calcium and iron. Fat comprises only 2 percent of the total calories in wheat; but, if properly grown, the oil will be high in omega-3 linolenic acid. Low-temperature milling and careful handling of wheat is necessary to preserve all the nutrients intact and prevent rancidity of precious oils. Wheat has the highest protein value of any of the cereals, but the protein is not complete. Wheat is particularly deficient in lysine. Furthermore, many people are allergic to wheat proteins resulting in celiac disease, which may be due either to a genetic defect or an acquired defect in the intestinal lining. Older varieties of hard wheat, such as spelt and kamut, may be more digestible than modern hybrids. SWF

Know Your Ingredients

Name This Product #27

Whole wheat, sugar, tricalcium and dicalcium (provides calcium), salt, malt extract, corn syrup, vitamin C (sodium ascorbate), zinc and iron (mineral nutrients), vitamin E (tocopherol acetate), trisodium phosphate, a B vitamin (niacinamide), a B vitamin (calcium pantothenate), annatto extract color, vitamin A (palmitate), vitamin B6 (pyridoxine hydrochloride), vitamin B2 (riboflavin), vitamin B1 (thiamin mononitrate), a B vitamin (folic acid), vitamin B12, and vitamin D. Freshness preserved with BHT.

See Appendix B for Answer

Kasha, or cracked buckwheat, is to Russia as bulgur is to the Middle East—the staple carbohydrate food used in numerous dishes but chiefly as a simple casserole.

Buckwheat is not technically a grain but the seeds of an herb, a relative of rhubarb. The seeds, or groats, form a dietary staple in northern climates, especially in Siberian Russia and in Brittany. Buckwheat is an important component of Jewish cuisine. It is high in lysine and calcium as well as vitamin E and the entire gamut of vitamin B complex. It is especially noted for its high nitriloside or B_{17} content, a vitamin that plays an important role in the body's defense against cancer. SWF

KASHA
Makes 4 cups

3 cups buckwheat groats

Sprout the groats in two jars according to instructions (page 114). Drain well, spread on a cookie sheet and bake at 150 degrees overnight or until the berries are well dried. Store the kasha in an airtight container in your refrigerator. As the kasha has been sprouted, it does not require soaking before cooking.

RUSSIAN KASHA
Makes 3 cups

1 cup kasha prepared according to
*   preceding recipe*
1 egg, beaten
2 cups chicken stock (page 124)
2 tablespoons butter
1 teaspoon salt
1/2 teaspoon pepper
2 tablespoons butter (optional)

The Russian method of preparing kasha, with egg, homemade chicken stock and butter, makes this casserole truly a meal in itself, nourishing fare for hardy peasants and modern sophisticates. Heat a heavy, cast-iron skillet, add kasha and cook, stirring, for about 5 minutes until kasha is toasted. Let cool. Mix toasted kasha with egg. Reheat the pan and pour in the kasha-egg mixture. Over medium-high heat, flatten, stir and chop the kasha with wooden fork until the egg has cooked and the kernels are hot and mostly separated, about 2 to 4 minutes. Meanwhile, bring chicken stock to a boil with butter and seasonings. Add kasha-egg mixture, bring to a boil, cover and turn heat to low. Cook about 30 minutes. Remove cover and fluff up with butter if desired.

KASHA CASSEROLE

Serves 4-6

1 cup whole buckwheat groats
1 1/2 cups filtered water
2 tablespoons whey (page 87)
2 medium onions, finely chopped
2 tablespoons butter
2 tablespoons extra virgin olive oil
1 1/2 cups potato quarters (page 400)
1/2 teaspoon sea salt
1/4 teaspoon pepper
1 cup boiling water

In a cast-iron skillet with a lid, or in a flameproof casserole, toast buckwheat groats over a medium-high flame, shaking occasionally. Remove from heat and mix with 1 1/2 cups water and whey. Cover and let stand in a warm place for at least 7 hours. Sauté onion in butter and olive oil. Add sautéed onion, potato quarters, salt, pepper and boiling water to skillet or casserole. Transfer to an oven preheated to 350 degrees and bake, covered, for about 25 minutes or until all liquid is absorbed.

KASHA NUT LOAF

Serves 8

3 cups Russian kasha (page 464)
2 tablespoons butter
2 tablespoons extra virgin olive oil
2 medium onions, finely chopped
1 cup celery, finely chopped
2 carrots, grated
2 cloves garlic, peeled and mashed
1 teaspoon dried thyme
1 teaspoon dried sage
1 teaspoon dried rosemary
6 eggs, beaten
3 cups crispy cashews (page 515), processed in
*   food processor to a coarse meal*
1 teaspoon cracked pepper
1 teaspoon sea salt
2-3 cups yoghurt sauce for garnish (page 143)

In 1956 over 300 middle-aged Englishmen, free of heart disease, were asked what they ate. The men were then studied for ten years. The researchers were astonished by what they found.

Men who consumed the most calories were found to have the least heart disease.

In addition, it was found that those men not prone to heart disease ate significantly more cereal fiber. However, it was found that fiber from other sources did not protect against heart disease. The author stated, "The composition of the diet (of the men on the high-fiber cereal) does not impress (one) as being particularly health conscious." Chris Mudd *Cholesterol and Your Health*

Since World War II, the food industry in the U.S. has gone a long way toward ensuring that their customers (just about all of America's children, as well as a good proportion of the adults) do not have to chew breakfast. The bleached, gassed, and colored remnants of the life-giving grains are roasted, toasted, frosted with sugar, embalmed with chemical preservatives, and stuffed into a box much larger than its contents. Fantastic amounts of energy are wasted by sales and advertising departments to sell these half-empty boxes of dead food—money back coupons, whistles and toy guns are needed to induce refined women to lift these half-empty boxes off supermarket shelves. William Dufty *Sugar Blues*

Rice is the staple food for peoples of the Orient. The Japanese and Chinese consume over 100 pounds of rice per person per year, while Americans eat less than 10 pounds. Macrobiotic enthusiasts consider rice the most perfect grain, in which the yin and yang energies are in equilibrium. But the Westerner should not necessarily adopt Oriental rice-eating habits. Asians have larger pancreas and salivary glands in proportion to body weight than Westerners, and these traits make them ideally suited to a grain-based diet. The Westerner who adopts the strict macrobiotic or Oriental diet, with rice at every meal, may develop serious health problems.

Nevertheless, whole rice in moderation has a place in most diets. As rice contains no gluten, a difficult-to-digest protein found in wheat, oats, rye and barley, it is often well tolerated by those with grain allergies. It is relatively low in phytic acid and so does not necessarily require overnight soaking before preparation. A long, slow steaming in mineral-rich broth is sufficient to neutralize most of the phytic acid content and results in a preparation that some people find more palatable than rice that has been soaked overnight.

Brown rice is highest of all grains in B vitamins and also contains iron, vitamin E and some protein.

Short grain rice is starchier and stickier than long grain rice. Basmati rice grown in the Himalayas, wehini rice grown in California and texmati rice grown in Texas are all noted for their rich flavor and aroma.

What about the accusation that "all brown rice is rancid?" Tests indicate that airtight packaging will protect rice from developing free radicals and off flavors. So buy brown rice in airtight containers or packages, not loose rice from bins. SWF

Sauté onions, celery and carrots in butter and olive oil until soft. Stir in garlic and herbs and cook another minute. Allow to cool slightly. In a large bowl mix kasha, eggs, cooked vegetables, salt, pepper and cashews. Press into a well-buttered loaf pan. Cover, set in a pan of hot water and bake at 350 degrees for 1 hour. Cool and invert onto a serving dish, blotting up any liquid with a paper towel. Slice and serve with yoghurt sauce. Ginger carrots (page 95) also go well with this dish.

Variation: Sautéed Kasha Loaf Platter

Cut loaf into slices and sauté until golden in *2-3 tablespoons each butter and olive oil.* Arrange on a platter and keep warm in oven until ready to serve. Serve with side dishes of yoghurt sauce (page 143) and ginger carrots (page 95).

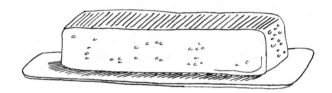

BASIC BROWN RICE I
(Unsoaked Rice)
Serves 6-8

2 cups long-grain brown rice
2 tablespoons butter
2 tablespoons extra virgin olive oil
3 cardamom pods
4 cups chicken stock (page 124) or combination
    of filtered water and chicken stock
1 tablespoon gelatin (see Sources), optional
1/2 teaspoon sea salt

In a heavy, flameproof casserole, melt butter and olive oil. Open cardamom pods and add seeds to the casserole. Sauté rice in butter and oil, stirring constantly, until rice begins to turn milky. Pour in liquid, add salt and optional gelatin and bring to a rolling boil. Boil, uncovered, for about 10 minutes until water has reduced to the level of the rice. Reduce flame to lowest heat, cover tightly and cook for at least 1 1/2 hours or as long as 3 hours. Do not remove lid during cooking.

Variation: Brown Rice and Bulgur

Use *1 cup long-grain brown rice* and *1 cup bulgur (page 460)* in place of 2 cups long-grain rice.

Variation: Basic Wehini or Texmati Rice

Use *2 cups wehini or texmati rice* in place of long-grained rice.

Variation: Coconut Rice

Use *1-2 cups coconut milk* (page 159), or *7 ounces creamed coconut (see page 160), melted,* as part of the 4 cups of liquid.

Variation: Liver and Rice

Add *2-3 ounces liver, grated or finely chopped,* to the rice as it cooks.

BASIC BROWN RICE II

(Soaked Rice)
Serves 6-8

2 cups long-grain or short-grain brown rice
4 cups warm filtered water plus 4 tablespoons whey,
   yoghurt, kefir or buttermilk (pages 83-87)
1 teaspoon sea salt
2-4 tablespoons butter

Place rice and warm water mixture in a flameproof casserole and leave in a warm place for at least 7 hours. (Note: Those with severe milk allergies can use *lemon juice or vinegar* in place of whey, yoghurt, kefir or buttermilk.) Bring to a boil, skim, reduce heat, stir in salt and butter and cover tightly. Without removing lid, cook over lowest possible heat for about 45 minutes.

During the building of the great wall of China, coolies were fed salted [fermented] cabbage with their rice to keep them strong and healthy. Salting [fermenting] preserved the cabbage in season and out, and it was the only vegetable they had to supplement their complete, unrefined rice. When the Mongols overran China, knowing a good thing when they tried it, they adopted salted [fermented] cabbage as a very practical traveling ration. The Mongol armies got as far as Hungary in the thirteenth century, where they introduced salted cabbage to Europe. As sauerkraut, it became one of the principal foods of Germany and eastern Europe.

Julius Caesar's legions, the most efficient fighting machine the world had ever known, ranged far from Rome. The sole provisions were sacks of grain—one for each man. Like the Viet Cong, Caesar's men did not have sugar or kitchens, nor did they have a medical corps, only surgeons for repairing wounds. They ate whole grains plain, on the march, or ground into Roman meal and supplemented with cabbage and any other vegetables they could scrounge. Pliny has said that cabbage kept Rome out of the hands of physicians for many centuries. It was the European armies traveling in the other direction that ran into trouble. In his history of the invasion of sugar-rich Egypt by the Crusaders of St. Louis in 1260, Sire Jean de Joinville described the funguous putrid bleeding gums, the hemorrhaging skin spots, and the swollen legs that plagued Christian armies and led to the ultimate defeat and capture of the holy knights and their commander. William Dufty *Sugar Blues*

At the beginning of World War II. . . . the British medical officer of Singapore, Dr. Scharff, made the same kind of hard decision that had saved Denmark in World War I during the German blockade. Polished white rice was forbidden by military decree. Only unpolished brown rice could be sold. British military authorities were influenced by one factor only: Inadequate supplies. They were worried about quantity; quality was of no concern. They simply didn't want any food riots on their hands. . . the aftermath was startling, incredible. Dr. Scharff had originally gone to Singapore with the mission of reducing infant mortality from malaria. When he arrived, the mortality rate was 420 per 1,000 births. He used herculean but orthodox medical methods. In less than a decade, the program had reduced the death rate of infants to 160 per 1,000, almost on a par with the existing rate in Britain. However, after a year on the brown rice diet enforced by military decree, there was a dramatic shift in vital statistics. Instead of 160 infants dying in their first year of life, only 80 died. The figure was cut in half without medical efforts. William Dufty *Sugar Blues*

In 1960, researchers at Ann Arbor University performed an interesting experiment on laboratory rats. Eighteen rats were divided into three groups. One group received cornflakes and water; a second group was given the cardboard box that the cornflakes came in and water; and the control group received rat chow and water. The rats in the control group remained in good health throughout the experiment. The rats receiving the box became lethargic and eventually died of malnutrition. But the rats receiving cornflakes and water died before the

BROWN RICE PILAF
Serves 6-8

1 1/2 cups long-grain brown rice
1 cup buckwheat or brown rice noodles,
*   broken into 1-inch bits*
1 medium onion, finely chopped
2 cardamom pods
1 teaspoon dried thyme or dill
grated rind of 1 lemon (optional)
2 tablespoons butter
2 tablespoons extra virgin olive oil
4 cups chicken stock (page 124) or combination
*   of filtered water and stock*
1 tablespoon gelatin (see Sources), optional
1/2 teaspoon sea salt

In a heavy, flameproof casserole, melt butter and olive oil. Open cardamom pods and add seeds to the casserole. Add onion and thyme or dill and optional lemon rind and sauté until onion is soft. Add noodles and sauté, stirring, until they turn brown. Add rice and sauté, stirring, until rice turns milky. Pour in liquid, add salt and optional gelatin and lemon rind and bring to a rolling boil. Boil, uncovered, for about 10 to 15 minutes until the water has reduced to the level of the rice. Reduce flame to lowest heat, cover tightly and cook for at least 2 hours or as long as 3 hours. Do not remove lid during cooking.

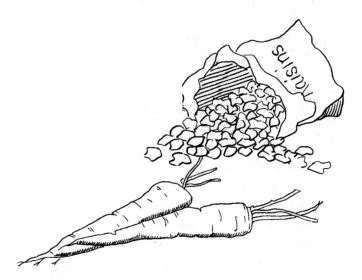

RICE AND CARROT CASSEROLE

Serves 6-8

2 cups long-grain brown rice
2 tablespoons butter
2 tablespoons extra virgin olive oil
1 medium onion, finely chopped
1 teaspoon dried thyme
4 whole cloves
3 cardamom pods
grated rind of 1 lemon (optional)
4 cups chicken stock (page 124) or combination
    of filtered water and stock
1 tablespoon gelatin (see Sources), optional
1/2 teaspoon sea salt
1 cup grated carrots
1/2 cup raisins

In a heavy, flameproof casserole, melt butter and olive oil. Open cardamom pods and add seeds to casserole along with thyme, cloves, optional lemon rind and onion. Sauté until onion is soft. Add rice and sauté until milky. Pour in liquid, add salt and optional gelatin and bring to a rolling boil. Stir in carrots and raisins. Boil, uncovered, for about 10 to 15 minutes until the water has reduced to the level of the rice. Reduce flame to lowest heat, cover tightly and cook for at least 2 hours or as long as 3 hours. Do not remove lid during cooking.

rats who were given the box—the last cornflake rat died on the day the first box rat died. Before death the cornflake rats developed schizophrenic behavior, threw fits, bit each other and finally went into convulsions. Autopsy revealed dysfunction of the pancreas, liver and kidneys and degeneration of the nerves in the spine—all signs of "insulin shock." The startling conclusion of this study is that there is more nourishment in the box that cold breakfast cereals come in than in the cereals themselves. Loren Zanier, designer of the experiment, actually proposed the protocol as a joke. But the results are far from funny. They were never published and similar studies have not been repeated. If consumers knew the truth about breakfast cereals, vast fortunes would be jeopardized. SWF

The U.S. adventure in Viet Nam was, by world consensus, a folly on many levels. Perhaps, on the basic level of human nutrition, it was one of the sorriest stories of all. . . . For years, the guerilla bands of the Viet Minh and Viet Cong sustained themselves with a food supply system as simple and primitive as that of the Roman legions of Julius Caesar. Each man carried a little sack of whole rice and some salt. They added manioc leaves, from the jungle, and fish when possible. For years they stymied the elaborately equipped and lavishly rationed armies of the West. . . . When the victorious Viet Cong armies overran Saigon, they were exposed for the first time—like the Crusader arriving in the Holy Land centuries before—to the pause that refreshes, the Coke machine, the candy counter. It is their turn to accustom themselves to gluttony and La Dolce Vita and to eat and drink sugar openly in the street without shame. William Dufty *Sugar Blues*

Sodium, in the form of sodium chloride (salt), plays an essential role in digestion, starting from the moment food enters your mouth. Salt . . . activates the primary digestive enzyme in the mouth, salivary amylase. . . . Further down the digestive tract, in the stomach, sodium continues its good work. Sodium chloride generates hydrochloric acid in the parietal cells of the stomach wall, an essential secretion for proper digestion. . . . Vegetarians have been led to believe that their vegies supply all the salt they need in their diet. This is completely false. Why are salt blocks provided for grazing animals? They are provided with this salt source because every farmer knows that without it his vegetarian animals will get sick. . . . Salt is the single element required for the proper breakdown of plant carbohydrates into usable and assimilable human food. A salt-free, vegetarian diet is a sure ticket to the hospital and a premature old age. Vegetarians are also prone to sugar addiction. The physiological explanation for this: Glucosides in grains are not digested without the presence of salt. As the body is denied these natural sugars, a deficiency develops and there is an insatiable desire to eat sweets. William Campbell Douglass, MD *Second Opinion*

INDIAN RICE
Serves 6-8

2 cups long-grain brown basmati rice
1 medium onion, finely chopped
2 tablespoons butter
2 tablespoons extra virgin olive oil
1 teaspoon cumin seeds
1 teaspoon fenugreek seeds
2 teaspoons turmeric powder
4 cardamom pods
2 bay leaves
1 teaspoon salt
1 tablespoon gelatin (see Sources), optional
4 cups chicken stock (page 124) or
　　combination of filtered water and stock

In a heavy, flameproof casserole, melt butter and olive oil. Open cardamom pods and add seeds to casserole along with onion, cumin and turmeric. Sauté until onion is soft. Add rice and sauté, stirring, until rice turns milky. Pour in liquid, add salt, optional gelatin and bay leaf and bring to a rolling boil. Boil, uncovered, for about 10 to 15 minutes until the water has reduced to the level of the rice. Reduce flame to lowest heat, cover tightly and cook for at least 1 hour or for as long as 3 hours. Do not remove lid during cooking.

MEXICAN RICE
Serves 6-8

2 cups long-grain brown rice
1 medium onion, finely chopped
2 tablespoons butter
2 tablespoons extra virgin olive oil
1 teaspoon annatto seeds (available in
　　Latin American markets)
1 teaspoon cumin seeds
1/4 teaspoon red chile flakes
1 teaspoon dried oregano
1 teaspoon salt

4 cups chicken stock (page 124) or
combination of filtered water and stock
1 tablespoon gelatin (see Sources), optional
1 clove garlic, peeled and mashed
2 tablespoons green olives, chopped (optional)

In a heavy, flameproof casserole, melt butter and olive oil. Sauté annatto seeds in oil for about 5 minutes, or until oil turns yellow, and remove with a slotted spoon. In the same oil, sauté onion with red chile flakes and cumin seeds until onion is soft. Add rice and sauté until milky. Pour in liquid, add salt, optional gelatin, oregano and garlic and bring to a rolling boil. Boil, uncovered, for about 10 to 15 minutes until the water has reduced to the level of the rice. Reduce flame to lowest heat, cover tightly and cook for at least 2 hours or as long as 3 hours. Do not remove lid during cooking. Just before serving, remove lid and stir in optional olives.

MEXICAN RICE CASSEROLE

Serves 8

4 cups basic brown rice (page 466)
1 1/2 cups grated Monterey Jack
or Cheddar cheese
2 bunches green onions, chopped
1/2 cup pitted black olives, chopped
1 cup pickled red peppers (page 99), chopped or
2 small cans green chile peppers, chopped
1 cup piima cream or creme fraiche (page 84)

This delicious dish is only for those with a high tolerance to milk products. Combine all ingredients except 1/2 cup grated cheese and pour into a buttered casserole. Top with cheese and bake at 350 degrees for about 30 minutes.

Despite the efforts of ACT [Action for Children's Television], 600 million dollars is now spent yearly on children's advertising, 30 million of it by the cereal industry. This advertising, which necessarily glosses over such drawbacks as tooth decay in peddling candy to children, is adroit at deception. In 1982 "Sugar Smacks" was rechristened "Honey Smacks," presumably because honey is healthier. Of course, both versions of the cereal contain 57 percent refined sugars.

Although the motto of the market place, supposedly, is to "give the people what they want," the reality is more a matter of giving the people whatever increases one's market share. Most parents are trying to wean their children from excessive sweets; yet supermarkets and drug stores across the country always have candy prominently displayed at checkout counters—where parents are stuck in line with restless, candy-craving children. Kroger's, a Cincinnati grocery chain that conscientiously established a no-candy lane, prompted a representative of the national Candy Wholesalers Association to object: "Discipline begins with the parent, and our attitude is the product should be available." So much for giving the people what they want. Joseph D. Beasley, MD and Jerry J. Swift, MA *The Kellogg Report*

Dr. Price was often called to the bedsides of dying individuals, when last rites were being administered. He brought with him two things—a bottle of cod liver oil and a bottle of high vitamin butter oil from cows eating growing grass. He put drops of both under the tongue of the patient—and more often that not the patient revived. He was puzzled by the fact that cod liver oil alone and butter oil alone seldom revived the dying patient—but the two together worked like magic. Research into prostaglandins may supply the answer. High vitamin butter may be rich in arachidonic acid (AA) and possibly other factors needed for the omega-6 pathway; and cod liver oil is rich in eicosapentaenoic acid (EPA) needed for the omega-3 pathway. In addition, the saturated fatty acids in butter help the unsaturated fatty acids in cod liver oil to work more efficiently.

Many delicious traditional dishes provide a synergystic combination of fatty acids of the omega-3 family with fatty acids of the omega-6 family and saturated fatty acids—lox and cream cheese, caviar and sour cream, liver and bacon, salmon and Bernaise sauce, dark green vegetables with butter, cream cheese and flax oil. In India, milk products provide AA and shorter chain fatty acids while insects provide the longer chain fatty acids of the omega-3 chain. Fish, pork and coconut oil provide all the necessary fatty acids in the Polynesian diet; American Indians valued fish, bear fat and oil of the evening primrose plant. Traditional combinations of rich foods, therefore, need not be avoided. They provide factors that open both lanes of the prostaglandin pathway, creating a wide and open highway to skip along for renewed vitality and vibrant health. *Tripping Lightly Down the Prostaglandin Pathways*

GREEK RICE
Serves 6-8

2 cups basic brown rice (page 466)
2 onions, finely chopped
2 sticks celery, finely chopped
3 tablespoons extra virgin olive oil
2 cloves garlic, peeled and mashed
2 tablespoons sesame seeds, toasted
2 tablespoons pepitas (page 513)
2 tablespoons crispy pine nuts (page 514)
1/4 cup freshly chopped mint
grated rind and juice of 1 lemon
1/2 teaspoon oregano
sea salt and pepper

Sauté onions, celery and garlic very gently in olive oil until soft. Mix together all ingredients and season to taste. Greek rice may be used as a stuffing in grape leaves, tomatoes, or eggplant, or served on its own.

ALGERIAN WEDDING RICE
Serves 6-8

3 cups basic brown rice (page 466)
1 cup dried apricots, cut into bits, soaked in
   filtered water about 1 hour and drained
1/2 cup crispy almond slivers (page 515), toasted
1/2 cup crispy pine nuts (page 514)
2 bunches green onions, chopped
4 tablespoons butter, softened
sea salt and pepper

Toss the cooked rice with remaining ingredients. Season to taste. Place in a buttered casserole and bake at 250 degrees for about 30 minutes.

RAINBOW RICE SALAD

Serves 8

4 cups basic brown rice (page 466)
1 red pepper, seeded and diced
1 green pepper, seeded and diced
1 bunch green onions, chopped
1 cup fresh pineapple, cut into small pieces
1/2 cup raisins
1 cup basic dressing (page 129)

Mix all ingredients together. May be pressed into a mold and inverted for serving.

ORIENTAL RICE SALAD

Serves 8

4 cups basic brown rice (page 466)
1 bunch green onions, chopped
1/2 cup crispy cashews (page 515), chopped
1 small can water chestnuts, drained and sliced
1 cup Oriental dressing (page 135)

Mix all ingredients together and let stand an hour or so before serving.

Perhaps one of the most remarkable aspects of the saturated fat issue is that the *trans* fatty acids were kept out of both government and private food composition data bases for several decades! *Trans* fatty acids were treated as a nonissue by most technical and government information sources and by the media for several decades, though that situation has now changed. The Harvard University School of Public Health has established a data base that includes the *trans* fatty acids for a large number of foods; at least one of the commercial food analysis programs has begun the inclusion of *trans* fatty acids in its data base; it was only in the mid 1990s that the U.S. Department of Agriculture's provisional table of *trans* fatty acids in foods surfaced. Mary G. Enig, PhD *Know Your Fats*

Know Your Ingredients
Name This Product #28

Enriched parboiled long grain rice (preserved with BHT), wild rice, hydrolyzed vegetable protein, monosodium glutamate, dried onion, salt, dextrose, beef extract, dried torula yeast, dried parsley, dried celery, dried garlic, partially hydrogenated vegetable oil, natural flavors, artificial flavor.

See Appendix B for Answer

Not technically a cereal grain, but the seed of a marsh-growing plant native to North America, wild rice was harvested by the North American Indians and formed an important part of their diet.

Wild rice is rich in protein, containing more lysine and methionine than most other cereals. It is high in B complex vitamins and rich in minerals including magnesium, potassium, phosphorus and zinc. Wild rice is relatively low in fat, so eat it with plenty of butter—or bear or beaver grease if you have them on hand! SWF

One school of thought tells us not to eat grains; another not to eat animal products. But both have been in the diet of mankind for millennia. Some of the oldest archeological finds show evidence that our caveman ancestors gathered and stored seeds, including wild grains. The cultivation of grains on a large scale made civilization possible.

And mankind has always depended on animal products. Our Paleolithic ancestors used meat and fat to nourish themselves, furs to keep warm, skins for housing, clothing and food storage, and bones for tools. Today animal products are used in many lifesaving drugs, household and building products, photographic supplies, shoes, luggage, tires, hydraulic brake fluid for cars, airplane lubricants--and flavorings for vegetarian foods. Even the most ardent vegans cannot escape dependence on animal products. SWF

WILD RICE
Serves 6-8

2 cups wild rice
4 cups warm filtered water plus 4 tablespoons whey,
  yoghurt, kefir or buttermilk (pages 83-87)
1 teaspoon sea salt
2-4 tablespoons butter

Place wild rice and warm water mixture in a flameproof casserole and leave in a warm place for at least 7 hours. Bring to a boil, skim, reduce heat, stir in salt and butter and cover tightly. Without removing lid, cook over lowest possible heat for about 45 minutes.

WILD RICE CASSEROLE
Serves 6-8

2 cups cooked wild rice
1/2 cup melted butter
1 bunch green onions, chopped
grated rind of 2 oranges
1/2 cup slivered crispy almond slivers (page 515)
  or crispy pine nuts (page 514)
1/4 cup parsley, finely chopped or
  1/2 cup cilantro, coarsely chopped

Mix cooked rice with remaining ingredients. Place in a buttered casserole and bake at 250 degrees for about 30 minutes.

Variation: Wehini Rice Casserole
Use *2 cups basic wehini rice (page 467)* instead of cooked wild rice.

Variation: Texmati Rice Casserole
Use *2 cups basic texmati rice (page 467)* instead of cooked wild rice.

ECUADORIAN QUINOA CASSEROLE

Serves 6-8

2 cups quinoa
6 cups warm filtered water plus 2 tablespoons whey,
    yoghurt, kefir or buttermilk (pages 83-87)
1 bunch green onions, chopped
2 tablespoons extra virgin olive oil
1 teaspoon annatto seeds
    (available in Latin American markets)
4 cups beef or chicken stock (page 122 or 124)
1/2 teaspoon sea salt
3 cloves garlic, mashed
2 medium potatoes, washed and sliced
1 bunch cilantro, tied together
1/2 cup piima cream or creme fraiche (page 84)
5 tablespoons cream cheese (page 87)

This authentic recipe, from a chipper centenarian living in Equador, incorporates all the basic principles for easy digestion and thorough assimilation—use of rich stock made by boiling bones for a long time, presoaking of grain and the addition of cultured cream and homemade cheese, rich in fat-soluble vitamins.

Soak quinoa in warm water mixture at least 12 hours. Rinse and drain well. Sauté annatto seeds in oil for several minutes, or until oil turns yellow, and remove with a slotted spoon. Sauté onions in the same oil, adding garlic at the last minute. Add quinoa and stock and bring to a boil. Skim, reduce heat, cover and simmer for 1 hour or more on very low heat. About 1/2 hour before serving, stir in the potatoes and salt. About 10 minutes before serving, add cilantro. To serve, remove cilantro and stir in cultured cream and cheese.

Quinoa is a staple food of the Incas and the Indians in Peru, Ecuador and Bolivia. During his pioneering investigations in the 1930's, Weston Price noted that the Indians of the Andes mountains valued gruel made of quinoa for nursing mothers. Quinoa contains 16 to 20 percent protein and is high in cystine, lysine and methionine—amino acids that tend to be low in other grains. It contains iron, calcium and phosphorus, B vitamins and vitamin E, and is relatively high in fat. Like all grains, quinoa contains antinutrients and therefore requires a long soaking as part of the preparation process. SWF

As an illustration of the remarkable wisdom of these primitive tribes, I found them using for the nursing period two cereals with unusual properties. One was a red millet, which was not only high in carotene but had a calcium content of five to ten times that of most other cereals. They used also for nursing mothers in several tribes in Africa a cereal called by them linga-linga. This proved to be the same cereal under the name of quinoa that the Indians of Peru use liberally, particularly the nursing mothers. The botanical name is quinoa. This cereal had the remarkable property of being not only rich in minerals but a powerful stimulant of the flow of milk. Weston Price, DDS *Nutrition and Physical Degeneration*

BREADS & FLOUR PRODUCTS

Housewives of old knew that the most delicious pancakes, muffins and cakes could be made by soaking flour in sour or cultured milk, buttermilk or cream. Our recipes for baked goods follow this format. Those who are allergic to milk products can use water to which a small amount of whey or yoghurt, or even vinegar or lemon juice, has been added, although the results will be less satisfactory. Flour products should be soaked at room temperature for at least 12 hours but better results may be obtained with a 24-hour soaking.

Because they are acidic, buttermilk, cultured milk, yoghurt and whey (as well as lemon juice and vinegar) activate the enzyme phytase, which works to break down phytic acid in the bran of grains. Sour milk products also provide lactic acid and *lactobacilli* that help break down complex starches, irritating tannins and difficult-to-digest proteins. Soaking increases vitamin content and makes all the nutrients in grains more available. This method has the further advantage of so softening whole meal flour that the final product is often indistinguishable from one made with white flour. Breads, muffins and pancakes that have been made with soaked whole wheat, kamut or spelt flour rise easily with baking soda alone; they do not require baking powder. And they are not characterized by the heaviness that can make whole grain products so unpalatable.

If you do a lot of baking, a home grain grinder is a must. Grains quickly go rancid after grinding, and optimum health benefits are obtained from freshly ground flour. Unbleached white flour may be used for dusting pans, rolling out doughs and kneading. We also allow unbleached white flour for pie crust.

Pancakes, muffins and soda breads are easy to prepare, although it should be noted that these soaked whole grain flour preparations take longer to cook than those made with white flour. For best results, use stoneware muffin tins and bread pans. (See Sources.) Sourdough breads take more dedication and time. They must be made with high-gluten flours, such as spelt, kamut, hard winter wheat or rye. While they have a delicious flavor, these breads may seem heavy to modern tastes. (For those who have neither the time nor the inclination for bread making, properly made sourdough breads are now commercially available. See Sources.) Soft wheat is better for casseroles and unleavened bread, such as Zarathustra bread (page 494).

We suggest avoidance of two grain products considered to be health foods—bran and wheat germ. Bran is high in phytates and wheat germ is extremely susceptible to rancidity. Eating the bran and germ separate from the starchy portion of grain presents as many problems as eating the starchy portion of grain separated from the bran and the germ. Traditional populations eat all parts of the grain together, freshly ground or milled and properly prepared.

BAKING WITH ALTERNATIVE GRAINS

Allergies to grains are widespread, especially allergies to wheat. Individuals with grain allergies often tolerate wheat products that have first been soaked, sprouted or fermented; but many must avoid wheat altogether even when it has been properly prepared. Older wheat varieties, such as spelt and kamut, are the first choice for substitutes because they mimic the properties of modern hybrid wheat; and no special adjustments are needed when substituting them for wheat in most recipes.

Many alternative flours are also available—not only those that contain gluten, such as rye, barley or oat, but also nongluten flours like corn, rice, millet, buckwheat, amaranth, quinoa, potato, tapioca, bean and tuber flours. All of these may be used for baked goods, such as muffins, pancakes, waffles and soda breads; but certain adjustments must be made to the recipes because these flours are heavier than wheat flour and do not rise as well. Specific recipes for alternate flours are beyond the scope of this book. However, the following guidelines should suffice.

In addition to baking soda, homemade baking powder should be added to alternative grain recipes in the proportion of 2 level teaspoons per cup of flour. Prepare by mixing *1 part potassium bicarbonate* (available from your pharmacist), *2 parts cream of tartar* and *2 parts arrowroot*. Store in an airtight glass jar. In addition, you may wish to add guar gum to your batter if it seems too runny— often the case with alternate flours as they do not absorb water as well as wheat or spelt. Use 1/2 teaspoon guar gum per cup of flour.

All flour products should be soaked in an acidic medium, such as buttermilk or water with whey or yoghurt added, for 12 to 24 hours. Baked goods made with alternate flours may take longer to cook than those made with whole wheat or spelt.

We must caution you against using soy flours. Soy contains a high phytate content as well as potent enzyme inhibitors. These are not inactivated by ordinary cooking methods, such as soaking, but only after a long, slow fermentation process that results in traditional fermented soy products, such as *natto, miso* or *tempeh*. The antinutrients in modern soy products and soy flour can inhibit growth and cause intestinal problems, swelling of the pancreas and even cancer. In addition, soy contains a high omega-3 content that quickly goes rancid when the bean is made into flour. Soy flour has a disagreeable taste that is difficult to mask—nature's way of telling us to avoid it. The phytoestrogens in soy have been promoted as panaceas but they are actually goitrogens that depress thyroid function.

PANCAKES
Makes 16-20

*2 cups freshly ground spelt, kamut
   or whole wheat flour*
2 cups buttermilk, kefir or yoghurt (pages 83-86)
2 eggs, lightly beaten
1/2 teaspoon sea salt
1 teaspoon baking soda
2 tablespoons melted butter

Soak flour in buttermilk, kefir or yoghurt in a warm place for 12 to 24 hours. (Those with milk allergies may use *2 cups filtered water plus 2 tablespoons whey, lemon juice or vinegar* in place of undiluted buttermilk, kefir or yoghurt.) Stir in other ingredients and thin to desired consistency with water. Cook on a hot, oiled griddle or in a cast-iron skillet. These pancakes cook more slowly than either unsoaked whole grain flour or white flour pancakes. The texture will be chewy and the taste pleasantly sour. Serve with melted butter and maple or sorghum syrup, raw honey, berry syrup (page 111) or apricot butter (page 110).

Variation: Corn Cakes
Use *1 cup freshly ground corn flour* plus *1 cup freshly ground spelt or whole wheat flour.* Soak in *2 cups limewater (see page 454) plus 2 tablespoons whey or yoghurt (pages 85-86).*

Variation: Buckwheat Cakes
Use *1 cup freshly ground buckwheat flour* plus *1 cup freshly ground spelt or whole wheat flour.*

Variation: Crispy Pancakes
Let pancakes dry out in a warm oven. These make delicious snacks with raw honey, apple or apricot butter (page 110) or homemade cream cheese (page 87). Small crispy pancakes may be used as a base for canapés (page 170).

On every continent, mankind has fermented grains, pulses, vegetables, milk, meat and fish. Up until the beginning of the 20th century, the French peasant made his bread, his cheese, his sausage, his sauerkraut (in the east), his olives (in the Midi), his vinegar and often his wine, cider or beer. Each time he directed this fermentation process empirically and by himself. Sometimes it was of short duration, as for his bread; sometimes long and complicated, as for wine and aged cheeses. Fermented foods were prepared by each family—in Russia cucumbers, in Poland sour soups, in Japan *miso* and lacto-fermented vegetables, in Indonesia *tempeh*, in Mexico *pozol*, in Equador fermented rice, in West Africa *soumbala*, to give just a few examples. Without realizing it, everyone put millions of microorganisms to work on his behalf.

Almost everywhere in the world people ate fermented foods on a daily basis. They often ate them for breakfast, no doubt because after a night of sleep the body needs something that is rapidly and easily digested.

The sour taste that characterizes so many fermented foods is found in every culinary tradition. Used in moderation, fermented foods satisfy the palate and fulfill a real physiological need, even if current nutritional practices fail to recognize this.

The practice of domestic fermentation still occurs in the Third World but is largely disappearing in industrialized countries, under the influence of Western life styles and eating habits. Claude Aubert *Les Aliments Fermentés Traditionnels*

DUTCH BABY PANCAKES

Serves 4-6

1 cup freshly ground spelt, kamut
*   or whole wheat flour*
1 cup buttermilk, kefir or yoghurt (pages 83-86)
4 eggs
1 teaspoon vanilla extract
1/2 teaspoon sea salt
1 cup filtered water
4 tablespoons butter
pinch of nutmeg (optional)

Soak flour in buttermilk, kefir or yoghurt in a warm place for 12 to 24 hours. (Those with milk allergies may use *2 cups filtered water plus 2 tablespoons whey, lemon juice or vinegar* in place of undiluted buttermilk, kefir or yoghurt.) Place eggs in food processor and process several minutes. Add flour mixture, vanilla, water and salt and process another minute. Place 2 tablespoons butter in a large skillet and cook in a 400-degree oven until it melts and sizzles. Pour half the batter (about 1 1/2 cups) into pan. Bake at 350 degrees until pancake is puffed and browned. Repeat for second pancake. Dust with nutmeg if desired. Serve with butter and honey, sorghum syrup or maple syrup.

Variation:

Fold *1 cup chopped fresh fruit* into the batter. Top with a dollop of *sweet cheese topping (page 541)*.

I know, too, that the body is affected differently by bread according to the manner in which it is prepared. It differs according as it is made from pure flour or meal with bran, whether it is prepared from winnowed or unwinnowed wheat, whether it is mixed with much water or little, whether well mixed or poorly mixed, overbaked or underbaked, and countless other points besides. The same is true of the preparation of barley meal. The influence of each process is considerable and each has a totally different effect from another. How can anyone who has not considered such matters and come to understand them possibly know anything of the diseases that afflict mankind? Each one of the substances of a man's diet acts upon his body and changes it in some way and upon these changes his whole life depends.

Hippocrates

Celiac disease stems from grain allergies—or, more precisely, allergies to the gluten and alpha gliadin components of grain. Those allergies cause malabsorption and, hence, a massive deficiency of vitamins B_1, B_3, B_{12}, folic acid and the mineral zinc. A serious deficiency in any one of those, if undiagnosed or untreated, can cause dementia. The allergies also cause malabsorption of essential minerals and trace elements, such as calcium, magnesium, iron and manganese. In addition, they allow the absorption of toxic metals, such as aluminum; and higher than normal concentrations of aluminium in the brain is one of the dementia-causing features of Alzheimer's disease. *PPNF Health Journal*

Modern commerce has deliberately robbed some of nature's foods of much of their bodybuilding material while retaining the hunger satisfying energy factors. For example, in the production of refined white flour approximately eighty per cent or four-fifths of the phosphorus and calcium content are usually removed, together with the vitamins and minerals provided in the embryo or germ. The evidence indicates that a very important factor in the lowering of reproductive efficiency of womanhood is directly related to the removal of vitamin E in the processing of wheat. The germ of wheat is our most readily available source of that vitamin. Its role as a nutritive factor for the pituitary gland in the base of the brain, which largely controls growth and organ function, apparently is important in determining the production of mental types. Similarly, the removal of vitamin B with the embryo of the wheat, together with its oxidation after processing, results in depletion of bodybuilding activators. Weston Price, DDS *Nutrition and Physical Degeneration*

WAFFLES
Serves 6

2 1/2 cups freshly ground spelt, kamut
    or whole wheat flour
2 cups buttermilk, kefir or yoghurt (pages 83-86)
2 egg yolks, lightly beaten
2-4 tablespoons maple syrup
2 tablespoons melted butter
1 teaspoon sea salt
4 egg whites
pinch of sea salt

Soak flour in buttermilk, kefir or yoghurt in a warm place for 12 to 24 hours. (Those with milk allergies may use *2 cups filtered water plus 2 tablespoons whey, lemon juice or vinegar* in place of undiluted buttermilk, kefir or yoghurt.) Stir in egg yolks, syrup, melted butter and salt. In a clean bowl, beat egg whites with pinch of salt until stiff. Fold into batter. Cook in a hot, well-oiled waffle iron. Serve with melted butter and maple or sorghum syrup, raw honey, berry preserves (page 111), apricot butter (page 110) or sweet cheese topping (page 541).

Note: These waffles are softer than those made with white flour. However, they will become crisp if kept in a warm oven for several hours.

BUCKWHEAT CREPES
Makes about 18

1 cup freshly ground buckwheat flour
1 cup freshly ground spelt, kamut
    or whole wheat flour
2 cups buttermilk, kefir or yoghurt (pages 83-86)
3 eggs, lightly beaten
1/2 teaspoon salt
about 1/2 cup melted butter

Soak flour in buttermilk, kefir or yoghurt in a warm place for 12 to 24 hours. (Those with milk allergies may use *2 cups filtered water plus 2 tablespoons whey, lemon juice or vinegar* in place of undiluted buttermilk, kefir or yoghurt.) Beat in eggs, salt and 1/4 cup melted butter and thin with enough water to achieve the consistency of cream. Beat several minutes with an electric beater and chill well. Heat a heavy skillet. Brush with melted butter and use a 1/4-cup measure to ladle batter into pan. Tip pan to distribute batter. Turn after two minutes and cook another minute. Keep crepes warm in the oven while making the rest, brushing the pan with butter between each crepe. Fill with raw honey, apricot butter (page 110), sweet cheese topping (page 541), grated raw cheese, ratatouille (page 384), crab filling (page 252) or chicken supreme (page 288). Crepes may be made ahead of time and reheated.

Variation: Crispy Crepes

Spread crepes on a platter and leave in a 150 degree oven overnight. Crepes will dry out and become crispy. These are delicious with butter and raw honey.

YORKSHIRE PUDDING
Serves 4

3/4 cup bulgur flour (page 461)
1 teaspoon sea salt
1/2 cup whole milk
2 eggs, well beaten
1/2 cup filtered water
1/3 cup beef tallow or suet

Yorkshire pudding made with sprouted wheat flour will not rise as well as pudding made with white flour, but the results are still very tasty.

All ingredients should be at room temperature. Sift flour and salt into a bowl. Stir in milk, eggs and water. Beat vigorously several minutes with a wire whisk. Cover and chill well about 1 hour. Meanwhile, heat the beef fat in a round pie plate placed in a 400-degree oven. When the fat is very hot, beat the batter again for several minutes and pour into the pan. Bake at 400 degrees for 1/2 hour and at 300 degrees for another 1 hour.

Traditional methods for preparing grains and legumes supply those factors that nature uses for neutralizing phytic acid in seeds so that they can then sprout and grow: warmth, moisture, time and slight acidity. Soaking whole grains and flour overnight in a medium like cultured milk or warm acidulated water activates the enzyme phytase, which then neutralizes phytic acid. Studies show that salt added to the soaking medium inhibits this process, so the time to add salt to porridges and batters is just before cooking, not during the soaking period.

Under the right conditions, phytase is also activated in the human intestine, which explains why some people do not develop mineral deficiencies on a high-phytate diet while others do. However, extrusion—which is a high-temperature, high-pressure process used to transform whole grains into breakfast cereals like bran flakes and shredded wheat—totally destroys phytase but leaves phytic acid intact. Thus, high-fiber cold breakfast cereals deliver a double whammy of mineral-blocking phytic acid without the phytase that can deactivate at least a portion of the phytic acid in the intestinal tract. Extrusion also renders certain proteins very toxic, essential oils rancid and many vitamins useless. Cooked breakfast cereals are far more nutritious, even when not soaked beforehand. Best of all are properly soaked and cooked whole grains eaten with quality fat in the form of butter or cream.

The fact that phytic acid is a strong chelator has led to claims that phytic acid can be used to remove toxic metals. This may well be true, but to avoid mineral deficiencies the use of high phytate foods for this purpose should be carried out only for a brief period—as the Jews ate high-phytate unleavened bread for a few days during Passover. SWF

As one stands in profound admiration before the stalwart physical development and high moral character of these sturdy Alpine mountaineers, he is impressed by the superior types of manhood, womanhood and childhood that Nature has been able to produce from a suitable diet and a suitable environment. Surely, here is evidence enough to answer the question whether cereals should be avoided because they produce acids in the system. . . when one has contrasted these people with the pinched and sallow and even deformed faces and distorted bodies that are produced by our modern civilization and its diets; and when one has contrasted the unsurpassed beauty of the faces of these children developed on nature's primitive foods with the varied assortment of modern civilization's children with their defective facial development, he finds himself filled with an earnest desire to see that this betterment is made available for modern civilization. Again and again we had the experience of examining a young man or young woman and finding that at some period of his life tooth decay had been rampant and had suddenly ceased; but, during the stress, some teeth had been lost. When we asked such people whether they had gone out of the mountain and at what age, they generally reported that at eighteen or twenty years of age they had gone to this or that city and had stayed a year or two. They stated that they had never had a decayed tooth before they went or after they returned, but that they had lost some teeth in the short period away from home. Weston Price, DDS *Nutrition and Physical Degeneration*

BASIC MUFFINS
Makes about 15

*3 cups freshly ground spelt, kamut
    or whole wheat flour*
2 cups buttermilk, kefir or yoghurt (pages 83-86)
2 eggs, lightly beaten
1 teaspoon sea salt
1/4 cup maple syrup
2 teaspoons baking soda
1 teaspoon vanilla extract
3 tablespoons melted butter

Soak flour in buttermilk, kefir or yoghurt in a warm place for 12 to 24 hours—muffins will rise better if soaked for 24 hours. (Those with milk allergies may use *2 cups filtered water plus 2 tablespoons whey, lemon juice or vinegar* in place of undiluted buttermilk, kefir or yoghurt.) Blend in remaining ingredients. Pour into well-buttered muffin tins (preferably stoneware), filling about three quarters full. Bake at 325 degrees for about 1 hour or until a toothpick comes out clean.

Variation: Raisin Muffins

Add *1/2 cup raisins* and *1/2 teaspoon cinnamon.*

Variation: Blueberry Muffins

Add *1 cup blueberries, fresh or frozen.* To prevent blueberries from falling to the bottom of the muffins, do not mix into batter but place 5-7 blueberries on top of the batter in each muffin tin.

Variation: Dried Cherry Muffins

Add *4 ounces dried cherries* (available at health food stores and gourmet markets) and *1/2 cup chopped crispy pecans (page 513).*

Variation: Fruit Spice Muffins

Add *2 ripe pears or peaches, peeled and cut into small pieces, 1/2 teaspoon cinnamon, 1/8 teaspoon cloves* and *1/8 teaspoon nutmeg.*

Variation: Lemon Muffins

Add *grated rind of 2 lemons* and *1/2 cup chopped crispy pecans (page 513).*

Variation: Ginger Muffins

Add *1 tablespoon freshly grated ginger* and *1 teaspoon ground ginger.* Omit vanilla.

BANANA BREAD

Makes 1 9-inch by 4-inch loaf

3 cups freshly ground spelt, kamut
*   or whole wheat flour*
2 cups buttermilk, kefir or yoghurt (pages 83-86)
3 eggs, lightly beaten
1 teaspoon sea salt
1/4 to 1/2 cup maple syrup
2 teaspoons baking soda
1/4 cup melted butter
2 ripe bananas, mashed
1/2 cup chopped crispy pecans (page 513)

Soak flour in buttermilk, kefir or yoghurt in a warm place for 12 to 24 hours—bread will rise better if soaked for 24 hours. (Those with milk allergies may use *2 cups filtered water plus 2 tablespoons whey, lemon juice or vinegar* in place of undiluted buttermilk, kefir or yoghurt.) Blend in remaining ingredients. Pour into a well-buttered and floured loaf pan (preferably stoneware). Bake at 350 degrees for at least 1 1/2 hours, or until a toothpick comes out clean.

Variation: Zucchini Bread

Use *2 zucchini* instead of 2 bananas and add *1 teaspoon vanilla extract.* Use the food processor to cut the zucchini into a julienne, toss with sea salt and let stand for 1 hour. Rinse, squeeze dry in a tea towel and stir into batter.

Variation: Banana or Zucchini Spice Bread

Add *1/4 teaspoon nutmeg, 1/2 teaspoon all-spice, 1/2 teaspoon cinnamon* and *1/4 teaspoon ground ginger* to either of the above recipes.

Variation: Apricot Almond Bread

Omit bananas. Use *1 cup unsulphured dried apricots, cut into pieces, soaked in warm water for 1 hour and drained, 1 cup chopped crispy almonds* (page 515) and *1 teaspoon vanilla.*

[Egyptian tomb scenes show] the processing of wheat grain into bread. One man we see pounding the grain with pestles in a solid cylindrical mortar. . . . A woman passes the coarse flour through a sieve into a tray to remove husks and a companion grinds it still further. . . other scenes show the grinding operation repeated by successive teams until all the grain had attained the desired fineness, through thirteen sieving procedures . . . [but] many other accounts imply that the vast majority of peasants and workers ate a whole grain bread. This means that possibly only the pharaohs and nobles managed enough workers to produce a white flour bread. . . . Mummy x-rays [show] curvature of the spine or scoliosis. . . . This wife of a pharaoh suffered arthritis of the spine, which would have been severely uncomfortable, and marked scoliosis, which would have made movement difficult and painful. This condition can be produced in rats born in laboratories today. While pregnant, the mother rats were fed a diet low in the trace mineral manganese. What does this have to do with ancient Egypt? When we remove the bran and germ from the whole grain as they were doing and as we do today, manganese diminishes greatly. . . . Buck teeth, or malocclusion and impacted wisdom teeth appear. No doubt Dr. Price would spot this as the result of a deterioration of the diet of the parents. Ruth Rosevear *PPNF Health Journal*

Besides skim milk, there is another important by-product resulting from the manufacture of butter, namely buttermilk. In butter making the fat globules are brought together by churning and removed, leaving a thin liquid. This buttermilk is very like skim milk in composition, but it has usually a milk-acid taste because the cream is generally allowed to sour before churning. Buttermilk is often used as a beverage. . . and is frequently fed to babies, especially in Holland, and is sometimes prescribed when the protein of ordinary milk proves indigestible. . . . Just as buttermilk represents the residue of milk from butter making, so whey represents what is left from cheese making and consists mainly of water, milk sugar and mineral matters. . . . In the "whey cures" for dyspeptics of which so much was heard some years ago, whey was usually combined with a simple vegetable diet. . . . Sour milk or clabber is a common article of diet in many parts of the United States and is wholesome and, to those who care for it, very refreshing and palatable . . . sour milk is much used in cookery, and adds materially to the nutritive value of the dish of which it forms a part. Before baking powders became so common, sour milk and baking soda were very commonly used to leaven doughs and batters of various sorts. Some cooks maintain that they can secure the best results by using only the whey of sour milk. R. D. Milner, PhD *The Use of Milk as Food* 1915

YOGHURT HERB BREAD
Makes 1 9-inch by 4-inch loaf

3 cups freshly ground spelt, kamut
*   or whole wheat flour*
2 cups plain whole yoghurt (page 85)
1/2 cup filtered water
3 large eggs, lightly beaten
1 teaspoon sea salt
2 teaspoons baking soda
1/4 stick melted butter
1/3 cup maple syrup
1 teaspoon dried dill
1/2 teaspoon dried oregano
1/2 teaspoon dried thyme
1/2 teaspoon dried basil
1/2 teaspoon dried tarragon

Mix flour with yoghurt and water, cover and leave in a warm place for 12 to 24 hours—bread will rise better if soaked for 24 hours. Place flour mixture in food processor and process for several minutes to knead the dough. Add remaining ingredients and process until well blended. Pour into a well-buttered and floured loaf pan (preferably stoneware). Bake at 350 degrees for at least 1 1/2 hours, or until a toothpick comes out clean.

BUTTERMILK BISCUITS
Makes about 1 dozen

3 1/2 cups freshly ground spelt, kamut
*   or whole wheat flour*
1 cup buttermilk (page 83)
4 tablespoons melted butter or lard
1 1/2 teaspoons sea salt
2 teaspoons baking soda
unbleached white flour

Mix flour with buttermilk to form a thick dough. Cover and leave in a warm place for 12 to 24 hours. Place in food processor and process several minutes to knead. Blend in remaining ingredients. Remove dough to a well-floured pastry cloth or board and sprinkle with unbleached white flour to prevent sticking. Roll dough to about 3/4 inch thickness. Cut biscuits with a glass and place on a buttered baking sheet. Bake at 350 degrees for about 40 minutes. Serve with butter and honey or mustard and cold meats.

Variation: Cheaters Biscuits

Use *1 cup unbleached white flour* and *2 cups spelt, kamut or whole wheat flour*. This makes a lighter biscuit.

Variation: Date Scones

Add *2 tablespoons Rapadura (see page 536)* to melted butter or lard and *1 cup chopped dates* to dough before removing from food processor. Blend in dates with a few pulses.

YOGHURT DOUGH

1 cup plain whole yoghurt (page 85)
1 cup (1/2 pound) butter, softened
3 1/2 cups freshly ground spelt or wheat flour
2 teaspoons sea salt
unbleached white flour

This excellent all-purpose dough recipe makes enough for two 10-inch, French-style tart shells. It cooks more slowly than dough made with white flour.

Cream yoghurt with butter. Blend in flour and salt. Cover and leave in a warm place for 12 to 24 hours.

Roll on a pastry cloth using unbleached white flour to prevent sticking. For a prebaked tart shell, prick well with a fork and place in a cold oven. Turn heat on to 350 degrees and bake for 20 to 30 minutes.

Whenever we open a book on medicinal plants, we are surprised to find there almost all the herbs that play a part in good cooking. These "good herbs" are above all plants for our health. It is no accident that at the same time they are essential elements in food that we eat with pleasure. Here is the proof that for the cook, the food provider, good health and good taste go together. Claude Aubert *Dis-Moi Comment Tu Cuisines*

Know Your Ingredients
Name This Product # 29

Enriched flour (wheat flour, malted barley flour, iron, niacin, thiamine mononitrate, riboflavin), water, corn bran, high fructose corn syrup, wheat gluten, whole wheat flour, wheat bran. Contains 2% or less of each of the following: Molasses, yeast, canola oil and/ or soybean oil, salt, soya flour, guar gum, calcium sulfate, dough conditioners (may contain one or more of the following: calcium and sodium stearoyl, lactylate, ethozylater mono- and diglycerides monocalcium phosphate, calcium carbonate, dicalcium phosphate), mono- and diglycerides, yeast nutrients (diammonium phosphate and/ or ammonium sulfate), calcium propionate (added to retard spoilage).

See Appendix B for Answer

While pellagra was being investigated as an interesting curiosity in Europe, it was becoming a way of life in the Southern United States. . . . The general diet consisted of cornmeal and grits, soda biscuits, corn syrup and fat salt pork; and even when they had enough bulk of food, the Southerners developed sore skin and mouths, became thin and listless, and suffered from depression, hallucinations, irritability and other mental disorders. The clinical description of the typical poor Southerner, any time between about 1900 and 1940, comes alive in the novels of William Faulkner—the brooding sullenness suddenly shattered by outbursts of irrational anger, persecution mania, the feeling of people living in a cruel and demented world of their own. . . . Doctors knew very well that diet was at the bottom of all the misery they saw around them, and that the disease could be kept at bay by a balanced food supply . . . . The Red Cross distributed dried yeast, already noted as a cure for the disease, or could sometimes lend a rural family a cow until the general health and earning power had improved; but it was not until 1937 that it was finally proved that pellagra was due to a shortage in the diet of the very simple compound nicotinamide [vitamin B$_3$]. . . . The discovery that such a simple material could have such profound effects not only on the body but on the mind set off a great wave of nutritional research. One mystery was soon solved: doctors had known for years that poor Mexicans who also lived mainly on maize might suffer from many other diseases but very rarely from pellagra. It emerged that there was, in fact, some nicotinamide in maize, but in a form that could not easily be absorbed. The

CORN BREAD
Serves 6-8

2 cups freshly ground cornmeal
1/2 cup freshly ground spelt, kamut
    or whole wheat flour
1/2 cup unbleached white flour
1 1/2 cups lime water (see page 454)
1 cup buttermilk or yoghurt (pages 83-86)
3 eggs, lightly beaten
1/4 cup maple syrup (optional)
1 teaspoon sea salt
2 teaspoons baking soda
1/4 cup melted butter

Soak cornmeal in lime water for about 7 hours. Stir in flour and buttermilk or yoghurt and let stand in a warm place for 12 to 24 hours—corn bread will rise better if soaked for 24 hours. (Those with milk allergies may use 1 1/2 cups water plus 2 tablespoons whey, lemon juice or vinegar in place of undiluted buttermilk or yoghurt.) Blend in remaining ingredients. Pour into a buttered and floured 9-inch by 13-inch pyrex pan. Bake at 325 degrees for at about 1 hour or until a toothpick comes out clean.

Variations: Chile and Cheese Corn Bread

Add 1 cup grated Monterey Jack or Cheddar cheese and 1 small can diced green chiles to batter.

CORNMEAL SPOON BREAD
Serves 8-10

2 cups freshly ground cornmeal
2 cups lime water (see page 454)
2 cups buttermilk, kefir or yoghurt (pages 83-86)
2 tablespoons butter
1 medium onion, finely chopped
5 egg yolks, at room temperature, lightly beaten
1 teaspoon sea salt
1/8 teaspoon cayenne pepper
2 teaspoons baking powder
5 egg whites, at room temperature
pinch of sea salt

Soak cornmeal in lime water for about 7 hours. Stir in buttermilk, kefir or yoghurt, cover and leave in a warm place for 12 to 24 hours. (Those with milk allergies may use *2 cups water plus 2 tablespoons whey, lemon juice or vinegar* in place of undiluted buttermilk, kefir or yoghurt.) Sauté onion in butter. Blend egg yolks into cornmeal mixture along with salt, cayenne pepper, sautéed onions and baking powder. In a clean bowl, beat egg whites with pinch of salt until stiff. Fold into cornmeal mixture and pour into a buttered 9-inch by 13-inch pyrex pan. Bake at least 45 minutes at 375 degrees.

POLENTA

(Italian Corn Casserole)
Serves 8-12

2 cups freshly ground cornmeal
1 cup lime water (see page 454)
4 tablespoons whey or yoghurt (pages 83-85)
3 cups water or chicken broth (page 124)
2 teaspoons sea salt
1 cup grated Parmesan cheese
1 medium onion, finely chopped,
    and sautéed in a little butter (optional)
2 tablespoon dried tomato bits,
    sautéed with the onions (optional)
1/2 teaspoon dried thyme (optional)

Soak cornmeal in lime water for about 7 hours. Add whey or yoghurt, cover and leave in a warm place at least 12 hours. Bring water or chicken stock and salt to a boil. Slowly add soaked cornmeal, stirring constantly with a whisk. Lower heat and continue stirring for another 15 to 30 minutes until liquid is reduced and polenta is so thick it comes away from the sides of the pan. Stir in cheese and optional ingredients and pour into a buttered 9-inch by 13-inch pyrex dish. Bake at 300 degrees for about 1 1/2 hours.

Variation: Polenta Triangles

Cut *chilled leftover polenta* into triangles and sauté in *lard* or a mixture of *butter and extra virgin olive oil.*

Mexican women had a custom taken from traditional Indian food preparation of soaking the corncobs in lime water before they made their tortillas. This apparently released the vitamin. It is an ironic thought that the adoption of one simple "primitive" custom might have saved the tens of thousands of ruined lives in the Southern states. Soon it was discovered that less of the vitamin was needed if there was plenty of protein in the diet, particularly protein containing the essential amino acid tryptophan. This knowledge might not have helped much in the worst periods of pellagra, because the people were too poor to buy much protein; and tryptophan is one of the rarest of the amino acids. However, it did explain why foods like milk and eggs, low in actual nicotinamide but rich in tryptophan, could keep pellagra away. Terence McLaughlin *A Diet of Tripe*

COUNTRY ITALIAN DINNER

Artichokes with Lemon Butter Sauce

Grilled Swordfish with Bagnat Sauce

Polenta Triangles

Broccoli

Merengue Marvel

The fermentation of vegetables (sauerkraut, kimchi, pickles), grains (sourdough bread, kvass, kiesiel, kisra, koji), beans (miso, natto, tempeh) and fish are experiencing renewed interest. The savings in refrigeration cost alone would warrant the return to a safer, saner and more savory taste. As the world's fastest and best quality foods, these are always ready to be consumed, cold or warmed. Ancient standard cookbooks never mentioned fermented fast foods for the simple reason that those cookbooks were written for the rich and famous. Reading these ancient texts, one gets the idea that our ancestors spent a great amount of time preparing those fancy and elaborate meals. The truth is, simple folks toiled in the fields long hours, had to be in good health and had little time for preparing moveable-feast style lunches to be quickly consumed in the furrows. These foods often had to stand all morning long in the heat of harvest without the benefit of refrigeration . . . . Sourdough breads, pickled olives, herrings and anchovies, lacto-fermented vegetables and beans and sometimes yoghurt or cheese were the everyday fare. . . . A properly elaborated sourdough loaf acquires an unsurpassed taste and an aroma that no cracker or porridge can ever match. Sauerkraut achieves a succulent gourmet savor that cole-slaw never reaches. If you taste Normandy country farm butter, churned from aged fermented sour cream, you will never again eat creamery butter. Jacques DeLangre *Seasalt's Hidden Powers*

CREAM CHEESE BREAKFAST PASTRIES

(Rugelach)
Makes 18-24

1/2 cup butter, softened
1 cup homemade cream cheese,
    softened (pages 87)
2 cups freshly ground spelt, kamut
    or whole wheat flour
1/2 cup Rapadura (see page 536)
1 tablespoon vanilla extract
1 teaspoon salt
1/4 cup melted butter
2 teaspoons cinnamon
1/4 cup crispy pecans (page 513), finely chopped

Mix butter, cream cheese and flour using an electric beater and leave in a warm place for 12 to 24 hours. Mix in Rapadura, vanilla and salt. Using unbleached white flour to keep from sticking, roll out dough on a pastry cloth to 1/4-inch thickness. Brush with mixture of melted butter and cinnamon and sprinkle with pecans. Roll up 1 1/2 turns and cut dough lengthwise. Roll another 1 1/2 turns and cut lengthwise. Repeat once more. You should now have three long rolls. Cut the rolls crosswise into 1-inch or 1 1/2-inch lengths. Place individual pastries on a buttered cookie sheet and bake at 300 degrees for about 45 minutes. These store well in freezer or refrigerator and the flavor improves with time. Reheat before serving.

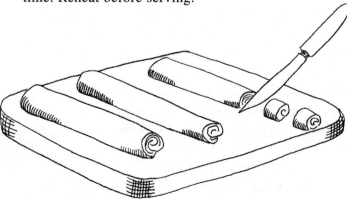

SOURDOUGH STARTER

Makes about 3 quarts

2 cups freshly ground rye flour
2 cups cold filtered water
cheesecloth
6 cups freshly ground rye flour
cold filtered water

Best results for sourdough starter are obtained from rye rather than wheat flour, perhaps because rye contains a lower phytate content than wheat. You will need two gallon-sized bowls. Total time to make the starter is 1 week.

Grind 2 cups flour and let it sit for a bit to cool. In one large bowl, mix flour with 2 cups of cold water. The mixture should be quite soupy. Cover with a double layer of cheesecloth secured with a rubber band—this will allow yeasts and bacteria to get in but will keep insects out. In warm weather, you may set the bowl outside in the shade if you live in an unpolluted area and no pesticides have been used in your garden. Otherwise, keep it in a warm open area indoors or on a patio.

The next day and every day for a total of 7 days, transfer the starter to the other clean bowl and add 1 cup freshly ground rye flour plus enough cold water to make a soupy mixture. Cover and let stand. After a few days the starter will begin to bubble and develop a wine-like aroma. It should go through a bubbly, frothy stage and then subside. After 7 days, the starter is ready for breadmaking. Use 2 quarts for a batch of sourdough bread (page 490) but save 1 quart for your next batch of starter. If not using remaining starter immediately, you may store it in airtight jars in the refrigerator or freezer.

Do not be tempted to add honey to your starter, as some recipes require. Honey encourages the proliferation of yeasts at the expense of lactic-acid-producing bacteria and may give you an alcoholic fermentation.

To start a new batch of starter, place the quart of leftover starter in a clean bowl. Add 1 cup freshly ground rye flour plus water each day, changing bowls, until 3 quarts are obtained. Note: See Sources for sourdough starters by mail order.

"But how do you make the sourdough?" Mrs. Boast asked.

"You start it," said Ma, "by putting some flour and warm water in a jar and letting it stand till it sours."

"Then when you use it, always leave a little," said Laura, "and put in the scraps of biscuit dough, like this, and more warm water," Laura put in the warm water, "and cover it," she put the clean cloth and the plate on the jar, "and just set it in a warm place," she set it in its place on the shelf by the stove. "And it's always ready to use, whenever you want it." Laura Ingalls Wilder *By the Shores of Silver Lake*

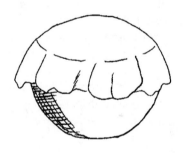

The history of bread making is a good example of the industrialization and standardization of a technique that was formerly empiric. . . . It was simpler to replace natural leaven with brewers yeast. There are numerous practical advantages: the fermentation is more regular, more rapid and the bread rises better. But the fermentation becomes mainly an alcoholic fermentation and the acidification is greatly lessened. The bread is less digestible, less tasty and spoils more easily. Claude Aubert *Les Aliments Fermentés Traditionnels*

Where do we find these lactic-acid-producing bacteria that cause milk to sour, that gives bread its aroma and that conserves vegetables? They are in the living soil and on healthy plants, in particular those that grow close to the soil. A protective coat of acid, truly an acid sheath, envelopes all higher organisms. In the mouth, the stomach, the intestine and in the reproductive organs one finds a flora that produces lactic acid. Annelies Schoneck *Des Crudités Toute L'Année*

No single substance will maintain vibrant health. Although specific nutrients are known to be more important in the functions of certain parts of the body, even these nutrients are totally dependent upon the presence of other nutrients for their best effects. Every effort should therefore be made to attain and maintain an adequate, balanced daily intake of all the necessary nutrients throughout life. Lavon J. Dunne *Nutrition Almanac*

Raw honey is noteworthy for having considerable plant amylase. The amylase does not come from the bee but is a true plant enzyme, concentrated from the pollen of flowers . . . . If you wish to predigest a starchy food, such as bread, spread some raw honey on it. The moment the honey and bread come into contact, the honey enzyme starts predigestion; and as you chew more digestion takes place. If the bread with its honey-enzyme coating is allowed to stand at room temperature for 15 minutes before you eat it, there will be less work for salivary amylase. Edward Howell, MD *Enzyme Nutrition*

SOURDOUGH BREAD

Makes 3 large loaves or 5-6 smaller loaves

2 quarts sourdough starter
13 cups freshly ground spelt, kamut
*   or hard winter wheat*
2 1/2 tablespoons coarse sea salt
about 1 1/2 cups cold filtered water

Traditional sourdough bread, prepared with a starter rather than with yeast, has a delicious flavor but tends to be heavy for modern tastes. Spelt gives the most satisfactory loaf.

Your starter should be at room temperature and have gone through the bubbling, frothy stage.

Place starter, salt and 1 cup water in a large bowl and mix with a wooden spoon until the salt crystals have dissolved. Slowly mix in the flour. Towards the end you will find it easier to mix with your hands. You may add the other 1/2 cup of water if the dough becomes too thick. It should be rather soft and easy to work. Knead by pulling and folding over, right in the bowl, for 10 to 15 minutes; or knead in batches in your food processor.

Without pressing down the dough, cut or shape loaves into the desired shapes or place into 3 large well-buttered loaf pans or 5-6 smaller loaf pans. Cut a few slits in the top of the dough, cover and let rise from 4 to 12 hours, depending on the temperature. Bake at 350 degrees for about an hour. Allow to cool before slicing.

The bread will keep for up to a week without refrigeration.

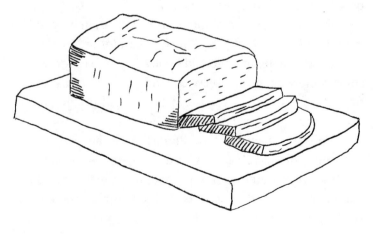

Variation: Sourdough Herb and Nut Bread

To each loaf, add *1 tablespoon rosemary* or *1 tablespoon dill* during kneading and *1/4 cup chopped crispy pecans or walnuts (page 513)* at the end of the kneading process.

Variation: Sourdough Cheaters Bread

Use *3 cups unbleached white flour* and *10 cups whole wheat flour* for a lighter loaf.

SPICE BREAD

(Pain d'Epices)
Makes 2 9-inch rounds

4 cups freshly ground rye or spelt flour
1 cup raw honey
2 cups filtered water
2 teaspoons ground cinnamon
1 teaspoon ground coriander
1 teaspoon ground fennel
1 teaspoon ground cumin
1 teaspoon sea salt
grated rind of 2 oranges
1/2 cup sourdough starter

Mix spices, orange rind and salt with flour in a large bowl. Meanwhile, gently heat the honey with the water until honey is dissolved. Let cool. Make a well in the flour and place the starter in it. Gradually add the honey-water mixture, stirring with a wooden spoon. The dough should be more liquid than bread dough. Line two well-oiled, 9-inch cake pans with buttered parchment paper and divide the batter between the two pans. Cover with a damp towel and let rise in a warm place for at least 12 hours. Bake at 350 degrees for 1 hour. Let cool slightly and remove from pan. Leave at room temperature, covered, a day or two before eating.

In books on baking and even in nutritional/medical writings, the two techniques [for making bread], natural leaven (sourdough) and baker's yeast, are often mingled and confounded. . . . Baking with natural leaven is in harmony with nature and maintains the integrity and nutrition of the cereal grains used. . . . The process helps to increase and reinforce our body's absorption of the cereal's nutrients. Unlike yeasted bread that diminishes, even destroys, much of the grain's nutritional value, naturally leavened bread does not stale and, as it ages, maintains its original moisture much longer. A lot of that information was known pragmatically for centuries; and thus when yeast was first introduced in France at the court of Louis XIV in March 1668, because at that time the scientists already knew that the use of yeast would imperil the people's health, it was strongly rejected. Today, yeast is used almost universally, without any testing; and the recent scientific evidence and clinical findings are confirming the ancient taboos with biochemical and bioelectronic valid proofs that wholly support that age-old common sense decision.

Jacques DeLangre

We may live without poetry, music and art. . . We may live without conscience and live without hearts. . . We many live without friends. . . We may live without books. . . But civilized man cannot live without cooks.

Athenaeus

The nutrition of the people of the Loetschental Valley, particularly that of the growing boys and girls, consists largely of a slice of whole rye bread and a piece of the summer-made cheese (about as large as the slice of bread), which are eaten with fresh milk of goats or cows. Meat is eaten about once a week. In the light of our newer knowledge of activating substances, including vitamins, and the relative values of food for supplying minerals for body building, it is clear why they have healthy bodies and sound teeth. The average total fat-soluble activator and mineral intake of calcium and phosphorus of these children would far exceed that of the daily intake of the average American child. The sturdiness of the child life permits children to play and frolic bareheaded and barefooted even in water running down from the glacier in the late evening's chilly breezes, in weather that made us wear our overcoats and gloves and button our collars. Of all the children in the valley still using the primitive diet of whole rye bread and dairy products, the average number of cavities per person was 0.3. On an average it was necessary to examine three persons to find one defective deciduous or permanent tooth. The children examined were between seven and sixteen years of age. Weston Price, DDS *Nutrition and Physical Degeneration*

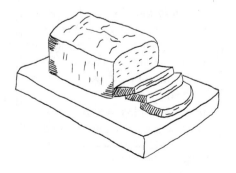

NATURAL YEAST BREAD
Makes 2 loaves

2 cups unwashed organic grapes, processed to pulp
4 cups freshly ground rye flour
1 tablespoon sea salt
7 cups freshly ground spelt, kamut
    or hard winter wheat flour
1 tablespoon sea salt
filtered water

This makes a slightly lighter sourdough loaf than the preceding sourdough recipe, but the bread is still too heavy for traditional sandwiches. The starter can be prepared in 3 days rather than 7.

Place 2 cups grape pulp and 2 cups freshly ground rye flour in a clean bowl. Mix well and cover with two layers of cheesecloth or a square of light cloth secured with a rubber band. Leave in a warm place. On day two, transfer to a clean bowl and add 1 cup rye flour and 1 cup filtered water. Mix well, cover with a cloth and leave in a warm place. On day three, transfer to a clean bowl and add the final cup of rye flour and 1 cup water. Mix well, cover with a cloth and leave in a warm place until starter gets frothy and subsides. You should have about 5 cups. Use 4 cups for making bread and save 1 cup in a jar in the refrigerator or freezer for a new batch of starter.

To make bread, combine 7 cups of flour with 4 cups starter, 1 tablespoon sea salt and about 1 1/2 cups water. Mix well with a wooden spoon or with your hands. To knead, process in two different batches in food processor and place each batch in a well-buttered loaf pan. Cut a few slits in the top of the dough, cover and let rise in a warm place at least 12 hours. Bake at 300 degrees for about 1 1/2 hours.

Variation: Natural Yeast Herb and Nut Bread
To each loaf, add *1 tablespoon rosemary* or *1 tablespoon dill* during kneading and *1/4 cup chopped crispy pecans or walnuts (page 513)* at the end of the kneading process.

Variation: Natural Yeast Cheaters Bread
Use *2 cups unbleached white flour* and *5 cups whole wheat flour* for a lighter loaf

YEASTED BUTTERMILK BREAD

Makes 2 loaves

*4 cups freshly ground spelt, kamut
      or hard winter wheat flour
1-1 1/2 cups buttermilk (page 83 or 85), warm
1/2 cup butter, melted
1/4 cup warm water
1 package dry yeast
2 tablespoons honey
1 teaspoon salt
1/2 teaspoon baking soda
1 cup unbleached white flour.*

This is a good compromise bread that can be sliced and used for sandwiches. Yeast is used, but the flour is soaked in buttermilk first.

Combine whole wheat flour, 1 cup buttermilk and butter in a food processor until a ball forms. If dough is too thick, add more buttermilk, but it should be thick enough to form a ball. Place in a bowl, cover with a towel and leave in a warm place for 12-24 hours.

Combine water, yeast and honey in a small bowl and leave for 5 minutes or until it bubbles. Add salt and baking soda and mix well. Place half the flour mixture, half the yeast mixture and 1/2 cup unbleached white flour in a food processor. Process until a smooth ball forms. Repeat with the other half of dough, yeast mixture and white flour.

Knead the two balls together briefly and place in a buttered bowl. Cover with a towel and let rise 2 hours, until doubled in bulk. Punch down, cut the dough in half and process each half in a food processor for 30 seconds each. Form into loaves and place in buttered loaf pans (preferably stoneware). Cover with a towel and let rise 1-2 hours, until doubled. Bake for 30 minutes at 350 degrees. Cool on racks.

Variation: Yeasted Buttermilk Rolls

Divide into about 24 balls instead of 2 loaves. Place in two buttered cake pans and let rise until doubled. Bake at 350 degrees for about 30 minutes. Cool on racks

Weston Price's studies convinced him that the best diet was one that combined nutrient-dense whole grains with animal products, particularly fish. The healthiest African tribe he studied was the Dinkas, a Sudanese tribe on the western bank of the Nile. They were not as tall as the cattle-herding Neurs groups but they were physically better proportioned and had greater strength. Their diet consisted mainly of fish and cereal grains. This is one of the most important lessons of Price's research—that a mixed diet of whole foods, one that avoids the extremes of the carnivorous Masai and the largely vegetarian Bantu, ensures optimum physical development. *Nasty, Brutish and Short?*

Some health writers claim that saturated fats in the diet inhibit the production of prostaglandins, localized tissue hormones that govern many processes on the cellular level. Actually the reverse is true. Saturated fats in the diet improve the body's utilization of essential fatty acids and protect them from becoming rancid. . . .

Lauric acid, a 12-carbon saturated fatty acid found chiefly in mother's milk and coconut oil, and in smaller amounts in butter, seems to improve prostaglandin production. When lauric acid is present in the diet, the long chain fatty acids accumulate in the tissues where they belong, even when consumption of essential fatty acids is low. Unfortunately, highly useful and beneficial coconut oil has been forced out of the food supply by adverse propaganda originating with the fabricated food industry, which would rather use cheap hydrogenated oils rather than more expensive coconut oil for shortening. *Tripping Lightly Down the Prostaglandin Pathways*

"How could we cook our daily bread without fire, Master?" asked some with great astonishment.

"Let the angels of God prepare your bread. Moisten your wheat, that the angel of water may enter it. Then set it in the air, that the angel of air also may embrace it. And leave it from morning to evening beneath the sun, that the angel of sunshine may descend upon it. And the blessing of the three angels will soon make the germ of life to sprout in your wheat. Then crush your grain and make thin wafers, as did your forefathers when they departed out of Egypt, the house of bondage. Put them back again beneath the sun from its appearing and, when it is risen to its highest in the heavens, turn them over on the other side that they be embraced there also by the angel of sunshine and leave them there until the sun be set. . . ."
Edmond Szekely, trans. *The Essene Gospel of Peace*

Many of our refined foods have additions of B$_1$ and B$_2$. The *British Medical Journal* in an article entitled "Imbalance of vitamin B Factors" reported: "Recent experiments have produced clear-cut evidence of the adverse effects that may be caused by the disturbance of the balance of the vitamin B factors in the diet." They have shown that the overloading of B$_1$, for instance, can produce a definite deficiency of vitamin B$_6$. It is becoming increasingly recognized that there is a need for caution in addition of a supplement of a single synthetic vitamin to food preparations. National Health Federation *Seven Myths Exploded*

ZARATHUSTRA BREAD

Makes 10 small loaves

3 cups soft wheat berries
1/4 cup nonirradiated sesame seeds
*   or caraway seeds (optional)*
filtered water
1 teaspoon sea salt
1/2 cup currants or raisins (optional)

There are many variations to Zarathustra bread—here is ours. Another version may be found in the *Book of Living Foods* published by IBS International, P.O. Box 849, Nelson, BC Canada V1L 6A5.

Place wheat berries and optional seeds in a bowl, cover with water and leave in a warm, dark place for 24 hours. Pour out water, replenish and leave another 24 hours. Test berries to see if they are soft. If they are still hard when pinched, replace water and leave another 24 hours. Pour off excess water, transfer berries with a slotted spoon to a food processor and process with sea salt until smooth. Add optional currants or raisins and pulse a few times. Form into balls and flatten slightly. Place on a stainless steel baking sheet brushed with olive oil or butter and bake about 12 hours in a 150-degree oven, turning after about 6 hours. If you live in a hot, dry climate, you can bake these in the sun—thus baked Zarathustra.

Variation: Essene Bread

Flatten the balls into flat rounds, about 1/4-inch thick. Bake on lowest oven heat, in a dehydrator or, in hot, dry climates, in the sun, turning once.

Variation: Essene Crackers

Brush two stainless steel cookie sheets with olive oil or butter and use a rolling pin to flatten dough into thin sheets on the pans. Bake in a 150-degree oven or in a dehydrator until crisp. Break up into crackers.

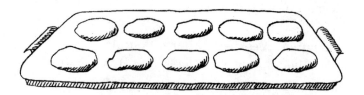

LEGUMES

Legumes or pulses, such as beans, chickpeas, lentils, peas, peanuts and cashews, have nourished mankind for centuries. Throughout the world, they have served as the poor man's meat. The combination of pulses, whole grains and a small amount of animal protein and good quality animal fat is the ideal low-cost diet. Legumes are rich in minerals and B vitamins. Recent research indicates that legumes contain several anticancer agents. All contain both omega-3 and omega-6 fatty acids. Kidney and pinto beans are high in omega-3 fatty acids; chickpeas are high in omega-6 fatty acids.

Traditional societies whose cuisines are based on legumes prepare them with great care. Beans are soaked for long periods before they are cooked. The soaking water is poured off, the beans are rinsed and, in the case of chickpeas, the skins picked off. As the legumes cook, all foam that rises to the top of the cooking water is carefully skimmed off. Sometimes water is replaced midway during the cooking process. Such care in preparation ensures that legumes will be thoroughly digestible, and all the nutrients they provide well assimilated because such careful preparation neutralizes phytic acid and enzyme inhibitors and breaks down difficult-to-digest complex sugars.

(Fava beans contain a substance, which is not neutralized by soaking, sprouting or fermenting, that can cause a type of life-threatening anemia in persons with an inherited susceptibility and are therefore best avoided.)

Asians have developed methods of inoculating soaked and cooked legumes, particularly soybeans, to produce products like *miso*, *tempeh* and *natto*. In fact, soybeans should be eaten *only* after they have been fermented. They are high in phytic acid and contain potent enzyme inhibitors, which can produce serious gastric distress, reduced protein digestion and chronic deficiencies in amino acid uptake. These phytates and enzyme inhibitors are not deactivated by ordinary cooking. We also do not recommend commercial soy milk because of its high-phytate and enzyme-inhibitor content, and because during processing carcinogens are formed.

Bland-tasting legumes marry very well with many sorts of spices, and they are particularly synergistic with sour foods. Always add lemon juice or the liquid from fermented vegetables to bean and lentil soups. Bean and lentil dishes go very well with sauerkraut and other lacto-fermented vegetables. In salads, beans and lentils are enhanced by copious amounts of onions.

What about canned beans? High temperatures and pressures used in the canning process do reduce phytate content, but the danger is that such processing overdenatures proteins and other nutrients at the same time. Canned beans are best eaten sparingly.

EL SALVADOREAN
TOSTADO FEAST

Basic
Black Beans

Mexican Chicken
Breasts

Grated Raw Monterey
Jack Cheese

Fried Tortillas

Guacamole

Cortido

Chismole

Watermelon Slices

Vegetable protein is also important and is found in largest quantities in whole grains, seeds, beans, legumes, peas, nuts, etc. Vegetable protein alone cannot sustain healthy life because it does not contain enough of all of the amino acids that are essential. There is only one plant that can be classed as a complete protein—the soybean; but it is so low in two of the essential amino acids that it cannot serve as a complete protein for human consumption. In fact, most all plants lack methionine, one of the essential amino acids. Vegetable protein, when supplemented properly by animal protein, makes an excellent combination. Health cannot be maintained on a diet that omits animal protein. H. Leon Abrams *Your Body Is Your Best Doctor*.

BASIC BEANS
Makes 8-10 cups cooked beans

2 cups black beans, kidney beans, pinto beans,
    black-eyed peas or white beans
warm filtered water
2 tablespoons whey (page 87) or lemon juice
4 cloves garlic, peeled and mashed (optional)
sea salt and pepper

Cover beans with warm water. Stir in whey or lemon juice and leave in a warm place for 12-24 hours, depending on the size of the bean. Drain, rinse, place in a large pot and add water to cover beans. Bring to a boil and skim off foam. Reduce heat and add optional garlic. Simmer, covered, for 4-8 hours. Check occasionally and add more water as necessary. Season to taste.

REFRIED BEANS
Serves 6

4 cups basic black or kidney beans, drained
about 3/4 cup lard or duck fat (page 295)

Mash beans with a potato masher. Melt lard or duck fat in a heavy, cast-iron skillet. Add beans and cook, stirring constantly, over a medium flame until all the fat is incorporated into the beans.

MASHED BEANS
Serves 6

2 cups small white beans
warm filtered water
2 tablespoons whey (page 87) or lemon juice
1 medium onion, coarsely chopped
1 medium carrot, peeled and chopped
1 medium parsnip, peeled and chopped
3 cloves garlic, peeled and crushed
1 medium onion, finely chopped
2 tablespoons butter
1 teaspoon paprika
sea salt and pepper

Cover beans with warm water. Stir in whey or lemon juice and leave in a warm place for about 24 hours. Drain, rinse and place in a pot with onion, carrot and parsnip. Add water to cover beans and bring to a boil. Skim off foam that rises to top. Reduce to simmer and add garlic. Cover and cook at least 4 hours. Remove in batches with a slotted spoon to food processor and purée, adding enough cooking liquid to achieve desired consistency. Sauté remaining onion until soft in butter. Stir in paprika and add onion-paprika mixture to the beans. Season to taste. Transfer to a heated serving dish.

BAKED BEANS

Serves 6-8

4 cups small white beans
warm filtered water
2 tablespoons whey (page 87) or lemon juice
2 medium onions
2 tablespoons butter
2 tablespoons extra virgin olive oil
1 small can tomato paste
3 tablespoons naturally fermented soy sauce
3 tablespoons vinegar
1/4 cup maple syrup
1/4 cup molasses
3 cloves garlic, peeled and crushed
1 teaspoon salt
pinch of red chile flakes

Cover beans with warm water. Stir in whey or lemon juice and leave in a warm place for 24 hours. In a flameproof casserole, sauté onion in butter and oil. Drain beans, rinse and add to casserole, with enough water to cover them. Bring to a boil and skim. Add remaining ingredients, cover and bake in a 350 degree oven for about 6 hours. Serve with sauerkraut (page 92), whole grain bread and turkey or lamb sausage (pages 363-364).

In *The Saccharine Disease (1975),* Cleave lays the blame for prevalence of diabetes on the doorstep of refined carbohydrates. He acknowledges the genetic basis of the disorder but "rejects unequivocally" the assumption that this is a "defect." "The hereditary features of the disease. . . do no more than reflect the inheritance of personal build, including that of the pancreas itself, rendering the persons concerned more vulnerable to the new environmental factor. . . . These features in no sense indicate hereditary defect. . . the body is not built wrongly but is being used wrongly." The more pronounced the genetic predisposition, according to Cleave, the earlier the onset of the disease, provided the triggering event occurs. In industrialized society, the triggering event appears to be the overload of sugar, white flour products, white rice and processed fruits and vegetables. "The consumption of refined carbohydrates. . . imposes unnatural strains upon the pancreas, either through overconsumption, or . . . rapidity of consumption and absorption, or. . . both." Joseph D. Beasley, MD and Jerry J. Swift, MA *The Kellogg Report*

By the mid 1980's, major changes were made in the food supply that were damaging to the image and markets of the naturally saturated fats. Some groups in the edible oil industry—particularly the soybean interests—and some of the consumer activist groups like Center for Science in the Public Interest (CSPI) further eroded the status of saturated fats when they sponsored the antisaturated fat, antitropical oils campaign in the mid to late 1980's. The activism of these groups resulted in wholesale economic boycotting of the so-called saturated fats; especially the palmitic-rich tallows and palm oil and the lauric-rich oils; this activism resulted in their ultimate removal from very many foods. As a result, the partially hydrogenated vegetable oils replaced the naturally saturated fats and there were major increases in the levels of unnatural *trans* fatty acids in popular food items in the U.S. and Canada, especially restaurant foods, bakery goods, snack chips and other widely consumed processed foods. Individual meals in fast food restaurants now provide many times more *trans* fatty acids than they did a decade ago; for example, a meal of the same foods showed 19.2 g *trans* fatty acids in 1992 versus 2.4 g *trans* fatty acids in 1982. This increase is largely due to the campaign waged by CSPI against the naturally saturated fats and oils.
Mary G. Enig, PhD *Know Your Fats*

FRENCH BEAN CASSEROLE

(Cassoulet)
Serves 12-16

6 cups small white beans
warm filtered water
3 tablespoons whey (page 87) or lemon juice
4 preserved duck legs and 4 preserved duck thighs
   (page 298), or 4 fresh duck legs
   and 4 fresh duck thighs (page 295)
2 medium onions, finely chopped
1 cup dry white wine
1/2 cup fresh lemon juice
several sprigs fresh thyme and 2 bay leaves,
   tied together
1/2 teaspoon ground cloves
6 cups beef or chicken stock (page 122 or 124)
4 cloves garlic, peeled and mashed
2 teaspoons sea salt
1 teaspoon dried green peppercorns, crushed
1 pound lamb stew pieces
1 large can tomatoes
2 cloves garlic, peeled and mashed
3 pounds garlicky lamb or chicken sausage
2 cups whole grain bread crumbs
1 cup grated Parmesan cheese (optional)
2 tablespoons butter
1/4 cup finely chopped parsley

This French version of baked beans and various meats makes a wonderful party dish. It is traditionally made with preserved duck legs but you may also use fresh duck pieces.

Cover beans with warm water. Stir in whey or lemon juice and leave in a warm place for 24 hours. In a flameproof casserole that is wide and shallow rather than deep, sauté the preserved or fresh duck pieces in their own fat until nicely browned on all sides. Remove and reserve. Sauté onion in duck fat. Add wine and boil down. Drain beans, rinse and add to the pot along with stock. Bring to a boil and skim. Stir in lemon juice, salt and pepper, garlic and thyme and bay leaf. Return the duck pieces to the casserole, cover and bake at 350 degrees for about 3 hours, stirring occasionally.

Meanwhile, brown lamb pieces in olive oil in a heavy pan. Place canned tomatoes in food processor, pulse a couple of times and add to lamb. Add garlic and season with salt and pepper. Cover and simmer for about 3 hours or until lamb is tender. About 1/2 hour before casserole is finished, add sliced sausage to beans.

When beans are tender, remove thyme and bay leaf and stir in the cooked lamb. Sauté bread crumbs in butter until browned. Mix with parsley and optional cheese and strew over casserole. Bake another 20 minutes, uncovered, at 350 degrees or until bread crumbs are crusty.

One objection frequently made to a diet based primarily on grains and pulses is that these foods contain phytic acid. Particularly abundant in the germ of grains and in the skins of pulses, it combines in the intestinal tract with calcium, iron, magnesium and zinc to form insoluble phytates that are then eliminated. According to some researchers, the elimination of these minerals in the form of insoluble phytates can lead to severe deficiencies in those who nourish themselves predominantly with grains, unless the whole grains have been soaked or fermented before they are consumed. The role of phytic acid has been most thoroughly studied in bread. In sourdough bread, with a long fermentation that is partially a lacto-fermentation, the phytic acid is almost completely destroyed. On the other hand, bread made with brewers yeast undergoes a rapid fermentation that is in large measure an alcoholic fermentation; and its phytic acid content remains largely intact. The phytase (enzyme needed to break down phytic acid) present in grains cannot do its work unless the pH becomes sufficiently low and the period of fermentation lasts a sufficiently long time. Claude Aubert *Les Aliments Fermentés Traditionnels*

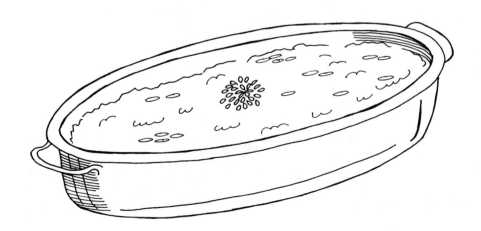

MARCH LUNCH

Baked Beans,
French Style

❀❀❀

Natural Yeast
Herb and Nut Bread
with Butter

❀❀❀

Caesar Salad

❀❀❀

Cashew Orange
Cookies

Primitive cultures showing a high immunity to dental disease and freedom from other degenerative processes had diets containing at least 10 times the vitamins A and D and at least 4 times the other vitamins and minerals found in a good modern diet. When the only foods available are unrefined and unprocessed, man must eat a wide variety and a large amount to meet his body's energy requirements. This usually supplies his body with the proper nutrients for good health and growth. Refining and processing of foods removes or destroys essential elements. It can make food a concentrated source of energy with little nutritional value. Modern man can easily fill his body's energy requirements without obtaining the nutrients for good health. When primitive man adopts the foods of modern society, his carbohydrate intake remains the same, but the form changes from whole grains and beans to sugar and other refined products. When primitive man adopts the foods of modern society, tooth decay and degenerative diseases follow. "Nutrition: The Appetite of Man" *PPNF*

BAKED BEANS, FRENCH STYLE
Serves 6-8

4 cups small white beans
filtered water
4 tablespoons whey (page 87) or lemon juice
1 cup extra virgin olive oil
1 small can tomato paste
4 cloves garlic, peeled and mashed
several sprigs fresh thyme, tied together
2 medium red onions, finely chopped
juice of 2 lemons
sea salt and pepper

This unusual and delicious recipe calls for cooking the beans in oil rather than in liquid. A long soaking is therefore essential or the beans will be too hard.

Bring a pot of water to the boil and pour over beans. Add 2 tablespoons whey and leave in a warm place for 12 hours. Pour beans into a colander, drain and rinse. Repeat the soaking process, leaving beans in a warm place another 12 hours. Pour beans into a colander, drain and rinse.

Heat olive oil in a pot and add beans, tomato paste, salt, thyme and garlic. Blend well. Bake at 300 degrees for about 6 hours, stirring occasionally to prevent burning. If beans seem too dry, add more olive oil. Beans are done when they are soft but they will not be mushy like beans cooked in liquid. Remove thyme, fold in onions and lemon juice, season to taste and serve.

BEANS AND RICE, JAMAICAN STYLE

Serves 6-8

1 cup red kidney beans
warm filtered water
1 tablespoon whey (page 87) or lemon juice
1 can coconut milk or
    7 ounces creamed coconut (see page 160)
1 bunch green onions, chopped
3 jalapeno peppers, seeded and chopped
3 cloves garlic, mashed
2 teaspoons dried thyme
2 teaspoons sea salt
1 teaspoon dried green peppercorns, crushed
1 cup brown rice, soaked at least 7 hours

Cover beans with warm water. Stir in whey or lemon juice and leave overnight in a warm place. In the morning, drain and rinse the beans and place in a pot. Add enough water to cover the beans, bring to a boil and skim. Add remaining ingredients except rice. (If using creamed coconut, stir until it is melted.) Cover and simmer for about 6-8 hours or until beans are tender. Drain the rice and add to the pot with enough filtered water to cover the rice and beans about 1/2 inch. Bring to a boil and cook, uncovered, until liquid has reduced to level of rice and beans. Cover and cook on lowest heat for about 30 minutes.

In the summer of 1965, I met a wise man from the East, a Japanese philosopher who had just returned from several weeks in Saigon. "If you really expect to conquer the North Vietnamese," he told me, "you must drop Army PX's on them—sugar, candy and Coca-Cola. That will destroy them faster than bombs." William Dufty *Sugar Blues*

Sir Robert McCarrison, M.D. of England, carried on elaborate experiments at Coonor, India, using over 2,000 clinical animals under controlled conditions.

Selecting out two of his experiments: The rats in one group were fed on the diet of the Hunzas of northern India. The Hunzas are large, strong and healthy, do physical work in their 80's and 90's and many live over 100 years. The diet of the Hunzas consists chiefly of whole grains, raw fruits and vegetables grown on organically fertilized soil and milk products from goats. The groups of rats fed on the Hunza diet grew large, were healthy, long-lived, docile and affectionate.

The rats of the second group were fed on the diet of the Madrasi of southern India. The Madrasi are small, puny ailing people with a life span of less than 20 years.

The Madrasi live on such foods as polished rice, tapioca, pulses, condiments, very little milk and few vegetables (mostly refined foods). The rats fed on this Madrasi diet were sickly, nervous, vicious and short-lived and had the diseases common to the Madrasi. R. Dean Conrad *The Great American Tragedy*

If you are having thyroid problems, check the amount of soy in your diet; or if you eat a lot of soy foods, watch your thyroid function. . . . This is the third strike against soy as the "health food" it has become, thanks to incessant propaganda by the huge agribusiness giants behind the world's biggest money crop.

Vegetarians have long championed soy foods as the "ideal" source of protein despite the scientific facts that disprove the notion. Textured soy protein, which is more widely used in packaged and refined foods and meat products (hamburger extender) than most of us ever imagined, now has three antinutrients that should make anyone think twice before making it a major part of the diet. The three antinutrients are: (1) a large amount of phytic acid, which binds up and prevents absorption of minerals, especially zinc, calcium and magnesium needed by the body; (2) trypsin inhibitors, which cannot be refined out of the soy mash (trypsin is an important enzyme in digestion); (3) isoflavones, genistein and daidzein, three phytochemicals that have now been shown to have antithyroid activity. . . [Researchers found] that soy isoflavones, which are now being especially hyped for possible anticancer activity, are the most potent of the thyroid inhibitors followed by daidzein and then genistein. In a previous study, the team of plant chemical researchers had found similar antithyroid activity in some known bioflavonoids, including . . . quercetin. Most of the bioflavonoids, however, have not been found to inhibit thyroid function to any detrimental degree. . . . No other dietary staple has so many antinutrient drawbacks as soy. Conversely, no other food has so many public relations firms and lobbyists working for it. Tom Valentine *True Health*

BLACK-EYED BEANS, PERSIAN STYLE
Serves 6

6 cups basic black-eyed beans (page 496)
4-5 bunches chard, washed and chopped
2 bunches green onions, finely chopped
1 bunch parsley, finely chopped
1 bunch cilantro, finely chopped
1 medium onion, chopped
2 tablespoons butter
2 tablespoons extra virgin olive oil
4-5 dried limes (available at Middle Eastern
    markets) or grated rind and juice
    of 3 fresh limes

Sauté green onions, parsley and cilantro in butter and olive oil, stirring constantly. Remove to a casserole. Sauté onion and add to parsley mixture. If you are using dried limes, open up and remove seeds and membranes. Add dried limes (including skins) or lime juice and rind, cooked beans (with their juices) and chopped chard to casserole. Cover and simmer about 20 minutes. Serve with basic brown rice (page 466).

SOUR CORN AND BEAN PORRIDGE

(Shuco)
Serves 6

1 cup black beans
1/2 cup lemon juice of whey (page 87)
filtered water
2 teaspoons sea salt
3 cups freshly ground cornmeal
3 cups lime water (see A Word on Corn, page 454)
1/2 cup pepitas (page 513),
    finely ground in a mini mill
cayenne pepper

This interesting fermented dish from El Salvador is said to be good for a hangover! Purple or black cornmeal is normally used, but yellow cornmeal will do.

Cover beans with warm water, add 1/4 cup whey or lemon juice and soak overnight. In the morning, drain and rinse the beans and place them in a pot with 1 teaspoon salt and water to cover them. Bring to a boil and skim off foam. Reduce heat, cover and simmer throughout the day.

In the evening, remove beans from the stove and leave them in their juice at room temperature overnight. Mix cornmeal with lime water and remaining 1/4 cup whey or lemon juice and leave overnight at room temperature.

In the morning, add 2 cups water to the soaked cornmeal. Stir in salt, bring the batter to a boil and cook about 5 minutes, stirring constantly.

To serve, stir the beans into the corn mixture and simmer, stirring constantly, until they are warmed through. Ladle into bowls and sprinkle with ground pepitas and cayenne pepper to taste. Although not strictly traditional, the *shuco* may be garnished with cultured cream.

Fatty acids are essential parts of all body tissues where they are the major part of the phospholipid component of the cell membrane and are not just stored energy. Lowfat diets that supply adequate calories are basically high-carbohydrate diets. When the body does not get enough fat from the diet, it makes fats "from scratch" from carbohydrates. The fatty acids that the body synthesizes are saturated fatty acids—exactly the same kind of saturated fatty acids found in butter, cream and animal fat—and monounsaturated fatty acids—exactly the same kind of fatty acids found in olive oil. The cell membranes are composed of a combination of saturated, monounsaturated and polyunsaturated fatty acids.

It happens that the more fat you consume in your diet the less your body tissues need to make from scratch. But when you consume high levels of polyunsaturated fatty acids, such as the kind found in commercial vegetable oils, the normal body synthesis of saturated fat is depressed and the ingested polyunsaturated fats are used for structural fatty acids, leading to an unnatural balance in the membranes. . . . When the fat that is eaten is more highly unsaturated, the fatty acids available for incorporation into the tissue phospholipids are more unsaturated than the body normally prefers; and this causes a number of differences in membrane properties that are thought to be detrimental to the regular body economy. High levels of polyunsaturates in the diet have been shown to increase cholesterol levels in tissues, increase fat cell synthesis in growing animals, alter the response of the immune system, increase peroxidation products such as ceroid pigment, increase gallstone formation and, of all things, decrease HDL cholesterol in the blood. Mary G. Enig, PhD *PPNF Health Journal*

Animal proteins (meat, fish, milk products, eggs) seem to present many drawbacks. . . . Why not, then, replace animal protein with vegetable protein? These are found in grains, vegetables, oily fruits and, above all, pulses. But they are less well balanced than animal proteins. By proper combining of grains and pulses, one can improve the overall quality of protein from vegetable sources. But many people assimilate vegetable proteins less well than animal proteins. This leads to the common sense conclusion, found widely in books on diet and health, that half of our protein should be of animal origin and half of vegetable origin. This rule really has no scientific foundation, as it is only necessary to eat a small amount of animal protein to aid the assimilation of vegetable proteins. Tradition and science confirm each other in this for once. The tradition: the French *pot au feu* (beef bouillon with bread), Italian pasta with Parmesan cheese, Spanish *paella*, Moroccan *couscous*, Indian *thali*, Japanese fish with rice—always the animal products, whether meat, fish or dairy product, were traditionally eaten in very small quantities.

By economic necessity? Perhaps . . . . But also perhaps due to an ancestral intuition. For research done with animals has confirmed the wisdom of these practices. In one of these studies conducted in Latin America, rats were give mixtures of corn and beans in various proportions, the two foods that form the basis of the diet of a large part of the population. In whatever proportions these foods were given, the growth of the rats was insufficient, even if theoretically the amount of protein was adequate. In contrast, it was sufficient to add just 2% of fish to the bean-corn mixture to considerably raise the growth rate of the animals (from 70%

BLACK BEAN AND CORN SALAD
Serves 6

2 cups basic black beans (page 496), drained
2 cups fresh corn kernels
2 jalapeno peppers, seeded and diced
1 red onion, finely chopped
1 cup basic dressing (page 129)
    or 1 cup lemon pepper dressing (page 134)

Mix all ingredients together. Chill well before serving.

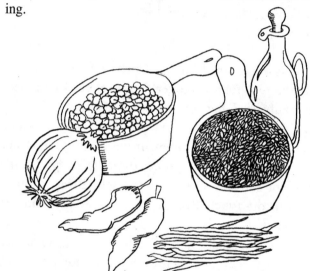

THREE BEAN SALAD
Serves 12

2 cups basic kidney beans (page 496), drained
2 cups basic chickpeas (page 505), drained
2 pounds cooked French beans (page 369),
    cut into 1-inch lengths
2 medium red onions, finely chopped
1/4 cup finely chopped parsley
1 red pepper, cut into a julienne
1 green pepper, cut into a julienne
juice of 1 lemon
1 cup garlic dressing (page 129)

Mix all ingredients together. Let stand 1 hour or more before serving.

BASIC CHICKPEAS

Makes 3 cups

1 cup dried chickpeas
warm filtered water
2 tablespoons whey (page 87) or lemon juice
1 teaspoon sea salt

Cover chickpeas with warm water. Stir in whey or lemon juice and leave in a warm spot for 24 hours. Drain, rinse and pick off skins. Transfer to a pot, add salt and water to cover and bring to a boil. Skim. Cover and simmer for about 6 hours or until chickpeas are very tender. Drain and use in salads.

CHICKPEA STEW

Serves 8

4 cups basic chickpeas (see above)
1 cup millet
2 cups warm filtered water mixed with
    2 tablespoons whey (page 87),
    lemon juice or vinegar
2 medium onions, finely chopped
2 tablespoons butter
2 tablespoons extra virgin olive oil
8 cups beef or chicken stock (page 122 or 124)
1/4 teaspoon cayenne pepper
1/2 cup currants
1 head broccoli, cut into flowerets
1 1/2 cups crispy cashews (page 515), chopped
3-5 tablespoons lemon juice
sea salt and pepper

Soak millet in warm water plus whey, lemon juice or vinegar for at least 7 hours. Drain in a colander. Sauté onions in butter and olive oil until soft. Add stock, bring to a boil and skim. Add millet, stirring with a whisk to prevent clumping. Add chickpeas, cayenne and currants, cover and simmer about 30 minutes. Add remaining ingredients and simmer a few minutes more or until broccoli is tender. Season to taste.

to 120% greater, according to the proportions of the two main ingredients).

The small supplement of fish cannot in itself explain these spectacular results. Undoubtedly the added animal protein has a synergistic effect on the assimilation of the vegetable protein. The amount of fish given to the rats was the equivalent of 30 grams for a man—just one sardine!—as the only animal protein for the whole day. Another interesting observation: The combination of corn and fish (without beans) never gave as good results, whatever the amount of fish, as the trilogy of beans, corn and fish. Claude Aubert *Dis-Moi Comment Tu Cuisines*

Chickpeas or garbanzo beans have been used for so long that they are unknown in their wild state. They form a staple of the diet in the Middle East and in Mediterranean countries. They are one of the most nutritious of all the legumes, high in calcium, phosphorus and potassium. They have an exceptionally high iron and vitamin C content and contain B complex as well. Like all pulses, they are rich in essential fatty acids. However, as chickpeas are high in omega-6 fatty acids compared to omega-3 fatty acids they should not be consumed to excess. Their bland taste marries well with onions, spices and sour foods. SWF

The first phase of digestion begins in the mouth where the enzyme amylase becomes mixed with the food we are chewing and begins to digest starches. The production of saliva and the activity of amylase are considerably stimulated by. . . several spices, notably pepper, ginger, hot pepper, curry and mustard. Research on the amount of saliva produced and the total activity of amylase shows that these spices and condiments can increase their activity by as much as 20 times. Claude Aubert *Dis-Moi Comment Tu Cuisines*

FALAFEL
(Chick Pea Patties)
Serves 8

2 cups chickpeas
filtered water
4 tablespoons whey (page 87) or lemon juice
4 cups parsley leaves, loosely packed
4 medium onions, coarsely chopped
4 large cloves garlic, peeled
1 teaspoon ground cumin
1 teaspoon ground coriander
1 teaspoon pepper
1 teaspoon sea salt
1 teaspoon cayenne pepper
1 teaspoon baking powder
about 1 cup extra virgin olive oil or lard

Here is yet another delicious ethnic dish in which the main ingredient is fermented—in this case the base is chickpeas. Falafel is a popular food throughout the Middle East.

Bring a pot of water to a boil and pour over chickpeas. Stir in 2 tablespoons whey or lemon juice and leave in a warm place for 12 hours. Pour off excess water and pour in more boiling water. Add remaining 2 tablespoons whey or lemon juice and leave in a warm place another 12 hours. Place 1 cup parsley in food processor and pulse until chopped. Add 1/4 of the chickpeas, 1 onion, 1 garlic clove, and 1/4 teaspoon each of the remaining ingredients (except olive oil or lard) and pulse until reduced to a coarse paste. The mixture should be finely ground enough to hold together but not entirely smooth. Repeat process three more times. Mix all batches together, cover and refrigerate for at least 1 hour. Form into patties and sauté in olive oil or lard. Serve with tahini sauce (page 148), sliced tomatoes, sliced cucumbers and pita bread.

BASIC LENTILS
Serves 6-8

2 cups lentils, preferably green lentils
warm filtered water
2 tablespoons whey (page 87) or lemon juice
3 cups beef or chicken stock (page 122 or 124)
2 cloves garlic, peeled and mashed
several sprigs fresh thyme, tied together
1 teaspoon dried green pepper corns, crushed
pinch dried chile flakes (optional)
1 teaspoon sea salt
juice of 1-2 lemons or
  3 tablespoons sauerkraut juice (page 92)

Lentils are excellent with sauerkraut and strongly flavored meats, such as duck, game or lamb.

Cover lentils with warm water. Stir in whey or lemon juice and leave in a warm place for about 7 hours. Drain, rinse, place in a pot and add stock. Bring to a boil and skim. Add garlic, thyme, peppercorns and chile flakes and simmer, uncovered, for about 1 hour or until liquid has completely reduced, stirring occasionally to prevent burning. Add lemon juice or sauerkraut juice and season to taste. Serve with a slotted spoon.

LENTIL SALAD
Serves 4

2 cups basic green lentils, drained
1 cup carrots, grated
1 bunch green onions, chopped
2 tablespoons parsley, finely chopped
3/4 cup basic dressing (page 129)

Mix all ingredients. Serve at room temperature.

Since the beginning of civilization, the lowly lentil has nourished healthy peoples across a wide portion of the globe. Dr. Weston Price considered the lentil the most nutritious of all legumes, due to its high phosphorus content. Lentils are also rich in calcium, potassium, zinc and iron as well as vitamin B complex. Lentils have a high molybdenum content, a mineral that plays a role in protein assimilation, iron absorption, fat oxidation and normal cell function. They are low in phytates as well and thus need only be soaked a few hours rather than overnight.

American markets usually carry brown lentils. Some markets carry the pretty red lentil, which is best used only for soups as it disintegrates during cooking. The French prefer the tiny green lentil, available in gourmet markets and specialty shops. These make the most satisfactory cooked lentils as they hold their shape very well. SWF

Know Your Ingredients
Name This Product # 31

Cooked beans, water, tomato puree, light brown sugar, sugar, invert sugar, molasses, cottonseed oil, high fructose corn syrup, salt, modified food starch, pork, onion powder, spice and apple concentrate

See Appendix B for Answer

Modern civilization is making a tragic mistake in getting away from the natural foods that are low in energy and high in minerals and increasing the intake of the heat and energy producing foods. This energy can be quantitatively expressed by the amount of oxygen that may be utilized when modern foods are burned either by the wet process within our bodies or by the dry process in special apparatus. We speak of this in terms of calories.

Most people need from 2000 to 3000 calories a day, according to the nature of their physical activities. Similarly, we need two grams of phosphorus and one and one-half grams of calcium a day in our food in order to keep up the body's daily requirements. Our problem, then, is to get enough of the minerals and vitamins without exceeding our limit in calories. . . . It is not wise to fill the limited space with foods that are not doing our bodies any particular good. You would be interested to know that while you would have to eat 7 1/2 pounds of potatoes or 11 pounds of beets or 9 1/2 pounds of carrots to get the daily phosphorus requirement, all of which would provide too high a number of calories, you would obtain as much phosphorus from 1 pound of lentils. This would also provide the calcium. You would also supply the entire day's requirement of minerals from 0.8 pounds of fish or 0.6 pounds of cheese. Milk is one of the best, if not the best single food, since you obtain the minerals rapidly in proportion to the calories. The main thing is to get the daily phosphorus and calcium requirement and sufficient of the vitamins, particularly the fat-soluble vitamins. Weston Price, DDS *Letter to His Nieces and Nephews* 1934

LENTIL-PECAN PATTIES
Makes about 1 dozen

1 cup green or brown lentils
2 medium onions, finely chopped
2 tablespoons butter
grated rind of 1 lemon
2 cloves garlic, peeled and mashed
1 cup crispy pecans (page 513), finely ground
2 eggs, lightly beaten
1 teaspoon sea salt
1/4 teaspoon cayenne pepper
1/2 teaspoon thyme
1 teaspoon dry mustard
about 2 cups whole grain bread crumbs
about 1/2 cup extra virgin olive oil or lard

Sprout lentils according to directions on page 115. Place in food processor and process to a paste. Sauté onions in butter until soft. Mix lentil paste with onions, lemon rind, garlic, pecans, eggs and seasonings. Form into balls and roll in bread crumbs. Sauté in olive oil or lard until golden. Serve with sour cream sauce (page 140) or a fermented condiment, such as sauerkraut (page 92), cortido (page 93), or ginger carrots (page 95).

INDIAN-STYLE LENTILS
(Dal)
Serves 8

1 1/2 cups brown lentils
warm filtered water
2 tablespoons whey (page 87) or lemon juice
1 teaspoon turmeric
1/2 teaspoon pepper
2 cloves garlic, peeled and mashed
1/4 cup clarified butter (page 150)
1 1/2 teaspoons cumin seeds
2 small hot red or green peppers,
*   seeded and chopped*
1/3 cup cilantro, chopped
sea salt

Cover lentils with warm water. Stir in whey or lemon juice and leave for about 7 hours in a warm place. Drain, rinse and place in a pot, add water to cover and bring to a boil. Skim. Add turmeric, pepper and garlic. Simmer, covered, for about an hour or until lentils are very soft. Off heat, beat with a wire whisk until lentils are creamy. Meanwhile, sauté cumin seeds and chiles in clarified butter until chiles are soft. Fold chile-cumin seed mixture and chopped cilantro into lentils. Season to taste.

INDIAN-STYLE DUMPLINGS

(Idli)
Serves 6-8

1 cup lentils
2 cups brown rice
warm filtered water
2 tablespoons whey (page 87) or lemon juice
2 teaspoons sea salt

These vegetarian "meatballs," cooked in an egg poacher, may be served with a variety of sauces. Wash lentils and rice well and place in separate bowls. Cover each with warm water, add 1 tablespoon whey or lemon juice to each and leave overnight in a warm place. Drain each in a colander and process separately in food processor with a little water until smooth. Blend lentil and rice dough together with salt—the dough should be rather firm. Cover and leave in a warm place for 24 hours. Fill well-oiled egg poaching cups with balls of rice-lentil mixture, cover and steam for 15 minutes or until a needle comes out clean. Serve hot with curry sauce (page 149), yoghurt sauce (page 143) or fruit chutney (page 106).

Variation: Indian-Style Spicy Dumplings
Just before cooking, add *1/2 teaspoon pepper, 1/2 teaspoon ground cumin, 1/4 teaspoon nutmeg* and *1 teaspoon grated ginger* to dough and mix well.

Variation: Indian-Style Picant Dumplings
Just before cooking, add *1 teaspoon fried mustard seed* and *2 tablespoons chopped cilantro* to dough and mix well.

In many countries around the world, lacto-fermented foods, or at least certain lacto-fermented foods, are valued for their medicinal properties. . . . In Europe during the 19th century, doctors prescribed sauerkraut for numerous diseases—for enlarged liver and spleen, hemorrhoids, constipation, nervous troubles and hysteria. In Germany and Poland sauerkraut juice and juice of fermented cucumbers are still used to treat enteritis.

The therapeutic value of yoghurt is well known, notably for the re-establishment of intestinal flora. . . . In India *idli* (lacto-fermented rice and lentils) is particularly recommended for children and people in a weakened condition; *dahi* (a fermented milk product similar to yoghurt) is recommended for dyspepsia, dysentery and various intestinal disorders. It is also recommended to stimulate the appetite and to increase vitality. In Mexico *pozol* (fermented corn) is used to counter diarrhea; it is also made into poultices to dress wounds. Mixed with water and honey, it is given to the sick to bring down fevers.

Pulque, a fermented drink inherited from the Aztecs and made with cactus juice, is used to treat kidney infections and to stimulate lactation. In Nigeria *ogi* (lacto-fermented corn) is given to babies, to the sick and to convalescents; it also is valued for stimulating lactation. In Greece and Turkey *tarhanas* (mixture of wheat and fermented milk) is consumed in large quantities by nursing mothers, by infants when they are weaned, by the sick and the very old. Claude Aubert *Les Aliments Fermentés Traditionnels*

INDIAN-STYLE PANCAKES
(Dosas)
Makes about 20

1 cup lentils
2 cups brown rice
warm filtered water
2 tablespoons whey (page 87) or lemon juice
1 teaspoon salt
about 1/3 cup clarified butter (page 150)

Food of the Indian *idli* type, acidified and leavened through fermentation by heterofermentative lactic acid bacteria, constitutes a very interesting group of cereal-based foods of considerable potential importance in the developing and also the developed world where it is largely unknown. Idli is closely related to sourdough bread of the Western world, but it does not depend upon wheat or rye as a source of protein to retain the carbon dioxide gas during leavening. Leavening is produced by bacterial rather than by yeast activity. The importance of idli lies in (1) its high degree of acceptability as a food in South India, (2) its protection against food poisoning and transmission of pathogenic organisms, because of its acidity, and (3) the fact that the idli fermentation can be used in many parts of the world using various combinations of cereal grains and legumes to produce acid, leavened bread or a pancake-like product. No wheat or rye flour is needed.

Idli and dosa . . . can be consume directly "out-of-hand" following steaming, or the cakes may be deliciously flavored with fried mustard seeds and chopped coriander leaves. The unflavored cakes are eaten with chutney and/or sambar, a thin spiced soup of dhal and vegetables. . . . These foods are an important source of protein and calories in the diet and nutrition of South Indians. Idli and dosa . . . constitute the breakfast of many South Indians, regardless of economic or social status. Because they are easily digested, they are often used as food for infants and invalids. Keith H. Steinkraus ed. p 131 *Handbook of Indigenous Fermented Foods* Courtesy Marcel Dekker, Inc.

Wash lentils and rice well and place in separate bowls. Cover each with warm water, add 1 tablespoon whey or lemon juice to each and leave overnight in a warm place. Drain each and process separately in a food processor with a little water until smooth. Mix lentils and rice together with salt and enough warm water to make a batter about the consistency of cream. Cover and leave another 24 hours in a warm place.

To cook, heat a heavy, cast-iron skillet and brush with clarified butter. Ladle about 1/4 cup into pan and tip pan to spread batter. Cook about 5 minutes per side. (You may further thin batter with water to make a paper-thin dosa, but it takes some practice to turn these without tearing.) Keep warm in oven while preparing remaining dosas. Brush pan with butter between each pancake. Serve hot or warm with curry sauce (page 149), yoghurt sauce (page 143) or fruit chutney (page 106).

Variation: Indian-Style Coconut Pancakes

Place *2 cups finely grated fresh or dried coconut, 2 tablespoon coarsely chopped ginger, 2 small green chiles, coarsely chopped, 2 small onions, coarsely chopped, 1/2 teaspoon salt* and *1 bunch cilantro* in food processor and process to a paste. Blend into batter, along with additional water if necessary to achieve desired consistency, and proceed with recipe.

Variation: Indian-Style Onion Pancakes

Sauté *2 onions, very finely chopped* and *2 teaspoons mustard seeds in butter.* Stir into batter, along with additional water if necessary to achieve desired consistency, and proceed with recipe.

SNACKS & FINGER FOODS

SNACKS &
FINGER FOODS

In an ideal world we would consume all our food at sit-down meals; nevertheless, snacks have their place in today's diet, especially for growing children and for those whose metabolisms require small frequent feedings. Wise parents will keep a variety of nutritious snacks on hand, but at the same time will see to it that they do not replace proper meals.

Many of our snacks call for nuts, such as almonds, pecans, cashews and peanuts, either plain, in mixes, or as a basis for nut butters and cookies. Nuts are an extremely nutritious food if properly prepared. Once again, the habits of traditional peoples should serve as a guide. They understood instinctively that nuts are best soaked or partially sprouted before eaten. This is because nuts contain numerous enzyme inhibitors that can put a real strain on the digestive mechanism if consumed in excess. Nuts are easier to digest, and their nutrients more readily available, if they are first soaked in salt water overnight, then dried in a warm oven. (You may also use a dehydrator.) This method imitates the Aztec practice of soaking pumpkin or squash seeds in brine and then letting them dry in the sun before eating them whole or grinding them into meal. Salt in soaking water activates enzymes that neutralize enzyme inhibitors. An excellent snack is crispy nuts with raw cheese.

Our cookie recipes feature nuts, butter or coconut oil, natural sweeteners and arrowroot or bulgur flour made from sprouted wheat. These recipes offer you the opportunity to discover the merits of coconut oil. Coconut oil is richer than butter in medium-chain fatty acids, which the body absorbs directly from the small intestine for quick energy. Research has shown that coconut oil, like butter, promotes normal brain development, is less likely to cause weight gain than polyunsaturated oils, contributes to strong bones and has anticarcinogenic and antimicrobial effects. (For arrowroot and unrefined coconut oil, see Sources.)

We have included a recipe for pizza—the perennial favorite—made with a yoghurt crust and fresh tomato sauce. All snacks feature whole, natural ingredients in contrast to empty calories—in the form of refined sweeteners, white flour and rancid and hydrogenated vegetable oils—that make up the vast majority of commercially produced snack foods. These empty snack foods, consumed in great quantities by our youth, have resulted in a generation of teenagers imbued with the vague feeling that they have been cheated—as indeed they have.

A popular "health food" snack we must warn you about is rice cakes, made from puffed or extruded rice. Although theoretically nutritious, because made from whole grains, they are grains that have been subjected to high heat and pressure to cause them to puff. Diets of puffed grains cause rapid death in test animals.

PEPITAS

(Crispy Pumpkin Seeds)
Makes 4 cups

4 cups raw, hulled pumpkin seeds
2 tablespoons sea salt
1 teaspoon cayenne pepper (optional)
filtered water

This recipe imitates the Aztec practice of soaking seeds in brine, then letting them dry in the hot sun. They ate pepitas whole or ground into meal.

Dissolve salt in water and add pumpkin seeds and optional cayenne. Leave in a warm place for at least 7 hours or overnight. Drain in a colander and spread on a stainless steel baking pan. Place in a warm oven (no more than 150 degrees) for about 12 hours or overnight, turning occasionally, until thoroughly dry and crisp. Store in an airtight container.

CRISPY PECANS

Makes 4 cups

4 cups pecan halves
2 teaspoons sea salt
filtered water

The buttery flavor of pecans is enhanced by soaking and slow oven drying. Mix pecans with salt and filtered water and leave in a warm place for at least 7 hours or overnight. Drain in a colander. Spread pecans on a stainless steel baking pan and place in a warm oven (no more than 150 degrees) for 12 to 24 hours, turning occasionally, until completely dry and crisp. Store in an airtight container. Great for school lunches!

Variation: Crispy Walnuts
Use *4 cups walnuts halves and pieces, preferably freshly shelled* instead of pecans. Store in an airtight container in the refrigerator.

If you eat substantial quantities of raw pecans, walnuts, Brazil nuts, filberts or others, you have a choice of swallowing enzyme capsules with them to neutralize their enzyme inhibitors or first germinating the nuts and letting nature do the job through increased enzyme activity resulting from germination. . . . In the year 1918 or thereabouts, I was imbued with the idea of trying to avoid cooked food because of the potential destructiveness of heat. . . . I thought that raw meat was unsuited for the human diet and that the protein and fat of palatable raw tree nuts would take its place. . . after a period of about two months, during which I consumed liberal quantities of raw tree nuts of several kinds, I began experiencing an unpleasant heavy sensation in the abdomen and a feeling of extreme fullness and some nausea. The symptoms were pronounced enough to force my giving up this tasty diet. Almost anyone can eat several nuts without feeling any effect. But it is common knowledge that nuts "are heavy on the stomach" if consumed in substantial quantity. The enzyme inhibitors in seeds explain the mystery, but they were not identified until 1944. Edward Howell, MD *Food Enzymes for Health and Longevity*

Nuts are rich sources of natural oils, ranging in total fat content from 60% to 80% of calories. Almonds, pecans, cashews, macadamia nuts and peanuts have a high content of stable oleic acid. Thus, they do not go rancid easily and once prepared by soaking and dehydrating may be stored for many months at room temperature in an airtight container. Walnuts, on the other hand, contain large amounts of triple unsaturated linolenic acid and are much more susceptible to rancidity. They should always be stored in the refrigerator. SWF

Pecans are the pride of the South. They grow on huge trees throughout the Mississippi River Valley, especially in Georgia, New Mexico and Texas. Pecan trees grow to 150 feet with trunks of 7 feet in diameter. Mature trees can produce up to 200 pounds of nuts per year.

Like all nuts, pecans contain enzyme inhibitors that can irritate the mouth and cause digestive problems. Native Americans understood instinctively that pecans had to be treated in some way before they were consumed. They ground the nuts and soaked them in water to make a nutritious milky drink, much as European farmers made a kind of milk from walnuts.

Pecans contain about 70 percent fat, most of it monounsaturated oleic acid. This stable oil protects pecans from rancidity and gives them good keeping qualities. Pecans contain calcium, iron, magnesium, phosphorus, potassium and selenium. They are an exceptionally rich source of manganese. Like all nuts from large trees whose roots extend far down into the earth, pecans are good sources of trace minerals. They contain B complex vitamins, carotenoids and vitamin C in small amounts.

Pecans will last about four months at room temperature. To keep them longer, store in refrigerator. SWF

HOLIDAY PECANS
Makes 4 cups

4 cups crispy pecan halves (page 513)
3 egg whites
pinch sea salt
1/2 cup maple syrup
1 tablespoon vanilla extract

Beat egg whites with salt in a clean bowl until stiff. Slowly beat in maple syrup and vanilla. Fold in pecans until well coated. Spread on two buttered, stainless steel baking pans and place in a warm oven (no more than 150 degrees) for several hours until the egg white coating hardens. Store in an airtight container in the refrigerator.

CRISPY PEANUTS
Makes 4 cups

4 cups raw peanuts, preferably skinless
1 tablespoon sea salt
filtered water

Mix peanuts with salt and filtered water and leave in a warm place for at least 7 hours or overnight. Drain in a colander. Spread on a stainless steel baking pan and place in a warm oven (no more than 150 degrees) for 12 to 24 hours, turning occasionally, until completely dry and crisp. Store in an airtight container.

Variation: Crispy Pine Nuts
Use *4 cups pine nuts* instead of raw peanuts.

Variation: Crispy Hazelnuts
Use *4 cups skinless hazelnuts* in place of peanuts. (To peel hazelnuts, place on a cookie sheet and bake at 300 degrees until skins turn dark and begin to crack. Place hazelnuts in a kitchen towel and wrap up tightly. Hold towel-wrapped nuts in your hands and rub and squeeze for several minutes. Open up towel—most of the skins should have come off.)

CRISPY ALMONDS

Makes 4 cups

4 cups almonds, preferably skinless
1 tablespoon sea salt
filtered water

Skinless almonds will still sprout, indicating that the process of removing their skins has not destroyed the enzymes. (The skins are probably removed by a machine process.) Skinless almonds are easier to digest and more satisfactory in many recipes. However, you may also use almonds with the skins on.

Mix almonds with salt and filtered water and leave in a warm place for at least 7 hours or overnight. Drain in a colander. Spread on a stainless steel baking pan and place in a warm oven (no more than 150 degrees) for 12 to 24 hours, stirring occasionally, until completely dry and crisp. Store in an airtight container.

Variation: Crispy Almond Slivers

Use *4 cups slivered almonds* instead of whole almonds.

CRISPY CASHEWS

Makes 4 cups

4 cups "raw" cashews
1 tablespoon sea salt
filtered water

Some care must be taken in preparing cashews. They will become slimy and develop a disagreeable taste if allowed to soak too long or dry out too slowly, perhaps because they come to us not truly raw but having already undergone two separate heatings. You may dry them in a 200 to 250 degree oven—the enzymes have already been destroyed during processing.

Soak cashews in salt and filtered water for 6 hours (no longer). Drain in a colander. Spread on a stainless steel baking pan and place in a warm oven (about 200 degrees) for 12 to 24 hours, turning occasionally, until completely dry and crisp. Store in an airtight container. Great for school lunches!

The cashew nut comes from a pear-shaped fruit called the cashew apple. Curiously, the nut grows outside of the apple and hangs down so that it can be easily harvested. A native of Brazil, where natives make the apples into preserves or liqueur, the cashew also grows in India. About 90 percent of our domestic supply of cashews comes from India.

Cashews are rich in protein as well as magnesium, phosphorus and potassium. They contain less fat than most other nuts.

Cashews contain a toxic oil called cardol between the inner and outer shell. This is released by cracking the nuts and roasting them at 350 degrees. They are then cracked and roasted once again. These are then marketed as "raw" cashews.

We recommend soaking "raw" cashews in salt water and then lightly toasting them to make them more digestible. Unlike other nuts which benefit from an overnight soaking, "raw" cashews should be soaked no longer than 6 hours.

Always buy whole cashews rather than pieces as they are less likely to be stale. SWF

One of Australia's best gifts to the world is the macadamia nut, sometimes called the Queensland nut. This delicious nut now grows in other areas of the South Pacific, particularly in the Hawaiian Islands.

Like all nuts, macadamias are rich in minerals, such as copper, iron, magnesium, phosphorus, potassium and zinc. They also contain B vitamins, particularly vitamin B_1. In addition, macadamias are extremely rich in vitamin B_{17} or nitrilosides, containing as much per gram as bitter almonds.

Macadamias have a unique fatty acid profile. About 80% of the total fat content is stable monounsaturated, of which more than 22% is the 16-carbon monounsaturated palmitolytic acid. This fatty acid has strong antimicrobial properties; that is, it protects us from viruses, pathogenic bacteria and yeasts in the gut. About 60% of the total fat is monounsaturated oleic, the same kind of fatty acid found in olive oil. About 15 % is saturated fat with the remaining 3% as polyunsaturated fatty acids, with the ratio of omega-6 to omega-3 exactly equal— an excellent balance.

Like all seed foods, macadamias contain numerous antinutrients such as enzyme inhibitors that can cause gastric distress and irritations to the mouth and throat. It's best to buy raw macadamia nuts and then soak them to remove antinutrients. SWF

CRISPY MACADAMIA NUTS
Makes 4 cups

4 cups raw macadamia nuts (see Sources)
1 tablespoon sea salt
filtered water

Mix nuts with salt and filtered water and leave in a warm place for at least 7 hours or overnight. Drain in a colander. Spread on a stainless steel baking pan and place in a warm oven (no more than 150 degrees) for 12 to 24 hours, turning occasionally, until completely dry and crisp. Store in an airtight container.

NUT BUTTER
Makes 2 cups

2 cups crispy nuts, such as peanuts, almonds or cashews
3/4 cup coconut oil (see Sources)
2 tablespoons raw honey
1 teaspoon sea salt

Place nuts and sea salt in food processor and grind to a fine powder. Add honey and coconut oil and process until "butter" becomes smooth. It will be somewhat liquid but will harden when chilled. Store in an airtight container in the refrigerator. Serve at room temperature.

ROSEMARY WALNUTS
Makes 2 cups

2 cups crispy walnuts (page 513)
2 tablespoons butter
2 tablespoons dried rosemary
1 teaspoon sea salt
1/2 teaspoon cayenne pepper

Melt butter with rosemary, salt and cayenne pepper. Toss with walnuts, spread on cookie sheets and bake at 350 degrees for 10 minutes. Store in an airtight container in the refrigerator.

TRAIL MIX
Makes 5-6 cups

1 cup crispy pecans (page 513)
1 cup crispy cashews (page 515)
1 cup raisins
1 cup dried unsulphured apricots, cut into pieces
1 cup carob chips (optional)

Mix all ingredients together. Store in an airtight container. If carob chips are included, store in the refrigerator.

CAROB CHIPS
Makes 1 cup

3/4 cup carob powder
1/4 cup Rapadura (see page 536)
1 cup coconut oil (see Sources)
1 tablespoon vanilla extract
1 teaspoon chocolate extract

Place all ingredients in a glass container and set in simmering water until melted. Mix together well. Spread mixture on a piece of buttered parchment paper (see Sources) and allow to cool in the refrigerator. When hardened, remove parchment paper and cut into chips. Store chips in an airtight container in the refrigerator.

TROPICAL DELIGHT TRAIL MIX
Makes about 6 cups

2 cups crispy macadamia nuts (page 516)
2 cups crispy cashews (page 515)
1/2 cup dried papaya, cut into small pieces
1/2 cup dried pineapple, cut into small pieces
1 cup large flaked dried unsweetened coconut

Mix ingredients well. Store in an airtight container

Know Your Ingredients
Name This Product #32

Corn syrup, enriched flour (niacin, iron, thiamine mononitrate, riboflavin, sugar, water, partially hydrogenated vegetable and/or animal shortening (contains one or more of: canola oil, corn oil, cottonseed oil, soybean oil, beef fat), eggs, skim milk, contains 2% or less of: whey, modified food starch, salt, leavening (baking soda, monocalcium phosphate, sodium acid pyrophosphate), mono- and diglycerides, lecithin, sodium stearoyl lactylate, and artificial flavors, artificial colors (red 40 and yellow 5), sorbic acid (to retard spoilage).

See Appendix B for Answer

It is very unwise. . . to depend on plant sources for vitamin A. This vital nutrient is needed for the growth and repair of body tissues; it helps protect mucous membranes of the mouth, nose, throat and lungs; it prompts the secretion of gastric juices necessary for proper digestion of proteins; it helps build strong bones and teeth and rich blood; it is essential for good eyesight; it aids in the production of RNA; and contributes to the health of the immune system. Vitamin A deficiency in pregnant mothers results in offspring with eye defects, displaced kidneys, harelip, cleft palate and abnormalities of the heart and blood vessels. *Vitamin A Vagary*

A diet high in unsaturated fatty acids, especially the polyunsaturated ones, can destroy the body's supply of vitamin E and cause muscular lesions, brain lesions and degeneration of blood vessels. Care must be taken not to include a large amount of polyunsaturated oil in the diet without a corresponding increase in the intake of vitamin E. Linus Pauling, PhD, p 155 *How To Live Longer and Feel Better*

Know Your Ingredients
Name This Product #33

Enriched wheat flour (contains niacin, reduced iron, thiamine mononitrate [vitamin B1], riboflavin [vitamin B2]), whole wheat, bleached wheat flour, vegetable shortening (partially hydrogenated soybean oil), rice, rolled oats, brown sugar, yellow corn meal, sugar, oat bran, barley flakes, salt, high fructose corn syrup, leavening (baking soda, yeast, calcium phosphate), modified cornstarch, malted barely flour, whey, onion powder, soy lecithin (emulsifier).

See Appendix B for Answer

WHOLE GRAIN CRACKERS
Makes about 5 dozen

2 1/2 cups freshly ground spelt, kamut, whole wheat
    or rye flour, or a mixture
1 cup plain yoghurt
1 teaspoon sea salt
1 1/2 teaspoon baking powder
2 tablespoons sesame seeds, toasted in oven
8 tablespoons butter, melted
unbleached white flour

Mix flour with yoghurt and leave in a warm place for 12 to 24 hours. Place soaked flour, salt, baking powder and 4 tablespoons butter in food processor and process until well blended. Add sesame seeds and pulse once or twice to blend. Roll out to about 1/8 inch on a pastry cloth, using unbleached white flour to prevent sticking. Cut into squares with a knife or rounds with a glass. Place on a buttered cookie sheet, brush with remaining melted butter and bake in a 150-degree oven (or a dehydrator) for until completely dry and crisp. Store in an airtight container in the refrigerator.

SPROUTED GRAIN CRACKERS
Makes about 2 dozen

3 cups sprouted soft wheat berries
    (page 114)
1/2 cup sprouted small seeds such as sesame, onion
    or poppy (page 115)
1 teaspoon sea salt
1 teaspoon dried dill, thyme or rosemary

Place all ingredients in food processor and process several minutes to form a smooth paste. Form into balls and roll into rounds on a pastry cloth, using unbleached white flour to prevent sticking. Place on a buttered cookie sheet and leave in a 150 degree oven (or a dehydrator) until completely dry and crisp. Store in an airtight container in the refrigerator.

SOFT TORTILLAS

6 sprouted whole wheat tortillas (see Sources)
3 tablespoons melted butter

Heat a heavy, well-seasoned skillet over a medium flame. Place one tortilla in the skillet for about 1 minute. Turn and cook for another few seconds. Remove to a platter and brush with melted butter. Repeat with other tortillas. Keep warm in oven. May be eaten with fajitas (page 432), or simply rolled up with some sliced avocado and a little grated raw cheese.

BAKED TORTILLAS

6 sprouted whole wheat tortillas (see Sources)
2 tablespoons butter
2 tablespoons extra virgin olive oil

Melt butter with oil. Brush tortillas with this mixture, arrange on cookie sheets and place in a 250-degree oven. Bake several hours until crisp. May be broken into "chips."

FRIED TORTILLAS

6 sprouted whole wheat tortillas (see Sources)
about 4 tablespoons extra virgin olive oil or lard

Using a heavy, cast-iron skillet, fry tortillas one at a time on both sides in olive oil or lard until crisp. Drain on paper towels and keep warm in oven. May be broken into "chips."

Know Your Ingredients
Name This Product #34

Corn, vegetable oil (contains one or more of the following: corn oil, canola oil, sunflower oil, cottonseed oil, partially hydrogenated canola oil, partially hydrogenated sunflower oil, and/or partially hydrogenated soybean oil) and salt.

See Appendix B for Answer

For years the B vitamins, vitamin E and octocosanol—as well as desiccated liver—have been spotlighted for their contributions to greater endurance in exercises and athletic games. And they deserve the spotlight. However, there's still another helpful nutrient for endurance that, until now, has escaped attention: magnesium. Two experiments at the University of California at Davis reveal that a magnesium deficiency lessens the ability to endure long periods of exercising

Foods richest in this mineral are blackstrap molasses, sunflower seeds, wheat germ, almonds, soybeans, Brazil nuts, pistachios, soy lecithin, hazelnuts, pecans, oats, walnuts, brown rice, chard, spinach, barley, salmon, corn, avocados and bananas.

Roughly 50 percent of magnesium in foods is absorbed.

It is well to remember that magnesium and calcium are removed from soft water, a good reason to drink bottled water with a high-mineral content. James F. Scheer *Health Freedom News*

Recent, preliminary evidence . . . suggests that partially rancid fats, rather than animal fat per se, may be one of the real villains responsible for atherosclerosis. Sources of stale fats include products such as bread, crackers, pastries and commercial cereals made from stored, processed flour. Granville Knight *Introduction to Nutrition and Physical Degeneration*

Know Your Ingredients
Name This Product # 35

Enriched corn meal, (corn meal, ferrous sulfate, niacin, thiamine, mononitrate and riboflavin), vegetable oil (contains one or more of the following: canola, corn, cottonseed, or partially hydrogenated [canola, cottonseed, soybean or sunflower] oil), whey, cheddar cheese (milk, cheese culture, salt, enzymes and calcium chloride), salt, sour cream, artificial flavor, monosodium glutamate, lactic acid, artificial colors (yellow #6, turmeric and annatto), and citric acid. No preservatives.

See Appendix B for Answer

ROUND CROUTONS
Makes about 1 dozen

1/2 loaf good quality commercial or homemade sourdough whole grain baguette
6 tablespoons melted butter

Slice loaf at 1/4 inch intervals. Using a cookie cutter, cut a round from each slice. (Save crusts for making bread crumbs.) Brush with butter. Bake at 250 degrees about 1 hour, until crisp.

TRIANGLE CROUTONS
Makes 1 dozen

6 slices sprouted or sourdough whole grain sandwich bread
6 tablespoons melted butter

Trim crusts off bread (save for making bread crumbs) and cut slices in half on the diagonal to form two triangles. Brush with melted butter and bake at 250 degrees for about 1 hour until crisp.

SALAD CROUTONS
Makes about 2 cups

3 slices sprouted or sourdough whole grain sandwich bread
6 tablespoons melted butter
1 clove garlic, mashed (optional)
1 teaspoon fine herbs (optional)
1/4 teaspoon paprika (optional)

Trim crusts off bread. (Save for making bread crumbs.) Mix optional garlic, herbs and paprika with melted butter. Brush on both sides of bread. Bake at 250 degrees for about 1 hour, turning once, until toasts are crisp. Allow to cool slightly and cut into small cubes.

PITA CHIPS
Makes 48

6 whole wheat pita breads
1/2 cup butter, melted
4 tablespoons extra virgin olive oil
grated rind of 1 lemon (optional)
1 mashed garlic clove (optional)

Cut pita breads across center into quarters. Open up and place pieces, inside part up, on cookie sheets. Mix remaining ingredients and brush on pita pieces. Place under broiler for a few minutes until lightly browned, or bake in a 250-degree oven for several hours until crisp.

POPCORN
Makes 8 cups

1/4 cup popcorn
2 tablespoons extra virgin olive oil
sea salt
1/4-1/2 cup melted butter or coconut oil (see Sources),
or a mixture

Popcorn is a nutritious snack enjoyed by young and old; but remember that it is prepared without the all important soaking or fermenting process, so don't overdo. Note: An electric popcorn popper is a good investment that makes popcorn-making fun and easy for children.

Place olive oil and corn in a large, heavy skillet. Cover tightly and cook over a medium flame, shaking constantly until popping starts. Lower heat slightly and cook, shaking, until popping dies away. (If using a popper, place olive oil and corn in the popper and proceed according to instructions.) Transfer popcorn to a large bowl. Dribble on melted butter or coconut oil or the mixture and shake on sea salt. Mix well and serve.

Variation: Cheese Popcorn

Add *1/4-1/2 cup finely powdered Parmesan cheese* to melted butter or coconut oil, or the mixture.

Variation: Sweet Popcorn

Add *1/2 cup maple syrup* to melted butter or coconut oil, or the mixture. Omit salt.

There are still those diehards who insist that a candy bar or a couple teaspoons of sugar in the tea will charge you up with more energy than anything else. Well, 'tain't so!

That's the word from Robert E. Thayer, Ph.D., psychologist at California State University, Long Beach, who ought to know because he conducted an experiment comparing energy generated from a candy-bar fix with ten minutes of brisk walking.

His finding? That rushing to the vending machine on a ten-minute break gives you a greater boost for sagging energy than a chocolate bar.

Thayer's test, involving 18 students over 12 days, compared energy levels from the exercise and from the candy bar without the exercise. Invariably the students felt greater energy at intervals of 20 minutes, one hour and two hours from the exercise than from the candy.

The energy boost from the candy bar lasted little more than 20 minutes and dropped off fast within two hours. Tension and stress usually mounted after the candy and decreased after the ten-minute walk.

So the next time you're tempted to reach for a sweet to beat fatigue, don't. Instead, go take a hike! James F. Scheer *Health Freedom News*

Patricia Hardman, Ph.D., Director of Woodland Hall Academy, a school for children with hyperactivity and learning disabilities in Maitland, Florida, says, "We can change a child's behavior dramatically by lowering his or her intake of sugar. If a child comes to school extremely depressed or complains that nothing is going right, or if he flies off the handle and can't be controlled, we ask him what he's been eating. It's almost always the case that the night before he had ice cream or soda or some other food with a lot of sugar."

"We had one child who was tested for his I.Q. and scored 140. Three days later he was tested and scored 100! It turned out that grandma had come for a visit and, that morning, had made the child pancakes for breakfast. Of course, they were smothered in store-bought sugary syrup. We waited another three days without sugar and tested him again. Sure enough, he scored 140. There's no doubt about it. Sugar makes children poor learners. At Woodland Hall, sugar is eliminated from the diet of every child." Gaynelle D'Arco *Health Freedom News*

CELERY WITH NUT BUTTER
Serves 4

several large stalks celery
1/2 cup nut butter made from cashews
*   or peanuts (page 516)*
1/4 cup dried sweetened coconut meat (page 159)
*   or commercial unsweetened coconut meat*

Wash celery well and cut into 3-inch lengths. Fill hollow with nut butter and sprinkle with coconut meat.

APPLE SLICES
Serves 4

2 apples, peeled, cored and cut into slices
juice of 2 oranges

Dip each slice of apple in the orange juice and arrange on a serving plate. The orange juice keeps the slices from turning brown and combines well with the flavor of apple.

CAROB-BANANA DELIGHTS
Serves 8

4 bananas
toothpicks
1 cup warm carob sauce (page 550)
1/2 cup finely chopped crispy pecans (page 513)

Slice bananas and stick a toothpick in each. Line a cookie sheet with waxed paper, place slices on it and freeze. Remove from freezer. Holding toothpick, dip each slice in carob sauce and then into the nuts. Place again on waxed paper, cover and freeze again.

PIZZA

Makes 2 10-inch pizzas

1 recipe yoghurt dough (page 485)
2 cups chunky tomato sauce (page 154)
2 teaspoons dried Italian herbs
3 cups grated mozzarella cheese

Roll out yoghurt dough and line two 10-inch, French-style tart pans. Prick well with a fork and partially bake at 300 degrees for about 30 minutes. Meanwhile, process tomato sauce in food processor until smooth. Stir in Italian herbs. Spread tomato sauce thinly on pizzas and top with grated cheese. Bake at 350 degrees for about 1/2 hour until crust fully cooks and cheese is melted.

Variations:

Add any of the following toppings to basic pizza:
sliced green peppers
sliced onion
anchovy pieces
cooked turkey sausage (page 363)
cooked lamb sausage (page 364)
broccoli pieces
fresh tomato slices
sautéed mushrooms

It is recognized that sugar present in chocolate milk, juice, soda, kool-aid, etc., as well as in solid forms, such as candies and cakes, can all interact with gastrointestinal yeasts to form fermentation products.

These fermentation products include alcohol, such as ethanol, as well as mold products. A combination of direct drug effect, as well as chemical intolerance in hypersensitization to mold products, has long been associated with mood changes including what appears to be a mild drunken state, hyperactivity, dyslexia and chemical imbalances that may refer to depression, hyperactivity, mania, etc. Gaynelle D'Arco *Health Freedom News*

The second reason I dislike microwave ovens is the more serious situation. What about the quality of the food that comes out of the oven and is immediately consumed—free radicals and all. With the depressed immune system of the average affluent American, the last thing we need is another increase in our free radicals. It is well documented that microwaves are powerful enough to rupture cell walls of the food matrix, and this is undoubtedly why protein molecules are altered from microwave cooking. Warren Clough *PPNF Health Journal*

The most remarkable dish among them, as well as all the other tribes of Indians in those parts, both Chipewyan and Cree, is blood mixed with the half-digested food which is found in the caribou's stomach, and boiled up with a sufficient quantity of water to make it of the consistence of pease-pottage. Some fat and scraps of tender flesh are also shred small and boiled with it. To render this dish more palatable, they have a method of mixing the blood with the contents of the stomach in the paunch itself, and hanging it up in the heat and smoke of the fire for several days; which puts the whole mass into a state of fermentation, which gives it such an agreeable acid taste, that were it not for prejudice, it might be eaten by those who have the nicest palates. *The Journeys of Samuel Hearne* 1768

Venison was a primary part of many of the Native Americans' diet. The deer meat was often roasted on spits, as was wild fowl. Venison was also used to make "pemmican," an early convenience food of the Indians. Pemmican was a mixture of thinly sliced lean venison (or buffalo meat) dried in the sun, pulverized and mixed with melted animal fat and dried berries or cherries. This preparation was packed in sacks of hide, handy to carry. The high-protein mixture would purportedly keep indefinitely. The name comes from the Cree "pemmikkan" associated with their word "pimiy" meaning "grease" or "fat." Northwestern Indians utilized salmon to make a similar concoction. Patricia B. Mitchell *The Good Land*

PIZZA TOASTS
Makes 8

8 *slices whole grain sourdough bread*
4 *tablespoons extra virgin olive oil*
4 *ripe tomatoes*
1 *teaspoon Italian seasonings*
1/2 *cup grated mozzarella cheese*

Slice tomatoes about 1/2-inch thick. Spread on paper towels placed on cookie sheets. Bake at 200 degrees for several hours until most moisture is evaporated or absorbed. Meanwhile, brush bread slices with olive oil, spread on a cookie sheet and bake at 200 degrees for an hour or so until just barely crisp. Arrange tomato slices on bread, sprinkle with seasonings and grated cheese and place under broiler for a minute until cheese just begins to melt.

POTATO SKINS
Serves 4

4 *large baking potatoes*
2 *tablespoons melted butter*
1 *cup grated raw Cheddar or Monterey Jack cheese*
1 *bunch green onions, finely chopped, for garnish*
piima cream or creme fraiche for garnish (page 84)
duck cracklings (page 295), optional, for garnish
chismole (page 184), optional, for garnish
guacamole (page 172), optional, for garnish

Wash and dry potatoes, brush with butter and bake according to master recipe (page 396) until soft. Split lengthwise and scoop out flesh. (Use flesh for potato and celery root purée, page 401, parsnip purée, page 393, or turnip purée, page 408.) Brush skins with butter, inside and out and bake at 350 degrees for about 1/2 hour or until skins become crisp. Serve with cheese, cultured cream and optional garnishes.

PEMMICAN

Makes 3 cups

3 pounds lean beef, such as brisket or bottom round
1 pound beef suet or tallow
1/2 cup dried cranberries (optional)
1/4 cup maple syrup (optional

Slice beef into thin strips, spread on oiled racks placed on cookie sheets and bake several hours in a 150-degree oven until well dried. (You may also use a dehydrator.) Meanwhile, cut suet or tallow into small pieces and place in a pan. Melt over medium-high heat and allow to boil until any pieces of skin, meat or gristle have become crisp. Pour the hot fat through a strainer into a glass measuring cup—you should have about 3/4 cup rendered fat.

Cut dried beef into pieces and process in batches in the food processor, several minutes per batch, until the beef is reduced to a coarse powder. In a bowl, mix powdered beef, warm fat, optional cranberries and optional maple syrup. Press into a quart-sized, wide-mouth mason jar and cover tightly. Pemmican may be stored at room temperature. Eat pemmican as is, or fry it up in a pan.

SALMON JERKY

Makes about 2 cups

1 1/2 pounds fresh salmon, skin removed
1/2 cup naturally fermented soy sauce
1 teaspoon freshly grated ginger
3 cloves garlic, peeled and crushed
1 teaspoon raw honey or pinch of stevia powder

Mix soy sauce with ginger, garlic and honey or stevia powder. Cut salmon into strips, about 3/8 inches by 4 inches. Dip into soy sauce mixture and place on a rack, set over a cookie sheet. Place in a 150-degree oven for about 24 hours or until dehydrated, or dry in a dehydrator. Store in an airtight container in the refrigerator.

Pemmican is controversial. . . a number of scientists are on record that pemmican is good in cold weather, unsuitable in hot climates. But Europeans first encountered this food invention of the Plains Indians in the Texan-Missouri-Dakota-Manitoba sector, where midsummer temperatures go above 120° in the shade occasionally and above 100° frequently. Pemmican was there chiefly a summer food—because it was a travel food, and journeys were usually made in summer. Its most impressive record as the exclusive diet, or nearly so, of large numbers of men for long periods is from transportation crews of the fur trade working twelve to eighteen hours a day and straight through the noon period with its scorching or steaming heat.

The extreme supporters of pemmican recommend it as the most concentrated food known to man or possible within the modern concepts of physiological and chemical science. They say that it is a complete food in the sense that it will keep a hard-working man in top form for any length of time in any climate. They maintain, indeed, that it is the only concentrated food which ever has been tried out by large numbers of men for long periods which has met these specifications. . . .

There appears to be no disagreement . . . that pemmican is among the most preservable of foods. Cases are on undisputed record where packages, shielded only by rawhide, were in good condition after ten, twenty and more years, without any preservative, such as salt, and without protection . . . other than that given by the leather covering. Vilhjalmur Stefansson *The Fat of the Land*

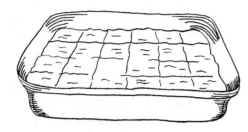

It's crystal clear that Americans . . . are paying for junk food addiction with their lives. The ones most devastated by the growth of the processed food industry are the populations of the underdeveloped nations. In their insatiable lust for sales, the food monsters are competing for overseas markets. They are pouring millions into Third World advertising campaigns, trying to convince the poor Brazilian farmer that "He Deserves a Break Today," and the starving child of Ghana that "Things Go Better with Coke" . . . . The food giants are certainly racking up a lot of victories in the Third World. Two noted food researchers, Frances Moore Lappe and Joseph Collins, have visited the tiny, rotting stores in the rural areas of poor countries and have found chewing gum sold by the stick, Ritz crackers sold one-by-one, and two-packs of Twinkies split up so the awful things can be sold separately. This demand for this poison has been generated by food conglomerate advertising which is doing a great job of teaching people in poor lands "that their traditional diets of beans, corn, millet and rice are worthless as compared to what Americans eat." To the food conglomerates, poor people turning from native, whole foods to processed junk means profit; to the people themselves it means death. Paul Stitt *Fighting the Food Giants*

SUNFLOWER SEED BROWNIES
Makes about 18

4 cups hulled sunflower seeds, freshly ground
1/2 cup carob powder
1/2 cup Rapadura (see page 536)
1/2 to 1 cup chopped crispy pecans (page 513)
1 tablespoon vanilla extract
3/4 cup filtered water

This unusual brownie recipe contains no flour but is based on ground sunflower seed. It is baked very slowly in the oven so that all the enzymes and antioxidants are preserved. The long period of baking, in which the sunflower meal is warm and moist, also neutralizes enzyme inhibitors. Use a grain mill, fitted with the stainless steel grinder, to grind the sunflower seeds.

Mix sunflower meal with carob powder, Rapadura and nuts. Mix vanilla with water. Pour liquid into sunflower seed mixture and blend well. Dough should be very thick. Line a 9-inch by 13-inch pyrex pan with buttered parchment paper (see Sources) and pat dough to a thickness of 1/2 inch. Bake at 150 degrees for about 12 hours, turn and bake another 12 hours. Allow to cool and cut into squares. Store in an airtight container in the refrigerator.

APRICOT TOASTS
Makes 4

4 thick slices sourdough whole grain bread
4 tablespoons butter, softened
6 apricots
6 teaspoons Rapadura (see page 536)

Plunge apricots about 10 seconds in boiling water, remove and peel. Cut in half and remove stones. Generously butter the bread and place 3 apricot halves, cavity side up, on each slice and press in. Sprinkle each half with 1/2 teaspoon Rapadura. Bake about 40 minutes at 300 degrees.

CAROB FUDGE

Makes about 1 dozen small squares

1 cup softened butter, preferably raw, softened
1 cup raw honey
1 cup carob powder
1 teaspoon vanilla extract
2 teaspoons chocolate extract (optional)
1/2 teaspoon sea salt

Place all ingredients in food processor and process until well blended. Line a large loaf pan with parchment paper (see Sources) and spread mixture about 1/2-inch thick. Wrap up in parchment paper and refrigerate several hours. Cut into small squares and store in an airtight container in the refrigerator.

CAROB CHEWS

Makes about 2 dozen small squares

1 cup crispy almonds (page 515)
1 cup crispy cashews (page 515)
1/2 cup carob powder
1/2 cup raw honey
1 tablespoon vanilla extract
1 teaspoon sea salt
1 cup dried sweetened coconut meat (page 159)
*   or commercial unsweetened coconut meat*

Place almonds and cashews in food processor and pulse until finely chopped but not pulverized. Meanwhile, place honey, carob powder, vanilla and salt in a container set container in simmering water until melted. Blend well. Add honey mixture and coconut to nuts in food processor and pulse a few times more. Line a cookie sheet with buttered parchment paper (see Sources) and spread mixture about 1/2-inch thick. Wrap up in parchment paper and refrigerate several hours. Cut into small squares and store in an airtight container in the refrigerator.

Native to North America, the sunflower was first grown and used by American Indians. It was introduced to Europe in the 1500's where cultivation became widespread, principally for sunflower oil. Sunflower seeds are loaded with nutrients, containing calcium, iron, magnesium, phosphorus and potassium. They are good sources of B vitamins and carotenoids. They contain 27 percent protein, but it is an incomplete protein so sunflower seeds and their meal should be eaten with grains, legumes or dairy products. They contain about 50 percent fat, much of which is linoleic acid so they should not be consumed in excess. For reasons unknown, sunflower oil is more stable than most other high omega-6 oils. SWF

Know Your Ingredients
Name This Product #36

Whole grain oats and wheat, brown sugar, raisins, corn syrup, rice, dried coconut, almonds, glycerin, partially hydrogenated cottonseed and/or soybean oil, modified corn starch, salt, cinnamon, nonfat dry milk, polyglycerol esters, malt flavoring. Vitamins and Minerals: Vitamin E (alpha tocopherol acetate), niacinamide, zinc (oxide), iron, vitamin B6 (pyridoxine hydrochloride), vitamin B2 (riboflavin), vitamin A (palmitate; protected with BHT), vitamin B1 (thiamin hydrochloride), folic acid, and vitamin D.

See Appendix B for Answer

Arrowroot flour, the only starch with a calcium ash, is a nutritious food, obtained from the fleshy root stock of a tropical American plant. It is an easily digested food well fitted for infants and the convalescent.

It resembles cornstarch in being white, fine and powdery. When heated in water in certain portions, it thickens to form a jelly, an excellent thickening agent. It is also considered more desirable for gravies, sauces and pastries than some of the more common starches and flours. It is used primarily for food in dietetic use, where it enjoys a reputation for smoothness and palatability.

Arrowroot was once widely used in baby formulas as a superior carbohydrate, experience having shown it agreed with babies better than any other starch or sugar. We now find the reason. It is the only starch product with a calcium ash. In this regard, the calcium chloride, in the form of calcium found in arrowroot starch, is very important for the maintenance of proper acid and alkali balances in the human body.

Arrowroot only thrives on tidal flats where the sea minerals are available. Its known health-building properties may be due to trace minerals from the sea, as well as from the calcium it gets from the sea water. If it is used in ice cream formulas in place of cornstarch, arrowroot imparts a vanilla-like flavor, a smooth texture. Arrowroot as it comes to you is not a refined product; it is simply the dried and powdered root. Royal Lee, DDS *Journal of the National Academy of Research Biochemists*

ALMOND COOKIES
Makes about 18

1 1/2 cups crispy almonds (page 515)
1/2 cup butter, softened, or coconut oil (see Sources)
1 cup arrowroot or 7/8 cup bulgur flour (page 461)
1/2 cup Rapadura (see page 536)
1/2 teaspoon sea salt
grated rind of 1 lemon
1 teaspoon vanilla extract
1 teaspoon almond extract
about 18 crispy almonds (page 515)

Place almonds in food processor and process to a fine meal. Add remaining ingredients, except 18 almonds, and process until well blended. Form dough into walnut-sized balls and place on buttered cookie sheets. Press an almond into each. Bake at 300 degrees for about 20 minutes. After 5 minutes in the oven, press cookies down lightly with a fork. Let cool completely before removing to an airtight container. Store in refrigerator.

Variation: Raspberry Jam Cookies

Omit 18 almonds and use *1/4 cup naturally sweetened raspberry jam*. After 5 minutes in the oven, press cookies down slightly, make an indentation and fill with raspberry jam.

Variation: Cashew Orange Cookies

Use *1 1/2 cups crispy cashews (page 515)* in place of 1 1/2 cups crispy almonds and *grated rind of 1 orange* in place of grated rind of 1 lemon. Omit almond extract and 18 crispy almonds.

Variation: Carob Cookies

Add *1/2 cup carob powder, 1 teaspoon chocolate extract* and an additional *1/8 cup softened butter or coconut oil*. Omit lemon rind, almond extract and 18 crispy almonds.

Variation: Pecan Cookies

Use *1 1/2 cups crispy pecans (page 513)* and *18 crispy pecans halves (page 513)* in place of almonds. Reduce butter or coconut oil by 1/8 cup and omit almond extract.

PEANUT COOKIES
Makes about 16

1 1/2 cups crispy peanuts (page 514)
1/2 cup butter, softened, or coconut oil (see Sources)
1 cup arrowroot or 7/8 cup bulgur flour (page 461)
1/2 teaspoon sea salt
1/2 cup Rapadura (see page 536)
2 teaspoons vanilla extract

Place peanuts in food processor and process to a fine meal. Add remaining ingredients and process until well blended. Form into walnut-sized balls and place on buttered cookie sheets. Bake at 300 degrees for about 20 minutes. After 5 minutes in the oven, press cookies down lightly with a fork. Let cool completely before removing to an airtight container. Store in refrigerator.

Variation: Peanut Coconut Cookies

Add *1/2 cup dried sweetened coconut meat (page 159)* to the dough along with an additional *1 tablespoon butter or coconut oil*.

A factor in young grass is apparently the same one as described by Dr. Weston A. Price, in the second edition of his book *Nutrition and Physical Degeneration*, which he called "Activator X" and was found only in butter from cows fed spring grass. "Activator X" seemed very susceptible to oxidation, being lost in the butter within a few months after its production. "Activator X" was shown to promote calcification and health of bones and teeth in human patients. It inhibited the growth of the *caries bacillus* . . . completely, one test showing 680,000 salivary bacterial count before the use of "Activator X" and none after.

[Research shows] that this grass factor supports the differentiation of sexual development. Animals not getting the grass factor (but getting tocopherol) required 23% more time to become sexually mature.

It is highly interesting to find that tests of oleomargarine feeding to human subjects in comparison with commercial butter (having relatively low content of the fragile "X" factor) had the same effect of failing to bring out the secondary sex characteristics; not only a delay, but a failure to promote sex changes in toto.

A characteristic effect of castration of the child is a stimulation of growth and greater height. The investigators say the results vindicated oleo. What do you say? Royal Lee, DDS *Butter, Vitamin E and the "X" Factor of Dr. Price* Royal Lee, DDS

After analyzing hundreds of food samples for *trans* fatty acids and calculating dietary information, I have concluded that there are many people in the U.S. who consume 20% of the total fat in their diet as *trans* fatty acids. On average, though, 10.9% of the total fat is the average amount that can be calculated from all the published analyses. In the U.S. typical french fried potatoes have about 40% *trans* fatty acids, and many popular cookies and crackers range from 30 to 50% *trans* fatty acids. Doughnuts have about 35 to 40% *trans* fatty acids. Since these are all high-fat goods, someone who eats a lot of them will get a large amount of *trans* fatty acids. Several years ago we documented nearly 60 grams of *trans* fatty acids in one typical daily diet. More recently, the diet of a young student was found to contain nearly 100 grams of *trans* fatty acids every day because the foods being consumed included a pound of snack chips made with partially hydrogenated vegetable oil. Mary G. Enig, PhD *Know Your Fats*

Cholesterol is especially important to our brains. That's right, today's "most hated" substance is essential to the human brain function. In fact, infants need a constant supply of cholesterol during brain development, which is why mother's breast milk is so high in it. Modern science tripped over itself somehow when it named cholesterol the bugaboo of heart disease. Nature doesn't make that kind of mistake—but man does. [Most soy-based infant formulas contain no cholesterol.] Tom Valentine *Facts on Fats & Oils*

GINGER SNAPS
Makes about 18

1 1/2 cups crispy almonds (page 515)
1/2 cup butter, softened, or coconut oil (see Sources)
1 cup arrowroot or 7/8 cup bulgur flour (page 461)
1/2 cup Rapadura (see page 536)
1 tablespoon water
1 1/2 teaspoons ground ginger
1 teaspoon cinnamon
1/4 teaspoon nutmeg
1/4 teaspoon ground cloves
1/2 teaspoon sea salt

Place almonds in food processor and process until finely ground. Add remaining ingredients and blend well. Form into walnut-sized balls and place on buttered cookie sheets. Bake at 300 degrees for about 20 minutes. After 5 minutes in the oven, press cookies down lightly with a fork. Let cool completely before removing to an airtight container for storage. Store in refrigerator.

SWEET POTATO COOKIES
Makes about 18

1 cup cooked sweet potato or squash
1/2 cup butter, softened
3/4 cup maple syrup
1 egg
1/2 teaspoon sea salt
1/2 teaspoon powdered cloves
1/2 teaspoon ground nutmeg
1 teaspoon cinnamon
1 teaspoon baking soda
2 cups bulgur flour (page 461)
1/2 cup raisins
1/2 cup crispy pecans, chopped (page 513)

Place all ingredients except pecans and raisins in a food processor and process until well blended. Transfer to a bowl and fold in raisins and nuts. Form into walnut-sized balls and place on buttered cookie sheets. Bake at 325 degrees for about 20 minutes. After 5 minutes in the oven, press cookies down lightly with a fork. Let cool completely before removing to an airtight container for storage. Store in refrigerator.

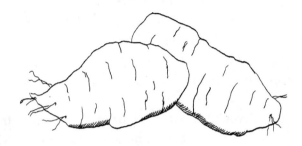

CAROB CHIP COOKIES

Makes about 18

1/2 cup butter, softened, or coconut oil
1/2 cup Rapadura (see page 536)
1 egg
1/2 teaspoon sea salt
1/2 teaspoon baking soda mixed with
*   1 tablespoon hot filtered water*
1 teaspoon vanilla extract
1 1/8 cups bulgur flour (page 461)
1 cup carob chips (page 517)
1/2 cup crispy pecans (page 513), chopped

Cream butter with Rapadura. Beat in egg, sea salt, baking soda with hot water, vanilla extract and bulgur flour. Fold in carob chips and chopped pecans. Form into walnut-sized balls and place on buttered cookie sheets. Bake at 325 degrees for about 20 minutes. After 5 minutes in the oven, press cookies down lightly with a fork. Let cool completely before removing to an airtight container. Store in refrigerator.

Variation: Date Nut Cookies
Use *1 cup chopped dates* in place of carob chips.

Know Your Ingredients
Name This Product #37

Sugar, enriched flour (contains niacin, reduced iron, thiamine mononitrate [vitamin B1], riboflavin [vitamin B2]), vegetable shortening (partially hydrogenated soybean oil), cocoa, (processed with alkali), high fructose corn syrup, corn flour, baking soda, chocolate, whey, soy lecithin (emulsifier), and vanillin, an artificial flavor.

See Appendix B for Answer

Suspected as a migraine causative for decades, chocolate has been cleared on the basis of insufficient evidence. Now things may be changing, thanks to new findings from a study by biochemist Vivette Glover . . . . Twenty heavy migraine sufferers volunteered for the study—12 eating real chocolate and eight eating a carob placebo made to taste identical to the chocolate.

Twenty-four hours after volunteers ate their test samples, five chocolate eaters experienced pounding migraines while the placebo eaters showed no symptoms. Asked what chemicals in chocolate brought on the migraines, Glover said that they had not as yet been isolated. Yet, two of the strongest suspects are catechin, also present in red wine, and theobromine, a biochemical cousin to caffeine in coffee. James F. Scheer *Health Freedom News*

It can be seen from a simple inspection [of the statistics] that cholesterol levels [are] apparently more closely related to sugar consumption than to fat consumption. For instance, it can be seen that two countries with the highest fat consumption, Spain and Ethiopia, had two of the lowest national blood cholesterol levels. However, these two countries with high fat consumption levels both had very low sugar consumption levels. On the other hand, two countries, Chile and Venezuela with high sugar consumption levels but with relatively low national fat consumption levels, had two of the highest national blood cholesterol levels. Chris Mudd *Cholesterol and Your Health*

RAISIN NUT COOKIES
Makes about 2 dozen

1/2 cup whole yoghurt (page 85)
1/2 cup butter, softened
1/4 teaspoon sea salt
1 1/2 cups freshly ground whole wheat,
*   kamut or spelt flour*
1 cup Rapadura (see page 536)
1 teaspoon vanilla extract
1/2 teaspoon cinnamon
1/2 cup raisins
3/4 cup crispy walnuts or pecans (page 513), chopped

Blend yoghurt, butter, flour and salt. Place in a bowl, cover and leave at room temperature for 12-24 hours. Beat in Rapadura, vanilla and cinnamon until dough is very smooth. Blend in raisins and walnuts. Drop by spoonfuls on buttered cookie sheets. Bake at 350 degrees for about 20 minutes. Let cool completely before removing from pan. Store in refrigerator.

MACAROONS
Makes 2 dozen

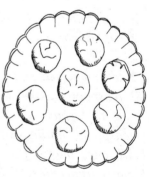

4 egg whites
pinch of sea salt
2 tablespoons arrowroot
1/2 cup maple syrup
1 tablespoon vanilla extract
2 cups commercial dried unsweetened
*   coconut meat, finely cut*

Line a baking sheet with buttered parchment paper (see Sources). Beat egg whites with salt in a clean bowl until they form stiff peaks. Beat in the arrowroot and slowly beat in syrup and vanilla. Fold in coconut. Drop by spoonfuls on parchment paper. Bake at 300 degrees for about 1/2 hour or until lightly browned. Reduce oven to 200 degrees and bake another hour or so until macaroons are completely dry and crisp. Let cool completely before removing from parchment paper. Store in an airtight container.

DESSERTS

DESSERTS

Sugary sweets are the bane of the civilized world, wreaking havoc on the health of young and old. Commercial sweets contain not only refined sweeteners—usually sugar or corn syrup—but also white flour along with highly processed and hydrogenated oils. And most contain little in the way of whole foods to compensate for these empty calories.

Yet it is perfectly possible to satisfy our inborn taste for sweet things with desserts that are nutritious. We offer here a selection of recipes featuring eggs, butter, cream, fruit, nuts and whole grains that have been soaked or fermented, along with moderate amounts of natural sweeteners. Natural sweeteners contain high amounts of minerals and other nutrients. Acceptable processed natural sweeteners are those in which the nutrients have been concentrated through boiling or dehydration rather than stripped away, as in white and brown table sugar, corn syrup or fructose.

Individual reactions to sweeteners, even and especially natural sweeteners, vary widely. Reseacher William H. Philpott found that many individuals experience a rapid rise in blood sugar when they consume one sweetener but not another. He cites the example of a patient whose blood sugar skyrocketed when she ate any corn product; but who could eat ordinary white sugar with no rise in blood sugar levels. (This does not mean that white sugar was good for her.) It is wise to test your pulse before and after eating various sweeteners to see if any provokes a reaction. Some physicians have found that fructose in corn syrup provokes more consistently severe reactions than sucrose in table sugar.

With sugar so cheap and plentiful, we have lost sight of the fact that desserts are something that you "deserve" and should not be eaten on a daily basis. Even naturally sweetened desserts should be eaten only occasionally. We recommend you limit your dessert-making to holidays and special occasions and perhaps one or two evening meals per week. A good idea is to make dessert on nights when you are serving fish or liver or some dish your children might be reluctant to eat, and offer dessert as the prize for clean plates.

Most authorities recommend that sweets be eaten after a meal and never on an empty stomach when the sudden infusion of sweetness can send the blood sugar racing upwards; however, a minority opinion asserts that sweet things, especially those containing milk products, like ice cream should only be eaten between meals, so that they have less time to ferment in the stomach. The best advice we can give in the face of these conflicting opinions is to limit your intake of sweets and never eat anything that is too highly sweetened. Finally, never eat sweet things without some fat to accompany them—whether it be cream on fruit or in ice cream, or butter and eggs in cakes and pies. Fats like butter, cream and egg yolks slow down the absorption of sugar into the bloodstream while providing fat-soluble nutrients that nourish those glands involved in the blood sugar regulation mechanism.

Avoiding sugar and keeping it away from your children is one of the most difficult things that parents are called upon to do in modern life. It is a challenge that requires discipline, planning, creative alternatives and cunning strategy. The following tips may help you in the never-ending battle:

- Don't keep sweets around the house, even if you yourself have the willpower to resist temptation. Children will find their way to candies, cookies and other sweet snacks if they are available.

- Never shop when you are hungry.

- If you crave sweets after meals, try a handful of crispy pecans or cashews (pages 513 and 515), both of which have a sweet taste. Author Nancy Appleton suggests brushing your teeth immediately after meals as the sweetness of toothpaste may be just enough to conquer cravings. A lacto-fermented beverage taken with meals also helps eliminate postprandial cravings.

- Don't forget to enlist the power of prayer in your battle against the sweet tooth.

- Make your children's school lunches. Unless their school policy is very enlightened, their school lunches will be loaded with sweet things.

- Never send a child to a birthday party or a sleep-over on an empty stomach; but fortify him beforehand with a large and nutritious sandwich or snack.

- Be resigned to that fact that you cannot keep sugar away from your children entirely. Don't make a fuss when they eat sweets and junk foods occasionally while they are with friends or you might give them good reason to rebel. You can protect them from occasional use of sugar by a diet that is consistently nutritious. When they are old enough, be sure to explain just why sugar is so bad for them. Remember that *your* example is your child's best guide to his adult eating habits.

GUIDE TO NATURAL SWEETENERS

"Natural sweeteners" may be defined as products sweet foods which the nutrients have not been removed, or may even be more concentrated due to boiling down and evaporation.

- **Raw Honey:** Honey that has not been heated over 117 degrees is loaded with amylases, enzymes that digest carbohydrates, as well as all the nutrients found in plant pollens. This makes it an ideal sweetener for porridge and toast, as the amylases in raw honey help digest grains. Glucose tolerance tests indicate that, for most people, honey does not upset blood sugar levels as severely as does refined sugar. Buy honey labeled "raw" and use it in desserts that do not require heating. Raw honey should not be given to infants as they lack sufficient stomach acid to deactivate bacteria spores.

- **Maple Syrup:** The concentrated sap of huge deciduous trees, maple syrup is rich in trace minerals, brought up from below ground by the tree's deep roots. It imparts a wonderful flavor to cream-based desserts and may be used in baked goods, such as muffins and pancakes. Unfortunately, formaldehyde is used in the production of most commercial maple syrup. See Sources for maple syrup that is formaldehyde free.

- **Rapadura:** Rapadura is the commerical name for is dehydrated cane sugar juice, which the people of India have used for thousands of years. It is rich in minerals, particularly silica. Rapadura has a wonderful flavor and closely mimics sugar in chemical properties. It gives the best results for cookies and cakes but be careful not to overdo—in large amounts Rapadura can upset the body chemistry just as much as sugar. (See Sources.)

- **Stevia Powder:** A sweet powder made from a South American herb, stevia can be used by those who are sensitive even to natural sweeteners. A little goes a very long way—a pinch of stevia powder will sweeten as effectively as a spoonful of sugar. As it does not add bulk, it is difficult to use successfully in baked goods; but stevia powder is a good sweetener for salad dressings, smoothies, whipped cream and pie crusts.

- **Date Sugar:** Made from nutritious dehydrated dates, it does not dissolve easily and is therefore unsuitable for many desserts. Its high tryptophan content makes it a good sweetener for hyperactive children, as this amino acid has a calming effect. Date sugar is delicious on porridge.

Molasses: A "waste" product from the production of refined sugar, molasses has a strong taste and moderate sweetness. If extracted from sugar cane grown in well fertilized soils, it will contain many minerals, especially iron, calcium, zinc, copper and chromium.

Malted Grain Syrups: Made with malted grains, usually barley, these syrups have been used for thousands of years, especially in the Orient. Sprouted grains are kiln-dried and the rootlets removed. The grains are then ground up, dipped briefly in an acid solution and heated with water to form malt syrup. Malt syrup is about 65 percent maltose, a disaccharide composed of two glucose molecules. (Sucrose is a disaccharide, composed of glucose and fructose.) Malted syrups contain small amounts of nutrients; but their real value is in the fact that they contain little fructose, which in large amounts is far more harmful than glucose.

Sorghum Syrup: A sweetener once popular in the Southern United States, sorghum syrup is made from sweet sorghum, a grain related to millet that grows on woody stalks to a height of 15 feet. The syrup is made by boiling the sorghum sap. It takes 8 to 12 gallons of sap to make one gallon of the syrup. Sorghum syrup contains B vitamins and minerals like iron, calcium and phosphorus. It can be used in place of maple syrup.

Naturally Sweetened Jams: Look for jams sweetened with dehydrated sugar cane juice rather than fructose or high fructose corn syrup.

The following sweeteners are used in many so-called health food products, but should be avoided.

Fructose and High Fructose Corn Syrup: These are highly refined products composed mostly of fructose. It is the fructose, not the glucose, moiety of sucrose that causes deleterious effects, especially in growing children.

Concentrated Fruit Juice: Fruit juices that have been boiled down are composed largely of fructose.

"Raw," "Natural," Turbinado and Sucanat Sugars and Florida Crystals: These are all refined sugars from which the nutrients have been removed. Small amounts of molasses may be added back to give a light brown color.

SWEETS for KIDS of ALL AGES

APRICOT COMPOTE
Serves 6-8

3 cups dried unsulphured apricots
1/2 cup maple syrup
1 cup water
1/4 teaspoon sea salt
2 cups piima cream or creme fraiche (page 84)
1/2 cup crispy almond slivers (page 515), toasted

Place apricots, maple syrup, water and salt in a sauce pan. Simmer, uncovered, for about 1 hour or until soft and most of liquid is absorbed or evaporated. Process in food processor until smooth and let cool. Fold piima cream into the apricot mixture and place in a serving dish, individual bowls or parfait glasses. Top with almonds. Serve well chilled.

STEWED RHUBARB
Serves 6

6 cups fresh rhubarb, cut into 1-inch pieces
1 tablespoon freshly ground ginger
about 1/2 cup filtered water
1/2-3/4 cups raw honey

Place rhubarb, ginger and water in a pan and bring to a boil. Reduce heat to a simmer and cook about 1 hour, stirring occasionally, until rhubarb disintegrates. Allow to cool and stir in honey to taste. Serve with whipped cream or sweet cheese topping (page 541).

The desire for sweet is inborn and instinctual. Research reveals that as increasing amounts of sugar are added to a newborn's bottle, the rate of sucking increases. Small children offered a choice between a healthy food and a heavily sweetened one will overwhelmingly choose the sweet. Our first food, mother's milk, is naturally sweet; and some say it is very sweet when considering the highly sensitive taste buds of an infant. From an evolutionary standpoint, our preference for sweets is highly advantageous for survival. Not only did it direct early hominids toward easily available ripe fruits and vegetables, it kept them away from poisonous plants, which are usually bitter in taste. No sweet foods are known to exist in nature that are poisonous. But the longing for sweets goes far beyond biology. It goes beyond the pleasure of taste and beyond the instincts of the body. Marc David *Nourishing Wisdom*

AMBROSIA

Serves 6-8

8 navel oranges
1 cup unsweetened date pieces
3/4 cup dried sweetened coconut meat (page 159)
1 cup crispy pecans (page 513), chopped

Peel and slice oranges. Place in a serving bowl and sprinkle on date pieces, coconut and pecans. Serve well chilled.

CAROB DIPPED STRAWBERRIES

Serves 8

24 large strawberries with stems
2 1/2 cups carob sauce (page 550)

Wash strawberries and drain on paper towels. Dip each strawberry in carob sauce and place on waxed paper. Chill well before serving.

FRIED BANANAS

Serves 8

8 very ripe large plantain bananas
*   16 small red bananas*
about 1/2 cup extra virgin olive oil or lard
1 cup fresh orange juice
1/3 cup honey
1 teaspoon cinnamon
piima cream or creme fraiche (page 84) for garnish

Peel bananas and cut lengthwise. Sauté in batches in olive oil or lard, transferring with a slotted spoon to an oblong pyrex dish. Make a mixture of orange juice, honey and cinnamon. Pour over the bananas and bake at 300 degrees for about 15 minutes. Serve in bowls with a dollop of cultured cream.

Refined white sugar carries only negligible traces of bodybuilding and repairing material. It satisfies hunger by providing heat and energy besides having a pleasant flavor. The heat and energy producing factors in our food that are not burned up are usually stored as fat. . . we have seen that approximately half of the foods provided in our modern dietaries furnish little or no bodybuilding or repairing material and supply no vitamins. Approximately 25 percent of the heat and energy of the American people is supplied by sugar alone, which goes far in thwarting nature's orderly processes of life. Weston Price, DDS *Nutrition and Physical Degeneration*

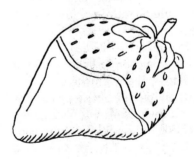

Yudkin analyzed the sugar consumption habits of men with atherosclerosis. . . the men who had heart attacks reported a sugar intake nearly twice as high as those not having the heart attacks; and, moreover, in patients with artery disease the degree of atherosclerosis was proportional to the amount of sugar consumed. . . . The statistical figures indicate the relationship between sugar consumption and heart attack and between sugar consumption and artery disease was extremely strong in this study. Chris Mudd *Cholesterol and Your Health*

In the spiritual tradition of India, it is said that if you could taste the soul, it would be sweet. Indeed, the human condition in some of its most precious moments is perceived as "sweet": "the sweet life," our "sweetheart," "sweet dreams," or "the sweet smell of success." Sweetness is an *experience*, and food is just one doorway that leads us there.

The Sufis believe that every object and sensation on the physical plane has a corresponding mirror image on higher planes. In their view the sweetness of food (on the physical level) is reflected in the sweetness of love (emotional), which is reflected in the sweetness of divine ecstasy (spiritual). Even though the sweetness of a chocolate truffle differs radically from the sweetness shared between lovers, the metaphoric connections still exist.

In fact, scientists have recently discovered a chemical compound in chocolate—phenylethylamine—believed to mimic the physiological sensations of love. Even more fascinating, in the religious traditions of the Hindus, Taoists, and Tibetan Buddhists, mystics have referred to an ecstatic state where a sensation of indescribable sweetness spontaneously arises in the mouth. Contemporary accounts of this phenomenon are widespread among meditators and practitioners of religious traditions of the East and the West. Furthermore, the Austrian philosopher-scientist Rudolf Steiner pointed out the role various foods have played in the evolution of consciousness in different historical epochs. Sugar is seen as a food that has had a powerful effect in helping to expand personality force, creativity, and self-consciousness. Even today historians are at a loss to understand why so many wars have been fought over sugar and different spices. I offer

SAUTEED APPLES
Serves 4

6 apples, peeled and cut into chunks
4 tablespoons butter

In a heavy skillet, sauté the apples in butter until golden. Serve with whipped cream (page 541).

Variation: Sautéed Asian Pears
Use *6 Asian pears, peeled and cut into chunks*, instead of apples. This is a delicious accompaniment to game!

ARISTOCRATIC APPLES
Serves 4

4 large tart apples
juice of 1 lemon
1 cup water
1/2 cup raisins, soaked in warm water
1/4 teaspoon saffron threads dissolved in
*   1 tablespoon water*
4 tablespoons butter
1/2 cup piima cream or creme fraiche (page 84)
3 tablespoons maple syrup
1/2 cup crispy almond slivers (page 515), toasted
1/4 teaspoon ground cardamom

Peel, quarter and seed the apples and place in water mixed with juice of 1 lemon. Heat butter in a heavy skillet. Remove apple quarters from lemon water, pat dry and grate into the melted butter. Cook gently until excess moisture is evaporated. Drain raisins and add to the pan along with remaining ingredients. Cook, stirring, until mixture is the consistency of thick applesauce.

APPLESAUCE

Makes 4 quarts

1/2 case organic tart apples
juice of 2 lemons
1 cup maple syrup
2 teaspoons cinnamon
1/2 teaspoon nutmeg

Cut apples into quarters and fill a very large enamel or stainless steel pot. Squeeze lemon juice over top and add about 2 cups of water to the pot. Bring to a boil and simmer, covered, for several hours until apples are very tender. Push down with a potato masher occasionally and check that the apples are not burning. Allow to cool and pass in batches through a food mill. (See A Word on Equipment, page 68.) Stir in syrup and spices. Store in refrigerator or freezer. Serve with whipped cream and toasted crispy almond slivers (page 515).

WHIPPED CREAM

Makes 2 cups

2 cups good quality heavy cream,
    preferably raw, not ultrapasteurized
1 teaspoon vanilla extract
pinch of stevia powder

Beat cream in a clean glass bowl with a whisk or an electric beater. When cream makes soft folds, beat in vanilla and stevia powder

SWEET CHEESE TOPPING

Makes 1 1/2 cups

1 cup cream cheese (page 87), softened
3 tablespoons raw honey

Place cream cheese and honey in a food processor and blend well.

this reason: Sugar and spices were the drugs of earlier cultures. When these foods were first introduced, their effect was even more powerfully narcotic and mind expanding than they are today.

When we eat sweets, our desire is not just for food. Our longing is for the *experience* of *sweetness*, something we can taste on the tongue, in the heart, or in our most sacred thoughts. However, because it is more difficult to find a sweetheart or sweet Jesus, the mind often considers sweet foods an acceptable substitute. Food happens to be the most available form of the sweet experience. Can you see how we instinctively crave sweetness on several different levels? Do you understand why it is a perfectly natural biological phenomenon?

Sugary food is one of the most popular forms of substitute love. Its effect is even more potent when combined with the love-inducing chemicals in chocolate. The downside of repeated substitution is the same for sugar as it is for drugs, alcohol, or cigarettes—dependency. We become mechanically bound to sugar because it fulfills an immediate need and exerts a powerful narcotic effect.

It is important to note that the need for the sweet experience is inborn; but as every nutritional scientist knows, there is no physiological requirement for refined sugar in the diet. Quite the contrary. Excess sugar in the diet promotes tooth decay and obesity and has been implicated in heart disease, diabetes, hypoglycemia, immune deficiency diseases, digestive disorders, and allergies. Perhaps the most fascinating and best kept medical secret about sugar is that excessive consumption causes calcium loss, which leads to a much publicized disease of our day—osteoporosis.
Marc David *Nourishing Wisdom*

Modern scientific inquiry has substantiated the old saying, "An apple a day keeps the doctor away." Studies have shown that regular apple-eating helps reduce the risk of strokes. Apples are rich in boron, which helps prevent osteoporosis, and they have a low glycemic index, which means that they do not cause a steep rise in blood sugar and therefore can be eaten safely by diabetics.

Apples are also rich in a type of fiber called pectin, which requires a cautionary note. Studies of rats on diets high in raw pectin show pathological changes to the villi of the small intestine. An apple a day may keep the doctor away, but lots of raw apples can cause digestive problems. Is this why macrobiotic adherents warn against eating raw apples? SWF

The current practice, encouraged by doctors and the American Heart Association, of increasing the consumption of vegetable oils in the diet is a nutritional disaster. Unsaturated fatty acids are needed only in small amounts in the diet. They are in adequate supply in vegetables, nuts and meat. It would be difficult, even in the average American diet, not to get adequate amounts of unsaturated fats.

Unsaturated fats found in vegetable oils increase the production of "free radicals," which are by-products of cellular chemistry. They are like tiny hand grenades that devastate body tissues, leading to degeneration and early aging. These little free radical killers lead to hardening of the arteries and cancer. In fact, the major cause of aging is probably "free radical" formation. William Campbell Douglass, MD
The Milk Book

BAKED APPLES
Serves 6

6 large baking apples
6 tablespoons butter, softened
1/2 cup Rapadura (see page 536)
grated rind of 2 lemons
juice of 2 lemons
1 teaspoon ground ginger
1/2 teaspoon ground cinnamon
1/4 teaspoon ground cloves
1/4 teaspoon ground cardamom
1/4 cup currants or raisins
1/4 cup coarsely chopped crispy almonds
(page 515), or crispy pecans (page 513)

Core apples from stem side through the center (but not entirely through) and peel from top to about 1/3 the way down. Cream butter and Rapadura. Stir in remaining ingredients and place a spoonful of stuffing in each apple. Place in a buttered baking pan with a little water. Bake about 2 hours at 325 degrees or until apples are tender.

APPLE COBBLER

Serves 6

8 tart apples
juice of 1-2 lemons
grated rind of 1 lemon
1 tablespoon arrowroot
2 tablespoons Rapadura (see page 536)
1/2 teaspoon cinnamon
3/4 cup crispy almonds (page 515)
3/4 cup arrowroot or bulgur flour (page 461)
6 tablespoons butter, softened
1/4 cup Rapadura
1/4 teaspoon sea salt
1 teaspoon vanilla extract

Peel and core apples and cut into slices. Toss with lemon juice. Mix Rapadura, lemon rind, arrowroot and cinnamon together and toss with the apples. Place in a buttered baking or souffle dish. Place almonds in food processor and process to a powder. Add butter, arrowroot or bulgur flour, Rapadura, vanilla and salt and process until smooth. Crumble this mixture on top of the apples. Bake at 350 degrees for 1 hour. Serve with whipped cream or sweet cheese topping (page 541).

Variation: Peach Cobbler

Use *8 ripe peaches* in place of apples and omit cinnamon.

Variation: Blueberry Cobbler

Use *6 cups blueberries* in place of apples and omit cinnamon.

Deficiency in manganese—which is widespread in the United States—can lead to defects in the metabolism of both fats and carbohydrates. Manganese activates dozens of enzymes throughout the body. It is involved in the formation of bone and cartilage, in blood clotting, in the effective use of insulin and in cholesterol synthesis. Rats on manganese-deficient diets develop fatty livers and show impaired production of fatty acids. Other signs of deficiency in animals include poor reproductive performance, growth retardation and abnormalities of bone and cartilage. In humans, lack of coordination, trembling hands and proneness to seizures may indicate manganese deficiency.

Manganese is absorbed with difficulty, but the body stores it in the bones and certain organs and excretes very little, thereby indicating that it is effectively recycled. Excess of calcium in the diet may inhibit manganese absorption.

Two native American foods are outstanding sources of manganese—blueberries and pecans. It is also found in other nuts, grains, ginger and cloves. SWF

We can summarize from the preceding data that the present enzyme-deficient diet may be responsible for the reduction in brain weight and size, unfavorable enlargement of the pancreas, wasting of the precursors of metabolic enzymes, and many degenerative trends. Added to the modern catastrophe called the stove are hundreds of food factories whose job it is to "refine" or denature foods. In almost every case refining eliminates much of the enzymes in foods and, in many cases, also adds potential carcinogens to them. Edward Howell, MD *Enzyme Nutrition*

Nutrition pioneer Weston Price considered the fat-soluble vitamins, especially vitamin A, to be the catalysts on which all other biological processes depend. Efficient mineral uptake and utilization of water-soluble vitamins require sufficient vitamin A in the diet. His research demonstrated that generous amounts of vitamin A ensure healthy reproduction and offspring with attractive wide faces, plenty of room for the teeth and strong sturdy bodies. He discovered that healthy primitives especially valued vitamin-A-rich foods for growing children and pregnant mothers. Working in the 1930's, he found that their diets contained ten times more vitamin A than the typical American diet of the time. This disparity is almost certainly greater today as Americans have forsworn butter and cod liver oil. In Third World communities that have come into contact with the West, vitamin A deficiencies are widespread and contribute to high infant mortality, blindness, stunting, bone deformities and susceptibility to infection.
Vitamin A Vagary

Know Your Ingredients
Name This Product #39

Skim milk, water, sugar, partially hydrogenated soybean oil, modified food starch, salt, sodium stearoyl lactylate, artificial flavor, color added (including FD&C yellow #5)

See Appendix B for Answer

ALMOND FOOL
Serves 4

2 cups crispy almonds (page 515)
2 teaspoons gelatin (see Sources), dissolved in
*   1/2 cup warm water*
1/4 cup Rapadura (see page 536)
2 teaspoons vanilla extract
1/2 cup water
2 cups whipped cream (page 541)
1 10-ounce package frozen berries
1/2 cup water
1/4 cup maple syrup

Pulverize almonds in food processor. Process with Rapadura, vanilla, water and gelatin mixture until smooth and fluffy. Fold whipped cream into almond mixture and chill well. Meanwhile, purée berries with water and maple syrup and chill in a separate bowl. To serve, spoon almond mixture into serving dishes and top with a generous spoonful of puréed berries.

TAPIOCA PUDDING
Serves 8

1 cup medium or small pearl tapioca
4 cups whole milk
3 eggs, separated, at room temperature
1/2 teaspoon sea salt
3/4 cup Rapadura (see page 536)
grated rind of 1 lemon
pinch of sea salt

Soak tapioca in milk overnight in the refrigerator. In a separate bowl, blend egg yolks, salt, Rapadura and lemon rind. Cook tapioca about 45 minutes in a double boiler over simmering water until very thick, stirring almost constantly with a whisk toward the end of thickening. Add a spoonful of hot tapioca to egg yolk mixture and then add warmed egg yolk mixture to the tapioca. Cook about 5 minutes more over simmering water, stirring constantly. Beat egg whites with sea salt until softly stiff and fold into tapioca mixture. Serve well chilled.

BAKED CUSTARD

Serves 5-6

1 cup whole milk
1 cup heavy cream, not ultrapasteurized
1/4 cup honey or Rapadura (see page 536)
5 egg yolks
1 teaspoon vanilla extract

Warm milk and cream gently over a low flame. Meanwhile, beat Rapadura or honey with egg yolks. Slowly add milk and cream mixture to eggs, beating constantly. Blend in vanilla and pour into individual custard cups. Place in a pan of hot water and bake at 325 degrees for about 1 hour, or until a knife inserted into the custard comes out clean. Chill well.

CAROB BAVARIAN CREAM

Serves 8

1 tablespoon gelatin (see Sources)
1/2 cup water
1/4 cup maple syrup
4 egg yolks
1 tablespoon vanilla extract
1/2 cup carob powder
1 tablespoon chocolate extract (optional)
4 egg whites
pinch of sea salt
2 cups heavy cream, not ultrapasteurized

Warm gelatin in water over very low heat until melted. Place egg yolks, carob, maple syrup, optional chocolate extract and vanilla in food processor. Blend about 1 minute. Add gelatin mixture while motor is running. Remove processing bowl to refrigerator. In a clean bowl beat egg whites with salt until stiff. Remove processing bowl from refrigerator and process egg yolk mixture once more. Whip cream and fold into egg yolk mixture and then fold egg whites into cream mixture. Place in a serving dish, cover and chill well.

Puddings of various sorts are a staple of the English diet. While these rich desserts are traditionally high in sugar, they also contain many ingredients that provide growing children with important nutrients—eggs, whole milk and cream.

Some researchers believe that boiled or cooked milk is actually easier to digest than pasteurized milk. Cooking causes complex proteins to unfold so that peptide bonds become more accessible to digestive enzymes, whereas pasteurization merely denatures large proteins in such a way that they are harder to break down. However, long periods of heat treatment, as in canning and spray drying, result in cross-linking in the protein chain which greatly lowers digestibility.

Both pasteurization and cooking destroy enzymes and lower vitamin availability. Puddings may be fine for an occasional treat but they are no substitute for clean, certified, whole, raw milk for growing children. SWF

It is easy—and much less costly—to produce a sugar rich in vitamins and minerals—and delicious as well—as they have done in India for thousands of years by a simple evaporation of sugar cane juice. It is true that this "poor man's sugar," as they call it in the Third World, is not immaculately white and that it is not "modern." Because of its color, white sugar is a perfect symbol of "progress" and of Western civilization, to which in these modern times all peoples unfortunately aspire. Claude Aubert *Dis-Moi Comment Tu Cuisines*

The overemphasis on unsaturated fats in the American diet, with vegetarians particularly, may lead to a brand new disease epidemic in the next 10-20 years. It is called Ceroid Storage Disease. Ceroid is a waxlike pigment that is formed from the heating of unsaturated fatty acids. . . . Let's look at a typical case of this new disease. A young man came to the emergency room complaining of bellyache. The operation revealed a spleen filled with ceroid. His history was interesting. He had been fed soybean milk as an infant. As an adult he followed a strict vegetarian diet for religious reasons. This diet consisted of soybean and wheat protein cooked in corn and Wesson oil. A perfect setup for ceroid storage disease. As pure vegetarianism becomes more popular, ceroid storage disease may be come more common. William Campbell Douglass, MD *The Milk Book*

Table sugar (sucrose) has been condemned by dentists, nutritionists, and physicians for scores of years. It is the greatest scourge that has ever been visited on man in the name of food. Endocrinologists agree that the endocrine system of glands and the nervous system cooperate to regulate the appetite so that the right amount of the right kind of food is taken in. Sugar spoils this fine balance. Being almost 100 percent "pure," this high-calorie dynamite bombs the pancreas and pituitary gland into gushing forth a hypersecretion of hormones comparable in intensity to that artificially produced in laboratory animals with drugs and hormones. Sugar is the culprit the endocrinologists have been looking for that has been throwing the finely regulated endocrine balance completely out of kilter. Edward Howell, DDS *Enzyme Nutrition*

MACADAMIA NUT PUDDING
Serves 8

1 1/2 cups crispy macadamia nuts (page 516)
1 cup piima cream or creme fraiche (page 84)
1/2 cup Rapadura (see page 536)
1 teaspoon vanilla extract
6 egg whites
pinch of sea salt

Prepare two 8-inch cake pans by cutting two rounds of parchment paper (see Sources) to fit into the pans. Place the parchment paper into buttered pans, and then butter the parchment paper. Flour the pans with unbleached white flour.

In a food processor, process macadamia nuts to a powder. Add the cultured cream, Rapadura and vanilla and process well. Place egg whites in a clean stainless steel or glass bowl with a pinch of salt and beat until stiff. Fold the macadamia nut mixture into the egg whites. Divide mixture between the two pans and spread gently so that it touches the sides. Bake at 325 degrees for about 40 minutes or until the layers pull away from the sides of the pan. To serve, let cool and place the two layers, one on top of the other, on a plate. You may "ice" the pudding with sweet cheese topping (page 541) and decorate with macadamia nuts or raspberries.

CAROB BROWNIES
Makes 24

3 cups freshly ground spelt, kamut
 or whole wheat flour
2 cups buttermilk, kefir or yoghurt (pages 83-86)
3/4 cup butter, softened
1 1/2 cups Rapadura (see page 536)
4 eggs
1 tablespoon vanilla extract
1 tablespoon chocolate extract (optional)
1 teaspoon sea salt
3/4 cup carob powder

1 tablespoon baking powder
1 cup chopped crispy pecans (page 513)

Soak flour with buttermilk, kefir or yoghurt for 12 to 24 hours in a warm place. (Those with milk allergies may use 2 cups water plus 2 tablespoons whey, lemon juice or vinegar in place of undiluted buttermilk, kefir or yoghurt.) Cream butter with Rapadura. Add eggs, extracts, salt, carob powder and baking powder. Blend in soaked flour and fold in nuts. Pour into a buttered and floured 9-inch by 13-inch pyrex pan. Bake at 350 degrees for about 40 minutes. Allow to cool thoroughly and cut into squares.

GINGERBREAD

Makes 16

2 2/3 cups freshly ground spelt, kamut
*   or whole wheat flour*
2 cups buttermilk, kefir or yoghurt (pages 83-86)
3/4 cup butter, softened
3 tablespoons freshly grated ginger
2/3 cup Rapadura (see page 536)
1/3 cup molasses
2 eggs
1/2 teaspoon cinnamon
1/2 teaspoon ground nutmeg
1/4 teaspoon ground cloves
1 teaspoon powdered ginger
1 teaspoon dry mustard
1/2 teaspoon sea salt
2 teaspoons baking powder

Soak flour with buttermilk, kefir or yoghurt for 12 to 24 hours in a warm place. (Those with milk allergies may use 2 cups water plus 2 tablespoons whey, lemon juice or vinegar in place of undiluted buttermilk, kefir or yoghurt.) Cream Rapadura with butter, molasses and eggs. Blend in remaining ingredients and blend this mixture with the soaked flour mixture. Pour into a buttered and floured 9-inch by 13-inch pyrex pan. Bake at 350 degrees for about 1 hour. Serve with whipped cream or sweet cheese topping (page 541).

. . . with normal food that carries all needed nutritional factors, the glands know just when the body has had enough and will shut off the appetite just as abruptly as one would shut off a water faucet. But when sugar gets into the mouth and begins its evil machinations, it throws the endocrine switchboard into helter-skelter. The glands know the organism has been loaded up with a lot of calories but, in spite of searching, the nutrients that normally go along with the calories cannot be found in the body. So an order to take in more food, in the expectation of getting the important vitamins, minerals, and enzymes, is issued in the form of increased appetite. Don't let it fool you, the increased appetite sugar induces is not a call for more sugar or the foods that it contaminates but for the missing nutrient factors that your body craves. Eating added sugar in various foods and drinks every day is a way of perpetuating chronic overstimulation of the pituitary and pancreas glands. The thyroid and adrenals also feel the brunt of the affront. The false craving and feeling of well-being sugar induces is on a par with the ecstasy experienced when dope takes command in a victim's body. Therefore, far overshadowing the damage resulting from sugar as a carrier of empty calories is its capacity to destroy the delicate endocrine balance and inaugurate a train of pernicious consequences. Edward Howell, MD *Enzyme Nutrition*

Sugared cereal products and hundreds of other items are made by sugarization, accounting for an average consumption of 100 pounds each year for every man, woman, and child in the USA. If the government outlawed sugar, it would shake the foundations of American business. It remains to be seen whether the ultimate damage to twenty-first century man will accrue more from today's sugar eating or from the consumption of artificial sweeteners, such as saccharine. Edward Howell, MD *Enzyme Nutrition*

The latest explosive evidence incriminating table sugar as the chief architect of heart disease comes from the University of Hawaii (1972). C. C. Brooks and his associates fed pigs high-sugar diets. Sixty-eight of the eighty pigs developed heart disease in the left half of the heart. This backs up the contention that Dr. Yudkin and others have been making for many years. A remarkable added finding was that in pigs in which 10 percent of the sugar was replaced by coconut oil or beef tallow the heart remained free from the endocarditis that afflicted the [other] animals. This may confound those who have been apprehensive about fat in the diet. Edward Howell, MD *Enzyme Nutrition*

COCONUT BARS
Makes 16

3/4 cup crispy almonds (page 515)
1/4 cup butter, softened or
    1/4 cup coconut oil (see Sources)
1/2 cup arrowroot or bulgur flour (page 461)
1/4 cup Rapadura (see page 536)
1 teaspoon vanilla extract
pinch sea salt
1 egg
1/4 cup piima cream or creme fraiche (page 84)
1/2 cup maple syrup
1 tablespoon vanilla extract
grated rind of 1 lemon
2 tablespoons arrowroot
pinch of sea salt
1 1/2 cups dried unsweetened coconut meat

Place almonds in food processor and process to a fine powder. Add butter or coconut oil, 1/2 cup arrowroot or bulgur flour, vanilla, Rapadura and salt and process until smooth. Press into a well-oiled 9-inch by 9-inch or 7-inch by 11-inch pyrex pan. Bake at 300 degrees for 20 minutes. Let cool. Beat egg with cultured cream, maple syrup, vanilla, lemon peel, 2 tablespoons arrowroot and sea salt. Stir in coconut and spread over almond pastry. Bake at 325 degrees for about 25 minutes. Let cool slightly before cutting into bars. Let cool completely before removing bars from the pan.

APRICOT BARS
Makes 24

3 cups dried apricots
1/2 cup Rapadura (see page 536)
2 cups crispy almonds (page 515)
5/8 cup butter, softened or
    5/8 cup coconut oil (see Sources)
1 1/2 cups arrowroot or bulgur flour (page 461)
1/2-3/4 cup Rapadura (see page 536)
1/2 teaspoon sea salt
1 teaspoon almond extract

Cook apricots in water until tender. Remove with a slotted spoon to food processor and process with 1/2 cup Rapadura. Set aside and let cool.

Meanwhile, process almonds to a powder in food processor. Add remaining ingredients and process until smooth. Press 2/3 of the almond mixture into a buttered 9-inch by 13-inch pyrex pan, making a thin crust. Bake about 15 minutes at 350 degrees. Spread apricot mixture over crust and distribute the remaining 1/3 almond mixture, crumbled, over top. Bake at 325 degrees for about 45 minutes. Let cool slightly before cutting into bars. Let cool thoroughly before removing bars from pan.

Dextrose, which is made by boiling corn starch with acid, should be reserved for occasional use as temporary intravenous medicine in hospitals. The indictment against both table sugar and dextrose is strong enough to demand that both be placed off limits to people. Let them be available only by prescription issued by a doctor. The chemists in the large food processing plants are very efficient people. They know their subjects from A to Z. But the last thing they can afford to be concerned about is the consumer's health. Oh yes, they will protect the public health from immediate poisoning and the like. But they do not worry about what goes on in a consumer's body after 20 years of eating their products. If the result is a killing disease, it is given a name on a death certificate as an established disease entity; and no one suspects that food had anything to do with it. Edward Howell, MD *Enzyme Nutrition*

ALMOND BARS

Makes 24

1 recipe flaky pie crust (page 557)
1 cup naturally sweetened raspberry jam
3 cups crispy almond slivers (page 515)
1 cup maple syrup
1 tablespoon arrowroot

Line a buttered 9-inch by 13-inch pyrex pan with flaky pastry. Prick the pastry well with a fork and place in a cool oven. Turn oven on to 300 degrees and bake about 20 minutes. Let cool and spread with jam. Bring syrup to a boil with arrowroot. Stir in almonds and spread mixture over jam. Bake at 325 degrees for about 30 minutes or until almonds become nicely browned. Let cool slightly before cutting into bars. Let cool completely before removing bars from pan.

Sometimes the eastern Iroquois squaws seasoned the cornmeal foods with berries, mushrooms or maple sugar. Maple syrup and maple sugar were, in fact, Indian favorites. The granulated sugar could be dissolved in water as a refreshing beverage; other uses of maple syrup and sugar were to season fruits, vegetables, cereals and fish. . . . Even when salt was available, Indians used it sparingly. . . because they believed that an excess of salt caused illness and an unnatural thirst. Patricia B. Mitchell *The Good Land*

Each isolated Swiss valley or village has its own special feast days of which athletic contests are the principal events. The feasting in the past has been largely on dairy products. The athletes were provided with large bowls of cream as constituting one of the most popular and healthful beverages, and special cheese was always available. . . their cream products took the place of our modern ice cream. . . it is reported that practically all skulls that are exhumed in the Rhone valley and, indeed, practically throughout all of Switzerland, where graves have existed for more than a hundred years, are found with relatively perfect teeth; whereas the teeth of people recently buried have been riddled with caries or lost through this disease. Weston Price, DDS *Nutrition and Physical Degeneration*

The Prodigal Son, at his lowest ebb, ate "the husks that the swine did eat." His food was the carob pod, for millennia a staple of the Middle Eastern diet. In recent decades the carob's standing has risen considerably as people have discovered in the powder made from this hard, dark brown pod an acceptable substitute for chocolate. Carob is an excellent source of calcium—containing three times more calcium than mother's milk! It also contains carotenoids, B vitamins, phosphorus and iron. It is naturally sweet, containing about 50 percent sugars. Unlike chocolate, carob contains no stimulants; it does, however, contain tannin, a substance that reduces the absorption of protein through the intestinal wall. Roasting neutralizes most of the tannins so buy only powder made from roasted carob pods. SWF

VANILLA ICE CREAM
Makes 1 quart

3 egg yolks
1/2 cup maple syrup
1 tablespoon vanilla extract
1 tablespoon arrowroot
3 cups heavy cream, preferably raw,
    not ultrapasteurized

Ice cream should be made with the best quality cream you can find, preferably unpasteurized. Never use ultrapasteurized cream.

Beat egg yolks and blend in remaining ingredients. Pour into an ice cream maker and process according to instructions. (See A Word on Equipment, page 68.) For ease of serving, transfer ice cream to a shallow plastic container, cover and store in the freezer. Serve with Carob Sauce or Raspberry Sauce.

Variation: Ginger Pecan Ice Cream
Add *1 tablespoon ground ginger* and *1/2 cup finely chopped crispy pecans (page 513).*

Variation: Carob Chip Ice Cream
Add *1/4 cup carob chips, finely chopped (page 517).*

CAROB SAUCE
Makes 2 1/2 cups

2/3 cup carob powder
1/2 cup butter
1/3 cup maple syrup
1 tablespoon vanilla extract
1 tablespoon chocolate extract (optional)
pinch of salt
1 cup cream, not ultrapasteurized

Place all ingredients in the top half of a double boiler. Cook gently, stirring occasionally with a wooden spoon, until well amalgamated.

RASPBERRY SAUCE

Makes 4 cups

1 12-ounce package frozen raspberries
1/2 cup maple syrup
1-2 cups water

Place partially thawed raspberries in food processor with maple syrup and process to make a thick paste. Gradually add water until desired consistency is obtained.

BERRY ICE CREAM

Makes 1 quart

2 cups fresh berries, such as raspberries,
    boysenberries, or blackberries, fresh or
    10 ounces frozen berries, partially thawed
2 egg yolks
1 tablespoon arrowroot
2 cups heavy cream, preferably raw,
    not ultrapasteurized
1/2-3/4 cup maple syrup

Process berries in food processor for several minutes. Add egg yolks, cream and arrowroot and process until well blended. Gradually add maple syrup until desired sweetness is obtained. Pour into an ice cream maker and process according to instructions. (See A Word on Equipment, page 68.)For ease of serving, transfer ice cream to a shallow plastic container, cover and store in the freezer.

Variation: Strawberry Ice Cream
    Use *2-3 cups fresh strawberries, washed and picked* and add *1/4 teaspoon almond extract.*

In the old days when ice cream was made of whole eggs, milk and sugar and laboriously cranked out in the old home freezer, a serving of ice cream was only an occasional family treat which didn't do much harm. Today in this mass producing, synthetic age, it is another matter entirely. Today you may be treating your family to poison! Ice cream manufacturers are not required by law to list the additives used in the manufacturing of their product. Consequently, today most ice creams are synthetic from start to finish. Analysis has shown the following:

DIETHYLGLYCOL: A cheap chemical used as an emulsifier instead of eggs is the same chemical used in antifreeze and in paint removers.

PIPERONAL: Used in place of vanilla. This chemical is used to kill lice.

ALDEHYDE C-17: Used to flavor cherry ice cream. It is an inflammable liquid also used in aniline dyes, plastic and rubber.

ETHYL ACETATE: Used to give ice cream a pineapple flavor—and as a cleaner for leather and textiles; its vapors have been known to cause chronic lung, liver and heart damage.

BUTYRALDEHYDE: Used in nut flavored ice cream. It is one of the ingredients of rubber cement.

AMYL ACETATE: Used for its banana flavor. It is also used as an oil paint solvent.

BENZYL ACETATE: Used for its strawberry flavor. It is a nitrate solvent.

The next time you are tempted by a luscious looking banana split sundae made with commercial ice cream, think of it as a mixture of antifreeze, oil paint, nitrate solvent, and lice killer; and you won't find it so appetizing.
PPNF Health Journal

It's almost as if the devil sat down and listed all the criteria of a substance man could use to destroy himself. It would have to be pleasing to the eye and taste. It would have to be pure white and easily available. It would have to appeal to all the people of this world. The destroying effects would have to be subtle and take such a long time that very few would realize what was happening until it was too late. The cruelest criteria of all is it would have to be supported and distributed by the kindest, most well-meaning people to the most innocent people.

So far the devil is winning. Did you ever go to a church cake sale conducted in a grade school? Bruce Pacetti, DDS *PPNF Health Journal*

Many people with sugar dependencies report that their need for sugar drops significantly when they cut down on meat.

Interestingly enough, we crave sugar also when there is not enough protein in the diet. The reason for this is that opposites, in their extremes, change into one another. Extreme pleasure becomes painful. Extreme light is blinding (darkness). And lack of protein or meat, an extremely expansive function, will cause us to crave the food we need least, an extremely expansive food like sugar. It is not unusual for people who switch to a vegetarian diet and have a lower protein intake to begin craving sweet foods. And vegetarians who eat too much refined sugar often have strong cravings for meat and fish. Marc David *Nourishing Wisdom*

FRUIT ICE CREAM
Makes 1 quart

2 cups fresh fruit, such as peaches, pears or plums, peeled and sliced
2 tablespoons lemon juice
4 tablespoons maple syrup
1 teaspoon gelatin (see Sources)
2 egg yolks, lightly beaten
2 cups heavy cream, preferably raw, not ultrapasteurized

Mix maple syrup with lemon juice and toss with fruit. Cover and let stand for 2 hours. Drain the fruit and combine 3/4 cup of the drained juice with the gelatin. Heat gently until the gelatin is dissolved. Place fruit in food processor with gelatin mixture and process until desired texture is obtained—either smooth or chunky. Stir in remaining ingredients. Pour into an ice cream maker and process according to instructions. (See A Word on Equipment, page 68.) For ease of serving, transfer ice cream to a shallow plastic container, cover and store in the freezer.

PERSIMMON ICE CREAM
Makes 1 quart

4-5 ripe persimmons, peeled and seeded
2 tablespoons lemon juice
1/2 cup maple syrup
2 egg yolks
1 tablespoon arrowroot
2 cups heavy cream, preferably raw, not ultrapasteurized

Place persimmons in a food processor and process to a smooth pulp. Add remaining ingredients and blend well. Pour into an ice cream maker and process according to instructions. (See A Word on Equipment, page 68.) For ease of serving, transfer ice cream to a shallow plastic container, cover and store in the freezer.

LEMON SHERBERT

Makes 1 quart

grated rind of 2 lemons
juice of 2 lemons
2 egg yolks
3 cups piima milk, kefir or
    buttermilk (pages 83-88)
1/2 cup maple syrup

Place all ingredients in food processor and process several minutes. Pour into an ice cream maker and process according to instructions. (See A Word on Equipment, page 68.) For ease of serving, transfer sherbert to a shallow plastic container, cover and store in the freezer.

PLUM SHERBERT

Makes 1 quart

2 pounds plums
1 1/2 cups water
1/2 cup maple syrup

This is an excellent dessert for those who cannot tolerate milk products in any form. Even though not made with cream, the sherbert will have a creamy texture.

Cut plums in half, remove seeds and cook with 1/2 cup water until soft. Lift out with a slotted spoon into a food mill and process plums to remove skins. (See A Word on Equipment, page 68.) Meanwhile, bring 1 cup water to a boil, add syrup and mix with a wooden spoon. Simmer for about 10 minutes. Let cool and add to plum mixture. Refrigerate plum mixture several hours until well cooled. Pour into an ice cream maker and process according to instructions. (See A Word on Equipment, page 68.) For ease of serving, transfer sherbert to a shallow plastic container, cover and store in the freezer.

It seems, therefore, that we Americans are bent on "refining" ourselves into a chromium deficiency; the ultimate result of which is a significant glucose intolerance in the human body. This rather unhappy distinction of the United States is not shared by other countries that do not refine their foods. In a series of tests on men between the ages of twenty and fifty-nine, the amount of chromium found in the heart artery was 1.9 parts per million (ppm) in American men, 5.5 ppm in African men, 11 ppm in men from the Near East, and 15 ppm in men from the Far East. This evidence is one source of speculation which proves that there is indeed a definite link between the overconsumption of refined foods and a chromium deficiency. William H. Philpott, MD *Victory Over Diabetes*

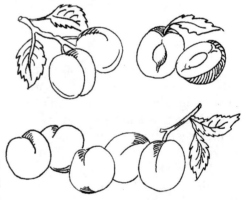

Sprawsen. . . observed that raw milk had specific effect on teeth of man, conferring considerable immunity to dental caries. It excelled pasteurized and sterilized milk in body-building properties. No incidence of dental caries showed in 40 children brought up on raw milk from the age of 4 1/2 months to an average age of 4 years, although they had been on diets rich in refined carbohydrates. Edward Howell, MD *Food Enzymes for Health and Longevity*

Know Your Ingredients

Name This Product #40

Water, corn syrup, hydrogenated coconut and palm kernel oils, sugar, sodium caseinate, polysorbate 60 and sorbitan monostrearate (for uniform dispersion of oil), natural and artificial flavors, xanthan gum and guar gum (thickeners), artificial color

See Appendix B for Answer

It used to be an apple a day that keeps the doctor away. Today, it's a banana. But who cares what healthful fruits or vegetables are used so long as you can keep illnesses and the doctor away?

Lewis Tobian, M.D., a professor of medicine at the University of Minnesota and a nutrition authority, really wants to keep other doctors away. He eats two bananas daily and indicates that due to their high potassium content—about 400 mg. of potassium per unit—they may lower blood pressure and keep cholesterol from building up in the arteries. . . .

However, bananas aren't the only potassium-rich foods. There are also apricots, avocados, dates, Brussels sprouts, lima beans, orange and grapefruit juice, carrots, tomatoes, potatoes, spinach and yoghurt. James F. Scheer *Health Freedom News*

BROWN RICE PUDDING
Serves 8-10

2 cups basic brown rice (page 466)
3 eggs
1 1/2 cups heavy cream, not ultrapasteurized
1/3 cup maple syrup
1 teaspoon vanilla extract
1/8 teaspoon sea salt
1/2 teaspoon cinnamon
2 cups raisins, preferably organic
3/4 cup crispy pecans (page 513), chopped

Beat eggs with cream, maple syrup, vanilla, salt and cinnamon. Stir in rice, pecans and raisins. Pour into a buttered casserole or soufflé dish. Bake for about 50 minutes at 325 degrees.

TROPICAL DELIGHT
Serves 8

1 cup crispy peanuts (page 514)
3/8 cup butter, softened, or 3/8 cup coconut oil
1 cup arrowroot or bulgur flour (page 461)
3/8 cup Rapadura (see page 536)
1/2 teaspoon salt
1 teaspoon vanilla extract
3/4 cup dried unsweetened coconut meat
3-4 fresh bananas
2 cups whipped cream (page 541)

Place peanuts in food processor and process to a powder. Add remaining ingredients, except bananas and whipped cream, and pulse until well blended. Butter and flour a 10-inch or 12-inch French-style tart pan. Press dough into pan, making an even layer. Bake at 300 degrees for about 45 minutes. Let cool. Cut into wedges and top with sliced fresh bananas and whipped cream.

FRUIT CUSTARD CAKE

(Clafoutis)
Serves 8

3 cups fresh fruit, such as pitted cherries,
*   sliced nectarines or peaches,*
*   or pineapple cut into chunks*
1/4 cup Rapadura
3 eggs
1/2 cup Rapadura (see page 536)
1/4 cup unbleached flour or
*   3 tablespoons arrowroot*
1 1/3 cup piima cream or creme fraiche (page 84)

This is a traditional French dessert, something between cake and custard. Sprinkle fruit with 1/4 cup Rapadura and set aside for about 1/2 hour. Remove with a slotted spoon to a buttered baking pan and bake at 250 degrees for an hour or more or until fruit is rather dry. Butter an easy-remove, 10-inch cake pan. Beat eggs with 1/2 cup Rapadura until smooth. Beat in flour or arrowroot and cream. Stir in fruit and pour batter into pan. Bake about 1 hour at 350 degrees. Let cool slightly before removing from pan.

NUT BUTTER MOUSSE
Serves 6

2 cups nut butter (page 516), at room temperature
3 egg whites, at room temperature
pinch sea salt
6 merengues (page 556)

In a very clean bowl, beat egg whites with a pinch of salt until stiff peaks form. Carefully fold in the nut butter and chill well. To serve, place merengues on individual serving plates and fill with a generous spoonful of nut butter mousse. Serve with fresh fruit.

Most dentists and physicians sincerely believe the destructive action on tooth enamel is only a local one that is caused by bacterial action upon carbohydrates, primarily sugar, sweets and refined grains.

It is agreed that this is the outward inciting cause, but the reason the bacteria and refined foods are able to attack the hard tooth enamel is due to changes that have taken place in the body and subsequently in the inside of teeth. . . . Though hard to imagine, this very hard tooth enamel of ours is porous. Two percent of its volume is water and it, too, can flow in either direction. However, the normal flow is from the pulp and the odontoblast cells outwardly through the dentin and then through the enamel.

Not only is this fluid movement measurable, but when laboratory rats are fed a high-sugar cariogenic diet the fluid movement is reversed and herein lies the reason teeth become susceptible to decay. . . .

In addition to the changes good and bad nutrition have on dentin tubule flow and function, dietary habits have numbers of other actions that are involved in the cause of tooth decay. One of these is how the food we eat affects the acid-base balance of the saliva. Under ideal dietary conditions the saliva is slightly alkaline. Like the blood it has a 7.4 pH. When it falls below a pH of 7.0, as it does to a considerable extent after sugar and refined grains are eaten, the saliva becomes more acid and environmental factors in the mouth are more conducive to the development of tooth decay and dental erosion. *PPNF Health Journal*

Researcher Richard Passwater states that of fourteen tests conducted all showed a high correlation between eating high amounts of polyunsaturates and the occurrence of cancer in both humans and animals. He states that a large percentage of the population is consuming an excessive amount of polyunsaturates in the form of corn oil, peanut oil, margarines, soybean oil, etc., and notes that presently Americans eat two to three times the amount of vegetable oils than were consumed sixty years ago. Passwater stresses that only from two to four percent of one's diet should consist of vegetable fats. H. Leon Abrams *Vegetarianism: An Anthropological/Nutritional Evaluation*

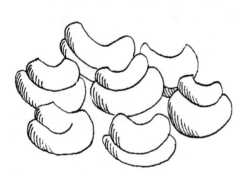

When a junkie dies, known or unknown, is it ever from "metabolic complications?" Of course not. Heroin is a killer. Junkies die of junk. Even when a drunk dies, he dies of his sins. But when a person dies of sugar blues, the mourners often serve sugar at the wake. Sugar-poisoning is a word wedding that rarely appears in print.

The same double standard is evident in the world of art and entertainment. Junkies die like flies every hour of every day on television. Many of these consoling sagas are brought to you by those wonderful people who push sugar and other products laced with sugar at every commercial break. William Dufty *Sugar Blues*

MERENGUES
Makes 6

6 egg whites
pinch of sea salt
3 tablespoons arrowroot
1/4 cup maple syrup
1 tablespoon vanilla extract

Merengues are a good way to use up leftover egg whites. They should cook overnight in a warm oven—about 150 degrees. Be sure to use a very clean bowl to beat your egg whites.

Line a cookie sheet with buttered parchment paper (see Sources). Beat egg whites with salt until they form stiff peaks. Beat in arrowroot. Slowly add maple syrup and vanilla, beating constantly. Place six blobs of egg white mixture on parchment paper and form a little hollow in each one. Cook overnight in a warm oven, about 150 degrees. Let cool before removing parchment paper. Store merengues in an airtight container until ready to use.

STRAWBERRY DELIGHTS
Makes 6

6 merengues
6 cups fresh strawberries
2 tablespoons Rapadura (see page 536)
2 cups whipped cream (page 541)

Wash strawberries and remove stems. Slice lengthwise into quarters. Sprinkle with Rapadura and let stand for 1 hour or more. Spoon strawberries into individual merengues and top with whipped cream. Serve immediately.

PIES & CAKES

FLAKY PIE CRUST

1 1/3 cups unbleached white flour
    or 1 1/4 cups sifted bulgur flour (page 461)
pinch of sea salt
pinch of stevia powder
1/2 cup (1 stick) butter, frozen
2 egg yolks
3 rounded tablespoons cold water

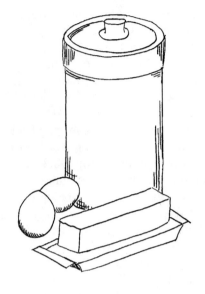

This is the only recipe in which we compromise somewhat on our principles. Bulgur or sprouted wheat flour can be used for pie crust, but the exacting gourmet will prefer to use unbleached white flour. This recipe will make a 9-inch pie shell with enough left over for lattice work; or two 8-inch French-style tart shells; or seven individual 4-inch tart shells.

Sift flour, sea salt and stevia powder into food processor. Place butter on a board and cut into about 16 pieces using a sharp knife. Distribute butter over flour. Pulse processor several times until butter is broken into pea-sized pieces and is well distributed. Beat egg yolks briefly with a fork, dribble over flour mixture and pulse once or twice. Have water ready. Turn on processor and immediately pour water in. Stop processor at once. (Butter should still be visible as pea-sized and seed-sized pieces.) Turn crust onto waxed paper, wrap up and squeeze together, forming a ball. Refrigerate several hours. Roll on a pastry cloth using unbleached white flour to keep from sticking.

When lining French-style tart pans (with removable bottoms) press dough firmly into sides and drape over the top. Roll a rolling pin over the top to trim crust evenly.

For a partially baked or fully baked tart shell, prick dough several times with a fork. Place in a cool oven and turn on heat. (Gradual warming will prevent the dough from excessive shrinking.) Bake at 300 degrees for 15 minutes for partially baked pastry and 25 minutes for a fully baked pastry—longer if using bulgur flour.

Know Your Ingredients
Name This Product #41

Enriched wheat flour containing niacin, reduced iron, thiamine mononitrate (vitamin B1) and riboflavin (vitamin B2), vegetable shortening (partially hydrogenated soybean oil), sugar, graham flour, brown sugar, corn syrup, salt, leavening (sodium bicarbonate, sodium acid pyrophosphate, monocalcium phosphate), malt, cornstarch, soy lecithin and artificial flavor.

See Appendix B for Answer

No other product has so profoundly influenced the political history of the Western world as has sugar. It was the nickel under the foot of much of the early history of the New World. The Portuguese and Spanish empires rose swiftly in opulence and power. As the Arabs before them had crumbled, so they, too, fell rapidly into decline. To what extent that decline was biological—occasioned by sugar bingeing at the royal level—we can only guess. However, the British Empire stood by waiting to pick up the pieces. In the beginning, Queen Elizabeth I shrank from institutionalizing slavery in the British colonies as "detestable," something which might "call down the vengeance of heaven" on her realm. By 1588 her sentimental scruples had been overcome. The Queen granted a royal charter extending recognition to the Company of Royal Adventurers of England into Africa, which gave them a state monopoly on the African slave trade. William Dufty *Sugar Blues*

Myth: Coconut oil causes heart disease.
Truth: When coconut oil was fed as 7% of energy to patients recovering from heart attacks, the patients had greater improvement compared to untreated controls and no difference compared to patients treated with corn or safflower oils. Populations that consume coconut oil have low rates of heart disease. Coconut oil may also be one of the most useful oils to prevent heart disease because of its antiviral and antimicrobial characteristics. (*JAMA* 1967 202:1119-1123; *Am J Clin Nutr* 1981 34:1552)

HAZELNUT PIE CRUST

1 cup crispy hazelnuts (page 514)
3/4 cup arrowroot or bulgur flour (page 461)
3/8 cup butter, softened, or coconut oil (see Sources)
1/4 cup Rapadura (see page 536)
1/4 teaspoon sea salt
1/2 teaspoon vanilla extract

This makes a delicious press-in type of pie crust, enough for one 9-inch pie pan.

Place hazelnuts in food processor and process to a meal. Add remaining ingredients and process until smooth. Press into a well-buttered and floured pie pan. For a fully baked pie crust, bake at 325 degrees for about 1/2 hour.

Variation: Pecan Pie Crust
Use *1 cup crispy pecans (page 513)* instead of hazelnuts. Reduce butter or coconut oil to 1/4 cup.

Variation: Almond Pie Crust
Use *1 cup crispy almonds (page 515)* instead of hazelnuts

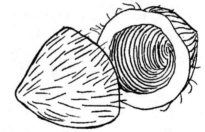

COCONUT PIE CRUST

1/2 cup melted butter or coconut oil (see Sources)
2 cups dried unsweetened coconut meat,
*   finely shredded*

Mix coconut with butter in a small bowl. Transfer to a buttered and floured 9-inch pie pan and press firmly and evenly against the bottom and sides. Bake at 300 degrees for 30 minutes or until crust is a dark golden color. Allow to cool to room temperature.

RASPBERRY TART

Serves 6-8

1 recipe flaky pie crust (page 557),
  fully baked as a 12-inch French-style tart
  or as individual tarts
2 cups naturally sweetened raspberry jam
1/2 cup pear or raspberry liqueur
3-4 cups fresh raspberries

Heat raspberry jam with liqueur and boil gently about 10 minutes. Brush pastry with melted jam. Arrange berries on top and drizzle remaining jam mixture over berries.

Variation: Raspberry-Carob Tart

Spoon *1 1/2 cups carob sauce (page 550)* over raspberry jam glaze and proceed with recipe.

Variation: Blueberry Tart

Use *3-4 cups fresh blueberries* instead of raspberries.

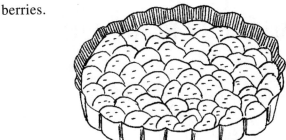

STRAWBERRY-PECAN TART

Serves 8

1 fully baked pecan pie crust
  in a 9-inch pie plate (page 558)
2-3 pints strawberries
2 tablespoons Rapadura (see page 536)
2 cups whipped cream (page 541)

Wash strawberries, trim off tops and quarter lengthwise. Toss with Rapadura and chill several hours. Just before serving, fill tart crust with strawberries. Serve with whipped cream.

Scientists at the Agriculture Department's U.S. Dairy Forage Research Center in Madison, Wisconsin, have been studying a substance called conjugated linoleic acid or CLA that occurs in butterfat. Many studies over the past 12 years have established that, at least in laboratory animals, CLA offers some protection against breast cancer and other malignancies, apparently through its role as a potent antioxidant. In addition to anticancer benefits, CLA also seems to dramatically reduce the deposition of fat. Livestock eating feed supplemented with CLA tend to lay down more lean tissue and dairy cattle ingesting CLA-enriched diets have greater milk productivity. "Much to their big surprise," scientists found that the highest level of CLA in milk was obtained with cows just eating pasture—nothing else, according to Larry D. Satter, director of the forage center. Satter finds the notion of pasture feeding "a far-out idea." Those familiar with the work of Weston Price know that pasture feeding is the *only* way to provide healthful, nonallergenic, nutrient-dense dairy products to the populace. Could it be that CLA in America's pasture-fed cows at the turn of the century not only protected against cancer but overweight as well and allowed mothers to nurse successfully because they had plenty of milk? Meanwhile, University of Wisconsin scientists are trying to figure out ways to mass produce CLA as a food additive. *PPNF Health Journal*

Supplies of vitamin A are so vital to the human organism that mankind is able to store large quantities of it in the liver and other organs. Thus, it is possible to subsist on a fat-free diet for a considerable period of time before overt symptoms of deficiency appear. But during times of stress, vitamin A stores are rapidly depleted. Strenuous physical exercise, periods of physical growth, pregnancy, lactation and infection are stresses that quickly deplete vitamin A stores. Children with measles rapidly use up vitamin A, often resulting in irreversible blindness. An interval of three years between pregnancies allows mothers to rebuild vitamin A stores so that subsequent children will not suffer diminished vitality.

One aspect of vitamin A that deserves more emphasis is its role in protein utilization. Kwashiorkor is as much a disease of vitamin A deficiency, leading to impaired protein absorption, as it is a result of absence of protein in the diet. High-protein, lowfat diets in children induce rapid growth along with depletion of vitamin A supplies. The results—tall, myopic, lanky individuals with crowded teeth and poor bone structure—are a fixture in America. Growing children in particular actually benefit from a diet that contains at least twice as many calories as fat than as protein. Such a diet, rich in vitamin A, will result in steady, even growth, a sturdy physique, and high immunity from illness. *Vitamin A Vagary*

BERRY PIE
Serves 8

1 recipe fully-baked hazelnut pie crust
in a 9-inch pie plate (page 558)
2 12-ounce packages frozen berries or
1 1/4 pounds fresh berries
1/2 cup water
1/4 cup maple syrup
2 tablespoons lemon juice
1 tablespoon gelatin (see Sources) dissolved in
3 tablespoons water over low heat

Place half the berries in food processor with water and maple syrup. Process until berries are liquefied. Add lemon juice and gelatin mixture while motor is running. Place remaining berries in cooled pie crust and pour gelatin mixture over them. Refrigerate several hours before serving.

CRANBERRY-PEAR PIE
Serves 8

1 recipe flaky pie crust (page 557)
12 ounces fresh cranberries
1 cup maple syrup
6 large pears
4 1/2 teaspoons arrowroot dissolved in
2 tablespoons cold water

Line a 9-inch pie plate with flaky pie crust dough and reserve the rest for making lattice. Place cranberries and maple syrup in a saucepan. Peel and core the pears and cut into 1/2-inch pieces, adding to maple syrup as you cut. Bring syrup to a boil and cook, stirring, for several minutes until cranberries begin to pop. Add the arrowroot mixture and cook another minute more, stirring constantly. Let cool slightly. Pour into pie shell. Make a lattice to cover the pear mixture and bake at 350 degrees for about 45 minutes.

COCONUT MOUSSE PIE

Serves 8

1 recipe coconut pie crust (page 558)
6 egg yolks at room temperature
1/2 cup honey
1 teaspoon vanilla extract
1 teaspoon coconut flavoring
6 egg whites at room temperature
pinch of sea salt
1 cup heavy cream, preferably raw, well chilled
1 cup fresh coconut, grated or 1 cup dried
     unsweetened coconut, finely shredded

Place egg yolks, honey, and extracts in the top of a double boiler over simmering water. Whisk constantly for about 10 minutes until mixture thickens. Remove from heat and chill in refrigerator for about 1/2 hour. Beat cream until stiff. In a separate clean bowl, beat egg whites with sea salt until stiff. Stir coconut into egg yolk mixture and fold coconut-egg yolk mixture into cream. Gently fold this mixture into the egg whites. Pour into pie shell and chill well.

RHUBARB PIE

Serves 8

1 recipe flaky pie crust (page 557)
4 cups fresh rhubarb, cut into 1/2-inch pieces
3/4 cup Rapadura (see page 536)
2 tablespoons arrowroot
grated rind of 1 orange
2 tablespoons butter

Toss rhubarb with Rapadura, arrowroot and orange rind and let stand for 15 minutes. Meanwhile, line a shallow pie plate with flaky pie crust, reserving enough to make a lattice-work top. Fill pie crust with rhubarb mixture, dot with butter and cover with lattice work. Bake at 450 degrees for 10 minutes. Reduce heat to 350 degrees and bake another 40-45 minutes. Serve with whipped cream or sweet cheese topping (page 541).

A well-nourished child, first of all, measures up to . . . standards of his age in height and weight. He has good color, bright eyes, no blue or dark circles underneath them and smooth glossy hair. His carriage is good, his step elastic, his flesh firm and his muscles well developed. In disposition he is usually happy and good natured; he is brim full of life and animal spirits and is constantly active, both physically and mentally. His sleep is sound, his appetite and digestion good, his bowels regular. He is, in short, what nature meant him to be before anything else: a happy, healthy young animal. L. J. Roberts 'What Is Malnutrition?' *U.S. Department of Labor Publication No. 59* 1944

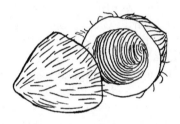

In mice with surgically or chemically induced brain lesions, as in the Marshall, et. al., study, the liver, heart, kidneys and pancreas become enlarged. In a piece of research work done by a team long before the Marshall work, continuous intravenous injection of large amounts of dextrose (glucose) into 20 dogs caused death in all of them in 1 to 7 days. It also caused severe hemorrhage and destruction in the pituitary gland and pancreas and marked liver enlargement. This and other experiments create a compelling reason to believe that the habitual use of refined sugars and other carbohydrates over long periods can create brain lesions similar to the brain lesions produced in the laboratory. Edward Howell, MD *Enzyme Nutrition*

The word for cinnamon is derived from the Greek word for Ceylon, which has been a source of this delicious spice since antiquity. It is made from the bark of a species of tree that grows in sandy soil beside rivers in warm wet zones. Today it is used to flavor everything from pickles to pipe tobaccos.

Cinnamon has many medical properties. It stimulates the digestive juices and has antiseptic properties. In China, a Taoist writer and alchemist of the fourth century AD wrote that if one took cinnamon along with the brains of toads for seven years a person could walk on water and avoid ageing and death! This hypothesis has not been tested. But studies do show that cinnamon stimulates insulin activity and thus helps the body process sugars more efficiently. Researchers found that three spices and one herb actually tripled insulin activity—cinnamon, cloves, turmeric and bay leaves, with cinnamon being the most powerful. Thus, cinnamon is an excellent spice to add to sweet desserts. SWF

PUMPKIN PIE
Serves 8

1 recipe flaky pie crust (page 557)
1 15-ounce can pumpkin purée
3 eggs
3/4 cup Rapadura (see page 536)
1 tablespoon freshly grated ginger
1 teaspoon cinnamon
1/4 teaspoon sea salt
1/4 teaspoon powdered cloves
1/4 teaspoon nutmeg
grated rind of 1 lemon
1 cup piima cream or creme fraiche (page 84)
2 tablespoons brandy (optional)

Line a 9-inch pie pan with flaky pie crust dough and pinch edge to make a border. Cream eggs with Rapadura. Gradually blend in other ingredients. Pour into pie shell and bake at 350 degrees for 35 to 45 minutes. Serve with whipped cream (page 541).

LEMON-ALMOND TART
Serves 8

1 recipe flaky pie crust (page 557)
3/4 cup crispy almonds (page 515)
3 eggs
3/4 cup Rapadura (see page 536)
grated rind of 3 lemons
3/4 cup lemon juice
4 tablespoons melted butter

Line a 10-inch French-style tart pan with flaky pie crust dough. In a food processor, process almonds into a fine powder. Add eggs and Rapadura and blend well. Blend in remaining ingredients. Pour into tart shell and bake at 350 degrees for 35 minutes.

Variation: Orange Tart
Use *rind and juice from 2 oranges* instead of lemons.

WALNUT TART
Serves 8

1 recipe flaky pie crust (page 557)
1 1/3 cup crispy walnuts (page 513)
4 tablespoons butter, melted
3/4 cup Rapadura (see page 536)
2 eggs
1 teaspoon coffee extract
2 tablespoons brandy (optional)
1 teaspoon vanilla extract
1/2 teaspoon sea salt

Line a 10-inch French-style tart pan with flaky pie crust dough. Process walnuts in food processor to a fine powder. Add remaining ingredients and process until smooth. Pour into tart shell and bake at 350 degrees for about 40 minutes.

Variation: Pecan Tart
Use *1 1/3 cups crispy pecans (page 513)* in place of walnuts.

WHOLE PECAN TART
Serves 8

1 recipe flaky pie crust (page 557)
4 tablespoons butter, softened
3 eggs
1/2 cup Rapadura (see page 536)
2 tablespoons piima cream
    or creme fraiche (page 84)
grated rind of 1 lemon
1 tablespoon vanilla extract
1 tablespoon arrowroot
2 cups crispy pecans (page 513)

Line a 10-inch French-style tart pan with flaky pie crust dough. Cream butter with eggs and Rapadura. Beat in cultured cream, vanilla, lemon rind and arrowroot. Fold in pecan halves. Pour into tart shell and bake at 350 degrees for about 35-45 minutes.

The walnut is a versatile and nutritious nut containing notable amounts of minerals, such as iron, magnesium, phosphorus, potassium and zinc. In earlier times, walnut "milk" made from pulverized walnuts soaked in water was served in European households that had no cow. Walnuts also contain about 60 percent fat, including a high proportion of omega-3 linolenic acid. This essential fatty acid is often deficient in the American diet, but its three double carbon bonds make it extremely susceptible to rancidity. You should therefore ideally only use walnuts that you have shelled yourself. Freshly shelled walnuts may be stored in the freezer. Fresh walnut oil, properly extracted and stored, is delicious and nutritious on salads but should never be heated. SWF

Western medicine and science has only just begun to sound alarm signals over the fantastic increase in per capita sugar consumption, in the United States especially. Their researches and warnings are, I fear, many decades too late. . . . I am confident that Western medicine will one day admit what has been known in the Orient for years: sugar is without question the number one murderer in the history of humanity— much more lethal than opium or radioactive fallout—especially to those people who eat rice as their principal food. Sugar is the greatest evil that modern industrial civilization has visited upon countries of the Far East and Africa. . . foolish people who give or sell candy to babies will one day discover, to their horror, that they have much to answer for. Sakurazawa Nyoiti
You Are All Sanpaku

In the 1940's, Dr. John Tintera rediscovered the vital importance of the endocrine system (especially the adrenal glands) in "pathological mentation"—or brain boggling. . . . Tintera published several epochal medical papers. Over and over he emphasized that improvement, alleviation, palliation or cure was "dependent upon the restoration of the normal function of the total organism." His first prescribed item of treatment was diet. Over and over again he said: "The importance of diet cannot be overemphasized." He laid out a sweeping permanent injunction against sugar in all forms and guises.

While Egas Moniz of Portugal was receiving a Nobel prize for devising the lobotomy operation for the treatment of schizophrenia, Tintera's reward was to be harassment and hounding by the pundits of organized medicine. William Dufty *Sugar Blues*

The mind truly boggles when one glances over what passes for medical history. Through the centuries troubled souls have been barbecued for bewitchment, exorcised for possession, locked up for insanity, tortured for masturbatory madness, psychiatrized for psychoses, lobotomized for schizophrenia.

How many patients would have listened if the local healer had told them that the only thing ailing them was sugar blues? William Dufty *Sugar Blues*

LEMON MERENGUE PIE
Serves 8

1 recipe flaky pie crust (page 557),
  lining a 9-inch pie plate and partially baked
grated rind of 2 lemons
1/2 cup lemon juice
3/4 cup maple syrup
4 tablespoons arrowroot mixed with
  6 tablespoons water
3 egg yolks
1 tablespoon butter
3 egg whites, at room temperature
pinch of sea salt
1/4 cup Rapadura (see page 536)
1/2 teaspoon vanilla extract

Place lemon rind, lemon juice, maple syrup and arrowroot mixture in a pan. Cook over medium heat, stirring constantly with a whisk, until mixture thickens. Let cool slightly and beat in egg yolks and butter. Meanwhile, beat egg whites with a pinch of sea salt in a clean bowl until softly stiff. Beat in vanilla and Rapadura. Pour lemon filling into partially baked pie crust and carefully cover with beaten egg whites. Bake at 325 degrees for about 20 minutes.

APPLE PIE
Serves 8

1 recipe flaky pie crust (page 557)
8-10 tart apples, peeled, cored and cut into chunks
2 tablespoons arrowroot powder
2 tablespoons Rapadura (see page 536)
grated rind of 1 lemon
1 teaspoon cinnamon

Line a 9-inch pie pan with flaky pie crust dough, reserving remaining pastry for the top of the pie. Mix arrowroot, Rapadura, cinnamon and lemon peel. Fill pie with apples, sprinkling arrowroot mixture on each layer. Cover pie with remaining pastry and pinch edges together. Poke a few holes in the pastry and bake for about 45 minutes at 375 degrees.

PEAR CUSTARD TART

Serves 8

1 recipe flaky pie crust (page 557) in a 12-inch
French-style tart pan, fully baked
4 ripe pears
1/4 cup fresh lemon juice
1/4 cup honey or maple syrup
1 quart filtered water
3 egg yolks
1/4 cup maple syrup
2 teaspoons vanilla extract
1 cup heavy cream, not ultrapasteurized
1 cup seedless naturally sweetened
blackberry jam
2 tablespoons pear liqueur

This is a complicated recipe but the results are wonderful. The pie crust, pastry cream, poached pears and jam should all be prepared in advance and well chilled. Assemble the tart just before serving.

Peel pears, cut in half lengthwise, core and immediately brush with lemon juice. Bring water to a boil with 1/4 cup honey or maple syrup and vanilla. Add pears and simmer, covered, for about 10 minutes until soft. Carefully transfer to a bowl, cover with cooking liquid and chill well.

Meanwhile, combine cream, 1/4 cup maple syrup and vanilla in a saucepan and bring to a boil. Remove from heat and allow to cool slightly. Place egg yolks in the top of a double boiler and beat for several minutes until pale. Over a low flame, add the cream mixture very gradually, stirring constantly until the mixture thickens and becomes almost too hot to touch. Remove from heat and chill well.

Place jam and pear liqueur in a saucepan, bring to a boil and cook several minutes, stirring constantly. Chill well.

To assemble, drain pear halves and pat them dry. Arrange in a ring on tart shell, cored side down. Spread pastry cream over pears and place a spoonful of jam mixture on each. Serve at once.

Man-refined sugar was introduced to Japan when the Christian missionaries arrived after the U.S. Civil War. At first, the Japanese used refined sugar in the way the Arabs and Persians had used it centuries before: as a medicine. Sugar was taxed as severely as imported patented medicines. By 1906, 45,000 acres of sugar cane were cultivated in Japan, compared with 7 million acres devoted to the cultivation of rice. Interestingly enough, in its war with Russia in 1905, the Japanese armed forces carried their own food in much the same way as the Viet Cong in the 1970's. Each man had enough dried rice to keep him going for three days. This was supplemented with salt fish, dried seaweed and pickled umeboshi plums. William Dufty *Sugar Blues*

The difference between sugar addiction and narcotic addiction is largely one of degree. Small quantities of narcotics can change body-brain behavior quickly. Sugars take a little longer, from a matter of minutes in the case of a liquid, simple sugar alcohol to a matter of years in sugars of other kinds.

The enduring American fantasy of the dope pusher—imbedded in law and myth—is a slimy degenerate hanging around school playgrounds passing out free samples of expensive addictive substances to innocent kids. This fantasy devil was created at the turn of the century by and for a country of booze and sugar addicts with an enduring nostalgia for the friendly country store where so many of them got *their* habit. William Dufty *Sugar Blues*

Refined sugar is lethal when ingested by humans because it provides only that which nutritionists describe as empty or naked calories. In addition, sugar is worse than nothing because it drains and leeches the body of precious vitamins and minerals through the demands its digestion, detoxification, and elimination make upon one's entire system.

So essential is balance to our bodies that we have many ways to provide against the sudden shock of a heavy intake of sugar. Minerals, such as sodium (from salt), potassium and magnesium (from vegetables) and calcium (from the bones) are mobilized and used in chemical transmutation; neutralizing acids are produced, which attempt to return the acid-alkaline balance factor of the blood to a more normal state. Sugar taken every day produces a continuously overacid condition, and more and more minerals are required from deep in the body in the attempt to rectify the imbalance. Finally, in order to protect the blood, so much calcium is taken from the bones and teeth that decay and general weakening begin. William Dufty *Sugar Blues*

Her majesty's government, with its vested interest in both slavery and sugar, spoke loftily of the Empire. Britain was the center of the sugar industry of the entire world. "The pleasure, glory and grandeur of England has been advanced more by sugar than by any other commodity, wool not excepted," said Sir Dalby Thomas. "The impossibility of doing without slaves in the West Indies will always prevent the traffic being dropped." William Dufty *Sugar Blues*

APPLE TART
Serves 8

1 recipe flaky pie crust (page 557) in a
*   12-inch French-style tart pan, fully baked*
8 tart apples
1/2 cup butter
1/2 cup Rapadura (see page 536)

Peel and core apples and cut into chunks. In a heavy skillet, sauté apples in butter until golden. Add Rapadura and sauté a few minutes more. Pour into baked tart shell. Serve with whipped cream (page 541).

ALL-RAW CHEESE CAKE
Serves 12-16

2 cups crispy almonds (page 515)
1 cup pitted dates
4 cups homemade cream cheese (page 87), softened
4 eggs, separated, at room temperature
1 1/4 cups milk, preferably raw
2 tablespoons gelatin
1/2 cup raw honey
1 tablespoon vanilla
pinch sea salt

In a food processor, process dates and almonds until they form a sticky mass. Press into a buttered 9-inch by 13-inch pyrex pan to form a crust.

Put egg yolks and milk in a sauce pan, beat lightly, sprinkle with gelatin and warm slightly until gelatin is dissolved. In a food processor, combine cream cheese, honey and vanilla and process until smooth. Add yolk mixture and process until smooth. Transfer to a bowl and place in refrigerator while beating eggs. Beat egg whites with a pinch of salt until stiff, fold into cream-cheese mixture and pour into crust. Chill several hours before serving.

ORANGE CAKE
Serves 12-18

2 1/2 cups freshly ground and sifted
    spelt, kamut or whole wheat flour
1 cup piima cream or creme fraiche (page 84)
1 cup whole plain yoghurt (page 85)
1/2 cup water
1 cup butter, softened
1 1/4 cups Rapadura (see page 536)
2 eggs
1 teaspoon baking soda
1/2 teaspoon sea salt
1 teaspoon vanilla extract
grated rind of 2 oranges and 2 lemons
1 cup crispy pecans, finely chopped (page 513)
juice of 2 oranges and 2 lemons
1/4 cup whey (page 87)
1/2 cup raw honey
1/4 cup brandy or dry sherry (optional)

This delicious cake incorporates the principles of both lacto-fermentation and enzyme nutrition. The flour is soaked in cultured cream and yoghurt and, after cooking, the cake is soaked for another day or so in a mixture of orange juice, lemon juice, raw honey, whey and brandy or sherry. This imparts enzymes to the cake along with flavor and moistness.

Mix flour with yoghurt, cultured cream and water. Cover and leave in a warm place for 12 to 24 hours. Cream butter with Rapadura and eggs. Beat in baking soda, salt, vanilla and grated rind. Gradually incorporate the soaked flour and fold in the nuts. Pour batter into a well-buttered and floured fluted bundt pan or angel food cake pan. Bake at 300 degrees for 1 1/2 hours or more, or until a toothpick comes out clean. Allow to cool. Place lemon juice, orange juice, honey, whey and optional sherry or brandy in a container and set in simmering water until honey is dissolved. Slowly pour this mixture over the cake until the liquid is absorbed. Cover with a towel and leave at room temperature for 1 or 2 days. To serve, loosen sides with a knife. Turn over onto a serving plate and tap pan until cake falls out.

CHRISTMAS DINNER

Duck and Chicken Liver Mousse

Round Croutons

Pickled Pearl Onions

Pickled Cucumber Slices

Rib Roast

Horseradish Sauce

Baked Tomatoes

Broccoli Timbales

Radicchio and Orange Salad

Orange Cake

It would be extraordinary if sugar and white flour, known to wreak havoc on the teeth, did not also have profound repercussions elsewhere in the body.

Coronary disease has heretofore been regarded as a "complication" of diabetes. Both coronary disease and diabetes have a common cause: White sugar and white flour. William Dufty *Sugar Blues*

Excess sugar eventually affects every organ in the body. Initially it is stored in the liver in the form of glucose (glycogen). Since the liver's capacity is limited, a daily intake of refined sugar (above the required amount of natural sugar) soon makes the liver expand like a balloon. When the liver is filled to its maximum capacity, the excess glycogen is returned to the blood in the form of fatty acids. These are taken to every part of the body and stored in the most inactive areas: the belly, the buttocks, the breasts and the thighs.

When these comparatively harmless places are completely filled, fatty acids are then distributed among active organs, such as the heart and kidneys, and these begin to slow down; finally their tissues degenerate and turn to fat. The whole body is affected by their reduced ability and abnormal blood pressure is created. . . the circulatory and lymphatic systems are invaded and the quality of the red corpuscles starts to change. An overabundance of white cells occurs, and the creation of tissue becomes slower . . . . Our body's tolerance and immunizing power becomes more limited, so we cannot respond properly to extreme attacks, whether they be cold, heat, mosquitoes or microbes. William Dufty *Sugar Blues*

POPPY SEED CAKE
Serves 8-10

1/4-1/3 cup poppy seeds
2 1/2 cups freshly ground spelt, kamut
*   or whole wheat flour*
1 cup piima cream or creme fraiche (page 84)
1 cup whole yoghurt (page 85)
1 cup butter, softened
1 1/4 cups Rapadura (see page 536)
2 eggs
1 teaspoon baking soda
1/2 teaspoon sea salt
grated rind of 1 lemon
1 tablespoon vanilla extract
1/4-1/2 cup water (optional)
juice of 1 lemon
1/4 cup whey (page 87)
1/2 cup raw honey
1/4 cup dry sherry (optional)

Mix flour and poppy seeds with yoghurt and cultured cream, cover and leave in a warm place for 12 to 24 hours. Cream butter with Rapadura and eggs. Beat in baking soda, salt, vanilla and grated rind. Gradually incorporate the soaked flour. Beat in 1/4 to 1/2 cup water to thin batter if necessary. Pour batter into a well-buttered and floured fluted bundt pan or angel food cake pan. Bake at 300 degrees for 1 1/2 hours or more, or until a toothpick comes out clean. Let cool slightly.

Place lemon juice, honey, whey and optional sherry in a container and set in simmering water until honey is dissolved. Slowly pour this mixture over the cake until all liquid is absorbed. Cover with plastic wrap and leave at room temperature for 1 or 2 days.

To serve, loosen sides with a knife. Turn over onto a serving plate and tap pan until cake falls out.

Variation: Irish Seed Cake
Use *1/4 cup caraway seeds* instead of poppy seeds and *rind and juice of 2 oranges* instead of 1 lemon. Omit water.

CARROT CAKE WITH CREAM CHEESE ICING

Serves 16-20

2 1/2 cups freshly ground spelt, kamut
    or whole wheat flour
1 cup piima cream or creme fraiche (page 84)
1 cup whole yoghurt (page 85)
1 cup butter, softened
1 1/4 cups Rapadura (see page 536)
4 eggs
2 teaspoons vanilla extract
2 teaspoons baking soda
1 teaspoon cinnamon
1 teaspoon sea salt
1 8-ounce can crushed pineapple, water packed
2 cups finely grated carrots
1 cup dried sweetened coconut meat (page 159)
    or commercial dried unsweetened coconut meat
1/2 cup crispy pecans, chopped (page 513)
2 cups cream cheese (page 87), softened
1/2 cup butter, softened
1 tablespoon vanilla
1/2-3/4 cup raw honey

Mix flour with yoghurt and cultured cream. Cover and leave for 12 to 24 hours in a warm place. Line a buttered 9-inch by 13-inch pyrex pan with buttered parchment paper (see Sources) and coat pan and parchment paper with unbleached flour. Cream butter with Rapadura. Beat in eggs, baking soda, cinnamon, vanilla and salt. Gradually add flour mixture. Fold in pineapple (with juice), carrots, coconut and nuts. Pour into pan and bake at 300 degrees for about 2 hours. Let cool slightly and turn onto a platter or tray.

To make icing, place cream cheese, butter, vanilla and honey in food processor and blend until smooth. Generously ice the top and sides of the cake. Decorate with flowers.

Variation: Stars and Stripes Cake

Use *blueberries* and *raspberries* to make an American flag on top of the cake.

It's a bit embarrassing to the lowfat people, as the truth is beginning to come out about vitamin A. A recent *New York Times* article noted that vitamin-A rich foods like liver, egg yolk, cream and shell fish confer resistance to infectious disease in children and prevent cancer in adults. A *Washington Post* article hailed vitamin A as "cheap and effective, with wonders still being (re)discovered," noting that recent studies have found that vitamin A supplements help prevent infant mortality in Third World countries . . . . Serious students of nutrition know that foods rich in vitamin A, like liver, eggs, and cod liver oil, are vital to good health. If you—or your children—don't like liver, eggs and cod liver oil, don't despair. Studies show that the best and most easily absorbed source of vitamin A is butterfat, a food relished by young and old alike. So use butter and cream liberally for good taste and wise nutritional practice. *Vitamin A Vagary*

In his comprehensive study. . . . Dr. Roberts concluded that a "significant source" of many unexplainable [automobile] accidents is that "millions of American drivers are subject to pathological drowsiness and hypoglycemia due to functional hyperinsulinism." He estimates that there may be as many as ten million drivers like that on the roads of America today. In other words, low glucose levels in the blood gum up brain functioning, perceptions and reactions. What causes this condition? The doctor's answer: "The apparent increased incidence of hyperinsulinism and of narcolepsy [abnormal attacks of drowsiness] during recent decades can be largely attributed to the consequences of an enormous rise in sugar consumption by a vulnerable population." William Dufty *Sugar Blues*

Food quality is first determined upon the farm by the way we interact with nature and its forces. The profit motivation does not lead to quality food production. This thesis can be proved by looking into the history of modern farming in the last 100 years and into the state of affairs with our processed foods. Farming differs here from the production and marketing of industrial goods. You cannot sell cars that have grave deficiencies for very long, but you can deceive mankind for a long time with deficient food. The consequences of a deficient car show up very rapidly, but the effects of deficient food—nicely colored and flavored with artificial ingredients—are much harder to discern and turn up mainly in the soul life of humanity or in the health problems of old age. Trauger Groh and Steven McFadden *Farms of Tomorrow Revisited*

Dr. Yudkin reports another recent experiment which pointed the other way. He persuaded seven young men each to swallow a tube first thing in the morning so that samples could be obtained of their gastric juices at rest; then, at fifteen minute intervals—after they had swallowed a bland test meal consisting mainly of pectin—further samples were taken. Samples were analyzed in the usual way, measuring the degree of acidity and digestive activity. Then the patients were put on a high-sugar diet for two weeks and tested again. Results showed that two weeks of a sugar-rich diet was enough to increase both stomach acidity and digestive activity of the gastric juices, of the kind one finds in people with gastric or duodenal ulcers. The rich diet of sugar increased stomach acidity by 20 percent or so and the enzyme activity was increased almost three times. William Dufty *Sugar Blues*

SPICE CAKE WITH BUTTER CREAM ICING
Serves 8-10

1/2 cup whole yoghurt (page 85)
1/2 cup butter, softened
1/4 teaspoon sea salt
1 1/2 cup bulgur flour (page 461)
1/4 cup water
1 cup Rapadura (see page 536)
1 teaspoon vanilla extract
1 teaspoon cinnamon
1 teaspoon ground ginger
1/2 teaspoon ground nutmeg
1/8 teaspoon ground cloves
1/4 teaspoon ground white pepper
2 teaspoons baking soda
4 egg whites, at room temperature
 pinch of sea salt
1 cup Rapadura (see page 536)
2 teaspoons vanilla extract
3/4 cup butter, softened

This is a moist cake composed of two thin layers and a rich butter icing. Blend yoghurt, butter, flour, salt and water. Beat in Rapadura, vanilla, spices and baking soda until dough is very smooth. Line two buttered 8-inch cake pans with rounds of parchment paper (see Sources). Butter the parchment paper and dust the pans with unbleached white flour. Divide the batter between the two pans, spread to fill the pans and bake at 300 degrees for about 1 hour. Loosen the layers immediately, but let layers cool before removing from pans. Carefully trim off any rough edges.

To make the icing, beat butter until smooth and creamy. In a very clean bowl, beat the egg whites with a pinch of salt until they form stiff peaks. Gradually beat in Rapadura and vanilla. Spoonful by spoonful beat in the butter. Chill well.

Assemble the cake on a decorative plate, applying icing between the layers and to the top and sides.

WALNUT TORTE WITH WHIPPED CREAM ICING

Serves 8-10

1 cup crispy walnuts (page 513)
1/4 cup Rapadura (see page 536)
6 large egg whites, at room temperature
pinch sea salt
1/2 cup Rapadura
1 teaspoon vanilla extract
2 cups good quality cream, not ultrapasteurized
1/2 cup piima cream or creme fraiche (page 84)
1/2 cup Rapadura (see page 536)
grated rind of 1 lemon
1/2 teaspoon vanilla extract
1 cup fresh berries, for garnish (optional)

This makes a three-layer rectangular merengue or torte, filled and iced with whipped cream icing.

Draw three 9-inch by 5-inch rectangles on parchment paper. (See Sources.) Turn over and place on baking sheets. Butter or oil the paper.

Process walnuts and 1/4 cup Rapadura in a food processor. Beat egg whites with a pinch of sea salt until foamy. Gradually add 1/2 cup Rapadura, beating until stiff and glossy. Beat in 1 teaspoon vanilla. Carefully fold in half the ground walnut mixture and then the other half. Spread merengue over the traced rectangles. Bake at 300 degrees for 1 1/2 hours. Turn oven off and leave merengues in the oven for another 1 hour.

To make the icing, place whipping cream, cultured cream, Rapadura, lemon rind and 1/2 teaspoon vanilla extract in a bowl and beat until stiff peaks form.

To assemble the torte, carefully trim any rough edges off the merengues. Assemble on a decorative plate, applying icing between the layers and over the top and sides. Decorate with optional berries. Chill well and serve.

The finding that an increased intake of polyunsaturated fatty acids, also called PUFA, can lower the serum cholesterol concentration in laboratory experiments has led to the belief that they would lower the risk of coronary heart disease also. Consequently, an increased intake of PUFA has been advised as an important part of the prudent diet. Initially, no limit was put to such intake, but by the years the limit has been lowered successively. Most recently, an upper limit of only 7 cal% was recommended because a high intake of PUFA has induced cancer, infections and testicular damage in rats.

There is little evidence that an increased intake of PUFA protects against heart attacks. In "Seven Countries," intake of PUFA was not associated with heart mortality, and studies of patients with coronary heart disease have shown that if anything, they eat more PUFA than do healthy individuals. Uffe Ravnskov, MD, PhD *The Cholesterol Myths*

The American Dietetic Association, which trains registered dieticians to direct the preparation of hospital and institutional food, has been soundly criticized for its association with the Sugar Association and companies like Coca Cola and M&M Mars. Such groups supply about 15 percent of the ADA's annual budget. A recent ADA nutrition fact sheet, which stated that people were not more likely to respond to MSG than to a placebo, was financed by an MSG manufacturer. The ADA has also actively promoted the use of margarine and polyunsaturated oils. *PPNF Health Journal*

"No cask of sugar arrives in Europe to which blood is not sticking. In view of the misery of these slaves, anyone with feelings should renounce these wares and refuse the enjoyment of what is only to be bought with tears and death of countless unhappy creatures."

Thus wrote French philosopher Claude Adrien Helvetius in the middle of the eighteenth century when France had moved into the front ranks of the sugar trade. The Sorbonne condemned him. Priests persuaded the court he was full of dangerous ideas; he recanted—in part to save his skin—and his book was burned by hangmen. The virulence of his attacks on slavery brought his ideas to the attention of all Europe. He said in public what many people thought in secret.

The stigma of slavery was on sugar everywhere but most particularly in Britain. Everywhere sugar had become a source of public wealth and national importance. Through taxes and tariffs on sugar, government had remained a partner in organized crime. Fabulous fortunes were being amassed by plantation owners, planters, traders and shippers; and the sole concern of European royalty was how they were to take their cut. William Dufty *Sugar Blues*

FLOURLESS CAROB CAKE
Serves 8

3/4 cup carob powder
1/2 cup plus 1 tablespoon butter
3 tablespoons water
1 tablespoon vanilla extract
1 tablespoon chocolate extract (optional)
5 egg yolks, at room temperature
1/2 cup Rapadura (see page 536)
5 egg whites, at room temperature
pinch of sea salt
1 cup carob sauce (page 550)

This is a delicious, moist and rich cake—indistinguishable from chocolate. (Well, almost.)

Butter and flour two easy-remove 9-inch cake pans. Place butter, carob powder, water and extracts in a glass container set in a pan of water over a low flame. Melt and blend well. Beat egg yolks with Rapadura for about 5 minutes with electric beater. In a clean bowl, beat egg whites with pinch of salt until stiff. Mix carob mixture with egg yolk mixture and then fold into egg whites. Divide batter between two pans. Bake at 350 degrees for about 25 minutes. Let cool completely before removing from pans. Remove one layer to a serving dish and place other layer on top. Frost top with carob sauce and let it dribble over the sides.

FLOURLESS ALMOND CAKE

Serves 8-12

4 egg yolks, at room temperature
1/2 cup Rapadura (see page 536)
grated rind of 1 lemon
1 teaspoon almond extract
1 cup finely grated carrots
1 cup crispy almonds (page 515),
     processed into a coarse meal
1 tablespoon arrowroot
1/2 teaspoon sea salt
4 egg whites, at room temperature
pinch of sea salt
2 tablespoons crispy pine nuts (page 514)

Butter and flour a 9-inch easy-remove cake pan. Beat egg yolks with Rapadura for about 5 minutes. Blend in lemon rind, almond extract, carrots, almonds, arrowroot and sea salt. In a clean bowl, beat egg whites with pinch of sea salt until stiff. Fold egg yolk mixture into egg whites and pour into cake pan. Sprinkle pine nuts on top. Bake at 350 degrees for about 45 minutes. Let cool completely before removing from pan.

BREAD AND RICE CAKE

Serves 8

3/4 cup basic brown rice (page 466)
3 slices whole grain bread, crumbled by hand
1 cup piima cream or creme fraiche (page 84)
1/2 cup raisins
4 tablespoons butter, melted
1/2 cup chopped crispy pecans (page 513)
3 eggs
3/4 cup Rapadura (see page 536)
grated rind of 1 orange
2 tablespoons brandy

Soak crumbled bread with cream. Using a wooden spoon, mix all ingredients. Pour into a buttered 9-inch easy-remove cake pan. Bake at 350 degrees for 1 hour or more. Let cool before removing from pan.

[Throughout the Azores and the West Indies] enormous quantities of wood were consumed in building the many sugar mills and converting the cane into sugar. Mills failed if their owners did not have access to large amounts of timber because as Gonzalo Fernandez de Oviedo, who spent many years on Espanola, observed, "You cannot believe the quantities of wood they burn without seeing it yourself." Experts in West Indian sugar production estimated that from six to eight slaves had to be constantly employed in carrying fuel in the forest and transporting it to the mill for optimum efficiency. To provide fuel for one mill stripped about ninety acres of forest land each year. John Perlin *A Forest Journey*

Know Your Ingredients
Name This Product #42

Sugar, bleached flour, egg whites, pineapple, non-fat milk, water, wheat fiber, modified cornstarch, baking powder (sodium acid pyrophosphate, baking soda, monocalcium phosphate), mono- and diglycerides, dextrin, natural & artificial flavors, oat fiber, maltodextrin, corn syrup, salt, dextrose, lemon puree, potassium sorbate (a preservative), beta carotene, sodium stearoyl lactylate, xanthan gum, guar gum, citric acid.

See Appendix B for Answer

GOURMET DESSERTS

Downey considered that gelatin was recognized as a valuable addition to the dietary because of its easy digestion, ready absorption, protein-sparing ability and supplementary protein value. He also noted that gelatin aided in the digestion of other foods, especially milk and milk products, and served as a base for many attractive and appealing dishes. N. R. Gotthoffer *Gelatin in Nutrition and Medicine*

Sugar, which had up to about 1600 been extremely expensive and only used for making luxury confectionery for the very rich, had fallen in price dramatically when the seventeenth century trade with the East opened up and was freely available for such dishes as fruit tarts and puddings. One immediate result of this was that the teeth of the well-to-do, who could afford to eat large quantities of the new sugary dishes, began to show rapid signs of decay, especially as the custom of cleaning the teeth was not very common. The courtiers, always the first with new fashions, were inevitably also the first to display the stigmata of excessive sweet-eating: a visitor to England in 1598, Paul Hentzner, who saw Queen Elizabeth arriving at the royal Palace of Greenwich, remarked on her black teeth, "a defect the English seem subject to, from their too great use of sugar." Terence McLaughlin *A Diet of Tripe*

VANILLA BAVARIAN CREAM WITH BLACKBERRY SAUCE
Serves 12

1 tablespoon gelatin (see Sources)
1/2 cup water
4 egg yolks, at room temperature
1/2 cup maple syrup
1 tablespoon vanilla extract
4 egg whites, at room temperature
pinch of sea salt
2 cups heavy cream, preferably unpasteurized
1 12-ounce package frozen blackberries
1/2 cup maple syrup
1-2 cups water
fresh blackberries for garnish

Mix gelatin with water and dissolve over low heat. Place egg yolks, syrup and vanilla in food processor and process until smooth. With motor running, pour in gelatin mixture and process briefly. Place food processor bowl and its contents in refrigerator while completing next steps. In a clean bowl, beat the egg whites with pinch of sea salt until they form stiff peaks. In a separate bowl, beat the cream until softly stiff. Return food processor bowl with gelatin mixture to machine, scrape down sides and pulse briefly. Fold gelatin mixture into cream and this mixture into egg whites. Pour into individual molds and chill for several hours.

Meanwhile, place partially thawed berries and syrup in food processor and process until smooth. Add water to achieve desired consistency. (Sauce should not be too thick.)

To serve, dip molds briefly in hot water and invert onto soup plates. Spoon sauce around molded Bavarian cream and decorate with blackberries.

HAZELNUT SHORTCAKE

Serves 8

1 1/2 cups crispy hazelnuts (page 514)
1 cup arrowroot
1/2 teaspoon sea salt
1/2 cup butter, softened
1/2 cup Rapadura (see page 536)
1 teaspoon vanilla extract
3 cups fresh berries, such as strawberries,
    blueberries, blackberries or raspberries
2 cups whipped cream (page 541)

Process hazelnuts in food processor to a fine meal. Add arrowroot, butter, salt, Rapadura and vanilla and process until well blended. Butter and flour a 12-inch French-style tart pan and press dough into the pan to make an even layer. Bake at 300 degrees for about 1/2 hour. Let cool. To serve, cut shortcake into wedges and top with fresh berries and whipped cream.

BERRY-CREAM CHEESE DELIGHT

Serves 8

2 cups homemade cream cheese (page 87)
1/2 cup raisins, soaked for 1 hour in water
grated rind of 2 lemons
1/2 cup cognac
1/4 cup raw honey
1 teaspoon cinnamon
3-4 cups fresh berries

Using a slotted spoon, transfer the soaked raisins to a pan. Add cognac and lemon rind and simmer for about 10 minutes. Mix cream cheese with honey and cinnamon in food processor. Blend in cognac and raisins with a wooden spoon. Line a strainer with a linen towel and place cream cheese mixture into the cloth. Tie into a bag, being careful not to squeeze, and hang the bag over a bowl to drain for several hours.

To serve, place 1/2 cup cream cheese mixture in eight individual bowls and place berries on top.

A study from the Netherlands has found that people older than 85 live longer if their cholesterol level is higher than "normal." More than 700 elderly residents of the town of Leiden had their cholesterol levels measured 10 years ago. In the ensuing decade, a majority died as expected, but the death rate for the people with a cholesterol reading higher than 251 was 44 percent lower than that of those whose cholesterol levels were below 194. The explanation is that cholesterol is not an enemy but a friend — the body's repair substance, a potent antioxidant and precursor to many important substances including vitamin D, bile salts for digesting fats and the whole family of protective steroid hormones. *PPNF Health Journal*

The startling interest in Viagra, a new drug that increases sexual potency in men, indicates that a huge number of American men are not satisfied with their sexual performance. Clues to the underlying cause come from the massive MRFIT study, in which men were encouraged to make substantial reductions in their fat intake. When fat intake was cut back, testosterone levels went down. Men with type A behavior—driven, aggressive, combative types—also show a greater decline in testosterone levels as they grow older. Could it be that lowfat, low-cholesterol diets cause men to be "driven, aggressive and combative," and then burn out by middle age? *PPNF Health Journal*

Defenders of pasteurization make little of enzymes and report that a large number of enzymes are completely destroyed in the process of pasteurization. They attribute little importance to this and point out that the complete destruction of the enzyme phosphatase is one method of testing to see if the milk has been adequately pasteurized. Phosphatase is essential for the absorption of calcium, *but the complete destruction of phosphatase is the aim of pasteurization!* William Campbell Douglass MD *The Milk Book*

SUET PUDDING
Serves 8

1/2 pound (1 packed cup) beef suet, grated
1 cup Rapadura (see page 536)
3 eggs
1 cup dark beer or ale
1 cup dates, finely chopped
1 cup dried pineapple, finely chopped
1 cup dried currants
1 cup crispy walnuts or pecans, chopped (page 513)
2 teaspoons grated orange rind
1 teaspoon ground ginger
1/4 teaspoon nutmeg
1/4 teaspoon sea salt
2 cups whole grain bread crumbs
2 teaspoons baking powder
2-3 tablespoons brandy

Beat suet with Rapadura to form a smooth paste. Beat in eggs and dark beer or ale. Stir in remaining ingredients except brandy. Pour pudding into a well buttered 6-cup ceramic bowl or mold and cover with 2 layers of greased parchment paper (see Sources), secured with a rubber band or string. To steam, place in a pan of simmering water with water coming one-third up the side of the mold. Steam for 5 hours, adding more water as needed. Allow to cool, remove parchment paper and pour brandy over the pudding. Cover again with ungreased parchment paper, secured with a rubber band or string, and keep in a cool, dry place for several days to several weeks. To serve, steam again for 2 hours, unmold onto a plate and serve with brandy butter.

BRANDY BUTTER
Makes 1 cup

1 cup butter, softened
1 cup Rapadura (see page 536)
4 tablespoons brandy

Beat butter until soft and light. Gradually beat in Rapadura and rum. Place in a bowl and chill.

BAKED PEARS

Serves 8

8 whole pears
1/2 cup lemon juice
1 cup red wine
1/2 cup honey or maple syrup
1/2 cup sweet cream sauce (page 578), optional

Combine lemon juice, wine and honey or syrup in a small pan. Bring to a simmer. Peel pears and core from the bottom end. Set on sides in a buttered pyrex dish and pour the wine mixture over them. Bake at 350 degrees for about 1/2 hour, turning and basting frequently. Carefully remove pears to a bowl and chill well. Meanwhile, pour syrup into a small saucepan and boil down until it thickens. Let cool.

To serve, place pears on individual plates and spoon sauce over. For a more elegant presentation, place pears on individual plates and place one large spoonful of thickened sauce on one side of the pear and one large spoonful of optional sweet cream sauce on the other side of the pear. Let the two sauces run together slightly for an interesting pattern.

Variation: Baked Peaches

Use *8 fresh peaches* instead of pears.

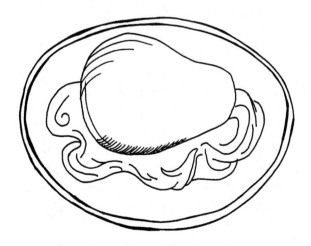

The pear is a relative of the apple and a native to the temperate regions of Europe and Asia. Pears are good sources of fiber and contain phosphorus and carotenoids as well as ellagic acid, a substance that protects against cancer. The ancient Chinese valued the pear for treatment of the stomach and lungs.

There are many delicious varieties of pears. The best for poaching and baking purposes are the bartletts. SWF

Know Your Ingredients
Name This Product #44

(Filling) milk, sugar, nonfat dry milk, corn syrup, microcrystalline cellulose, mono and diglycerides, natural and artificial flavor, sodium carboxymethylcellulose, guar gum, locust (carob) bean gum, polysorbate 80, carrageenan, salt (Wafer) enriched bleached flour (contains niacin, reduced iron, thiamine mononitrate, and riboflavin), sugar, mono- and diglycerides (with BHA and citric acid), caramel color, dextrose, polydextrose, corn syrup, glycerine, leavening (sodium bicarbonate, sodium acid pyrophosphate), calcium sulfate, cocoa, cellulose fiber, food starch-modified, salt, water, artificial flavor, artificial color including FD&C yellow No. 6, sodium bisulfate.

See Appendix B for Answer

Lasby and Palmer. . . found the bones of rats fed on raw milk had a slightly higher percentage of ash and a slightly higher content in calcium and phosphorus than the bones of rats fed on pasteurized milk. Edward Howell, MD *Food Enzymes for Health and Longevity*

Know Your Ingredients

Name This Product #45

86% water, 4.8% corn syrup, 2.5% sucrose, 2.1% soy oil, 2.0% soy protein isolate, 1.4% coconut oil, 0.14% calcium citrate, 0.13% calcium phosphate tribasic, potassium citrate, potassium phosphate monobasic, potassium chloride, mono- and diglycerides, soy lecithin, magnesium chloride, carrageenan, ascorbic acid, l-methionine, potassium phosphate dibasic, sodium chloride, choline chloride, taurine, ferrous sulfate, m-inositol, alpha-tocopherol acetate, zinc sulfate, l-carnitine, niacinamide, calcium pantothenate, cupric sulfate, vitamin A palmitate, thiamine chloride hydrochloride, riboflavin, pyridoxine hydrochloride, folic acid, manganese sulfate, potassium iodide, phylloquinone, biotin, sodium selenite, vitamin D3 and cyanocobalamin.

See Appendix B for Answer

SWEET CREAM SAUCE
(Creme Anglaise)
Makes 3 cups

2 cups heavy cream, preferably raw,
    not ultrapasteurized
1/2 cup maple syrup or honey
1 tablespoon grated ginger, optional
1 tablespoon vanilla extract
5 large egg yolks

Combine cream, syrup or honey, optional ginger and vanilla in a bowl. Heat until quite warm, but not burning, to the touch by placing the bowl in a pan of simmering water. Meanwhile, place egg yolks in a double boiler and beat for several minutes until pale. Over a low flame, add the warm cream mixture to yolks very gradually, stirring constantly, until the mixture thickens slightly. Chill well. Serve with fresh berries or other fruit.

POACHED PEARS WITH CAROB SAUCE
(Poires Belle Helene)
Serves 8

8 ripe pears
1/2 cup fresh lemon juice
1/2 cup honey or maple syrup
1-2 quarts filtered water
1 tablespoon vanilla extract
2 1/2 cups warm carob sauce (page 550)
1 cup crispy almond slivers (page 515), toasted

Peel pears, cut in half lengthwise, core and immediately brush with lemon juice. Bring water to a boil with honey and vanilla. Add pears and simmer, covered, for about 10 minutes until soft. Carefully transfer to a bowl, cover with cooking liquid and chill well.

To serve, remove pears from liquid, pat dry and place two halves on individual serving plates. Spoon carob sauce over them and sprinkle with almonds.

BERRY GRATIN

Serves 6

6 cups mixed berries
3 cups sweet cream sauce (page 578)
3 tablespoons Rapadura (see page 536)

Arrange berries on six flameproof dishes and place 1/2 cup sweet cream sauce on each. Sprinkle with Rapadura. Place under broiler for 3 or 4 minutes until Rapadura melts. Serve immediately.

SUMMER FRUIT COMPOTE

Serves 8

1 1/2 cups filtered water
3 tablespoons honey
4-inch stick of cinnamon
freshly ground nutmeg
4 medium pears, peeled and quartered
4 medium peaches, peeled and quartered
2 cups dark cherries, pitted and halved
1 1/2 cups sweet cheese topping (page 541)

In a medium saucepan bring water to boil with honey, cinnamon and nutmeg. Add fruit and simmer, covered, for 3 minutes. Remove fruit to a bowl and chill in refrigerator. Remove cinnamon stick and reduce sauce to about one-third by boiling down. Let cool, pour over fruit and chill well. To serve, place fruit in individual bowls and top with sweet cheese topping.

[In order to beat Britain's sugar blockade] Benjamin Delassert found a way to process the lowly Babylonian beet into a new kind of sugar loaf at Plassy in 1812. Napoleon awarded him the Legion of Honor. Napoleon ordered sugar beets planted everywhere in France; an imperial factory was established for refining; scholarships were granted to schools for starting courses in sugar beet crafts; 500 licenses were created for sugar refineries. By the very next year, Napoleon had achieved the herculean feat of producing eight million pounds of sugar from homegrown beets. When Napoleonic armies set out for Moscow, their sugar rations were ensured. Like the Moors before them, they were turned back while traveling north. The mighty French army, in the unaccustomed climate, had met their match and more, including the armies of a backward people who had not yet accustomed themselves to sugar in their tea. William Dufty *Sugar Blues*

New evidence points a sharp finger at sugar as a food item that makes us grow older faster!

The quick rush of sugar into the bloodstream is probably what does it . . . . In much the same way as a steak turns brown and toughens on the barbecue grill, a reaction between sugar and protein called the "brown- ing effect"—sugar reacts with protein in human cells—occurs, particularly as human cells age. . . .

Aging seems to be accelerated when the body must cope with exces- sive sugar and is unable to do it—as in diabetes.

[Scientists] now feel that col- lagen, which glues our trillions of cells together, is affected by glucose, which acts upon DNA causing mutations in this genetic material that permit the start and spread of cancer. . . . Any sudden rush of glucose into the blood- stream—from a candy bar, a glass of orange juice, or a couple teaspoons of granulated sugar in the coffee— stresses the pancreas to produce more insulin. Excessive sugar making the rounds of the bloodstream brings about cross-linking and aging. James F. Scheer *Health Freedom News*

LEMON MOUSSE
Serves 6

6 egg yolks, at room temperature
1/2 cup raw honey
grated rind of 2 lemons
strained juice of 2 lemons
6 egg whites, at room temperature
pinch of sea salt
1/2 cup heavy cream, preferably raw,
*   not ultrapasteurized, well chilled*

Place egg yolks, honey, lemon rind and lemon juice in the top of a double boiler over simmering water. Whisk constantly for about 10 minutes until mixture thickens. Remove from heat and chill in refrigerator for about 1/2 hour. Beat cream until stiff. In a separate clean bowl, beat egg whites with sea salt until stiff. Fold lemon mixture into cream and then egg whites into cream mixture. Spoon into individual parfait glasses and chill well before serving.

Variation: Lime Mousse

Use *rind and juice of 3 limes* instead of lemons.

APRICOT SOUFFLE

Serves 4

1/2 pound dried unsulphured apricots,
*   cooked in water until tender*
2 tablespoons honey or Rapadura (see page 536)
2 egg yolks, at room temperature
2 tablespoons heavy cream, not ultrapasteurized
5 egg whites, at room temperature
pinch of sea salt

The secret to a successful desert soufflé is to make it in small quantities. This unusual soufflé will fill a quart-sized souffle dish or four smaller soufflé ramekins. If you double the recipe, use two quart-sized soufflé dishes, not one larger one.

Transfer cooked apricots with a slotted spoon to food processor and process with honey or Rapadura, egg yolks and cream. In a clean bowl, beat egg whites with pinch of salt until stiff. Fold in apricot mixture thoroughly, but as quickly and as lightly as possible. Pour into a buttered quart-sized soufflé dish or four smaller ones and bake at 350 degrees for about 25 minutes. Check progress by peeking though the oven window—not by opening the door. Serve immediately

Variation: Fruit Soufflé

Use *2 cups fresh berries or other fruit* instead of apricots. Sprinkle with *2 tablespoons Rapadura* and mash with a fork. Let stand about 1/2 hour. Meanwhile, blend honey, egg yolks and cream. Using a slotted spoon, transfer fruit to egg yolk mixture and fold in. Proceed with recipe.

The people of Hunza have lived in relative isolation high in the Himalaya Mountains for over 2,000 years, following a way of eating and thinking that has lengthened their lives and reduced their susceptibility to the diseases of civilized man. In this tiny country many Hunzas live to be over 100 year of age, physically healthy and mentally alert. Men in their 90's play polo and volleyball and father children. These sturdy people often walk over a hundred miles a day, go barefoot in the snow or swim in icy water. The mortality rate of infants is very low, and death usually comes to the very aged in their sleep with no specific cause. The whole body just finally wears out. The secret of their healthy life is found in their simple and natural diet, vigorous outdoor life and freedom from mental worry. These mountain dwellers eat little meat but large amounts of whole goat milk products. They also eat vegetables and fruits grown on their intricately terraced mountain sides, wheat cakes (*chapattis*) and mineral-rich, milky colored glacier water. They flavor their food with mint, salt, green pepper, ginger and curry. Herb tea, with salt, is enjoyed as well as grape wine. Apricots are very important in the Hunza diet. The fruit is dried and stored for winter use, and the oil extracted from the pits is used in cooking and is a major source of fat in their diet. Food is scarce so everyone eats sparingly. However, no one ever starves. There is no tooth decay, cancer or respiratory disease in Hunza. "Nutrition: The Appetite of Man" *PPNF*

MERENGUE MARVEL
Serves 10-12

12 egg whites, at room temperature
pinch sea salt
1/2 cup arrowroot powder
3/4 cup Rapadura (see page 536)
1 teaspoon vanilla extract
4 cups whipped cream (page 541)
2 tablespoons brandy (optional)
1 cup carob chips (page 517), chopped
1 cup crispy almond slivers (page 515), chopped

Draw two circles, about 11 or 12 inches in diameter, on parchment paper (see Sources) and cut them into rounds. Place each on a cookie sheet and butter them well.

In a very clean stainless steel or glass bowl, beat egg whites with pinch of salt until softly stiff. Gradually add the arrowroot while beating continuously. Gradually add the Rapadura while beating continuously. Add vanilla extract and beat a minute more. Divide the egg whites between the two rounds, spread to the edges and smooth the tops.

Bake at 150 degrees for about 12 hours or until completely dry and crisp. To avoid the merengues becoming stale, place each on a plate and cover tightly with plastic wrap until ready to assemble.

Shortly before serving, place one merengue on a decorative plate and spread with half the whipped cream. Sprinkle with 1 tablespoon optional brandy, 1/2 cup carob chips and 1/2 cup chopped almond slivers. Place second merengue on top and repeat with remaining whipped cream, brandy, carob chips and almond slivers.

Variation:
Use *2-3 cups blueberries or raspberries* in place of carob chips.

BEVERAGES

BEVERAGES

It is difficult to think of a popular beverage that is healthy—tea, coffee, soft drinks, alcoholic beverages and even fruit juice—all should be avoided because they contain caffeine, concentrated sugars or large amounts of alcohol. Our collection of beverages offers unique alternatives to all of these. They feature dilute fruit juices, seeds, nuts and yoghurt; all enhanced by the process of lacto-fermentation to make their nutrients more available and to supply lactic acid and *lactobacilli* to the intestinal tract. The heartier drinks made from grains and nuts qualify as foods; the others, as refreshing pick-me-ups and digestive aids. We offer the theory that the craving for both alcohol and soft drinks stems from an ancient collective memory of the kind of lacto-fermented beverages still found in traditional societies. These beverages give a lift to the tired body by supplying mineral ions depleted through perspiration and contribute to easy and thorough assimilation of our food by supplying *lactobacilli*, lactic-acid and enzymes.

A survey of popular ethnic beverages will show that the fermentation of grains and fruits to make refreshing and health-promoting drinks is almost universal. Usually these drinks are very mildly alcoholic, the result of a fermentation process that is both alcoholic (by the action of yeasts on sugars) and lactic acid forming (by the action of bacteria on sugars). Beers made from millet, corn, barley and wheat are ubiquitous: *tesquino*, an Aztec beer, is made from corn; *munkoyo*, a beer of Zambia containing less than 0.5 percent alcohol, is consumed in large quantities by young and old; *kaffir beer*, a thick brew made from millet with a very short shelf life, is the national drink of Blacks in South Africa; *chicha*, a beer used by the Incas during religious festivals, is made from little balls of dough that have been chewed to inoculate them with saliva; very mildly alcoholic beers made from rice are found throughout Asia; *kvass*, the Russian national drink made from various cereal grains and fruits, contains less than 1 percent alcohol and is used to treat the sick; a similar Middle European drink called *kiesel* is made from oats or rye. Wines and ciders made from fruits, such as grapes, bananas, apples, pears and watermelon, are also found throughout the world: *pulque*, a Mexican drink, is made from juice of a cactus plant; palm wine, found throughout tropical countries, contains less than 2% alcohol and is made from spontaneous fermentation of palm sap; natives of British Guyana make a drink called *fly* from sweet potatoes and cassava; and fermented tea is found throughout Asia and Europe. The American Indians made a drink from crushed soaked pecans while European peasants made a similar beverage from walnuts. In Colonial America we find spruce beer, brewed from spruce leaves and a variety of seeds and berries. The Indians taught the explorer Cartier that a similar beverage made from hemlock leaves would relieve the symptoms of scurvy. It was for the same reason that Washington included "one quart of spruce beer per day" in the rations of the Continental Army.

Although most of these traditional beverages were mildly alcoholic, we have found that alcoholic fermentation can be minimized by the addition of whey and a little sea salt to our beverage preparations. The results are pleasantly acidic drinks, sometimes slightly bubbly, with complex flavors, especially if allowed to age for several weeks or more. Be sure to use homemade whey (see page 87), not concentrated or powdered whey sold at health food stores. Use only Celtic sea salt for lacto-fermentation (see Sources).

The use of whey to make nutritious drinks is not so much an innovation as a revival of an ancient method found throughout the British Isles and probably in other European countries since very ancient times. Medical treatises written during the 17th and 18th centuries extol the virtues of whey-based drinks including "wine whey" (wine mixed with whey) and "whey whig" (a beverage made of whey flavored with herbs).

We also offer one grain-based drink in which the culture is a mixture of bacteria and yeasts derived from bread making. Such "small beer" (as opposed to alcoholic "strong beer") was consumed throughout Europe and the Middle East in earlier times.

Throughout the world, these lactic-acid-containing drinks have been valued for medicinal qualities including the ability to relieve intestinal problems and constipation, promote lactation, strengthen the sick and promote overall well-being and stamina. Above all, these drinks were considered superior to plain water in their ability to relieve thirst during physical labor. Modern research has discovered that liquids containing dilute sugars and electrolytes of minerals (mineral ions) are actually absorbed faster and retained longer than plain water. This research is used to promote commercial sports drinks that are merely high-sugar concoctions containing small amounts of electrolytes. But natural lactic-acid fermented drinks contain numerous valuable minerals in ionized form and a small amount of sugar, along with lactic acid and beneficial *lactobacilli*, all of which promote good health in many ways while at the same time cutting the sensation of thirst.

Both soft drinks and alcoholic beverages—and even plain water—are poor substitutes for these health-promoting beverages. Taken with meals they promote thorough and easy digestion of food; taken after physical labor they give a lift by replacing lost mineral ions in a way that renews rather than depletes the body's reserves. The day when every town in America produces its own distinctive lacto-fermented brew, made from the local products of woods and fields, will be the day when Americans see the dawning of a new age of good health and well-being, as well as a new era of economic vitality based on small-scale local production rather than on large-scale monopolistic control of the food-processing industry.

To make beverages you will need some 2-quart-sized glass containers with tops or lids that seal tightly. A juicer is needed for the production of grape cooler (page 588) and apple cider (page 587).

Now the sun and the wind were hotter and Laura's legs quivered while she made them trample the hay. She was glad to rest for the little times between the field and the stack. She was thirsty, then she was thirstier, and then she was so thirsty that she could think of nothing else. It seemed forever till ten o'clock when Carrie came lugging the jug half full.

Pa told Laura to drink first but not too much. Nothing was ever so good as that cool wetness going down her throat. At the taste of it she stopped in surprise and Carrie clapped her hands and cried out, laughing, "Don't tell, Laura, don't tell till Pa tastes it!"

Ma had sent them ginger-water. She had sweetened the cool well-water with sugar, flavored it with vinegar, and put in plenty of ginger to warm their stomachs so they could drink till they were not thirsty. Ginger-water would not make them sick, as plain cold water would when they were so hot. Such a treat made that ordinary day into a special day, the first day that Laura helped in the haying. Laura Ingalls Wilder *The Long Winter*

Modern ginger ale has two ancestors. One is ginger beer, brewed and bottled at home like root beer. A fermented, bubbly drink, it was sometimes alcoholic, mostly not. The other is ginger water or "switchel," as New Englanders called it, a nonalcoholic drink prepared for farmers during long, hot days of scything in the hayfields. By Laura Ingalls Wilder's day, ginger drinks were flavored with sugar rather than with natural sweeteners, such as maple syrup or honey; and the tart taste was obtained from vinegar rather than from lacto-fermentation. SWF

GINGER ALE
Makes 2 quarts

3/4 cup ginger, peeled and finely
*   chopped or grated*
1/2 cup fresh lime juice
1/4-1/2 cup Rapadura (see page 536)
2 teaspoons sea salt
1/4 cup whey (page 87)
2 quarts filtered water

This is a most refreshing drink, taken in small amounts with meals and as a pick-me-up after outside work in the sun.

Place all ingredients in a 2-quart jug. Stir well and cover tightly. Leave at room temperature for 2-3 days before transferring to the refrigerator. This will keep several months well chilled.

To serve, strain into a glass. Ginger ale may be mixed with carbonated water and is best sipped warm rather than gulped down cold.

RASPBERRY DRINK
Makes 2 quarts

2 12-ounce packages frozen raspberries
*   or 24 ounces fresh raspberries*
juice of 12 oranges
1/4-1/2 cup Rapadura (see page 536)
1/4 cup whey (page 87)
2 teaspoons sea salt
about 1 1/2 quarts filtered water

Place raspberries in food processor and blend until smooth. Mix in a large bowl with remaining ingredients. Cover with a cloth and leave at room temperature for 2-3 days. Skim any foam that may rise to top. Strain through a strainer lined with a tea towel. Pour into a 2-quart glass container, cover tightly and store in refrigerator.

APPLE CIDER
Makes about 1 gallon

about 4 dozen organic apples
1 heaping tablespoon sea salt
1/2 cup whey (page 87)

As it is becoming increasingly difficult to obtain unpasteurized apple juice, we recommend starting from scratch with organic apples. Wash the apples, cut into quarters, remove the cores and pass them through a juicer. A great deal of foam will rise to the top of the juice—remove as much of this as possible with a spoon. Strain the juice into a very clean large bowl and stir in salt and whey. Cover with a cloth and leave at room temperature for 3 days. Skim off any foam that may have risen to the top. Pour into two 2-quart-sized glass containers, cover tightly and refrigerate. Flavors will develop slowly over several weeks. The cider will eventually develop a rich buttery taste and may become slightly effervescent. The sediment will fall to the bottom of the containers and should remain there if the cider is poured out carefully.

ORANGINA
Makes 2 quarts

juice of 12 oranges
2 teaspoons sea salt
1/4 cup whey (page 87)
1/2 teaspoon orange extract
1 3/4 quarts filtered water

Place all ingredients in a 2-quart glass container and stir well. Cover tightly. Leave at room temperature for 2 days before transferring to refrigerator. In several days the juice will develop an interesting banana-like flavor. Stir before pouring.

Soviet cancer researchers determined to find out why, where and how this dread disease [cancer] had increased so dramatically following World War II. . . . There in the midst of dreadful cancer statistics two districts in the region of Perm, on the Kama River in the central western Ural mountains, stood out like neon lights. The districts of Solikamsk and Beresniki had hardly any cancer cases reported, and those few with cancer often turned out to be people who had only recently moved into the area from elsewhere. How could this be? Environmental conditions were not any better than other districts—in fact, the region had potassium, lead, mercury and asbestos mining with production facilities spewing plenty of pollution. In fact, trees in the area and fish in the Kama were dying.

. . . two teams of scientific investigators were set up, one in Solikamsk, the other in Beresniki. They probed into private lives and investigated and analyzed. In the end they were puzzled. . . the people of these two districts drank as much vodka as other Russians but did not seem to have the social drunkenness problems, nor the poor work record usually associate with drinking. The problem was finding an explanation for this curious improvement.

Then it happened that one of the scientific team leaders personally visited the home of a family selected to be studied. It was a warm summer day and the family was away—only an elderly "babushka" was at home. The old woman offered Dr. Molodyev a refreshing beverage. . . . It turned out that Dr. Grigoriev in Beresniki also stumbled across tea kvass at about the same time, and it was soon confirmed that nary a home in the region was without the fermenting crocks of kvass or kombucha. Tom Valentine *Search for Health*

Fruits contain protective substances, above all fiber and vitamin C. Berries (strawberries, raspberries, blackberries, gooseberries and cassis) are particularly rich. Grapes contain a phenol—ellagic acid—that reduces the effects of carcinogens. Johanna Brandt, author of a well-known book, cured herself of metastasized cancer with grapes and fasting. Her book contains numerous testimonies of other cancer victims who were cured by her method. Claude Aubert *Dis-Moi Comment Tu Cuisines*

In an American Cancer Society study of 78,000 women, those who consumed artificially sweetened foods gained more weight over a one-year period than those who consumed sugar sweetened products. In another study students were hungrier after drinking artificially sweetened liquids than sugared ones. If sugar is a substitute for "the sweet experience," then artificial sweeteners are a substitute for a substitute. It's like using counterfeit money to buy fake diamonds. David Marc *Nourishing Wisdom*

Know Your Ingredients
Name This Product #48

Water, sucrose, glucose syrup solids, citric acid, natural lemon flavor with other natural flavors, salt, sodium citrate, monopotassium phosphate, caramel color, ester gum, brominated vegetable oil.

See Appendix B for Answer

GRAPE COOLER
Makes 5-6 quarts

1 case organic red grapes, about 16 pounds,
1/2 cup whey (page 87)
1 tablespoon sea salt

This delicious and refreshing drink is an excellent substitute for wine, containing all the nutrients of grapes found in wine, including many enzymes, but none (or at least very little) of the alcohol.

Remove grapes from stems, wash well and pass through a juicer. Place liquid in a large bowl with salt and whey and stir well. (Reserve pulp to make natural yeast bread, page 492). Cover with a cloth and leave at room temperature for 3 days. Skim off any scum that may rise to the top and strain juice through a strainer lined with a tea towel. Store grape cooler in airtight glass containers in refrigerator. Delicious flavors will develop over time. Best served diluted—half water, half grape juice.

The sediment will fall to the bottom of the containers and should remain there if the grape cooler is poured out carefully. However, you may also filter the cooler again by pouring it through a strainer lined with a tea towel.

PUNCH
Makes 2 quarts

juice of 6-8 lemons
1/2 cup Rapadura (see page 536)
1/2 cup whey (page 87)
1/2 teaspoon grated nutmeg
2 quarts filtered water

Punch comes from the Hindu word meaning "five," because it was made with five ingredients. During colonial days in America, the five ingredients were water, sugar, lemons, tea and liquor. The earliest description, in a poem thought to have been written by Samuel Mather in 1757, calls for water, sugar, lemon juice, grated nutmeg and a small amount of "spirit." We substitute Rapadura (which was the type of sugar used in India) for sugar and whey (which would have been readily available in India) for "spirit." The result is a delicious nonalcoholic fermented drink—a kind of Hindu lemonade.

Place all ingredients in a 2-quart glass container. Cover tightly and leave at room temperature for 2-3 days. Skim off any foam that may have risen to the top. Cover tightly and refrigerate. The punch will develop more flavor over time.

ROOT BEER
Makes 2 quarts

3-4 cups sassafras root shavings
1/4 cup whey (page 87)
1 teaspoon sea salt
1/2 cup Rapadura (see page 536)
1/4 cup molasses
1/2 cup fresh lime juice
1/2 teaspoon coriander seeds, crushed
1/4 teaspoon ground allspice
filtered water

Sassafras, with its distinctive root-beer-like smell, grows all along the eastern seaboard. You'll need to dig up a piece of root and turn it into coarse shavings. Homemade root beer made from the root, rather than an extract, has little resemblance to syrupy sweet commercial varieties. Its taste is somewhat medicinal but not unpleasant. You may wish to dilute it with sparkling mineral water.

Place shavings in a pan with about 4 cups of filtered water, bring to a boil, reduce heat and simmer about 2 hours. Strain into a measuring cup. You should have about 1 cup of sassafras concentrate. Let cool and combine with remaining ingredients in a 2-quart glass container, adding enough filtered water to make 2 quarts. Cover tightly and leave at room temperature for about 2 days. Transfer to refrigerator for several weeks before serving.

You can eat a diet that has no enzymes and still live for many years, even to ripe old age, though each generation you would produce inferior offspring; and, eventually, reproduction would be impossible. Would it not be better to let outside enzymes do some of the work and save your own enzymes for cellular work? Is it possible that cellular enzyme exhaustion is the root cause of what ails us? Victoras Kulvinskas *Introduction to Food Enzymes for Health and Longevity*

Sassafras was one of America's first export crops, a bigger seller than tobacco in the 17th century. Its leaves are in season from spring to fall, but the root is edible all year long. The Indians valued infusions of sassafras root for the blood and as a traditional spring tonic. American colonists and Europeans used it to treat a long list of complaints including arthritis, gout, colds, fevers, blood pressure, urinary problems, kidney stones, eczema and other skin disorders and intestinal problems. Safrole, an ester derived from the root, was valued for menstrual discomfort and the pain of childbirth.

When research showed that astronomical quantities of artificial safrole caused cancer in rats, the U.S. Food and Drug Administration had a convenient excuse for removing sassafras from health food stores. One suspects that the FDA was more concerned about eliminating competition for the drug and soft drink industries than in protecting the populace from a carcinogen. Americans had enjoyed sassafras as a tea and in root beer with no ill effects for centuries. SWF

The world today relies on just one hundred fifty food plants, and only twenty of those produce 90 percent of our food. Nine are widely used and account for three-quarters of the human diet. Of these, just three—rice, corn and wheat—account for half. These are truly slim pickings, considering that there are thirty thousand to eighty thousand edible plants . . . . ninety percent of the people who have ever lived were hunters and gatherers who spent just about three weeks a year collecting a year's worth of grains. Wild food was abundant and people were not. The diet was truly diverse. People grazed on three thousand to five thousand plants. The biologist Gary Naghan estimates that Native Americans in the Southwest regularly sampled eleven hundred plants. . . . A second Green Revolution is at hand; but this time it is a Green Gene Revolution, a bioengineered food system based on the ingredients of privatized germ plasm and the menu of monopoly. Poised on the two-headed cusp of the biotechnology revolution, the seed genetics industry comprehends the depth of public controversy it could provoke. Scientists are reporting to work today at the gene bank and the cell library. Using tissue culture technology, they take cellular samples of a plant and grow it out in the laboratory. They cook up large batches of plant embryos and bathe them in liquid fertilizers and pesticides. Then they ready them for sale to farmers and gardeners, eliminating all the chancy, costly, time-consuming vagaries of agriculture and seed production. . . . The Green Gene Revolution is mutating from monocultures to clonal cultures. Entire fields will be planted in monocultures of identical clones derived from the cell tissue of a single plant, chemical fed and lab bred. Kenny Ausubel *Seeds of Change*

SWEET POTATO SODA
(Fly)
Makes 1 gallon

2 large sweet potatoes
1 tablespoon mace
1 gallon filtered water
2 cups Rapadura (see page 536)
1/2 cup whey (page 87)
grated rind of 2 lemons or 3 limes
juice of 2 lemons or 3 limes
pinch of nutmeg
pinch of cinnamon
2-3 cloves
2 egg whites
pinch of salt
shells from 2 eggs, crushed

This interesting fermented drink comes from Guyana. Place mace and 1 cup filtered water in a pan, bring to a boil and allow to cool. Meanwhile, peel and grate sweet potatoes. Place in a strainer and rinse well with running water. Place sweet potatoes, boiled mace, Rapadura, whey, spices, remaining water and rind and juice of lemons or limes in a bowl and mix well.

In a clean stainless steel or glass bowl, beat egg whites with pinch of salt until stiff. Fold in crushed egg shells and spread gently on top of the liquid. Cover with a cloth and keep at room temperature for 3 days. Pour through a strainer into glass containers, cover tightly and store in the refrigerator.

HAYMAKERS' OAT WATER
Makes 1 gallon

1 gallon filtered water
1 cup rolled oats
1 cup lemon juice or raw apple cider vinegar
1 cup molasses (optional)

Mix all ingredients and keep at room temperature several hours or overnight, stirring occasionally.

GINGER BEER
Makes about 8 quarts

14 teaspoons ground ginger
14 teaspoons white sugar
filtered water
3 cups Rapadura (see page 536)
juice of 4 lemons

Genuine ginger beer begins with a "bug" made by feeding 2 teaspoons ground ginger and 2 teaspoons white sugar to a culture for seven days. White sugar is used for the small quantity needed to make the "bug," but Rapadura is used for the larger quantity that goes into the beer.

Place 1 1/2 cups water, 2 teaspoons ground ginger and 2 teaspoons white sugar in a jar. Cover, shake well and leave at room temperature for 24 hours. Feed the culture with 2 teaspoons each of sugar and ground ginger every day for 7 days, leaving culture at room temperature. On the seventh day, it should produce bubbles. If not, throw away and start again.

Dissolve Rapadura in 10 cups boiling water. Place in a very large bowl or stainless steel pan. Add lemon juice and 20 more cups water. Carefully pour off the liquid from the "bug" and add to the bowl, reserving the sediment. Mix well, cover the bowl tightly and leave for about 7 days. Transfer to eight quart-sized bottles with wire-held corks or stoppers. Let stand 14 days at room temperature before drinking.

To make a new "bug," throw half of the ginger-sugar sediment away and reserve the rest. Add 1 1/2 cups water and feed with 2 teaspoons each sugar and ginger for 7 days, as before.

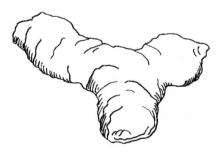

This supply [of enzymes], like the energy supply in your new battery, has to last a lifetime. The faster you use up your enzyme supply, the shorter your life. A great deal of our enzyme energy is wasted haphazardly throughout life. The habit of cooking our food and eating it processed with chemicals and the use of alcohol, drugs, and junk food all draw out tremendous quantities of enzymes from our limited supply. Frequent colds and fevers and exposure to extremes of temperature also deplete the supply. A body in such a weakened, enzyme-deficient state is a prime target for cancer, obesity, heart disease or other degenerative problems. A lifetime of such abuse often ends in the tragedy of death at middle age. Stephen Blauer *Introduction to Enzyme Nutrition*

Throughout the British Isles, grains were traditionally fermented into various sorts of ales and lagers—either by the housewife or in alehouses that existed in almost every town. These beers were an excellent source of nutrients including B vitamins, minerals and enzymes. Small beer, which contained only a small amount of alcohol, but large amounts of lactic acid and beneficial enzymes, was traditionally consumed in the morning, accompanying a heavy breakfast of fish or cold meat, bacon and eggs. Strong beers, with their high content of alcohol, were recognized as providing "comfort for the poor." The poet John Taylor recorded a total of nine different ales served at the same meal, during a visit to Manchester in 1618. Eight of them were herbal ales, flavored with hyssop, wormwood, rosemary, betony and scurvygrass. *Merrie Olde England*

SMALL BEER

Makes 3 quarts

1 cup whole barley or rye
1/2 cup sourdough bread culture
(page 489 or see Sources)
1 cup freshly ground whole wheat, kamut,
spelt or rye flour
filtered water
1 cup dried hops (available in the herb department
of health food stores)

Sprout barley or rye berries according to directions (page 114). After 2 days, rinse sprouts well, drain and spread on a stainless steel baking sheet. Bake at 150 degrees for at least 12 hours until complete dehydrated. Raise heat to 400 degrees and roast the berries for about 15 minutes until they turn dark brown, shaking them occasionally to avoid burning. Grind the berries coarsely in a grain grinder.

While the rye or barley is sprouting, "refresh" the sourdough culture by adding 1/2 cup flour and 1/2 cup warm filtered water. Cover with a cloth and leave for 12-24 hours in a warm place. Repeat the process by adding an additional 1/2 cup flour and 1/2 cup warm water and leaving in a warm place for 12-24 hours.

Soak hops in warm water for 1/2 hour. Remove with a slotted spoon and place in a large bowl with 1 cup sourdough culture, the ground rye or barley and 3 quarts water. (Reserve remaining sourdough culture in the refrigerator for future batches.) Stir well, cover with a cloth and leave at room temperature for 3-4 days, removing cover occasionally to stir vigorously.

When the small beer has developed a sour taste, remove the hops with a slotted spoon and pour carefully through a strainer, leaving most of the sediment in the bowl. Transfer the strained liquid to three quart-sized bottles with wire-held corks or stoppers. Keep in a cool place for at least one week and up to four weeks. It may be stored another month or so in the refrigerator. The final product should be sour and may be slightly bubbly.

Prince: Belike then my appetite was not princely got; for, by my troth, I do now remember the poor creature, small beer. But, indeed, these humble considerations make me out of love with my greatness.
William Shakespeare
Henry IV Part II

One theory proposed that the common occurrence of being exposed to aluminum could cause Alzheimer's dementia. . . . In recent years. . . the aluminum hypothesis has been gaining respect. For example, studies have discovered a direct association between the level of aluminium in municipal drinking water and the risk of Alzheimer's dementia.

We also know that serum aluminum concentrations increase with age. Aluminum may accumulate slowly over our lifetimes, or we may absorb it more easily as we age. Moreover, there is evidence that people with probable Alzheimer's disease have serum aluminum levels that are often significantly higher than those people with other types of dementia, as well as healthy people of similar ages.

Further evidence that aluminum fosters the development of Alzheimer's dementia comes from a scientific (placebo-controlled) trial of desferrioxamine, a drug that removes aluminum from the body by binding with it. While regular administration of the drug failed to stop the disease from progressing, desferrioxamine did significantly reduce the rate of decline in the ability of a group of people with Alzheimer's dementia to care for themselves. Melvyn R. Werbach, MD *The Natural Activist* Citizens for Health

RICE MILK

Makes 2 quarts

1/2 cup brown rice
8 cups filtered water
1 teaspoon sea salt
1/4 cup whey (page 87)
1/4 cup raw honey
1 teaspoon cinnamon

This recipe comes from Egypt, but similar recipes can be found throughout the Middle and Far East. Fermented grain drinks were traditionally prescribed to nursing mothers.

Cook rice in water, covered, for several hours until rice becomes very mushy. Pass rice and liquid through a food mill. (See A Word on Equipment, page 68.) Place in a 2-quart jug with salt and whey. Cover tightly and leave at room temperature for 2 or 3 days. Transfer to refrigerator. (A certain amount of separation is normal.)

To serve, blend with honey and cinnamon and enough water to achieve desired consistency.

Variation:
Use other grains, such as *oats, rye* or *barley.*

Variation: Nursing Mothers Tonic
Use *1/2 cup quinoa*, soaked 12 hours in warm water, rinsed and drained.

ALMOND DRINK

Makes 2 quarts

2 cups skinless almonds
warm filtered water
2 teaspoons sea salt
1/4 cup whey (page 87)
1/8 cup raw honey or Rapadura (see page 536)
1 teaspoon vanilla extract
1 teaspoon almond extract
filtered water

The traditions that surround the life of Gautama Buddha include this one: that on the evening when he seated himself beneath the Bo tree and began the meditation that led to his enlightenment, he dined on rice milk offered to him by a peasant woman. His death occurred 45 years later, around 480 BC, when he ate some poisonous mushrooms that the smith Cunda served him by accident. In pain on his death bed, he commanded his companions to tell Cunda that of all the meals he had eaten in his lifetime, two brought him great blessings. One was the meal of rice milk that nourished him during his meditation under the Bo tree; the other was Cunda's meal that took him to Nirvana. SWF

Hominy Corn Drink: Shell corn, soak in lye until the skin can be removed. Beat the corn in the corn beater until it is the size of hominy. Sift the meal from the corn particles. Cook the corn particles until they are done, thicken this a little with meal. Drink this hot or wait until it sours and drink it cold. The drink may be kept for quite a while unless the weather is very hot. This was the customary drink to serve to friends who dropped by for a visit. *Cherokee Cooklore*

What a strange drink. . . a drink obtained by allowing an infusion of tea to ferment with the aid of a special inoculation and a little sugar. One finds this drink in many countries of Asia and Europe (China, Japan, Indonesia, Russia, Bulgaria, Poland and Germany) called by various names: *Tesschwamm, tea fungus, kombucha, wunderpilz, hongo, cajnij, teekvass.* This tea possesses antibiotic properties that are used in medicine in Russia. Claude Aubert *Les Aliments Fermentés Traditionnels*

What's inside the cupboard is competing strongly with what's inside the medicine cabinet for managing various physical ailments. Now word from out of Denmark informs us that ginger has been found to be effective in relieving common symptoms of rheumatoid arthritis: pain, inflammation and stiffness.

Dr. Krishna C. Srivastava, of the Institute of Odense, gave arthritis patients a bit less than a tablespoon of ginger daily for three months, and patients reported "significant relief." Doctor Srivastava fed the patients either five grams of fresh ginger root or from one-half gram to a gram and one-half of ginger powder. Both forms worked equally well. Every one of the patients noted marked improvement: ability to get around better, less swelling and less start-of-the-day stiffness. James F. Scheer *Health Freedom News*

Irish moss is a red algae that the Irish have gathered and made into refreshing drinks and desserts. It contains a gel, similar to agar, called carrageenan that has many uses. Unfortunately, some individuals have adverse reactions to carrageenan, particularly in commercial preparations. This may be because, like all seaweed, carrageen moss contains long-chain sugars that some people have difficulty digesting. Seaweed can also be overused, providing a surfeit of iodine that can cause thyroid problems just as much as a deficiency.

But the Irish have always valued their carrageen moss as a health food. Used in moderation as a tea, Irish moss seems to be helpful for digestive disorders, including ulcers, kidney ailments, heart disease and glandular irregularities. It is high in carotenoids, iodine, iron, sulphur, sodium, copper and numerous trace minerals. SWF

Soak almonds overnight in warm water. Pour off water and process in food processor to a smooth paste. In a 2-quart jug mix almond paste with other ingredients and enough water to fill the jug. Cover tightly and leave at room temperature for 2 days before transferring to refrigerator. Stir well before serving.

Variation: Pecan or Walnut Drink

Use *2 cups freshly shelled walnuts* or *pecans* instead of almonds

GINGER TEA
Makes 4 cups

1 tablespoon freshly grated ginger
4 cups filtered water
1 tablespoon raw honey

Place ginger in a teapot. Bring water to a boil and pour over ginger. Let stand several minutes and stir in honey. Strain into teacups or mugs

CARRAGEEN TEA
Makes 4 cups

1 cup carrageen moss (Irish moss)
3 cups filtered water
juice of 1 orange
juice of 1 lemon
1 tablespoon raw honey

Place Irish moss, water, orange and lemon juice in a pan and bring to a boil. Simmer for about 10 minutes. Let cool slightly. Strain into teapot and stir in honey. Serve in teacups or mugs.

YOGHURT DRINK

(Dahi)
Makes 3 quarts

1 quart plain whole yoghurt (page 85)
juice of 12 limes
1/2 cup raw honey
filtered water

Place yoghurt, lime juice and honey in food processor and blend well. Dilute with filtered water to desired consistency.

KVASS

Makes 2 quarts

4-5 slices whole grain sourdough bread
    (page 490)
2 quarts filtered water
1/4 cup whey (page 87)
2 teaspoons sea salt
1/2 cup raisins
2 apples, peeled and quartered

Place bread in warm oven until dried out. Place in a large bowl. Bring water to a boil and pour over bread. Let cool before adding salt and whey. Cover with a cloth and leave at room temperature for 2-3 days. Remove bread and strain into a 2-quart container. Add raisins and apples, cover tightly and store in refrigerator for about 1 month before drinking. Kvass is ready when the fruit floats—a sign that sufficient lactic acid has been produced.

QUICK SPORTS DRINK

Makes 8 ounces

8 ounces filtered water
juice of 1 lemon
1/4 teaspoon sea salt
1/2 teaspoon Azomite powder (see Sources)
2-4 tablespoons whey (page 87)

Mix all ingredients together in an 8-ounce glass.

The particular activator which is chiefly requisite for the utilization of calcium and phosphorus. . . comes to us chiefly through fats of plant and animal origin, the two chief of the latter are the fats of marine forms of life and the butterfat of milk. Thus, many of the great civilizations of the world have been built around sources of seafoods and the dairy animals, chiefly the cow, as adjuncts to plant foods. . . . We have not recognized the marvelous similarity between milk and blood. The milks of many mammals carry calcium and phosphorus in practically the same ratios as they are found in the bloods of mammals, though differing in concentration of the blood. Human milk and cow's milk carry calcium and phosphorus in a concentration about ten times that found in mammalian blood. Weston Price, DDS *Journal of the American Association of Medical Milk Commissions*

The potentially large amount of glucuronic acid in the beverage is especially exciting to us, just as it was to Soviet scientists and cancer researchers. . . . Glucuronic acid is not readily commercially synthesized, but the healthy human liver makes large amounts of it to detoxify the body. In the liver the glucuronic acid binds up all poisons and toxins—both environmental and metabolic—and rushes them to the excretory system. Toxins once bound by glucuronic acid cannot be resorbed into the system so we are rid of them. Tom Valentine *Search for Health*

The Soviet experience is part of the large body of documentary evidence that the beverage made from kombucha fermentation of tea and sugar is, indeed, a dramatic immune system booster and body detoxifier. Tom Valentine *Search for Health*

It seems surprising, even ironic, to conclude a health food cookbook, in which we have warned against sugar, yeasted foods and tea, with a tonic made from sugar, yeast and tea! But the kombucha "mushroom" (which is actually a symbiotic colony of yeast and bacteria) acts on sugar and tea to produce not only acetic and lactic acid but also small amounts of a potent detoxifying substance, glucuronic acid. Normally this organic acid is produced by the liver in sufficient quantities to neutralize toxins in the body—whether these are naturally produced toxins or poisons ingested in food and water. However, when liver function becomes overloaded, and when the body must deal with a superabundance of toxins from the environment—certainly the case with most of us today—additional glucuronic acid taken in the form of kombucha is said to be a powerful aid to the body's natural cleansing process, a boost to the immune system and a proven prophylactic against cancer and other degenerative diseases.

More importantly, kombucha is the cure for a hot day—it tastes delicious and refreshing. A fizzy, dark colored, energizing beverage, at the same time acidic and slightly sweet, this gift to the world from the Ural mountain region of Russia qualifies as the soft drink of the twenty-first century, the answer to the scourge of cola drinks that now wreaks havoc with the health of Western populations. SWF

KOMBUCHA
Makes 1 gallon

3 quarts filtered water
1 cup sugar
4 tea bags of organic black tea
1/2 cup kombucha from a previous culture
1 kombucha mushroom (see Sources)

Bring 3 quarts filtered water to boil. Add sugar and optional salt and simmer until dissolved. Remove from heat, add the tea bags and allow the tea to steep until water has completely cooled. Remove tea bags. Pour cooled liquid into a 4-quart pyrex bowl and add 1/2 cup kombucha from previous batch. Place the mushroom on top of the liquid. Make a crisscross over the bowl with masking tape, cover loosely with a cloth or towel and transfer to a warm, dark place, away from contaminants and insects. In about 7 to 10 days the kombucha will be ready, depending on the temperature. It should be rather sour and possibly fizzy, with no taste of tea remaining. Transfer to covered glass containers and store in the refrigerator. (Note: Do not wash kombucha bowls in the dishwasher.)

When the kombucha is ready, your mushroom will have grown a second spongy pancake. This can be used to make other batches or given away to friends. Store fresh mushrooms in the refrigerator in a glass or stainless steel container—never plastic. A kombucha mushroom can be used dozens of times. If it begins to turn black, or if the resulting kombucha doesn't sour properly, it's a sign that the culture has become contaminated. When this happens, it's best to throw away all your mushrooms and order a new clean one.

Note: White sugar, rather than honey or Rapadura, and black tea, rather than flavored teas, give the highest amounts of glucuronic acid. Non-organic tea is high in fluoride so always use organic tea.

A word of caution: Some individuals may have an allergic reaction to kombucha. If you have allergies, start with a small taste to observe any adverse effects. If you react badly, use beet kvass (page 608) several weeks to detoxify and then try again.

FEEDING BABIES

FEEDING BABIES

Any effort to ensure optimal nutrition of your baby must begin long before he or she is conceived. The wisdom of primitive peoples is vastly superior to our own in this regard, in that a common practice among isolated groups is the feeding of special foods to both men and women for a period of time before conception occurs. Dr. Weston Price's studies revealed that these foods—including organ meats, fish heads, fish eggs, shell fish, insects and animal fats—were rich in fat-soluble vitamins A and D as well as macro- and trace minerals. Couples planning to have children should eat liberally of organic liver and other organ meats, fish eggs and other seafood, eggs, and the best quality butter, cream and fermented milk products they can obtain for at least six months before conception. A daily cod liver oil supplement is also advised. (See note on cod liver oil, page 618.) Organic meats, vegetables, grains and legumes should round out the diet, with a special emphasis on the leafy green vegetables rich in folic acid, which is necessary for the prevention of birth defects like spina bifida.

A good rule for pregnant women is liver once a week, at least two eggs per day and 1 teaspoon cod liver oil daily. Appropriate amounts of superfoods, such as high-vitamin butter oil, evening primrose, borage or black currant oil, bee pollen, mineral powder, wheat germ oil and acerola powder, will provide optimal amounts of nutrients for your unborn child. Beet kvass (page 610) and kombucha (page 596), with their liver-supporting properties, are useful in preventing future morning sickness—as are foods rich in vitamin B_6, such as appropriately prepared raw fish and raw meat (pages 231-242).

A cleansing fast, undertaken six months or more before conception, is a good idea, but during the six months before conception and nine months of pregnancy it is vital to consume nutrient-dense foods. Every attempt should be made to enhance the digestibility of the diet through meat broths and the inclusion of lacto-fermented grains, beverages and condiments. All empty calories and harmful substances should be eliminated—sugar, white flour, hydrogenated and rancid vegetable oils, excess of polyunsaturated oils, tobacco, caffeine and alcohol. Oral contraceptives should be avoided during this preparatory period as these deplete many nutrients, particularly zinc, the "intelligence mineral."

The importance of breastfeeding your baby, especially during his first few months, cannot be overemphasized. Breast milk is perfectly designed for your baby's physical and mental development. Breastfed babies tend to be more robust, more intelligent and freer from allergies and other complaints, especially intestinal difficulties, than those on formula. In addition, colostrum produced by the mammary glands during the first few days of a baby's life helps guard him against colds, flu, polio, staph infections and viruses.

It must be emphasized, however, that the quality of mother's milk depends greatly on her diet. Sufficient animal products will ensure proper amounts of vitamin B_{12}, A and D as well as all-important minerals like zinc in her milk. Lactating women should continue with a diet that emphasizes liver, eggs and cod liver oil. Whole milk products and stock made from bones will ensure that her baby receives adequate calcium.

Pesticides and other toxins will be present in mother's milk if they are present in the diet, so all care should be taken to consume organic foods of both plant and animal origin during pregnancy and lactation. Organic foods also provide more omega-3 fatty acids needed for baby's optimal development. Hydrogenated fats should be strictly avoided as these result in reduced fat content in mother's milk. *Trans* fats accumulate in mother's milk and can lead to decreased visual acuity and learning difficulties in the infant.

Breastfeeding should ideally be continued for six months to a year. If mother's milk is not adequate or of good quality, or if the mother is unable to breast feed for whatever reason, a homemade baby formula, rather than a commercial formula, can be used. Commercial infant formulas are highly fabricated concoctions composed of milk or soy powders produced by high-temperature processes that overdenature proteins and add many carcinogens. Milk-based formulas often cause allergies while soy-based formulas contain mineral-blocking phytic acid, growth inhibitors and plant forms of estrogen compounds that can have adverse effects on the hormonal development in the infant. Soy-based formulas are also devoid of cholesterol, needed for the development of the brain and nervous system.

Fortunately, it is possible to compose a formula that closely resembles mother's milk. Whenever possible this formula should be based on raw organic milk, from cows certified free of tuberculosis and brucellosis. The milk should come from cows that eat food appropriate to cows, which is green grass in the warm months and hay and root vegetables in the winter, not soy or cottonseed meal. Ideally, the milk should come from Jersey or Guernsey cows, rather than Holsteins, so that it has a high butterfat content. This may be purchased at the farm in some states. Of course, such milk should be produced under the cleanest possible conditions and stored in sterilized containers. But the milk should be unheated. Properly produced raw milk does not pose a danger to your baby, in spite of what numerous public health propagandists may assert. Raw milk contains enzymes and antibodies that make it less susceptible to bacterial contamination than pasteurized milk, while many toxins that cause diarrhea and other ailments survive the pasteurization process. Your nose will tell you if raw milk is contaminated or spoiled—but pasteurized milk may be seriously contaminated with no telltale warning odor. Raw milk is easier for your baby to digest than pasteurized and less likely to cause cramps, constipation and allergies. If it is not possible for you to obtain certified raw milk, begin with the best quality pasteurized whole milk you can find, milk that is not homogenized, and culture it for 12 hours with piima culture or kefir grains to restore enzymes lost through pasteurization (pages 83 and 88). Or, you may prepare a milk-free formula made from organic liver. Organic liver should also be added to formula made from goat milk, as goat milk is deficient in iron, folic acid and vitamin B_{12}.

Both our milk-based and meat-based formulas have been designed to provide maximum possible correspondence with the various components of human milk. Our milk-based formula takes account of the fact that human milk is richer in whey, lactose, vitamin C, niacin, manganese and long-chain polyunsaturated fatty acids compared to cows milk but leaner in casein (milk protein). The addition of gelatin to cow's milk formula will make it more digestible for the infant. The liver-based formula also mimics the nutrient profile of mother's milk. Use only truly expeller-expressed oils (see Sources) in the formula recipes, otherwise they may lack vitamin E.

A wise supplement for all babies—whether breast fed or bottle fed—is an egg yolk per day, beginning at four months. Egg yolk supplies cholesterol needed for mental development as well as important sulphur-containing amino acids. Egg yolks from pasture-fed hens or hens raised on flax meal, fish meal or insects are also rich in the omega-3 long-chain fatty acids found in mother's milk but which may be lacking in cow's milk. These fatty acids are essential for the development of the brain. Parents who institute the practice of feeding egg yolk to baby will be rewarded with children who speak and take directions at an early age. The white, which contains difficult-to-digest proteins, should not be given before the age of one year. Small amounts of grated, raw organic liver may be added to the egg yolk after six months. This imitates the practice of African mothers who chew liver before giving it to their infants as their first food. Liver is rich in iron, the one mineral that tends to be low in mother's milk.

A pinch of sea salt added to the yolk will also facilitate brain development. Salt is necessary to activate the formation of glial cells in the brain, the cells that make connections and help us think faster. Unfortunately, salt is often left out of commercial baby food, in the mistaken belief that salt should be avoided. As you add other foods to baby's diet, be sure that they are salted with unrefined sea salt.

An unfortunate practice in industrial societies is the feeding of cereal grains to infants. Babies produce only small amounts of amylase, needed for the digestion of grains, and are not fully equipped to handle cereals, especially wheat, before the age of one year. (Some experts prohibit all grains before the age of two.) Baby's small intestine mostly produces one enzyme for carbohydrates—lactase, for the digestion of lactose. (Raw milk also contains lactase.) Many doctors have warned that feeding cereal grains too early can lead to grain allergies later on. Baby's earliest solid foods should be animal foods as his digestive system, although immature, is better equipped to supply enzymes for digestion of fats and proteins rather than carbohydrates.

Carbohydrate in the form of fresh, mashed banana can be added after the age of six months as bananas are rich in amylase enzymes and thus are easily digested by most infants. Some preindustrial societies give a gruel of cereal grains, soaked 24 hours, to babies one year or older. Soaking in an acidic medium neutralizes phytates and begins the breakdown of carbohydrates, thus allowing children to obtain optimum nourishment from grains. It also provides lactic acid to the intestinal tract to facilitate mineral uptake.

At the age of about ten months, meats, fruits and vegetables may be introduced, one at a time so that any adverse reactions may be observed. Carbohydrate foods, such as potatoes, carrots, turnips, etc., should be mashed with butter. (Don't overdo on the orange vegetables as baby's immature liver may have difficulty converting carotenoids to vitamin A. If your baby's skin develops a yellowish color, a sign that he is not making the conversion, discontinue orange vegetables for a time.) Lacto-fermented taro or other roots (page 102) make an excellent carbohydrate food for babies. It is wise to feed babies a little buttermilk or yoghurt from time to time to familiarize them with the sour taste. Above all, do not deprive your baby of animal fats—he needs them for optimum physical growth and mental development. Mother's milk contains over 50 percent of its calories as fat, much of it saturated fat, and children need these kinds of fats throughout their growing years.

It is unwise to give baby fruit juices, especially apple juice, which provide only simple carbohydrates and will often spoil an infant's appetite for more nutritious foods. Sorbitol, a sugar-alcohol in apple juice, is difficult to digest. Studies have linked failure to thrive in children with diets high in apple juice. High-fructose foods are especially dangerous for growing children. The best beverage for a growing child is whole raw milk, which can be introduced slowly as the baby is weaned from the breast or from homemade formula.

Remember that babies should be chubby and children should be sturdy and strong, not slim. Babies need body fat to achieve optimum growth. The fat around their ankles, knees, elbows and wrists is growth fat that ensures adequate nourishment to the growth plates at the ends of the bones. Fat babies grow up into sturdy, well-formed adults, neither too tall nor too short and either slender or stocky depending on genetic heritage.

Keep your baby away from processed junk foods as long as possible—but do not think that you can do this indefinitely. Unless you lock your child in a closet—or live in a closed community of like-minded parents—he will come in contact with junk foods sooner or later. His best protection is the optimal diet that you have given him during his infancy and your loving example and training in later years.

During the process of digestion, lactose breaks up into two other sugars, glucose (dextrose) and galactose. In myelin there is a large amount of galactolipids in the nature of phrenosin (cerebrosides) of various kinds. Cerebrosides are compounds found in the brain. Galactose is one of the constituents of this material. . . . Mother Nature must have intended that the young infant have this important substance, so amply provided for it in breast milk. . . . I have long held the opinion that the tremendous use of various [other] sugars in milk formulas over the years could be an important factor in the high percentage of mental and nervous breakdowns in our civilian population, not to mention the alarming numbers of such cases that have been reported in the military. The demyelination of the nerves is what makes the dread disease multiple sclerosis so crippling. This disease was quite rare in the days of breast-feeding. Emory W. Thurston, PhD *Nutrition for Tots to Teens*

Alexander and Bullowa . . . observed that the casein of milk was an irreversible colloid and that it could be protected by the addition of a reversible colloid, such as gelatin. They pointed out, moreover, that woman's milk was higher in albumen or protective colloid than cow's milk and that the curd obtained from the coagulation of woman's milk was softer and more easily digested. When gelatin was added to cow's milk, a curd of equally desirable characteristics was formed. In addition, gelatin . . . served not only to emulsify the fat but also, by stabilizing the casein, improved the digestibility and absorption of the fat. . . . Experimental feeding tests show that milk containing gelatin is more rapidly and completely digested in the infant. N. R. Gotthoffer *Gelatin in Nutrition and Medicine*

MILK-BASED FORMULA
Makes 36 ounces

*2 cups organic, certified clean raw milk
    or organic pasteurized, nonhomogenized piima
    milk (page 83), preferably from pasture-fed
    Jersey or Guernsey cows*
1/4 cup homemade liquid whey (page 87)
4 tablespoons lactose (see Sources)
1/4 teaspoon bifodobacterium infantis (see Sources)
*2 tablespoons good quality cream
    (not ultrapasteurized)*
*1/2 teaspoon high-vitamin cod liver oil
    (see note on cod liver oil, page 618)*
1 teaspoon unrefined sunflower oil (see Sources)
1 teaspoon extra virgin olive oil
2 teaspoons coconut oil (see Sources)
2 teaspoons brewer's yeast
2 teaspoons gelatin (see Sources)
1 7/8 cups filtered water
1/4 teaspoon acerola powder (see Sources)

Add gelatin to water and heat gently until gelatin is dissolved. Place all ingredients in a blender and blend well. Transfer to a very clean glass or stainless steel container and mix well. (Note: If milk is from Holstein cows, add an additional 1-2 tablespoons cream.)

To serve, pour 6 to 8 ounces into a very clean glass bottle, attach nipple and set in a pan of simmering water. Heat until warm but not hot to the touch, shake bottle well and feed baby. (Never, *never* heat formula in a microwave oven!)

Variation: Goat Milk Formula

Although goat milk is rich in fat, it must be used with caution in infant feeding as it lacks folic acid and is low in vitamin B_{12}, both of which are essential to the growth and development of the infant. Inclusion of brewers yeast to provide folic acid is essential. To compensate for low levels of vitamin B_{12}, add *2 teaspoons organic raw chicken liver, frozen for 14 days, finely grated* to the batch of formula. Be sure to begin egg-yolk feeding at four months.

MEAT-BASED FORMULA

Makes 36 ounces

*3 3/4 cups homemade beef or chicken broth,
    (page 122 or 124)*
2 ounces organic liver, cut into small pieces
5 tablespoons lactose (see Sources)
1 teaspoon bifodobacterium infantis (see Sources)
1/4 cup homemade liquid whey (page 87)
1 tablespoon coconut oil (see Sources)
1 teaspoon cod liver oil
    (See note on cod liver oil, page 618)
1 teaspoon unrefined sunflower oil (see Sources)
2 teaspoons extra virgin olive oil
1/4 teaspoon acerola powder (see Sources)

Simmer liver gently in broth until the meat is cooked through. Liquefy using a handheld blender or in a food processor. When the liver broth has cooled, stir in remaining ingredients. Store in a very clean glass or stainless steel container. To serve, stir formula well and pour 6 to 8 ounces in a very clean glass bottle. Attach a clean nipple and set in a pan of simmering water until formula is warm but not hot to the touch, shake well and feed to baby. (Never heat formula in a microwave oven!) Note: It is very important to include the coconut oil in this formula as it is the recipe's only source of antimicrobial saturated fatty acids.

Milk-based commercial formulas are bad enough, but formula based on soy protein should never have been brought to market. This list of toxins in soy is a long one: phytic acid, which blocks absorption of minerals, especially zinc; protease inhibitors which block the digestion of protein; and high levels of aluminum, fluoride, MSG and manganese, all of which can have adverse effects on the brain and nervous system.

But it is the phytoestrogens or isoflavones in soy that give the most cause for concern. These compounds not only depress thyroid function, they also can have profound hormonal effects, especially at the levels to which the soy-fed infant is exposed. A recent study of infants fed soy formula found that they had concentrations of estrogen compounds at levels 13,000 to 22,000 times higher than infants on milk-based formula or breast milk. Infant boys go through a "testosterone tide" during the first six months of their lives, during which they normally have testosterone levels nearly equal to those of mature men. This early surge of male hormones programs the reproductive system, brain and other organs to take on male characteristics at puberty. Researchers are now wondering whether the feeding of estrogen-rich soy formula to infant boys interferes with this process and is a partial explanation the increase in learning disabilities and maturation problems in boys. Soy infant feeding may also explain why so many girls are developing breasts and other sexual characteristics before the age of eight years old.

Anecdotal reports of other adverse effects include extreme emotional behavior, learning difficulties, immune system problems, irritable bowel syndrome and depression. SWF

Both gelatin and [lactic] acid when added to cow's milk seem to make the milk more digestible to the ordinary infant. This is evidenced by the fact that both vomiting and constipation appeared to be reduced when either of these substances was added, and a better rate of gain was made on the low curd tension milks. Similarly, it was noted that a much smaller percentage of the children developed diarrhea on the modified milks than on the unaltered cow's milk. Attention is called to the lower incidence of upper respiratory infections in the gelatin milk group. N. R Gotthoffer *Gelatin in Nutrition and Medicine*

It is a remarkable fact that the young of most, including man, have weak digestive fluids; particularly do they have low amylase content in the saliva. The suckling animal or infant does not need to secrete a great quantity of enzymes because milk, its first food, does not demand so many of them for its digestion as it has quite a complement of its own enzymes. Edward Howell, MD *Food Enzymes for Health and Longevity*

Soy-based infant formula may adversely affect hormonal development in neonatal infants and should not be sold commercially. Soya is the richest dietary source of phytoestrogens, a plant form of the female hormone estrogen. Neonatal infants are particularly vulnerable to estrogens and insufficient research on the long-term health effects of phytoestrogens warrants a ban on the nonprescription sale of soy formula. *New Zealand Medical Journal*

FORTIFIED COMMERCIAL FORMULA

Makes about 35 ounces

1 cup Mead Johnson low-iron,
*   milk-based powdered formula*
29 ounces filtered water (3 5/8 cups)
1 large egg yolk from an organic egg,
*   cooked 3 1/2 minutes (page 605)*
1 teaspoon cod liver oil
*   (see note on cod liver oil, page 618)*

This stopgap formula can be used in emergencies, or when the ingredients for homemade formula are unavailable. Place all ingredients in a blender or food processor and blend thoroughly. Place 6-8 ounces in a very clean glass bottle. (Store the rest in a very clean glass jar in the refrigerator for the next feedings.) Attach a clean nipple to the bottle and set in a pan of simmering water to heat gently. (Never, *never* heat formula in a microwave oven!)

DIGESTIVE TEA FOR BABY

about 2 cups fresh anise leaves
about 2 cups fresh mint leaves
2 quarts filtered water

This is a folk remedy for treating constipation and intestinal gas in infants.

Bring water to a boil and pour over the herbs. Let steep until water cools. Strain. Give tepid tea to baby, about 4 ounces at a time.

Note: When a nursing mother drinks this tea, she passes along the benefits to her colicky baby!

EGG YOLK FOR BABY

1 organic high-omega-3 egg
*   or egg from a pasture-fed hen*
pinch sea salt
1/2 teaspoon grated raw organic liver,
*   frozen for 14 days (optional)*

Boil egg for 3 1/2 minutes. Place in a bowl and peel off shell. Remove egg white and discard. Yolk should be soft and warm, not hot, with its enzyme content intact. Sprinkle with a pinch of salt.

If you wish to add liver, grate on the small holes of a grater while frozen. Allow to warm up and stir into egg yolk.

CEREAL GRUEL FOR BABY

Makes 2 cups

1/2 cup freshly ground organic flour of spelt,
*   kamut, rye, barley or oats*
2 cups warm filtered water plus 2 tablespoons whey,
*   yoghurt, kefir or buttermilk (pages 83-87)*
1/4 teaspoon sea salt

Mix flour with water mixture, cover and leave at room temperature for 12 to 24 hours. Bring to a boil, stirring frequently. Add salt, reduce heat and simmer, stirring occasionally, about 10 minutes. Let cool slightly and serve with cream or butter and a small amount of a natural sweetener, such as raw honey. Note: Do not give cereals or raw honey to infants before the age of one year.

Many cultures recognize that eggs are a brain food and encourage pregnant and nursing mothers to eat as many as possible. In China, nursing mothers who can afford it eat up to ten eggs per day!

Unfortunately, most commercial eggs available in the supermarkets are inferior, nutritionally speaking, to the eggs from free-range hens of yesteryear. The typical supermarket egg from battery hens given grain feed contains nineteen times more omega-6 fatty acids than omega-3 fatty acids.

Studies have shown that hens fed flax meal or fish meal rich in omega-3 fatty acids have equal amounts of omega-6 and omega-3, a very beneficial balance. Eggs from hens allowed to eat bugs and graze on green pasture would also have this favorable balance. In addition, these eggs are richer in certain special long-chain fatty acids needed for the optimal mental development of the infant's brain, nervous system and visual acuity. These fatty acids include arachidonic acid (AA), eicosapentaenoic acid (EPA) and docosahexaenoic acid (DHA). Many researchers, most notably the eminent Dr. David Horrobin, have warned that adequate EPA and DHA in the diet of infants is needed to prevent learning disabilities and defects in visual function.

Egg yolks also provide cholesterol needed for the optimal development of the nervous system.

So do not hesitate to give your infant his or her daily egg yolk, starting at four months. It is the yolk that contains the beneficial fatty acids. The proteins in the white of the egg may be difficult to digest until baby is older. SWF

TIPS FOR SUCCESSFUL BREASTFEEDING

❧ The right diet is the key to having a good supply of nourishing milk. It should be followed from before conception and contain high levels of healthy animal fats. Follow the suggestions given in pages 598-601 and be sure to eat plenty of food. When you are pregnant or breastfeeding, it is no time to diet!

❧ Avoid *trans* fatty acids, found in margarines, vegetable shortenings and almost *all* processed foods. *Trans* fats lower the overall fat content of mother's milk, depriving the baby of important nutrients and reducing the chances for successful breastfeeding.

❧ Try to arrange to have good help for the first four weeks after the baby is born so that you will have adequate rest. Husband or partner, grandparents, relatives, friends, housekeepers or even a professional baby nurse should be on hand so that the nursing mother can concentrate on getting optimal nourishment and plenty of sleep.

❧ Fermented foods and beverages, and porridges of soaked grains, are said to increase milk supply.

❧ Consume plenty of liquids in the form of whole milk (preferably raw), stock or soups based on stock, and lacto-fermented beverages.

❧ If you have *any* qualms or fears about not having enough milk, assemble the ingredients for homemade formula, and purchase the Lact-Aid breastfeeding support system so that you have what you need to provide a nourishing supplement, if that is required. The Lact-Aid (see Sources) allows you to breastfeed while giving a homemade supplement to your baby. Sometimes just a few days of supplementing using this device can increase milk flow, and just having the supplies on hand can be enough to give you the peace of mind that allows your milk to keep flowing. While you are pregnant, be sure to scout out the best quality milk available in your area—you will need this for yourself, and for the baby after weaning, even if the breastfeeding goes well.

❧ If, in spite of these measures, your milk supply is inadequate, don't feel guilty. Lack of adequate milk supply is relatively common, especially as baby grows and his appetite increases. You have done the best you could and your baby can still grow up healthy, strong and smart on a homemade, whole-food baby formula.

TONICS & SUPERFOODS

TONICS

The following tonics are offered for their medicinal rather than epicurean qualities. They are useful for fasting and detoxification. Caution: Fasting should only be undertaken under a doctor's supervision. Consult a qualified health practitioner for the treatment of all serious disease conditions.

BIELER BROTH

Makes 2 quarts

4 medium squash (zucchini, yellow or summer)
washed, ends removed and sliced
1 pound string beans, ends removed
2 sticks celery, chopped (optional)
2 bunches parsley, stems removed (optional)
fresh herbs, such as thyme or tarragon,
tied together with string (optional)
1 quart filtered water
whey (page 87), optional

Maverick physician Henry Bieler recommended this broth for fasting, for energy and for overall health. He felt that this combination of vegetables was ideal for restoring acid-alkaline and sodium-potassium balance to organs and glands, especially the sodium-loving adrenal glands. Bieler broth is highly recommended for those under stress or suffering from stress-related conditions, such as back pain and ligament problems. (A more epicurean version is found on page 226.)

Place water, vegetables and optional herbs in a pot. Bring to a boil, skim, lower heat and simmer, covered, for about 1/2 hour. Remove herbs. Vegetables may be eaten whole with cooking water, or blended into a thick soup with a handheld blender. One tablespoon whey may be added to each cup of soup.

POTASSIUM BROTH

Makes 2 quarts

4 potatoes, preferably organic, well scrubbed
3 carrots, peeled and chopped
4 celery sticks, chopped
1 bunch parsley
4 quarts filtered water
whey (page 87)

This is a wonderful pick-me-up, drunk warm like tea; a great rejuvenator for those who have been sick or are recovering from childbirth.

Peel potatoes. Place peelings, carrots and celery in a pot with water. Bring to a boil, lower heat and simmer, covered, for about 1/2 hour. Add parsley and simmer 5 minutes more. Allow to cool and strain into a 2-quart glass container. Store in refrigerator and reheat in small quantities as needed. Add 1 tablespoon of whey to each cup of warm broth—this will greatly facilitate the absorption of potassium and other minerals.

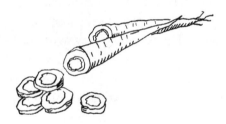

CARROT JUICE COCKTAIL

Makes 8 ounces

1 pound carrots, peeled
2 tablespoons cream

Cream added to carrot juice helps the body to convert carotene efficiently into vitamin A (retinol). This remedy is used with success in European clinics for the treatment of cancer, psoriasis and many other diseases. Use only the best quality cream you can find—preferably raw but never ultrapasteurized.

Process carrots in a juicer. Stir in the cream. Sip slowly.

When a toxemia is present without symptoms of a specific disease but with liver impairment, a short fast on vegetable broth or soup is a natural and efficient treatment that will relieve the liver of its congestion and restore it to normal function. Henry Bieler, MD *Food Is Your Best Medicine*

Sometimes the patient, unlike the horse, knows the "lifesaving water" is there; but his professional life is so arranged that he cannot (or so he believes) stick to his therapeutic diet. Many of the motion-picture stars I have treated, for instance, travel to faraway places or must attend many public functions and have meals at irregular hours; thus, they find it difficult to eat properly. But when they return home, ill, exhausted, filled with tension, they immediately go on what they call "Bieler broth"—a combination of lightly cooked string beans, celery, zucchini and parsley. . . . Even one correct meal aids a toxin-saturated body. Henry Bieler, MD *Food Is Your Best Medicine*

> Accuse not Nature;
> she hath done her part; do
> thou but thine.
> *Milton*

Professor Zabel observed that sick people always lack digestive juices, not only during the acute phase of their illness but also for a longtime afterwards. In addition, he never saw a cancer victim that had a healthy intestinal flora. . . . Thus, the different lacto-fermented foods are a valuable aid to the cancer patient. They are rich in vitamins and minerals and contain as well enzymes that cancer patients lack. Of particular value are lacto-fermented beets, which have a very favorable effect on disturbed cellular function. Many scientific studies have demonstrated that beets have a regenerating effect on the body. Annelies Schoneck *Des Crudités Toute L'Année*

No Ukrainian home was ever without its "beet kvass." The kvass was always handy and ready when a pleasing, sour flavour had to be added to soups and vinaigrettes. Lubow A. Kyivska *Ukrainian Dishes*

Truly the vegetable kingdom contains our best medicines. . . . [The vegetables] are not only beautiful to look at but filled with healthful properties, chief of which are their natural vitamins and trace elements. But only if they are used. Did you know that a stalk of celery or a serving of fresh salad greens has more vitamins and minerals than a box of synthetic vitamin tablets? Henry Bieler, MD *Food Is Your Best Medicine*

BEET KVASS
Makes 2 quarts

*3 medium or 2 large organic beets,
    peeled and chopped up coarsely*
1/4 cup whey (page 87)
1 tablespoon sea salt
filtered water

This drink is valuable for its medicinal qualities and as a digestive aid. Beets are just loaded with nutrients. One 4-ounce glass, morning and night, is an excellent blood tonic, promotes regularity, aids digestion, alkalizes the blood, cleanses the liver and is a good treatment for kidney stones and other ailments. Beet kvass may also be used in place of vinegar in salad dressings and as an addition to soups.

Place beets, whey and salt in a 2-quart glass container. Add filtered water to fill the container. Stir well and cover securely. Keep at room temperature for 2 days before transferring to refrigerator.

When most of liquid has been drunk, you may fill up the container with water and keep at room temperature another 2 days. The resulting brew will be slightly less strong than the first. After the second brew, discard the beets and start again. You may, however, reserve some of the liquid and use this as your inoculant instead of the whey.

Note: Do not use grated beets in the preparation of beet tonic. When grated, beets exude too much juice resulting in a too rapid fermentation that favors the production of alcohol rather than lactic acid.

FLAX SEED DRINK

Makes 1 cup

1 tablespoon organic flax seeds
1 cup filtered water

Flax seeds are relatively low in phytic acid. When taken in small amounts, they do not require soaking.

Grind flax seeds in a mini mill and mix with water. Drink immediately. This supplies omega-3 fatty acids in the freshest possible state; the fiber is an excellent antidote to constipation.

VEGETABLE JUICE COCKTAIL

Makes 1 quart

1 green pepper
2 carrots, peeled
2 sticks celery
1 bunch parsley
1/2 zucchini or yellow squash
6-8 string beans
4 tablespoons whey (page 87)

Run all vegetables through a juicer. Thin with a little filtered water, if desired, and stir in whey. Recommended for detoxification and fasting.

RAW MILK TONIC

Makes 2 cups

1 1/2 cups whole, certified clean raw milk,
  at room temperature
1/4 cup cream, not ultrapasteurized
2 tablespoons molasses
2-4 egg yolks
1/2 teaspoon vanilla extract

Blend ingredients together with a whisk.

Typhoid fever is an acute infectious disease excited by specific bacteria which attack the mucous membranes lining the intestinal tract. . . . The character of the diet is at first liquid, then passes to a bland, smooth-residue diet, free from all fiber, to (1) prevent irritating an already inflamed intestinal tract, (2) assure ease of digestion and a more complete absorption of food and (3) prevent stimulation of peristaltic action. . . . A successful diet developed by Dr. Coleman is the ""milk diet" which is made up of milk, cream and lactose and furnishes from 1000 to 3000 calories per day. . . .

Pulmonary tuberculosis is a specific inflammatory disease of the lungs manifested by continual wasting of the tissues, exhaustion, fever and cough. . . . In the adjustment of the high-caloric diet for tuberculosis, the sugars and other carbohydrates are not stressed to the same extent as the simple digestible fats (cream and butter) and the diet is more diversified than is possible in cases where the seat of infection and inflammation is in the intestinal tract, as in typhoid fever. . . . Because the tubercular patient needs all the resistance he can get from food, etc., additional vitamins should be given in the form of cod liver oil and other vitamin concentrates if the high-caloric diet does not provide enough to protect the patient. Fairfax T. Proudfit *Nutrition and Diet Therapy* 1945

Fasting is an ancient traditional method of restoring health, based on the principle of sparing the digestion through greatly reduced food intake (or a monodiet composed of one easy-to-digest food like raw milk) so that the energies of the body can be directed towards healing and rebuilding. Many fasts call for the exclusive use of plant foods, usually in the form of juices, broths or purées. Such diets can be very useful in the short term for healing and detoxifying, particularly if coupled with gentle methods of removing toxins, such as coffee enemas or colonic irrigations. Fasting should only be carried out under the supervision of a qualified health practitioner and never be allowed to continue for too long.

Fasting may be likened to applying mops and brooms to the body temple. All buildings, even the magnificent edifice of the human body, need an occasional cleansing; but they are built strong and kept in good repair with bricks and mortar—the fats and proteins supplied by nutrient-dense animal foods. SWF

Of course, using food as medicine is ancient. The pharmacopeia of ancient Egypt, Babylonia, Greece and China as well as those of the Middle Ages was based on food. Only in this century has society become almost exclusively dependent on manufactured pills to cure our miseries. But now that pharmaceutical model is breaking down as a panacea for today's plague of chronic diseases, such as cancer, arthritis, and heart disease; and the ancient wisdom about food's medicinal powers, newly confirmed by twentieth century scientific research, is increasingly infiltrating mainstream medicine. Jean Carper *The Food Pharmacy Guide to Good Eating*

POTTENGER LIVER COCKTAIL
Makes 1 cup

1 small chunk pasture-fed beef or lamb liver,
frozen for at least 14 days
4-6 ounces tomato juice
dash of tabasco sauce
squeeze of lime juice
1 tablespoon whey (page 87)

Dr. Francis Pottenger, author of the famous cat studies, recommended this tonic for the health and stamina-building properties of raw liver and gave it to patients at his sanitorium suffering from tuberculosis and other respiratory diseases. This is a great tonic for athletes. The liver you use should come from pasture-fed cows.

Grate liver finely to obtain about 1-2 teaspoons. Mix with tomato juice, whey and seasonings. Drink immediately.

RAW LIVER DRINK
Makes 1 cup

1/4 pound raw beef liver,
frozen for 14 days and thawed
1/2 cup cold water
pinch sea salt
juice of 1 lime
1/2 cup freshly squeezed orange juice
1 teaspoon Rapadura (see page 536), optional
1 tablespoon whey (page 87)

Wash liver, chop finely and soak for 2 hours in water and sea salt. Press through a fine strainer. Mix with the remaining ingredients and drink immediately.

BARLEY WATER

Makes 1 quart

4 tablespoons pearled barley
1 quart filtered water
juice of 1 lime
Rapadura (see page 536) to taste
1/4 cup whey (page 87)

Wash barley, cover with cold water, heat to boiling and discard this water. Place barley and 1 quart water in top of double boiler and simmer for 2 hours. Strain and add remaining ingredients after barley water has cooled. May be drunk warm or cold.

MARY'S SWAMP JUICE

Makes 6 ounces

1 tablespoon freshly ground flax seed
1 teaspoon spirulina powder
1/4 teaspoon dolomite powder (see Sources)
6 ounces fresh orange juice

Mix all ingredients thoroughly and drink immediately.

IODINE GARGLE

Makes 1 cup

1 cup filtered water
2 teaspoons sea salt
7 drops atomidine, an iodine solution
    (see Sources)

Add salt to water and bring to a boil. Allow to cool and add atomidine. Use when the gargle is still quite hot but not hot enough to burn. Great for sore throats, hoarseness and tonsillitis.

Primitive tribes in both Africa and the New World consumed algae in the form of "pond scum," which they dried in the sun. Rich in chlorophyll, protein, beta carotene, omega-3 fatty acids, minerals, enzymes and nucleic acids, dried microalgae have been used successfully to treat everything from leprosy to AIDS. The nutritive value of these products depends in part on the minerals available in the water in which they are grown. Toxins will be present if the growing medium is polluted. Look for algae that have been processed by freeze drying, rather than heat, and that are cultivated in pure, mineral rich waters.

There are three main type of dried algae available. Spirulina is said to be the easiest to digest and absorb, partly because its cell walls are composed of mucopolysaccharides rather than indigestible cellulose. Chlorella needs special processing to improve the digestibility of a tough outer cell wall but is valued for its ability to bind with heavy metals and pesticides and carry them out of the body. Wild blue-green algae is said to have remarkable healing properties but can transform into an exceptionally toxic plant under certain conditions. Freeze drying is said to denature these toxins. SWF

Throughout history, ocean salt has earned a hallowed reputation. Our ancestors saw it as an element that regenerates blood, a principle of equilibrium and life. To this day names of towns ending in "lick" still attest to the fact that our early ancestors were drawn to the seashores or the rock salt deposits of the earth. In England town names ending in "wich," in Germany "saal" as in Salzburg, remind us of its neolithic origins. Early settlements grew up around these salt beds and springs. Jacques DeLangre *Seasalt's Hidden Powers*

Using cheese whey as a beverage in human nutrition, especially for therapeutic purposes, can be traced back to the ancient Greeks. Hippocrates, in 460 BC, prescribed whey for an assortment of human ailments. In the Middle Ages, whey was recommended by many doctors for varied diseases; and by the mid 19th century, whey cures reached a high point with the establishment of over 400 whey houses in Western Europe. As late as the 1940's, in spas in Central Europe, dyspepsia, uremia, arthritis, gout, liver diseases, anemia and even tuberculosis were treated with the ingestion of up to 1500 grams of whey per day. V. H. Holsinger *Whey Beverages: A Review*

Cabbage is an unusually rich source of vital nutrients, particularly vitamin C and carotenoids. Vitamin C is required by the body for the integrity of blood vessels, connective tissue, bones and every essential biochemical activity including immune function.

Cabbage juice is highly valued as a folk remedy. Its healing powers may be related to its high sulphur and chlorine content, which in combination is said to exert a powerful cleansing action upon the mucous membranes of the intestinal tract. Cabbage juice has been used in the treatment of arthritis, gastrointestinal ulceration, skin disorders and obesity. "Cabbage water for the complexion," is a truism among the Irish.

Even better than plain cabbage juice is the juice of fermented cabbage, with is content of lactic acid and enzymes. German folk wisdom values both cabbage juice and cucumber pickle juice for digestive disorders, infectious illnesses and many other complaints. SWF

WHEY DRINK
Makes 4 ounces

1/2 cup whey (page 87)
1/2 cup filtered water
juice of 1 lemon

Mix all ingredients together and drink immediately.

MORNING TONIC
Serves 1

2 tablespoons noni juice (see page 617 and Sources)
1 teaspoon cod liver oil
1 heaping teaspoon Azomite mineral powder (see page 615 and Sources)
18 drops 3% hydrogen peroxide
1/4 cup filtered water

Mix all ingredients together and drink immediately.

CABBAGE JUICE TONIC
Makes 2 quarts

1/4 organic green cabbage
1 tablespoon sea salt
1/4 cup whey (page 87)
filtered water

This should be taken in small amounts throughout the day to improve intestinal flora.

Shred cabbage finely with a stainless steel knife and pound briefly with a meat hammer or a wooden pounder. Place in a 2-quart jug with salt, whey and enough water to fill the container. Cover tightly and leave at room temperature for 2 days before transferring to refrigerator.

Variation: Spiced Cabbage Juice

Add *1/4-1/2 teaspoon cayenne pepper* to 4 ounces cabbage juice tonic for a gargle and sore throat remedy.

REJUVELAC
Makes 6 quarts

2 cups organic soft spring wheat berries
filtered water
cheesecloth

This tonic was popularized by Ann Wigmore, the first of American practical nutritionists to recognize the importance of enzymes and lacto-fermented food in the diet. Rejuvelac should be yellowish, cloudy and tart, without being too sour, and slightly carbonated.

Place wheat berries in a 2-quart glass jar. Fill with water and cover top with cheesecloth held in place by a rubber band. Soak at room temperature for 8 to 10 hours. Drain through the cheesecloth, rinse and drain again. Place jar at an angle and leave for 2 days, rinsing two to three times per day, while the berries begin to sprout. After 2 days, rinse thoroughly and fill jar with water. Soak 48 hours. Pour off the rejuvelac and store in a glass container in the refrigerator. A layer of white foam may form at the top, which should be gently lifted off with a spoon.

A second batch may be made by filling the jar and soaking for 24 hours; and a third batch, by filling again and soaking another 24 hours. After that the berries will be spent and may be put outside for the birds.

No sooner had we concluded the formalities of taking possession of the island than people began to come to the beach. . . . They are very well-built people, with handsome bodies and very fine faces, though their appearance is marred somewhat by very broad heads and foreheads, more so than I have ever seen in any other race. Their eyes are large and very pretty. . . . These are tall people and their legs, with no exceptions, are quite straight; and none of them has a paunch. They are, in fact, well proportioned. . . . These lands are very fertile. They are full of *niames* [sweet potatoes], which are like carrots and taste like chestnuts. They *have beans very different from ours*. . . . These fields are planted mostly with *ajes* [manioc, yuca or tapioca]. The Indians sow little shoots, from which small roots grow that look like carrots. They serve this as bread, by grating and kneading it, then baking it in the fire.

More than 120 canoes came to the ships today. They all brought something, especially their bread and fish, small earthen jars of water, and seeds of many good kinds of spices. Some of these seeds they put in a gourd full of water and drank it; and the Indians with me said that is very healthy. . . . I think that another 500 swam to the ships because they did not have canoes, and we were anchored 3 miles from land! Robert H. Fuson, trans. *The Log of Christopher Columbus*

SUPERFOODS

Superfoods—as opposed to vitamins or supplements—are foods that naturally concentrate important nutrients. Unlike dietary supplements or vitamins taken in isolation, superfoods provide many nutrients that support each other and prevent the kind of imbalances that often occur when vitamins are taken singly.

Do we need superfoods? In theory, if the diet is good, we should need nothing more to supplement our diet; but can even the most conscientious among us say that his or her diet is, or has been, perfect? With the depletion of our soils, the widespread use of additives and the prevalence of sugar, refined carbohydrates and rancid vegetable oils, which all of us have invariably ingested—if not in adulthood, at least in our youth—no one living in an industrial society today can say that his diet has been perfect. For those unwilling or unable to give up bad habits like caffeine, alcohol or smoking, a daily supply of superfoods is essential.

Even those who live in isolated primitive societies seek out special foods for optimum health—foods high in fat-soluble vitamins, such as fish eggs and organ meats, to ensure reproduction and strong healthy children, soaked grains for strength and stamina, and herbs to prevent certain diseases.

The following short list is not meant to be exhaustive but only to provide a few examples of superfoods that can, in general, be taken by everyone. Herbal products for specific ailments are best taken with the advice of a holistic health practitioner. To purchase hard-to-find superfoods, see Sources.

Acerola Powder: A berry rich in ascorbic acid, acerola provides vitamin C with numerous cofactors, including bioflavonoids and rutin, to optimize the body's uptake and use of ascorbic acid. Vitamin C, the most important dietary antioxidant, was popularized by Linus Pauling who recommended taking pure ascorbic acid in amounts up to 15 grams a day for a variety of ailments. But large quantities of vitamin C may be harmful to the kidneys and can lead to deficiencies in bioflavonoids. Small quantities of natural vitamin C occurring in whole foods can provide the same protection as large amounts of pure ascorbic acid, without the side effects.

Amalaki Powder: This is another excellent source of natural vitamin C. The amalaki fruit grows in India and is used in Ayurvedic medicine. The powder is very sour. About 1/4 teaspoon mixed with water is a good daily dose—an excellent treatment for allergies. Amalaki powder is an extremely economical source of natural vitamin C.

- **Azomite Mineral Powder:** This powdery mineral supplement, containing montmorillonite clay and many other compounds, comes from an ancient seabed. It is an excellent source of silicon, calcium, magnesium and the gamut of trace minerals. Clay also has detoxifying effects as the negatively charged clay particles attract positively charged pathogens and take them out of the body. Technically sold as an anticaking compound and originally available only in 40-pound bags, Azomite is now available in consumer-friendly, economical 2-pound containers. Take a heaping teaspoon mixed with water daily as an insurance of adequate macro- and trace-mineral ingestion in these days of soil depletion through intensive farming. (It's also great as a soil amendment for the garden and compost pile.)

- **Bee Pollen:** Bee pollen has been popularized by famous athletes who take it regularly for strength and endurance. It has been used successfully to treat a variety of ailments including allergies, asthma, menstrual irregularities, constipation, diarrhea, anemia, low energy, cancer, rheumatism, arthritis and toxic conditions. A Russian study of the inhabitants of the province of Georgia, where many live to 100 years and a few to age 150, revealed that a large portion of these centenarians were beekeepers who often ate raw, unprocessed honey with all its "impurities," that is, with the pollen. Bee pollen contains 22 amino acids including the eight essential ones, 27 minerals and the full gamut of vitamins, hormones and fatty acids. Most importantly, bee pollen contains more than 5,000 enzymes and coenzymes. It is the presence of enzymes, many of which have immediate detoxifying effects, that sometimes provokes allergic reactions in those taking bee pollen for the first time. If this happens, start with very small amounts and slowly build up to a tablespoon or so per day. Some brands are more easily tolerated than others. Avoid pollen that has been dried at temperatures higher than 130 degrees. Bee pollen can be taken in powder, capsule or tablet form—or in raw unprocessed honey mixed with cereal or spread on toast.

- **Blue-Green Algae, Spirulina and Chlorella:** Blue-green micro algae, and its cousins spirulina and chlorella, grow on inland waters throughout the world—visible as greenish scum on still lakes and ponds. The Aztecs of Mexico ate it as a staple food, dried and spread on tortillas. Africans of the Sahara region also use dried spirulina with grains and vegetables. These algae are high in protein, carotenoids and minerals. Beware, however, of claims that they can provide vitamin B_{12} in vegetarian diets. Nevertheless, the high mineral and protein content of the various algae make them an excellent superfood, a good supplement to the diet and a useful product for the treatment of a variety of health problems. Of the three main types of algae, spirulina is said to be the easiest to digest and absorb, because its cell walls are composed of mucopolysaccharides rather than indigestible cellulose. Chlorella needs special processing to improve digestibility of a tough outer cell wall but is valued for its ability to bind with heavy metals and carry them out of the body. Wild blue-green algae is said to have remarkable healing properties but can transform into an exceptionally toxic plant under certain conditions. Freeze drying is said to denature these toxins.

Bitters: Herbal extracts of bitter, mineral-rich herbs are a traditional tonic for stimulating the bile and increasing digestion and assimilation of fats. They often are the best remedy for calming a queasy stomach. One such product is made by Floradix. Another is Swedish Bitters, originally formulated by Paracelsus and later "rediscovered" by a Swedish scientist. Bitters supply nutrients from bitter leaves that are often lacking in the Western diet. Many cultures, including the Chinese and Hindu, value bitter herbs for their cleansing, strengthening and healing properties.

Butter, High-Vitamin and High-Vitamin Butter Oil: Deep yellow butter from cows feeding on rapidly growing green grass in the spring and fall supplies not only vitamins A and D but also the X Factor, discovered by Weston Price. The high-vitamin oil is made by centrifying butter at a low temperature; the process concentrates the nutrients in the oil. Use high-vitamin butter or butter oil as a supplement to regular dietary butter, particularly during winter and early spring.

Cod Liver Oil: Once a standard supplement in traditional European societies, cod liver oil provides fat-soluble vitamins A and D, which Dr. Price found present in the diet of primitives in amounts ten times higher than the typical American diet of his day. Cod liver oil supplements are a must for women *and* their male partners, to be taken for several months *before* conception, and for women during pregnancy and lactation. Growing children will also benefit greatly from a small daily dose. Cod liver oil is also rich in eicosapentaenoic acid (EPA). The body makes this fatty acid from omega-3 linolenic acid as an important link in the chain of fatty acids that ultimately results in prostaglandins, localized tissue hormones. It is very important for the proper function of the brain and nervous system, and for visual acuity. Those individuals who have consumed large amounts of polyunsaturated oils, especially hydrogenated oils, or who have impaired pancreatic function, such as diabetics, may not be able to produce EPA and will therefore lack important prostaglandins unless they consume large amounts of oily fish or take a cod liver oil supplement. Studies indicate that the unsaturated fatty acids in cod liver oil may be toxic in large amounts so don't overdo—2 teaspoons per day is a good rule for adults, 3 teaspoons for pregnant and nursing mothers and 1 teaspoon for babies and children. It's easy to take when stirred into a small amount of fresh orange juice or water. (Use an eye dropper to give it to infants.) Dr. Price always gave cod liver oil together with high-vitamin butter oil, extracted by centrifuge from good quality spring or fall butter. He found that cod liver oil on its own was relatively ineffective but combined with high-vitamin butter or butter oil produced excellent results. Your diet should include both cod liver oil and good quality butter from grass-fed cows.

- **Colostrum:** The first milk of cows, colostrum is high in components that stimulate and protect the immune system and that aid healing in many ways. Colostrum was highly prized in traditional societies. If you have access to fresh colostrum, do avail yourself of this source. Powdered colostrum can also be used. Look for a product that has been processed at low temperatures and is non-defatted.

- **Evening Primrose Oil, Borage Oil or Black Currant Oil:** These oils contain a fatty acid called gamma-linolenic acid or GLA, which the body produces from omega-6 linoleic acid by the action of special enzymes. In many individuals the production or effectiveness of this enzyme is compromised, especially as they grow older. Malnutrition, consumption of hydrogenated oils and diabetes inhibit the conversion of omega-6 linoleic acid to GLA. GLA-rich oils have been used to treat cancer, premenstrual syndrome, breast disease, scleroderma, colitis, irritable bowel syndrome and cystic fibrosis. They have been shown to increase liver function and mental acuity.

- **Glandular and Organ Extracts:** Dried tissue from the glands and organs of animals has been used successfully to treat the same gland or organ in human beings including thyroid, adrenal, pituitary, liver, thymus, spleen, kidney and eye tissue. Those who do not like the taste of fresh liver, particularly athletes and those suffering from chronic fatigue, should consider taking dried liver capsules on a daily basis. Look for products that have been freeze dried rather than processed at high temperatures.

620

Glandulars are best taken under supervision of a qualified health practitioner.

- **Kelp:** Like all sea vegetables, kelp provides minerals found in sea water, especially iodine and trace minerals that may be lacking in our depleted soils. For Westerners unaccustomed to including seaweed in the diet, a small daily supplement of kelp in tablet or powdered form is a good idea, but don't overdo—excess iodine may also cause thyroid problems.

- **Noni Juice:** Juice of the Tahitian noni fruit is revered by the Polynesians for its curative powers, possibly due to the presence of an alkaloid precursor called proxeronine, which contributes to the effectiveness of proteins on the cellular level. Noni juice has been used successfully to treat diabetes, injuries and pain, digestive disorders, depression and many other ailments. It should be taken on an empty stomach.

- **Wheat Germ Oil:** Expeller-expressed wheat germ oil is an excellent source of natural vitamin E, which is our best natural protection for the cell membrane. The Shute brothers of Canada demonstrated that vitamin E supplements are an effective protection against heart disease. In their studies they used wheat germ oil, not synthetic vitamin E preparations.

- **Yeast, Nutritional:** Dried nutritional yeast is an excellent natural source of B complex vitamins (except for B_{12}) plus a variety of minerals, particularly chromium, so important for the diabetic. Yeast does not contribute to candida as has been claimed—candida feeds on refined carbohydrates, not yeast. The late eminent physician Dr. Henry Bieler treated many cases of chronic fatigue with nutritional yeast supplements. Unfortunately, most commercial brands of nutritional yeast contain high levels of MSG—formed during high-temperature and chemical processing from the glutamic acid naturally present in the yeast. (Actually, high levels of natural glutamic acid in yeast make it an excellent superfood for alcoholism and sugar cravings.) Look for yeast that has been processed at low temperatures. It should be a light yellow color and dissolve easily.

Appendix A
LIMITED-TIME
LIMITED-BUDGET
GUIDELINES

No one in modern America deserves more sympathy than the working parent on a limited budget. Finding the time, energy and means to prepare nutritious meals for oneself and one's children poses a real challenge, especially as the temptation to opt for convenience foods is very great. The first step to meeting that challenge is the realization that fast foods are a terrible trap that, in the long run, leads to diminished vitality and, hence, even greater restrictions on one's time, energy and budget—not to mention the tragedy of serious disease.

While it is not necessary to spend long hours in the kitchen in order to eat properly, it is necessary to spend *some* time in the kitchen. Simple, wholesome menus require careful planning rather than long hours of preparation. Much can be accomplished in the way of advanced preparation by dedicating just one block of four to five hours per week to food, which might include shopping, starting a large pot of stock to last the week, putting up a jar of fermented vegetables, making a batch of cookies for school lunches and preparing a large casserole of soup or stew that can last for several meals. Simple, nutritious meals can be prepared very quickly when one lays the groundwork ahead of time. If your present schedule allows no time at all for food preparation, you would be wise to re-examine your priorities.

- Don't buy boxed cold breakfast cereals, even those made of whole grains. They are very expensive, poor in nutrients and difficult to digest. A serving of the best quality organic oatmeal costs half the amount of the average boxed breakfast cereal and is infinitely more nutritious. For optimum nourishment, you need to think ahead and soak your oatmeal overnight (page 455).

- Make your own salad dressing. You can make your own dressing using the finest ingredients for about the same cost as the average bottled dressings, most of which contain rancid vegetable oils, *trans* fatty acids and numerous additives. With practice, it takes no more than a minute to produce a delicious dressing for your salad (pages 127-135).

❧ Always buy butter. Margarine and shortening may cost less but it is a false economy, one that leads to numerous impoverishing diseases. If the cost of butter is prohibitive, use lard.

❧ Make stock at least once a week. Meat stocks have formed the basis of nourishing peasant diets for millennia. They cost very little to make (often a good fish merchant will give you fish carcasses for free), are very nourishing and have a protein-sparing effect. That means you can get by with very little meat in the diet when you use properly made stock for soups and stews. Use congealed fat from stocks for cooking and leftover meat for soups, meat salads and other dishes.

❧ It's better to put your money into whole foods than vitamins. However, most benefit from a daily teaspoonful of cod liver oil, one of the least expensive supplements on the market, and from Azomite powder, a very inexpensive mineral supplement. Lacto-fermented beet kvass (page 608) contains a large array of nutrients in easily assimilated form and is simple and inexpensive to make.

❧ Good quality dairy products are worth the price. If you live in the country, look into an arrangement for keeping a Jersey cow or goats.

❧ The less expensive vegetables include some of the most nourishing— potatoes, cabbage, carrots, zucchini, onions, broccoli, chard, beets and kale—and they are easy to prepare. Always prepare or serve vegetables with butter for best assimilation of the minerals they contain.

❧ If you can't afford caviar (and very few can), buy fish roe in the spring. Uncured roe from a variety of fish can be had from a good fish merchant at a reasonable price—possibly even for free. Use it to make roe cakes (page 316), or add to fish cakes (page 267). You can buy roe in quantity and store in the freezer to use throughout the year. Fish roe is just loaded with nutrients and was always prized by healthy primitive peoples.

❧ Don't forget eggs as a nourishing, low-cost alternative to meat. It pays to buy the best quality.

❧ Make soups part of your repertoire. Blended soups can be put together in very little time and are extremely nourishing. Invest in a handheld blender (which costs about $25) so you can blend your soups right in the pot, thereby saving time and dishes to wash.

- Don't forget to eat liver occasionally. It is not expensive but is worth its weight in gold, nutritionally speaking.

- Leftovers can be turned into delicious treats. Leftover puréed vegetables can be made into pancakes (page 412); leftover oatmeal is delicious fried (page 457); tender meat reserved from making broth can be added to soups or used for meat salads and sandwiches.

- A judicious choice of recipes will make a little go a long way. Budget stretchers include stir-fry stews (pages 286, 294 and 339), fish cakes (page 267), ground meat dishes, kidney-rice casserole (page 306), chicken gumbo (page 289) and lamb shanks (page 346). For special meals, consider leg of lamb, one of the more economical meat cuts, which can provide several days of leftovers in the form of leg-of-lamb soup (page 208).

- Buy organic whole grains in bulk and store them in 5-gallon covered plastic buckets, available at paint stores.

- If you can't afford a grain grinder, buy whole grain flours at your health food store or supermarket and store in the refrigerator. Use them to make easy and low-cost pancakes, muffins, gingerbread, brownies, crackers, etc. If you have the time, you can save money by making your own bread. Otherwise, try to buy good quality sourdough or sprouted grain breads.

- Learn to make basic brown rice (page 466). It is delicious, economical and nutritious. Leftovers make wonderful salads (pages 473).

- Children love our cookies (pages 528-532)—adults do too. Peanut cookies are the most economical. Arrowroot powder is rather expensive. (Asian markets often carry it at a good price.) Bulgur flour (page 461) is more economical but takes time to prepare.

- Make kombucha! It cost less than 20 cents per quart; and the taste is better than the most expensive soft drink, beer or wine.

- Try not to overeconomize on food. Instead cut out all the junk food—prepared cookies and cakes, soft drinks, frozen foods, fast foods, etc.—and use the savings to buy good quality whole foods. Above all use good quality fats—they keep you healthy during times of stress.

Appendix B
KNOW YOUR INGREDIENTS ANSWERS

Our "Know Your Ingredients" quizzes should demonstrate that certain ingredients recur in processed foods. The first of these is sugar in its many forms and guises—white sugar, corn syrup, fructose, etc. When sweeteners form the main ingredient of a processed food, manufacturers often use several so they do not need to list any one sweetener as the first ingredient. Next on the list is processed and hydrogenated vegetable oils, which allow the manufacturer to claim "no cholesterol"; third is refined flour often listed as "wheat flour," which a hasty reader may misinterpret as "whole wheat flour"; and, finally, numerous additives, coloring agents and artificial flavors. Note that many so-called "diet" and "lowfat" foods are composed of skim milk (formerly considered a waste product by dairymen), sugar and hydrogenated or highly processed vegetable oil, a highly dangerous combination; and that MSG and hydrolyzed protein, both neurotoxins, serve as substitutes for properly made meat broths. We hope that this exercise will convince our readers that when we enrich the food conglomerates by buying their impoverished concoctions, we jeopardize our own health and personal prosperity.

1. Cross and Blackwell Hot Mango Chutney
2. Wyler's Bouillon Cubes
3. Wish Bone Thousand Island Dressing
4. Seven Seas FREE Ranch Nonfat Dressing (Fat Free & Cholesterol Free)
5. Miracle Whip
6. Lipton Rice and Sauce (Asparagus with Hollandaise Sauce)
7. McCormick Green Pepper Sauce Blend
8. Town House Fancy Tomato Catsup
9. Thank You Brand Creamy French Onion Dip
10. Hearty Cup O'Noodles
11. Campbell's Homestyle Vegetable Soup
12. Campbell's Healthy Request Cream of Mushroom Soup
    (99% Fat Free, 1/3 less salt, low cholesterol, 60 calories, no MSG)
13. Farm Rich Non-Dairy Breakfast Creamer (100% cholesterol Free)
14. Lean Cuisine Lasagna with Meat Sauce (98% fat free, 35% less sodium)
15. Weight Watchers Beef Broth Mix
16. McCormick Brown Gravy Mix
17. Hamburger Helper (Macaroni & Cheese Type)
18. Utz Sour Cream and Onion Flavored Potato Chips

19. Del Monte Vegetable Classics, Garden Duet
    (Less than 300 calories per package, no preservatives added,
    a source of fiber)
20. Kellogg's Poptarts (Strawberry with Smuckers Real Fruit;
    fortified with 6 vitamins and iron, complex carbohydrates 21 grams,
    sucrose and other sugars 16 grams)
21. Land-o-Lakes Light Sour Cream
22. Patio Chicken Burrito
23. Slender Diet Meal for Weight Control (Chocolate Flavor)
24. Second Nature No Cholesterol Egg Product
25. Nature's Cupboard Hearty Granola Bread
26. Post Honey Bunches of Oats
27. General Mills Whole Grain Total
28. Rice-a-Roni, Long Grain and Wild
29. Mrs. Wright's Lite reduced calorie wheat bread
    (40 calories per slice, 33 1/3 less calories than regular wheat,
    30% less carbohydrates than regular wheat)
30. Quaker Chewy Granola Bars, Raisin and Cinnamon,
    (no cholesterol, no tropical oils)
31. Campbell's Baked Beans
32. Hostess Twinkies
33. Nabisco Harvest Crisps, 5 grain crackers
    (low fat, low salt, no cholesterol)
34. Santita's Corn Chips
35. Cheetos (Made with real cheese)
36. Kellogg's Low-Fat Granola (Half the fat of leading granolas)
37. Nabisco's Oreo Cookies
38. Pepperidge Farm Wholesome Choice Soft Cookies, Cranberry Honey
    (low fat)
39. Hunts Snack Pack Pudding (No preservatives, no cholesterol)
40. Cool Whip
41. Keebler Ready Crust
42. Entemann's Fresh Baked Pineapple Crunch Cake
    (Fat free, cholesterol free, with less than 100 calories per serving)
43. Slim Fast (Chocolate Royal Flavor)
44. Weight Watchers Vanilla Sandwich Bar
45. Isomil Soy Protein Formula with iron
47. Jello Pudding and Pie Filling
46. Weight Watchers Chocolate Mousse
48. Gatorade Thirst Quencher, Lemonade Flavor

Appendix C
SOURCES

Acerola Powder: Radiant Life (888) 593-8333, radiantlifecatalog.com.

Amalaki Powder: Bazaar of India (800) 261-7662.

Arrowroot Powder: Natural Lifestyle (800) 752-2775; Bob's Red Mill (503) 654-3215, bobsredmill.com; Azure Standard (541) 467-2230, azurestandard.com; Radiant Life (888) 593-8333, radiantlifecatalog.com.

Atomidine (iodine solution): Heritage Store (800) 862-2923, caycecures.com.

Azomite Mineral Powder: Peak Minerals (877) 296-6483, azomite.com.

Baby Bottles, Glass: Radiant Life (888) 593-8333, radiantlifecatalog.com.

Baby Formula Products: All products for homemade baby formula may be ordered from Radiant Life (888) 593-8333, radiantlifecatalog.com.

Bee Pollen: Vitamin Shoppe (888) 880-3055, vitaminshoppe.com.

Bifidobacterium Infantis: Life Start by Natren (800) 992-3323; Radiant Life (888) 593-8333, radiantlifecatalog.com.

Biodynamic Products (including fruit and vegetables): Spiritual Food for the New Millennium (888) 384-9642 or (301) 654-4899; for a list of certified biodynamic farms, the Demeter Association (315) 364-5617, demeter-usa.org.

Bitters: Survival Enterprises (800) 753-1981, survival.com; Life's Vigor, (661) 589-1818, lifesvigor.com.

Breads: Sourdough breads made with Celtic sea salt can be ordered from Mountain Eagle Bakery (406) 222-3617; Grain & Salt Society (800) 867-7258; or Miller's Bakery (530) 532-6384.

Butter, Grass-Fed and High-Vitamin: See classified ads in *Wise Traditions*, journal of the Weston A. Price Foundation (202) 333-HEAL, westonaprice.org.

Butter Oil, High-Vitamin (X-Factor): Radiant Life (888) 593-8333, radiantlifecatalog.com.

Buttermilk Culture: New England Cheesemaking Supply (413) 628-3808, www.cheesemaking.com; the *fil mjolk* culture from Sweden, which is similar, is available from G.E.M. Cultures (707) 964-2922.

Coconut Oil: Radiant Life (888) 593-8333, radiantlifecatalog.com; Carotec (800) 522-4279.

Cod Liver Oil: High-vitamin cod liver oil from Radiant Life (888) 593-8333, radiantlifecatalog.com; lemon-flavored cod liver oil from J.R. Carlson Laboratories (800) 323-4141.

Colostrum: Low-temperature dried colostrum from pasture-fed cows from Radiant Life (888) 593-8333, radiantlifecatalog.com.

Corn Mill: Lehman's (888) 342-2387.

Corn, Dried Kernels: Community Mill and Bean (800) 755-0554; Spiritual Food for the New Millennium (888) 384-9642 or (301) 654-4899.

Creamed Coconut: Available in Asian and Indian food shops; P.A. Tropical Products (718) 763-5888 supplies creamed coconut to retailers.

Cutco Knives: (800) 633-8323, cutco.com.

Dolomite Powder (Calcium Carbonate): NEEDS (800) 634-1380.

Dr. Bronner's Sal Suds: (760) 743-2211, drbronner.com.

Flax Oil: Omega Nutrition (800) 661-3529, omeganutrition.com; also Barlean's brand available in health food stores.

Gelatin: Bernard Jensen Gelatin (made from beef) available from Radiant Life (888) 593-8333, radiantlifecatalog.com. (See note on use of gelatin, page 126.)

Ghee, Organic: Grain and Salt Society (800) 867-7258.

Glandular and Organ Extracts: Carotec (800) 522-4279; Douglas Labs (800) 245-4440; J.R. Carlson Laboratories (800) 323-4141; Standard Process (available through health care practitioners) (414) 495-2122.

Grain Mills: Jupiter grain mill may be ordered from New Market Naturals (800) 873-4321, newmarketnaturals.com; other mills are available from Lehman's (888) 342-2387 and Radiant Life (888) 593-8333, radiantlifecatalog.com.

Grain Roller: New Market Naturals, as an attachment to the Jupiter grain mill (800) 873-4321; or from Lehman's (888) 342-2387; or with other attachments (slicer, meat grinder) from Radiant Life (888) 593-8333, radiantlifecatalog.com.

Grains, Biodynamic: Spiritual Food for the New Millennium (888) 384-9642.

Grains for Sprouting: Jaffe Brothers Natural Foods (760) 749-1133.

Grains, Organic: Natural Lifestyle (800) 752-2775; Community Mill and Bean (800) 755-0554.

Honey, Raw: Really Raw Honey (800) REALRAW.

Jet Stream Oven: Ozark (800) 835-8908.

Kefir Grains: G.E.M. Cultures (707) 964-2922.

Kefir Powder: Body Ecology (866) 533-4748.

Kombucha Mushrooms: Laurel Farms (941) 351-2233; G.E.M. Cultures (707) 964-2922; A. F. Kombucha (877) 566-2824, kombucha2000.com.

Kombucha (ready made): A. F. Kombucha (877) 566-2824, kombucha2000.com.

Lact-Aid Breastfeeding Support System: (423) 744-9090 www.lact-aid.com.

Lactose: The Apothecary (301) 530-1112; Radiant Life (888) 593-8333, radiantlifecatalog.com.

Macadamia Nuts: Raw macadamia nuts are available at Trader Joe markets and occasionally at Fresh Fields Whole Foods markets.

Maple Syrup (organic, non-formaldehyde): Grain & Salt Society (828) 299-9005; Coombs Vermont Gourmet (888) 266-6271, maplesource.com.

Meat, Pasture-Raised: See classified ads in *Wise Traditions*, the journal of the Weston A. Price Foundation (202) 333-HEAL, or contact a local chapter, listed at www.westonaprice.org; see also eatwild.com.

Milk, Raw: www.realmilk.com or contact a local chapter of the Weston A. Price Foundation, listed at www.westonaprice.org, (202) 333-HEAL.

Minerals (for adding to water): ConcenTrace, Radiant Life (888) 593-8333, radiantlifecatalog.com; Azomite (877) 296-6483, azomite.com.

Miso: South River Miso Company (413) 369-4057.

Noni Juice: Screaming Eagles (714) 921-0525.

Olive Oil (organic, extra virgin): Pietro del Marco (914) 723-5850; Bariani Olive Oil from Radiant Life (888) 593-8333, radiantlifecatalog.com.

Organic Foods: National Organic Directory (800) 852-3832.

Parchment Paper: Baker's Catalogue (800) 827-6836.

Pickling Lime: Mrs. Wages pickling lime (800) 647-8170, precisionfoods.com

Piima Culture: Send a $5 check for one or $20 check for five packages to Piima, PO Box 2614, La Mesa, CA 91943 along with your mailing information; G.E.M. Cultures (707) 964-2922 carries the Finnish *vili* culture, which is similar.

Rapadura: (800) 207-2814, rapunzel.com.

Sauerkraut Crocks: Goldmine Natural Foods (800) 475-3663; Radiant Life (888) 593-8333, radiantlifecatalog.com.

Sea Salt: Grain & Salt Society (800) 867-7258; Radiant Life (888) 593-8333, radiantlifecatalog.com.

Seaweed, Unsprayed: Maine Seaweed Company (207) 546-2875.

Sesame Oil: Omega Nutrition (800) 661-3529, omeganutrition.com

Sunflower Oil: Radiant Life (888) 593-8333, radiantlifecatalog.com.

Sourdough Bread Cultures: G.E.M. Cultures (707) 964-2922.

Soy Sauce, naturally fermented: South River Miso Company (413) 369-4057.

Spices and Herbs (nonirradiated): Frontier (800) 669-3275, frontierherb.com.

Sprouted Wheat Tortillas: Available wholesale from Alvarado Bakery (707) 585-3293.

Stevia Powder: (800) 4STEVIA; Radiant Life (888) 593-8333, radiantlifecatalog.com.

Stainless Steel Baking Pans and Cookie Sheets: Natural Lifestyle (800) 752-2775; Health Classics (805) 898-0089, www.healthclassics.com.

Stoneware: Bread pans and muffin tins available from the Pampered Chef (630) 261-8900 or (248) 656-0808, pamperedchef.com.

Sun Dried Tomato Bits: Timber Crest Farms (707) 433-8251.

Water Filters: Reverse osmosis system that restructures and remineralizes the water and the Doulton ceramic filter with additional fluoride filter both available from Radiant Life (888) 593-8333, radiantlifecatalog.com.

Yeast Flakes, Nutritional: Frontier brand (800) 669-3275, frontierherb.com, also available from Radiant Life (888) 593-8333, radiantlifecatalog.com.

Note: Sources and contact information are subject to change. Updates will be posted at www.newtrendspublishing.com.

Appendix D
THE WESTON A. PRICE FOUNDATION

The Weston A. Price Foundation was founded in 1999 to disseminate the research of nutrition pioneer Dr. Weston Price, whose studies of isolated nonindustrialized peoples established the parameters of human health and determined the optimum characteristics of human diets. Dr. Price's research demonstrated that humans achieve perfect physical form and perfect health generation after generation only when they consume nutrient-dense whole foods and the vital fat-soluble activators found exclusively in animal fats.

The Foundation is dedicated to restoring nutrient-dense foods to the American diet through education, research and activism and supports a number of movements that contribute to this objective including accurate nutrition instruction, organic and biodynamic farming, pasture feeding of livestock, community supported farms, honest and informative labeling, prepared parenting and nurturing therapies. Specific goals include establishment of universal access to clean, certified raw milk and a ban on the use of soy formula for infants.

Local chapters of the Foundation help people find oragnic and farm-raised foods in their locality, particularly meat, eggs and dairy foods from animals on pasture.

The Foundation seeks to establish a laboratory to test nutrient content of foods, particularly butter produced under various conditions; to conduct research into the "X" Factor, discovered by Dr. Price; and to determine the effect of traditional preparation methods on nutrient content and availability in whole foods.

The board and membership of the Weston A. Price Foundation stand united in the belief that modern technology should be harnessed as a servant to the wise and nurturing traditions of our ancestors rather than used as a force destructive to the environment and human health.

The Foundation's quarterly journal, *Wise Traditions in Food, Farming and the Healing Arts*, is dedicated to exploring the scientific validation of dietary, agricultural and medical traditions throughout the world. It features illuminating and thought-provoking articles on current scientific research; human diets; nontoxic agriculture; and holistic therapies. The journal also serves as a source for foods that have been conscientiously grown and processed.

For subscription, chapter and membership information contact:

The Weston A. Price Foundation

PMB 106-380, 4200 Wisconsin Avenue, NW   Washington, DC 20016

(202) 333-HEAL

website: www.WestonAPrice.org   email: WestonAPrice@msn.com

Appendix E
SUGGESTED READING

Periodicals: The following publications translate nutritional research into laymen's terms and have in common a history of balanced and rational presentation of the dietary fat issue. New discoveries and ideas often receive their first airing in these publications.

- *Wise Traditions in Food, Farming and the Healing Arts*
  Quarterly journal of the Weston A. Price Foundation
  PMB 106-380, 4200 Wisconsin Avenue, NW
  Washington, DC 20016   (202) 333-HEAL

- *Real Health*
  Dr. Douglass' Real Health
  819 N. Charles Street, Baltimore, MD 21201 (978) 514-7851

- **Books:** The following recommended books may be ordered from Radiant Life at (888) 593-8333. A portion of the proceeds from sales of these books is donated to the work of the Weston A. Price Foundation.

- *Nutrition and Physical Degeneration* by Weston A. Price, DDS: The classic study of isolated populations on native diets and the disastrous effects of processed foods and commercial farming methods on human health. Published in 1939, Dr. Price's findings have as much relevance today as they did 60 years ago. The book includes Price's unforgettable photographs showing the superb dentition and facial development of peoples living on nutrient-dense foods. All who plan to bear children and everyone in the practice of medicine should read this book. Now available in affordable soft cover.

- *The Cholesterol Myths* by Uffe Ravnskov, MD, PhD: A physician and researcher looks at all the research and demolishes the myth that cholesterol and saturated fats cause heart disease. Includes a discussion of the dangers of cholesterol-lowering drugs. Available from (877) 707-1776.

Excitotoxins: The Taste That Kills by Russell L. Blaylock, MD: Exposes the truth about monosodium glutamate (MSG), hydrolyzed vegetable protein (HVP) and aspartame, all potent neurotoxins that are pervasive in the food supply. Contains well-documented explanations of how these substances destroy nerve and brain cells, especially in the young and elderly, and tips for minimizing your exposure and sensitivity to these dangerous substances.

Solved: The Riddle of Illness by Stephen Langer, MD: Well-documented work on the importance of a healthy thyroid gland. Dr. Langer itemizes the maladies that can result from the often-misdiagnosed problem of an underactive thyroid and delineates important nutrients for the health of this all-important organ, including sufficient fat-soluble vitamins.

Enzyme Nutrition by Edward Howell, MD: Pioneering work on the role of food enzymes in diet and health. Reveals the dangers of diets composed entirely of cooked foods and problems posed by pasteurization of dairy products. Dr. Howell's work led to a renewed interest in lacto-fermented foods.

Food Enzymes for Health and Longevity by Edward Howell, MD: Recently republished volume contains more of Dr. Howell's fascinating research on food enzymes in human and animal diets.

Sugar Blues by William Dufty: Classic work on the dangers of sugar, written in a highly entertaining style.

Farms of Tomorrow Revisited by Trauger Groh and Steven McFadden: A handbook for communities and groups that want to support organic and biodynamic farming and have access to nutrient-dense produce and dairy products.

Appendix F
A CAMPAIGN FOR HEALTHY FATS

All of us pay a price for the widespread use of *trans* fatty acids—margarine, shortening and hydrogenated oils—in the food supply, even if we ourselves avoid processed and fast foods, because all of us collectively pay for the plague of cancer, heart disease and other chronic illness that the use of *trans* fatty acids has engendered. We pay with our pocketbooks in the form of increased health costs and lower productivity, and we pay with the lives of our loved ones. Informed consumers may not eat potato chips, cookies, crackers, prepared foods and french fries, but their children and grandchildren probably do. The tragedy is that hydrogenated fats are unnecessary—food processors have many alternatives for fried foods, baked goods, cookies and other processed foods. These include the tropical oils—coconut, palm and palm kernel—along with butter and other animal fats. These are safe and healthy alternatives to *trans* fatty acids.

Does it make you angry that food processors and fast food outlets use dangerous hydrogenated fats to save money while promoting them to the gullible consumer as health foods? If so, then join us in a letter-writing and phone-in campaign to the major food processing and fast food companies. No new laws are necessary to rid ourselves of the *trans* fatty acid menace—just the full weight of outraged public opinion.

FAST FOOD COMPANIES

McDonald's Corporation
1 Kroc Drive, Oak Brook, IL 60521   (708) 575-3000, 575-5512 fax

Burger King Corporation
PO Box 52078, Miami, FL 33142   (305) 378-7011, 378-7262 fax

Pizza Hut Worldwide
9111 East Douglas, Wichita KS 67207   (619) 681-9000, 681-9869 fax

Taco Bell Worldwide
17901 Von Karmon, Irvine CA 92714   (714) 863-4500

Wendy's
PO Box 256, Dublin, OH 43017   (614) 764-3100, 764-3459 fax

Hardee's
1233 Hardee's Blvd., Rocky Mount, NC 27804   (919) 977-2000, 977-8655 fax

Kentucky Fried Chicken
PO Box 32070, Louisville KY 40232   (502) 456-8300

Little Caesar Enterprise, Inc.
2211 Woodward Avenue, Detroit, MI 48201-3400   (313) 983-6000, 983-6197 fax

International Dairy Queen, Inc.
PO Box 39286, Minneapolis, MN 55439-0286   (612) 830-0200, 830-0480 fax

FOOD PROCESSING COMPANIES

Nestle USA, Inc.
800 N. Brand Blvd., Glendale CA 91203   (818) 549-6000, 549-6952 fax
(Carnation, Raisinettes, Butterfinger, Chunky, Stauffers and Lean Cuisine labels)

Philip Morris
120 Park Avenue, New York, NY 10017   (212) 880-5000
(Kraft, General Foods, Entemanns, Stove Top Stuffing and Coolwhip labels)

Grand Metropolitan
30 St. James Square, London, England SW1Y4RR   (44-71) 321-6000
(Pillsbury and Hungry Jack labels)

RJR Nabisco
1301 Ave. of the Americas, New York, NY 10019   (212) 258-5600
(Nabisco, Fleishman's, Planter's Peanuts, Stella d'Oro and Chun King labels)

Sara Lee
Three First National Plaza, Chicago, IL 60602   (312) 726-2600
(Baked goods)

Frito-Lay
7701 Legacy Drive, Dallas, TX 75035   (214) 351-7000
(Chips and snack foods)

CPC International
International Plaza Box 8000   (201) 894-4000, 894-2186 fax
Englewood Cliffs, NJ 07632
(Bran'nola, Arnold's, Hellman's, Mazola and Skippy labels)

Kellogg's
PO Box 3599, Battle Creek, Michigan 49016   (619) 961-2000
(Kellogg's, Eggo, Le Gout and Mrs. Smith's labels)

Campbell Soup
Campbell Place, Camden, NJ 08103   (609) 342-4800
(Campbell, Swanson and Pepperidge Farm labels)

Safeway
P.O. Box 28846, Oakland, CA 94604   (510) 891-3000
(Townhouse, Mrs. Wright's, Manor House, Bel Air and Lucerne labels)

Continental Baking Company
    Checkerboard Square, St. Louis, MO 63164   (314) 392-4700
(Wonderbread and Hostess labels)

UTZ Quality Foods
    900 High Street, Hanover, PA 17331   (717) 637-6644
(Chips and snack foods)

Quaker Oats Company
    321 North Clark Street, Chicago, IL 60610   (312) 222-7111
(Quaker Oats and Aunt Jemima labels)

Proctor and Gamble
    PO Box 599, Cincinnati, OH 45201   (513) 983-1100
(Duncan Hines label)

Van Den Bergh Foods Company
    2200 Cabot Drive, Lisle, Illinois 60532   (800) 955-5532
(Imperial Margarine, I Can't Believe It's Not Butter, Ragu and BakerSource labels)

Lance, Inc.
    PO Box 32368, Charlotte, NC 28232   (704) 554-1421
(Cookies and crackers)

Keebler Company
    One Hollow Tree Lane, Elmhurst, IL 60126   (708) 782-2630
(Cookies and crackers)

Sunshine Biscuits, Inc.
    100 Woodbridge Center Drive, Woodbridge, NJ 07095   (908) 855-4000
(Cookies and crackers)

SUBJECT INDEX

N

RECIPE INDEX

M

MENU INDEX

The authors thankfully acknowledge permission to print excerpts from the following books:

From AGELESS REMEDIES FROM MOTHER'S KITCHEN by Hanna Kroeger, Copyright © 1981. Reprinted by permission of the estate of Hanna Kroeger.

From THE BODY ECOLOGY DIET by Donna Gates, Copyright © 1996. Reprinted by permission of the author.

From BY THE SHORES OF SILVER LAKE by Laura Ingalls Wilder, Copyright © 1939 by Laura Ingalls Wilder. Copyright renewed in 1967 by Roger L. MacBride. Used by permission of Harper Collins Publishers.

From CHOLESTEROL AND YOUR HEALTH by Christopher Mudd, MS, JS, Copyright © 1990. Reprinted by permission of the author.

From THE CHOLESTEROL MYTHS by Uffe Ravnskov, MD, PhD, Copyright © 1999. Reprinted by permission of the author.

From COCONUT COOKERY by Valerie MacBean, Copyright © 1996. Reprinted by permission of the author.

From DES CRUDITES TOUTE L'ANNEE by Annelies Schoneck, Copyright © 1988. Reprinted by permission of Association Terre Vivante, Mens, France.

From A DIET OF TRIPE by Terence McLaughlin, Copyright © 1978. Reprinted by permission of David & Charles, Publishers.

From DISMANTLING A MYTH: THE ROLE OF FAT AND CARBOHYDRATES IN OUR DIET by Wolfgang Lutz, MD. Reprinted by permission of the author.

From DIS-MOI COMMENT TU CUISINES, JE TE DIRAI COMMENT TO TE PORTES by Claude Aubert, Copyright © 1987. Reprinted by permission of Association Terre Vivante, Mens, France.

From DR. NEWBOLD'S TYPE A TYPE B WEIGHT LOSS by H.L. Newbold, MD, Copyright © 1991. Reprinted by permission of NTC Contemporary Publishing Group, Lincolnwood, IL.

From EAT YOUR CHOLESTEROL by William Campbell Douglass, MD. Reprinted by permission of the author.

From ELECTRONS by Maha Chohan. Reprinted by permission of the Ascended Master Teaching Foundation, P. O. Box 466, Mount Shasta, CA 96067.

From ENZYME NUTRITION by Edward Howell, MD, Copyright © 1985. Published by Avery Publishing Group, Inc., Garden City Park, NY, 1-800-548-5757. Used by permission.

From THE ESSENE GOSPEL OF PEACE, Edmond Bordeaux Szekeley, translator, Copyright © 1981. Reprinted by permission of the International Biogenic Society, P. O. Box 849, Nelson, BC, Canada V1L 6A5.

From EXCITOTOXINS: THE TASTE THAT KILLS by Russell L. Blaylock, MD, Copyright © 1997. Reprinted by permission of Health Press, Santa Fe, NM.

From FARMER BOY by Laura Ingalls Wilder, Copyright © 1933 by Laura Ingalls Wilder. Copyright renewed in 1961 by Roger L. MacBride. Used by permission of Harper Collins Publishers.

From FARMS OF TOMORROW REVISITED by Trauger Groh and Steven McFadden, Copyright © 1997. Reprinted by permission of the Biodynamic Farming and Gardening Association, Inc.

From THE FAT OF THE LAND by Vilhjamur Stefansson, Copyright © 1956 by Vilhjamur Stefansson. Reprinted by permission of McIntosh & Otis, Inc.

From FIGHTING THE FOOD GIANTS by Paul Stitt, Copyright © 1990. Reprinted by permission of the author.

From FOOD IS YOUR BEST MEDICINE by Henry G. Bieler, MD Copyright © 1965 by Henry Bieler, MD. Reprinted by permission of Ballantine Books, a Division of Random House, Inc.

From THE FOOD PHARMACY GUIDE TO GOOD EATING by Jean Carper, Copyright © 1991 by Jean Carper. Used by permission of Bantam Books, a division of Random House, Inc.

From FOOD ENZYMES FOR HEALTH AND LONGEVITY by Edward Howell, MD, Copyright © 1994 National Enzyme Company, Forsyth, Missouri. Reprinted by permission of Lotus Brands, Inc.

From A FOREST JOURNEY: THE ROLE OF WOOD IN THE DEVELOPMENT OF CIVILIZATION by John Perlin. Copyright © 1989 by John Perlin. Reprinted by permission of W.W. Norton & Company, Inc.

From SEASALT'S HIDDEN POWERS by Jacques DeLangre, Copyright © 1992. Reprinted by permission of The Grain & Salt Society.

From SEEDS OF CHANGE by Kenny Ausubel, Copyright © 1994 by Kenny Ausubel. Reprinted by permission of HarperCollins Publishers, Inc.

From SOLVED, THE RIDDLE OF ILLNESS by Stephen E. Langer, MD and James Scheer, Copyright © 1995. Reprinted by permission of NTC Contemporary Publishing Group, Lincolnwood, IL.

From SUGAR BLUES by William Dufty, Copyright © 1975. Reprinted by permission of the author.

From YOUR BODY IS YOUR BEST DOCTOR by Melvin E. Page, DDS and Leon Abrams, Jr., PhD, Copyright © 1991. Reprinted by permission of NTC Contemporary Publishing Group, Lincolnwood, IL.

From ULYSSES by James Joyce. Reproduced with the permission of the Estate of James Joyce © Estate of James Joyce.

From THE USE OF GELATIN IN NUTRITION AND MEDICINE by N. R. Gotthoffer, Copyright © 1945. Reprinted by permission of Grayslake Gelatin Company.

From VICTORY OVER DIABETES by William H. Philpott, MD and Dwight K. Kalita, PhD, Copyright © 1983. Reprinted by permission of NTC Contemporary Publishing Group, Lincolnwood, IL.

From YOU ARE ALL SANPAKU by Sakurazawa Nyoiti, English version by William Dufty, Copyright © 1965. Reprinted by permission of William Dufty.

The authors thankfully acknowledge permission to print excerpts from the following articles, magazines and journals:

From "Adding extra bacteria. . . ," *New Scientist*. Reprinted by permission of The New Scientist.

From "Animal Pharm," by Mark Purdey. Reprinted by permission of the author.

From "Butter, Vitamin E and the 'X' Factor of Dr. Price," by Royal Lee, DDS, published in the *Price-Pottenger Nutrition Foundation Health Journal*. Reprinted by permission of the Price-Pottenger Nutrition Foundation, P. O. Box 2614, La Mesa, CA 92041 (619) 574-7763.

From "Can Aluminum Cause Alzheimer's Disease?" by Melvyn R. Werbach, MD, *Natural Activist*, March 1998. Reprinted by permission of Citizens for Health, Boulder, CO.

From "Can Foie Gras Aid the Heart? A French Scientist Says Yes," by Molly O'Neill, *The New York Times*, November 17, 1991, Copyright © 1991 by the New York Times Co. Reprinted by Permission.

From "Corn: Builder of Cities," by Mary Talbot, *Newsweek,* Fall/Winter 1991, Copyright © 1991, Newsweek, Inc. All rights reserved. Reprinted by Permission.

From "Facts on Fats and Oils," by Tom Valentine. Reprinted by permission of the author.

From "Fish Sauces Add a Subtle Grace Note," by John Willoughby and Chris Schlesinger, *The New York Times*, March 9, 1994, Copyright © 1994 by the New York Times Co. Reprinted by Permission.

From "Free radical pathology in age associated diseases: Treatment with EDTA chelation therapy, nutrition and antioxidants" by E.M. Cranton, MD and J.P. Frackelton, MD, *Journal of Holistic Medicine* ,Spring/ Summer 1984. Reprinted by Permission of Kluwer Academic/Plenum Publishing Corporation.

From "A Fresh Look at Dietary Recommendations," by Michael Gurr, PhD, *Inform Magazine*, April 1996, Vol. 7, No. 4. Reprinted by permission of the American Oil Chemists Society.

From *Health Freedom News*. Reprinted by permission of the National Health Federation.

From "Health Realities," by Sam Queen, MA, Winter 1997, Copyright © 1997. Reprinted by permission of Queen and Company Health Communications, Inc., Colorado Springs, CO.

From "Heart Rot, the Amish and Homeostasis," by Mark Purdey. Reprinted by permission of the author.

From "Hydrophylic Colloid Diet" by Francis M. Pottenger, Jr., MD, published in the *Price-Pottenger Nutrition Foundation Health Journal*. Reprinted by permission of the Price-Pottenger Nutrition Foundation, P. O. Box 2614, La Mesa, CA 92041 (619) 574-7763.

From "In the Beginning, There Was Broth," by Andrew Schloss, *The Washington Post*, May 14, 1998. Reprinted by permission of the author.

From "Life, Liberty and the Pursuit of Wellness," by John D. MacArthur. Reprinted by permission of the author.

From "Lower cholesterol increases risks of violent death." Reprinted by permission of Reuters.

ABOUT THE AUTHORS

Sally Fallon combines a background in nutrition with training in French and Mediterranean cooking. A creative and innovative cook, she has studied gourmet culinary techniques in both Paris and the United States and has devoted many years to researching genuine versions of traditional cooking methods. She brings a wide range of knowledge drawn from the areas of literature, anthropology, history and comparative religion to the fascinating subject of ethnic and modern diets. She is a popular speaker and the author or coauthor of numerous articles appearing in holistic health publications, including "Vitamin A Vagary," "The Ploy of Soy," "Tripping Lightly Down the Prostaglandin Pathways," and "The Oiling of America." She has served as editor of the *Price-Pottenger Nutrition Foundation Health Journal* and is the founder of A Campaign for Real Milk. In 1999, she founded The Weston A. Price Foundation in Washington, DC and serves as editor of the Foundation's quarterly journal, *Wise Traditions in Food, Farming and the Healing Arts*. The Foundation is dedicated to education, research and activism in the field of nutrition and food production. Mrs. Fallon is the mother of four healthy children and resides in Washington, DC.

Mary G. Enig, PhD is an expert of international renown in the field of lipid chemistry. She has headed a number of studies on the content and effects of *trans* fatty acids in America and Israel and has successfully challenged government assertions that dietary animal fat causes cancer and heart disease. Recent scientific and media attention on the possible adverse health effects of *trans* fatty acids has brought increased attention to her work. She is a licensed nutritionist, certified by the Certification Board for Nutrition Specialists; a qualified expert witness; nutrition consultant to individuals, industry and state and federal governments; contributing editor to a number of scientific publications; Fellow of the American College of Nutrition; and President of the Maryland Nutritionists Association. She is the author of over 60 technical papers and presentations, as well as a popular lecturer. Dr. Enig is currently working on the exploratory development of an adjunct therapy for AIDS using complete medium-chain saturated fatty acids from whole foods. She is the author of *Know Your Fats*, a primer on the biochemistry of dietary fats. She is the mother of three healthy children and resides in Beltsville, Maryland.

CONVERSION TABLES

U. S. COOKING MEASURES

3 teaspoons	= 1 tablespoon	= 1/2 ounce
4 tablespoons	= 1/4 cup	= 2 ounces
1 stick butter	= 1/2 cup	= 4 ounces
2 cups	= 1 pint	= 1 pound
1 pint	= 16 ounces	= 1 pound
4 cups	= 1 quart	= 2 pounds
4 quarts	= 1 gallon	= 8 pounds

MEASUREMENT CONVERSIONS

U.S.	BRITISH	METRIC
1 teaspoon	= 1 teaspoon	= 5 grams
2 teaspoons	= 1 dessertspoon	= 10 grams
1 tablespoon	= 1 tablespoon	= 15 grams
1/2 cup	= 4 fluid ounces	= 113 grams
1 cup	= 1 teacup	= 226 grams
2 cups (1 pint)	= 4/5 imperial pint	= .45 liters
1 quart	= 4/5 imperial quart	= .90 liters
1 gallon	= 4/5 imperial gallon	= 3.6 liters
1 pound	= 1 pound	= 454 grams

Note: 1 U.S. pint = 16 ounces and 1 U.S. gallon = 8 pounds
1 imperial pint = 20 ounces and 1 imperial gallon = 10 pounds

OVEN TEMPERATURES

FARENHEIT	CELSIUS	HEAT	GAS NO.
150	65	Warm	Pilot Light
225	107	Very Slow	1/4
250	121	Very Slow	1/2
275	135	Very Slow	1
300	149	Slow	2
325	163	Slow	3
350	177	Moderate	4
375	191	Moderate	5
400	204	Hot	6
425	218	Hot	7